# Fundamentals of Management

## Second Edition

Second Edition

# Fundamentals of Management

Mike Smith

## McGraw-Hill
## Higher Education

London   Boston   Burr Ridge, IL   Dubuque, IA   Madison, WI   New York   San Francisco
St. Louis   Bangkok   Bogotá   Caracas   Kuala Lumpur   Lisbon   Madrid   Mexico City
Milan   Montreal   New Delhi   Santiago   Seoul   Singapore   Sydney   Taipei   Toronto

Fundamentals of Management, Second Edition
Mike Smith
9780-07-712693-3
0-07-712693-9

# McGraw-Hill
# Higher Education

Published by McGraw-Hill Education
Shoppenhangers Road
Maidenhead
Berkshire
SL6 2QL
Telephone: 44 (0) 1628 502 500
Fax: 44 (0) 1628 770 224
Website: *www.mcgraw-hill.co.uk*

**British Library Cataloguing in Publication Data**
A catalogue record for this book is available from the British Library

**Library of Congress Cataloguing in Publication Data**
The Library of Congress data for this book has been applied for from the Library of Congress

Acquisitions Editor: Leiah Batchelor
Development Editor: Jackie Curthoys
Marketing Manager: Alexis Thomas
Production Editor: Alison Davis

Text Design by Hardlines
Cover design by Adam Renvoize
Printed and bound by CPI Group (UK) Ltd, Croydon, CR0 4YY

ISBN-13 9780-07-712693-3
ISBN-10 0-07-712693-9

The McGraw-Hill Companies

## Dedication

To my valiant and wonderful wife, Pam

# Brief Table of Contents

# Detailed Table of Contents

# Preface

Over many years I have taught the fundamentals of management to more than 12000 students. They have taught me the importance of good information given in a straightforward way. Unusually for an academic and researcher, I have been fortunate to experience management at first hand: junior manager in a knitwear factory in Leicester, director of a quoted company in London and chairman of a small company in Manchester. This has taught me the need to focus on what is practical and relevant. Consultancy work in Europe, Australasia, South Africa and Asia have also taught me lessons. It has made me aware of the need for a clear and straightforward text which combines a broad, classic framework with a deeper treatment of contemporary management topics.

## Who is this book for?

This book is focused on three groups of readers.

- *First* are students embarking on a course of business studies and management at university or college. They face the danger that individual courses dealing with specific areas give a disjointed view that lacks perspective. This book aims to provide an integrating framework that places other specific courses within the context of management as a whole.

- *Second* are students of other subjects, perhaps engineering, IT or languages, who are taking one or two courses in management as subsidiary subjects. Even if they never become managers themselves they will need to interact with those who do. This book aims to give an understanding of management that will enable them to relate effectively with managers.

- The *third* group of readers are those already working in organisations who have started, or are thinking of starting, a managerial career. This book is designed to provide them with an authoritative, high-quality text which will help guide their decisions. This group also includes people who are about to embark on an in-company course or, perhaps, an MBA after many years away from education. This book aims to be pre-course reading that gives a head start.

## Explicit knowledge, tacit knowledge and critical thinking

Knowledge can be divided into two types – explicit and tacit (this is explained further in Chapter 18). The much greater part of this book is devoted to the *explicit knowledge* about management that is formally set out in texts and academic writings. It contains many references to both classical writings and up-to-date papers. Each chapter ends with a short, annotated list of recommended readings so that readers can explore this explicit knowledge in more depth. Inevitably, a book presents information in a linear form. But, management knowledge is far from linear and parts of the same topic are often best placed in different places. For example, "strategy" is clearly a part of the planning process but certain aspects of strategy are better placed within decision-making and marketing. A unique system of signposting cross-references has been developed to help readers navigate their way through the multidimensional nature of the explicit knowledge about management.

*Tacit knowledge* is the informal, less codified information that is held in "managers' heads". Many texts ignore tacit information. But readers find tacit knowledge very engaging. It also provides a background that makes it easier to understand and apply explicit knowledge. I have made a conscious effort to provide tacit knowledge of management by including many **cases and examples** which, appropriately, are written in a less formal, more accessible style. Each chapter contains an opening case study to help readers recognise instantly what sort of information the chapter is going to cover. Development of critical thinking is a major concern of all education and development. The **critical thinking boxes** included throughout the chapters are a distinctive feature of this book which aims to develop these skills. Hopefully, they are thought-provoking – they are often disputatious and divergent. If readers are prompted to criticise my critical thinking . . . wow! Job done!

## The book's structure

There are significant differences from the first edition in terms of both the content and pedagogy: all sections of the book have been updated and many recent references have been included, while numerous cases and critical thinking boxes have been added throughout. The structure of the book has also been reinforced to reflect a coherent and logical picture of management.

It was tempting to structure the book by starting with chapters on popular topics (e.g. strategy, leadership and organisational change), and work down to less fashionable areas such as control, and even omitting important but less conducive topics such as budgeting. That assembly is flawed. It is incomplete. It fails to convey what is a clear and coherent structure for the fundamentals of management. Further, this scrapbook approach would ignore a basic psychological principle: material within a meaningful framework is easier to remember. The framework of this book is formed by four giant girders: definition, processes, functions and personal perspective.

## Definition of management

The starting point for a book on fundamentals of management is obvious – a definition of management with some idea of the types of managers (level, entrepreneurs, line managers, etc.) and the skills and characteristics managers need. But, managers do not exist in a vacuum. So, it is important to understand the contexts in which managers work (types of organisation plus the organisational, national and international cultures). Rightly or wrongly, the historical legacy, perhaps two centuries old, exerts an indelible influence on modern management. Further, history teaches an eternal lesson: social, economic, technical and intellectual zeitgeists shape the management methods of their era – but there is often a time lag. A knowledge of history may help managers identify trends that are shaping, and will shape future management practices. At a banal level a survey of the history of management also provides an excellent way to introduce key ideas such as "scientific management" or "contingency theory".

There have been three major changes to Part 1 which aims to answer the question "What is Management?".

■ Management career pathways have been integrated into the first chapter, demonstrating the diversity of management.

■ Sections on culture, both organisational and national, have been expanded significantly and now have their own chapter devoted to the organisational context of management (Chapter 2). Globalisation is now integrated into this chapter as an integral aspect of the context of modern management.

■ Fordism is included

## Management Processes

*All* managers use processes to transform resources into more valuable outputs. The large number of management processes can be bewildering. So, our framework requires a subframe of lintels. Very early in my teaching, I found that Fayol's subframe (planning, organising, staffing, etc.) is much better than most. It is widely known. The acronym (POSDCRB) is easy to remember. Above all else, it is very, *very* widely used and understood by practising managers throughout the world. Sure, it is an old subframe but it has proved its strength and it fully supports up-to-date topics. For example, strategy fits perfectly within Fayol's process of planning and it benefits from being placed in this context: it can be seen as an important part of a larger chain of activities that includes, say, organisational visions and management by objectives (MBO). Fayol's (updated) subframe gives a very comprehensive coverage of the processes that all managers must perform. In contrast, for example, some organisational behaviour frameworks give the impression that managers need pay little attention to, say, controlling or budgeting.

The new edition has changed to give greater emphasis to:

■ organisational change, which now has its own chapter

■ leadership, which also has its own chapter

■ strategy – especially PESTLE

■ teamworking

## Management Functions

Most organisations have functions that involve specialist cadres which deploy specialist knowledge and expertise. Most managers work within a specific function. But it is impossible for them to be successful without some awareness of others. There are at least 12 functions. It is impossible to describe all of them in a book of this kind. A good solution is to list all functions and place them within another substructure (line, facilitating and controlling). Substantive chapters then describe each of the "Big Five" functions: marketing, operations, human resources management (HRM), finance and the information function (IT). The distinction between management processes and management functions is clearly understood by practising managers but it can cause confusion for students. Sometimes, for example, staffing is wrongly equated with HRM while budgeting is wrongly equated with finance. In essence, *processes* are activities performed by almost all managers at an individual level. *Functions* are specialist activities performed by groups or organisations (the management). The structure of this book makes this distinction clear and explicit.

The structure of Part 3 has changed significantly. It now starts with a short introduction which puts management functions into context and then deals with the *five* main management functions. The major change has been to devote a substantive chapter on the knowledge function which covers the IT(updated), e-commerce and knowledge management. The section describing knowledge management has been expanded significantly and moved to this part. Other important additions involve: marketing (marketing orientations, market planning and sales); operations (supply chain management, business process re-engineering) and HRM (employee engagement, the psychological contract).

## Personal Perspective on Management

Management processes and functions are the bread-and-butter of the fundamentals of management. But important issues are personally relevant to individual managers themselves. Some of these personal perspectives are covered in other chapters. For example, Chapter 1 has a section relevant to personal careers and Chapter 7 has a section on training and development which is relevant to personal improvement. Further, most chapters end with toolkits, development activities and recommended readings which an individual can use to extend their personal competencies. However, two major personal issues need chapters of their own: social and ethical responsibility plus scientific attitudes. These topics may not be a part of introductory courses on management but they are an essential background. It is very useful to be able to point students to a readily available source. The subjects of both chapters are inherently interesting. Some students will read them spontaneously.

Many management texts scatter aspects of *social responsibility and ethics* among several chapters. This demonstrates that ethics apply to most areas of management but the approach is unsatisfactory. It makes it difficult for students to form an integrated and coherent view. A separate chapter, on the other hand, allows social responsibility and ethics to be viewed as a whole. Many texts only cover the organisational perspective of ethics. However, practising managers also need to be ethical in their own job as well as ethical and socially responsible as consumers and members of society.

Chapter 20 "Management Fads, Gurus, and Research" is another distinctive feature and it was very enjoyable to write! It aims to encourage a scientific attitude to the study of management. There is a lot of bad management advice and research. Few texts give help in separating the wheat form the chaff. A prime responsibility of educationalists is to develop critical and evaluative abilities. I hope the final chapter enables readers to adopt a scientific approach so that they can recognise management fads, evaluate management research and differentiate between good and bad advice.

There have been major changes to Part 4. The material illustrating HR issues (diversity and bullying) has been moved to the website. This reluctant change liberated space that could be devoted to other topics such as organisational change, leadership and knowledge management. The material illustrating commercial issues has been shortened and moved to other chapters ("e-commerce" to information function and "globalisation" to management contexts).

## Pedagogical Features

A good text should always lead readers to extend their knowledge and abilities. The role of the critical thinking boxes in developing the ability to evaluate research and ideas has already been noted. Each chapter has up to five features to encourage students to broaden their understanding.

- **Toolkits** highlight the practical implications of the preceding chapter so that readers can apply the knowledge they have gained. Toolkits also have a half-hidden agenda: to provide models so that students will, themselves, learn to draw practical implications from academic writings.

- The main role of **Essay plans** is self-explanatory – to develop the ability to structure material to serve a given (academic) purpose. The website provides model answers for essay plans suggested for early chapters. Later chapters do not. They can be set as the title for assignments. Only a masochistic tutor who enjoys marking scores of near identical essays would set a title where a model answer is available!

- **Web activities** serve a number of pedagogical purposes. Early Web activities direct readers to structured exercises which are contained in the website that accompanies this book. Later activities generally aim to encourage students to search for additional information and specific examples of ideas or management practices.

- **Experiential activities** aim to give readers a personal, subtle and nuanced appreciation of the softer, subjective facets of management. Many Web activities require readers to relate a chapter's contents to their own lives. Some of the experiential activities can be tailored to provide the basis of good seminars or tutorials.

- **Annotated recommended readings** aim to lead students to study at a wider or deeper level. I hope that the annotations are sufficiently intriguing and informative to entice students to follow them up. Almost all recommended readings should be downloadable using a college or university's subscriptions to literature databases. The readings offer a wide range of difficulty – from easy magazine articles to difficult journal articles. The difficulty level is often flagged and a little guidance is often given in how to approach difficult articles.

There is lots more that I would like to include, but one of the key aims of this text is to avoid the mass of unwieldy and expensive detail that is seen in many introductory management texts. However, this disciplined approach resulted in a tighter focus on key aspects of management. Fortunately, extra material is available on the website associated with this book.

I hope that readers find the book is clearly written and logically structured. I hope that you find it adds value by being both interesting and "profitable".

Good luck.

Mike Smith
January 2011

# Guided Tour

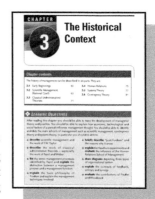

## Learning objectives

Each chapter opens with a set of learning objectives clearly summarising what knowledge, skills and understanding readers should acquire from each chapter.

## Cases

Each chapter includes numerous boxed examples illustrating how well-known organisations and real individuals tackle management issues in practice, including new opening cases which introduce readers to the chapter topic with an instant lively insight into the issues.

## Cross-reference icons

New to this edition, links between related topics are made clearly with marginal cross-reference icons indicating where the topic is explained elsewhere in the book.

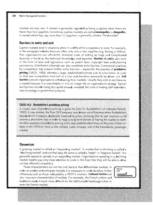

## Critical thinking boxes

New to this edition, this unique feature encourages readers to question "accepted wisdom". Lively and thought provoking, these boxes help the reader to develop the skills of critical thinking.

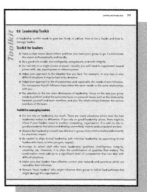

## Toolkits

Many chapters end with a toolkit which provides succinct guidance to applying the ideas to practical situations.

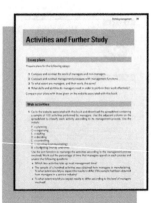

## Activities and further study

Each chapter ends with this section which gives the reader ample opportunity to test, apply and develop their understanding in a variety of ways:

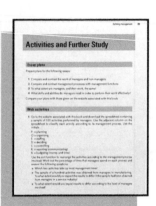

## Essay plans

Practice essay questions with feedback provided on the book's website at www.mcgraw-hill.co.uk/ textbooks/mikesmith

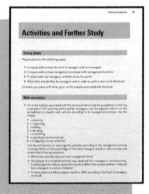

## Web activities

Guided activities for further research on the Web.

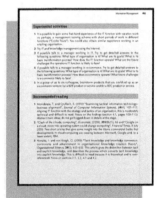

## Experiential activities

An opportunity for individual or group work to apply the chapter's ideas.

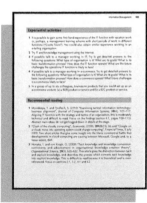

## Recommended reading

Annotated suggestions chosen as the ideal starting point for any additional reading or further research on the chapter's themes.

# Technology to Enhance Learning and Teaching

### Visit www.mcgraw-hill.co.uk/textbooks/mikesmith

This textbook is accompanied by a range of learning and teaching materials which have been created to help students to learn and assist lecturers in delivering their Management module.

## The Student Centre

The Student Centre for this title provides access to a number of helpful, completely free, learning resources designed to support Management students. These include:

- hints for studying Management
- tips for getting good grades for your assignments
- additional activities to support your learning
- self-test questions and guidance for essay questions

## The Lecturer Centre

The Lecturer Centre for this title contains

- PowerPoint presentations for each chapter
- a bank of test questions
- tips on structuring a course in management, and other helpful resources for teaching.

The Lecturer Centre is for lecturers only and as such is password-protected. In order to request the password to access the Lecturer Centre, please fill in your details at *www.mcgraw-hill.co.uk/he/password* or contact your McGraw-Hill representative.

## Custom Publishing Solutions: Let us help make our content your solution

At McGraw-Hill Education our aim is to help lecturers to find the most suitable content for their needs delivered to their students in the most appropriate way. Our **custom publishing solutions** offer the ideal combination of content delivered in the way which best suits lecturer and students.

Our custom publishing programme offers lecturers the opportunity to select just the chapters or sections of material they wish to deliver to their students from a database called CREATE™ at *www.mcgrawhillcreate.com*.

CREATE™ contains over two million pages of content from:

- textbooks
- professional books
- case books - Harvard Articles, Insead, Ivey, Darden, Thunderbird and BusinessWeek
- Taking Sides - debate materials

across the following imprints:

- McGraw-Hill Education
- Open University Press
- Harvard Business Publishing
- US and European material

There is also the option to include additional material authored by lecturers in the custom product - this does not necessarily have to be in English.

We will take care of everything from start to finish in the process of developing and delivering a custom product to ensure that lecturers and students receive exactly the material needed in the most suitable way.

With a Custom Publishing Solution, students enjoy the best selection of material deemed to be the most suitable for learning everything they need for their courses – something of real value to support their learning. Teachers are able to use exactly the material they want, in the way they want, to support their teaching on the course.

Please contact your *local McGraw-Hill representative* with any questions or alternatively contact Warren Eels e: *warren_eels@mcgraw-hill.com*.

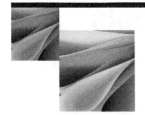

# Make the Grade!

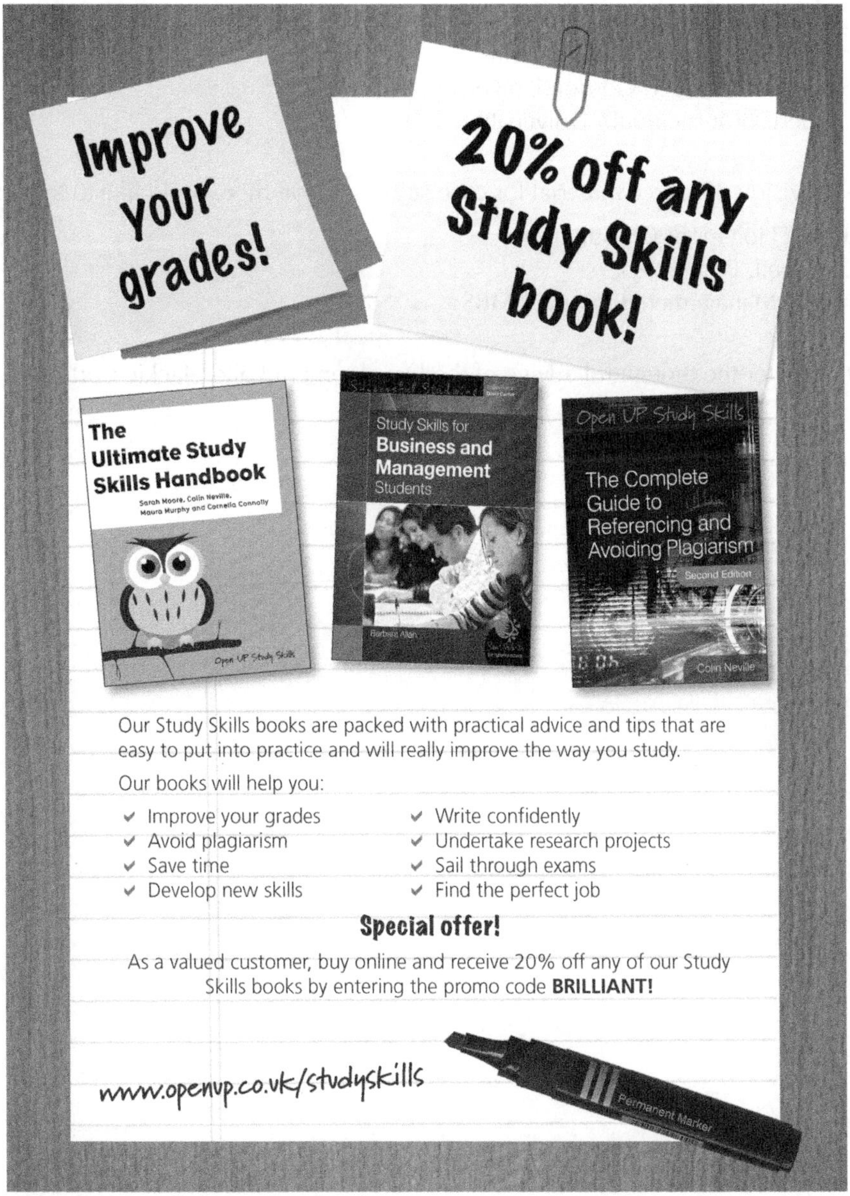

# Acknowledgements

The author and the publishers would like to thank the following reviewers for their comments at various stage of the book's developement:

Sukhvir Manak, Coventry University
Phil Johnson, Keele University
Guy Brown, University of Northumbria
Linda Strangward, Robert Gordon University
Simon Roberts, Bournemouth University

For the provision of source material for case studies, the author would like to thank:

Dave Banks, Holymoor Consultancy
Glen Campbell, BodyCheck
John French, Management Librarian, MBS

Many thanks for the thoughtful advice of the Development Editor, Jackie Curthoys.

# About the Author

Dr Mike Smith has researched and taught management for many years. He has experience of managing in several UK organisations, as well as consulting in management in UK, Australasia, South Africa and Asia. He was formerly Senior Lecturer at Manchester Business School.

# PART 1
# What is Management?

CHAPTER

# Defining Management

## ❖ LEARNING OBJECTIVES

After studying this chapter you should have a general overview of management and managers. In particular you should be able to:

❖ **define**\* the essential role of management and differentiate managers from operatives and specialists

❖ **explain** the concepts of transformation, added value and organising people

❖ **distinguish** between management processes and management functions

❖ **compare and contrast** different types of managers when classified by ownership, relation to line functions, seniority etc

❖ **identify** three general management skills and explain how their

importance changes at different levels of management

❖ **list** three characteristics of management work and 10 management roles

❖ **list** the three competences sought most frequently by employers

❖ **describe** the main psychological characteristics of typical managers

❖ **compare** the approach and management style used several decades ago with the approach and management style used today

\* *Explanation of terms such as define, describe, describe briefly, compare and contrast, list, analyse etc. are given on the website associated with this book.*

**CASE 1.1** *Managing birds or bytes?*

Arthur Darfor is an owner-manager of an ostrich farm at Oudtshoorn in South Africa. He is responsible for the work of eight farmhands who need to be allocated work such as feeding or moving the birds to breeding paddocks. At times their work needs to be monitored closely to ensure that the correct temperatures and hygiene standards are maintained in the incubators. Since breeding is seasonal, Arthur needs to plan his flock carefully so that his farm is fully utilised throughout the year. He also needs to plan the supply of "lucerne", which is a key part of the birds' diet. Many of his decisions are routine, but the timing of sending the birds to market is a key judgement as the prices for both feathers and ostrich meat need to be predicted. The income produced must be budgeted carefully to ensure that cash is available to meet labour and other costs until another flock of birds is sent to market.

Karen Bede is the team leader of a group of six computer programmers working for a software company based in Berkshire, near Windsor Castle. Every week she allocates the parts of a larger program to each programmer and checks the code they produce. The work needs careful planning to ensure that the parts fit together and the costs stay within the budget agreed with the client. Karen often needs to juggle demands and prioritise tasks in order to meet deadlines. A considerable amount of her time is spent writing progress reports and attending meetings so that the middle managers in her organisation can integrate the work of several teams like hers.

Managers play a very important role in our society but, unlike many other occupational groups, such as teachers, builders or doctors, managers do not form a single homogeneous group. They work in many different ways, at many different levels in many different types of organisation. It is therefore important to understand both the similarities and the variations in management. This chapter aims to do this by answering, the question "What is management?" in four sections:

## 1.1 Definition of management

### The basic transformational role of management

A simple definition of management is "using resources in an efficient and effective way so that the end product is worth more than the initial resources". This definition has the advantage that it focuses upon the crucial role of management to transform inputs into outputs of greater value. This is shown in Figure 1.1.

The simple definition has a drawback: it is too inclusive. According to this definition, a cow chewing the cud would be an excellent manager since it eats a cheap resource, i.e. grass, and converts it into a more valuable product (milk). The definition includes practically every adult: a vagrant collecting cigarette stubs, a student working in a library and a lone programmer debugging information technolgy (IT) code would qualify as a manager. A definition so wide is useless because it does not differentiate a subset of people who are

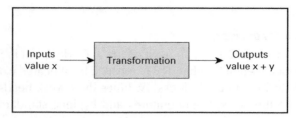

**FIGURE 1.1** The fundamental transformation process

clearly managers. Many people identify the management of *other people* as the defining characteristic of management. Mary Parker Follett (1941) defined management as:

> ❝ Getting things done by other people. ❞

More recently Stewart (1967) described a manager as:

> ❝ Someone who get things done with the aid of other people. ❞

This emphasis on the management of other people provides a good way to differentiate between managers, operatives (workers who work directly upon raw materials or information or who directly provide personal services) and specialists (workers who use their skills and knowledge to enable other people to do things). Specialists such as neurologists, lawyers or financial analysts may have equal or higher status and salaries than managers. However, they will not be managers until they are responsible for the work of other people such as a clinical team or a group of junior investment analysts.

The simple definition of a manager needs a final improvement. It needs to specify what is meant by "more value". Resources can be combined in ways that merely make the workers feel happy or they can be combined in ways that merely give managers pleasure. However, managers work within organisations and the phrase "more value" means "more value" in terms of the organisation's goals. When all these ideas are taken into account management can be defined as:

> ❝ the activity of getting other people to transform resources so that the results add value to the organisation in terms of reaching its organisational goals. ❞

As we saw in Case 1.1, despite the fact that Arthur and Karen are working in very different environments (different countries, different industrial sectors and different technologies), the processes they use – planning, organising, staffing, deciding, budgeting – are very similar. The only major difference is that Karen spends time reporting and communicating to others. In both cases, these managers are using other people to transform resources so that the end product has greater value than their inputs.

## Indices of managerial effectiveness and types of transformations

In the commercial world organisational goals are usually framed in monetary terms. The effectiveness of managers is often gauged by the percentage return on capital. For example, a manager who uses £1 million of resources to produce a product worth £1.2 million will, other things being equal, be a better manager than one who uses £1 million to produce a product

## CRITICAL THINKING 1.1 *Is management necessary?*

People in many organisations, such as hospitals, frequently complain that there are too many managers and management has major **disadvantages**:

- *It consumes a great deal of working time.* Time spent in meetings means that there is less time for direct work. Policy documents and memos also consume time. Further, reports and records are often viewed as distractions.

- *It is expensive.* Managers are often highly paid. It is often argued that it would be better to use this money to employ more operatives, buy better equipment or pay higher salaries.

- *It pursues selfish goals.* Sometimes managers take decisions that benefit their own interests and status (e.g. empire building) rather than adding or behaving fairly.

Sometimes, even effective management is a bad thing because it is used to pursue evil ends such as improving the efficiency of gas chambers or the marketing of fraudulent financial services. A management guru, Peter Drucker, once commented, "So much of what we call management consists in making it difficult for people to work". 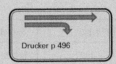 Drucker p 496

Although these arguments are persuasive, management has two *huge* **advantages:**

- *It enables big achievements.* Management often enables the work of very large numbers of people to be co-ordinated so they can achieve things beyond the reach of individuals or small amorphous groups.

- *It increases efficiency and reduces waste.* This means that resources can be conserved or used to create extra value.

These huge advantages mean that management is clearly necessary. If management is abandoned totally our lives would revert to a Neathandrial existence. So, it is best to use management with care. Leading thinkers such as Peter Drucker conclude that management is an evil necessity!

worth £1.1 million. Similarly, a managing director who takes over a company that is valued at £50 million and turns it into a company worth £55 million after one year is, other things being equal, a better managing director than one who takes over the same company and destroys value so that it is worth only £45 million one year later. 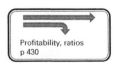 Profitability, ratios p 430

In many situations, financial indices are far too crude. They need to be supplemented by other information such as the number of people managed. The value added per employee is a common index of a manager's efficiency. For example, a manager who employs five people to convert £1 million of resources to products worth £1.2 million is probably doing a better job than a manager who employs 20 people to convert £1 million of resources to products worth £1.2 million – even though they add the same value (£200 000). Each person employed by the first manager is adding £40 000 value per year, while each person employed by the second manager is adding only £5 000 – probably not enough to cover their wages and other costs. Unless the second manager is able to obtain a subsidy from the government or other parts of the organisation, their unit will not be viable and the 20 jobs will eventually disappear – with enormous consequences for the 20 employees and their families.

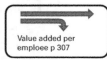

Value added per emploee p 307

These examples have been drawn from the commercial world because they are clear. Similar indices can be used in other types of organisation but value will be expressed in non-monetary units. For example, in the university sector a unit of performance will be FTE (full-time equivalent) per member of staff, in the theatre the unit of performance may be the number in the audience per performance, while in the health sector a hospital manager may be judged on the number of successful operations per surgeon per year. Table 1.1 lists some of the transformations where managers can add value to resources they consume.

| Industry | Transformation | Means of transformation |
|---|---|---|
| Education | Makes students more valuable by adding to their knowledge, intellectual ability, skills and, perhaps, enjoyment of life | Lectures, tutorials, practicals, books, webinars, tests, exams, etc. |
| Transport and communication | Alters the position of physical things to a location where they are more valuable | Air-flights, lorry journeys, courier services, postal system |
| Media | Transmits information from the mind of originator to the mind of someone who finds it valuable | Newspapers, radio, TV, computer games, the Internet |
| Manufacturing | Changes the physical form of objects or chemicals into a more valued shape | Bending, cutting, joining, heating, assembling, etc. |
| Storage and warehousing | Holds things until a time when they are more valuable | Warehouses, depots, data stores |
| Exchange | Transfers the ownership of an object or commodity to someone who places a higher value upon it | Wholesale and retail organisations, merchanting organisations, exchanges such as the Stock Exchange, legal conveyancing |
| Health care | Removing or ameliorating illnesses | Hospitals, clinics, surgeries |
| Government | Improving security and infrastructure for the population | Parliaments, councils, armed forces, police services, Quangos |

**TABLE 1.1** Examples of various management transformations

## Management processes, management functions and other perspectives of management

Once the basic concept of management (as the process of organising other people to transform resources so value is added) is understood, many questions arise:

- who are managers?
- where do they work?
- what processes are used to transform resources?
- what are management functions?
- what is involved in a management career? Etc.

This book divides the topic of management into four parts.

In *Part 1* we take **a broad look at managers and the context in which they work**. It considers different types of managers: all managers are not identical and it is essential to know the different types. It also considers the skills that managers need. The next chapter concerns contexts in which managers work:

- the institutional context
- the organisational context
- the international and the global context

There is a fourth important context – the historical context. This is so big that, for convenience, it is given a chapter on its own (Chapter 3).

*Part 2* covers **management processes**. They are the *activities* performed by the majority of individual managers in order to transform resources. For example, almost all managers make plans and supervise their staff. The main management processes are planning, organising, staffing and making decisions. Often management processes can be performed adequately without detailed levels of specialist knowledge. For example, a manager may be able to motivate staff without having studied psychology to degree level.

*Part 3* covers **management functions**. These are distinct areas *of management practice* that involve only a fraction of all managers. For example, in most large organisations less than 10 per cent of managers are directly involved in marketing or looking after the organisation's money. People working within a management function will usually need specialised training or experience in order to perform the intricate, high-level tasks within their function. For example, a manager in the human resource (HR) function will need specialised training in order to devise an appraisal system that will be applied to the whole organisation. Managers working within a function often belong to relevant professional organisations. For example, a manager working within the HR function is likely to belong to an institute of personnel and will have studied for its qualifications. Similarly a manager working within the finance function is likely a member of an institute of accountancy. The main management functions are marketing, operations, HR, finance and the information function. It is vital to keep the distinction between management process and management functions clear. Some academics use the words interchangeably. But there is a clear distinction in the minds of practising managers. **Management processes** are the activities which individual managers use in order to get other people to transform resources to a greater value. **Management functions** are the ways that managers are grouped within an organisation to achieve specialist tasks.

*Part 4* covers two issues that are personal to an individual manager's understanding of management. It includes topics such as behaving ethically, avoiding management 'cons' and evaluating the scientific merit of articles and papers that are written about management.

The interrelationships between these topics is shown in Figure 1.2, which, in effect is a plan of this book. In principle, all management processes are relevant to all management functions, which is why there is a shaded area in Figure 1.2 connecting processes to functions. However, some management processes are particularly relevant to certain functions For example, a manager working within the HR function is likely to spend a large proportion of his or her time on staffing processes, while a manager working within the finance function will spend a large part of their time dealing with budgeting processes – which is why there are arrows indicating explicit links between, say, staffing and HR and budgeting and finance.

Even the complicated structure shown in Figure 1.2 is a simplification. A further perspective is needed – the viewpoint of academic disciplines that underlie many management processes, functions and topics. The main management disciplines are sociology, psychology, economics and quantitative methods. Marketing, for example draws on each discipline. A manager in the marketing function may use economics and sociology to identify unexploited markets. He or she may use psychology to ensure that advertisements

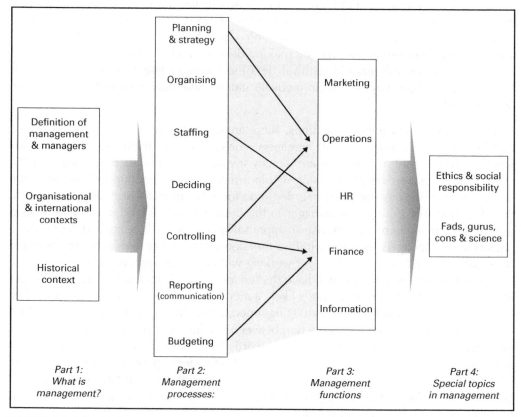

**FIGURE 1.2** Relationship between management processes, functions and topics

have the maximum impact in the minds of customers. He or she may also use quantitative methods to predict the number of future sales. Unfortunately, even a superficial treatment of academic functions is impossible in a book of this size. However, textbooks covering academic disciplines are readily available elsewhere. Often these topics are the subject of specific courses at college or university. On their own, these courses can appear fragmented, but if they are related back to Figure 1.2 a unifying framework for the study of management will be clear.

## 1.2 Varieties of manager

Many schools of management tend to assume that all managers are the same. In fact there are many different kinds of manager. The types of managers can be classified in many ways. The main ones are:

1 *relationship to ownership*: owner managers, entrepreneurs and intrapreneurs

2 *levels in organisation*: junior, middle, senior

3 *relationship to operations*: line, specialist and project managers, and functional and general managers

### Managers categorised by *ownership*: owner-managers, entrepreneurs and intrapreneurs

"**Owner-managers**" are, perhaps, the archetypal form of manager where the management and the ownership of the organisation is the same. It was probably the dominant form of management before the Industrial Revolution. However, with the rise of limited companies and government organisations, a specialist cadre of people emerged to manage organisations on behalf of other people. People can own an organisation even when they are patently unsuitable to manage it. Walker and Webster (2006) note that "for many small business owners . . . managerial skills may not be well developed and, more importantly, the recognition of the need to participate in skills development may not be obvious, even though the chances of business survival are higher in business owners who have participated in some form of training or skills development". Perhaps these people have inherited an organisation from previous generations. Perhaps such people have saved money all their lives and have used their savings to purchase an organisation in order to provide an income in retirement. Professional managers, on the other hand, can be selected and trained specifically for the job.

Today most owner-managers exist in small firms and will be involved in most, if not all, activities. They keep their finger on the pulse by walking round the firm and directly observing the state of affairs. As an organisation grows beyond, say, 50 employees, the demands and the complexity of communication are too much for one person to control directly and the organisation will tend to hire professional managers.

Many, but not all, owner-managers started as **entrepreneurs**. An entrepreneur is someone who identifies a business opportunity – by seeing a gap in the market, a technological development or a commercial change. Once the opportunity is identified an entrepreneur will take a moderate risk to initiate a business venture to exploit it. A classic example of an entrepreneur would be James Dyson. He noted that current vacuum cleaners became less efficient as the dust bag filled. He developed a new type of vacuum cleaner that did not need a dust bag. Dyson took a calculated risk and used his own money to fund the early developmental stages. Then he spent considerable time and effort convincing bankers who specialise in funding new developments (venture capitalists) to provide further funds that would pay for later development and the set-up costs for a factory. Other examples of entrepreneurial successes are Amazon book distribution, and Lastminute.com travel reservations. Perhaps the most successful entrepreneur of all time has been Bill Gates, who founded the software colossus Microsoft. There are also many examples of successful entrepreneurs in China and Singapore (Dana, Hamilton and Wick, 2008; Tang, 2010).

### CASE 1.2:  *A modern entrepreneur – Peter Cuddas*

Peter Cuddas was born in Hackney. His father was a meat porter and his mother an office cleaner. Peter left school at 15 and went to work in the telex room at the Western Union where he would type out instructions to transfer money from one country to another. He learned two important things: how to type and how financial markets worked. He became a trader and prudently saved his bonuses. By the time he was 36 he had paid off the mortgage on his house. He spotted a gap in the market. Most trades in foreign exchanges were so complicated and expensive that few people were able or willing to engage in them. Peter Cuddas invested £10 000 of his savings to set up CMC, an innovative firm that simplified trading and which lowered the cost. In the mid-1990s he grasped the potential of Internet trading. He invested £½ million in IT and broadened its scope to include trading in commodities, shares and currencies. His fairly simple trading system also allowed investors to dabble in more risky products such as contracts for difference. The commission he charges can be as low as 0.1 per cent. Simplicity and low charges attracted huge numbers of customers. His business grew, around the globe. Peter Cuddas is believed to be the richest man in the City of London and he enjoys a very opulent lifestyle. He has also made generous charitable donations and has established a foundation which makes grants to charities that help disadvantaged young people.

Small firms (under 500 employees) account for a disproportionate number of innovations. Birch (2000) suggests that small firms are responsible for 55 per cent of all innovations and 95 per cent of radical innovations. Fast-growing businesses, sometimes nicknamed "gazelles", produce twice as many product innovations per employee as larger firms. Unfortunately, entrepreneurs do not have a guarantee of success. Small entrepreneurial organisations have a high failure rate. Perhaps 60–80 per cent of small businesses fail within five years.

In recent years the importance of entrepreneurs to the economic well-being of a country has been more appreciated. Many large employers have been investing in machinery or moving their factories to countries where labour costs are low. Governments have been looking to entrepreneurs to start up new businesses which will replace the jobs being lost from large organisations.

Entrepreneurs frequently set up businesses in two sectors: business services and restaurants – presumably because the "entry costs" are low in these sectors. They are often "corporate refugees". They have either been the victims when a large organisation has downsized or they are people who feel uncomfortable with the restrictions imposed by corporate life. Whatever their background, entrepreneurs follow one of five main tactics:

1  **Start a new business**: this means the entrepreneur is in total control and can form the business in any way he or she prefers. Starting a new business can take a long time to produce a profit.

2  **Buy an existing business**: an existing business can be obtained fairly cheaply if the former owner wishes to retire or sell the business for other personal reasons. Existing businesses carry much less risk. However, it will be more difficult for entrepreneurs to mould these to their own preferences.

3  **Buy a franchise**: in a franchise an entrepreneur buys the right to produce or distribute a product or service which has already been developed. Franchises carry much less risk than marketing a totally new product (Castrogivanni and Justis, 2007). However, the person taking on the franchise will have much less freedom because he or she will need to operate procedures determined by the owners of the product. Perhaps the most famous franchises are McDonald's, and some hotel chains such as Holiday Inns.

4  **Be incubated**: some venture capitalists, government organisations and universities have incubator units where a number of entrepreneurs are gathered in close proximity, probably in a "science park". The parent organisation provides facilities such as premises and secretarial support in return for a share in the equity. The proximity of other entrepreneurs means that they can share information and business leads.

5  **Be spun off**: sometimes good ideas emerge within organisations. However, it may not be appropriate for the large organisation to exploit the idea. The large organisation may therefore produce a spin-off company which is staffed by its former employees. They usually buy their materials and, perhaps, patents from the parent organisation. The parent organisation may provide support such as guaranteed sales for the entrepreneur's output. A typical spin-off situation would be where an employee of a large glass producer develops a new type of double glazing. A double-glazing unit or division would provide the glass producer with a distraction that could mean a loss of focus from its core activity. The double-glazing company could, however, be spun off. The new company might use the parent as a source from which to buy raw materials and, maybe, to identify contacts as potential customers.

Obtaining sufficient finance is a significant problem for most entrepreneurs. In essence there are two sources of finance: debt financing and equity financing. In **debt financing** (see page 415) an entrepreneur will approach a bank, other institutions or wealthy individuals and obtain the required capital at a rate of interest. Sometimes the money is borrowed from family and friends. If the money is borrowed from commercial sources, the rate of interest may be high because the risk of failure may also be high. Commercial sources of finance are likely to demand extra surety such as a claim on the entrepreneur's house. In **equity financing** (see page 417) money is obtained in exchange for a share in the ownership of the new organisation. Often the funds are provided by venture capital firms such as 3i. If the firm fails the venture capitalists lose money, but if it succeeds they make big profits. Usually a venture capital company will only provide money if it has reasonable expectations of a high rate of return. This is because the return from successful companies must outweigh the losses they might make from unsuccessful ones. However, using a venture capital company brings the additional advantages of advice, It would be wrong to think that all entrepreneurs work in small companies. Some large organisations realise that it is often necessary to act like a small firm. They value the entrepreneurial spirit and give entrepreneurs scope to work (Drucker, 1985). Entrepreneurs who work within a large company are called **intrapreneurs**. Some large organisations take proactive steps to encourage intrapreneurs. They set up small units where groups of people are able to work on new ideas creatively and without formality. Sometimes, these units are called "**skunk works**". Perhaps the best-known skunk work was a fiercely independent and sometimes anarchic unit set up by Apple Computers that developed the famous Macintosh computer which was state-of-the-art and user-friendly.

Financing p 413

## Managers categorised by *level* in organisation: first-line managers, middle managers and senior managers

Managers may be divided into first-line managers, middle managers and senior managers.

**First-line managers** are also called junior managers, supervisors, overlookers, team leaders or foremen/women. First-line managers are responsible for directing the day-to-day activities of operatives. They have substantial spans of control but their range of responsibility is quite narrow. Their responsibility is restricted to ensuring that their team of operatives is achieving performance targets. Often first-line managers will be directly responsible for machinery and materials. The objectives of first-line managers are usually clear. Their success in achieving objectives is clear-cut and apparent within a short period of time (i.e. their **time span of discretion** is low). First-line managers frequently work at a frenetic pace, often needing to attend to a new issue every one or two minutes. An important part of the role of a first-line manager is to listen to the concerns of the people they manage (their **direct reports**) and relay these concerns to more senior managers. Similarly, they need to be aware of the wider organisational objectives and translate these into terms that are relevant and understandable by their direct reports. First-level managers are usually recruited from the ranks of operatives. They would be expected to be able to perform the job they supervise as well as manage it.

**CRITICAL THINKING 1.2** *Why do business schools ignore first-line managers?*

First-line managers are the most junior level of management. And their contribution to an organisation cannot be overstated. However, their contribution is often taken for granted or ignored – especially by business schools and theorists.

▶ Look in the index of most management texts and magazines – junior managers are hardly mentioned except in passing. Why is this so? Perhaps the writers lack the practical experience to understand what first-line managers do? Perhaps, writers and academics are a bit snobbish or megalomaniac. Perhaps, the simple truth is that it is easier to write about grand things such as strategy without appreciating the need for someone to translate the strategy into action.

Recently, the role of first-line managers has expanded. They are now expected to perform many of the activities previously required of middle managers. The main reasons are flatter organisational structures, greater use of computer information systems and a marked trend to better training and recruitment of first-line managers.

**Middle managers** manage first-line managers. They will have titles such as Head of Recruitment or Head of Payroll or even Head of Procurement! One of the major trends in recent years has been reduction in the number of middle managers. Their number has often been reduced by as much as 30 per cent. This has been achieved by using computers to do many middle-management tasks and by training first-line managers to do some (hitherto) middle-management tasks.

The key activities of middle managers are co-ordination and liaison. They transmit information up and down the hierarchy and across the various functions in the organisation. They convert the strategies and objectives set by senior managers into specific actions and plans which must be implemented by first-line managers. Often they are required to find creative ways to achieve objectives. They will have a fairly wide remit and will spend most of their time on organisational activities rather than operations. Middle managers will spend a great deal of time in meetings with other middle managers. The pace of middle management work is less frenetic. Typically they will have about nine minutes to concentrate on a problem before they need to attend to another matter. In some large organisations there may be several layers of middle managers. The four excellent vignettes of middle managers given by Rouleau and Balogun (2010) are a good read!

**Senior managers** are sometimes called "top managers" or "C-suite managers". They will generally have the word "Chief" in their job title – such as Chief Executive Officer (CEO), "Chief Financial Officer" (CFO) or "Chief Knowledge Officer" (CKO). Senior managers are often called directors, president, chief officer or controller. Except in very large organisations they will report to the most senior person in the organisation, such as the Chairman or the President or the Principal. Senior managers are primarily concerned with future strategy and developing a "vision" for the organisation. They then need to communicate their vision effectively *so that other people within the organisation are motivated towards its achievement.*

Senior managers are responsible for the performance of large units or the organisation as a whole. They need to be particularly sensitive to trends and developments in the outside environment. Much of their time is spent in meetings with other senior managers, important people from the external environment and middle managers, as well as acting as figureheads for the organisation.

CRITICAL THINKING 1.3 *C-suite inflation*

Job titles containing the word "Chief" are very desirable and they seem to be multiplying like rabbits! *The Economist* (2010, 6/26/2010 p 70) calls it "job title inflation". It notes that some companies have *four* CEOs. Southwest Airlines has a Chief Twitter Officer (CTO), Kodak, Coca-Cola and Marriott hotels have Chief Blogging Officers (CBOs) and Kodak also has a Chief Listening Officer (CLO). Someone could offer a prize to the first organisation with both CXO and CZO – whatever they may be.

## Managers categorised according to their *relationship with production*: line and specialist managers

**Line managers** are directly responsible for producing goods or services. Sometimes, they are called "production managers" or "operations managers" but this title should not be interpreted narrowly since most line managers these days produce services rather than material goods. In a factory, the line manager will be the supervisor, the head of the production department or the head of the manufacturing unit. In a call centre, line managers will be the section supervisor, the floor manager and the call centre manager. Line managers' actions play a clear, identifiable part in the performance of the organisation. Often line managers have large spans of control. Many line managers regard themselves has being at the "sharp", "front end" of management.

**Specialist managers** are sometimes called staff managers or enabling managers. Typically they are found in finance, HR, purchasing or technical service functions. Specialist managers often have only a narrow range of expertise but, within that restricted range, their knowledge is deep and detailed. For example, a line manager will be one of the first people to notice that productivity has declined and will use their working knowledge to eliminate possible causes (e.g. poor operative training) and to identify obsolete machinery as the major problem. Engineering specialists and financial specialists will then be involved to design a better machine and to obtain necessary money to fund it, although the line manager will retain the central role of co-ordinating their specialist efforts. Some specialist managers may have formal authority over line managers. These usually involve control functions designed to prevent errors – especially when environmental health and safety are involved. They have the power to overrule line managers and, if necessary, shut down production. Similarly, quality control managers will have a right to overrule line managers if they feel that the output is below the required standard.

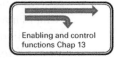

Enabling and control functions Chap 13

New initiatives and major changes are usually developed and brought to fruition by a **special project team**. For example, a financial services organisation that decides to offer a new tele-banking service would probably set up a team consisting of a line manager from its existing services, an HR specialist, a legal specialist and an IT specialist. This team would meet on a very regular basis to produce plans, organisational structures, procedures and training systems until the new service was up and running. It would then hand over to a line manager and disband. When the organisation undertakes another project a fresh team of different members would be constituted. The person in charge of such a team is usually called a "**project manager**". Sometimes organisations hire special managers who are employed by the organisation only for the time (the interim) it takes to finish a project. This usually occurs when the project requires specialist expertise which is not provided by anyone in the organisation. **Interim managers** are also used when people cannot be spared from their other duties. Interim managers may also be used to substitute for existing managers if they suddenly become unavailable due to ill health or other causes. Interim managers usually have a considerable track record in management which has given them a wide range of experience which they can deploy rapidly and effectively when they are called into a company. Interim managers need to "hit the ground running".

## 1.3  Skills and abilities needed by managers

The skills needed by managers have been studied by a large number of researchers. Probably the most influential studies have been carried out by Katz, Mintzberg and McClelland. Other important studies have centred upon management competencies and the psychometric qualities of managers.

### Katz's three broad skills and management level

Katz (1974) divided management skills into three broad groups:

1 **Conceptual skills**: the ability to view situations broadly, think analytically and to solve problems. Often conceptual skills involve breaking problems into smaller parts and understanding the relationships between these parts. Sometimes this is called a "helicopter view".

2 **Interpersonal skills** involve the ability to work effectively with other people and teams within the organisation. They involve listening carefully to the views of other people and tolerating differing perspectives. Communication is a very important interpersonal skill but others include the ability to motivate people and generate the appropriate psychological atmosphere. Interpersonal skills also embrace political acumen – which is needed to be able to build a power base, establish the right connections and the ability to enhance one's own position.

3 **Technical skills** consist of specialised knowledge of an industry or a process. Technical skills can involve engineering, scientific, financial or legal knowledge. Knowledge of IT systems, markets and commercial procedures are also kinds of technical skill. Often technical skills are obtained initially through formal education and are then developed by formal training.

Figure 1.3 shows how the mix of these three skills changes according to a manager's position in the hierarchy.

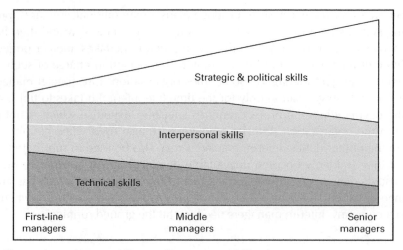

**FIGURE 1.3** Changes in management skills according to managerial level

*First-line managers* require high technical skills in order to get their operatives to transform resources into more valuable products. Good technical skills are often the *basis* for a higher career. However, as a manager rises in the hierarchy, detailed technical skills become less important. A computer programmer, for example, must know the ins and outs of the computer language that is used. However, a chief executive needs a less detailed understanding but he or she must understand the contribution which IT can make to the organisation.

The most important skills for *middle managers* are the interpersonal skills. Many technically competent people who are promoted into middle management fail because their interpersonal skills are insufficient. Sometimes people with brilliant financial skills rise to high positions within an organisation only then to fail because they antagonise so many people that their position becomes untenable. While interpersonal skills assume their maximum importance at middle management level they are also very important at all other levels.

Conceptual and political skills are highly important at *senior levels*. Managers at the top of the organisation encounter complex, ambiguous, longer-term problems. They need to be able to understand the many components of a problem and find accurate, long-term, solutions.

Changes in the skills needed at different management levels cause much heartbreak. First-line managers who have exceedingly good technical ability can become very frustrated when they are passed over for promotion in favour of a colleague who has better interpersonal skills. Similarly, very successful middle managers may be promoted to senior levels only to find that they no longer enjoy their jobs because they do not have conceptual skills.

Katz's analysis has important implications for management training and education. It suggests that introductory courses should focus on technical skills with an appreciation of interpersonal and conceptual skills. Courses for senior managers, however, should focus upon conceptual skills.

## Mintzberg and the nature of managerial work

Probably the most famous study of the skills needed by managers was conducted by Henry Mintzberg (1973). His study is a classic example of research using **structured observation**. He observed each of five chief executives for five days. Mintzberg noted that the work of the chief executives was characterised by three features: brevity, variety and fragmentation.

Management work primarily consists of a series of *brief episodes*. Mintzberg carefully recorded the duration of each episode. He found that, on average, each episode would last nine minutes. Less than 10 per cent of managerial episodes last longer than an hour. The average for chief executives included six minutes for each of numerous telephone calls. This was counterbalanced by scheduled meetings which tended to last 68 minutes. By some standards nine minutes is a long time. Previous research into the work of first-line managers (foremen) suggested that they attended to 583 incidents per day – less than one minute for each incident. The duration of a managerial episode seems closely related to the level of management. The more senior the level, the longer the duration of an activity. This is in sharp contrast to the assumptions made by many management educators who emphasise that managers should spend extended periods of analysis and reflection before they take action.

Management work is also characterised by *variety*. This is in contrast to many other jobs such as a general practitioner (GP) The average time a GP devotes to each patient is about nine minutes. But for each patient the GP will be dealing with a medical problem. However, each nine-minute episode completed by a manager is likely to vary from the previous one: the first episode may involve a financial problem; the second may involve a customer; the third may involve disciplining a subordinate; and the fourth may involve a mechanical problem that is affecting production. The range of activities which managers need to complete suggests that their education should be broad and multidisciplinary with a wide range of knowledge and skills.

The third characteristic of managerial work is *fragmentation*. Managers are rarely able to complete a task in one go. Often, they will spend nine minutes dealing with a problem – perhaps by ascertaining the nature of the situation and requesting further information. They will then deal with several totally different issues. Later in the day they may return to the initial problem, absorb the new information and request further clarification. The problem will be revisited, perhaps during the next day, when a decision will be made. Mintzberg also noticed that managers *prefer live* action. They much prefer talking to people and observing situations. They dislike static, formal and written work. Much of this dislike was based upon the fact that formal media are slow. With the possible exception of email, by the time a written report is composed, typed and checked it is likely to be out of date. Further, people are more circumspect when writing things down: they are more likely to be diplomatic and disguise the true facts and causes.

Mintzberg noticed that managers routinely perform 10 major roles. He groups the roles under three major headings:

**Interpersonal** roles centre upon dealing with other people:

1 **Figurehead**: this is probably the most basic managerial role. Most managers act as a symbol of their unit because they have the formal responsibility. They are therefore

obliged to perform a ceremonial duties such as welcoming guests or presenting retirement presents. In other cases a manager must formally sign legal documents.

2 **Leader**: it is a manager's responsibility to induce people to do things they would otherwise let lapse. They must inform, motivate and guide subordinates to perform activities that contribute to the organisation's goals. A manager must act as a role model for his or her subordinates.

3 **Liaison**: managers have a vital function in linking their own group to other groups. Their role in vertical communication (forming a channel between their own subordinates and senior management) is demonstrated in most organisational charts. With middle and senior managers the vertical communication role is masked by the importance of horizontal communication. A large proportion of a middle manager's time is taken up by liaising with other middle managers in the same organisation. A large proportion of a senior manager's time involves liaising with senior people from other organisations. Often this is a source of complaint from junior managers who frequently feel that senior managers should spend more time liaising with them.

**Informational** roles involve the key management activities of obtaining and receiving information. Once information has been obtained it must be passed on to people who can use it. Informational roles are:

4 **Monitor**: managers are continuously seeking information about the performance of their **area of responsibility (AoR)**. They do this by making frequent, informal tours of inspection (walking the job), discussions with other people and by reading trade press. Further, they are bombarded with information from suppliers, customers, regulatory authorities (e.g. health and safety) and other stakeholders. They must sift information to identify relevant trends.

5 **Disseminator**: once information has been collected it must be transmitted to subordinates for action.

6 **Spokesperson**: a spokesperson is similar to a disseminator but, while the disseminator directs information internally within the organisation, a spokesperson directs information outside the organisation to keep the general public informed. The chances are it will be a manager, and probably a senior manager, who performs this task.

**Decisional** roles concern the choices made in the allocation of resources, the direction to follow and how to negotiate with other organisations.

7 **Entrepreneur**: a manager often acts as an initiator and designer of change. Often the entrepreneurial roles stem from a manager's ability to authorise action. This allows them to spot opportunities and to galvanise their unit into appropriate action.

8 **Disturbance handler**: unforeseen events may send progress violently off-target. A disturbance handler takes action to get progress back on track. Typical disturbances are sudden departure of staff, accidents such as a fire or when a major customer takes their business elsewhere. Disturbances usually have a sudden onset and managers usually give them priority. Often the first reaction is to "buy time", which is used to find a solution.

9  **Resource allocator**: usually a manager has more possibilities than their resources can match. They therefore exercise judgement when allocating resources to some activities and not to others. This power gives a manager ultimate control without the necessity of being involved in the detailed preparatory work. The process of delegation involves considerable power because it contains the authority to choose one individual over another. The choice process communicates to the whole unit the preferences a manager will reward. Delegation is a clear manifestation of power because the manager can give the work to a second person if the first choice does not live up to expectations.

10  **Negotiator**: a manager will nearly always be involved in a major negotiation with an external organisation. Normally the manager will lead the other negotiators. In part the negotiation role flows from the role of figurehead, but it also involves the spokesperson and the resource allocator roles since only a manager can commit the resources that are implicit in the negotiated solutions.

## McClelland and managerial needs

David McClelland (1971) was interested in managers' needs. He was particularly interested in achievement motivation. Achievement motivation is the need to do something quicker, better or more efficiently. McClelland maintained that if a society had a high proportion of people who were motivated by achievement the society would grow faster. Using an ingenious method of gauging motivation by analysing street ballads he was able to show that the Industrial Revolution in the UK was preceded, 50 years earlier, by a surge in the level of achievement motivation of the British population. Similarly, the relative economic decline of Britain in the first part of the twentieth century was preceded, 50 years earlier, by a fall in the level of achievement motivation in the British population.

McClelland studied achievement motivation in executives of companies in the USA, Finland, the UK, India and Australia. He obtained a very robust finding. Companies who had executives with high level of achievement motivation made more innovations, filed more patent applications and grew faster. McClelland was also interested in the motives for power and affiliation. He found that people who rose to senior levels in large organisations showed a distinct motivational pattern which he called the **Leadership Motivation Profile** (**LMP**). People who rise to the top of large organisations tend to have a high need for power, a moderate need for achievement and a low need for affiliation.

## Managerial competencies

During the 1980s many organisations were keen to identify the skills, abilities, attitudes and other characteristics which made managers competent at their jobs. Boyatzis (1982) called these attributes "competencies". Organisations tried to determine the competencies needed so that they could recruit people who already had the required competencies or who could be trained to achieve them. Many organisations produced their own list of competencies. The lists used different words to describe the competencies but often they were referring to the same attributes. Bristow (2001) analysed the lists which were used by over 60 different organisations. Table 1.2 is based on his results.

| Competency | Components | % |
|---|---|---|
| 1 Communication | Written communication, oral communication | 97 |
| 2 Self-management | Personal effectiveness, self-control, self-discipline, self-confidence, resilience | 75 |
| 3 Organisational ability | Organisational awareness, delegation, control, structure | 68 |
| 4 Influence | Impact others, networking, negotiation | 67 |
| 5 Teamwork | Team membership, team leadership | 60 |
| 6 Interpersonal skills | Relationships, dealing with individual people | 58 |
| 7 Analytical ability | Conceptual thinking, problem-solving | 58 |
| 8 Results orientation | Achievement focus, concern for effectiveness | 55 |
| 9 Customer focus | Customer service, customer orientation | 53 |
| 10 Develop people's potential | Enabling others, coaching | 53 |
| 11 Strategic ability | Vision, breadth of view, forward thinking | 52 |
| 12 Commercial awareness | Business acumen, market awareness, competitor awareness | 48 |
| 13 Decision-making | Decisiveness, evaluating options | 48 |
| 14 Planning | Planning and organising, action planning, task planning | 40 |
| 15 Leadership | Providing purpose and direction, motivating others | 40 |
| 16 Self-motivation | Enthusiasm for work, achievement drive, commitment, energy, drive, will to win | 35 |
| 17 Specialist knowledge | Expertise, professional knowledge, functional expertise, operational understanding | 35 |
| 18 Flexibility | Adaptability, mental agility | 32 |
| 19 Creativity | Innovation, breakthrough thinking | 32 |
| 20 Initiative | Proactivity | 31 |
| 21 Change orientation | Change management, openness to change | 23 |

| 22 Dealing with information | Information gathering, information processing | 20 |
|---|---|---|
| 23 Concern for quality | Quality focus, concern for excellence | 20 |
| 24 Reliability | Accuracy, disciplined approach, procedural compliance, attention to detail, systematic | 18 |
| 25 Ethical approach | Integrity, commitment to social and economic equity, valuing people | 13 |
| 26 Financial awareness | Financial judgement, cost awareness | 12 |
| 27 Negotiating skills |  | 7 |
| Other |  | 15 |

**TABLE 1.2** Competencies demanded of graduates

Interpersonal skills dominate the competencies a manager needs. (This conclusion is supported by the Chartered Institute of Personel Development's *Learning and Development Survey 2009* (CIPD, 2009a) which identify interpersonal and communication skills as the most important attributes for recruits.) Seven of the top 10 competencies concern relations with other people. Communication skills are particularly important and tower above all other competencies. This suggests that the priority in both self-development and management training should be given to interpersonal and intra-personal skills. Once these competencies have been developed, precedence should then be given to organisational skills, analytical ability and a results orientation.

## Psychometric profiles of managers

Managers have been completing psychometric tests of intelligence and personality for many years as part of a selection procedure or career counselling. The results reveal a consistent pattern.

Managers need to be more intelligent than average and their intelligence score correlates with their managerial level. The average IQ score for the population as a whole is 100. Typically, a first-line manager will have an IQ of about 109 which would put them in the top 27 per cent of the population. A typical middle manager will have an IQ of about 119 (top 10 per cent of the population) while a typical senior manager will have an IQ of about 124 (top 5 per cent of the population). This pattern is not perfect and there will be a spread of scores either side of these averages. Nevertheless, "tests of cognitive ability", commonly known as intelligence tests, are good predictors of management ability. Personality tests are moderately good predictors of managerial performance but there is a wider spread of scores about the averages. Personality is more complex and difficult to measure. Research indicates that there are five main aspects of personality. They are:

- extroversion (relating to people)
- stability (feelings and emotions)

- conscientiousness
- tough-mindedness
- openness to new ideas

---

### CRITICAL THINKING 1.4 *What? No Freudian personality?*

You might be surprised that this section on the personality of managers makes no reference to the ideas such as the id, the ego and the superego that were "invented" by Sigmund Freud. Today, few psychologists regard Freud as much more than a historical curiosity. Indeed, some such as Crews (2003) regard Freud as an unscientific fraud who "reconstructed" a few famous case studies to fit his theories. For example, it is claimed that he mis-diagnosed a case of tuberculosis as a psychological illness (conversion reaction). Medawar (1975) suggested that the psychoanalytic theory of personality was a most stupendous intellectual confidence trick of the twentieth century. Nevertheless, some academics continue to promulgate his theories despite the lack of substantial evidence. Old theories die hard – especially when they tell a simplified but interesting story. Another example of a theory which persists without much empirical support is Maslow's hierarchy of needs, which is discussed in Chapter 7.

---

Typically managers, especially production managers, tend to be *moderate extroverts*. They are lively and sociable without going "over the top". Moderate extroverts enjoy jobs involving a variety of tasks and where they need to make quick practical decisions involving people. This is consistent with Mintzberg's view that the managerial job involves brevity, variety and fragmentation. There are, however, some exceptions to this rule. Managers of specialist functions such as R&D, quality control or finance may be less extroverted and perhaps even a little introverted.

Managers are usually *emotionally stable*. This enables them to cope with a torrent of emotional situations and gives them the resilience to bounce back after setbacks. Again, there are some exceptions to this rule. Project managers and some managers in the finance function may have average stability and may even be a little "touchy".

Almost all managers are *conscientious*. They have a sense of duty and they have a clear self-image to which they adhere. This often means that they are reliable and their work is well organised and considerate of other people. The few exceptions to this rule are usually seen in managers working in highly competitive, dealing or merchanting situations.

Finally, managers tend to be moderately *tough-minded* – they are prepared to take responsibility, push proposals through and get things done. They will face conflict but they will not actively seek it.

The level of *open-mindedness* is often related to the industry in which they work. Traditional industries which are "close-coupled" to the market and which produce a fairly standard product with high efficiency and at low cost tend to suit people with a personality that is down to earth and focuses on concrete information. On the other hand, academia, the media, advertising and fashion industries tend to favour a personality that exults in new ideas.

Writers such as Dumaine (1993) believe that the skills needed by managers are changing in order to match contemporary demands. Table 1.3 shows the contrasts between what Dumaine calls the old manager and the new manager.

| Old manager | New manager |
|---|---|
| Thinks of self as manager or boss | Thinks of self as sponsor, team leader or internal consultant |
| Follows chain of command | Deals with anyone necessary to do job |
| Works within existing structure | Changes structure according to environment |
| Makes decisions alone | Involves others in decisions |
| Hordes information | Shares information |
| Masters single discipline, e.g. finance or marketing | Masters broad array of disciplines |
| Demands long hours | Demands results |

**TABLE 1.3** Differences between old and new managers

## 1.4  Careers in management

Understanding management careers is important because the behaviour of managers differs according to their career stage. Furthermore most management careers have had drastic changes in the last decade and these changes have had big impacts on individual and organisations. Indeed, career development is a major preoccupation of most managers. In 2007 Velthouse and Kadogan asked managers to rank management issues in order of importance. Career development was in seventh place out of 22 issues – higher than planning, ethics and diversity. A good understanding of the importance of careers can be obtained by first studying traditional careers and then studying modern management careers.

### Traditional management careers

Traditional management careers tended to follow a standard path such as those described by Super (1990), Levinson (1986) or Schein (1978) and they are described in more detail on the website that accompanies this book. Super's career stages are the best known and they are shown in Figure 1.4.

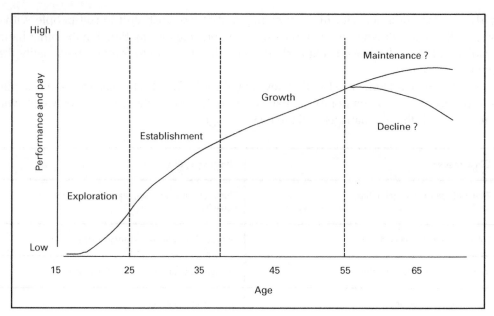

**FIGURE 1.4** Super's career stages

Super envisaged adult careers as passing through four main stages. From the age of leaving education until about the age of 25 many people explore a range of jobs without much commitment. Super calls this stage the stage of exploration. At about the age of 25 people settle down and build up experience as individual performers in, say, a single management function. In the mid-thirties people have often shown their ability and they are promoted to managing a group of people. They extend the range of their expertise into, say, two additional functions so that by the time they are 47 they will be regarded as broad-based managers who are knowledgeable in three or more functional areas. From the age of 47 the upward trajectory continues for a while but there is soon a divergence. People either continue to maintain their position or they start to decline. Those who maintain their position will expand their experience into extra functions, slowly arriving at the point when they have *some* experience in a majority of functions. Alternatively, those who decline will lose out in relative terms as the organisation and the world moves on. They will be analogous to the person who steps off an escalator that is moving onwards. Often the clearest examples of Super's stages were seen in bureaucracies where there is a strict ladder of promotion and progression. Such careers are known as **bureaucratic careers**.

Management functions Chap 13

## Modern management careers

Super, Levinson and Schein formed their ideas in middle of the twentieth century when careers were fairly predictable, stable and **bureaucratic** careers. However, the rate of organisational change in the 1980s and 1990s bought about major changes. Modern careers are much less stable. People often stay in a job for less than four years before they either change employer or type of work. Nowadays people can expect as many as 10 job changes and several episodes of redundancy during a career. Handy (1989) likened today's world of work to a shamrock in which there are three types of worker (Figure 1.5). There is a small group that forms an inner core of an organisation. They have permanence and stay with an organisation over long periods. They largely conform to the traditional pattern of bureaucratic careers. There is also a contractual fringe of people who are employed on a fee-paying basis for specific pieces of work. Often, they are employed on a repeat-contract basis, working for many organisations. Finally, there are the hired helps – people who are employed on a casual basis, when and where the need arises.

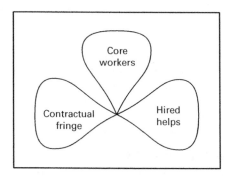

**FIGURE 1.5** Handy's shamrock

This relative impermanence of employment has important implications. In the past long-term employees were key organisational assets. It was in the organisation's interests to develop and improve their skills and abilities. Nowadays, this logic is less forceful. Why spend money on developing managers when, in four year's time, they will be working for someone else? The responsibility has shifted. Today, it is the individual who must ensure that their skills and experience improve so they will be able to obtain the next job or contract. People need to ensure their own "**employability**".

Arthur and Rouseau (1996) used the term **boundaryless** to describe such careers because there seemed to be few boundaries – there is high job mobility across employers and between different types of employment. People would use their networks of contacts to find different and new employment. Often, career moves were lateral rather than upwards. Many people in boundaryless careers enjoyed less certainty and gave less loyalty. A boundaryless career is characterised by two dimensions: physical mobility (from employer to employer); and psychological mobility (from one type of work to another). Hall (1996) observed the same trends but characterised careers in a slightly different way. He identified a **protean career** – after the Greek sea-god who would change his character in order to avoid someone capturing him and telling him what to do. A protean career is the one where the person, not the organisation is in charge. As in Schein's work a person's subjective core values are the main criteria. A protean career is also characterised by two main dimensions: the degree to which it is driven by *values* and the degree to which it is *self-directed*. The progress of protean careers is shown in Figure 1.6 (Based on Hall, 1996), which can be compared with Super's career stages given in Figure 1.4.

A typical career span has now shifted upwards and spans, say 20–70 years rather than 15–65. Also there are four or more related but distinct sub-careers. Each sub-career shows a recurrent sequence of exploration, trial, establishment, mastery and further exploration in

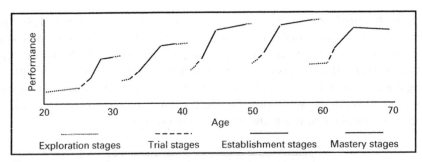

**FIGURE 1.6** Protean careers

anticipation of the next career move. There are, however, subtle differences in the stages at different ages. For examples, the trial stage during a person's twenties is likely to be longer than in later years and the establishment stages are particularly steep during a person's forties and fifties.

### CASE 1.3:  *Duncan Bannatyne's protean career?*

The career of Duncan Bannatyne, entrepreneur and celebrity "angel" on BBC's *Dragon's Den*, is usually quoted as an example of a career that does not follow a customary path. From a relatively modest background he joined the Navy at the age of 15 but was dishonourably discharged at the age of 20. He then tried a number of jobs which included welding, bakery and the car trade. At the age of 29 he started his entrepreneurial career by purchasing an ice-cream van. He grew this business and sold it at a profit. He then moved on to other areas such as nursing homes and finally health clubs, bars, hotels and property. He has also worked as a writer and television star. In addition, he has made notable contributions to charities such as a hospice for Romanian orphans and Comic Relief. Certainly his career has been restricted by few boundaries. Further, proteus-like, he has changed his career in a fluid and flexible way.

However, it can also be claimed that his career has followed a trajectory in line with Super's career model – exhibiting great flexibility *exploring* many different kinds of career up to the age of 29. Then he became an entrepreneur and an entrepreneur he has remained the rest of his life. Perhaps he was a little late settling down: many men make their fundamental choice of career at about the age of 25. Bannatyne *established himself* as an entrepreneur during that time when he owned the nursing homes. The main period of *growth* in his fortune occurred between his late thirties and his mid-fifties. In the last five years he has been successful in *maintaining* and even improving his career.

This introduction to managerial careers has been very brief and has only focused upon crucial concepts. Practical advice on topics such as:

- getting a job
- managing your boss
- getting promotion

## CRITICAL THINKING 1.5 *What's the use of management books?*

Superb managers such as Bolton, Watt or Richard Branson, were very successful even though they have never read a management book or studied management at college or university. Catastrophic managers, such as Skilling, CEO of Enron (USA's largest corporate failures) and Stanley O'Neill (CEO who steered Merrill Lynch into the disastrous sub-prime market), read many management texts while studying for their MBAs at Harvard Business School

**Practical experience** influences about a third of managerial success by giving direct exposure to management situations. In particular, it teaches how to implement specific projects and procedures. However, practical experience has two major disadvantages:

- *It is often very slow* and it takes many years to amass enough, especially when practical experience is accumulated in just one or two organisations.
- *It may provide a very limited perspective.* Managers may become very proficient in a limited range of situations but have little knowledge of other circumstances. They may develop a bigoted view that their limited perspective is universal. This may reduce their ability to adapt.

Management texts can play a small role in developing practical experience by giving practical cases and "toolkits" of practical tips.

**Management texts** usually contain a great deal of information which reinforces lectures and seminars and they can help obtain higher grades. They also give a wide, more flexible, view of management. Good textbooks have two further advantages:

- *They develop critical thinking which is a paramount skill.* Texts can give examples of flawed thinking and can outline scientific principles to evaluate management research.
- *They explain principles of ethics and social responsibility* that are often unclear when embroiled with practical, day-to-day activities.

Management texts have a useful role, especially for students who are keen to obtain good grades. In practice, however, texts need to be supplemented by experience and a substantial helping of good luck.

- making success of a promotion
- winding up a career

is given in the website *www.mcgraw-hill.co.uk/textbooks/mikesmith* that accompanies this book.

This chapter has focused closely upon the essential nature of management work, the ways that the different types of managers can be classified. It has also described some of the key characteristics that managers need. These are absolutely crucial elements in understanding management. Despite their importance they are inadequate. Management does not occur in a vacuum. It occurs within various contexts and these contexts play a very important part in determining the shape and form that management takes. There are at least four important contexts:

- the types of organisation in which managers work
- the organisational context
- the international context
- the historical context

Each of these contexts needs to be understood in greater detail. The types of organisation, the organisational context and the international context are discussed in Chapter 2. Dumaine's work highlights the fact that management is not static. It changes over time. In order to understand management it is necessary to have a basic knowledge about its history and how it has changed in the past. The historical context of management is discussed in Chapter 3.

# Activities and further study

## Essay plans

Prepare plans for the following essays:

1  Compare and contrast the work of managers and non-managers.

2  Compare and contrast management processes with management functions

3  To what extent are managers, and their work, the same?

4  What skills and abilities do managers need in order to perform their work effectively?

Compare your plans with those given on the website associated with this book.

## Web activities

1  Go to the website associated with this book and download the spreadsheet containing a sample of 100 activities performed by managers. Use the adjacent column on the spreadsheet to classify each activity according to its management process. Use the initials:

P = planning
O = organising
S = staffing
D = deciding
C = controlling
R = reporting (communicating)
B = budgeting (money and time)

Use the sort function to rearrange the activities according to the management process involved. Work out the percentage of time that managers spend on each process and answer the following questions:

- Which two activities take up most management time?

- The sample of a hundred activities was obtained from managers in manufacturing. To what extent would you expect the results to differ if the sample had been obtained from managers in a service industry?

- To what extent would you expect results to differ according to the level of managers involved?

Compare your answers with those given on the website associated with this book.

2 Use the Web to research the career of an entrepreneur in whom you are interested.

3 Self-management is a key skill which is not covered in depth in this book. Spend an hour surfing Youtube viewing appropriate clips. Remember, time management is an important skill. Some appropriate clips might be:

- how to keep a job: self management skills
- Daryl Cross – time management
- time management and the 80–20 rule
- 10 time management tips
- YP – Young Professional Time Management Tips
- why time management doesn't work

## Experiential activities

1 Form a discussion group to examine one or more of the following topics:

- the changes that have occurred in management work during the past 40 years (i.e. during the working life of someone who is just retiring)
- the changes that are likely to occur in management work during the next 40 years (i.e. during the working life of someone who is just starting a career)
- the skills needed for management work (start by brainstorming the skills and competencies needed) and writing them on a flip chart. Then list the skills and competencies according to their importance. Finally, compare your group's list with list of competencies from organisations – for example, see the list on page 20

2 Interview a manager (use your network of friends and relatives to identify someone who would help) and ask about:

- the people they supervise
- the people to whom they are responsible
- the way they spend their time at work

On the basis of this information decide whether they are junior, middle or senior managers. Also decide whether they are general or specialist managers. You should also identify the function (e.g. marketing, operations, finance, HR, etc.) in which they work. Check your decisions by asking your interviewee to name their management level and their management function.

3 Arrange (perhaps with the help of your college, university or careers service) to observe a practising manager at work for one or two days. In advance of your visit read Henry Mintzberg's (1973) book *The Nature of Managerial Work* (or at least a summary of it!). Keep notes on the roles that the manager occupies and the duration of his or her "working episodes". Compare your notes with the findings by Mintzberg.

## Recommended reading

Recommended readings will improve your understanding and be useful for assignments, seminars and tutorials. They will also guide your personal development and career.

1 Mintzberg, H.H. (1973) *The Nature of Managerial Work*, New York: Harper and Row. An old but classic text that has stood the test of time. It is usually sufficient to:

- quickly read the sections on the different management schools. Make a mental note of the general contents so that you can refer to them in the future
- read (but do attempt to memorise) the sections describing the 10 major management roles
- read the sections on brevity, variety and preference for action

A long read – at least four hours – interesting and of average difficulty. Highly recommended.

2 Rouleau, L. and Balogun, J. (2010) "Middle managers, strategic sense making and discursive competence", *Journal of Management Studies*, early view, 30 March. Gives four vignettes of entrepreneurs and the tasks of middle managers. Useful for seminars.

3 Katz, R.L. (1974) "Skills of an effective administrator", *Harvard Business Review*, **52** (94). Another classic text, which will help you understand the different levels of management and the skills that they require.

4 Hall, D.T. (1996) "Protean careers of the 21st century", *Academy of Management Executive*, **10** (4), 8–16. An excellent article which contrasts careers as viewed by Super with modern careers. Particularly good for developing your own career and understanding modern management.

5 Hindle, T. (2008) *Guide to Management Ideas and Gurus*, London: Economist Books. This is like an encyclopedia where management topics and leading thinkers are arranged in alphabetical order. It is easy reading. Highly recommended and relevant to all chapters. If you are studying management for more than a year, this book would be a good buy!

# CHAPTER 2

# The Organisational Context

## ❖ LEARNING OBJECTIVES

After reading this chapter you should have a clear knowledge of the world in which managers work. You should also have some appreciation of how the management context influences the way that managers work. In particular you should be able to:

❖ **list** at least five types of commercial organisations, three types of voluntary organisation and three types of public sector organisation. You should be able to name two specific examples of each

❖ **briefly describe** the advantages and causes of organisational culture

❖ **define** organisational culture and list, with examples, two main components

❖ **briefly describe** one- and two-dimensional ways of categorising organisational culture

❖ **describe** the work of Hofstede and Trompenaars and give some examples of the differences they found between countries

❖ **briefly describe** the difference between high context cultures and low context cultures

❖ **give** five examples of possible cultural misunderstanding in non-verbal communications

❖ **identify** four different types of legal systems and outline the impact this has on judicial and financial systems

❖ **define** globalisation and list the possible problems of globalisation

❖ **identify** five different stages of globalisation and put them in order on a scale simple–complex

Most aspects of management are generic, and good managers can use their skills in a wide range of situations. Managers do not operate in a vacuum and they need to adjust the way they work according to:

- the *type of organisation* where they work, e.g. sole trader, conglomerate or charity
- the *culture of the organisation* where they work
- the *national culture* of the unit or organisation where they work
- *globalisation* and its impact on organisations

These contexts have an important influence on what managers do, how they do it and the quality of both home and work life. A sole trader will need to cope with all aspects of management from basic operational activities to long-term strategic activities. The first part of this chapter outlines the different types of organisation where managers work. The simplest type involves sole traders. Sole trader, Dave Banks, is unusual because his work is very specialised and technical. But in many other ways he is typical of sole traders.

---

### CASE 2.1: *Dave Banks – an interesting sole trader*

Dave Banks is a sole trader specialising as a geological consultant in hydrogeological aspects of ground water. For example, he measures the purity of wells, streams and ponds, and advises how to eliminate impurities such as copper or zinc from the acid drainage caused by abandoned mines. He also uses deep boreholes to circulate water within strata where heat can be extracted. He has worked in London, Durham, Merseyside, Anglesey, Sudan, Zambia and Bucharest. A part of his work consists of training courses and research – in collaboration with the universities of Newcastle upon Tyne, Leeds and Tomsk, Russia. Like many "high-end sole traders" the visibility in all his work is promoted by authoring books (Banks, 2008).

His history shares many characteristics with "high-end" sole traders. He obtained a BA in natural sciences from Cambridge and went on an MSc in hydrogeology at Birmingham. He then gained practical experience at Thames Water authority in Reading and became a hydrogeologist. He obtained wider experience as a senior hydrogeologist in a global engineering consultancy that helps design infrastructure projects such as London Crossrail and hydroelectric projects in Laos. That company played an important role in the construction of the Mulberry harbours that were vital in the D-Day landings. Sole traders need a wide range of experience. In Dave Banks's case this included a review of water supply and sanitation in Darfur, Sudan. From 1998 until 2008 was a sole trader under the name of Holymoor, based in Chesterfield, Derbyshire. In 2008, the business grew sufficiently to justify converting Holymoor to a limited company, still operating out of Dave's home.

---

The way Dave works and his career are quite different to, say, that of a sales manager in a multinational organisation such as Rekitt-Benckisser (see Case 2.4). However, both travel extensively. They both experience many different national cultures and the impact of globalisation.

A junior manager in a pharmaceutical firm and a junior manager in a charity will share many attributes: they both need to transform resources so that they add value, they will both have frenetic pace of work – attending to a new thing every few minutes – and they will both have noticeably above average intelligence. However, their contexts, one in a leading edge technology puplic limited company (PLC) and the other in a world-class charity, will mean that they must manage differently. The former will have a lot of authority because he or she has formal power over wages or promotion. The latter will have little power over volunteers and he or she must be more aware of social and ethical issues. Similarly, there will be many similarities between a senior manager in a UK public enterprise and a similar organisation in, say, the Middle East. They will both be responsible for strategic decisions and have long timescales of discretion. However, cultural differences will mean that the former will be able to take decisions quickly, based on detailed written sources whilet the senior manager in the Middle East will need to proceed much more slowly in negotiations and to take non-written information such as family relationships or the location of meetings into account.

The other main contextual perspective on management, the historical context, is so big that it is described separately in the next chapter.

## 2.1 Types of organisation

Managers work in many different kinds of institutions. In broad terms these institutions can be grouped into three categories: commercial, voluntary and public sector. Below is a list of the main types of institutions in each group. Many of the types are well known or self-explanatory. Readers familiar with this subject can merely scan the list and perhaps read some of the more unusual entries such as limited partnerships, conglomerates and virtual organisations.

### Commercial institutions

- **Sole traders** (often 'called Fred in a shed') are people who run a one-man or a one-woman band. They handle all aspects of the organisation and are responsible to only themselves. Often, sole traders work from home. Sole traders are personally responsible for the debts they incur. Technically, sole traders are not managers: they are not usually responsible for the work of others – unless, of course, their trade is organising events and other people.

- A **franchise** is an arrangement between the owner of a product or service and a franchisee who owns the limited rights to make or sell it. The product is usually unique or has a strong brand image. The franchisee is relieved of the risk of developing and marketing the product, and often benefits from advice and supervision. However, the franchisee usually has to pay a substantial purchase price and a continuing proportion of the profits. Perhaps the best-known franchise in the world is the McDonald's fast-food chain.

- **Owner-managers** – the main difference between owner-managers and sole traders is that the former will employ other people. There are a large number of owner-manager organisations, especially in retailing. Most owner-managers employ up to 50 people. Above this limit it becomes increasingly difficult for one person to control all aspects of an organisation. Consequently, when organisations employ more than 50 people, it is likely that professional managers will be employed.

- **Partnerships** involve two or more people who jointly act as owner–managers. The key aspect of a partnership is the personal and unrestricted liability of each partner for the debts and obligations of the firm – whether or not he or she specifically agreed to them. One partner can be made personally liable for the business debts incurred by another partner. Partnerships are common in organisations providing professional services in architecture, accountancy and law. Many management consultancies are partnerships and there may be dozens or even hundreds of international partners. Generally, however, the number of partners is fewer than six. A well-known partnership, the John Lewis Partnership, is quite unusual since all employees who have a substantial length of service are partners. Many large organisations started as partnerships. Examples include Hewlett & Packard, Goldman & Sachs and Marks and Spencer. Eisner (2010) examines 10 effective partnerships and the reasons why they succeeded.

- **Limited partnerships** have existed in continental European countries and the USA for some time. They now exist in the UK. In limited partnerships each partner is only liable for the organisations debts to the extent of the capital they may contribute or agree to contribute.

- **Private companies** are owned by a small number of shareholders and the shares are not traded to the public. Private companies have the advantage that they are not required to make stringent disclosures of financial information. This involves less cost and it gives greater confidentiality. Many private companies start as owner-manager organisations. The original owner-manager may have passed some ownership to friends, family and business acquaintances. One of the most famous private companies is the BMW organisation.

- **Public limited companies** are owned by thousands of shareholders and the shares are traded to the public. In order to protect the public these organisations are required to submit detailed, stringent accounts. Public companies are often traded on national stock exchanges such as LSE (London) and NYSE (New York). Sometimes the stock exchanges specialise in various sectors of the economy such as technology (NASDAQ). Some public companies are set up merely to trade in the shares of other companies. These are usually called investment trusts. Large public companies, usually in the top 100 companies, are referred to as "blue-chip" companies. Obtaining a quotation is a long and costly procedure that involves establishing a track record and producing Articles of Association that regulate the way a company is governed. This elaborate process inhibits small or medium-sized organisations from obtaining a quotation. Consequently, small and medium companies are often listed on the Alternative Market (AIM). Belonging to the Alternative Market is less onerous and acts as a halfway house to a full listing.

- **Holding companies** are organisations that own a number of other companies. Often they have assets of many billions of pounds or dollars but they employ only a small number of people – most of the work is performed by the employees of subsidiary organisations. Most holding companies own subsidiaries that are related in some way. Sometimes there is a vertical structure whereby, for example, one subsidiary mines the raw materials, another subsidiary processes the raw material and a third subsidiary retails the product to the public. Sometimes there is a horizontal structure whereby, for example, one subsidiary manufactures a product in the southern region, another manufactures it in the northern region' etc. Conglomerates are usually large organisations and are often called corporations or groups. They are usually a type of holding company where the subsidiaries are involved in different industrial sectors. Conglomerates are usually formed when one company takes over several other companies in order to diversify risk, improve its market position or make additional use of plant and machinery. The formation of conglomerates was frequent between 1960 and 1980. Well-known conglomerates include AEG-AG, Agfa-Gevaert Group, Lever Brothers, Broken Hill Proprietary Company (BHP) and Virgin.

---

### CASE 2.2:  *A Virginal conglomerate*

In 1970, with pizazz and razzmatazz, Richard Branson founded Virgin Mail Order. The Virgin Record Shop, in Oxford Street followed close on its heels in 1971. Since then it has grown into a mature conglomerate. At the centre, Virgin Management Ltd consists of a relatively small number of people who are organised into specialist teams in London, New York and Sydney. They attend to three main activities:

- fastidiously number crunching the conglomerate's financial ratios to ensure assets get the best return

- analysing markets and spining public relations to maximise the value of the Virgin brand

- managing human resources so that Virgin's units are able to attract talented employees

The brand proved very successful and flexible. Today the Virgin conglomorate has more than 300 companies worldwide and employs many people in over 30 countries. The subsidiaries operate in a very wide range of sevice sectors. They include:

- transport (Virgin Atlantic Airways, Virgin Trains)
- telephone (Virgin Mobile India, Virgin Mobile France, etc)
- media (Virgin Radio International, Virgin Megastore, Virgin Books)
- vacations (Virgin Holidays, Virgin Experience Days, Virgin Balloon Flights, etc)
- finance (Virgin Money, Virgin Money Giving, Virgin Voucher)
- beverages(Virgin Drinks, Virgin Wines)

The Virgin conglomerate aims to provide better value than established competitors. Its name implies purity and lack of sexual experience. Some businesses, such as Virgin Bride – selling wedding dresses – were not successful. The oxymoronic subsidiary 'Virgin Condoms' was withdrawn after it failed!

---

- **Multinational corporations** are organisations that maintain significant, simultaneous, operations *in several countries* but are based in one home company. Well-known examples of multinational companies include the Kerry Group (Ireland), Shell Oil (Britain and Netherlands) and Nestlé (Switzerland).

---

**CASE 2.3:** *The Kerry group – an Irish multinational*

The Kerry group originated as a federation of farmer of co-operatives in County Kerry, western Ireland. In 1972 it joined forces with a state-owned dairy company and a US company that specialised in milk protein. The new company financed a new factory and initially focused on dairy processing. It grew organically over four decades and now has annual sales of about €4.5 billion.

It is not a conglomerate because it is focused in a single industrial sector, food products. A major advantage is its technological lead in the manufacture of food ingredients and flavours, which means that it sells products to other manufacturers who make crisps, sauces and beverages. The Kerry group also manufactures consumer goods that are well-known brands such as Wall's Sausages, Denny, Mattessons and Cheesestrings.

The Kerry group's headquarters remains in the delightful town of Tralee but it has a global reach. It employs over 20,000 people in 140 countries that cover Europe, North America, South America, Australasia and Asia. It has factories in over 20 countries.

---

■ **Virtual companies** are a relatively new kind of organisation. They occur when the various departments or components of an organisation are physically divided and separated by distances of miles. The component units may be separately owned. The separate components are linked together by computers and IT connections, which means that the separate components can work together as if they were one organisation. For example, a bookseller could set up a central computer that receives Internet orders. The computer could then search the inventories of several book wholesalers to locate a copy of the relevant book. It could then initiate the wholesaler's dispatch of the book to the customer. Finally, the computer could arrange to debit the customer's bank account. As far as the customers are concerned, they would be dealing with a large bookseller holding a huge inventory of books. In fact, they are dealing with a sophisticated computer system that links various components.

■ **Mutual organisations and co-operatives** are business association created for the mutual benefit of members. Often these are trading associations or financial institutions. In the UK they are sometimes called building societies or unit trusts. In the USA they are often called mutual funds. A co-operative is a legal entity that is owned and controlled by those who work for it or use it. There is usually some form of profit-sharing and the directors and managers are accountable to the members.

## Voluntary institutions

■ **Charities** are institutions or organisations set up to provide help, money and support to people and things in need. Many charities are small and are staffed by volunteers.

However, some charities have huge turnovers equalling those of substantial commercial organisations. Examples of large charities are the National Trust, Oxfam and Médecins sans Frontières. Much more about managing charitable institutions is given on the website associated with this book.

- **Clubs and associations** exist to increase the enjoyment of members. Some are managed by volunteers and are quite small. However, some clubs are large and employ professional managers. Some famous clubs are the MCC (Marylebone Cricket Club), the Garrick, the Liverpool Athenaeum and the Royal Channel Islands' Yacht Club. Some clubs become huge commercial successes and convert into commercial organisations. Typical examples include Manchester United Football Club and the Automobile Association.

- **Trade associations** and **professional bodies** are organisations which seek to protect and foster the interests of certain occupational groups and companies. To some extent they are very similar to political pressure groups since their aim is to increase the power of their members. These organisations can be substantial and wield considerable influence. They may also employ numerous managers. Associations fostering the interests of trades are usually called unions. Typical examples include the Communication Workers Union, and UNISON. Professional bodies tend to be called associations or societies. Typical examples include the Law Society, the British Psychological Society and the British Medical Association. Companies which share similar interests usually form a trade association to protect and foster their interests. Frequently they are called associations, federations or chambers. Typical examples include the Knitting Industries Federation, the Building Material Producers National Council and the Newspaper Publishers' Association. Usually trade associations and professional bodies start off as voluntary organisations but as their reputation and power increase it becomes virtually compulsory for members of the trade to enrol. For example, it is virtually impossible for a doctor or lawyer to practise unless they are a member of their professional body.

- **Political parties** and **pressure groups** aim to obtain sufficient power to change society. They aim to persuade other people to adopt and support their views so that they are then able to control resources they do not actually own. Senior managers in these organisations usually need a high level of charisma.

## Public sector organisations

- **Government departments** employ many managers. Usually these managers are responsible to representatives who are directly elected. The range of government departments is enormous. They include the diplomatic service, the armed forces, revenue collection, education and health. Usually government organisations are divided into two groups: central government and local government.

- **Public enterprises** are created by statute to govern nationalised businesses. Perhaps the most famous public enterprise is the Bank of England. Other public enterprises include the German Federal Railway and the Tennessee Valley Authority. These organisations do not have share capital and are owned by the government.

■ A **quango** is a quasi autonomous non-governmental organisation. They are semi-public administrative bodies which are set up by a government to achieve a "public good". Some are financed directly by a government and others are financed by a levy, which is often compulsory. A key feature of quangos is that the members are appointed, directly or indirectly, by the government and thus provide the government with huge powers of patronage. Quangos are often called agencies, commissions or councils. Typical examples of quangos are Health Service Trusts, the Health and Safety Executive, the Commission for Racial Equality and the Equal Opportunities Commission. Some lesser-known and esoteric quangos include the Crofters Commission, the Home Grown Cereals Authority and the Unrelated Live Transplant Regulatory Authority.

## 2.2 Organisational cultures

Apparently similar organisations can have quite different cultures. For example, a manager of a provincial newspaper will have quite a different work environment from that of a manager of a national newspaper based in London – even though they work in the same industry, produce a similar product and use similar technology. A great deal of the difference can be explained by the culture of the two organisations. One of the best-known definitions is given by Schein (2004):

> 66 the pattern of basic assumptions that a given group has invented discovered or developed and therefore taught to new members as the correct way to perceive think and feel in relation to problems. 99

In other words, culture is "the way we do things round here". Schein's definition focuses upon the intangible aspects of culture. However, as Figure 2.1 shows, it has both tangible and intangible components.

Tangible aspects of culture include the physical layout of the organisation. For example, an organisation with a culture that emphasises status might have separate canteens for

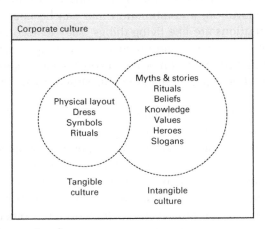

**FIGURE 2.1** Components of corporate culture

managers and workers. The intangible aspects of culture are usually more important and more numerous. They include shared values, shared knowledge and a fund of shared stories of past events and heroes.

Organisational cultures perform very **useful functions**. They help integrate the organisation and make sure that all members are "on the same wavelength". They help communication and give a sense of purpose. It has been claimed that a strong corporate culture helps to increase performance efficiency. However, research by Kotter and Heskett (1992) suggests that the relationship between corporate culture and performance is weaker than earlier claims suggest.

Corporate cultures do not happen at random. Schneider (1987) believes that the main *cause of a culture* is the personality and style of the person who sets up the organisation. If the founder has a fluid, ethical style with an interest in basics (e.g. Anita Roddick, founder of Bodyshop) the organisation will be imbued with a fluid, ethical culture that emphasises products. This initial culture is then transmitted to future generations by the ASA process: first, the organisation attracts applications from people who hold similar values. It then selects those who adhere most closely to its cultural norms. Finally, there is a process of attrition whereby employees who do not fit into the culture are encouraged to leave. Schneider's ASA theory does not fully explain the *transmission of organisational culture*. There is a socialisation process by which newcomers are taught the appropriate way of doing things and receive rewards, such as promotion, when they perform according to the organisation's culture.

## Organic versus mechanistic cultures

Half a century ago Burns and Stalker (1961), identified two main kinds of organisational culture: mechanistic and organic. In **mechanistic cultures** the organisation is like a machine with everything tightly controlled and very predictable. Jobs are closely defined and highly specialised. Efficiency is paramount. These organisations were often appropriate in the mass-production and relatively stable environments of the first half of the twentieth century. However, mechanistic organisations have one big disadvantage: they are often inflexible and stifle innovation; a combination that can be fatal in a rapidly changing world. **Organic organisations** are like living things. They tend to grow and develop into new forms, they respond to their environments and, perhaps, may be a little messy or chaotic. Organic organisations thrive on problem-solving and innovation. Jobs are defined loosely and many regulations are informal. Organic structures are better adapted to a fast-changing world.

In the1960s and 1970s organisational psychologists identified many dimensions of organisational culture. Some are shown in Table 2.1. The list is still relevant today: it gives dimensions that can be taken into account when writing assignments or preparing discussions on organisational culture. The list is too long to be used in its entirety: it will be necessary to focus on three or four of the most relevant factors. Questionnaires to measure these organisational characteristics are described by Smith (1981). Generally it is better to use established questionnaires in projects rather than develop something new. It will then be possible to compare results between studies.

| Organisational characteristic | Authors of relevant questionnaires |
|---|---|
| Organisational context (history, origin) | Pugh and Hickson (1976) |
| Location, geographical distribution, size, ownership and control, etc. | Pugh and Hickson (1976); Litwin and Stringer (1968) |
| Organisational structure | Reimann (1974); |
| Role variety; specialisation | Tyler (1973) |
| Role conflict; role ambiguity | Rizzo, House and Lirtzman (1970); Hage and Aiken (1968); Reimann (1974) |
| Centralisation | Reimann (1974); Hage and Aiken (1968); Pugh and Hickson (1976) |
| Decision-making style (participation, timeliness, level, etc.) | Likert (1967); House and Rizzo (1972); White and Ruh (1973) |
| Control processes and tolerance of error | Likert (1967); House and Rizzo (1972); Hage and Dewar (1973); Payne & Pheysey (1971) |
| Orientation towards the wider community | Payne and Pheysey (1971) |
| Innovation and risk | Litwin and Stringer (1968); Payne and Pheysey (1971) |

TABLE 2.1 Some aspects of organisational culture

## Strong versus weak cultures

A number of writers (Collins and Porras, 1994; Deal and Kennedy, 1982; Perrow, 1979; Schein, 2004) suggest that one of the most important distinction concerns **strong** and **weak** cultures (Table 2.2).

| STRONG organisational cultures | WEAK organisational cultures |
|---|---|
| ■ Most people have basic beliefs and values that *agree* with the organisation's values | Subcultures or people within an organisation have values and beliefs that are different or conflict with the organisation's values |
| ■ Values and beliefs are *consistent* and coherent | Values are vague or contradictory |
| ■ Values and beliefs are *comprehensive* and cover most things | Values are patchy |

TABLE 2.2 A contrast between strong and weak organisational cultures

A strong culture has been defined by Robbins (1998) as

66 one that is internally consistent, is widely shared, and makes it clear what it expects and how it wishes people to behave 99

It was generally thought that strong organisational cultures were better than weak ones – especially in volunteer organisations and charities. A strong culture means that people are "on the same wavelength". They can communicate speedily, they act as a cohesive group, they do not challenge organisational decisions and so these decisions can be made very quickly. Often, strong cultures are led by charismatic leaders. However, some writers such as Schein (2004) have noted that strong cultures can be dysfunctional. The strong structure tends to foster a conservative approach. New ideas have difficulty gaining a foothold and people therefore have difficulty thinking "outside the organisational box". Others have noted that "groupthink" is prevalent in strong organisational cultures. Perrow (1979) believed that strong organisational cultures could be coercive and manipulative because aggressive behaviour may be used to enforce conformity.

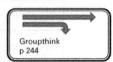
Groupthink p 244

In an organisation with a weak culture people follow their own ideas beliefs and customs. This may be beneficial in innovative organisations or those organisations whose environment changes rapidly. This can work effectively *provided* that there are clear common goals – otherwise there may be little sense of direction as different parts of an organisation pull in different directions. The organisation may respond to this situation by using rules or extra supervision – which may alienate many employees.

## The competing values framework (Cameron and Quinn)

Cameron and Quinn (2006) developed a framework based on the idea that organisational cultures largely arise from two values, each of which have two poles that compete with each other: they are:

| | | |
|---|---|---|
| ■ Flexibility, dynamism and discretion which is important in organisations that must change and adapt | *versus* | ■ Control and stability which is important in organisations that succeed by operating in a standard, structured and predictable way |
| ■ External orientation which is seen in organisations who are sensitive to the external environment and external competitors | *versus* | ■ Internal orientation where building unity and integration are major concerns |

In the time-honoured way beloved by many organisational theorists, Cameron and Quinn placed two dimensions on a grid to produce four quarters. Each quarter was said to represent an organisational culture, as shown in Figure 2.2.

A **clan culture** is sometimes called a collaborative culture. A well-documented example is given by the courier company, DHL (Chan, 1997). It often gives the feeling of a family firm.

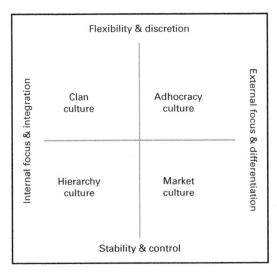

**FIGURE 2.2** Cameron and Quinn's competing values framework

Goals are achieved by consensus and agreement by involving as many people as possible in decision-making. Loyalty and cohesion are highly valued. In return, the organisation looks after employees – frequently helping them to develop their potential for promotion. An organisation with a clan culture tends to have a flat structure with diffused authority. Co-ordination is achieved via shared ideas and values rather than rules and regulations. Clan relationships engender a feeling of safety which, in turn, encourages flexibility and growth. Most employees prefer clan cultures. A classic example of an organisation with a clan culture is the John Lewis Partnership.

**Hierachy cultures** are sometimes called *control cultures*. They tend to be seen in large or bureaucratic organisations such as tax offices or government. They may also be seen in large manufacturing organisations such as Toyota and McDonald's. People in these organisations will use standard operating procedures (SOPs) to produce large numbers of products or services that have a lot of similarity. Also, it is likely that there are a large number of clearly defined management levels. Promotion often depends upon an employee's ability to know and navigate their way around a set of rules. These organisations tend to occur in stable business environments,

**Adhocracy cultures** are sometimes called *creative cultures*. They tend to be seen in organisations that transform ideas and data rather than things (e.g. Google) and in entrepreneurial organisations. They are also seen in aerospace, IT, the media, consultancy and advertising. Organisational charts are either transitory or non-existent. Similarly the allocation of office space changes very frequently. In an adhocratic organisation the management tends to respond to urgent problems rather than planning to avoid them. Adhocractic cultures have very little structure and are very flexible. This enables them to exploit new ideas and technologies so that they quickly capture market share.

Organisations with **market cultures** are sometimes called *competitive organisational* cultures. They value stability and control but they focus closely on the external market.

Often they face severe competition from organisations at home or abroad. They are transactional. Astute relations with suppliers, customers, unions and law-makers are vital. They strive to compete by being excellent in managing relations through partnership and positioning. Performance, in terms of profitability, market share or customer base is paramount!

For convenience, this discussion of organisational culture has assumed that all organisation show only one, pure, culture. Nothing could be further from the truth. In fact, most organisations are amalgams of different cultures, albeit one type of culture might predominate. Further, different parts of the same organisation may have different cultures. For example, the finance function may, rightly, have a hierarchy (control) culture, while the salesforce have a market (competitive) culture. Divisional managers will have the unhappy task of reconciling such differences. Finally, this discussion has focused on the major trends in thinking on organisational cultures. However it should be noted that other writers consider issues such as risk-taking, teamwork, attention to detail, time orientation and a proactive approach to change to be important issues.

## Relevance of organisational culture

Academic writings on organisational culture are relevant for three reasons:

- **Managers need to understand the culture of the organisation that employs them.** Even if they are technically proficient, intelligent and have the "right" personality and skills, they need to deploy these assets in a way that is appropriate to their organisational culture. For example, managers in an adhocratic organisation may be brilliant in devising rules and procedures but they are unlikely to succeed. Using their intelligence to be creative and adaptive would be better.

- **Managers need to foster an organisational culture that is appropriate to their business environment.** For example, a manager in an industry that is stable and where the unit costs are vital should encourage a control culture rather than an adhocracy.

- **Organisational culture matters in mergers and acquisitions.** A large proportion of mergers and acquisitions fail. The main reason for such failures is incompatible organisational cultures. When mergers or acquisitions are contemplated, due attention must be given to the congruence between organisational cultures or the ways in which the cultures of one (or both) organisations can be changed.

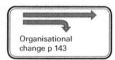

Organisational change p 143

## 2.3 National cultures

A large organisation such as IBM will have its own organisational culture but, since it operates in many countries, it will also need to take international cultures into account. The dominant western management style focusing on the achievement of overt results in the shortest possible time does not go down well in some countries. It is impossible to follow the western pattern of working 9 a.m. to 5 p.m., Monday to Friday in many parts of the world. In some countries a siesta is taken between noon and 4 p.m. and work then continues until, say, 8 p.m. In other countries Friday or Saturday are holy days when businesses are closed. In many western countries enthusiastic shaking of hands between negotiators is a sign that a deal has been reached; in some countries in the Middle East it is a sign that serious negotiations are about to begin. These differences are of great interest to multinational organisations. IBM, for example, commissioned a Dutchman, Geert Hofstede, to study such differences in 72 countries. His book *Culture's Consequences*, published in 1980 made him the most famous researcher in the field. Hofstede (2005) likens national cultures to "software of the mind". In essence he claims that there are five main dimensions to international cultures, which are fully described on Hofstede's website: *www.geert-hofstede.com*. In approximate order of size, they are:

- **Power distance (PD)** – the extent to which a culture accepts an unequal distribution of power. In high power distance cultures some people in an organisation will have much more power than others and this will be accepted.

- **Individualism (IDV)** – the opposite of collectivism. In individualistic cultures, the ties between individuals are loose and everyone is expected to look after themselves and their families.

- **Masculinity (MAS)** – the extent to which people are assertive, ambitious, competitive and wanting to accumulate wealth or possessions.

- **Uncertainty avoidance (UA)** – a culture's dislike of uncertainty and risk. It indicates the extent to which a culture programs its members to avoid unstructured, unusual, unknown situations.

- **Long-term orientation (LTO)** only emerges from data from students in 23 countries – mainly those with a Confucian heritage. When detected, it concerns perseverance over a long time. Things do not need to be rushed and another opportunity is to be expected – *mañana!*

Hofstede and other researchers have collected scores for many countries and they are available from his website. Figure 2.3 illustrates the results from the UK, Australia, Brazil, the Middle East and China.

It is no surprise that the cultures of the *UK* and *Australia* are very similar. They are characterised by a very high scores on individualism. This indicates that individual rights are very highly valued and that individuals tend to form a large number of looser relationships. The high score on masculinity suggests that people will be assertive and competitive. Low scores on long-term orientation suggest that punctuality is expected and that decisions can be made fairly rapidly (but not as rapidly as in the USA). Change can also be made more rapidly than in many countries. *China* has a very high score for long-term orientation, which means that people feel little need to rush when making decisions or friends. China also has a low score on individualism and things tend to be seen from a group perspective. Loyalty to one's group or family is paramount The high power-distance scores suggests a high level of inequality of power in Chinese society. Large power-distance and uncertainty avoidance indicates a society that has restricted upward mobility. Rules, laws and regulations are developed by those in power to reinforce their own control. In an effort to eliminate uncertainty, strong rules and regulations are often implemented. *Brazil* has a cultural profile similar to other Latin American countries. It has a very low

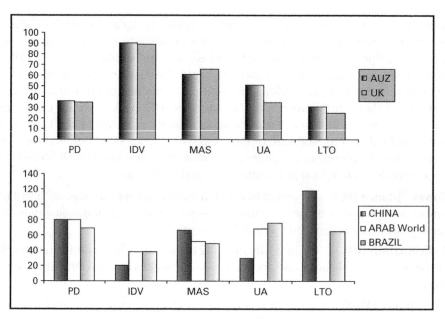

**FIGURE 2.3** Scores of selected countries on Hofstede's cultural dimensions

individualism score which indicates a collectivist approach to many things. Further, it is a society that tries to eliminate uncertainty, sometimes using strict rules and regulations. The moderately high score for power-distance suggests an acceptance of inequality in society. Contrary to the "macho" stereotype of South American countries, Brazil's moderate score on masculinity is not of particular note. An excellent site containing Hofstede profiles for many countries is *www.cyborlink.com*.

## CRITICAL THINKING 2.1 *Hofstede's critics*

Hofstede's work on international cultures is not universally accepted. There are five main criticisms (Jones, 2007 – a good read!):

- Surveys are not sufficiently sensitive measures of deep values. Hofstede (2002) rebutted this criticism by pointing to supporting studies using other methodologies.

- Cultures are not homogeneous – most nations are made up of subcultures whose characteristics are hidden when national averages are used. Hofstede attempted to rebut this by asserting national averages are usually the only data that are available and they are better than nothing.

- Some dimensions, especially masculinity, change according to "political influences" from time to time. Hence results change from decade to decade and results of Hofstede's 1980 study are now obsolete. Hofstede's rebuttal points out that the roots of a culture are centuries old and do not change significantly within a few decades.

■ Results were based on one company (IBM) and could not provide information on the cultural system of a country. Hofstede attempted to rebut this by claiming that differences between national cultures were apparent by studying the same organisation in different countries.

■ Four or five dimensions are not enough to capture the richness of cultures. Hofstede replies that many of the additional suggestions correlate highly with his dimensions and therefore amount to the same thing. More cultural dimensions are possible but they will be less important.

■ The analysis was inadequate because some questions were used on more than one scale and many statistics were based on a small sample of 40 datapoints (countries). This means correlations are multiplied and subject to huge random error. However, other people have replicated Hofstede's work and found four dimensions that were very similar.

Jones concludes that the majority of Hofstede's findings have weathered the storms of time and will be a good guide to culture.

Hofstede's work has been so influential that it has overshadowed other important work on international culture. For example, the dimensions of international culture have also been studied by Trompenaars (1993). Trompenaars's research was more systematic and scientific. It involved 15 000 people from 47 countries. He came to the view that cultures differed in three main ways: relationships between people, attitudes towards time and attitudes towards the environment.

*Relationships between people* is the most complex way that cultures differ. Trompenaars differentiated five sub-dimensions:

■ **Universalism vs particularism** reflects a culture's emphasis on rules and their consistent application (universalism) or its emphasis on flexibility and bending the rules depending upon the person and his or her circumstances (particularism).

■ **Individualism vs collectivism** concerns the emphasis a culture places upon the individual and his or her rights and responsibilities (individualism) or the interests of the group and achieving a consensus of opinion (collectivism).

■ **Unemotional vs emotional** is the degree to which a culture stresses detachment and objectivity in decision-making (unemotional) or whether subjective feelings are a part of decisions (emotional). This dimension may be related to universalism versus particularism.

■ **Specific vs diffuse** is the extent to which a culture stresses in-depth, intense relationships (specific) or a wider range of superficial relationships (diffuse). Again this may be an aspect of universalism versus particularism; universalism is more likely when there are diffuse relationships.

■ **Achievement vs prescription** reflects the extent to which a culture rewards people on the basis of their achievement or their social standing, celebrity and connections.

Trompenaars' second major dimension of cultural differences was the *way that time was viewed* – particularly the way that the present is viewed in relation to the past. Western cultures tend to see time as a linear **synchronic** dimension. There is a clear past, present and future. Present time is precious and must not be wasted. Decisions need to be taken quickly without losing time. In **sequential** cultures, time is a passing series of recurring events where opportunities will recur. Consequently there is a relaxed attitude to time and appointments – a philosophy of *manyana*.

Trompenaars' third dimension of cultural differences focuses on the *relationship with the environment*. In **inner-directed** cultures people see themselves as separate from the environment and attempt to control it for their personal benefit. On the other hand, in **outer-directed** cultures people see themselves as a part of nature. They try to live in harmony with nature and are more likely to "go with the flow".

Hall (1976) also studied international cultures and divided them into low-context and high-context cultures. **Low-context cultures** are typified by the UK, Canada, Germany and the USA. Important communication uses the written and spoken word. A message will be encoded very precisely. To decode the message the recipient needs to listen and read very carefully. **High-content cultures** include Japan and many Mediterranean countries. Only a part of the message is communicated in words. The rest must be inferred from contextual cues such as physical setting, the body language and even previous history. High-context communication takes considerable time. People from low-context cultures may not understand this and they may be perceived as pushy, hurried and even rude.

Other researchers contrast the way that different countries view **conflict** and **harmony**. Some organisations, especially those based in Australia and the UK, regard disagreement as a healthy sign. Employees are encouraged to discuss openly their reservations and conflicting views. There is a cultural belief that suppressing disagreements leads to longer-term problems and prevents good ideas from being adopted. Some organisations based in Asian countries have cultures that emphasise harmony. There is a cultural belief in preserving present methods and fostering traditional social relationships. Organisational cultures may also differ in a way that they deal with severe competition from home and abroad.

At a more specific and practical level differences in verbal and non-verbal communication can plague meetings where people from different national cultures are present. Some examples (see Dubrin, 2003) are:

■ UK managers understate positive emotions. The comment "not bad at all" is likely to be interpreted by Americans as lack of enthusiasm.

■ UK managers dislike personal questions and tend to stand further from people during business meetings.

■ French managers expect to be greeted by formal titles for a number of meetings until everyone is well acquainted.

■ The American "OK" symbol using the thumb and fore finger is a vulgar gesture in Spain and many Latin American countries.

- Attempts to impress Brazilian managers by greeting them in Spanish will be counterproductive. The language of Brazil is Portuguese!
- Shaking hands or embracing at the start of the meeting is considered offensive by the Japanese.
- Presenting small gifts when conducting business with Japanese managers is acceptable but it is offensive behaviour when conducting business with Chinese managers.
- In Arab countries, it is rude to sit down in a way that shows one's host the bottom of your feet or shoes.

## National legal and financial contexts

International managers must also work within the context of national differences in legal and accounting systems. Briefly, there are four main types of legal system:

- **Codified law** is sometimes called civil law where a nation sets up a legislature to devise a comprehensive set of laws based upon their view of justice and morality. Countries with codified law include Brazil, France, Germany, Japan, Mexico, the Netherlands and Switzerland. Civil law starts with abstract ideas that aim to formulate general rules for the future. These general ideas become more specific and practical as they are developed. It is a "top-down system". The archetypal example is the Roman code set up by Emperor Justinian. Napoleonic and Germanic codes are other examples. Trials are dominated by an elite of judges who have a high level of independence from politicians. Juries are sometimes used in important cases.

    *Financial context*: countries with codified law tend to favour raising finance by credit: from banks, rich families or the state. Gearing is usually high. Often, even listed companies rely heavily on these sources. The banks etc. usually appoint several board members. Consequently, they will have inside knowledge of an organisation's financial situation. The need for legal safeguards and formal financial reports is usually less. Therefore, in these countries there are fewer accountants and accounting rules give greater focus to taxation issues (Nobes and Parker, 2006).

- **Common law** is mainly developed by judges who make specific decisions in response to specific situations. These decisions are taken into account in making further judgements, i.e. they set a precedent for future cases. Gradually a consistent system is built up to cover most situations. Sometimes the legislature will intervene to systematise judgements and remove anomalies. It is a "bottom-up" system. In the courtroom, career layers are as influential as career judges and they are very independent from politicians. Juries are very important in deciding matters of fact. Countries using a system of common law include the UK, Australia, Cameroon, Ghana, India, Ireland, Malaysia, New Zealand, Pakistan and the USA.

    *Financial context*: countries using common law tend to favour raising finance by offering equity such as via the stock market. For example, for every million Germans there are 7.9 listed companies whereas there are 44.4 listed companies for every million people in the UK. Consequently, gearing will be relatively low (107 per cent for the UK but 236 per cent for Germany). In order to protect shareholders, requirements for reporting a company's finances will be high and it will be necessary to employ hordes of accountants who need to grapple with *both* taxation and financial issues.

■ **Islamic law** is sometimes called **religious law** and it is based in religious writings such as the Qur'an. Lawyers play a relatively minor role and the judges have religious training as well as legal training. Juries are not allowed and the courts are not very independent of religious leaders. Sharia law has some similarities to common law in the sense that it is based on previous cases and precedent. Indeed, it has been suggested that English common law was inspired by Islamic law. There are two main branches of Islamic Law; Sunni and Shia. The classic example of a legal system based on Islamic law is Saudi Arabia but there are many other examples in the Middle East and northern and eastern Africa.

*Financial context*: for many years the development of financial institutions in countries that adopted Islamic law was severely restricted by the sharia's prohibition against payment or collection of interest. However, experiments with Islamic banking during the 1960s has resulted in over 300 Islamic banking institutions. A number of ways are used to overcome the ban on interest. For example, instead of charging interest on a loan to buy property, the lender buys the property and then sells it back at a higher price (the original price plus the equivalent of interest) and the original owner repays this higher price over a number of years. Other approaches involve banks giving depositors "a gift" or paying "rent" rather than interest.

■ **Socialist law** is sometimes called communist law, which, like codified law, is based on statutes devised by a legislature. Party members play an important part in deciding disputes so the courts have only limited independence from politicians and juries are rarely used for important cases. The primary example of a country using socialist law is the Soviet Union.

*Financial context*: in a pure socialist state, the state owns and controls all financial resources. However, it was usually convenient for the state to set up several banks. Usually there would be at least a state bank, such as the Russian Gosbank (which handled all significant transactions) and a people's savings bank such as the Russian Sberbank. There may be other banks for specific purposes such as construction (Stoybank) and foreign trade (Vneshtorgbank). However, most socialist states now also have commercial banks or at least have allowed investors to purchase a share in previously state-owned banks (e.g. a Hong Kong billionaire was allowed to buy a 20 per cent stake in the Bank of China). Despite such relaxation the state still controls the economy and may fiercely restrict foreign control. For example, in China there are A and B shares. Foreigners have a restricted ability to trade in A shares which are more numerous.

To make matters more complex some countries have a mixture of the two systems. For example, most of Canada adopts common law while Quebec uses codified law. Scandinavian countries have a system that is a *mélange* of common law and codified law, as does Scotland. China has a mixture of socialist law and codified law (derived largely from the German version) and Hong Kong follows the English common law.

Yet more complications are added by specific pieces of legislation, especially in employment legislation where there may be differences in legal aspects of industrial relations, security of employment, equal opportunities and health and safety. There are also major differences in company law.

## 2.4 The global context and globalisation

This chapter has set out the contexts in which managers need to work. It started with the relatively small issues of the type of organisation and the organisational context and worked its way up to international contexts. A generation ago, this would have been sufficient. Few managers would have to work or deal with more than two or three countries. Today things are different. It is not unusual for managers to deal with a dozen countries across several continents because trade has become global.

### Definition and history of globalisation

There are many definitions of globalisation such as:

> A de-coupling of space and time, emphasising that with instantaneous communications, knowledge and culture can be shared around the world simultaneously.

> A process in which geographic distance becomes a factor of diminishing importance in the establishment and maintenance of cross-border economic, political and socio-cultural relations.

A more succinct definition by Fitzroy (2001) defines globalisation as:

> A worldwide drive towards a globalised economic system dominated by supranational corporate trade and banking institutions that are not accountable to democratic processes or national governments.

These definitions highlight the strong influence of communications, the shrinking of geographical distances and the flow of resources across national boundaries, together with globalisation's impact on political systems. They reflect the impact that globalisation has on virtually every person on the planet. As early as 1962 McLuhan recognised that the world had become "a global village". In the past, humankind existed in villages where they had personal knowledge of other people and events. McLuhan, considering the spread of radio communications in the 1920s, claimed that with the new media we could have the equivalent knowledge of people on the other side of the world. Today, we learn of far-off events, such as an earthquake in Haiti, almost as quickly as we learn of events in our own community. In this sense, the world is now one large village.

### Reasons for and advantages of globalisation

The reasons for globalisation are simple. Different countries have different advantages that allow them to make things more cheaply and better than other countries. For example,

Saudi Arabia can produce oil, Australia cannot. Australia can graze sheep, Saudi Arabia cannot. It makes sense for Saudi Arabia to concentrate on extracting oil and buying sheep from Australia. If all countries focus upon what they do best and trade with other countries for things they do less well, the whole world is better off: petrol gets cheaper and so do lamb chops! Barriers to trade make the world less efficient. While these principles are true, the real situation is more complex.

The reasons for globalisation at the *organisational level* are similar but they show themselves in the form of economies of scale, bigger markets and exploitation of resources:

- In many situations there are **economies of scale** if a service or product is made in high volumes. Often the market in one country is not big enough so organisations try to get customers from other countries. Indeed, in some industries it would not be economic to attempt *any* production on the basis of national demand. For example, despite the fact that it is situated in the USA, the biggest single market for aircraft, Boeing would not have developed the 747 if other markets were closed. Even if it captured 100 per cent of the American market it would not have sold enough aircraft to cover development costs. At a more mundane level there are huge advantages if global suppliers, such as Rekitt Benckiser, produce fast-moving consumer goods.

### CASE 2.4: *Reckitt Benckiser – a truly globalised company*

When Isaac Reckitt rented a starch mill in Hull, on the east coast of England, in 1840 he could not have dreamt that he would be a founding father of one of the most globalised companies on the planet. Today, Reckitt Benckiser is a very successful player in the fast-moving consumer goods (FMCG) market. Fast-moving consumer goods are low-cost products that sell very quickly. They include toiletries, cleaners and soft drinks. The market is very competitive and Reckitt Benckiser's competitors include giants such as Unilever, Procter & Gamble and Colgate-Palmolive. People may not have heard of Reckitt Benckiser but it is almost certain that they have used its products. The company derives about 80 per cent of its income from 17 "power products" which include Dettol, Clearasil, Strepsils and Harpic. Fifteen million of its products are sold every day.

The company's headquarters is in Slough, near London Airport. However, its reach is truly global. Its products are sold in approximately 200 countries and it has offices and factories in over 60 countries. The C-suite executives (those who have the word "Chief" in their job title) has a global composition too. The chief executive is Dutch. This is not particularly exceptional since a substantial proportion of global companies have CEOs from the Netherlands. (The country has a historical global outlook. One of the first global organisations was the Dutch East India Company. Perhaps people from a small country are forced to think internationally!) Further, the nine-member executive committee includes seven different nationalities.

In an article for the *Harvard Business Review* (Brecht, 2010, p.103 – a good read) the CEO, Bart Brecht, describes how they built a company "without borders". In every country Reckitt Benckiser has employees of many nationalities: the UK business is run by an Italian;

the German business is run by an American; the American business is run by a Dutchman; the Russian business is run by a Frenchman and so on. Forty-nine different nationalities are represented in the top 400 managers. This level of globalisation among senior executives requires streamlined organisational policies. There is only one employment contract and there is only one set of rules covering the remuneration, pension rules, medical plans, etc. However, Reckitt Benckiser funds whatever schooling an employee chooses for their children. All this makes international transfers easily. The company has a distinct approach with students who have studied in a "foreign country". It may help them get work permits in the country where they have been studying because the fact that they have travelled to study mean they are internationally minded. Many companies assume that, after a "tour" abroad "expats" will return home. Reckitt Benckiser does not make this assumption. It focuses on placing executives in the best job for them, regardless of country.

A major advantage of the international variety at Reckitt Benckiser is the synergy to develop new projects. For example, a brand manager in Korea noticed that some stores were using an automatic scent disperser. It was crude but he thought it could form a new product. Further development was a substantial gamble for Reckitt Benckiser. The price would be higher than existing products; the company would have to develop expertise in electronic interval timers. Consumer tests were very positive. Within 12 months Air Wick Freshmatic was "flying off the shelves" in 30 countries and Reckitt Benckiser had overseen the building of a new factory in China where it could be mass produced. There are now many variations that are sold in 85 countries and the product generates well over £200 million per year for the company.

- Other organisations "go global" when they have **saturated their home market**. McDonald's is a classic example. It had fully exploited the economies of scale when there were, say, five or six restaurants within a 50-mile radius of any sizeable town and the American market was saturated. The only alternative to stagnation was to establish restaurants abroad in the UK, Australasia, Hong Kong and even, eventually, in France and Russia.

- Some companies "go global" in search of **cheaper resources**. The colonial powers established their empires in order to have cheaper access to gold, sugar, cotton, tobacco, tea or rubber. A few companies still establish overseas operations in order to have cheap access to physical resources such as gasoline, aluminium or timber. However, today firms may "go global" to gain access to cheap labour for, say, call centres or producing trainers.

    Relocations are usually greeted warmly by recipient countries. Although the wages paid by multinational companies are usually much lower than in an organisation's "home" country, they are usually significantly higher than wages in the recipient country – bringing advantages for both workers and their country. In other cases organisations have moved production facilities to less-developed countries because they have less onerous regulations. For example, Union Carbide has been accused of having lower safety and environmental standards at its plant in Bhopal than in a similar plant in West Virginia.

■ Some organisations "go global" to **provide a 24-hour service**. By siting offices in each of the three main time zones (London, New York and Tokyo) they will be able to trade throughout the day.

---

### CASE 2.5: *Footloose and in search of cheaper labour*

In the past few decades firms such as Nike, Bennetton, Gap, Motorola and Dyson have moved manufacturing units to places such as Taiwan, the Philippines, Mexico and Malaysia in search of cheaper labour. More recently many manufacturing organisations have moved their production plants to China where labour costs are only a fraction of those in the developed world. Another example of an organisation seeking lower labour costs is Volkswagen's decision to move the production of its Polo cars to Bratislava, Slovakia. Years previously it moved production of Ibiza cars to Spain in order to avoid the high costs of labour in Germany. By 2002 Spanish labour costs had risen. Volkswagen then decided to move some production to Bratislava. Similarly, many American corporations such as Microsoft sited administrative centres dealing with billing and issuing licences in Ireland in order to take advantages of lower labour costs and government inducements. However, now that Irish labour costs have risen, these companies are relocating their administrative centres to Asia. Indeed, in 2004 Ireland became the second largest exporter of technology jobs worldwide. The most globalised countries in the world are Belgium, Austria, the Netherlands and Switzerland (KOF, 2010).

---

## Stages of globalisation

Organisations rarely jump from domestic operations to operations on a truly global scale. Usually a company's path follows a discernible pattern with six main stages, but companies do not necessarily pass through all six stages.

The first step is usually **importing** supplies from another country. Nowadays, this is very easy. Later an organisation may **export** goods by setting up a **website** or **advertising** in another country. More proactively, it can employ **agents**. Employing an agent needs to be managed with care so that the agent is motivated towards selling the organisation's products rather than promoting a large number of other products – including those of a competitor!

In a **licence agreement** a local company is allowed to use specialised knowledge and processes (e.g. a patent) to make a product or produce a service. Licensing agreements offer a relatively easy method of global expansion. Licences are operated by people from the second country who use their own resources and capital. However, when the agreement expires, the second company may set up as a competitor. A **franchise** is a special kind of licence.

**Joint ventures** represent the next stage of globalisation and they often give companies quick access to new markets because they can use existing distribution channels. They also provide quick access to increased production capacity. Possibly the main advantage of a joint venture is sharing the risk. Unfortunately, about half of all joint ventures experience difficulties. These usually arise if there is a large imbalance in the expertise, where one partner's contribution is disproportionate or where integration and control is poor.

---

### CASE 2.6: *Examples of joint global ventures*

Airbus is a classic example of a large-scale joint venture. The American giant, Boeing, was so dominant that companies outside the USA were not be able to mount an effective challenge. However, large aircraft manufacturers in France, Germany, England and Spain formed a joint venture that would be able to build a new series of aircraft (such as the super jumbo A380) and overtake Boeing in world markets. Bilateral joint ventures, where one company finds one partner in a host country, are more usual. For example, in 2004 Siemens Mobile signed a contract with Shenzhen Huawei Technology Company, one of China's leading telecommunication equipment manufacturers, to develop wireless-based communication products.

---

**Acquisition** is a bold globalisation strategy. It involves buying an existing organisation in another country. For example, a relatively small UK oil exploration company Paladin PLC was able to expand into the Timor Sea off north-west Australia by purchasing existing interests from the Australian multinational BHP Billiton. Acquisitions provide very speedy and full control over resources in another country. These include trained personnel, their tacit knowledge, an existing customer base and, perhaps, well-known brands. Unfortunately, acquisitions frequently fail.

Finally, an organisation may expand by starting and **developing their own foreign operations**. For example, when, in 1911, the Ford Motor Company wanted to expand outside the USA it set up an entirely new manufacturing operation at Trafford Park in Manchester. Today such developments are often called greenfield ventures. Greenfield ventures have the advantage that the new organisation can be set up in exactly the way the parent organisation wishes. Governments will often offer substantial inducements. The main disadvantage with a greenfield venture is that it takes a considerable time to mature.

When more than 25 per cent of an organisation's sales are derived outside its country of origin it is known as a **multinational corporation (MNC)**. Technically, a multinational corporation is the same as a **transnational corporation (TNC)**. However, the latter term tends to be used with large organisations operating on a truly global scale and where the majority of their income is outside the country of origin. A classic example of a transnational organisation is Nestlé, where over 98 per cent of its income is generated outside its country of origin, Switzerland. Philips is another example of a transnational company. It is estimated that Philips earns over 94 per cent of its income outside the Netherlands.

## CRITICAL THINKING 2.2 *Pitfalls of globalisation?*

Organisations that operate in several countries encounter difficulties. In many countries the *infrastructure* of roads, telecommunications and education may make production difficult. In parts of the world such as some African countries political *instability* can pose a threat. A change in the composition of the ruling faction can wipe out a huge investment or make trading difficult.

*Languages* can cause problems – especially in marketing and advertising. Some excellent examples of advertising gaffes are given in Table 2.3.

| Product | Intended message | Translated message |
|---|---|---|
| Coors Beer | "Turn it loose" | "Drink Coors beer and get diarrhoea" |
| Budweiser Beer | "Drink Bud light" | "Filling, less delicious" |
| General Motors car | "Body by Fisher" | "Corpse by Fisher" |
| Nova car | Nova | "Doesn't go" (Non Va) |

**TABLE 2.3**  Unintended cultural misunderstandings (see New Mexican, 1994; Ricks and Mahajan, 1984)

*Toolkit*

## 2.5 Globalisation toolkit

Managers cannot afford to adopt an ethnocentric view that their own country's business methods are superior. The best approach is to retain the best from their own culture but also benefit from good things in other cultures. There are three main implications of globalisation: implications for organisations, implications for managers abroad and implications for negotiations.

### Organisational implications of globalisation

The implications of globalisation for organisations divide into opportunities and challenges. A major opportunity is the ability to source raw materials from around the world. This gives greater choice and possibly higher-quality inputs at a lower price. Another opportunity is access to markets in other countries. An organisation that operates in another country must:

- Choose the **correct form of presence**: licensing, franchising, joint ventures, acquisition or greenfield development.
- Be familiar with **local customs, beliefs and laws**. In particular, organisations must be familiar with the local law governing workers.
- Use the organisation's **networks of contacts** to obtain informal information about the destination country, e.g. neighbouring organisations that are already operating in the destination country.
- be prepared to **modify** the organisation's management style to provide a better fit with the culture of the host country
- provide existing employees with **language training**. Managers should be given *acclimatisation training* to minimise "culture shock". Further details of content of acclimatisation training is given on the website associated with this book. Significant public announcements or **advertisement**s in another language should be *checked with at least two local speakers* who do not know the expatriate manager's home language

### Implications of globalisation for managers

The implications of globalisation for managers sent to a **host** country mirror many of the implications for organisations. *Managers* should attend acclimatisation training to learn about the culture of the host country. It is important that they adapt to the local culture rather than try to re-create their home culture. An individual manager will need

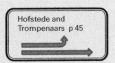

Hofstede and Trompenaars p 45

to adapt his or her management style to take into account differences on the dimensions identified by Trompenaars and Hofstede.

### Implications of globalisation for negotiators

Implications of globalisation for **negotiators** are fewer but more acute since they have a relatively short time to achieve success. They must remember that other cultures have different perspectives on time. Negotiations in a host country will probably take longer than equivalent negotiations at home. There may be a protracted period of establishing friendship and rapport that is punctuated by ceremonial occasions such as giving gifts or formal meals. It is vital that negotiators familiarise themselves in advance with local custom and the formalities of introductions, visiting the homes of their counterparts and closing negotiations. Negotiators should also familiarise themselves with the local euphemisms that their counterparts may use to say "no" or to decline an offer.

# Activities and further study

## Essay plans

Prepare plans for the following essays:

1 Compare and contrast *one, named* unidirectional classification of organisational cultures with Cameron and Quinn's classification.

2 Compare and contrast Hofstede's analysis of national cultures with Trompenaar's classification.

3 What are the main reasons why organisations "globalise"?

4 What are the main difficulties facing organisations that globalise. Illustrate your answer with at least three specific examples.

## Web activities

1 Use *Yellow Pages* or the Web to locate two specific examples, preferably from your own area or region, of the following types of organisations in which managers work. Enter their names in a table such as the one that follows:

| Type of organisation | Example 1 | Example 2 |
|---|---|---|
| Franchises | | |
| Limited partnerships | | |
| Holding companies | | |
| Conglomerates (not Virgin!) | | |
| Multinational corporations | | |
| Virtual companies | | |
| Trade associations | | |
| Quangos | | |

2 Choose two countries that you think you might visit, or work in, in the future. Visit Geert Hofstede's website (www.geert-hofstede.com) and look up the the cultural profile of these countries. Compare these profiles with that of your own country.

3 Visit www.cyborlink.com, scroll down to bottom of page and choose the two countries you nominated in the previous exercise. Using this information make a list of two important things that you would have to adapt concerning each of:

- your appearance
- your behaviour
- communications
- doing business

Look at the page for your home country. Using the same headings, list three things you think might surprise foreign visitors.

## Experiential activities

**1** Form a discussion group that contains students from other countries.
  - Write a list of things you would expect foreign student to find unfamiliar or difficult about coming to your country. Then ask the foreign students to list things they actually found different or difficult. Compare and discuss the two lists
  - Write a list of the things that you would expect to find difficult if you were to stay in the foreign students' country. Ask them to produce a list of the things they would expect you to find difficult. Compare and discuss the two lists

**2** Read Chan's (1997) article ("The corporate culture of a clan") to obtain a fuller understanding of a clan culture.

**3** Choose four organisations you know – preferably organisations where you have worked. Consider each in turn. Decide whether each had a culture of adhocracy, hierarchy, clan or market.

**4** Choose four family members or friends who are working. Read them the sections of this chapter that describe adhocracy, hierarchy, clan or market cultures. Ask them to decide the type of subculture where they work.

## Recommended reading

**1** Brecht, B. (2010) "Building a company without borders", *Harvard Business Review*, April, 103–106. Gives useful insights into globalisation and how a major multinational, Reckitt Benckiser, operates.

**2** Schneider, B. (1987) "The people make the place", *Personnel Psychology*, **40** (3), 437–453. A classic paper explaining how organisational cultures arise and persist. It contain useful sections on career choice. Hard in places but the sections on Mischel can be skipped.

**3** Chan, A. (1997) "Corporate culture of a clan", *Management Decision*, **35** (2) 94–92. A description of the organisational culture of the DHL parcel delivery company (in Hong Kong).

**4** Jones, M. (2007) "Hofstede – culturally questionable?", Oxford Business and Economics Conference, Oxford, 24–26 June, http://ro.uow.edu.au/commpapers/370. Follow the link to a good précis of Hofstede's work and its critics. Good references.

## CHAPTER 3

# The Historical Context

## Chapter contents

The history of management can be described in six parts. They are:

## ❖ LEARNING OBJECTIVES

After reading this chapter you should be able to trace the development of managerial theory and practice. You should be able to explain how economic, technological and social factors of a period influence management thought. You should be able to identify and date the main schools of management such as scientific management, contingency theory and systems theory. In particular you should be able to:

❖ **describe** scientific management and the work of F.W. Taylor

❖ **describe** the work of classical administrative theorists – especially the work of Fayol and Weber

❖ **list** the seven management processes identified by Fayol and **explain** the distinction between a management process and a management function

❖ **explain** the basic philosophy of Fordism and explain the management techniques involved

❖ **briefly describe** "post-Fordism" and the reasons why it arose

❖ **explain** the Hawthorn experiments and **evaluate** the influence of the Human Relations School of Management

❖ **draw diagrams** depicting three types of organisational system

❖ **explain** the concepts of feedback, entropy and synergy

❖ **evaluate** the contributions of Fiedler and Woodward

**CASE 3.1:** *PROTON City of the future – or of the past?*

Malaysian car manufacturer Perusahaan Otomobil Nasional Berhad (better known as PROTON) is currently building Proton City (tagged "City of the future") which is due to be completed in 2020. Its vision statement is "To be a self-contained eco-sensitive, intelligent city with superior technological and educational capabilities . . . which provide . . . living environment that enriches its multicultural community". Proton City is a vision of a futuristic city combining work, education, health care, but the idea may not be new at all. In the early nineteenth century Robert Owen, an enlightened Scottish mill owner, who set up a textile mill in New Lanark, south of Glasgow. New Lanark combined improved working and living conditions and an enlightened attitude towards its employees which produced a rise in productivity and profitability. Like Robert Owen's vision, Proton City is a community where the workforce lives and works in conditions to nourish their productivity. It features:

- enlightened and fair working conditions
- modern, living accommodation
- state-of-the-art amenities including healthcare (hospitals etc.) and education (schools, universities, etc.) that instill the company's vision and enlightened ethos

Proton City may be hundreds of years and thousands of miles from New Lanark, but it is the historical descendant of Robert Owen's ideas in its aims of providing a progressive model of industry that benefits workers, owners and the country.

Henry Ford once famously said that "History is bunk". Recent writers have suggested that history is like driving using the rear-view mirror. At a superficial level these views may be true – history tells us about the past. Most people, especially managers, are more concerned with the present and the future. However, there are three good reasons why managers need a basic grasp of the history of their profession. First, it is important to learn the terms and ideas that are used by other managers. A brief study of the history of management is a good way to learn what they mean. Further, knowing how the terms arose helps to ensure that they are used intelligently and within their proper context. Second, history allows management to be seen in perspective. This has two advantages. It stops people taking a narrow view of management where their actions are based on limited personal experience. History also helps managers identify and react to longer-term trends. Third, managers in the past have learned from both mistakes and sucesses. Knowledge of history can mean that some of these lessons can be learned without the inconvenience of making them. Avoiding mistakes is useful but it is even better to reduce the waste of "reinventing the wheel" and cherry-picking past successes.

## 3.1 Early beginnings

Management is not new. It has existed ever since humans started to undertake tasks in groups. The hunting of mammoths by groups of Neanderthals required some managerial activity. The high priests of the Sumerian Empire managed agricultural estates and developed writing specifically to record resources for purposes of taxation. The Egyptians used fairly advanced management techniques to build the pyramids. Druids used management skills to build Stonehenge.

The Romans were great and systematic managers. Their soldiers were organised into cohorts, managed by senior centurions, which in turn were organised into legions and armies. The Roman Catholic Church (in terms of longevity, the most effective organisation of the western world) adopted a management structure leading from the parish priest to the Pope.

Machiavelli tried to improve the management skills of his bosses, the Medici princes of Renaissance Florence. Jay (1967) believes Machiavelli's works are "bursting with urgent advice and acute observations for top management of the great private and public corporations all over the world". All these historic examples of management were unsystematic. Management became more rigorous with the start of scientific management.

## 3.2 Scientific management (rational goal)

Scientific management is sometimes known as the Rational Goal School of Management and it emerged with the Industrial Revolution. There were three reasons why management became more important as the Industrial Revolution progressed:

- Larger units of economic activity became more common. Previously the family or a group of families was the predominant unit of economic activity. Large organisations were exceptional and usually associated with government, armies or religion.

- Industry requires greater specialisation of labour. Industrial processes were more complex and required high expertise. Employment in agriculture depended upon a few generic skills which most agricultural workers could perform as and when they were required.

- Factories and machinery were costly and often could only be financed by the combined savings of groups of people. This led to the development of the limited company where investors' liability was limited to the money they had staked in the institution. The person managing the enterprise may or may not have been the same as the person or people who owned it.

Many of the management techniques that are taken for granted today were developed by the grandfathers of scientific management, such as Bolton and Watt or Arkwright.

---

**CASE 3.2:** *Management ideas that can be traced back to Bolton and Watt*

Bolton and Watt, the grandfathers of scientific management were pioneers. They built a factory to manufacture steam engines in Birmingham in 1800. Existing systems of manufacturing were based on the craft workshops, which were disorganised and inefficient. Bolton and Watt adopted a scientific, analytical approach to increase productivity by making work easier to perform:

- They made a systematic analysis of the market for steam engines and the rate at which steam engines needed to be produced.

- They designed their factory to provide an efficient flow of work on the basis of these estimates. The speeds of the various machines were studied and adjusted to provide the desired rate of output. Each stage was broken down into a series of minor operations which could be analysed systematically. The basics of time-and-motion study were developed at Bolton and Watt's factory.

- They developed a wage system which was based on the work done. The output for each job was estimated and workers who exceeded the estimate received a bonus while those who did not achieve the estimate received a wage cut. This system can be thought of as the forerunner of later piece-rate systems.

- They introduced an accounting system which kept track of material costs, labour costs and finished goods. The accounting system also recorded indirect costs. It also allowed management to pinpoint inefficiencies and waste so that productivity could be improved.

Another grandfather of scientific management was Richard Arkwright whose contributions to management are described on this book's website.

---

## F. W. Taylor – the father of scientific management

The scientific approach was taken up with enthusiasm in the USA, where workers were often seen as mere parts of a large machine. One of the pioneers of scientific management was Frederick W. Taylor. Taylor is most famous for his work at Midvale Steel and then the Bethlehem Steel Company. He studied jobs more scientifically than Bolton and Watt. He determined how much work could be expected from an operative each day. Previously management had relied upon tradition and workers had kept their output low to reduce the demands on them. Taylor used a more scientific approach to establish what a good worker should achieve. In one case, Taylor studied men loading pig iron into railway wagons: the average was 12.5 tonnes per day. Taylor calculated that if men worked 42 per cent of the time they should be able to achieve 47 tonnes per day. Taylor then chose a man called "Schmidt" and supervised him very closely, telling him exactly what to do and when. Note that Taylor was a reasonable man. He did not expect labourers to graft 100 per cent of the time. He scheduled substantial rest periods. At the end of the first day Schmidt had loaded 47.5 tonnes of pig iron. After a short period of training other men on the shift also achieved the target of 47 tonnes. Another experiment at Bethlehem Steel concerned shovelling iron ore and coal. When men were working with iron ore the load was very heavy but when they were working with coal the load was much lighter. Taylor's experiments showed that most material was moved when the shovel load was 21 lb. At that time workers provided their own shovels and they tended to use the same one irrespective of the material moved. Taylor provided a series of shovels – a small one for heavy material and a larger one for lighter material – so that the load was always constant at 21 lb. The average tonnage moved per labourer per day rose from 16 to 19. At a consequence the number of labourers needed fell from about 400 to 140. Taylor was sufficiently enlightened to pass on some of the increased productivity to the labourers. Wages increased from $1.15 per day to $1.88 – a rise of 63 per cent. In 1911 Taylor wrote his classic book *Principles of Scientific Management* and in 1912 he spoke before a congressional committee investigating systems of management. On the basis of these achievements Taylor was named the "father of scientific management".

### CASE 3.3: *Taylor's lectures on management, 1907–1915*

Wrege (2008) gives a delightful and very readable description on the background to Taylor's lectures on management. Taylor built an opulent Georgian mansion with beautiful gardens and large rooms near Philadelphia in 1905. In 1906, Taylor's health was poor and he was advised to work only two-and-half-hours per day. In 1907 he started giving lectures at his home and they continued until his death in 1915.

Taylor's friend Maurice Cook arranged for his lectures to be recorded by a court stenographer and eventually they became the basis for a chapter of Taylor's (1911) well-known book *Principles of Scientific Management*. The lecture was highly standardised and was virtually identical each of the frequent times it was delivered – but no matter how often it was heard, it was always interesting and stimulating and showed a progressive viewpoint.

Lilian Gilbreth attended many times and described it carefully. The audience assembled in the early morning in the beautiful large living room and was greeted by Taylor and then his two young sons. The lecture lasted two hours and Taylor very much objected to interruptions, but he did allow questions when he had finished. He took one-and-a-half hours talking about handling pig iron and shovelling, with which everybody was familiar. Taylor then spent 15 minutes talking on slide rules where the audience was bombarded with terms such as "cuts", "gears", "variables", "formulas", etc. until the audience was in a muddled frame of mind.

Some of the sons and daughters of the scientific management movement were Frank Gilbreth and his wife Lillian, a psychologist. The Gilbreths studied the hand movements of bricklayers in minute detail. By eliminating repetitions and movements which served no purpose they were able to reduce the number of movements needed to lay a brick from 18 to 5. Some movements were eliminated by training bricklayers, others by improving materials (e.g. making sure that the mortar was at the proper consistency so that bricklayers did not need to "tap down" each brick) and by providing equipment such as a stand to hold the bricks so that the bricklayers did not need to stoop to pick up each brick. These improvements meant that the number of bricks a person could lay in an hour rose from 120 to 350. The analyses conducted by the Gilbreths were so detailed that they needed to use slow-motion photography. Gilbreth and his wife developed a system which characterised all operative work in terms of 17 basic motions such as "reach", "grasp", "hold" and "position". They called these basic movements "Therbligs".

## Fordism and post-Fordism

### *Fordism*

Henry Ford was another son of the Scientific Movement of Management. His major contributions were between, say, 1903 and 1926. At that time technology had devised attractive new products such as the motor car, but they were expensive luxury items built by craftsmen. Even though "the masses" of America were more prosperous than ever, a motor car was beyond their reach. In 1901 Ransom Olds used a stationary production line to bring down costs and produce the first mass-produced car, the "Oldsmobile". Henry Ford refined these ideas and developed a new line of thought. If better production methods could reduce costs, more people could buy the product. If more people bought a product, the economies of scale would bring costs down further and demand would grow. More people would be employed so more people could afford cars and so on. There would be an accumulation of wealth and economic activity. The idea of efficient mass production and mass consumption lies at the heart of Henry Ford's contribution to management. A number of things were necessary in order to reduce costs so that "the masses" could afford products. They were:

- **Standardisation, interchangeability and precision**. Henry Ford sought to standardise as much as possible. Every component would be designed to be as efficient and as economical as possible. It would have very exact specifications so that its performance would be precise and employees would not have to spend time making adjustments for each individual item. Any one of a specific component could be fitted to any car. If one proved defective, it could be replaced by one that worked well. Components could be manufactured in very large numbers, at low costs. Ford's standardisation is epitomised by his statement that the consumer could have "any colour of car so long as it was black" – he had established that black paint dried quicker than other colours. This together with bulk buying of only one colour shaved costs so that the price of cars could be brought within the reach of more people.

- **Simplicity and specialisation.** Henry Ford analysed the manufacturing process in fine detail. Even complex assemblies were divided into a series of very simple actions such as (1) placing an axle in position, (2) putting a wheel hub on the axle, (3) tightening two top screws and (4) tightening two bottom screws. Workers would be trained to perform just one of these specialist actions. This reduced training costs and it could be accomplished by less skilled workers. Further, time was not wasted changing tools – again reducing costs. Specialisation was extreme. An employee would have only one task, such as putting a bolts on a wheel. He did not order parts, repair equipment, check quality, keep the work area clean or even understand what the assemblers on either side were doing (Womack, Jones and Roos, 1990).

■ **Syncronisation and conveyor belt production.** Because production was broken down into small standardised steps they could be syncronised into a smooth, efficient sequence. One of Henry Ford's innovations was **the conveyor belt system** which is also called a **production line**. Previously, mechanical power, such as in the textile industry, had been produced by huge central steam engines or even waterwheels. It was transmitted to the workplace by cumbersome and inefficient systems of gears and belts. Henry Ford used electric motors. This energy could be placed much nearer the workshop and could power a series of conveyor belts. The belt brought work to the workers – saving the cost of the time they would take to walk between units. Further, the speed of the belt could be set at a pace which just, and only just, allowed enough time for workers to complete their small, monotonous tasks. However, it saved the time that workers might spend idling.

All of these innovations were implemented at Ford's Model-T plant at Highland Park in Michigan in 1914. Productivity increased tenfold and the price of cars was halved – bringing their purchase within reach of more people-volume increased and so did economies of scale and profits. The workers benefited too. Wages rose from $2.34 per day to a breathtaking $5.00 per day. So more workers could afford to buy cars for themselves – thus increasing volumes, the economies of scale and profits. The Ford Motor Company quickly became the biggest company in the world and retained that position for decades.

A business model yielding such fantastic results could not be ignored. It was copied with enthusiasm by competitors and many other industries in the USA. Ford already had a factory near Manchester and the techniques were quickly transferred to the UK before the factory was relocated to Dagenham in 1931.

Other countries rushed to adopt Ford's principles. This was especially true in Germany (some of Ford's ideas were based on Prussian principles of administration) and, ironically, the anti-capitalist state of the Soviet Union (standardisation, uniformity and the promise of a better future for the masses, if properly planned and controlled, were especially appealing to Stalin and his colleagues). It also attracted attention in Italy. In about 1929 an Italian Marxist philosopher, jailed by the Fascists, noted the spread of Ford's influence. Gramasci (see Levy and Egam 2003) considered the Ford "model" to be a ploy by the bourgeoisie to obtain hegemony by making concessions. He termed the phrase "Fordism". Fordism, fuelled by the demands of war and subsequent aspirations of "the masses" for a more affluent life swept into its heyday, say, 1950–1970, when it was very dominant as large corporations provided masses of people with many standard products at prices they could afford. It could not last. Fordism, in all its mighty glory had inherent problems.

> **CRITICAL THINKING 3.1** *What was wrong with Fordism?*
>
> There were at least two major problems with Fordism:
> **Inflexibility resulted from centralisation and specialisation.** Changes needed to be referred to HQ and this took time. Alfred P Sloan, chairman of rival General Motors allowed divisional managers to make decisions. They came up with a bigger range of products, and quicker decision-making meant better adjustment to changes. Customers wanted more choice and many preferred cars, made by competitors, that were not black. General Motors overtook Ford as the number one car-maker in the late 1920s.
> **Working practices were monotonous.** There were considerable hidden personal and social costs. Large numbers of "bored" workers were easy to organise into unions to stand up for their rights. Strikes could cause mayhem in a rigid and tightly scheduled assembly line. The negative aspects of monotonous working practices were satirised by Charlie Chaplin in the film *Modern Times*.

### Post-Fordism

Among others, a Russian economist, Nilolai Kondratiev (1935), controversially noted that there are long-term economic cycles lasting about 54 years. This is the time it takes for a major set of innovations to pass through four phases: prosperity following the innovation, recession, depression and recovery. He identified three waves in modern times:

- Kondratiev wave 1: c.1800–50, cotton processing technology
- Kondratiev wave 2: c.1850–1900, steam power, railways, steel, etc.
- Kondratiev wave 3: c.1900–50, motor cars, petrochemicals, etc.

So, it should have been no surprise that a major change, from Fordism, was due in the 1960s. Almost on cue, major changes started and they became very apparent in the 1970s. This led to an era called post-Fordism. The changes were fuelled by several developments:

- The market for cars, petrochemicals and electricals became mature and saturated. Additional volumes to provide greater economies of scale were hard to find. People wanted more and better services rather than material possessions.
- Boundaries between social classes became less important. Many blue-collar workers became more affluent than many white-collar workers. The many different groups were not satisfied with a limited range of products.
- Computers and IT made it easier to identify a myriad of trends and to set up production to cater for these trends. Modern robotics meant that the production line could be easily modified, Indeed, modern robotics mean that production could be achieved without assembly lines of the type built by Ford.

Post-Fordian managers developed flexible organisations with fewer managerial levels, smaller corporations, where many activities were outsourced. This was Kondratiev's fourth wave and it was based on electronics and consumer goods. Kondratiev's fifth wave started in the 1990s and it was based on the Internet, wireless technology and biotechnology. It is expected to reach its high point about now!

### The continuing contribution of scientific management

Writers today tend to minimise, or even disparage, the contribution of scientific managers. However, their great contribution is clear when it is set against the historical context of their times when industry was very labour intensive and productivity was very low. Scientific managers, and Henry Ford, tackled the most pressing managerial problem – to increase efficiency and productivity. Today we take their efforts for granted. We automatically assume that workers will be properly selected, trained and equipped. Scientific managers were primarily concerned with productivity of manual workers in heavy industry. The importance of heavy industry to the economy has decreased substantially in the century since the heyday of Taylor, Ford and Gilbreth. Nevertheless, scientific management retains an important role. The Gilbreths' contributions are an integral part of operations management and industrial engineering. Their ideas are fascinating and still used in many different ways. If they were alive today Frank and Lillian Gilbreth would be overwhelmed to see how much their work is the foundation for a great deal of contemporary management (Mousa and Lemark, 2009).

Equipment manufacturers conduct studies to ensure that their products are suited to people's capabilities. For example, designers of computer software will check that screen images are legible. Similarly, manufacturers of mundane military equipment such as boots and socks will conduct studies to ensure that their products are designed to allow soldiers to march long distances without producing footsores. Designers of control panels for complex chemical plant will go to great lengths to ensure that the control displays are easy to understand and that warnings of danger are unmistakable. Today studies in scientific management are usually covered by the discipline of ergonomics – the science of work.

## The quantitative school of management

Scientific management and the basic ideas of Taylor reached a second peak, in a slightly different form, between 1940 and 1980 and it operated under different names such as the **Quantitative School** or **management science**. There were, however, important differences. Taylor was largely concerned with physical work, whereas the Quantitative School focused upon managerial decisions. While Taylor used very straightforward analytical techniques, the Quantitative School used very sophisticated methods of analysis. In many areas the Quantitative School is still strong today.

During the Second World War garguantian quantities of men and material were deployed against the enemy. Governments were keen to obtain a military advantage by deploying men and materials in the most effective way. They employed scientists, mathematicians and statisticians to study a problem in a rational, quantitative, scientific way. For example, it was imperative to defeat the U-boats' menacing convoys. Depth charges were a main method of attack. Many questions needed to be answered for a destroyer to make a successful attack.

How many depth charges should be used against a single submarine? Too few might not result in a "kill" while the use of too many might mean there were insufficient to attack other submarines in the pack. At what depth should the fuses be set to explode? What would be the most efficient pattern of scattering the depth charges? Scientists and mathematicians studied the kill rates for various situations and derived an attack plan which would result in the greatest number of submarine kills per depth charge. More recent, civilian, problems are illustrated by a retail organisation which wants to know the optimum density for its outlets. If each outlet serves a large area, a large number of consumers will be within range and profits will be high – except for the fact that large catchment areas involve high transport costs and management supervision becomes costly and difficult. Further, wide spacing of outlets might allow competitors to establish themselves. On the other hand, retail outlets too close to each other yield small catchment areas. The question arises "what is the optimum density of retail outlets". The company might conduct a study and its mathematicians might produce the formula:

$$\text{Profit (in millions)} = r \times 2 + (r^2 \times \pi) - (r^3 \times 0.5)$$

It is then possible to construct the following table:

| Catchment radius (miles) | 1 | 2 | 3 | 4 | 5 | 6 | 7 | 8 | 9 |
|---|---|---|---|---|---|---|---|---|---|
| Expected profits (£m) | 23 | 49 | 75 | 98 | 116 | 125 | 122 | 105 | 70 |

From the table it is clear that the catchment area of retail outlets should have a radius of 6 miles. Therefore shops should be set 12 miles apart so that the catchment areas touch but do not overlap.

   The Quantitative School of Management had a great influence upon quality management which emphasises setting standards, samples, measurement and the use of statistical methods to detect batches that were faulty. This developed into a very numerically based statistical process control (SPC) and a six sigma approach which aims to ensure that there are less than four defects per million products (see Fisher and Nair, 2009). The Quantitative School of Management also had important influences on the development of queuing theory and "just-in-time" production methods. The Quantitative School uses algorithms and game theory to reach solutions. It aims to provide the best possible decision and it is usually applied to problems that are too complex to be solved by common sense. When managers are asked to solve complex problems without the aid of qualitative models they tend to settle for solutions which are satisfactory (**satisficing**) rather than the best possible solution (**optimising**).

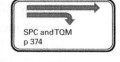

SPC and TQM
p 374

   The quantitative approach is often called **operations research** (**OR**). The quantitative approach is characterised by three features:

■ *mathematical models*, linear programs and statistical trend analysis to identify patterns that can be projected into the future to make forecasts

- *simulations* to determine the impact of different decisions – often these simulations take the form of spreadsheets to examine "what if" scenarios where the impact of several variables can be studied
- *specialised techniques* such as algorithms, critical path analysis and just-in-time methods to help managers determine key dates and identify likely bottlenecks

The Quantitative School is a far cry from the techniques developed by Taylor. Nevertheless they share the aim of making behaviour more predictable, more productive and more machine-like. The quantitative approach has made enormous contributions to management decisions, especially decisions concerning planning and control.

## CRITICAL THINKING 3.2 *Problems with quantitative methods*

Quantitative methods are not as perfect as they seem.

- They may be less precise than they seem. They often rely on data which are estimated by managers and other people who may have a vested interest in providing distorted information. These estimates can be substantially awry and unreliable.

- The assumptions used in the models developed by the quantitative managers may be wrong. Because these assumptions appear scientific they are difficult to identify and correct.

- Quantitative methods may place an unreasonable emphasis on economic effectiveness. They may miss more subtle goals such as satisfaction, enjoyment and justice because intangible psychological states are very difficult to quantify.

Some critics go further and complain that the Quantitative School gives too narrow a view of management. Other critics maintain that it is not a school at all. Mathematics and statistics are used in many sciences such as engineering and medicine but they are not a school of thought.

## 3.3 Classical (administrative) theorists

Scientific managers, and Ford, were concerned predominantly with managing operatives and labourers. They said very little about management itself. The classical theorists were largely senior managers in large organisations who turned their minds to analysing the processes of management.

## Henry Fayol

Probably the most important classical theorist was Henry Fayol. Fayol was the general manager of a large French mining company. He was primarily concerned with "administrative principles" that apply to the organisation as a whole. Fayol identified the key processes which managers needed to perform. If a manager performed these functions properly, he would be effective. The main processes of management according to Fayol were: planning, organising, commanding, co-ordinating and controlling. Since his time Fayol's list has been amended and the main processes of management are now seen to be:

- planning
- organising
- staffing
- deciding
- controlling
- reporting
- budgeting

The processes can be remembered by the acronym POSDCRB. Each of the processes will be considered in much greater depth in Part 2 on management processes. Fayol also identified a number of management principles. It has been argued (Yoo, Lemak and Choi, 2006) that they are important constituents of modern competitive strategies – cost leadership and differentiation (CL and DF respectively below). Fayol's management principles were were:

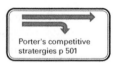

Porter's competitive stratergies p 501

- **Division of labour** – up to a point people should specialise in performing certain tasks so that they can build a high level of expertise (CL).

Specialisation p 114

- **Authority and responsibility** – the right to give orders and expect them to be obeyed. Authority usually arises from a manager's role. Sometimes, authority arises from the person's abilities such as intelligence, expertise, charisma or general character. This kind of authority is sometimes known as "informal" or "personal" authority. A good manager should have both formal and informal sources of authority. Fayol was keen to link authority with responsibility. When a manager uses power to issue an instruction, he or she is responsible for the consequences. If the course of action leads to success, the manager should be rewarded and if it leads to failure the manager should be punished. Later writers referred to Fayol's concept as the *"parity of authority and responsibility"* (CL).

Types of power p 195

- **Discipline** – involves obedience, diligence, energy, correct attitude and respect.
- **Unity of command** – everyone should have one, and only one, boss (CL).
- **Scalar chain of command** – there should be a clear hierarchy which runs from the bottom of an organisation through to the top. This ensures the integrity of the organisational structure and unity of command. Generally, communications should follow the hierarchical route. However, Fayol recognised that if every piece of information needed to go from the bottom of an organisation to the top and then down again to the bottom,

the delays would be unacceptable. Fayol therefore introduced the "gang-plank" principal whereby people at the same level within an organisation could communicate with each other (CL).

- **Unity of management** – efforts and plans should be in pursuit of the same objective.
- **Subordination of individual interests to the common good** – the goals of the organisation should take precedence over the goals of individuals or groups.
- **Remuneration of staff** – employees should be fairly rewarded for what they do.
- **Centralisation** – the degree of initiative which is left to individuals or groups. Centralisation is neither good nor bad: it depends on the organisation, its environment and goals. Every organisation must strike the appropriate balance
- **Order** – the correct position for equipment should be determined and equipment should be kept in that position (a place for everything and everything in its place).
- **Equity** – managers should be friendly and fair. They should show good sense and good nature.
- **Stability of staff** – staff turnover is disruptive and incurs costs. It should be minimised so staff can develop required skills and commitment to the organisation (modern thinking is that excessive stability produces rigidity and should therefore be carefully controlled) (DF).
- **Initiative** – employee initiative is an asset to all organisations, especially when times are difficult. Initiative is the ability to conceive and execute a new plan when existing plans are not satisfactory.
- *Esprit de corps* – refers to the harmony among people within the organisation so that morale is high (DF).

## Max Weber and bureaucracy

Max Weber was a classical theorist who focused on administrative processes. Weber was struck by the inefficiencies of the old semi-feudal structures where people had loyalties to their patrons rather than to the organisation. This led to conflict and inefficiency. Weber attempted to provide guidelines for a rational organisation which had rules so that the organisation performed predictably and consistently. He envisaged organisations managed in an impersonal, rational way. He called these organisations "bureaucracies". Weber attempted to improve routine office operations in a way similar to Taylor's improvement of labour operations. According to Weber an ideal organisation would be characterised by six facets:

- Jobs are **specialised** and have **clear definitions** of their authority.
- Jobs are arranged in **hierarchical order** in which each successive level has greater authority and control.
- Personnel are selected and promoted on the basis of **merit**. Personnel are given adequate training.
- Acts and decisions are **recorded in writing**. Proper records form the memory of an organisation and the use of precedents ensures equality of treatment.

- A **comprehensive set of rules** which cover almost all eventualities. Employees are expected to keep to the letter of these rules and apply them impartially – irrespective of the rank and position. This meant that employees, customers and citizens would not be subject to the whims of individual employees and people would be treated fairly.
- **Management is separate from ownership** of the organisation.

Bureaucratic organisations have been heavily criticised because they become inflexible. Rules confine initiative and lead to demotivated employees. Some writers have identified the phenomena of **bureau pathology** in which unrealistic and irrelevant rules are set. When employees fail to observe these rules, yet more rules are developed to control non-conformance. The additional sets of rules alienate employees further and provoke more non-conformance – which triggers yet more detailed rules and so on. Over time, the original purpose of the rules is forgotten and the rules become ends in their own right. Strict observance of the rules may serve administrative officials well because it offers security – as long as they obey rules they are safe from criticism. However, the rules may not be in the interests of the organisation's clients. Weber is also famous for his identification of the link between prosperity and the Protestant work ethic. He noted that according to Protestant culture and dogma hard work was sanctified by God. Thus Protestant people work harder. A scattergram where countries are positioned on two axes, the proportion of the population that is Protestant and the gross domestic product (GDP) per head of population shows a clear trend. There is a clear correlation between Protestantism and national wealth. Protestant countries such as the UK, the USA and Germany tend to be wealthier than countries such as Mexico, Italy and Spain.

## CRITICAL THINKING 3.3 *Was Weber wrong?*

A paper by Becker and Ludger (2009) suggest that Weber was mistaken. The Protestant ethic emphasised the importance of individuals studying and reading the Bible. This meant that Protestant countries had a higher rate of literacy which in turn meant people were more productive. Becker and Ludger tested their hypothesis by studying the percentage of Protestants in provinces of Prussia, the level of literacy and average income. When literacy is taken into account there appears to be no relationship between Protestantism and economic success.

This is a very good example of the great problem of interpreting correlations. There may be a clear relationship between two things but this does not mean that one thing (e.g. Protestantism) necessarily causes another (e.g. economic success). There could be a hidden, unsuspected phenomena (e.g. literacy) that is more important. Further, a causal relationship might be the other way around. For example, higher incomes could make it more favourable for people to be literate, and more inclined to be Protestant.

## 3.4 Human relations

Scientific managers thought of employees as machines. They sought to improve the efficiency of the "human" machines. Even during the heyday of scientific management, some people were not convinced that human beings were like machines. They argued that human beings had special characteristics. The human relations school goes back at least to the days of Robert Owen, a Scottish mill owner, who criticised contemporary managers for buying the best machines and then hiring the cheapest labour. He set up a textile mill in New Lanark, south of Glasgow, where he established better working conditions for his employees and noted a rise in productivity.

The work of Robert Owen was influential but it did not employ techniques that were explicitly scientific. One of the first people to use scientific methods to investigate the characteristics of human beings in work situations was a German, Hugo Munsterberg. He noted that the scientific managers emphasised physical skills but ignored mental skills. Munsterberg was way ahead of his time. During the first decade of the 1900s he identified the major trend in the nature of work which is still evident today: work becoming less dependent on physical skills and more dependent on mental skills. Munsterberg developed tests which could identify workers who had the mental skills demanded by a job – especially higher-level jobs. Munsterberg also tried to establish the psychological conditions that produce highest productivity. In many ways Munsterberg was the link between the scientific managers and the human relations school of management.

### Elton Mayo and the Hawthorne experiments

Elton Mayo followed Munsterberg's lead. He tried to find psychological conditions that would give higher levels of productivity among workers at the Hawthorn electrical plant near Chicago which, among other things, manufactured light bulbs. The work of Mayo and his colleagues has been described by Roethlisberger, Dixon and Wizght. (1939) and criticised by Parson (1974), Adair (1984) and Diaper (1990). The company was keen to prove that good lighting improved the performance of operatives. Mayo and his colleagues established two groups of workers. One was a control group. The other was an experimental group and the level of illumination at their workplace was varied. As the level of illumination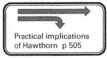

Practical implications of Hawthorn p 505

rose so did productivity. However, most people were surprised when productivity also rose when illumination was reduced. Evidently, the actual level of illumination was not a key factor. Other experiments suggested that workers were responding not to the levels of illumination but to the attention which management was devoting to workers. These studies are famous for identifying the "Hawthorne effect".

The Hawthorne effect was a very, very important discovery. However, a second finding from the Hawthorne studies was equally important. Mayo and colleagues observed workers in the bank wiring room where connections on electrical equipment were soldered (nowadays such connections are a part of microchip's design). The time-and-motion department established that an efficient worker should be able to solder 7312 connections per day. However, workers generally completed about 6300. Mayo and his colleagues wondered why output was lower than expected – was it because the time-and-motion department had set a target that was too high? Mayo came to the conclusion that **informal social norms** were responsible. The men, and indeed their immediate supervisors, believed that 6300 connections was a fair day's work. If anyone made significantly more connections than 6300, they were called a "rate buster" and were punished by sarcastic comments and a hard punch on the top of their arm – a process called "binging". If anyone made fewer than 6300 connections they were called a "chiseller" and subjected to similar sanctions. This was not the machine-like behaviour that scientific managers expected. Machines do not form coalitions to set and enforce their own standards of output. The work of Mayo in the bank wiring room showed that managers need to take account of social and psychological factors such as social norms and group dynamics. The bank wiring room studies pointed to the importance of teamworking.

Teamworking
p 121

## Barnard and Follett

Other experts refined and developed ideas demonstrated in the Hawthorn studies. Mary Parker Follett (1941) argued that the management of people was the very essence of management. She defined management as "getting things done by other people". She advocated abandoning traditional bureaucratic organisations and their demotivating disadvantages. She argued, we should harness the potential of people. She suggested that management's main task is to encourage people to form self-governing groups that are empowered to solve commercial and industrial problems. This advice contradicted the principle of "specialisation" advocated by the scientific managers. Mary Parker Follet also offered advice on conflict resolution. Whereas scientific managers believed senior managers should work out the best possible solutions to the problem and then cajole employees to implement that solution, she suggested it is better to bring conflicting groups together and allow them to work out their own solutions.

Chester Barnard was president of the New Jersey Bell Telephone Company. He stressed the need for managers to obtain the co-operation of employees so that they would work towards adding value to the organisation rather than their own goals. He maintained that the best way of obtaining employee co-operation is to communicate effectively and hence create a harmonious working atmosphere. Again, this was in direct contradiction to Taylor and Ford's approach which implied that working atmosphere is irrelevant to the performance of machines.

The Human Relations School has had an enormous, evangelical impact on management practice. Nevertheless, it is open to criticism.

---

**CRITICAL THINKING 3.4** *What were the weaknesses of the Human Relations School?*

Many of the early experiments were less scientific than they seemed. For example, the Hawthorn studies were very poorly controlled and many factors were left to vary at random. In other cases the changes introduced for human relations reasons were introduced at the same time as other changes such as higher wages.

Consequently, it is not possible to identify with certainty the causes of improvements. Other critics point out that the Human Relations School has too narrow a focus, which excludes aspects such as equipment, planning and organisations that are an undoubted part of management.

## 3.5 Systems theory

During the 1950s people became increasingly suspicious of theories which, while true, only explained a part of the management task. In 1961 Koontz complained that there was "a management theory jungle". Systems theorists aimed to correct the situation by considering organisations as a whole in the same way medics need to consider the human body as a whole rather than a collection of separate functions such as excretion, breathing and thinking. Each part of an organisation would have an impact on other parts. *The whole organisation can only work effectively if the individual parts work effectively and co-operate.* A system is usually defined as a set of interrelated parts that function as a whole to achieve a common purpose.

The simplest system is a **closed system** that operates in isolation to its environment. A closed system is depicted in Figure 3.1. Closed, simple, systems tend to be called "linear systems ". In linear systems events occur as management plans them without too much interference from the outside environment.

This means that the outside environment is usually stable and, with effort, can be understood and predicted. In a linear system it is usually clear what actions (levers) must be taken in order to achieve a given goal.

Many early management theories tended to operate on the basis that organisations were closed, linear, systems. As an approximation, this was almost true. A century ago technological developments were relatively slow to make an impact. Communications and ideas travelled slowly. Further, physical barriers and tariffs meant that outside competition was low. Modern organisations tend to be complex **open systems.** The defining characteristic of an open system is that it interacts with its environment via feedback loops. This is shown in Figure 3.2.

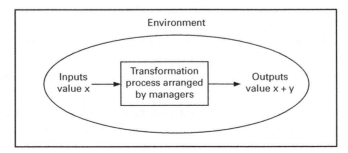

**FIGURE 3.1** A simple closed system

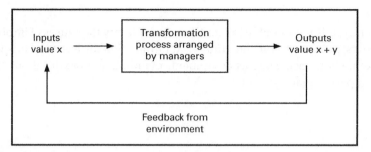

**FIGURE 3.2** A simple open system

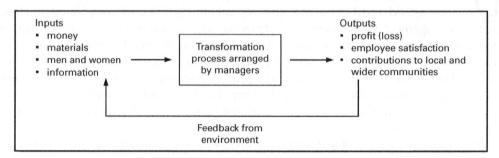

**FIGURE 3.3** An open system showing some inputs and outputs

Systems theorists spend considerable effort specifying inputs and outputs in detail. Often inputs are specified in classical terms of money, machines and men and women. However, information resources are important to most modern organisations and are added as an important input. Traditionally the main output of an organisation has been its profit (or loss).

However, a modern list would also include employee satisfaction and contribution to the local and wider community. A modern systems view is given in Figure 3.3.

Figure 3.4 shows a very simplified view of the environment. In reality the environment is complex. On the **supply side**, managers need to be alert to the demands of employees, suppliers, shareholders and lenders. On the **demand side** they need to be aware of markets, pressure groups, new competitors and changes in consumer tastes. There are also a number of factors that might affect both the demand side and the supply side. For example, a poorer economic climate might mean that there are fewer customers, which will make the managerial task more difficult. However, a poorer economic climate might also aid managers by making suppliers and employees more co-operative. Similarly, government regulations and new technology can also affect the inputs and the outputs of an organisation.

Figure 3.4 illustrates the concept of **stakeholders**. A stakeholder is any person or group that is affected by an organisation's activities. As the diagram shows, stakeholders include employees, suppliers, customers, clients, pressure groups, the local community, competing organisations and government. These are in addition to the more obvious stakeholders

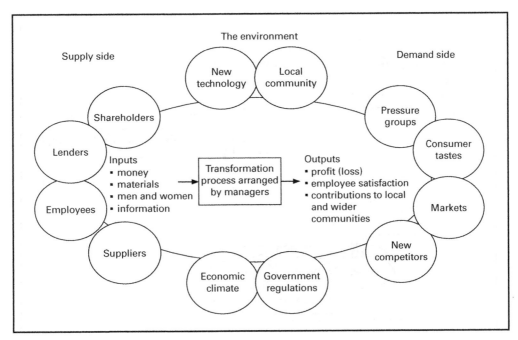

**FIGURE 3.4** A complex open system

who have a formal financial interest – the shareholders, lenders and creditors. In many ways managers, especially senior managers, need to achieve a successful balance between competing demands of the organisation's stakeholders.

Closed systems tended to be linear systems in which the outcome of any action would be highly predictable. Complex open systems, such as that shown in Figure 3.5, are generally non-linear systems with less certainty. In a non-linear system managers may be able to predict the short-term consequences within their organisation but it is very difficult for them to predict wider, longer-term consequences.

Open systems contain feedback loops. They are much less predictable and decisions can have quite unexpected consequences. Figure 3.5 represents only a fraction of the complications that exist: it shows only one organisation, one competitor and one government. However, there are feedback loops both within, and between, the three organisations.

Suppose there is a major technological advance. Suppose also that organisation A detects the technological change and uses it to improve production so that quality is increased by 50 per cent and costs are reduced by 50 per cent (not an unlikely scenario in the computer industry!). In a closed system this would bring enormous benefits to organisation A because it would be able to dominate its market with superior goods at a lower price. However, in an open system the situation may be quite different. A competitor would be more likely to monitor websites, newspaper articles and the promotional literature and to detect organisation A's actions. The competitor might respond in a number of ways. If it was larger and richer it might engage in a **predatory price war** designed to starve organisation A of funds so that it could not exploit the new product. Alternatively, the competitor could

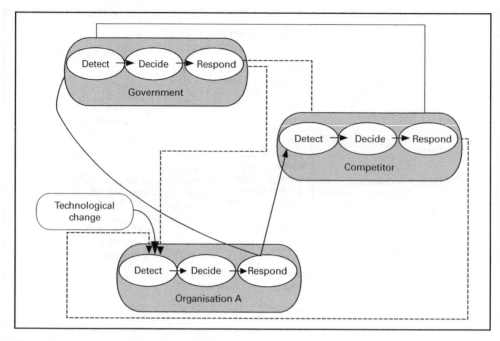

**FIGURE 3.5** An open system showing competitors, government and feedback

decide to meet the challenge "head on" by embracing the same technological advance and developing a similar product. Finally, the competitor could abandon hope, exit that market and concentrate on its other products. Organisation A is unlikely to know which of these alternatives its competitor will choose.

Government would also detect increased revenues and it would decide upon some course of action. It might decide to levy a windfall tax; it might decide to write off organisation A's extra capital expenditure on favourable terms. In the interests of greater employment the government could also offer organisation A help in developing export markets. It will be difficult for organisation A to predict exactly which combination of decisions will be made by its competitor and the government. Most modern organisations tend to be more like non-linear systems than linear ones.

Feedback mechanisms are generally believed to be good. As organisations put more information on the Internet, or intranet, the rate of feedback both within and between organisations has accelerated. However, **excessive feedback** can, as any acoustic engineer will verify, be dysfunctional. The feedback mechanisms can amplify the consequences of each decision so that the level of noise in the system is so great that it becomes intolerable. The systems approach to management emphasises three other concepts: entropy, synergy and subsystems.

**Entropy** is the tendency for a system to run down, decay and become chaotic unless it receives energy, regular inputs and maintenance. The duration of decay will be influenced by the organisation's size: small organisations usually reach the point of extinction before larger ones (survival of the fattest). **Synergy** is the extra value that is produced when two parts of a system interact. For example, in isolation, even an excellent production department will not generate extra value, because it will have to rely on customers calling in person to buy a product. In isolation even a superb sales team will not generate extra value, because it will have nothing to sell. However, the combination of an excellent production department and a superb sales department can add considerable value.

Except for one-person concerns, organisations are not amorphous structures where all parts perform the same tasks in the same way. Usually they are split up into **subsystems**. For example, some people in an organisation will attend to financial matters, others to purchasing supplies and materials and others still will attend to personnel matters, and so on. Technically sub-systems are defined as relatively homogeneous parts of a system that depend on one another. Sub-systems must be managed and co-ordinated and the impact of one sub-system have upon other systems must be understood. Unfortunately several sub-systems may conflict and the conflict may divert energy

Organisational functions pp 316–436

## 3.6 Contingency theory

The systems approach to management emphasises that most modern organisations are open systems which need to respond to their environment. Contrary to the ideas of scientific management, administrative management and the human relations schools (which all implied there was one best way to manage – *if only it could be identified*) systems theory implies that the style of management needs to be responsive to (contingent upon) an organisation's environment.

To an extent the contingency theory of management has its roots in research into leadership. Many research programmes were conducted but they tended to produce different results. It was concluded that the style of leaders is contingent upon the circumstances of their group. (Later re-analyses suggest that, to an extent, this was false. There is a clear tendency for leaders to be more intelligent, stable, conscientious and assertive than most people.)

### Fiedler's contingency theory of leadership

Fiedler, Chemers and Mahar (1978) measured whether members of a group had good or poor *relationships* with each other. They also measured whether the group had a clear *task* or an ambiguous task. Finally, they measured the extent of the leader's *formal power*. Fiedler categorised groups into eight types. He then looked at the leadership styles that were preferred by each kind of group. The results are shown in Figure 3.6.

| Group relationships | Good | Good | Good | Good | Poor | Poor | Poor | Poor |
|---|---|---|---|---|---|---|---|---|
| Tasks structure | High | High | Low | Low | High | High | Low | Low |
| Position power | High | Low | High | Low | High | Low | High | Low |
| Situational control | Very high | | | | | | | Very low |
| Appropriate leader style | Task-oriented style | | | | Relationship-oriented style | | Task-oriented style | |

**Figure 3.6** Fiedler's contingency theory of leadership style

Fiedler's results indicate that when the situational control is either very high or very low a leader should emphasise the task which faces the group. However, when the situational control is in the middle range a leader should emphasise the maintenance of good relationships among group members.

## Woodward

Another classic investigation which supports the contingency view of management was conducted by Woodward (1965). She investigated three groups of manufacturing companies. One group was classified as "unit and small batch production". In this group products were made in small quantities – often to the specifications of individual customers. The products included designer furniture, luxury yachts and specialist cars. In some ways these firms were like craft organisations because they relied heavily upon individual skills and the quality of the products. The second group was termed "large batch and mass production". These organisations made large quantities of standard products such as computer disks, standard cars and everyday washing machines. The work was heavily mechanised and routinised. The third group were termed "continuous process". Highly sophisticated machines did most of the work, which continued 24 hours a day. Employees had the task of maintaining and checking the machines. This group included brewers, oil refineries and steel-makers. Woodward and her colleagues collected a wide range of data about the organisations. They noted systematic differences in managers' spans of control (see Figure 3.7).

The differences in spans of control could be explained readily by the differences in the complexity of information involved. In the continuous process manufacturing work was high level, intricate and each worker undertook separate tasks. Hence, managers could only keep track of the activities of a relatively few number of employees. In mass production most workers were producing similar or identical products. Hence managers could keep track of a relatively high number of employees.

Many of the terms and ideas introduced in this brief history of management are still in use today. For example, most management courses and texts use terms such as "span of control", "open systems" and "stakeholders". The management processes first outlined by

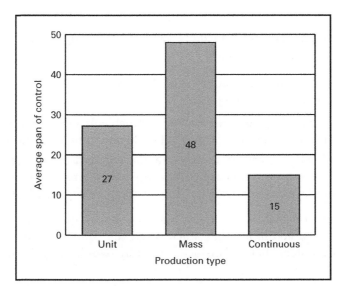

**FIGURE 3.7** Span of control and type of production

Fayol are still considered important – even though the details have been heavily modified and improved. Consequently, the next part of this book is devoted to providing a more up-to-date and detailed description of planning, organising, staffing, deciding, controlling, reporting and budgeting.

## CRITICAL THINKING 3.5 *Management history – not bunk for Bill Smith*

When presented as a mere chronology of past events, history conforms to Ford's dictum that "history is more or less bunk". It is a phrase that enables many consultants to charge high fees for reinventing the wheel. Good history is more than a chronology. It involves the integration of past events, people, situations and understandings into theories that explain *why* the events occurred. Intelligent use of these theories helps managers understand their current situations. This understanding can help them make successful improvements that are more effective than random restarts.

For example, Bill Smith looked into the history of quality management which included individual topics such as quality control, total quality management (TQM) and zero defects outlined by previous pioneers such as Deming, Juran, Ishikawa and Taguchi. He cherry picked key historical ideas such as the importance of:

- measurement of important things
- continuous improvement

- entire organisational commitment to quality – especially top management
- statistical process control (SPC)

Bill Smith was not content to simply mimic historical ideas, he integrated and built on them. History stimulated him to add:

- a focus on achieving measurable and quantifiable financial returns and making decisions made on the basis of verifiable data rather than guesswork
- methods of ensuring leadership structures that emphasised strong and passionate support for quality – a hierarchy of quality champions that included "yellow quality belts", "black quality belts" and "master black quality belts".

Bill Smith built on history to devise the "six sigma" quality system that was implemented in Motorola and has since saved the company billions of dollars. The "six sigma system" born of history is used by two-thirds of Fortune's top 500 companies.

# Activities and further study

## Essay plans

Prepare plans for the following essays:

1 Compare and contrast the contribution of F.W. Taylor (scientific management) with those of Elton Mayo.

2 Explain why the management schools of scientific management, administrative theorists, human relations and contingency theory evolved when they did.

3 Evaluate the extent to which modern managers use scientific management, administrative theory and human relations theory.

4 Was Fordism good or bad?

5 Outline the main aspect of systems theory and relate the concepts to a specific organisation that you have researched.

Compare your plans with those on the website site associated with this book.

## Web activities

Use the Web to locate:

1 The first example of measuring the time it took workers to perform certain operations.

2 The contribution of Eli Whitley to an efficient factory system.

3 Who studied the economies achieved from specialisation of labour by studying workers manufacturing pins?

4 Why were civil servants in the USA forbidden to use stop watches (until 1949) after F.W. Taylor was questioned by a special committee of the US House of Representatives (1911–12)?

5 The company that first used a "production line".

6 Page 68 describes three 'long-term' or 'Kondratiev' waves. There has since been a fourth wave and it is said we are starting a fifth wave. Use the Web to identify details of these later waves: what they are, their technological base, and their start and end dates.

7 To whom the concept of "operational research" is attributed. Where did he work?

8 What is Fielder's "cognitive resource theory". To which school of management does it belong?

## Experiential activities

1 Draw a time line stretching from 1800 to the year 2000. Position the following schools of management onto this time line: contingency theory, operational research, scientific management, human relations and administrative theory.

2 Choose an organisation you know well and identify all the possible stakeholders. Then classify the stakeholders into three types: supply side, demand side and others.

3 Arrange a debate with other students to discuss the motion "On the whole, observing bureaucratic principles brings benefits to an organisation".

4 Hold a seminar discussion on "the value of studying the history of management".

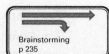
Brainstorming
p 235

5 Hold a brainstorming session on "the likely developments in management practice in the next 30 years".

## Recommended reading

1 Wrege, C.D. (2008) "F. W. Taylor's lecture on management, June 4, 1907", *Journal of Management History,* **14**(3), 209–213. A delightful, very readable description of the background to Taylor's lectures on management.

2 Becker, S.O. and Ludger, W. (2009) "Was Weber wrong? A human capital theory of Protestant economic history", *Quarterly Journal of Economics*, **124**(2), 531–566. A long and tedious paper but it is a good example of how sociologists can empirically examine and revise historical ideas.

3 Hartford, T. (2009) "How social science ends up as urban myth; the undercover Economist", *Financial Times*, 13 June; and Economist (2009) "Finance and economics: light work: questioning the Hawthorne effect", *Economist*, 6 June, **391**(8634), 74. Some of the well-established management ideas (e.g. the Hawthorne effect) are less solid than we think because their imperfections are forgotten.

# PART 2
# Management Processes

## Part Contents

# CHAPTER 4

# Planning and Strategy

## Chapter contents

Classical management theorists (see Chapter 3) identified seven main management processes. The first process is planning. It can be considered under eight main headings:

## ❖ LEARNING OBJECTIVES

After studying this chapter you should have a clear understanding of the planning process. You should be able to see the topic of "strategy" in its context as a key and early part of a bigger chain of activity. You should also be able to make a balanced judgement on the advantages and pitfalls of planning. In particular you should be able to:

* **define** planning and **list** the five main stages in the planning process
* **define and differentiate** between mission and vision statements
* **differentiate** strategic plans from tactical and operational plans
* **produce** SWOT and PESTLE analyses for an organisation you know well
* **compare and contrast** the dangers of three strategies: choose one strategy concerning size, one concerned with customers and one strategy concerned with adaptation

* **explain** the nature of tactical plans and their place in the planning cycle
* **explain** the nature of operational plans and their place in the planning cycle
* **explain the reasons** for using PERT charts and **draw** an illustrative example
* **describe briefly** single-use, standing and contingency plans
* **discuss in detail** the advantages and disadvantages of planning

---

**CASE 4.1:** *Advantages of planning an assignment*

Imagine you've been set a student assignment to produce a report within a week on the impact of computers on marketing. If you dislike planning, you might immediately start work by borrowing a library book on computers and then spend the next two days extracting relevant information. You then need to borrow a book on marketing, but find that it is on loan and the recall will take two days. After the book becomes available, it takes a day to extract and integrate the relevant information and to word process the assignment. Unfortunately, on the evening before the deadline you discover that your printer has run out of ink and paper. By the time you've got your hands on ink and paper the deadline has passed. By contrast, one of your fellow students has carefully noted the future deadline, anticipated the need for both books and ordered them from the library simultaneously. At the same time this student checks the supplies of ink and paper and tops up her stocks in advance. Consequently she does not waste three days' waiting time. The assignment is submitted on the fourth day and the remainder of the week is free to spend on leisure activities.

---

## 4.1  Definition of planning and the various types of plan

A plan is a scheme which specifies the future resources and actions that an organisation needs in order to perform in an efficient way. It involves anticipating future requirements and challenges. It also involves sequencing future resources and actions to minimise the delay and waste which could arise if events were allowed to take their natural pace and chronological order. A basic but relevant example of how planning increases effectiveness was given in Case 4.1, which illustrated the essential features of planning. They are:

- a goal – the desired future states an organisation intends to achieve
- an analysis of resources and stages
- an arrangement of the stages to minimise delay and waste

There are six main kinds of plan. Figure 4.1 shows they are linked together in a consistent and logical way.

The whole planning process should start with an analysis of the organisation's mission and this feeds into successive types of plan which become increasingly more detailed and practical. The diagram wrongly implies that planning is a top-down process. Indeed, the planning process may start that way. But all stages of the process need to be influenced by consultation and feedback from subsequent stages. Once the general framework has been established, each of the main kinds of plan needs to be considered in more detail.

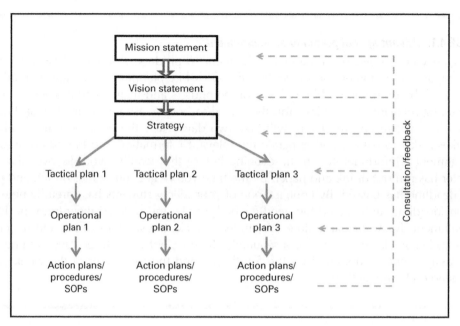

**FIGURE 4.1**  The relationship of the six main kinds of plan

## 4.2  Mission statements and visions

Mission statements and visions are often mistaken for each other or the terms are used interchangeably. Even when a distinction is made some people believe that planning should start with a mission statement while others believe it should start with a vision. Generally, planning should start with an organisation's **mission statement**, which is a succinct statement of *the reason for the organisation's exisitence*. Sometimes this is called the organisation's *overarching purpose*. When a mission statement refers to a group of related organisations it is often called a **team charter**. A mission statement should be short (three or four sentences) and it should form a memorable image which gives focus to the organisation's activities and employees. The mission statement usually refers to the present purpose of the organisation and is intended for use by all stakeholders, both internal, such as employees, and external, such as customers, suppliers and the government. A mission statement often contains:

- a statement of core values or ethics
- target customers or market and, sometimes, corporate relationships
- the products or services offered and the geographical region of availability
- expectations for growth or profitability

Mission statements should avoid hyperbole and bragging. Some inspired mission statements include the following:

- "High Quality Care for All" – British National Health Service
- "Make People Happy" – Disney Corporation
- "Ford will democratize the automobile" – Ford Motor Company (*circa* 1920)

A **vision statement** is a picture of what the organisation is likely to be at a time in the future when it is performing its mission in an effective way. It sets out the organisation's chosen way of achieving its purpose. It is perfectly possible for two organisations to have identical missions but very different visions. A good example is different churches. They may have identical missions, e.g. to redeem as many souls as possible by bringing people nearer to God. However, one church may have a vision of doing this by providing hostel accommodation to "down-and-outs" while another church may have a vision of achieving the same purpose by reading bible stories and providing Sunday services. Vision statements are longer and may, for a large and complex organisation, stretch to several pages. They are powerful pieces of communication that attempt to inspire employees. Indeed, the main readership will be employees and others (such as suppliers or regulators) who have a close and enduring contact with the organisation. Vision statements will often have specific dates stating when various components of the vision will be realised. All this should help the organisation communicate its core values and sense of direction to active stakeholders. Much criticised, but highly readable, research by Peters and Waterman (1988, see page 500) suggests that a key feature of outstanding companies is that employees share a core ideology and sense of direction.

## CRITICAL THINKING 4.1 *Problems with mission and vision statements*

Mission and vision statements are usually full of lofty language, superlatives and rhetoric which aim to position an organisation on high moral ground. However, they have been criticised as a managerial fashion of the 1990s. Many reek of condescension and give the impression of "the great and the good" hypocritically setting moral standards for the "lower social orders".

Enthusiasm for vision statements and strategy can be overdone. For example, KPMG (a global organisation providing accountancy and other services and which employs over 140 000 professional people in 146 countries) takes vision statements and strategy very seriously. So seriously that, in 2001, a company song was written and sung at a consultants conference in Frankfurt. The chorus went

> KPMG – We're as strong as can be
> We dream of power and energy
> We go for the gold, together we hold
> Onto our vision of global stratergy

The other verses and some rather scathing comments on the song can be accessed on http://www.theregister.co.uk/2001/03/08/kpmg_rocks_the_world_not/.

▶
> Boddy (2002a) points out that vision statements can fail to recognise an organisation's capabilities. Unrealistic statements can blind an organisation to commercial realities. They may also make employees cynical of management claims.

Mission and vision statements are often confused. Table 4.1 contrasts the two types of statement.

| Facet | Mission statement | Vision statement |
|---|---|---|
| Order in planning sequence | First | Second |
| Length in sentences | 3 or 4 sentences | 5 or more sentences |
| Whether factual or inspirational | Factual | Inspirational |
| Primary readers | All stakeholders | Mainly employees and close partners |
| Time orientation | Present statement of intent | Future statement of organisation |

**TABLE 4.1** Mission statements contrasted with vision statements

Once missions and visions have been formed, it is possible to get down to the nitty-gritty of planning. In principle, there are three other major types of plans:

- strategic plans
- tactical plans
- operational plans

These are covered in some detail in the next sections. Other, more specialised types include standing plans, single-use plans and contingency plans and are described later.

## 4.3 Strategic plans

### What are strategic plans?

Strategic plans specify the major objectives of an organisation. They are derived from the vision statement. Strategic plans may be thought of as an organisation's overall master plan that will shape its destiny and achieve its vision. They indicate the direction an organisation needs to take. Indeed, some people call strategic plans "directional plans". Strategic planning is a complex and multidimensional activity that can be viewed in many ways. Figure 4.2 indicates the way the topic is structured in this book. The figure shows that strategy is fundamentally a part of planning.

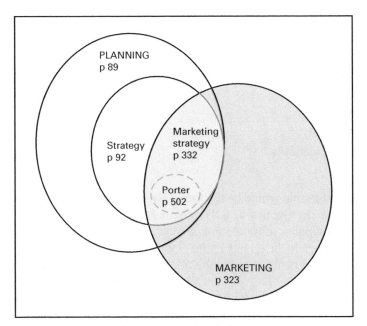

**FIGURE 4.2**  The relationship between planning, strategy and marketing

Treated separately, strategy is emasculated: it can be irrelevant if it is not related to an organisation's mission or goals and it has little effect if there is no follow-through with tactical and operational plans. Yet, strategy is also a vital part of marketing and much of the research on strategy has been written by marketers. So, even though strategy belongs within planning, there is an overlap with marketing. We explore marketing strategy more fully on pages 332–336.

Within marketing strategy there is the very important contribution of guru Michael Porter. His contribution to strategy is best seen in the context of other management gurus. Porter's excellent contribution to strategic planning is therefore described in Chapter 20.

To avoid cluttering Figure 4.2, other aspects of planning such as missions, visions, tactical and operational plans, etc. have been omitted (see pages 332–336). Similarly, important aspects of strategy such as methods of producing strategies or types of organisational strategies have been omitted from the figure (see pages 94–97).

The aim of any strategy is to guide the organisation to areas where the organisation will find it easiest to achieve its objectives and where it can resist challenges from competitors. To do this it must identify its **competitive advantages** which are sometimes **key success factors**. They are also sometimes called **core competences** or **critical success factors**, depending upon the consultant giving the seminar! A competitive advantage is a medium- or long-term factor where the organisation has such strength that its competitors are deterred from entering its market. Ideally, organisations should have several layers of competitive advantage so that other organisations can see that even if they penetrate or neutralise one they still face a daunting challenge. Ideally, the competitive advantage should be restricted to just one organisation or only a small group of organisations. Competitive advantages give an organisation an edge over its rivals. They enable an organisation to transform resources more efficiently than similar organisations. An organisation with a competitive advantage may be able to achieve superiority, so that it is difficult for other organisations to copy. Competitive advantages are those facets of the organisations which are costly and time-consuming for others to develop so that a competitor's "entry price is high". Typical competitive advantages are:

- cost leadership
- brand recognition
- technological superiority
- uniqueness

Examples of cost leadership would be the John Lewis Partnership, "who are never knowingly undersold" and the do-it-yourself, (DIY) chain B&Q, who refund 110 per cent of the difference if a local supplier sells the same item at a lower price. Marks & Spencer once had a competitive advantage in the quality of their clothes. IBM also had a competitive advantage in the field of mainframe computers, but this advantage evaporated when personal computers became common.

The last two examples illustrate that competitive advantages are not permanent. Companies may seek to sustain a competitive advantage by using patents, trademarks and copyrights. However, the most effective methods of maintaining a competitive advantage include:

- improvements and innovations to produce "layers of technological advantage"
- economies of scale which allow for cost-cutting
- "strategic alliances" with suppliers which deny raw materials to competitors

All of these approaches seek to make the entry price for competitors daunting.

Counteracting threats to a competitive advantage requires a system of **competitive intelligence** that scans the business environment for information about the activities of competitors. The vast majority of competitive intelligence is available from public sources. The expansion of the Internet means that information on new competitor activities is available much more quickly!

Another major aim of strategic planning is to direct an organisation towards promising markets. Consequently, marketers have devised additional methods of identifying aids to strategic planning which include the BCG matrix, the GE matrix and the Ansoff matrix. Michael Porter's work on the way that organisations and nations can develop a strategy for achieving competitive advantage is very important.

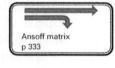

Ansoff matrix p 333

A good example of a strategic plan is given by Luton and Dunstable Hospital which is highlighted in Case 4.2.

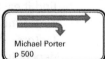

Michael Porter p 500

## Methods of producing strategic plans

Strategists use many methods to identify an appropriate strategy. Probably the best-known method is a **SWOT analysis** which covers four main features that involve internal and external factors.

## CASE 4.2: *Strategic planning in the NHS*

The British National Health Service (NHS) is a huge organisation. It employs more people than any organisation on the planet except the China's People's Liberation Army. The NHS is a stable organisation: it has a steady income, no competitors and the demands placed on it are relatively easy to predict. However, changes (such as building a new hospital or department) take many years to complete. All these factors mean that the NHS must produce strategic plans, and any strategic plan is unlikely to be overturned by sudden changes in its environment.

Luton and Dunstable are two large towns situated either side of the main motorway, about 30 miles north of London. In 2005 the area (population of about 300 000) is served by a medium-sized hospital which offers an accident and emergency (A&E) department, specialist treatments (such as neurophysiology or intensive care of babies) and minor medical procedures (such as removal of some skin growths).

Luton and Dunstable Hospital draws up a strategic plan every five years (sometimes called "quinqennial planning"). The 2006–10 strategic plan includes:

- Providing services for a catchment population of 500 000. The increase reflects two factors: natural population growth and offering specialist services to a wider area – in the neighbouring county of Hertfordshire.

- Making the A&E department quite separate from other services. This specialisation will increase expertise and make A&E provision more accountable.

- Providing more treatments away from the hospital, in places that are more convenient to patients. More patients, especially the elderly, will be treated in their own homes or in their own communities, such as their local GP surgeries.

- There will be an effort to add more value by constraining costs to a level that can be afforded.

The "architects" of Luton and Dunstable Hospital's strategic plan needed to take account of many different factors. It might be useful to pause and think of the factors you would take into account if you were one of the planners.

Factors *internal* to the organisation:

1  **Strengths** may include closeness to customers, management expertise and other skills, financial strength, branch network, market position and brand image.

2  **Weaknesses** are often the opposite of the strengths. They may include poor reputation, out-of-date equipment, inadequate R&D, difficult markets, poor industrial relations and poor communications.

Factors in the *external* environment:

3  **Opportunities** can arise from either strengths or weaknesses. Often they occur from a change in technology, legislation or markets where there is a gap.

4 **Threats** usually arise from competition – especially new entrants in the market and substitution products, shortage of resources (including skilled labour) and new government regulations.

SWOT analysis is easy to use, especially by those with little knowledge of strategic planning. However, it can be unsystematic and it is easy to miss important factors. **PESTLE analysis** is more comprehensive and gives a good checklist of important strategic factors. PESTLE is not in opposition to SWOT. Indeed, the PESTLE factors can be used to identify strengths, weaknesses, opportunities or threats. The PESTLE checklist has six main factors:

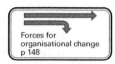

Forces for
organisational change
p 148

1 **Political factors** such as government stability, privatisation/, government regulation and control, or health issues

2 **Economic factors** such as phases of the business cycle, economic growth, interest rates, inflation, labour costs and unemployment rates

3 **Sociocultural factors** include population trends, educational levels, lifestyles and changes in consumer tastes and values

4 **Technological factors** include new discoveries, new production methods, better communications, technology transfer

5 **Legal factors** include changes in the law concerning employment, companies or business regulation

6 **Environmental factors** include discovery of new supplies of energy or raw materials, shortages of water, etc. climate change nationalisation

Sometimes PESTLE analyses is too involved. Consequently some organisations, such as UNISON and the Highways Agency, use an abbreviated version called PEST analysis.

---

**CASE 4.3:** *Unison's PEST analysis*

In Chapter 2 it was noted that trade associations and unions employ significant numbers of managers. Unison is Europe's largest public sector trade union and it has over 1.3 million members working in jobs such as librarians, social workers, secretaries and school meals supervisors. In order to represent the interests of its members it needs to develop a strategy key areas. For example, Unison used PEST analysis to develop its strategy towards immigration:

■ **Political factors** are important because immigration is an emotive issue that can generate sensational press coverage which can lead to actions by politicians. Political pressures are greatest in locations where the migrant population is high and can impact on, say, the provision of housing, health and education. Government decisions such as reducing funding for legal aid can have unanticipated effects on the ability of migrant workers to uphold their rights.

■ **Economic factors** play an important role in developing a strategy towards immigration. For example, most migrants come to the UK from countries that pay lower wages. Further, it is claimed that immigration adds 0.5 per cent to the UK's gross domestic product (more than £6 billion). The level of immigration is correlated to the business cycle – highest in booms and lowest in recessions.

- **Social factors** relevant to immigration include an ageing population which without immigration would mean a smaller number of workers to support pensioners. Difficulty in communicating in English is often another significant social factor relevant to immigration.
- **Technological factors** have a huge impact on the actions of immigrants and the appropriate strategy. For example, automation has reduced the demand for less skilled workers, transport to the UK is much cheaper and improvements in telecommunications have made it easier for immigrants to discover job opportunities and maintain contact with their home countries.

This PEST analysis has helped Unison develop an effective strategy to help immigrants. This includes political lobbying, disseminating statistics, shaping employment legislation and providing information in 11 different languages.

*Source*: based on *Times 100 Case Studies*.

## Alternative strategies

Once an organisation has analysed position and competitive advantages, it must decide upon the appropriate strategy. Many different kinds of strategy have been identified by writers such as Miles and Snow (1978), Mintzberg (1987) and Porter (1996, 2001). The following section categorises the main types of strategies according to size, focus, customers and adaptation/innovation. In addition there are some miscellaneous strategies.

Strategies concerned with size:

- **Globalisation:** expanding into other countries.
- **Industry dominance:** capturing such a large part of a market that there is little room for competitors.
- **Growth:** to obtain economies of scale and market dominance. Growth can be:
  - organic (natural) growth of present business
  - acquisition (takeover) of other organisations
  - merger with other organisations.
- **Retrenchment** is a defensive strategy aimed at increasing efficiency by reducing the size of an organisation. It takes several forms including:
  - downsizing – usually by removing middle managers and support staff
  - selling parts of the organisation to refocus on core competences
  - liquidation – closing parts of an organisation to eliminate debt (bankruptcy) or to realise assets (asset stripping).

Strategies concerning focus aim to stop an organisation spreading itself too thinly:

- **Core competences:** restricting activities to those the organisation does best. Often this means selling minor parts of the organisation.
- **Geographical focus:** restricting activities to a well-defined area so that regional dominance is achieved.

Strategies concerning *customers* focus on building a clear difference from its competitors in the minds of its consumers:

- **Product differentiation**: making a product appear different to others.
- **Cost leadership**: offering a product or service cheaper than competitors – by increased efficiency or "squeezing" suppliers.
- **Imitation**: following the ideas of a market leader and not incurring risk or development costs.
- **High speed**: delivering services to customers more quickly than competitors.

Strategies concerning *adaptation and innovation* reflect how the organisation intends to respond to changes:

- **Prospectors** innovate and follow new opportunities. They bear a risk in return for prospects of substantial growth.
- **Defenders** attempt to hold a position in a declining market by emphasising existing products. This strategy may end in terminal decline.
- **Analysers** "follow the leader when things are good". These organisations usually maintain the stability of their key products while expanding a few promising areas pioneered by others. Analysers will also follow the imitation strategy and make goods that are clones of the market leaders' products.
- **Reactors** only respond to competitive pressures when there is a danger to their survival. Reactor organisations often do not have any other strategy and only change as a last resort.

Miscellaneous strategies:

- **Employee talent** involves finding and retaining able people.
- **Strategic alliances** involve collaborating with other organisations – especially in marketing and sales where the same infrastructure can be used to sell non-competing products from different companies.

Strategies are not mutually exclusive. Many organisations, especially large ones, will use a combination. For example, they may retrench older and less profitable parts while expanding more profitable parts.

Some people are sceptical of strategic plans, they suggest that such plans are only useful in hindsight. Advocates of strategic plans forget those that have gone wrong. For instance, one of the biggest business failures in recent decades has been the fall of the Marconi Company, a fall which has been blamed on bad strategy. This is explored in Case 4.4.

## CASE 4.4: *Strategies that failed – Marconi and the Royal Bank of Scotland*

Under the chairmanship of Arnold Weinstock the General Electric Company (GEC) was a jewel in the crown of British industry: steadfast, calculating every risk with precision and making oodles of money out of such things as defence contracts. It had a cash pile of more than £2 billion – a massive sum in 1999. Lord Arnold Weinstock retired and was succeeded by George Simpson, who was keen on grand strategies. He saw GEC's future in terms of the high-technology communications market. His intention was to exploit the use of micro mirrors as optical switches to bounce signals around the Internet and become a serious rival to the likes of Cisco, the American computer colossus.

The bold strategic plan had everything – selling off the old defence businesses, rebranding with the new name Marconi, relocation of the communication business's headquarters to Pennsylvania in order to be nearer the world's largest communications market. The plan was implemented with gusto. High-technology communication companies were bought as if they were gold mines.

Simpson was so dazzled by the strategic plan, he failed to notice that communications companies were actually going out of fashion! The dotcom bubble burst. Worse, customers such as such as BT were short of cash after bidding for hugely expensive mobile phone licences and were cutting back on equipment purchases. Other companies such as Nortel and Ericsson were not blinded by their strategic plan. They saw the downturn and reacted appropriately. Simpson did not. The Marconi spree continued. Inevitably, the share price crashed. The company had a debt pile of £2.5 billion and many underperforming assets. A former GEC executive commented "as destructions of shareholder values go, I cannot think of another case that even approaches this". Simpson was replaced. Thousands of innocent workers lost their jobs and wished ruefully for the profits made in the boring old days before Simpson's "innovative", "exciting", "far-seeing" strategic plan.

The Royal Bank of Scotland (RBS) was founded in 1727 and under prudent management grew steadily to become a major British bank. In the late 1990s Sir Fred Goodwin (known as 'Fred the shred' because of his reputation for ferocious cost-cutting) joined the company and subsequently became CEO. Sir Fred and colleagues developed a strategy of aggressive expansion. In 2000, Fred led a successful hostile takeover of NatWest, a bank that was three times the RBS's size. Fred's Napoleonic strategy of expansion led to a $1.6 billion minority stake in the Bank of China. Analysts regarded his strategy as risky in case of inclement financial weather. Some shareholders accused him of megalomania. Goodwin promised to avoid further acquisitions and to focus on growing the group organically. But a harsh financial winter, the global liquidity crisis, developed in 2007. Goodwin and his colleagues continued the strategy of expansion and took over parts of a large Dutch Bank, ABN Amro. The victory stretched the RBS's resources beyond the limit. ABN Amro had underwritten many dodgy debts in America. The RBS was in real trouble, and was bailed out by the British government. 'Fred the shred' was shredded – he resigned but refused to forfeit any of his (circa £700 000 per annum) pension.

The two cases have remarkable similarities. Both were very respected and stable organisations before they adopted aggressive strategic planning. The strategies were championed by powerful and dominating men. In both cases the strategies were continued even though there were clear signs that the business environment had changed. Alas, in both cases, thousands of loyal workers lost their jobs and shareholders such as pension funds lost a lot of money. In the RBS's case the taxpayer, including the families of readers of this book, were hard hit too!

## CRITICAL THINKING 4.2 *Criticisms of strategic planning?*

Mintzberg (1994) suggests that strategic planners often make fallacious assumptions:

1 They assume an organisation can, with sufficient skill, *predetermine the future*. In fact, the business environment is so dynamic and interactive that the future cannot be estimated with any precision. It is likely that a strategic plan will be blown off course. Strategic plans reached their zenith in times of greater stability. They are less useful in today's turbulent environment.

2 They assume that *planners have an objective view*, detached from current political intrigues and beliefs of the organisation. In fact, strategists are as immersed in subjectivity and political intrigues as anyone else. Their strategies are not as objective as they would wish.

3 They adopt a formal approach involving ticking boxes on checklists in the belief that *standard procedures will produce the best plans*. In fact, a good strategy requires flair, imagination, insight and creativity, which tend to be stifled by a formal approach. It is necessary to think "outside the box".

Mintzberg acknowledges that organisations may have deliberate, *intended strategies* but these will be buffeted and blown about by forces that subsequently emerge in the environment. The *realised strategy,* the events that actually happen, may be quite different. Perhaps the most sensible approach is an *incremental strategy*. An incremental strategy occurs when an organisation takes sensible, case-by-case decisions that gradually merge to form a strategy. An incremental strategy emerges via unstructured, unpredictable, organic processes rather than a series of clinical steps. This organic approach often produces the strategy that is more appropriate to the environment.

Kay (1996) suggests that strategic planning has a formal impossibility. If good strategic planning can be reduced to a set of procedures and checklists, most organisations would be able to produce a good strategy. If all organisations have good strategies then there is little or no competitive advantage in having one!

## 4.4  Tactical plans

Tactical plans are also called *functional plans* or *intermediate plans*. They translate a firm's strategic plan into specific goals for organisational subunits. For example, a strategic plan may call for a 10 per cent increase in the market share. This depends on detailed tactical plans for each of the sales, production and finance departments. Tactical plans are usually concerned with *how* things are done whereas strategic plans are usually concerned with *what* is done.

Tactical plans need to be co-ordinated with each other and with the strategic plan. They usually have a timescale of one to five years. This contrasts with strategic plans and visions which generally have a timescale of 10 years or more. Strategic plans primarily involve top managers, whereas tactical plans primarily involve middle managers.

One of the main tools of tactical planning is the Gantt chart. These are particularly useful because they show how related operational plans are progressing. An idealised Gantt chart associated with a marketing department's tactical plan to increase sales by 10 per cent is given in Figure 4.3.

This example is highly simplified but it does demonstrate the main features of a Gantt chart. A complete Gantt chart would include holidays and other activities. It would also show progress to date and other events. Often each of the main programmes shown on a Gantt chart would be accompanied by a detailed action plan.

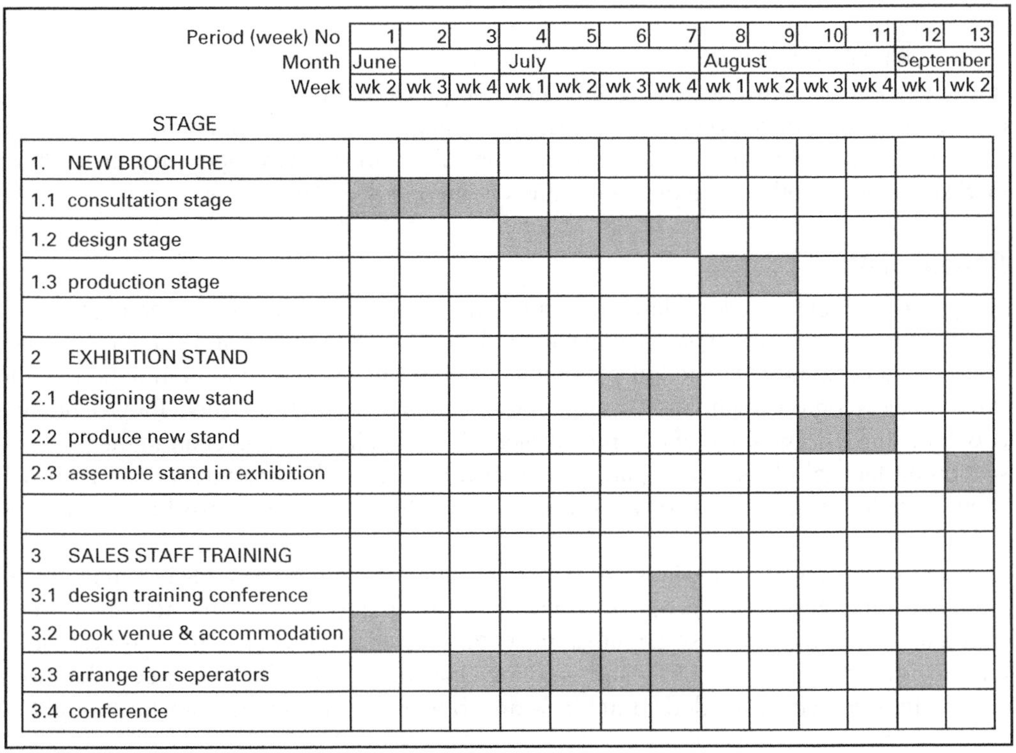

| Period (week) No | 1 | 2 | 3 | 4 | 5 | 6 | 7 | 8 | 9 | 10 | 11 | 12 | 13 |
|---|---|---|---|---|---|---|---|---|---|---|---|---|---|
| Month | June | | | July | | | | August | | | | September | |
| Week | wk 2 | wk 3 | wk 4 | wk 1 | wk 2 | wk 3 | wk 4 | wk 1 | wk 2 | wk 3 | wk 4 | wk 1 | wk 2 |
| **STAGE** | | | | | | | | | | | | | |
| 1.  NEW BROCHURE | | | | | | | | | | | | | |
| 1.1 consultation stage | ▓ | ▓ | ▓ | | | | | | | | | | |
| 1.2 design stage | | | | ▓ | | ▓ | | | | | | | |
| 1.3 production stage | | | | | | | | ▓ | ▓ | | | | |
| | | | | | | | | | | | | | |
| 2  EXHIBITION STAND | | | | | | | | | | | | | |
| 2.1 designing new stand | | | | | | ▓ | ▓ | | | | | | |
| 2.2 produce new stand | | | | | | | | | | ▓ | ▓ | | |
| 2.3 assemble stand in exhibition | | | | | | | | | | | | | ▓ |
| | | | | | | | | | | | | | |
| 3  SALES STAFF TRAINING | | | | | | | | | | | | | |
| 3.1 design training conference | | | | | | | ▓ | | | | | | |
| 3.2 book venue & accommodation | ▓ | | | | | | | | | | | | |
| 3.3 arrange for seperators | | | ▓ | ▓ | ▓ | ▓ | | | | | | ▓ | |
| 3.4 conference | | | | | | | | | | | | | |

**FIGURE 4.3** An example of a Gantt chart

Much less research and thought has been devoted to tactical plans than to strategic plans. The reasons are open to speculation. Perhaps it is because academics, writers and researchers find the heady world of high-level strategy much more exciting. Perhaps they do not have sufficient practical knowledge – an essential requirement for tactical planning.

## 4.5 Operational plans

### Definition of operational plans

Operational plans are sometimes called **action plans** or **production plans**. They are the most detailed level of planning, and specify the actions or results which individuals or small groups must achieve. Operational plans are very specific. For example, they may specify that a production line should produce 150 objects per week, a sales representative should obtain orders worth £100 000 per month or that a consultant should recruit two new clients every quarter. Operational plans should be linked to tactical plans. Operational plans are short term. They have a time span of several months but they can involve time intervals that are as short as a week or less. Operational plans involve first-line managers and should incorporate suggestions and input from employees at lower levels.

Good operational plans are essential to the efficient functioning of an organisation. They affect all employees on a day-to-day basis. They state the results which must be achieved so that tactical and strategic plans come to fruition. Clear, unambiguous communication of operational plans is essential. While strategic plans and tactical plans are not altered over long periods, operational plans constantly change – even though much of this change is cyclical. Operational plans often incorporate rules and **standard operating procedures (SOPs)**. These procedures are often contained in an operations handbook.

### Action plans

The prime tool for operation planning is the action plan. These first divide large goals into small discreet stages, which are then placed in the optimum sequence and completion dates are estimated. Sometimes, action plans allocate responsibility for the completion of the stages. Table 4.2 gives a simplified example of an action plan, starting 1 June, for producing a new brochure. This was one of the three projects included in the Gantt chart in the previous section on tactical plans. A comparison between the Gantt chart and the action plan will shows that the latter is more detailed and specifies the results that must be achieved by individuals.

Gantt charts and action plans are fairly simple and popular methods but may not be adequate for complicated projects where there are many interrelated activities. **PERT charts** are often used in these circumstances. PERT is an acronym of Program Evaluation and Review Technique. A PERT chart is a flowchart that shows the sequences, durations and timings of events needed to achieve an objective. PERT charts can be thought of

| Action plan for new brochure | | | |
|---|---|---|---|
| **Stage** | | **Completion date** | **By** |
| 1 | Review present brochure | 1 June | MA |
| 2 | Discuss needs and ideas with sales force and small number of customers | 21 June | MA & MD |
| 3 | Discuss needs and ideas with marketing director | 28 June | MA & MD |
| 4 | Produce specifications for new brochure and submit to marketing director for approval | 7 July | MA & MD |
| 5 | Produce draft brochure | 21 July | CW |
| 6 | Discuss draft brochure with marketing director, sales force and small number of customers | 28 July | MA & MD |
| 7 | Dispatch revised draft to printers | 1 Aug | MA |
| 8 | Correct proofs | 14 Aug | MA |
| 9 | Receive copies of new brochure from printer | 21 Aug | MA |

**TABLE 4.2** Example of action plan
MA = marketing assistant MD = marketing director CW = copywriter

as complicated versions of Gantt charts which are complicated and are produced by computer programs. PERT charts consist of activities which have a start, duration and completion point. Usually completion points are called "milestones". The start point of an activity is usually governed by the completion of a previous activity. Events which govern the start of an activity are usually called "**dependencies**". The preparation of a lecture provides a simple example of the process of structuring a PERT chart. The activities are shown in Table 4.3.

A computer can compile the information into a PERT chart such as that shown in Figure 4.4.

A key feature of a PERT chart is the "critical path" which indicates the shortest time in which the project can be completed. The critical path is emphasised by thicker lines or use of colour. Activities along the critical path *must* be completed to time. If they are not, the project will not finish on time. The timing of activities that are not on the critical path is less crucial. Some delay can be tolerated. The tolerable level of delay is called "**the float**". In our example, the timing of locating own books is not crucial. It can be performed any time before the library books are obtained. In fact there is a float of two and a half days.

| Activity | Duration | Dependency |
|---|---|---|
| A. Check syllabus | ½ day | None |
| B. Order and collect library books | ½ day | Activity A |
| C. Locate own books | ½ day | Activity A |
| D. Read and note relevant material | 3 days | Activity B,C |
| E. Write lecture notes | 3 days | Activity D |
| F. Prepare visual aids | 1 day | Activity E |
| G. Prepare handouts | 2 days | Activity E |
| H. Duplicate handouts | ½ day | Activity F |
| I. Assemble all materials | ¼ day | Activities E, F, H |
| J. Deliver lecture | 1hr | Activity J |

**TABLE 4.3** Data for a PERT chart

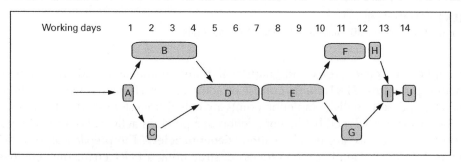

**FIGURE 4.4** Example of a simple PERT chart

## Other plans: single-use plans, standing plans and contingency plans

Sometimes it is useful to distinguish between single-use plans and standing plans:

**Single-use plans** are devised to meet unique situations and are never used again. For example, a pharmaceutical company setting up a new production plant will have elaborate plans covering the construction of buildings, the cash flow and the recruitment of employees. Even if another production plant is commissioned, the circumstances will have changed so much that the original plans will be useless.

**Standing plans** are used when a task reoccurs. For example, the pharmaceutical company may make a range of medicines, manufacturing a stock of each medicine on a cyclical basis. Thus, for example, it will have a standing plan for the manufacture of an anti-cancer medicine, a standing plan for the manufacture of a medicine to combat high blood pressure and a standing plan to manufacture a medicine to reduce inflammation of joints. Standing plans have the advantage of ensuring consistent standards and methods.

**Contingency plans** are needed because the business environment can change rapidly, making it difficult to plan for the future with certainty. Hence, many organisations develop parallel plans to cover likely eventualities. Two or more parallel plans which are in place and activated if certain conditions arise are called contingency plans. For example, a company that is extending its production facility may have two contingency plans: one will come into operation if the new plant is ready on time, while the other will be used if there is a significant delay. Similarly, a company bidding to take over another company will have two plans: one will be used if the takeover bid is successful and the other will be used if its bid fails. Contingency plans enable organisations to respond to events in a flexible way.

## 4.6  Management by objectives (a synthesis of types of plan?)

Strategic, tactical, operational, single-use, standing and contingency plans do not add value unless they are co-ordinated. Management by objectives (MBO) is a system which aims to integrate all types of plans into a coherent system where each is linked explicitly to the level above and ultimately, to an organisation's mission. Management by objectives, was embraced very enthusiastically in the 1970s. Today it is ubiquitous but implemented in a more subtle and less mechanistic way.

Management by objectives starts with the goals of someone's boss – often called "key results". The boss' key results are examined and the ways that a worker should contribute to them is identified. These are developed into key results for the worker. If he or she has subordinates, the worker's key results are examined to identify the subordinate's key results and so on. Therefore, MBO is a top-down system where one person's goals are linked to the goals of their boss and the goals of any subordinates. Ultimately everyone's goals are linked to organisational mission.

For example, an organisation's strategic plan may lead to a service manager's key result of servicing 100 customers per month. If there are four service units, the service manager will discuss their key result with each of the four first-line managers. Taking other factors such as the stringency of service contracts and the availability of service providers into account, the service manager and first-line managers will agree individual targets. For example, the four first-line managers may agree to service 30, 30, 25 and 15 customers, respectively. The first-line managers with the highest targets may have agreed an above-average contribution because they are in charge of a production lines with up-to-date equipment and experienced staff. The first-line manager with the lowest target may manage services staffed by trainees and where much machine maintenance is needed. However, as a group, the four first-line managers will service the 100 customers the service manager needs in order to achieve his or her key result that is linked to the organisation's mission.

At the end of the month each manager and subordinate will meet to discuss performance. Any shortfall is examined and its reason identified. The shortfall may not be the fault of the subordinate. It could be that the initial target, or perhaps the strategy, are too ambitious – in which case they should be reduced. It could be the shortfall was caused by an unreliable supplier – in which case the purchasing department would be asked to improve the supply chain. Finally, it could be that the manager omitted to communicate a key piece of information – in which case the manager should seek to improve communication skills. In some cases it is important to note the five characteristics of MBO, and extra information about them is given on the website associated with this book.

## Research results and MBO

Management by objectives is consistent with research by occupational psychologists such as Locke *et al.* (1981), which proposed that people perform better when they are given specific goals that are moderately, but not excessively, challenging. However, many people are unenthusiastic about the effectiveness of MBO. Research concerning participation in decision-making is less positive. It would seem that the level of the difficulty of the goals is much more important than the way the goals are set (Latham and Saari, 1979). In general, research indicates that MBO is highly effective and is likely to produce productivity gains in over 90 per cent of cases (Rogers and Hunter, 1991). Rogers and Hunter's study emphasised the importance of top-management commitment. When their commitment to MBO was high the average productivity gain (56 per cent) was higher than the productivity gain when top-management commitment was low (6 per cent).

### CRITICAL THINKING 4.3 *Weaknesses of MBO*

The original enthusiasm for MBO is somewhat diluted because it has at least five *weaknesses*:

1   MBO distorts an organisation by focusing upon measurable things which are not necessarily important things. Behaviour linked to targets increases but the gains may be at the expense of equally important, less measurable activities such as setting a good example or helping others. Often, these activities are called "corporate citizenship".

2   Implementation and operation of MBO absorbs a great deal of managerial effort. Sometimes MBO produces excessive paperwork and managers may spend more time devising criteria, drawing up action plans and preparing for appraisal meetings than actively managing others.

3   In the longer term, MBO encourages managers to set lower goals. Once managers realise that successive cycles of MBO will result in ever-increasing targets, they become wise and set themselves easier goals.

4   MBO might work in the UK, the USA, the Netherlands and Australia where there is a high work ethic and where people are accustomed to working towards goals in an independent way. However, there is doubt whether it works in other cultures that have different values (Hofstede, 1980).

5   MBO does not work well where rapid change is the norm. MBO was developed in the 1950s when there was a more stable business environment. Nowadays a dramatic, overnight change can make such plans obsolete.

## 4.7  Advantages and disadvantages of planning and strategy?

Most people agree that the advantages of planning far outweigh the disadvantages. Plans are *advantageous* because they:

- **Give direction and focus to organisational activities** – provided the plans are well communicated. Without plans people will make decisions in isolation and ignore the goals that need to be achieved.
- **Indicate the required standard of performance**.
- **Improve speed of decision-making**. Instead of referring matters higher and waiting for a reply, a manager can consult a plan and make a quicker decision.
- **Plans allow lower levels of staff to participate in making decisions**.
- **Give context** and an explanation of many decisions which are handed down from senior management.
- **Minimise waste and redundancy** by foreseeing future difficulties and therefore taking action to circumvent them.
- **Focus attention on the future** and the way an organisation must marshal its resources. Without plans people may be content to "rest on their laurels".

However it is clear that plans and strategies have *three disadvantages:*

- Strategies are **only useful with hindsight.** Advocates of strategy ignore strategic plans that have gone wrong. For example, two of the biggest business failures in recent decades has been the fall of the Marconi Company and the RBS. The falls of Marconi and the RBS were explored further in Case 4.4.
- Strategies **consume large quantities of management time** and effort that would be better spent elsewhere. If the organisation operates in a very turbulent environment or if it operates in a very predictable and constraining environment, strategies have limited value. It is better to simply make sure that the organisation is very adaptable so that it can respond appropriately whatever happens.
- Strategies can **induce rigidity**, because their designers become too committed to them. Instead of responding to the environment, strategists are likely to argue that their plans will work "if only" the organisation will provide more resources. Continued failure may lead to the claim that the strategy is correct and the difficulties are only short-term aberrations. Yet further failure may lead to the claim that the strategy is fine but it was implemented in the wrong way. Eventually it dawns that a new strategy is needed but by that time the organisation may have "done a Marconi or an RBS!"

The inevitable conclusion is that managers *must* use plans to their full advantage. Nevertheless, they should beware of devoting too much time perfecting plans to the nth degree and they should abandon plans when there is clear evidence that they are inadequate or if the environment has changed. Plans are excellent servants but are very dangerous masters!

## 4.8  Planning toolkit

- Most disadvantages of planning are because of *inflexibility*. Hence planners should ensure a flexible environment which values learning and continuous improvement.

- The goals contained in plans are important. *Goals should be ambitious but not unreasonable*. The goals will be more practical and easier to understand if the people required to implement the plans are involved in setting the goals. Generally speaking, plans should be constructed "bottom-up" rather than "top-down".

- *Timescales of plans should be realistic*. They should take account of:
  - illnesses and holidays
  - staff training
  - daily, seasonal and other variations in workload
  - rotation of staff into different jobs so that versatility and motivation are enhanced

- *Planning specialists should not be aloof experts* working in a distant planning department. Rather, they should be facilitators who assist a group to formulate their own workable plans.

The importance of planning was identified very early in the history of management. However, tasks need to be organised into jobs. Jobs must be organised into a coherent structure. Staff must be willing and able to implement the plans and the plans must be communicated effectively. The next chapters describe other important management processes such as organising, staffing and communicating.

# Activities and further study

## Essay plans

Prepare plans for the following essays:

1 Compare and contrast two methods of producing organisational strategies.
2 Select a local organisation (perhaps your college or university department, perhaps a charitable organisation or club that you know well) and conduct both a SWOT analysis and a PESTLE analysis for that organisation.
3 Compare and contrast mission statements and vision statements.
4 Compare and contrast strategic plans, tactical plans and operational plans.
5 Evaluate the benefits and disadvantages of planning.

## Web activities

1 People often confuse mission statements and vision statements. Log on to the website associated with this book and and access "Web Based Exercise 2: Missions and Visions". Then complete the table that contrasts the two types of statement. When you have finished compare your answer with the model which is also given on the website.
2 Log on to the website associated with this book and access "Web Based Exercise 3: Planning Techniques". Follow the instructions and produce an action plan and a Gantt chart. When you have finished compare your work with the model answer which is also given on the website.
3 Search the Internet for mission statements – perhaps the mission statement of your employer, university or college. To what extent do you think people in the organisation find a mission statement useful in achieving organisational goals? Ask six members of the organisation whether they are aware the mission statement exists. Ask those who are aware of its existence what the mission statement contains.
4 Search the Internet for more information about the Marconi case study (hint: wikipedia. org and news.bbc.co.uk are good places to start).

## Experiential activities

1 Write a mission and vision statement for yourself!

2 Imagine that you are a member of a consultancy group that helps other organisations install management by objectives. You have received an enquiry from a small organisation that employs 100 people and has 12 managers. They invite you to give a 20-minute presentation to explain MBO. Prepare this presentation and deliver it to a group of fellow students.

3 Make a list of the six most important goals you wish to achieve in the next year. Examine these goals critically for their technical merit as objectives:

● Are they clear?

● Are they quantifiable?

● Are they realistic, etc.?

(Hint: it may be useful to visit websites such as www.smc.qld.edu.au/goals.htm or www.goal-setting-guide.com/smart-goals.html.)

4 Visit the Preactor website (http://www.preactor.com/online-demo/data/english/ standard%20demo/online-demo.html) to gain an impression of the complexity of operational planning. After a wooden introduction the demonstration shows how complex Gantt charts are set up to control production.

## Recommended reading

1 Porter, M.E. (1996) "What is strategy?", *Harvard Business Review*, 61–78. November– December, A long, tedious paper which is a little outdated. Nevertheless it gives a clear distinction between effectiveness and strategic positioning. It also give many examples of company strategies. Highly recommended.

2 Collins, J.C. and Porras, J.I. (1996) "Building your company's vision", *Harvard Business Review*, September–October, 65–77. This article outlines the construction of vision statements and examples from well-known companies.

3 Furst, P. (2010) "Planning is the architect", *Industrial Engineer*, **42** (2), 44–50. A practical example of the importance of planning. Read from page 46 onwards.

4 Stoller, J. (2010) "The world according to Gantt", *CMA Management*, **84** (5), 33–35. This article outlines the significance of Gantt charts in managing projects and helping stakeholders communicate with each other. It also gives details of IT packages which can construct Gantt charts.

# Organisational Structures and Teamwork

**5**

## ❖ LEARNING OBJECTIVES

After studying this chapter you should be able to suggest ways of structuring jobs, managing teams and arranging them into an organisation. In particular, you should be able to:

❖ **define** the organising process and **differentiate** between formal organisational structures and informal ones

❖ **explain** how you would design a job using the concepts of: division of labour – authority and responsibility– span of control – ergonomics

❖ **describe** the types of teams, team roles and the factors that make teams effective

❖ **describe** the following ways of scheduling work: flexitime – compressed working week – homeworking and teleworking – job sharing – contingency working – office sharing and hoteling

❖ **briefly explain** the concept of functional organisational structures and **differentiate** between tall and flat structures

❖ **briefly explain** the concept of divisional structures and **itemise** the three main ways of creating divisions

❖ **draw a diagram** of a matrix organisational structure

❖ **draw a diagram** of network organisational structures

❖ **explain** the concepts of learning structures and itemise their five main characteristics

❖ **draw up a substantive table** that systematises the advantages of functional, divisional, matrix and team structures

❖ **itemise** four ways of co-ordinating the activities teams within an organisation

❖ **itemise** five main dimensions of organisational structure

---

**CASE 5.1:** *Organisational restructuring at Pilkington in Australia*

Pilkington is a world-renowned maker of glass, now owned by Nippon Sheet Glass. One of its manufacturing plants is in Dandenong, Australia.

The factory had a very traditional organisational structure with workers at the bottom and senior managers at the top. The normal flow of information was from the top downwards. Top management set standards and objectives which were then communicated down the hierarchy. This structure resulted in many employees feeling they were given orders by managers who had little knowledge of things that were happening on the "factory floor". The hierarchical structure was largely responsible for strong divisions between "them and us". Labour relations were poor and at the time the plant was shut by strike action. The plant was also losing its competitive advantage against other glass-makers.

Pilkington decided to implement major changes in the organisation at Dandenong. Work was reorganised into three business units: making, cutting and warehousing. Within these divisions employees were organised into work teams which participated in setting standards and working methods. The main information flow was reversed and passed from employees to team leaders to team supervisors and upwards to the plant manager.

An evaluation showed that the changes in organisational structure had resulted in higher morale, greater industrial harmony, higher customer satisfaction and increased employee productivity.

*Source*: based on B. Barrett, C. Cook and M. Williams Pilkington, "An organisation in transition" http://www.thomsonlearning.com.au/higher/management/waddell/2e/media/ Case_Pilkington.pdf.

---

In a one-person set-up there is no need for organisation: the one person does everything. As soon as more people are involved the process of organising becomes essential–otherwise people will complete tasks at random using whatever resources are at hand and in ignorance of what others are doing. Chaos will ensue. While *planning* determines *what* tasks need to be done in what sequence, *organising* determines *who* completes the tasks and the *resources needed*. Planning and organising are interrelated. For example, many action plans involve a certain amount of organising.

The subject of organising includes a number of interesting topics such as team-working, organisational change and organisational structures which can be studied in isolation. However, it is much better to cover them in a logical order. The obvious starting point is to *define the process of organising* and to *recognise the two main branches, formal and informal organisation*. The most basic aspects of work are the activities that need to be performed in order to add value. Hence, the most basic aspect is to organise these activities into jobs (i.e. *job design*). The next stage is to arrange the jobs into coherent groups that can be performed by *teams of people*. In their turn, teams of people can be placed within an *organisational structure* that helps deliver its strategy. Unfortunately, the world is not static and even a good initial organisational structure will need to be amended to suit a different business environments. Hence the subject of organising does not finish with a study of the

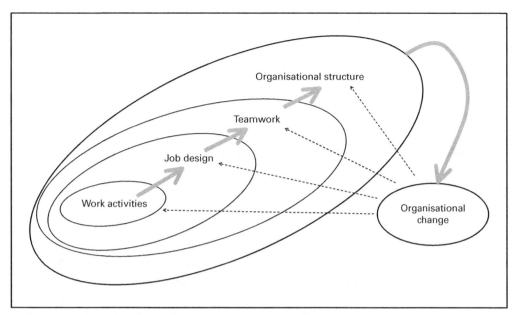

**FIGURE 5.1** The relationship between the subtopics of the organisational process

organisational structure. It finishes, instead, with the topic of *organisational change*. This logical arrangement of organising is shown in Figure 5.1.

The topics interact with each other. For example, organisational change will influence the activities that are performed, the way that teams function and the way an organisation is structured. The six topics cover a great deal of information. In order to make it easier to absorb, they are split into two chapters. This chapter covers the first four of these topics. The next chapter deals with organisational change and all its uncertainties.

## 5.1 Definition of organising and organisational structures

Many definitions do not make the distinction between planning and organising sufficiently clear. One of the clearest definitions is:

> 66  Organising is the process of determining who will perform the tasks needed to achieve organisational objectives, the resources to be used and the way the tasks will be managed and co-ordinated.  99

Four points from this definition need to be noted. Organising:

- **Is *not* primarily concerned with specifying goals and tasks**. However, the way in which things are organised will have a bearing on the tasks which can be attempted and the degree to which they are achieved.
- **Is concerned with the allocation of the tasks** to specific people or groups of people.

- **Is concerned with the co-ordination of the efforts** of several people needed to complete large tasks.
- **Concerns resources and other people**. It may involve budgets, territories, production facilities or intellectual abilities.

Many of the issues concerning organisational structure were illustrated in Case 5.1.

## 5.2  Formal and informal organisational structures

An *organisation chart* is a representation of an organisation's formal structure – the official arrangement of work positions within an organisation. The distinction between the *formal* organisation and the *informal* organisation is important but, when set up, they may be very similar. In practice the formal structure is soon modified by friendships, the personalities of individuals and the networks which develop. The "grapevine" is an important component of an informal organisation. The informal organisation often allows people to use shortcuts

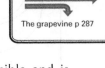
The grapevine p 287

and obtain information or take action which would otherwise be impossible and is particularly important during times of change and stress. The informal organisation meets the psychological needs of individuals. However, the informal side of organisations has disadvantages: it may take on a life of its own and work towards goals which are different from the formal goals: information "on the grapevine" may be inaccurate or distorted; and informal organisation can be used to exclude certain people and their ideas. The formal organisation is made up of jobs and the structure in which the jobs are placed. The first step in understanding the formal structure of an organisation is to understand the fundamentals of job design.

## 5.3  Job design

The most fundamental aspect of organising is to decide what people are required to do as part of their job. This process is called *job design*. Six main aspects need to be considered:

1  specialisation
2  authority
3  span of control
4  ergonomics
5  work schedules and
6  worker involvement in job design

### Specialisation and division of labour

Job design assumes that some workers will specialise in certain activities while other workers will specialise in different ones. *Specialisation* means that each worker only does a part of what is needed to make a product, deliver a service or complete a task. It is sometimes called *division of labour*. Up to a point it leads to greater efficiency and economies of scale because:

- Individuals can quickly develop high level of skills in certain activities.
- People can be employed in those activities where they have natural ability. Their potential can be exploited more fully.
- Employees do not waste time changing from task to task.
- Jobs are often simplified and can be allocated, at less cost, to workers with lower skills.

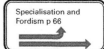

Extreme specialisation is seen in some assembly lines where employees are required to do a single task, repetitively, but with a high level of speed and efficiency. Unfortunately, high levels of specialisation have disadvantages:

- Highly specialised jobs are boring and tend to demotivate people. Employees rarely see a finished product; they tend to have no pride in their work.
- Teamwork and creativity are inhibited.
- Employees only have a restricted range of skills. They cannot be redeployed to deal with bottlenecks elsewhere. Further, these employees are vulnerable to changes. When changes occur these employees are likely to be dismissed or need retraining.

In general, job design seeks to achieve a balance between the advantages and disadvantages of specialisation. Figure 5.2 indicates that optimum productivity is achieved at intermediate levels of specialisation.

Jobs should be designed to avoid negative effects of specialisation and include factors which motivate workers. Hackman and Oldham (1980) suggest that people will be motivated if a job:

- Requires the use of different skills rather than the repetitive use of one or two skills (*skill variety*).

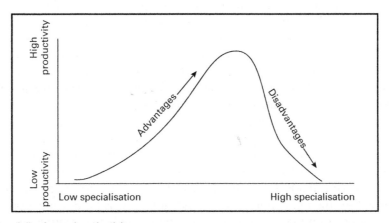

**FIGURE 5.2** Specialisation and productivity

- Allow a person to do a complete job rather than a small part. Workers are then more likely to be motivated by a sense of pride (*task identity*).

- Allows people to understand the contribution their work makes to the goals of the organisation or its importance to colleagues or customers (*task significance*)**.**

- Gives freedom, discretion and independence in the way that the work has to be done – providing that the correct results are achieved (*autonomy*).

- *Provides feedback* on a worker's effectiveness. Sometimes feedback is *extrinsic* in the sense that people are told by others how well they are performing. In other jobs feedback is *intrinsic* because the job itself provides information about success or failure.

Often these principles are applied to improve specialised jobs which are believed to be demotivating. The jobs are examined using a special questionnaire and those areas that are found to be deficient are improved by, say, including new activities or developing a systematic method of feedback.

It is widely recognised that, nowadays, the greatest asset of most organisations is the knowledge generated and held by its employees. Many jobs should therefore be designed so that expanding and recording the organisation's knowledge base is an explicit component. Knowledge management is explained in more detail in Chapter 18.

Knowledge
management p 452

## Authority and responsibility

Authority is the formal power to make decisions, marshal resources and give instructions to others. Authority is a characteristic of a job rather than a characteristic of an individual – it remains the same even if a job is held by a different person. Early management theorists considered authority in depth. They viewed from a feudal perspective: all authority was held by top management and it was successively delegated to lower ranks. Authority was therefore determined by one's position in a management hierarchy.

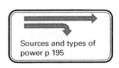

Sources and types of
power p 195

The modern view of authority is rather more complicated. Subordinates often refuse to obey the authority of a superior who is incompetent. Subordinates may join forces and use the informal organisational structure to thwart the authority of a new or insecure manager. Subordinates who have particular expertise may exercise more authority than those in superior positions. For example, a chief executive may follow the judgement of a human resource (HR) manager when selecting key members of staff because the HR manager has a higher level of expertise. Job descriptions usually specify limits of authority. For example, a job description might state that a manager can only authorise overtime up to a certain level.

Traditionally authority was closely guarded. It was believed that employees at lower levels were basically idiots who could not be trusted. This meant that time was wasted because subordinates repeatedly referred matters to their superiors and waited for decisions. Many decisions were made by superiors who had neither up-to-date information nor specialist expertise. The modern trend is to push authority as far down the organisation as possible so that decision-making is quicker and based on better information. This trend is called **empowerment.**

**Responsibility** is the converse of authority. A manager's "area of responsibility" (AOR) is the domain of resources over which she or he has authority. It is the duty of a subordinate to perform a task that has been given to him or her. However, this duty only exists if the employee, in turn, has authority over the resources needed to do the job. Job design must achieve the correct relationship between authority and responsibility.

## Span of control

Responsibility for the work of other employees is a special kind of authority. The number of employees supervised is called the "span of control". Traditionally it was argued that about six subordinates was the optimum span of control. If a manager is responsible for more employees there is the danger of "communication overload". However, research has indicated that the span of control depends upon a number of factors such as environmental stability. In highly stable situations with few complexities and exceptions, the span of control can be higher, perhaps extending to 20, 30 or even 50 subordinates. The latter situation occurs on production lines making highly standardised products. High spans of control are possible when an organisation has a clear system of values, where a boss and subordinates work in close proximity, or where there is an efficient computer system that captures and collates key management information. The increasing use of information technology may be one of the reasons why, in recent years, the spans of managerial control have increased. In more changeable situations, where different products are made to meet the needs of individual customers, smaller spans of control may be better.

## Ergonomics and job design

**Ergonomics** is a specialised area of psychology. It aims to ensure that jobs are designed in a way that makes them suitable for human beings to perform. This means that workplaces should minimise harmful effects. Machines should be designed in a way which makes accidents impossible. For example, a metal-cutting machine can avoid accidental amputation of a hand by making sure that the cutting blades do not operate until a guard is in place and the worker's hands are safely out of the way while pressing two buttons that are placed well outside the danger area.

Ergonomics plays an important role in the **design of instrument displays**. For example, the pilot of an aircraft must monitor many dials. Many scientific experiments have been conducted to ensure that a cockpit display is laid out to maximise the ease of reading and to minimise the risk of confusion. One of the most recent concerns of ergonomists is the design of computerised workplaces. They should be constructed so that the working position does not create problems from poor posture, glare or repetitive actions that result in repetitive strain injury (RSI).

Ergonomists try to establish the patterns of **shiftwork** which do least damage to long-term health. Working very long hours (48 hours or more per week for more than nine weeks) carries long-term health risks. Studies conducted as long ago as 1918 showed that the output of people who work very long hours is less than those who work to a more reasonable schedule.

## Work schedules

In traditional agricultural economies work schedules were determined by seasonal cycles of night and day. With the Industrial Revolution and invention of artificial lighting, work schedules tended to involve long shifts of 12 hours or more. Such long hours were often counterproductive and shorter hours with more holidays became the norm. In the middle of the twentieth century the stereotypical work schedule followed a "nine to five" pattern – although probably only a small proportion of the working population actually worked that schedule. In the closing decades of the twentieth century work schedules became more varied and included flexible working hours, a compressed working week and homeworking.

- **Flexitime** is probably the most common variation on the "standard" working week. It allows workers some autonomy and discretion in the hours that they work – provided that the total hours worked is sufficient. Flexitime employees must usually be present for certain core hours such as 10.00 a.m. to 3.00 p.m. It is very popular with secretarial and administrative staff. Flexitime often increases productivity because it decreases absenteeism and lateness. *Employees* like flexitime because it allows them to balance the competing demands of work and home. However, some *managers* may question an employee's motivation and commitment if they use flexitime too liberally.

- **Compressed working week** is another variation on the "standard" working week. Employees have longer working days in return for more days when they do not work. The most common form is for employees to work ten hours for four days in return for having a weekend break of three days. Some employees then choose to take a second job. The compressed working week is ideally suited to the domestic arrangements of some employees. However, many people are fatigued during the last two hours of the 10-hour working shifts and their concentration and attention may suffer.

- **Homeworking** and **teleworking**. Working at home, or in the fields near to home was once the most common form of work. In many industries, such as assembling small products or packing goods, working from home persisted for many years. The increasing availability of computers has led to a new variety of homeworking–teleworking. In teleworking an employee works at home but is linked to "the office" via the Internet. In addition, they attend "the office", say, one day a week for meetings and social events. The archetypal form of telecommuting is employees who are engaged in data input. Some *advantages* of teleworking are:

  - *Low overheads* – a firm does not have to provide office space, heating and lighting. These costs are usually borne by the teleworker.

  - *Reduction of labour shortages* – firms can employ people who would otherwise be outside the labour market. Teleworking often allows employers to recruit people with domestic responsibilities or who do not wish to commute to work.

  - *Increased productivity* – research suggests that teleworking can increase productivity by 25 per cent. Part of this saving is due to lower absenteeism and lower labour turnover. Some of the saving may be due to a reduction in time spent on social activities at work and the fact that employees are not fatigued by commuting.

Some *disadvantages* of teleworking are:

- Teleworkers may feel that their *careers suffer* because they are not as visible to important people in the organisation.
- *Home circumstances may interfere* with teleworking and increase the stress placed upon teleworkers. Teleworkers may find the *home-work interface* very difficult and will work very long hours in order to complete assignments.

■ **Job sharing** – the concept of job sharing is self-explanatory. The duties involved in one job are shared, usually, by two people. Sometimes they work on different days of the week. Sometimes one person works in the morning while the other person works in the afternoon. Frequently the people who share the job are friends, indeed, sometimes husband and wife. If the job is complex, it is important to arrange a "handover" period where the sharers co-ordinate. From the employee's point of view job sharing may be an excellent way of combining work with domestic responsibilities or leisure. From the employer's point of view job sharing reduces the impact should an employee fall ill. Some people maintain that there is an increase in productivity because each person will achieve more than their proportionate share of the job. Apparently this is particularly true when the job involves creative work: a job shared between two people may well produce 20 per cent or more ideas than a single employee.

■ **Contingent workers** – casual workers who are hired as and when there is sufficient demand are called contingent workers. There is nothing new about contingent working. In agricultural economies many people were hired during the harvest period and their employment ended once the crops were gathered. In the past, dockyard workers were employed when ships arrived and dismissed when cargoes had been unloaded. Universities employ large numbers of contingency seminar leaders to cope with increased student numbers. Managers who are hired for specific projects are often called "interim managers".  The provision of many contingent office workers is highly organised by "temping agencies". Many contingent workers are paid low wages but the temporary nature of their work may be convenient for them. Costs of using contingent workers from an agency may be high because an agency charges a sizeable commission to cover the expense of recruiting and maintaining a register of temporary employees. Nevertheless, the costs of employing "temps" may be an efficient way of meeting peaks in demand.

■ **Office sharing and hoteling**. Providing employees with a workplace or office is expensive. It is particularly expensive if the workplace requires specialist equipment or if it is located in the centre of a major city. To make matters worse, individuals may only use their workplace for a part of the time. For example, a sales manager may only use his or her office during the mornings. During the afternoon he or she may be accompanying sales representatives "on the road". Therefore it may be possible to allocate an office to two sales managers. One uses it in the morning and is "on the road" during the afternoon while the other is "on the road" during the morning and in the office during the afternoon.

Operational planning p 102

*Hoteling* takes the idea a step further. A firm can have a number of desks or offices. Staff can book a desk or an office when it is needed in a way that is analogous to booking a hotel room when it is needed for a day or, for some purposes, only an hour! These arrangements are often used by major consultancy firms that have premises in prestigious but expensive centres of major cities. Providing consultants with their own accommodation would be prohibitively costly. Each might occupy an office for only a few hours each week since most of their time is spent at the premises of their clients. The system of booking an office or desk space for short periods is called **"hot-desking"**.

---

### CRITICAL THINKING 5.1 *Hot desks and employer commitment*

A hot-desking employee will be given a trolley to keep files and other equipment. It will be stored, cheaply, in a depot. When the consultant needs an office one will be reserved, the trolley will be taken from the depot to the allocated desk and a computer will route telephone calls to them. When they complete their work the desk will be vacated, the trolley returned to the depot and the desk space allocated to another consultant. From the firm's point of view, hot-desking is an excellent proposition – it slashes accommodation costs. Further, it inhibits employees wasting time luxuriating in their own office rather than spending time with clients on work that generates fees. However, the impact on employees can be very negative. Hot-desking may generate annoyance. Time is often wasted by the process of reserving a desk, and trollies may arrive late or be delivered to the wrong desk. Perhaps the most damning criticism of hot-desking is that it hardly engenders a feeling that the organisation has a long-term commitment to an employee. Hot-desking may reduce organisational commitment. After all, if the organisation provides them with so little back-up, they may as well become a "Fred in a shed" and "poach" clients from his or her employer.

---

The way that jobs are designed has changed. In the past jobs were usually designed by managers who then explained them to workers. Nowadays, workers are often encouraged to be proactive and take the initiative in shaping their own job designs. It is perhaps surprising that people at lower organisational levels seem to have the greatest freedom in shaping their own jobs. There is evidence that jobs have become more stressful. In addition, interaction with other people form important activities. Daniels and de Jonge (2010) suggest that workplace social support and job control help to reduce excessive job demands. An excellent source of recent findings on a job design is given in a special issue of *Journal of Organisational Behaviour* (see Grant *et al.*, 2010).

### *Worker involvement in job design*

In the classical view of job design a job is objectively defined, in great detail, by management so that a job is objective and independent of the person who performs the work. This may have been accurate the days of Ford when mass production required people to produce identical things with great efficiency. Today, this is rarely the case. Jobs are conceived as broad roles which give incumbents a great deal of latitude and allow them to interpret and perform the work. Workers are usually involved in the process of producing a job description: indeed many workers are allowed to define their own jobs. It is commonplace for organisations to encourage workers to "sculpt" their jobs by stretching and contracting its boundaries, often redefining it in idiosyncratic ways. This has advantages: it motivates workers and it makes them more flexible. However, it can lead to "untidy organisational structures" that are difficult to communicate and it makes some activities such as equitable appraisals quite difficult (see Lievans, Sanchez, Bartram and Browne, 2010). Further, management needs extra vigilance to ensure that all essential activities are covered.

In some jobs, such as sales, an individual works predominantly on their own, occasionally reporting to their boss and perhaps delegating work to an assistant. However, such jobs are rare. Most jobs involve working with other people in a team. Therefore, once a job has been properly designed, the next step is to arrange jobs into groups that can be performed by teams and it is important to describe how these teams can work.

## 5.4  Teams and teamwork

Teams exist in most organisations but, as Elton Mayo discovered in the bank wiring room at the Hawthorne electrical plant, they can restrict output and productivity. However, the opposite can also be true. A good team that is well managed can be very good at transforming resources into more valuable products. Clearly every manager needs a good understanding of teams and teamwork. The topic can be divided into five major sections:

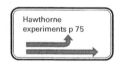
Hawthorne experiments p 75

- advantages and disadvantages of teams
- types of teams
- composition of teams and team roles
- stages of team development
- characteristics of effective teams

We now consider each of these sections in greater detail.

### Advantages and disadvantages of teams

Teams exist in most organisations because they have many *advantages*. The main ones are:

- Groups of people working in co-operation can often *achieve more* than the same number of people working individually. This was discovered thousands of years ago when men learnt that they could hunt and kill more and bigger animals when they worked as a group.

- People can *learn new skills* from other people. This means that ideas which benefit an organisation can spread faster. Further, in teams, the ideas of one person can *stimulate* other people to have more and better ideas (synergy)

- Working in teams satisfies human "belongingness needs" and this may increase worker motivation.

A major *disadvantage* of teams is the *time and effort it takes to weld individuals into a team*. Energy needs to be spent communicating the organisation's objectives and methods, and inculcating organisational values. More time is needed to maintain a group. Time must be allowed for team members to communicate with each other – mainly at meetings. Time will also be spent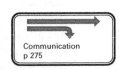

Communication
p 275

on meeting the social and emotional needs such as resolving arguments or arranging social events. The energy taken to form and maintain a team means, inevitably, that there is less energy to complete the team's task. There is a third disadvantage of teamworking: **social loafing**. Some members of the team "do not pull their weight". They make the calculation they can get away with doing less work and yet receive full pay. Social loafing can be reduced by good leadership and incentives such as team bonus schemes.

## Types of teams

Teams take many forms. Sometimes, as in the airline industry, a team takes the form of a **crew** – a group of people who have rarely met but they can work effectively because they have been thoroughly trained and understand their duties. These teams may only last as long as a work shift. Sometimes, teams take the form of **project teams** who are dedicated to a particular objective. Often the members of these teams are drawn from different department so that they encompass a wide range of skills. Project teams are frequently used to develop new products or services. They are frequently found in the IT industry where, say, they will be tasked to devise a system and write a computer program for a client. Quality circles are another kind of project team where a major role is to communicate and advocate new ideas. The duration of a project team will depend on the precise project but, in general, they last 3–15 months. **Production teams** are a group of people who produce an established good or service, in considerable quality. They usually last a long time, perhaps years (see CIPD, 2009b). Classic examples are construction teams or healthcare workers. A more specialist example might be legal teams who work together to deal with the legal side of, say, a merger or acquisition.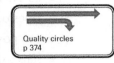

Quality circles
p 374

Virtual teams** are a relatively new and have come into prominence because of the Internet or Intranet. Members of virtual teams may rarely meet and may work in different buildings, countries or continents. They will communicate by telephone, computer or teleconferencing. The geographical distances between members means that managing virtual teams is particularly difficult: they are prone to misunderstandings on fundamental issues. **Self-managing teams** are another, relatively new, form of teamworking. They are also called **semi-autonomous workgroups** and **self-directed teams**. A self-managing team is given a task where quantity, quality and cost are clearly specified. The team then decides, by

## CASE 5.2: *The C-suite teams at Goldman-Sachs etc.*

The C-suite team (senior people whose job title includes the word "chief") is probably the most important team in any organisation. A classic example emerged in the financial giant, Goldman Sachs. In 1976 the managing director died and his position was filled by two people, John Weinberg and John Whitehead. They were friends and they found it easy to co-operate to run the firm for eight years and set a precedent. Henry Paulson was member a later C-suite who ran Goldman Sachs with two chief operating officers (COOs) and then he became US Treasury Secretary. Similar C-suite teams are seen in many other major companies, such as Coca-Cola, Microsoft and Wal-Mart. Starbucks once had an H2O team made up of three chiefs whose Christian names were **H**oward, **H**oward and **O**rrin. The C-suite team in Seagate (disk-drive maker) has four members: CEO, COO, CFO and a vice-president in charge of marketing and strategy.

Small, high-ranking, teams are necessary because a single person does not have enough ability to focus attention, acquire new capabilities, process information or take on the diverse roles needed at the head of a large organisation. Bruce Chizen, CEO of Adobe Systems has said, "my job is simply too big for any one person".

Members of a C-suite team are usually *complementary*. Generally the CEO is good at dealing with external matters such as politics and public relations, while the COO is good at dealing with internal matters such as procedures and operational matters. Often, one or more members of a C-suite team will act as a diplomat and a "good cop" while others act aggressively as "bad cops". Similarly, one member of a team acts as a "guardian" who preserves what is good in the organisation, who tries to *pull* things together within the organisation, while another member acts as an entrepreneur who tries to *push* the organisation into new things. Members of C-suite teams usually have complementary expertise. Although they are general managers they only have detailed experience in one or two business functions such as sales and marketing or, say, R&D plus operations. Some *advantages* of C-suite teams are:

- There is a diversity of thought and talent.
- While decisions take longer to make, they are usually superior.
- There is an effective constraint on strong egos that are found at the top of organisations.

C-suite teams also have *disadvantages* such as:

- Members may pursue incompatible goals and they may have incompatible styles.
- People lower down the organisation sometimes wonder to whom they should talk or listen.
- It is much more difficult to make changes at the top because members of a C-suite team are likely to join forces to resist changes they dislike.

*Source:* based on Miles, S.A. and Watkins, M.D. (2007) "The leadership team: complementary strengths or conflicting agendas?", *Harvard Business Review*, **85** (4), 90–97.

themselves, how to fulfil the task – e.g. the order and pace at which sub-tasks are completed and which team members perform different roles. Self-managing teams can be thought of as the opposite of the assembly-line system where managers decided, in minute detail, the sequence in which a car should be assembled. *Individual workers* would then be give specific tasks to perform at a pace determined by the conveyor belt which was controlled by management. A classic example of self-managing teams is Volvo's production system at their Uddvalla plant in the 1960s where a team of assemblers stayed with a car as it moved through the assembly process on a special jig. The team put the whole car together and they obtained much higher job satisfaction.

## CRITICAL THINKING 5.2 *What is wrong with self-managed teams?*

In the closing decades of the twentieth century most management thinkers romanticised the virtues of teamworking – especially the virtues of self-management teams. "However, most of these experiments, even in Volvo, have been terminated and traditional assembly systems have been reintroduced" (Contu, 2007). The reversion to traditional assembly systems has been attributed to lower productivity in self-managed workgroups but variability in quality also played a part in their demise. Higher unemployment in Sweden meant that it was easier to get employees to work on assembly lines and vested interests in traditional methods were happy to reassert themselves. Others have pointed out that, even in their heyday, most self-managed teams had limited discretion and could not, for example, hire or fire workers, nor could they change suppliers or redesign components.

Barker (1993), for example pointed out that teamworking has a darker side and that managers were using teams as an invisible form of control. Group dynamics were doing management's job for them. Peer-group pressure was being harnessed to shape a worker's behaviour so that it was in line with the organisation's objectives. Team members themselves would identify and discipline colleague who failed to meet targets. Time and motion study may have been formally abandoned but "the stopwatch" still resides in the team (see Alder, 1993).

## Composition of teams and team roles

A team will consist of a relatively small (about 6–12) number of workers drawn from relevant functions. Generally, it is better to choose members who share the same goals and that those goals are consistent with the organisation's goal. Within this basic constraint, it is better that the team members are quite diverse so that many different types of expertise and viewpoints are available. For example, in IT, an ideal software development team would contain someone who is good at structuring systems (an "IT architect"), someone who is good at detailed logical thinking (an analyst), someone who is good at graphics and design and someone who is good at implementing the final result and deploying the software in different business locations. The exact composition of members will depend on the task facing the team.

Teams needed to complete management tasks have been studied extensively, especially by R.M. Belbin (2004). He identifies nine team roles – which he defined as "a tendency to behave, contribute and interrelate with others in a particular way". Three of the nine roles are *outward oriented and creative*:

- **Plants** are managers who sow the seeds of an idea within the group. They then encourage the seed to develop into a flower. Plants are good at solving problems, are imaginative but sometimes unorthodox. However, they may not pay sufficient attention to detail and they may be so wrapped up in their ideas that they do not communicate them to others.

- **Resource investigators** forage inside and outside the organisation for opportunities and useful contacts. They are usually enthusiastic extroverts who like to communicate with others. Unfortunately they can be over-optimistic and they may not follow through with projects, skipping from idea to idea.

- **Shapers** make a team "shape-up" to challenges and the task ahead. Left on their own, other team members will be happy to have a good time. Shapers are happy to challenge this. They are also prepared to challenge established ideas or people. They are dynamic and thrive on pressure. They have the drive and courage to tackle obstacles. Unfortunately they may offend people and provoke anger. A team containing two or more shapers is likely to be turbulent!

Two of the nine roles are oriented to *dealing with people:*

- **Co-ordinators** make good chairpersons, clarifying goals and encouraging sound decision-making. They are usually good at delegating tasks to others. However, they can offload too much work to others and they may be very manipulative.

- **Teamworkers** help maintain good relations in a group and they help to repair damage caused by disagreements. They listen carefully to others. They are perceptive, diplomatic and avoid friction. In addition they are happy to give up some of their own interests in order to co-operate with others. However, teamworkers may be indecisive in a crisis.

The remaining four roles are oriented towards the *tasks facing the team:*

- **Monitor-evaluators** weigh up situations in a sober way that takes account of the major options. They take a long-term view and avoid distraction by minor issues. They have good judgement. However, they may give the impression that they lack drive and their balanced, careful approach means they are unlikely to enthuse or inspire other people

- **Specialists** are often technical people who provide expert knowledge and skills. They will be single-minded and dedicated to their profession or trade. Specialists may only contribute on technical points where they are sure of themselves – indeed they may dwell too much on technicalities

- **Implementers** are organised, reliable and efficient. They are good at dealing with the practicalities of turning ideas into results. Dependability and discipline are their watchwords. However, they may be slow to respond to new ideas and they can appear to be inflexible.

■ **Completer-finishers** are team members who are concerned with things that may go wrong. They are painstaking and conscientious in searching out errors or omissions. They will focus themselves and other team members on deadlines. Unfortunately, they may be anxious and worry too much. This may lead them to keep things under their own control rather than delegating them.

Most managers will be good at two or more of these roles. It is important to avoid teams where everyone suits the same role. Indeed, in an ideal team, every role would be covered by at least one member.

## Stages of team development

Tuckerman (1965) and Tuckerman and Jensen (1977) reviewed a number of studies of small teams and noted that team behaviour was not the same throughout the time the team existed, but would pass through a sequence of five stages:

■ Stage 1: **forming** is the initial stage when the team first comes together. Team members are forming impressions of each other and trying to ensure that they are being accepted. During this stage the team will be trying to establish the details of their task and the ways they can operate in order to achieve objectives. The team will look to the formal team leader for guidance and direction. Substantial resources will be directed towards interpersonal issues and team productivity will be mediocre.

■ Stage 2: **storming** occurs as team members start to vie with each other for position or to get their ideas accepted. They may openly challenge each other and the leader. Alliances may form and cliques may battle for supremacy. Conflict and confrontation rule the day and productivity is low. The team gains a better understanding of itself and its task. Eventually, compromises are made and the team is ready to progress to the next stage.

■ Stage 3: **norming** happens as the team clarifies its task and starts to develop its own way of doing things. They come to value each others' different strengths. There is a growing sense of togetherness and there may be some social activities which will repair the damage to relationships that arose during the storming stage. There is less need to devote resources to clearing ambiguity or conflict. Productivity rises to reasonable levels.

■ Stage 4: **performing** is the stage where the team is free to concentrate on the task in hand. There is synergy between team members. Although disagreements occur, there will be accepted ways of reconciling them so that they are only a minor distraction from the task. Members get on with their jobs with only a low level of instruction or communication. Most of the team's energy is focused on the task and productivity is high.

■ Stage 5: **mourning** is sometimes called "adjourning" or "deforming". This final stage was added by Tuckerman and a colleague after an analysis of more research. Having completed the task, the team members go their separate ways, being redeployed to other teams. They will probably be proud of their achievements and happy to have made new friends. They may feel a sense of loss when the team ends. Sometimes there may be a reluctance to move on to new things.

Some teams omit certain stages. Experienced airline cabin crew rarely go through the storming or mourning stages. Similarly some teams become mired in the storming stage and never reach the performing stage – especially when there are two or more members who consider themselves "prima donnas". Sometimes teams go backwards. For example, if there are new team members a high-performing team may revert to the storming stage. Nevertheless, Tuckerman's stages are very useful. Managers need to remember that team performance is a process and that one of the aims of a good leader is to help the team pass quickly and easily through the first three stages. Managers should also be watchful in case a team regresses – in which case some action will be needed to get the team back to the performing stage. In some cases, managers may need to remind colleagues who loiter too long in the mourning stage that it is time to move on.

## Characteristics of effective teams

There has been a great deal of speculation about the characteristics of an effective team. Many writers suggest that effective teams should be small since social loafing is more prevalent in large teams. Others have argued that trust between members is the hallmark of a good team. It has also been argued that a key characteristic is group cohesion. It is easy to see why a group that sticks together may be effective *provided* its values and goals coincide with the values and goals of the organisation. If a cohesive group's values and goals are antagonistic to the organisation, it will hinder an organisation achieving its aims. In the 1960s and 1970s a great deal of industrial strife arose, partly, because highly cohesive groups pursued goals that were contrary to the goals of management.

Ground-breaking research by Campion, Papper and Medsker (1996) and Campion Medsker and Higgs (1993) involved high-quality empirical studies. They found that the main characteristics of effective teams were, in order, the:

- **Processes used by the group.** Teams which: (1) believed that they were efficient and could be effective; (2) who supported each other when difficulties arose; (3) shared work in a way that ensured little social loafing or "free-riding"; and (4) where there was good communication and co-ordination between members, tended to be very effective teams.

- **Interdependence** was, according to Campion *et al.*, the second most important factor in determining a team's effectiveness. This includes such things as whether bad performance by one person would have knock-on effects for the work of other team members (task interdependence) and goal interdependence. It also covers the interdependence of the feedback that each team member receives.

- **Task design.** Teams whose work was structured according to the principles of researchers such as Hackman and Oldham (1980) were also likely to be effective teams. These teams were allowed a high degree of self-management and there was a high level of participation by all team members. Their work also involved a variety of tasks rather than a monotonous concentration on a single tasks.

- **Group context** in terms of their training, the support given by management and the level and quality of communication with other teams was the fourth most important determinant of group effectiveness.

■ As expected the **composition of the team** was related to effectiveness but the strength of the relationship was weaker than the relationship for the previous factors. There was a weak tendency for heterogeneous teams and flexible teams to be more effective. The results concerning group size were a little more complex. It would appear that team size is important with lower-level jobs but much less so at higher levels.

Very few organisations have only one team. Indeed, large organisations may have hundreds of teams. They cannot be structured in a random way. The next section explains the different ways that teams can be arranged into an organisational structure.

## 5.5 Types of organisational structure

Even when jobs are properly defined and work groups assembled they cannot be arranged at random. It is necessary to put jobs and work groups in a structure so that they do not duplicate each other and, collectively, they cover all the things an organisation needs to do in order to add value. A good organisational structure also helps communication and the sharing of knowledge. If there is a good organisational structure it much easier to establish "who should be told about what". There are many ways of structuring jobs. The main ones are:

■ functional structures
■ divisional structures (regional, product, client)
■ matrix structures
■ network structures
■ learning structures

Business process re-engineering (BPR) is a detailed way of looking at how an organisation is structured and then restructuring it to be more efficient. It was a popular management fad of the 1990s (Micklethwaite and Wooldridge, 1996). Further details of BPR are given on the website associated with this book.

### Functional structures

The usual way to organise jobs is to group them according to their function. A function is an intended purpose. For example, the purpose (function) of the brain is to think and the purpose (function) of the skeleton is to support the body. Similarly, the function of the production department is to make goods or services while the function of the sales department is to sell those goods.

Most organisations have a number of functions. The major functions are marketing and sales, operations (production), human resources, finance and the knowledge function. These are covered in detail by later chapters. Most organisational functions are based on jobs that share a similar purpose. For example, the common purpose of selection, training, personnel planning and safety is the management of human beings. Hence, an interviewer, a management trainer, the personnel planning officer and a safety officer might be grouped into the HR function. Similarly, the common element of paying suppliers, paying employees, raising money on the stock market and obtaining payment from customers all concern money, and the people whose jobs involve these activities might be grouped into the financial

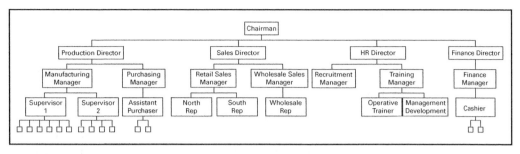

**FIGURE 5.3**  A flat functional structure

function. A functional structure brings together people with similar expertise. This means that they can advise and support each other. A functional structure normally engenders loyalty in its members. Organisation by function is depicted by a classic organisation chart of a small manufacturing business, shown in Figure 5.3.

This organisation has a *flat structure* and is typical of many manufacturing organisations with large spans of control and where a small number of people manage the work of many operatives. Some administrative and clerical organisations also have flat structures. For example, in government departments collecting taxes a few senior officials will supervise the work of many people who process tax returns.

Some organisations have *tall structures* where each manager has only one or two subordinates. Tall structures are found in specialist organisations where the activities of one person are interrelated with to the activities of others. A typical tall structure is depicted in Figure 5.4. It would be characteristic, for example, of a consultancy designing software.

Functions differ from organisation to organisation. A manufacturing organisation will have functions similar to those shown in the first organisational structure. In a retail organisation such as Homebase there will be no production function but a very large sales function. In a regulatory organisation, such as the the Health and Safety Executive, there will be neither a production nor sales function but there will be large technical and legal functions. Functional structures work well when an organisation recurrently processes large batches of a few standard products.

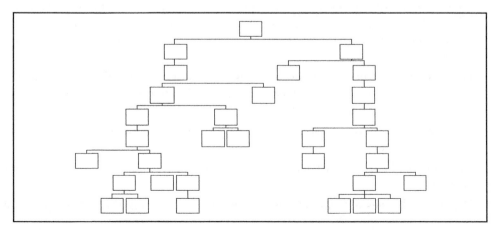

**FIGURE 5.4**  A tall functional structure

Functional organisational structures have a number of *advantages*:

- **Operational efficiency is high**. There is tight, centralised control. Responsibilities are clearly defined and understood.
- **Similar jobs are grouped**. People doing similar tasks can support each other and develop considerable expertise. Work groups are cohesive.
- **Employees have a clear career structure.**
- **Economies of scale are obtained**. Resources are used efficiently. Specialised equipment is located where it is needed most and fewer items of equipment need to be bought.

Unfortunately, functional structures also have *disadvantages*. Loyalties develop to the function rather than to the organisation. People put the goals of their own groups before the goals of the organisation. Functional groups may develop narrow perspectives that lead to conflict with other functions. For example, the sales function may blame the manufacturing function for producing poor products, while the manufacturing function may blame the sales function for not selling products energetically. The narrow viewpoints of functions are often called "functional chimneys" that lead to a "blame culture" and poor communication. Decision-making slows because choices are referred to higher levels where responsibilities for the functions converge.

Functional structures also lead to "empire building" by managers. They enhance the prestige of their jobs by expanding the numbers inside their function – irrespective of the contribution extra workers might make.

## Divisional structures

Large organisations are often structured into self-sufficient divisions. Divisions are often like mini-businesses within a larger business. For example, in a bank there may be a retail division, an Internet division and a commercial banking division. Similarly, a large legal partnership may have separate divisions for different types of legal work, such as commercial property, intellectual property, litigation and family law. Divisions have a number of *advantages*:

- **Clear identification** of costs, profits and the contribution a product is making to an organisation's success. The responsibility for poor performance can be pinpointed. Managers of a division are highly motivated to respond to their customers and their environment.
- **Justification of dedicated facilities**. Decision-making is speeded up and changes to customer needs can be met quickly. An organisation that is divided into divisions is likely to be flexible and adaptable.
- **Co-ordination within divisions** is usually easy because a division is likely to consist of a small number of units and employees (Baron and Greenberg, 1990).
- **Divisions can focus on particular areas of business** and build up the specific expertise needed.
- **Structural changes are easier**. Failing divisions can be closed and new, profitable, divisions can be opened.

- **Divisions provide a training ground for general managers**. Each division will have managers who are concerned with integrating a whole business unit. When a new manager is needed at corporate level, there are likely to be a number of suitable candidates in the various divisions.

Divisional structures have *disadvantages*:

- **Facilities are duplicated**. For example, a New Zealand organisation structured into regional divisions may have three separate accounts departments: one in the North Island and one in the South Island and a further accounts department at corporate headquarters. It might be more efficient to have one accounts department for the whole country.

- **Divisions may become too autonomous**, following their own vision and strategy rather than those of the organisation.

- **Divisions may also be subject to "empire building"**. "Divisional chimneys" may develop.

In large organisations the advantages of structuring operations into divisions usually outweigh the disadvantages. The divisions can be based upon many characteristics – mainly region, product, customer and process. Usually there is a hybrid structure combining an appropriate mix of divisional structures. However, it is useful to know the pure types:

- **Regional divisions** are based on geographical proximity. They are very common in organisations involved in retailing, distribution and transport. They are also common in service organisations such as hospitals, highway maintenance and schools. Multinational organisations are often organised on a regional basis such as North America, Europe, Middle East and Asia and Australia. Organisations structured into regions have the key advantage that decisions can be made at a local level where personnel have first-hand local knowledge. Further, they often reduce transport costs. Unfortunately, regional structures may not give managers the wider, general experience needed to operate at a national or global level: they only have experience of their own region. A typical regional structure is shown in Figure 5.5.

- **Product divisions** group activities making similar products or services. They have a major advantage that a business unit can specialise in a technology or market and develop a high level of expertise. Figure 5.6 gives an example of a chemical organisation structured according to its products.

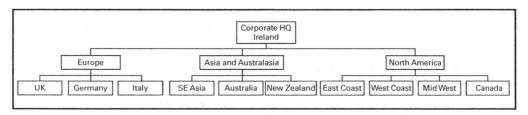

**FIGURE 5.5** A regional divisional structure

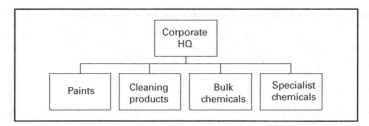

**FIGURE 5.6** A product divisional structure

- **Client divisions** group jobs and activities according to their customers. This is common in service organisations such as hospitals and prison services. It is also common in consultancies and organisations making sophisticated equipment. For example, a hospital may be structured into A&E, paediatrics, obstetrics and geriatrics. Organisations supplying a handful of powerful clients will set up a division for each client. Client divisions are able to serve the special needs of customer groups. In a commercial setting, an organisation structured into divisions may be able to build customer loyalty which gives them a competitive advantage. A major disadvantage of client divisions is that many clients have common needs, yet the divisions duplicate facilities when meeting the needs of each separate group.

## Matrix structures

Matrix structures aim to avoid functional and divisional chimneys by making sure that subunits co-operate. At the same time they try to maintain the advantages of specialisation. In many ways, matrix structures can be thought of as a mixture of functional and divisional structures. They have been defined as "a structure in which the tasks of the organisation are grouped simultaneously along two organising dimensions". Figure 5.7 shows a typical matrix structure where functions are shown along the top of an organisation chart while divisions, in this case product divisions, are placed down the side.

A distinctive feature of a matrix organisation is that each person appears to have two bosses. They have a function boss who is in charge of their function and who has authority over professional matters such as promotions and salary, and they have an operational boss who has day-to-day authority relative to working on a specific project. The operations boss and function boss need to co-ordinate their demands. Some matrix structures are even more complex. They attempt to place employees in a three-dimensional matrix of, say, functions, products and client base. Such complex matrix structures are often impractical.

Many medium and large organisations have adopted a matrix structure. The main *advantages* are:

- **Co-ordination is increased and gross duplication is avoided**. Often a matrix structure enables an organisation to achieve several objectives simultaneously.
- **Employees have varied work and they gain wide experience**. Matrix structures may allow a higher level of worker participation.
- **A cohesive organisation** results from the interaction of employees from different functions or divisions.

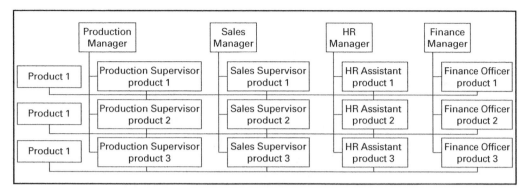

**FIGURE 5.7** A matrix organisational structure

■ **A more adaptable and flexible organisation** results from the richness of the contacts between employees. It can readily adapt to changes in the business environment.

The major *disadvantages* of a matrix organisation are:

■ **Confusion arises** when a functional boss and a project boss fail to co-operate or, worse, when they engage in a power struggle. People in a matrix structure are sometimes confused about where their main responsibility lies.

■ **Much time is consumed** by complexities of co-ordination. Matrix structures may lead to more discussion than action.

■ **Employees feel isolated** from the colleagues with whom they have a natural or professional affinity.

## Network structures

Network structures are a modern innovation. They are sometimes called "boundaryless organisations". They have similarities with "strategic alliances" and "partnering arrangements".

In a network structure (see Figure 5.8), a small core of employees has responsibility for the general organisation, communication, finance and perhaps one other function where it excels, such as design. All other aspects are subcontracted to outside suppliers. Core workers co-ordinate the outside suppliers so that the final product can be delivered. For example, an entrepreneur may invent a new self-sealing can that prevents fizzy drinks going flat. Instead of setting up a sizeable organisation to manufacture and market the product, the entrepreneur enters an arrangement with an existing Malaysian manufacturer.

This saves expense. There is no need to acquire expertise in container manufacturing. The entrepreneur could also enter into an alliance with a sales and marketing organisation based in New York – saving the time and trouble of setting up a sales organisation. The entrepreneur would also hire three or four core workers who would manage relationships with the suppliers. Naturally, the training and salary administration of the core workers would be outsourced to a specialist agency based in Delhi.

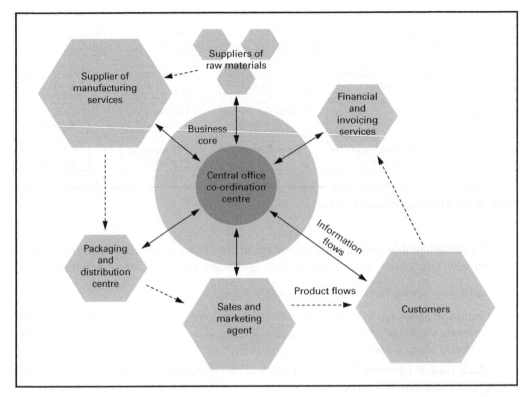

**FIGURE 5.8** A network organisational structure

Network organisations are particularly common in the clothing, computer and publishing industries. Network or boundaryless organisations are free to find subcontractors anywhere in the world. The network can be changed rapidly in response to market demand. If a product is not selling, a contract with the producer can be terminated. A new contract can be struck with another producer who makes a more profitable or attractive product. In a sense, a network structure is a **modular organisation** where the components can be removed or added according to demand.

There are three main kinds of network structures:

1 **Internal networks** exist within large organisations that need to retain full control in order to achieve high quality or to meet statutory requirements. They often set up subgroups with responsibility for supplying various products or services to "internal customers". The subgroups operate like mini-organisations. Usually they act independently as a separate profit centre. They negotiate prices and conditions of supply with their internal customers. However, the organisation maintains sufficient control to prevent them defecting to another organisation or refusing to supply their internal customers. Most of the power is with the internal customers since they are usually free to source their requirements from the open market.

2 **Stable networks** rely on outsourcing. Suppliers are chosen with care. The objective is to establish strong, long-standing relationships. Suppliers have a high level of loyalty and

commitment to the core organisation, which in turn will act in a slightly paternalistic way to ensure the health of their key suppliers. The core organisation may give help with financing and research and development. These relationships may be called "organisational partnerships". But the power lies with the core organisation. When necessary, the core organisation switches to a cheaper supplier. The partner supplier, on the other hand, usually becomes too dependent upon the core organisation to resist their demands.

3 **Dynamic networks** are characterised by outsourcing most operations. They consist of many alliances and partners. Partners change rapidly and there is little loyalty.

The physical headquarters of a network structure may be small: in extreme cases it may simply consist of a room with a computer and communications equipment. This type of network structure is often called a "**virtual organisation**". Virtual organisations can locate and relocate very quickly in any country that suits their temporary requirements. The supreme example of a virtual organisation is eBay where a relatively small number of people manage a computer and financial system which links to huge numbers of buyers and sellers.

Small entrepreneurial firms may find that a network structure enables them to match the power of large organisations since they are able to "buy in" facilities and services at will. Other organisations adopt a network structure in order to concentrate on key strengths (core competences) and will leave other aspects to outside organisations chosen on the basis of core strengths that complement the strengths of the central organisation.

The main *advantages* of network structures are that they:

■ **Enable organisations to manufacture and market globally**. A network structure can often achieve large results from meagre resources.

■ **Give flexibility to redefine an organisation rapidly** in the search for markets.

■ **Enable efficiency**. A network organisation will have little administration and low overheads. There may be no need for a traditional hierarchy.

The *disadvantages* of a network structure include:

■ **Loss of control**. Many decisions will be made by subcontractors. Further, actions will be fragmented amongst subcontractors. Long-term suppliers may be unstable because subcontractors are able to switch to another organisation who can offer better terms. Loss of control often means an increase in uncertainty. Long-term projects may become difficult to plan and organise. Loss of control may mean loss of key components overnight.

■ **Employee loyalty may decrease** because there is little identification with the central core.

## Learning structures and knowledge management

Management gurus such as Peter Drucker (1997) (see pages. 497–505) suggest that for today's organisations, the knowledge they contain is their major asset. This knowledge includes patents, copyrights, trade secrets and contacts. The majority of such knowledge is inside the heads of employees. Senge's (1990) book, *The Fifth Discipline*, emphasised the need to structure an organisation in a way that maximises its ability to increase the capital of knowledge it holds by adopting a "learning structure". A learning structure uses its people, values and systems continuously to change and improve performance-based experience (Senge, 1990). This places a high value on learning from the experience of customers, suppliers, partners and contractors. Learning structures seek out learning opportunities whenever and wherever they can.

A learning structure shows five main characteristics:

- **Employees share the same vision of the organisation**. They will have participated in the formation of the vision and will therefore be willing to consent to the actions needed to bring it about. If the vision is clear, people are able to identify and solve problems in order to achieve that vision.

- **Employees understand how the whole organisation operates**. Understanding how the organisation works as a system helps individuals work in a succession of project teams while maintaining a sense of perspective.

- **Employees are willing to discard the old ways** – in particular, views on controlling staff change. Managers in learning structures think of control as a co-operative process. Rather than having control *over* subordinates, managers exercise control *with* subordinates. People are not a cost that needs to be minimised. Their knowledge, experience and creativity are regarded as the organisation's main asset. An atmosphere of respect and trust creates an environment where it is safe to experiment. Mistakes are accepted not punished. They are an inevitable part of taking necessary risks needed to learn, grow and improve. People are expected to "push the envelope" on the understanding that sometimes things will go wrong and they will not be blamed.

- **Employees feel confident of their position** within the organisation. They are able to discuss ideas openly and frankly, without taking defensive positions. Features which emphasise status differences (car-parking spaces, separate restaurants and differences in dress) are eliminated.

- **Information is distributed widely**. Everyone can obtain information about budgets, expenses, schedules and other databases. People can see for themselves how their actions and ideas contribute to organisational goals. Communications are fluid. People can email any other person in the organisation.

Although learning structures are particularly efficient at generating knowledge, in fact, it is generated in all organisations and in many cases it is the organisation's most valuable asset. Hence it must be managed as effectively as an organisation's human resources or finances. Knowledge management is explained in more detail in Chapter 18.

Knowledge
management p 452

## Co-ordination within organisational structures

Structuring an organisation involves placing people in groups and then arranging the groups into some kind of logical order. On its own, this is not enough. There must be some mechanism that enables the groups to relate to each other so that their activities harmonise.

This process is called "co-ordination". In this context it refers to the quality of collaboration between groups or departments. All organisations require some co-ordination. In very small organisations this can be provided by one person, usually the owner, who directly supervises all activities. In large organisations, especially international ones, specific methods of co-ordination need to be built into the organisational structure. The main methods are:

- **A hierarchical arrangement of authority** means that someone is available to tell groups what they must do in order to work harmoniously with other groups. The higher authority arbitrates in disputes and issues plans or instructions to ensure that groups work towards the organisation's goals in a mutually helpful way.

- **Standardisation** helps co-ordination by simplifying the situation so that compatibility and interchangeability are increased. Standardisation covers procedures, inputs and outputs.

- **Personal contact**, where one person speaks to people from other groups, allows each group to be aware of events in the other group. This means that they are able to adjust their own activities in a way that helps themselves, the other group and the organisation as a whole. Often personal contact is formalised and certain people are given the specific responsibility of keeping one group informed of events in another group. These roles are usually called "liaison posts". For example, one member of the engineering department may have an official responsibility for liaising with the sales department.

- **Computer information systems** are playing an increasingly important role in the co-ordination of organisations. Data from one group can be automatically passed to other groups that need to be kept informed. Indeed, with automated information-sharing, a receiving department has data almost as quickly as the group that generates it. Moreover, the information on organisational intranets often allows every employee to see the progress an organisation is making towards it production, sales or financial targets.

## 5.6 Major organisational dimensions

The characteristics of an organisation can vary in many ways. The main variations concern size, role variety, centralisation, formalisation, mechanistic or organic systems, and environmental uncertainty. Often these factors are related. For example, large organisations tend to be more mechanistic than small ones. Each of the six major characteristics of organisations needs further explanation.

### Size

Size is a very significant, self-explanatory, organisational dimension. Large organisations tend to have a more formal structure, usually based on functions or departments. Large organisations also tend to have many hierarchical levels. The size of an organisation is usually measured in two ways: the number of employees or its financial value (usually **market capitalisation** which is the value of a single share on the stock exchange multiplied by the number of shares in existence).

## Role variety

Some organisations are very simple and have only two jobs: the manager and the aides who do all kind of work, as and when needed. Other organisations have many different jobs which are quite distinct. Sometimes, role variety is also called "specialisation". Role variety centres upon interchangeability. If many employees can be substituted there is little role variety. Tyler (1973) developed a mathematical index of role variety.

## Centralisation

Centralisation is the concentration of power. The opposite is "decentralisation", "autonomy" or "participation". If all power is in the hands of one person the organisation is highly centralised. If members of an organisation have equal power the organisation is highly decentralised. A highly centralised organisation is characterised as follows:

- Decisions, even quite minor ones, will be referred to senior managers.
- Plans, even operational plans, will be drawn up without the participation of junior staff.
- Information will be "hoarded" by managers and only be given reluctantly to subordinates.
- There will be stringent control procedures to ensure that operations are carried out exactly in the prescribed way. Employees have little discretion.

## Formalisation

Formalisation (see Reimann, 1974) is the extent to which expectations and norms are made explicit. In theory, formalisation applies to both written and oral communication. In practice, formalisation is the level to which rules, procedures, instructions and other communications are written. Formalisation is related to concepts such as routinisation (Hage and Aiken, 1968, 1969) and standardisation. Routinisation is the degree to which roles are structured. Roles are routinised when tasks are simplified and repeated. The degree of standardisation in an organisation can be measured by counting the number of repetitive sequences.

## Mechanistic or organic systems

Burns and Stalker (1961) noted that organisations often operate in one of two ways. Some operate much like an efficient machine devised by scientific managers and administrative theorists. In these **mechanistic organisations** tasks are divided into small parts that are organised in a logical sequence. Senior levels of management exercise downward control using precise instructions and rules which minimise discretion. Boundaries of responsibility are clearly defined and often related to technical expertise and knowledge. Mechanistic organisations seem to work well in stable situations – especially when products or services are mature and produced in high volume. In the second type of organisation things are less predetermined. In these **organic organisations** there is a degree of disorganisation and fluidity that is analogous to the flexibility seen in the cells of living material. There are few prescriptive job descriptions, rules and regulations are kept to a minimum and employees are often expected to use their initiative. Communications within these organisations tend to be horizontal between colleagues rather than upwards towards senior management. Organic organisations seem to work best in volatile situations where the market or technology is changing rapidly and frequent adjustments mean that long production runs are infrequent.

## Environmental uncertainty

Lawrence and Lorsch (1969) maintain that a major difference between organisations is the uncertainty of their environments. Organisations, such as manufacturers in the computer industry, operate in an uncertain environment where new developments and market trends can emerge overnight and then completely change the organisation's operations. Ambiguity is often highest in the political arena where political leaders do not spell out their requirements clearly. Public services also suffer from competing demands. A prison service, for example, must strike a balance between the need to restrict the activities of prisoners in order to make the community safer and the need to expand the activities of prisoners in order to rehabilitate them into society. A final component of environmental uncertainty includes the quality and speed of feedback. In an uncertain environment it is vague and slow.

Other significant dimensions of an organisation's culture are its attitude towards risk (to what degree it will tolerate actions that might go wrong), innovation (the emphasis it places on making improvements) and rules (the number of rules it has, whether they are written down and the severity of punishment when rules are broken). Space constraints mean that they cannot be described here but details can be found in the website associated with this book.

## 5.7 Organising toolkit

- Design jobs carefully. Do not over-specialise. Make sure the job has motivating elements. In management jobs, make sure the span of control is reasonable – especially in organisations that produce complex, interrelated product or services (pages 114–121).
- Make the authority and responsibilities of every job crystal clear (pages 116).
- Make sure that all equipment, including IT equipment, is ergonomically designed (page 117).
- Choose appropriate work schedules for each job. Consider adopting less traditional schedules such as teleworking, job-sharing, contingent workers, office-sharing and hoteling (page 118).
- Organise jobs into teams. With lower level jobs, keep teams relatively small. Help them to be effective by making sure they adopt the right processes, their work is interdependent and contextual factors are right (page 127).
- Make sure teams share the same basic outlook but then choose members so that they have a wide range of backgrounds and experience (page 128).

- Check the styles of team members. Make sure that they do not all have the same style. If possible, choose members so that there is at least one person who can discharge each of the major roles (page 128).
- Choose an organisational structure that suits your organisation's size, product and methods. Do not ignore newer structures such as network structures (page 133)
- Using five-point scales (very high, high, middle, low, very low), indicate where your organisation would lie on the six major organisational dimensions. Next estimate where your organisation is now. If there is any discrepancy between the two, sketch out ways of reducing the discrepancy (page 137).

# Activities and further study

## Essay plans

Prepare plans for the following essays:
1 What are the advantages and disadvantages of work specialisation?
2 Do charities have organisational structures?
3 What are the different ways in which work can be scheduled?
4 What are recent trends in structuring organisations and why have they changed from traditional structures?

## Web activities

1 Search the Internet for organisational structures. You should try a number of organisations including governmental and charity organisations. Some useful examples of organisational structure are given by:
   - Parker Pens – a structure very largely based on geographical regions – why? Try www.competition-commission.org.uk.
   - Gillette – a complicated structure which uses both product group and geographical regions.
   - Nomura Research Institute – a service organisation largely based on customers and products. Try http://www.nri.co.jp/english/company/org.html.
   - Serious Fraud Office – a governmental structure based on procedural responsibilities. Try http://www.sfo.gov.uk/about/structure.asp.
   - For a really complex organisational structure look at the organisation chart for Microsoft, which can be found at: http://www.directionsonmicrosoft.com/sample/DOMIS/orgchart/sample/orgchart. html.
2 You might also try to locate the organisational structure for a "virtual organisation" such as Amazon or eBay.
3 Log on to the website associated with this book and access the file containing the organisation chart exercise. Examine the chart, locate the errors and a draw a new chart which does not contain errors.

## Experiential activities

1 Draw up a job description for your role as a student. Compare your result with the model answer given on the website associated with this book.

2 With a group of fellow students discuss the different ways that work can be scheduled. Allocate one of the following roles to each member of the group:

- single unmarried worker
- married worker
- married worker with young children
- worker who is a single parent with young children

Each person should then examine the following work schedules and describe the impact it would have on their work and domestic lives:

- traditional nine to five schedule
- flexitime schedule
- compressed working week
- job share

## Recommended reading

1 Oldham, G.R. and Hackman, J.R. (2010) "Not what it was: the future of job design research", *Journal of Organizational Behaviour*, **31** (2/3), 463–480. These veterans of job design speculate on the future of research and theory of organisational design. A difficult read but highly recommended. This issue of the journal is devoted to job design.

2 Miles, S.A. and Watkins, M.D. (2007) "The leadership team: complementary strengths or conflicting agendas?", *Harvard Business Review*, **85** (4), 90–98. This considers the way that top management should work as a team. There is a good section on succession planning and transitions within senior management teams.

3 Barker, J.R. (1993) "Tightening the iron cage: concertive control in self-management teams", *Administrative Science Quarterly*, **38** (3), 408–437. This makes the point that high commitment of a team increases demands on members. This article won an award for its scholarly contribution. It is a long read (two hours or more) which delves into the concept of organisational control.

4 Ortenblad, A. (2004) "The learning organisation: towards an integrated model", *The Learning Organisation*, **11** (2/3), 129–144. An excellent discussion of concept and vagueness of "learning organisations", this offers a good review of literature on: organisational learning; learning at work; learning climate and learning structure. A challenging read; stop at page 135.

## CHAPTER 6

# Organisational Change

## Chapter contents

## ❖ LEARNING OBJECTIVES

After reading this chapter you should be able to recognise the need for organisational change and the different types of change that may be necessary. You should also be aware of some of the stages of change and the methods that change agents may use. You should be able to identify some of the factors that may make organisational change effective. Finally, you should be aware of some of the criticisms levelled against writers and researcher on the subject of organisational change. In particular, you should be able to:

❖ **explain** why organisational change may be necessary

❖ **list** at least four covert ways that people can sabotage organisational change

❖ **describe** at least four dimensions of change situations and suggest at least one way that these dimensions may converge

❖ **describe** in detail Lewin's three phases of organisational change and describe at least one other writer's categorisation of the phases of change

❖ **explain** the ethical issues that may be involved in organisational change

❖ **list** three techniques of changing the way an organisation analyses and solves problems, and two techniques of changing organisational structures

❖ **describe** at least four techniques of changing behaviour in organisations

❖ **describe** the role of change agents

❖ **explain** the difficulties of evaluating the success of organisational change

❖ **list** at least six factors that are thought to help the success of organisational change

❖ **explain** at least three serious criticisms of research into organisational change

Organisational change is in itself not new. The following statement may sound familiar.

> 66 We trained hard . . . but it seemed that every time we were beginning to form
> into teams we would be reorganised. I was to learn later in life that we tend to
> meet any new situation by reorganising; and a wonderful method it can be for
> creating the illusion of progress while producing confusion, inefficiency and
> demoralisation. 99

You may be surprised to discover that its author is believed to be a Roman soldier, Petronius Arbiter. No doubt the builders of the pyramids and the scribes of Hammurabi voiced similar complaints. However, the business environment always changes and an organisation that does not change with it will encounter great difficulties. This can be true of high-technology and nimble organisations such as Nokia.

---

### CASE 6.1: *Nokia's organisational change – from manufacturing galoshes to mobile phone behemoth to ailing multinational*

Many owners of Nokia phones produced by the largest Finnish company will be amazed at the changes that it and its organisation have experienced. They will also be amazed at the changes it needs to make in order to survive in the face of recent commercial developments.

In brief, Nokia was founded (near the Nokianvita river) in 1896 as a manufacturer of rubber galoshes. Shortly after the First World War, it took over an insolvent electricity company, in order to ensure its electricity supply. Over the next few decades it changed its organisation to focus upon the manufacture of electricity cables. It reorganised again after 1967 when it became an industrial conglomerate. When mobile telephone technology developed in the 1990s, the organisation changed by divesting many peripheral products to concentrate on the manufacture of mobile phones. This was a shrewd organisational change and by 1998 it became the world's largest mobile phone manufacturer. Its handset (Nokia 1100) was the world's best selling mobile phone – indeed the world's best consumer electronics product. The company reorganised again after troubles in the network equipment division. It shed large numbers of staff and moved production from a factory with high costs in Germany to a factory with lower costs in Romania.

Shortly after the appointment of a new CEO (Olli-Pekka Kallasvuo – known as OPK) in 2006 the behemoth encountered a storm that threatens it hegemony. Six months later Apple unveiled the smart mobile phone, the iPhone. Since then Nokia has been on a downhill run and its profit margins have dived from 15 per cent to 7 per cent. Google and Blackberry produced competing products. Nokia took time to unveil the N8 model which despite its spin, is perceived as a mere "catch up". Nokia's slowness to change its organisation in response to a commercial challenge is blamed on its CEO's cautious and inward-looking approach. However, the people of Finland share some of the blame because they are unwilling to condone drastic changes in an organisation they deem to be a national treasure.

Nokia can regain ground. If it skilfully uses the techniques of organisational change, it can produce an equivalent transformation of its change from making rubber shoes to a leading manufacturer of mobile phones. The challenges facing the senior management of Nokia are discussed in the Schumpeter column of the *Economist* 8 July 2010, 396 (8694), page 65.

Obviously, managers need the skills, described in the preceding chapter, such as designing jobs, encouraging teamwork and devising an organisational structure which are vital to establishing an organisation. But, even if they establish a perfect organisation, it will only be a matter of months before they need to use their understanding of how to change their organisation to cope with changes in their environment.

## 6.1  Definition and reasons why organisations change

Change simply means "altering the state or direction of something". It does not necessarily imply either innovation or improvement. Change can be for better or for worse. It can also be backwards. Organisational change therefore means:

66    Altering the state and direction of an organisation – for better or for worse,
      forwards or backwards                                                                99

While technically correct, this definition is somewhat cynical. Although many changes are bad and regressive, probably a larger number are good and progressive and lead to progress. This means that change should be generally welcomed but we should be wary of adopting changes that follow "the flavour of the month" or "changes that are made for "change's own sake".

When organisations are set up they are usually fit for purpose and in step with their environment. Forces soon emerge which tend to slow the organisation down so that it starts to lag behind the environment. Organisations must change – otherwise they become outdated, uncompetitive and eventually they are either taken over or disbanded.

### CRITICAL THINKING 6.1  *Is change faster nowadays?*

It is often claimed that the pace of change is faster today than ever. This claim needs to be taken with a pinch of salt – *cum grano salis* as Petronious might have said! The dissolution of the monasteries was a huge change that took only five years. The urbanisation of Manchester saw its population grow from 22 000 in 1772 to 75 000 (an increase of 340 per cent) just 28 years later. Colonialisation of the Australian continent was assured in a generation or two. The rate of change imposed upon Japan after its defeat in 1945 was phenomenal. It would seem that each generation believes that its rate of change is the fastest in history. The belief that today's change is faster than ever is bolstered by writers and consultants who have a vested interest in increasing their opportunities and fees. Any bets that Petronius and his colleagues were claiming financial allowances because the Empire was expecting so many changes of them?

Organisational change is not rare. It is estimated that a typical establishment is reorganised every three years (CIPD, 2010). Petronius may have had an easy time in his day!

## Resistance to change

Vested interests are a force that prevents organisations changing at a pace to match their environments. For example, if a change means that Manager B's department is likely to grow faster than Manager A's department, Manager A may hinder the change. Inertia is another force that retards change. Change requires extra effort and some individuals will not want to put in the extra energy. Some people interpret a request to change as a criticism of their current methods. Still others will be reluctant to change because the end result is less predictable – the uncertainty makes them anxious. Paradoxically, one of the most powerful forces against change is an existing, very efficient organisation. Tim Mannon a senior executive with Hewlett Packard is widely quoted (e.g. Hoff, 1995) as saying, "The biggest single threat to our business today is staying with a previously successful business model one year too long". Managers of a successful business will usually be perplexed when they are told they need to change!

There are two main *foci of resistance* to change: content and process.

1 *Content resistance* occurs when workers object to what is being changed such as a new salary structure, new equipment, new job descriptions or the introduction of new pension arrangements.

2 *Process resistance* occurs when workers are content to accept the change but object to the way it is being introduced: they may be prepared to adopt new working methods but object to them being imposed without discussion. Similarly, they may be content with a new salary system but object if it is applied too quickly.

The *form of resistance* can vary widely. Sometimes change will be resisted on an *individual* basis by not attending meetings where change is discussed or simply continuing with old ways despite instruction to use new methods. Sometimes *groups* can resist change. Workers can form alliances to protest against change or they can collectively withhold useful information. In extreme situations trade unions may organise strikes in protest at "new working practices". Resistance can also be *passive* where workers quietly refuse to respond to initiatives. More seriously it can be *active* where workers sabotage attempts to change by spreading false information or misusing or damaging equipment. The difference between direct and indirect resistance is an important distinction. **Direct resistance** in terms of protests, arguments or withdrawal is uncomfortable but at least the change agents know it exists. Subtle **indirect resistance**, is a more dangerous foe. Change agents may not even realise that information is being withheld or that "political manoeuvring" is going on behind the scenes.

### CRITICAL THINKING 6.2 *How to spot change blockers*

Resistance to change is quite common so it is important to be able to recognise it and take appropriate action. Keen (1981) identified seven tactics people may use to block change. They are:

1 **Divert resources** to other projects so that the change is starved of support. Staff involved in the change are given competing priorities. At a crucial moment

essential equipment has to be shared with another department – preferably a department in a remote location. Superb diversions include commissioning research, writing long reports, holding many meetings and arranging fact-finding tours – preferably abroad.

2 **Insist enthusiastically that the project is "done properly".** Everyone's views must be canvassed and reconciled. Contradictory views will emerge and a heated conflict between rival proponents will slow or kill a project.

3 **Be vague.** Use long, convoluted communications couched in general, grandiose and abstract terms. At all costs, avoid specific goals with specific timetables.

4 **Encourage inertia** by commissioning research, waiting for the completion of another project, waiting until the "time is ripe" or until an important (and preferably very, *very* busy) person is consulted and persuaded to back the project.

5 **Ignore interpersonal issues** during the early stages. This will ensure that misunderstanding and animosities incubate and grow to the point where they later jeopardise success.

6 **Damage the credibility of those leading the change.** Spread gossip concerning those championing the project. It is particularly important to spread the gossip among supportiers of the project champion. This can be done very skilfully by pretending to be outraged by a scurrilous rumour and pretending to defend the project champion.

7 **Avoid overt hostility to the change.** Overt hostility alerts change champions and allows counter-measures to be deployed.

Whatever the reason, focus or form, resistance acts as a kind of magnetic force that retards the rate at which the organisation moves forward with its environment. Inevitably, it begins to fall behind.

## Forces in favour of change

Kurt Lewin (1951), a seminal management theorist, developed "field theory" which posited that for change to occur there must be a stronger force in favour of change and this force must be felt by the people in an organisation. He called this "perceived need for change". There are two main types of factors that can create a perceived need for change: internal forces and external forces. **Internal forces for change** are factors within the organisation. Some are inevitable. The people within the organisation change: they grow older; they get bored with current methods; they learn that some current methods do not work; some powerful people get weaker and some weak people gain confidence; new recruits arrive with new ideas or demands. Other internal forces for change are less certain. The values of the organisation may change so that, for example, it may wish to foster more equal opportunities or adopt a more collaborative management style. The organisation might also decide to change its mission. Further, it is possible that the R&D department devises a new method or product.

Every author has their own list of **external forces for change**. It seems best to offer a more organised list, given in Table 6.1, which is based on the PESTLE model of strategic planning.

PESTLE strategic analysis p 96

| PESTLE category | Examples of external forces for organisational change |
|---|---|
| *Political* | ■ Change of government favouring, e.g. private sector or expenditure on, say, rail infrastructure<br>■ Decrease in size of traditional working-class vote<br>■ Decrease in power of trade unions<br>■ Collapse of communism in Russia<br>■ Opening up of market in China |
| *Economic* | ■ Credit crunch<br>■ Cuts in government expenditure<br>■ Greater regulation of banking and lending<br>■ More equal/unequal distribution of wealth<br>■ New competitors, international competition<br>■ Capital markets and exchange rates |
| *Social* | ■ Ageing population<br>■ Higher levels of education<br>■ Greater emphasis on equality |
| *Technical* | ■ New technologies and production methods<br>■ New products and services |
| *Legal* | ■ Changes in safety legislation<br>■ Changes in employment legislation<br>■ Local planning constraints<br>■ International treaties |
| *Environmental* | ■ Climate change and recycling<br>■ Better transport and communications<br>■ Stricter regulation of pollution |

**TABLE 6.1** Forces attracting organisations to change

The balance between the three forces is crucial. Figure 6.1 illustrates Lewin's **field force analysis**.

If the forces of resistance are bigger than the combined internal and external forces for change, it is unlikely that the organisation will change. Indeed, in a few situations the organisation might regress to a previous form. However, if the combined forces for change are bigger than the forces of resistance, then it is highly likely that organisational change will ensue.

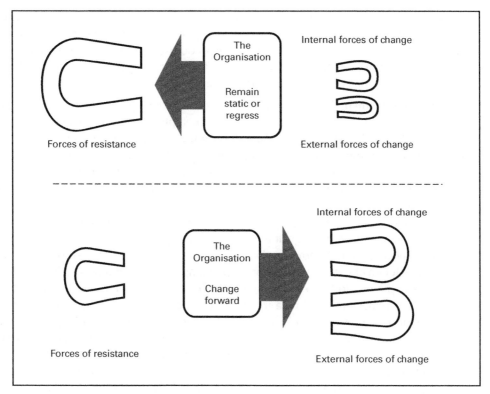

**FIGURE 6.1**  An illustration of Lewin's field force analysis

## 6.2  Types of organisational change

Organisations may attempt many different types of change. For example, one organisation may, foolishly, attempt a total reorganisation in a matter of three weeks while another, only slightly less foolishly, may only strive to accomplish one piffling change in a decade. The different types of organisational change can be classified into five main groups – which are not mutually exclusive:

1  **Episodic versus continuous change** (Weick and Quinn, 1999) is probably the most important concept concerning types of change. Most of the present discussion has implied episodic change where there is organisational inertia and where infrequent major decisions are made to institute a specific changes. This is not the ideal situation. In a perfect organisation, change would be a process of continual adaptation. *Episodic change* tends to be dramatic and is largely driven by external events. It usually follows Lewin's three stages of organisational change and there is one or more champions at senior level who initiate and propel the change throughout the whole organisation.

Lewin's three stages of change p 152

2  **Continuous change** is self-explanatory: it is like evolution. It is an endless process of constant modifications in day-to-day work practices that is driven

by pragmatic sensitivity to the work environment. Changes tend to emerge from the situation and usually amount to a redirection of what is already under way – but the cumulative effect can be huge. Change agents adopt the role of a sense-maker who recognises and reframes the current situation. The change agent will also spend time enabling a wide range of people to improvise and learn.

3  **Minor versus incremental change** (Marshak, 1993) lists four types of change in ascending order of how drastic they were: he called them metaphors. A *fix and maintain* change is not very drastic. It involves tweaking the system with minor adjustments or perhaps adding a few extra resources to cope with a minor problem. It does not involve anything fundamental. It is analogous to running repairs on your car. A *build and develop* type of change is also based on the belief that the present structure is fine but it is capable of improvement – which can be achieved by learning and consultation. For example, an organisation may improve production methods by enriching jobs, empowering workers or using new technology. It is analogous to improving your car's aerodynamics by fitting a new spoiler. A *move and relocate* change involves a transition that alters basic parameters within the organisation. Top management is certain to be involved. An obvious example would be to move the headoffice to a cheaper, out of town location. Similarly, the changes that follow a merger or outsourcing a function, such as payroll, would count as a move and relocate change. It is analogous to replacing your car with a new one with four-wheel drive to enable you to travel across country. A *liberate and re-create* type of change is the most drastic. The organisation is transformed by a complete rethink of mission vision and methods. The organisation almost reinvents itself. A good example would be when IBM changed drastically from a manufacturer selling mainframe computers to large organisations to a manufacturer of personal computers sold to private individuals. Sometimes such changes are called "morphing". A liberate and create change is analogous to giving up car travel in favour of helicopter transport.

4  The **organisational level** of the change can also be used to classify changes. This classification is often related to the "minor versus radical" dimension described in the previous paragraph. Some changes affect only individual jobs (micro-change) whereas others might affect a department and still others might affect the organisation as a whole (macro-change). Unfortunately, the situation is not so simple because changes at organisational level are very likely to produce changes in individual jobs – and vice versa. It may be better to view this categorisation of changes as a categorisation of where the changes start (Child, 2005). Sometimes this way of characterising changes is called **narrow vs broad changes**.

5  The distinction between **planned change** and **emergent change** is made by many writers (see Burns, 2004a). Early writers on organisational change, such as Kurt Lewin, focused on planned change which usually starts at the top. As described in the previous chapter, top managers devise a strategy to achieve the change which is then translated into tactical plans and, ultimately, action plans. Often, management will appoint or hire a change agent who has responsibility of ensuring the change takes place. In essence, planned change is "top-down change" where senior managers decide how their organisation must develop – although they will use participation and consultation to achieve their aims.

During the 1980s it became apparent that planned change had a number of shortcomings. For example, planning takes a great deal of time and the time needed is not available in turbulent environments when change is rapid and continuous: a few managers at the top of an organisation need a lot of time to understand all the complexities. By the time plans are finalised, the situation has changed!

Consequently attention turned to *emergent change* where a decentralised organisation continually changes itself. Weick (2000) notes, "Emergent change consists of ongoing accommodations, adaptations, and alterations that produce fundamental change without *a priori* intentions to do so". It occurs when workers devise new methods in their day-to-day work dealing with problems and opportunities. Often these changes go unnoticed. Emergent change is predominantly "bottom-up". A good explanation of planned and emergent change, together with a case study showing that the two approaches are not mutually exclusive is given by Burns (2004b)

As Table 6.2 shows, there are many similarities between these characterisations. It seems that authors have been using different words to write about the same things.

| Types of change | | |
|---|---|---|
| **Planned change** | **Major proponent** | **Emergent change** |
| **Name** | | |
| ■ Episodic change | (Wieke and Quinn, 1999) | ■ Continuous change |
| ■ Radical change | (Marshak, 1993) | ■ Incremental change |
| ■ Top-level change | (Child, 2005) | ■ Lower-level change |
| ■ Planned change | (Burns, 2004b) | ■ Emergent change |
| **Characteristics** | | ■ Constant and small |
| ■ Major and infrequent | | ■ Micro-change |
| ■ Macro-change | | ■ All levels – many people to share information and avoid overload. May therefore be quicker to react |
| ■ Top management – who may experience information overload. May therefore be slow to react | | ■ Individual learning |
| ■ Organisational learning | | ■ Easy acceptance |
| ■ Acceptance problems | | |
| **Suggested name** | | |
| **Command change** | | **Devolved change** |

**TABLE 6.2**  A synthesis of the types of organisational change

Clearly, different authors have been describing the same dimension where, at one end, is a centralised type of change that originates with senior managers – and all that implies. This can be called *command change*. At the other end of the dimension, change is initiated - more or less spontaneously – by many people throughout the hierarchy. This can be called *devolved change*.

An interesting, rather different, and pragmatic classification of change has been suggested by Senior and Flemming (2006). Organisational change is classified according to:

1 the rate at which change occurs (discontinuous, continuous, etc.)

2 how it comes about (planned, emergent, etc.)

3 the scale of the change (fine-tuning, incremental adjustment, etc.)

Their book is a useful practical guide that gives greater detail than could be given in this wider-ranging text.

## 6.3 The phases of change

Change rarely happens instantly. It usually occurs over a period of time and it is likely to pass through phases. Writers (surprisingly perhaps) agree what these phases are! This section first describes the grandfather of change phases – Lewin's three-phase model – and then outlines some others which have particular merit.

### Lewin's three phases of organisational change

The most frequently quoted stages of the change were developed long ago by Kurt Lewin (1947). He said there are three stages of change: unfreezing, changing and re-freezing.

**Unfreezing** aims to dissolve existing attitudes and positions. Essentially, it involves emphasising and strengthening the need to change so that the forces for change outweigh those in favour of the status quo. The main techniques for the unfreezing stage involve communication and can be described as three stages:

- *First*, many reasons for the change are assembled. These reasons will then be translated into words, examples and images which resonate with employees. The reasons to resist change will also be mentioned, because research suggests that giving both sides of an argument is more persuasive and much more effective against subsequent counter-arguments.

- *Second*, reasons for change are communicated by many media, such as meetings, memos, newsletters and presentations. It is important that employees should not be passive recipients. It is better if they play an active part. A standard tactic is to co-opt likely opponents of change to the planning and delivery of the change (provided the opponents are neither numerous nor powerful).

- *Third*, negotiations will be needed with powerful figures who resist the changes. It may be necessary to offer a trade or compromise which compensates for any negative effects. If all else fails, the bad consequences of blocking change can be pointed out. Explicit or implicit coercion carries enormous risks but it may be appropriate where speedy change is necessary.

Once a situation has been unfrozen, the **actual change** can start to take place. Change agents and organisational development (OD) consultants have evolved techniques to help. The main techniques include: survey feedback, team-building and process consultation plus large-group interventions. Some of these techniques are described in the next section.

The change stage sometimes uses small-scale projects in which the new methods can be perfected and the results used to reassure other employees.

When actual change has taken place it must be consolidated – otherwise the organisation may drift back to earlier methods. Lewin called this the **re-freezing phase**. It may involve altering the organisation's pay systems to reward adherence to the new situation. The organisation's culture may need to be altered to support the new system. Above all, the new systems and methods must be routinised so that they become habitual.

---

**CRITICAL THINKING 6.3** *What is wrong with Lewin's stages?*

Lewin's stages contain a great deal of sense but they are not perfect. There are two major criticisms:

1 While it is useful for planned (command) change, it does not cope well with emergent (devolved) change. It is easy to envisage how to unfreeze, change and re-freeze applies when the process is being directed from the top towards a clear set of objectives. It is exceedingly difficult to see how 'unfreeze, change and refreeze' applies when there are lots of small impromptu, continuous changes. Most organisations desire continuous change. Re-freezing will only store up problems for the future. Currently, emergent change is probably more important than planned change.

2 Lewin's three-stage process is incomplete. It ignores, for example, the vital, opening part of change – deciding what to change and how. Similarly, it ignores the closing parts of a change process – checking how effective the change has been and whether it was the correct change in the first place.

---

## Other models of the stages of change

The shortcomings of Lewin's three-stage process led many others to develop their own list of stages. It is easy to produce a list, and numerous writers have risen to the task. Many of the lists have modest scientific merit; they are only conjecture and experience from a few case studies. Hussey (2000) produced a six-stage approach to organisational change using the mnemonic "EASIER":

1 **E**nvisioning – developing a coherent view of the future
2 **A**ctivating – making sure others understand and share vision
3 **S**upport – helping people overcome the problems they encounter
4 **I**mplementing – planning and executing the change process
5 **E**nsuring – checking that the change is being implemented
6 **R**ecognising – and rewarding those involved

Kotter (1995) divides organisational change into eight stages The first two stages and the last stage are omitted from many models. Kotter's stages are derived from errors observed in organisational change projects. Kotter's eight stages and the errors associated with them are:

1 **Establish urgency**: identify crises, potential crises or opportunities. (Error – not kick-starting the change project.)
2 **Create guiding coalition**: establish a powerful group, encourage them to work as a team. (Error – not getting a critical mass of organisational power to support the changes in a coherent way.)
3 **Develop vision and strategy**. (Error – with no clear aims and objectives the change process will drift and meander.)
4 **Communicate the vision of change**: use all media, the guiding coalition act as role models. (Error – seriously under-communicating to people who are essential to the changes.)
5 **Broad-based action**: remove obstacles, encourage new ideas, risk-taking. (Error – allowing obstacles, especially recalcitrant managers, to remain.)
6 **Generate short-term, visible, wins**: reward the people involved. (Error – people become demotivated and cynical if they have to wait years to see positive results.)
7 **Consolidate gains and use them to produce more change**: use increased credibility to hire, promote and develop those who will help change and reinvigorate the process with new projects etc. (Error – declaring victory too soon can undermine future change.)
8 **Anchor changes in the organisational culture**: articulate links between changes and success, ensure leadership succession. (Errors – failing to make the link between success/survival and the changes; not ensuring the next generation of managers support the changes.)

Hannagan (2002) presents four stages of the change process, with has a different perspective. Instead of providing a "road map" for the change agents it focuses upon the emotions of the people involved:

1 **denial** that change is needed
2 **resistance** to change
3 **exploration** of the possibilities offered by change
4 **commitment** to the new changes

Bullock and Batten (1985) reviewed the literature and generated a general list of stages of change. Parker, Wall and Jackson (1998) outline the stages of a change process involving job design.

The time taken for an organisation to pass through all of these stages varies widely, depending on the change attempted, the people involved and the change techniques that are used. However, change usually takes much longer than people estimate – often more than twice as long. Managers face the challenge of shortening the time taken to change but without an undue rush that may jeopardise the whole process.

## 6.4 Techniques of changing organisations

Change agents and others do not simply "swan about" saying nice things to workers and even nicer things to top management. They employ a number of Organisational Development techniques. An Internet search will reveal hundreds of techniques but many come down to standard techniques that have been given a unique "spin" by consultants in order to appeal to prospective clients. OD techniques can be divided into three categories: problem analysis, changing structure and changing behavior. The final category is much bigger than the others.

### OD techniques for analysing problems

Briefly, OD techniques of problem analysis and diagnosis include surveys and **focus groups** as well as forcasting and planning techniques such as "what if" scenarios of **contingency planning**. They also include **business process engineering**.

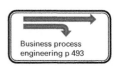
Business process engineering p 493

### OD techniques for structural change

**Role analysis** examines the expectations inherent in worker's positions. Roles are scrutinised to identify ambiguities such as reducing costs while also maintaining customer satisfaction. **Analysing the structure of jobs and enriching** them is another important OD technique. The outcomes of these processes help change roles and jobs for the better.

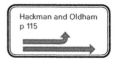
Hackman and Oldham p 115

### OD techniques for behavioural change

Changing behaviour always involves ethical issues. If people will be affected by a change, perhaps losing their job, they should at least be allowed to participate in the decisions. Indeed, in many countries there is a legal requirement to involve workers in any large change that could result in redundancy. Further, changing people's behaviour can become mere Machiavellian manipulation. If exploitation is to be avoided, worker participation should be on the basis of informed consent. Participation usually helps the change process because it helps gain support. Further, it helps communicate people's role in the change process and what the new structure will require from them. But, participation has grave dangers. It is inevitably time-consuming and it gives determined opponents an opportunity to slow or sabotage the change. Assuming that the ethical and practical problems are resolved, behavioural change can be achieved by one or more techniques such as action research, team-building exercises and process consultation, large-group interventions and survey feedback.

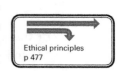
Ethical principles p 477

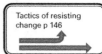
Tactics of resisting change p 146

### Action research

Action research was pioneered by Lewin. It sprang from the idea that much academic research led only to the production of books which were of limited practical use. He suggested that a small group of workers (and often, an academic from a local university) study a practical issue at the place of work.

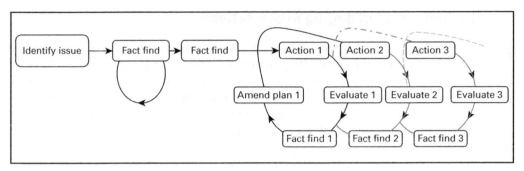

**FIGURE 6.2** Lewin's action research cycle

Their work proceeds in cycles. The first step is to identify an issue. The second is to obtain as much relevant information as possible. When this is reviewed, gaps are identified and more fact-finding may be undertaken. When the group is happy with their knowledge they make a plan to solve the issue and initiate the first step of action. After a short time, the consequences are evaluated. More information is obtained, the plan is revised and the cycle is continued, as shown in Figure 6.2.

The essence of action research is that managers learn from experience and that it inculcates managers with a scientific approach. It teaches them to work in groups, 'theorise' and then test their theories in a flexible empirical way.

## CRITICAL THINKING 6.4 *What is wrong with Lewin's action learning cycle?*

The action research approach has been criticized by writers such as Elliot (1991) and Winter (1987) They argue that action research:

- gives insufficient emphasis to analysis and it implies that fact-finding and implementing are straightforward processes
- is not very rigorous in scientific terms. People who undertake action research often have insufficient training. Action research is often used in a partisan way to further someone's self-advantage
- tends to ignore the cultural and psychological context of the issues explored. In itself, correct knowledge does not lead to change

## Team-building

Team-building is designed to weld people into a cohesive group which works effectively, and is particularly important when changes bring together collections of strangers. Indeed, many change processes in mergers and acquisitions bring together people who were previously competitors or even enemies. It is essential to remove old attitudes or rivalries. Team-building involves providing information about how effective teams function. Also, it will usually include sessions on behaviours that make teams ineffective. Participants who are taught these skills are organised into groups and given a "team task". They are observed by a facilitator who leads a discussion on how well the group operated as a team.

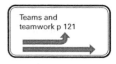

Teams and teamwork p 121

## Process consultation

Process consultation is nothing to do with production processes. It is an aspect of team-building. It is generally used when a team is inefficient. The team analyses how it can improve the way it works. It examines how group norms are formed, how the group members perceive each other's roles and how decisions are made. For example, a facilitator might start by observing the way that a team tackles a specific problem. The facilitator then guides a team's discussion of its performance. It is important to note that the facilitator will not diagnose the problem unilaterally. Their role is to help the team diagnose its own problems. However, the facilitator will ensure that the team does not overlook important facts. They will also help the team to recognise and correct its own prejudices. For example, the facilitator might point out that the team spent a lot of time obtaining information which was already known to an unpopular member who was excluded. The team might then conclude that its effectiveness was being diminished because of personal prejudices and informal cliques. An examination of the team's prejudices and social structure follows before deciding on remedial action.

Team-building and process consultation are expensive: they require a high number of facilitators. They generally produce permanent changes in specific, but small, areas of an organisation. These techniques often produce gradual, incremental changes.

## Large-group interventions

As the name suggests, these are often used in big organisations where it would be expensive and take too much time to cover everyone in a series of small groups. Organisational development consultants have developed ways of intervening on a large scale (Dannemiller and Jacobs, 1992). Large-scale interventions aim to change a whole system in a relatively short period. They bring together, say, 300 participants for three days in a large hotel. Participants are drawn from all sections of the organisation and may, sometimes, include suppliers or clients. There will usually be a number of set presentations which aim to give as much information as possible about the nature of the change. There will also be a number of group discussions led by facilitators. Often these events finish in activities where participants are required to show their commitment to the change and in the development of personal action plans which will help the change.

Because large-scale interventions involve many people, they can bring about major and profound changes in favourable situations where there is basic agreement on the content and processes of change. They can harness pressures to help change because everyone in the organisation will have been involved and everyone will be involved at the same time. Momentum for change can be established. However, large group interventions are not good at removing deep-seated objections to change.

## Survey feedback

Survey feedback is one of the most powerful OD techniques. It has five stages. *First*, the main worries about the change are identified. *Second*, a questionnaire is designed to measure people's attitudes. *Third*, the questionnaire is given, on an anonymous basis, to a large sample. In fact, the questionnaire is usually sent to all employees. This makes it clear that the change will affect the whole organisation. *Fourth*, replies are analysed and the main results are distributed to everyone. *Fifth*, results are discussed by groups of employees, who are asked to produce recommendations.

Survey research has an obvious role in clarifying employees' views. However, its feedback also has useful by-products. The construction of the questionnaire forces an organisation to clarify the main issues. Further, completing the questionnaire helps to educate employees. In addition, the process emphasises the importance of participation and it allows people to feel that they have been consulted. Survey research works best when the findings of the survey lead to specific actions which can then be reported back to those who took part – especially reporting back "quick wins". Survey feedback is a relatively cheap way of involving a large number of people. It can lead to a rapid change.

## Change agents

Many organisations employ outsiders (third parties) to help them implement change. They are often called change agents and there are two main types: commercial consultants and academics – although some change agents may be "in-house" professionals from headquarters. The main *advantages* of using external change agents is that they appear neutral (they have not been involved in previous inter-organisational power struggles) and their specialist expertise (they will have gained experience from their involvement with change in other organisations). The main *disadvantages* of external change agents may depend upon whether they are consultants or academics. Some consultants may have a hidden agenda to create more work for themselves and some may seek to impose a standard solution, used with previous clients, rather than developing a tailor-made solution. Some academics, on the other hand, may have a poor grasp of the realities of working life and their teaching or research commitments may mean they cannot devote sufficient time to the change project. Change agents, as outsiders, may encounter hostility from workers who may see them as either mercenaries or management lackeys. Kanter (1984) identified three sets of skills needed by change agents. *First*, good change agents must have a thorough knowledge of the types and techniques of change. They must also be good at adapting their knowledge to the needs of particular organisations. *Second*, they need to have good communication skills (acting, listening and speaking) to persuade people to adopt change – writing reports, giving presentations or taking part in group exercises. They are also likely to be good at understanding and using the power structure within the organisation. *Third*, a good change agent will be good at managing problems that arise from interventions such as participation. These skills determine whether a change program is successful. However, as the next section shows there are other factors involved in success or failure.

## Success factors in organisational change

Organisational change is a very risky business. Some writers estimate that about 70 per cent of attempts at organisational change fail. This grim statistic, however, raises the question: "what is meant by success of organisational change?" Following the major theme of this book that management is "organising people so they add value", the success of organisational change is:

 changing the structure, behavior or culture of an organisation so that the new form adds more value than the old form.

However, this simplistic definition conceals problems:

1 It requires measuring the added value to an organisation both before the change and after the change. This rarely happens. The better pieces of research, however, may take two measures of a restricted range of indicators but miss other areas. For example, they may measure an increase in the value of the profit made but omit damage to the firm's reputation or the environmental impact of the change.

2 It begs the question, "value to whom?" An organisational change may increase value to shareholders and even other employees but it may also make other workers redundant. For example, in 2009, the John Lewis Partnership changed the location of its distribution centre from Stevenage to Milton Keynes. Undoubtedly this added value for customers and other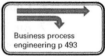

Business process engineering p 493

partners. But, did it add value for the "partners" who thought they were secure but who lost their jobs? Such changes can be justified on the *ethical* grounds of the greater benefit to a large number of people. But, does this amount to a violation of "partners" rights and the "tyranny of the majority"? Reports suggest that the John Lewis move was a success. In the 1990s many people in many organisations lost their jobs as a result of business process engineering. Many of these change programmes were not successful and people lost their jobs needlessly.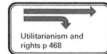

Utilitarianism and rights p 468

Many evaluations of organisational change ignore these wider considerations and focus upon the question: "did the change bring about the aims that were stated at the start of the change?" Using this limited criterion many people have sought to identify *critical success factors*. Moss Kanter (1983) looked at the success of organisational change in 10 companies. Her sample was miniscule. However, she came to the momentous conclusion that there are two main approaches to change: integrative and segmental. In the **integrative approach** organisations welcome change as an opportunity and are prepared to adopt a high level of change. They foster new ideas and view change in a holistic way: they are prepared to attempt change that might affect the whole organisation. In the **segmental approach** organisations tend to attempt change only within certain limits or certain segments of the organisation. Change is divided into easily managed and predictable compartments. Kanter found that organisations with an integrative approach were better at assimilating innovative ideas.

A quick Internet search yields an endless and disorganised array of lists of specific factors that lead to successful change. The following selection is based on By's excellent paper

(2005) which compared Kanter, Stein and Jick's (1992) "Ten commandments for executing change", Kotter's (1996) "Eight-stage process for executing change" and Luecke's (2003) "Seven Steps". The requirements of successful organisational change appear to be:

1 **A good change strategy** that is based on the analysis of the organisation and its need for change. Energy and commitment should be mobilised through joint identification of business problems and their solutions.

2 **A shared vision and a common sense of direction** is developed and widely communicated.

3 **A sense of urgency** where a clear line is drawn under the organisation's past shape and methods.

4 **Political support** is marshalled by forming a guiding coalition of powerful people and then identifying and supporting strong leaders.

5 **A detailed implementation plan.** This will include developing enabling structures (new posts, new committees, new communications, etc.) and empowering people to take action.

6 **Communicate, communicate, communicate** – in a direct and honest way.

7 **Anchor the new approaches in the organisation**. Reinforce the change by rewarding those who develop and maintain it. Institutionalise the change with formal policies, systems and organisational structures.

Other important aspects of successful organisational change include generating short-term wins and focusing on results rather than activities. Luecke (2003) suggests starting by changing the periphery of the organisation and allowing changes to spread to other units without undue pressure from the top. Naturally, an important feature of organisational change is to monitor and adjust both the strategy and the methods in response to problems and issues that emerge.

## CRITICAL THINKING 6.5 *The Wild West of organisational change*

In some ways the topic of organisational change is like the Wild West: everyone agrees that it is important and contains many riches, but it is chaotic, lawless and contains lots of cowboys and cowgirls!

It certainly contains many riches. For example the UK's spending watchdog, the National Audit Office (2010) reported that the central government machinery, as recommended by management gurus, is in a constant state of change. There were 90 reorganisations in four years at a cost of more than £1 billion. Yet, the National Audit Office found that these expensive changes could not demonstrate value for money. The situation is likely to be worse, but hidden, in the private sector where there is no parliamentary opposition and no public scrutiny by an equivalent of the National Audit Commission. A cynic might wonder how much longer we can afford the mania for change.

Research in this area seldom reaches the scientific standards set out in Chapter 19. *First*, the sample sizes used in research are often miniscule. Moss Kanter's (1983) study is highly respected but is based on a sample of merely 10 organisations. While it may be difficult to obtain large samples of *organisations*, it remains true that conclusions based on small samples are highly unstable and often incomplete. For instance, had Kanter used a larger sample she might have detected more than two (integrative and segmental) approaches to innovation.

*Second*, measures used by researchers are sometimes weak and amount to little more than subjective opinions. Even when objective scales or questionnaires are used, their reliability and validity are not established. In many studies there are no checks on the validity of questionnaires and we are left relying on the words of the researchers.

*Third*, the views we do have are organised in a chaotic way. For instance, many researchers produced multiple lists of the stages of organisational change (seven were duly listed on pages 152 – 154). Each list has some differences and similarities with other lists. This gives unnecessary confusion and duplication. It is as though each researcher has found some nuggets – some real gold, some fools' gold. Nobody has had the sense to separate them and then give true nuggets a consistent name. It is equivalent, but less obvious, to calling the same thing "gold", "aurum" and "bullion". In scientific terms the topic of organisational change is pre-Linnaean and pre-Mendeleevian.

In the end, the management processes of planning and organising are useless unless the organisation has people who are willing and able to implement the plans and fill the roles within the organisation. The management process of "staffing" aims to ensure that the organisation has employees that will do these things and is the subject of the next chapter.

Toolkit

## 6.5  Change toolkit

- Identify the major "environmental change" that has affected your work in the past six months. Identify a change that you must make in order adapt to the altered work environment. If the change you have chosen is negative, regressive or unethical choose another one.

- Identify *sources* of resistance (content and process) to the proposed change. Identify the *tactics* of resistance which opponents might use.

- Identify an appropriate change stratergy (Lewin or Hussey or Kotter, or Hannagan?).

- If possible, choose an integrative approach to change that affects several aspects of your organisation.

- Choose appropriate OD tools to bring about the change.

- Ensure that the change process will produce at least two "short-term wins".

- Communicate, communicate, communicate – especially the vision and urgency.

- Make sure you have the support of powerful people in your organisation.

- Have a detailed plan for implementing the change.

# Activities and further study

## Essay plans

Prepare plans for the following essays:

1 To what extent is the topic of organisational change a coherent academic subject?
2 Evaluate the contributions of Kurt Lewin to the topic of organisational change.
3 Compare and contrast the different types of organisational change.
4 Describe and synthesise at least three different writers' analysis of the phases of organisational change and explain why these are important to managers.
5 Describe and compare the OD techniques of action research, team-building and survey feedback.
6 What factors would help to make an organisational change project successful?

## Web activities

1 Kurt Lewin has been called the grandfather of organisational change. Use the Internet to find information about him and to build up a picture of his contribution to the topic.
2 Enter the terms "success factors" and "organisational change" into your search engine and locate the lists produced by a number of organisations. Compare these lists and evaluate their scientific basis. Decide whether each list is more like a marketing tool or a scientifically based list.
3 Search for an example of organisational change in your local area or in a sector of the economy that interest you. Appropriate search terms might be the name of your area, retailing, manufacturing and "organisational change". Searching a database of newspapers or journals will produce the best results.

## Experiential activities

1 Choose an organisation that you know well and think of a change that it might consider (your present educational establishment or an organisation where you have worked would be good choices). List the following forces:

- possible forces of resistance against the change
- possible internal forces in favour of the change
- possible external forces in favour of the change

2  Think of a change that you would like to make in an organisation that you know well. Decide how you would evaluate whether such a change is successful. List the OD techniques that you would use in order to bring this change about.

3  Find someone (friend or family) who has recently experienced an organisational change in the place where they work. Ask their opinions about:

- the need for change
- the phases the change went through
- the various OD techniques that were used
- the contribution and effectiveness of any external change agents (if any)
- their evaluation of the effectiveness of the change
- their view of the fairness of the change

4  Organise a mini-debate on the motion that "Most organisational change is motivated by senior management's need to be seen doing things rather than a genuine need for change". Speakers for and against the motion have a maximum of five minutes to make their cases. The maximum contribution from other people is two minutes. A vote is taken at the end of the mini-debate.

## Recommended reading

1  By, R.T. (2005) "Organisational change management: a critical review", *Journal of Change Management*, **5**(4), 369–380. This article describes the different types of change, the characteristics of change and how it comes about. Integrates these aspects with the work of major theorists.

2  Bacon, N., Blyton, P. and Dastmalchian, A. (2010), "The impact of organizational change on steelworkers in craft and production occupational groups", *Human Relations*, **63**(8), 1223–1248. A difficult paper which is an antidote to the belief that organisational change is easy. It gives a detailed analysis of the impact of organisational change in steelworks at Teeside and Scunthorpe. Start reading at the new section on page 1227 – and the section on research sites. Then read result sections on: team design; attitudes; job quality; work pressure and job satisfaction. Do not get bogged down in statistics or complicated tables.

3  Boomer, G. (2010) "Managing change: clarity reduces resistance", *Accounting Today*, July–August, p. 32. Common sense advice for accountants on how to manage change.

## CHAPTER 7

# Staffing – Selecting, Developing and Motivating People

## Chapter contents

## ❖ LEARNING OBJECTIVES

After studying this chapter you should be able to **explain** the importance of three of the four main staffing processes (the way all managers relate to staff) and **make a preliminary distinction** from human resource management (the specialist activities undertaken by a group of experts). You will also be able to **outline** the main ways in which managers recruit, train and motivate their staff. In particular you will be able to:

❖ **list** the four main stages involved in selecting employees

❖ **evaluate** the advantages and disadvantages of four scientific methods of selection – especially their accuracy

❖ **list** three main categories of training methods

❖ **describe briefly** each of six methods of "off the job" training

❖ **explain** the difference between training and development

❖ **describe briefly** the concepts of learning skills, self-awareness and 360-degree feedback

❖ **explain** the importance of motivating employees

❖ **compare and contrast** three theories of motivation

Once an organisation's strategic plans have been laid and an appropriate structure devised, the next step is to fill the organisation with workers and to treat them in a way which maximises their contribution. This latter stage is called **staffing**. It is also called **people management** but a pedant would point out that this alternative term is misleading since managers are only responsible for maximising the performance of their staff, not people in general.

---

### CASE 7.1: *Investing in People at Eversheds*

Eversheds is a huge law firm which employs more than 2000 lawyers and advisers in more than 20 locations in the UK, Europe, the Middle East, Africa and Asia. It recognises the importance of managing all its staff as effectively as possible and has achieved recognition by Investors in People (IIP) - which promotes high standards in staffing procedures. With the aid of an organisation-wide survey, Eversheds identified the key areas in managing its staff. Among other things, the organisation uses the following methods to harness their employees' talents:

- comprehensive induction programmes
- regular development reviews
- training and development
- a wide range of internal communications such as intranet and briefing sessions
- a "Careers Pathway" scheme for non-lawyers
- 360° feedback

For four years in a row, Eversheds has been voted as one of the top UK employers (*Sunday Times* annual surveys). Its internal employee survey indicates that 78 per cent of its staff believe the firm is a great place to work.

---

Most analyses of management work show that dealing with staff is *the* main management process. No matter whether they work in operations, sales, marketing or even IT, *all* managers need to maximise the potential of workers. It will be an exceptional day if a manager does not meet at least one member of their staff. This contrasts with other processes such as planning, organising and budgeting. At certain times of the year a manager can go for days without performing any of these processes. Staffing may be divided into four major topics: selecting, training, motivating and leading. The first three are discussed in this chapter, while leading is covered in Chapter 8.

There are important reasons why these topics do not appear in Chapter 16 which covers human resource (HR) management. Selecting, training, motivating and leading are management processes that *every* manager must perform. The primary responsibility for each aspect of staffing lies with the manager not the organisational function. Of course, the HR department can help with facilities or technical advice, but it is the manager's responsibility to select suitable people, to give them proper training and to motivate them and, as the next chapter shows, it is vital that the manager gives his or her team proper leadership. The message is loud and clear: selection, training, motivation and leadership of staff is the primary responsibility of the manager. Although there are close links between staffing and HR there are additional dangers in treating them together. First, there may be confusion about who is responsible for what. Managers might be able to blame poor motivation on the HR department, while the HR department might blame managers for poorly designed *systems* of appraisal or remuneration. Further, if staffing is simply considered as an aspect of HR, it will be difficult to compare and contrast its contribution relative to other processes such as planning or organising. Similarly, it will be more difficult to compare and contrast the contribution of the HR function with that of other functions such as marketing or finance.

## 7.1 Definition and introduction to the staffing process

The purpose of the staffing process is to produce effective workers. Figure 7.1 shows that the process starts with designing a job and then producing a job description. The next stage is to select workers who have most of the skills that are needed. However, it is probably impossible to find employees that have exactly all the right skills. Further, jobs change and, usually, extra skills are needed in the future. It is necessary to fill the gap between the skills that workers have and the skills that they need by training and development. When these

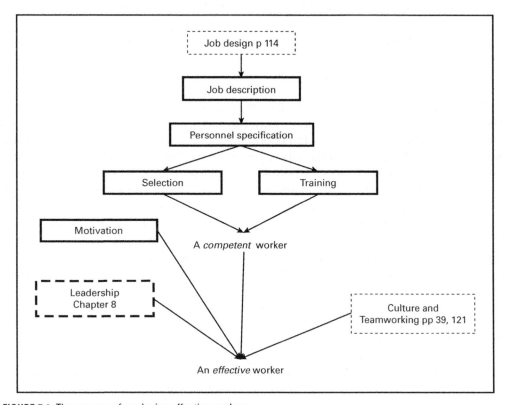

**FIGURE 7.1**  The process of producing effective workers

steps are completed effectively, the organisation will have competent workers that are able to do the job. However, workers may not use their abilities to the full. Their managers need to motivate them and lead them for their potential to be realised. In addition, the manager needs to provide a conducive organisational climate and an effective team.

This chapter briefly explains job descriptions and personnel specifications. It then gives substantial details on the selection, training, motivation and leadership of workers. More information on designing jobs, providing a conducive organisational climate and managing an effective team are covered elsewhere in this book as indicated in Figure 7.1.

## 7.2  Job descriptions and personnel specifications

The production of job descriptions and personnel specifications does not arise out of thin air. They are based on the way that jobs are designed. Technically, job design is a part of the organising process described in an earlier chapter. In practice jobs are usually designed with a combined effort of the HR and the operations functions – with perhaps a contribution by the finance function. Once jobs have been designed it is necessary to fill them with suitable workers. The first stage is to produce a **job description** which sets out what workers need to do. The purpose of the job description is to set out the key results a worker must achieve. A job description also covers the type of workplace, pay and other conditions of employment, and it will indicate where the job fits into the organisational structure (e.g. identifying the manager to whom the worker is responsible). In most countries, it is a legal requirement to give an employee a written job description. It should be noted that job descriptions are about the *job to be done*, not the people who occupy the job.

Job design p 114

**Personnel specifications** are based upon the job description and they concern the *people* who occupy the job. They identify the knowledge, skills, abilities and other characteristics which a person must have in order to perform the job in a competent way. In other words they specify the ideal person for the job. A personnel specification can take many formats. One very basic method of producing personnel specification uses Roger's seven-point plan (Roger,1953), which groups requirements under seven headings. The job description is used to identify the essential and desirable characteristics of workers. *Essential characteristics* are those which are central to the job and which would be difficult or expensive to develop by training. *Desirable characteristics* are those which are important to the job but which might be developed with appropriate training. A table which gives a simplified personnel specification for a sales representative of a software company is given on the website which accompanies this book.

Great care should be taken to avoid unfairness and discrimination. For example, it would generally be unfair to include a candidate's height in a personnel specification. Men are generally taller than women and a height requirement would differentially exclude more women than men. This would normally constitute unfair discrimination but there are exceptions if a person's height is relevant to performing the job. Similarly, personnel specifications should not imply that women candidates might be unsuitable because they would be responsible for the care of children.

## CRITICAL THINKING 7.1 *When height is a valid qualification for a job*

In a famous case in the USA it was declared illegal for a police force to demand that recruits should be taller than 1.75 m (5 feet 10 inches) because this would exclude many women and members of some ethnic groups such as Hispanics who could be competent police officers. However, the police force *was* allowed to demand that recruits should be taller than 1.65 m (5 feet 6 inches) since shorter officers might endanger themselves and colleagues because they would not be sufficiently tall to shoot a pistol over the top of a car (this is America!).

## 7.3 Recruiting and selecting (employee resourcing)

Recruitment and selection concerns the supply of suitable employees and is sometimes referred to as **employee resourcing**. Good recruitment and selection can easily raise productivity by 10 per cent and give an organisation a competitive edge. Good selection has two stages:

- attracting a field of candidates
- choosing among candidates

In addition, good selection often involves giving applicants a realistic preview of the job.

### Recruitment

The aim of recruitment is to attract about eight credible applicants for each post. If there are fewer than eight there might not be enough to allow a good choice. If there are many more, it will be difficult to give each candidate full and proper consideration. Some ways of attracting applicants are:

- internal notices and emails
- government employment agencies
- private employment agencies
- headhunters (executive search agencies)
- advertisements in the local press, national press and professional journals
- careers fairs and college visits

The choice of media will depend upon the exact situation. Many senior management jobs are advertised in the national press and professional journals. Very senior management posts will seek applicants using executive search agencies. The use of "headhunters" is very expensive (about 33 per cent of the first-year salary). But the service is very confidential and it is most likely to locate able people who are not actively searching for the job – because they are busy being successful in their present job. Whichever medium is chosen, care must be taken to ensure that the advertising is fair. Advertising a job solely in a magazine such as *FHM* or *GQ* is likely to be unfair because, presumably, few women read these magazines. Advertising a vacancy using internal notices or by word of mouth of existing employees may also be discriminatory since it is less likely that minority groups will learn that a vacancy exists.

---

**CASE 7.2:** *Selection of technical managers*

Bristol-Myers Squibb is a world-famous pharmaceutical company. It has a large production plant near Dublin airport in Ireland. A major expansion meant it needed to employ more than 40 technical managers who would be responsible for producing medicines to impeccable quality standards. Because requirements were so high the company decided to engage in a textbook selection exercise in order to obtain the best possible recruits.

First, the jobs of technical managers were analysed to identify the precise characteristics the managers would need. This was a substantial exercise involving more than 60 interviews with senior managers and currently successful managers. A selection system was devised to measure the exact characteristics needed to perform the job.

Applicants were first screened on the basis of their application forms. Those who survived were invited to a mini-assessment centre where they completed:

- two tests of high-level mental ability (verbal reasoning and numerical reasoning)
- a personality test to check, among other things, conscientiousness and emotional stability
- an in-tray test to check how well they could handle written administrative tasks
- a group discussion to check their ability to communicate and work in a team
- a situational interview seeking their reactions to realistic situations they might face
- a technical interview with the potential line manager to check their technical knowledge

The system proved very successful and it was used with hundreds of applicants. It was calculated that the improved selection system saved the organisation over €6 million during the time that the cohort of technical managers would work for the company.

---

## Selection

When a field of candidates has been assembled, it is necessary to **choose the best person** for the job. Many selection methods exist. Cook (2009 ) noted that three methods predominate. They are known as **the classic trio**:

1  application forms and CVs
2  interviews
3  references

While these methods are widely used they are not very accurate. A traditional interview, for example, is about 4 per cent better than chance in selecting the best candidate. References

**CRITICAL THINKING 7.2** *Lies, damn lies and cvs*

A good example of a deceitful CV is the nutritionist who advised the England football captain, Alan Shearer, for two years. When she tried to negotiate a sponsorship deal with Lucozade, a sharp-eyed executive noted that her documents were false. Due to ill health she had dropped out of a degree course and subsequently forged degree and diploma certificates. She obtained work at *two* private health clinics before joining Newcastle United.

Another example is an eye surgeon who was sacked on the spot when it was discovered that his application had omitted to mention a disciplinary offence and had covered it up by supplying two false references. Medical and allied professions seem particularly prone to this problem. One organisation that vets the applications of nurses found 24 bogus claimants within a period of nine months.

In 2002 a leading English clergyman, dean of Portsmouth Cathedral, resigned because he had falsely claimed a PhD.

Lies on CVs and application forms are tragic. They are discovered by reference checks. The perpetrator is disgraced and suffers the financial penalty of unemployment and subsequent reduction in earning power.

are no better but they are a useful way of checking basic facts, dates and job titles of previous employment. Perhaps surprisingly, it is estimated that about one in seven CVs contains blatant lies: the original copies of licences, certificates or diploma's, etc. should be inspected.

Because the classic trio of selection methods are so poor, many organisations use more modern methods such as psychometric testing which we discuss shortly. But just because the classic trio are flawed does not mean that they should not be used at all – they do fulfil other purposes. If candidates know that references will be checked, they tend to be more truthful when filling out application forms or writing CVs. Candidates expect to be interviewed and feel cheated if they are not given a chance to make their own case (even if, in doing so, they do themselves a disservice). Further, interviews are fairly efficient at giving candidates information about the job and starting their orientation towards the organisation. One of the best solutions is to put any interview at the very end of the selection process where it can do the least damage, since at that stage any of the surviving candidates will be reasonably well qualified.

**CRITICAL THINKING 7.3** *The long-known weakness of traditional interviews*

The lack of accuracy of traditional interviews has been known since 1929 when Hollingworth asked 12 experienced sales managers to interview 56 applicants. He ensured that the interviewers ranked the applicants independently. If interviews are any good, there should be some correspondence between the ratings – for example if an applicant is in the top 10 for one interviewer they should be in the top 10 for other interviewers. The actual results were appalling. There was very little correspondence between the rankings. For example, one applicant was top of one interviewer's ranking but fifty-third on the ranking of another interviewer. The conclusion is clear: with traditional interviews your chances of being offered a job very much depend on who is your interviewer.

## Modern selection methods

Psychologists and others have been developing better selection methods for almost a century. Some of the most accurate methods of choosing employees include psychometric tests, work samples, structured interviews and biodata. However, as Table 7.1 shows, no single method is perfect and it is usually better to use a combination of methods in, say, an assessment centre. Methods used to select among candidates must be sensitive, reliable, valid and fair.

### Psychometric tests

These are samples of behaviour which are highly standardised so that everyone is given precisely the same instructions and time to complete the same tasks. The answers are also evaluated in a standard way. Psychometric tests are more objective than other methods. Broadly speaking, two kinds of tests are used in selection: tests of mental ability and tests of personality.

- **Mental ability** is the ability to *process information quickly and accurately*. It is fairly stable after the age of about 18. Tests of mental ability have been used for 100 years or more. They are highly reliable (a typical reliability correlation is 0.9 – about the same relationship as the length of your right arm to your left arm). Scores of mental ability tests usually correlate about 0.53 with future success. In managers the correlation is higher at about 0.58. Mental ability is a vital factor in job success because it enables people to learn the job more quickly and to respond better to changes or unusual events.

- **Personality** is the *style in which things are done* and is moderately stable after the age of about 30. Tests of personality are rather less reliable than ability tests. A typical test–retest correlation will be about 0.75. Personality tests are useful predictors of job performance and correlate about 0.4 with future job success. Personality is less accurate than mental ability in predicting job performance because equal success can be achieved by people with different styles. Further, up to a point, people can mould jobs to suit their personality. Honesty tests are a particular type of personality test. They attempt to predict whether a future employee will participate in theft or other antisocial activity such as drug-taking. Honesty tests are most frequently used in retail organisations.

| | Use | | Accuracy/Validity | |
|---|---|---|---|---|
| **100%** | | **1.0** | | |
| 90% | Traditional interviews | 0.9 | | |
| 80% | CVs and letters of application | 0.8 | | |
| 70% | | 0.7 | | |
| | | | *Intelligence* and *integrity* | (0.65) |
| 60% | | 0.6 | *Intelligence* and *structured interviews* | (0.63) |
| | | | *Intelligence* and *work sample* | (0.60) |
| | | | Work sample tests | (0.54) |
| 50% | | 0.5 | Intelligence tests | (0.53) |
| | | | Structured interviews | (0.51) |
| 43% | References | | Job knowledge tests | (0.48) |
| | | | Integrity tests | (0.40) |
| 40% | | 0.4 | Personality tests | (0.40?) |
| | | | Assessment centres | (0.37) |
| 30% | | 0.3 | Biodata | (0.33) |
| | | | Conscientiousness | (0.31) |
| 22% | Mental ability tests | | References | (0.25) |
| 20% | Personality tests      18% | 0.2 | Traditional interviews | (0.15) |
| 13% | Work samples | | Years education | (0.15) |
| 13% | Graphology | 0.1 | Interests | (0.14) |
| 8% | Assessment centres | | Years job experience | (0.09) |
| 2% | Astrology | | Graphology | (0.0) |
| 0% | | 0.0 | Age | (0.01) |

**TABLE 7.1** The use and accuracy of methods of selection

### Work samples

These are carefully worked out exercises which aim to be mini-trials of the job. For example, an applicant for the job of a carpenter would be provided with a standard piece of wood and a standard set of tools. A set time is allowed to produce a piece of work entailing a range of joints and cuts. The exact nature of the task is determined by a prior analysis of the joints and cuts which differentiates between good and bad carpenters. Work samples for management jobs include:

- **Written analysis** of a business problem on the basis of a set of files.
- **A presentation** on a business topic to an audience.
- **A group exercise** which mimics a management meeting.
- **A role play**, e.g. a candidate is asked to study an errant employee's file and conduct a disciplinary interview with that employee.

Work samples are among the best methods of selection and usually correlate 0.54 with subsequent job performance.

### Structured interviews

These are much better traditional interviews. Structure means *all candidates are asked more or less the same questions* and, consequently, better comparisons can be made. Further, structured interviews are based on the job description and *only ask questions concerning work behaviour*. For example, an applicant sales representative might be asked how they would respond to the following, realistic, situation:

> 66   You have arranged to see an important customer. You arrive on time only to be told that the customer is busy. You wait for 30 minutes. Just as you are about to leave for your next appointment your customer emerges from her office with the sales representative from a rival company . . . what would you do?   99

The applicant's answer would be compared to a carefully calibrated set of model responses and a score would be allocated. An applicant would be asked how they would respond to five or six of these situations. This particular kind of structured interview is known as a "situational" interview. If properly prepared, situational interviews can be good predictors of future job performance and can rival work samples in their accuracy. Some people say that situational interviews are "verbal work samples".

### Biodata

This is a way of collecting information, usually by a questionnaire, about the course of a person's life. Typically the data include educational qualifications, hobbies, memberships and work experience. The data are then used in a carefully derived formula that calculates a person's probability of success. Credit scoring and the calculation of insurance premiums are specific varieties of biodata. Biodata has a moderately good correlation with future job performance. It is very useful as a first sift when there are many applicants for a job.

### Assessment centres

Many organisations, especially large ones, use a combination of methods. Candidates are asked to attend for a whole day when they will be asked to, say, complete tests of mental ability and personality, take part in a discussion group, write a report and participate in a situational interview. Combinations of methods such as this are called **assessment centres**. At senior management level they may be more intensive and last two days or even a week. Because assessment centres use several methods, the weaknesses of individual methods have chance to iron themselves out. However, assessment centres are expensive and may cause disruption to both the candidates and the assessors within the organisation.

Because there are so many methods of selection the question arises "which one to use?" A consultant graphologist would probably claim that graphology is best; a firm specialising in interview training would probably suggest using interviews; while a pychometrician might recommend psychometric tests. Before an organisation can choose the best candidate, it must decide on the characteristics that make a good method. The four main characteristics of good selection are:

- **Sensitivity**: it must differentiate between different candidates. If a method gives the same score to every person it is useless. References, for example, are often not very helpful because a very large majority of referees maintain that their applicant is very good.

- **Reliability**: it must give consistent results – otherwise the choice of candidate would depend upon the day on which they were chosen. Reliability is often measured using a correlation. A correlation of 1.0 means that a candidate will always achieve the same score, while a correlation of 0.0 will mean that the scores of a candidate will vary at random. For example, the scores of ability tests are very reliable and achieve a correlation of 0.9 or more. This means that a candidate will achieve a very similar score if they complete an ability test a second time. The reliability of traditional interviews is much less, and a typical correlation would be 0.3. This means that, while there would be a slight trend for candidates to obtain similar scores, far more would depend upon the person who interviewed them.

- **Validity**: does the selection method accurately predict which candidates will be successful? Validity is usually established by collecting scores at the selection stage and correlating them with the later job performance.

- **Fairness:** does not necessarily mean that all groups can do their job equally well. However, it does mean that those people from different groups who are likely to be equally good at doing a job are equally likely to be selected. For example, perhaps only 10 per cent are women who are able to carry a human body down a long ladder; however, these women should have an equal chance of being hired as a firefighter as men who can do the same thing.

Occupational psychologists have been studying the use and accuracy of different methods of selection for over 90 years and are able to provide the general results contained in Table 7.1.

It will be little surprise that the traditional methods of interviews, application forms or letters and references (Cook's classic trio) are the most frequently used methods of selection. There are, however, interesting national differences. In most countries the use of graphology is rare, at about 3 per cent. However, in France approximately 40 per cent of organisations use this technique and this has a marked effect upon the average figure shown in Table 7.1.

Indeed, the use of graphology outside France is largely restricted to subsidiaries of French companies. On average, references are used as a part of selection in 43 per cent of cases; there are, however, notable national differences. The use of references in the UK is very prevalent and is used by about 74 per cent of companies, but its use is much less common in other countries.

The right-hand side of Table 7.1 indicates the accuracy (validity) of the methods of selection. It is based largely upon the paper of Schmidt and Hunter (1996). Results gathered over the last 90 years indicate that the traditional and most prevalent methods of selection are not very accurate (valid). Traditional interviews, for example, have a validity of about 0.15.

More modern methods such as work samples, intelligence tests and situational interviews are far more accurate and have validities in excess of 0.50. While this is a big improvement, it should be noted that modern methods of selection are still far from perfect and many selection errors are still made.

The selection process should give applicants **a realistic preview of the job**. In other words, at the end of the selection process a candidate should have a realistic picture of what the job involves. If they have an unrealistic picture of their future jobs they are likely to leave within a few weeks and the organisation will have to bear the extra costs of recruiting another replacement. Realistic job previews (RJPs) can be provided by giving applicants information in brochures or handouts. An RJP can also be arranged by asking candidates to watch a video or by providing a tour of the workplace and allowing questions to existing employees.

## 7.4  Training and development (employee development)

The aim of selection is to ensure that employees arrive with the skills, knowledge and abilities (competencies) that are needed. However, selection is never perfect. Usually new employees have most, but not all, the required competencies. Managers must arrange training and development as a way of making up the gap between actual and required competencies. Training and development (nowadays there is a tendency to call this **employee development**) can be divided into five major topics. Managers need to know sufficient about each topic in order to follow a systematic approach and choose the most appropriate approach such as the best method of off-the-job training. The training and development of employees should follow a systematic process, shown in Figure 7.2.

In practice, training and development involves five major aspects:

1  assessing training needs

2  induction training

3  on-the-job training

4  off-the-job training

5  management development

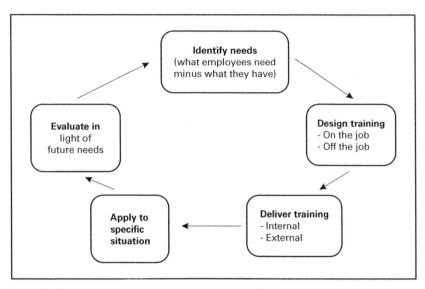

**FIGURE 7.2** The systematic training system

## Assessing training needs

Assessing *training needs* usually proceeds in three stages.

1 The *strategic plan is inspected and the major HR implications are identified*. For example, a strategic plan may aim for a 20 per cent increase in market share. To achieve the increase it may be necessary to arrange training for existing sales staff, recruit four extra sales representatives and seven production operatives together with two additional administrative staff. Sometimes, this process is called **human resource planning**.

2 Capabilities of existing or new employees are evaluated against the capabilities that will be needed. The difference is often called **the training gap**.

3 Arrangements are made to **provide the training and development** which will close the training gap. Most external recruits will need induction training. In essence, other training is into on-the-job training and off-the-job training. Managers need to know enough about the methods and their advantages and disadvantages in order to make appropriate choices.

## Induction training (orientation training)

Induction training aims to familiarise a newcomer with the organisation. It usually covers details which are taken for granted by existing employees. It may include arrangements for receiving wages, conditions of employment, grievance procedures, refreshment facilities and car-parking arrangements. It aims to remove initial problems for new employees and reduce the probability that they leave within the first few weeks. Induction training will usually include information about the company, its history, its structure and products. This information is an important element of fostering company loyalty and ensuring that a new employee becomes an effective employee. Finally, induction training usually tries to communicate the culture and ethos of the organisation.

## On-the-job training

On-the-job training is the oldest and simplest type of training. Since time immemorial new female recruits were told to "sit by Nellie" and watch what Nellie does and male recruits have been told to "stand by Sid" and be similarly observant. On-the-job training requires little preparation and there are few obvious costs. Further, it is very realistic so there are no transition problems when a trainee is transferred to production. Nevertheless, this type of training has major problems: it is inefficient and costly. Costs are, however, hidden and secrete themselves in lower production by Nellie and Sid and longer training times. In addition, Nellie or Sid may teach the trainee bad habits!

Other forms of on-the-job training are better and are very useful after initial training. Their success depend on careful planning and availability of a **mentor** who discusses work with the trainee and ensures appropriate lessons are drawn. First, the mentor determines what the trainee already knows. Often the mentor will then demonstrate the job to the trainee. In other cases the mentor will arrange for someone else to give instruction. Instruction will cover one point at a time. The trainee will be asked questions to check learning has taken place. When the trainee has fully understood the task, he or she will be asked to try it out by themselves. Once the trainee has gained confidence further guidance can be given. Finally, the trainee is left to perform the job unaided. Initially the performance of the trainee should be monitored at regular intervals but later this can be reduced.

This basic approach to on-the-job training is used in two main contexts: job rotation and special assignments. **Job rotation** is useful with new recruits, such as graduates, who have little previous experience of work or the organisation. It involves moving trainees through a series of jobs in different departments. For example, a graduate trainee may spend the first month in the production department, the second month in the sales department, and so on. Job rotation is an excellent way of allowing new recruits to build up knowledge of the organisation. It produces a flexible workforce and allows trainees to make informed decisions about the direction of their future careers.

**Special assignments** are used with longer-serving employees. Generally a review of training needs for a specific employee reveals a development need. An assignment, different to present duties, which allows new knowledge and skills to be acquired is found. For example, the strategic plan of a financial service company may envisage expansion into foreign markets. A review may reveal an existing personnel manager has no experience of foreign cultures. The organisation may therefore arrange a special assignment in which the individual is seconded for six months to the personnel department in, say, Singapore. Sometimes it is possible to arrange a special assignment in another organisation.

## Off-the-job training

Many managers shun off-the-job training that is conducted away from the workplace and outside their immediate control. This can disrupt the normal flow of work. Off-the-job training may strain their budget with substantial out-of-pocket expenses. Further, off-the-job training involves decisions about how it should be delivered such as:

- night school
- day release

- block release
- special seminars and workshops
- correspondence courses
- online, interactive training

The most appropriate method depends upon circumstances. For example, a day-release course for printing-machine engineers may be appropriate for trainees who work close to a suitable college. However, commuting and travelling times would make day release inappropriate for similar engineers who work in outlying areas. They might find block release courses (a week's residential course, for example) more suitable. Similarly, much will depend on the ability and motivation of trainees. Generally, night-school courses and correspondence courses are only suitable for people who are *very highly* motivated.

Off-the-job training may involve a wide range of instruction methods. The main methods are:

- **Lectures** are a very cost-effective method because their size is limited only by the size of the lecture theatre. Lectures can be very good at introducing a topic, identifying the structure of a subject and highlighting the key points. Lectures are not a good medium for consolidating detailed learning. Lectures have an intrinsic drawback: they are usually boring. Communication between lecturer and learner is usually one-way only. **Classes and seminars** are costly. Their size is usually limited to a maximum of about 16 students. Classes are based upon the question and answer technique. They are interactive and are able to maintain interest while consolidating detailed learning. **Role plays** require trainees to act out situations – usually situations involving decisions or interpersonal reactions. **Discussion groups** are used when training focuses upon changing or developing attitudes. A relevant topic will be introduced by a skilled leader. The group will then be invited to discuss the topic. The leader inconspicuously rewards positive attitudes and ignores negative ones. For example, a training session on ethnic diversity might include a discussion group on racial prejudice. Whenever a participant expresses tolerant attitudes, the discussion leader signals approval and encourages the participant to amplify their ideas. The contributions of participants with intolerant attitudes are accepted politely, but with minimal comment.

- **Case studies** are a very popular method of management development. Students are given background data and the details of the specific problem. They are then asked to discuss the situation and recommend a course of action. The actions actually taken and their actual consequences are then revealed. Students are able to compare their suggestions with the action actually taken. They also try to analyse the situation to evaluate why the organisation's actions did, or did not, work.

- **Online training** is a medium that has many potential advantages. Typically, trainees can use online training at any time convenient to them. The flexibility of online training means that there is no disruption of the normal workflow. At its simplest, online training will involve a screen containing text. When this has been read, the trainee completes, say, a multiple-choice test and they are immediately given a score which shows whether the material has been learned successfully. Online training can have more sophisticated features. For example, a video clip can be used instead of text. In some situations, online training can be highly interactive and it can branch according to decisions made by the trainee. Online training is very useful when there is a clear set of objective "facts"

CRITICAL THINKING 7.4 *Are case studies shared ignorance?*

Although the case study method is used in many top management courses, it has strong critics who maintain that the method results in "shared ignorance". There is an assumption that the person who creates a case study is an objective and knowledgeable expert. In fact, most problem situations involve a number of explanations. The person who creates a case study will choose the explanation which suits her or his purposes and it can never be known whether or not they have chosen the correct explanation.

Students like case studies because they *seem* realistic. In fact, most case studies are oversimplifications and the solutions proffered rarely have empirical evidence of their effectiveness. Indeed, shortly before its collapse in shame and ignominy, business schools around the world used more than a dozen Harvard Business School case studies that hyped and praised the innovation of Enron and the Enron business model (Curver, 2003). In effect, these case studies were teaching bad business methods. More details of the Enron collapse are given in Chapter 19. This is not an isolated example. Case study writers from Harvard Business School extolled the virtues of the "new architecture" formed by the Royal Bank of Scotland after its acquisition of NatWest Bank (Fred the shred, again!) – within a short time the bank was in trouble and had to be rescued by the British government (Broughton, 2008).

It is highly likely that readers of this book will be required to critique at least one case study during a management course. Some guidance on evaluating case studies is given on pages 505–506.

that a trainee must learn. For example, audiovisual training is a good way of training computer programmers to diagnose problems and faults. However, the set-up costs are high. This means that it is only appropriate where there are many trainees. The high set-up costs also mean that this training is appropriate only where the material is unlikely to change for a significant period of time. Indeed, critics complain that audiovisual training is inflexible, because the costs of making adjustments are so high. Initially, trainees like online training. However, the most able trainees quickly become bored and complain that it is too repetitive and pedestrian.

## Management development

Training implies learning *specific knowledge, procedures or skills* to meet *existing* challenges. Development implies the *improvement of a more general capability* which can be used to meet *future* situations. Management development is therefore a broader concept than management training. In most circumstances people in the first two years of their management career should spend at least four weeks on development courses. Thereafter, experienced managers should spend about two weeks per year on development activities. The two most prominent aspects of management development are **learning skills** and **self-awareness**.

**Learning skills** are an important aspect of "knowledge management". In a dynamic and rapidly changing world it is impossible to specify and train people to solve all the problems they might encounter. It is much better to train people in *ways* of solving problems so that they can solve-problems themselves, as and when they arise. This means that managers need to be aware of their own style of learning and any of their weaknesses in problem-solving. Probably the most famous analysis of problem-solving was made by Kolb and Fry (1975). They viewed problem-solving as a continuous cycle (Figure 7.3) with four main stages:

- **Concrete experience** occurs when a person performs an action and then directly experiences the results of that action in their specific situation.
- **Observation and reflection** follow from concrete experience. An individual tries to understand why the result followed from the action in that particular situation.
- **Abstract conceptualisation** involves extending the lessons from a particular situation to a more generalised idea of how the action and the result might be linked in a wide variety of situations.
- **Active experimentation** involves seeking out new circumstances in which to test the general ideas generated in the previous stage.

Active experimentation produces a new set of concrete experiences which set the cycle in motion again. According to this analysis management learning is a continuous cycle in which ideas become more and more accurate. Kolb found that individuals differed in their approach to problem-solving. Some would emphasise concrete experience while others would emphasise active experimentation, etc. However, effective learners need to be proficient at all stages of the cycle. A weakness at any one stage will slow down the whole learning process. It is therefore important for managers to locate their area of weakness

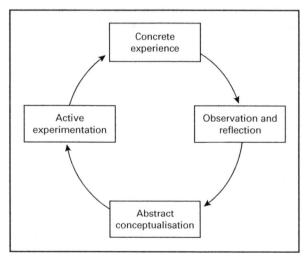

**FIGURE 7.3** Kolb and Fry's learning cycle

and develop it to the level of their ability at the other stages. A number of people including Honey and Mumford (Honey, 1982) have adapted Kolb's ideas.

**Self-awareness** is very important in leaders (see Chapter 8). It can be developed in a number of ways. Sometimes it is achieved by special training courses (**T groups**) where a workgroup sets aside, perhaps, two days to discuss their perceptions of each other. Each group member becomes, in turn, the focus of the training. The other group members give their frank and open views of that person and any inaccurate perceptions are challenged and discussed. Often the sessions are stormy but, it is claimed, at the end of the training the workgroup will have fewer personal misunderstandings. Self-awareness training can sometimes make vunerable participants upset and distraught – if you are trying hard but only just succeeding it does not help if others repeatedly tell you so!

**360-degree feedback** is another way of increasing a person's awareness of their strengths and weaknesses. A questionnaire measuring the competencies the organisation believes are necessary is produced. The questionnaire is then circulated to a person's boss, their colleagues and their subordinates and it is completed anonymously. The results are compiled and fed back to the individual so that she or he will be aware of how they are perceived by other people. The feedback will clearly indicate areas where other people believe they are strong and where they are weak. A manager will then be in a position to take action to improve areas of weakness.

## 7.5 Motivating

Motivation is the *energy* which enables people to achieve an organisation's objectives. Motivations are sometimes called **drives**. An organisation can recruit and select very able people and train them so that they have the appropriate knowledge: the result (as we saw in Figure 7.1) is a competent worker who is able to do a job. But without motivation they will do nothing – their skills and abilities need to be activated by some kind of motivation. Motivation determines the *goals* a person attempts to achieve, the *energy* that is devoted to attaining the goal and the *persistence* with which the goal is pursued.

Motivation can be increased in many ways. Probably the most effective way is to design a job so that people derive intrinsic enjoyment in their work and are keen to do it. This aspect of motivation was covered by the section on job design in the previous chapter on organisational processes. However, it is often necessary to use other techniques to add extrinsic motivation to a job. Extrinsic motivation can be provided by factors such as pay, recognition or social pressure. Extrinsic motivation can also be provided by a person who is either a formal or informal leader of a group.

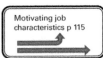

Motivating job characteristics p 115

### Theories of motivation

Many theories of motivation have been put forward. Some popular theories, such as Maslow's (1970) hierarchy of needs and Herzberg's two-factor theory, have not been supported by scientific evidence. However, equity theory, expectancy theory and goal-setting theory are particularly relevant to managers.

## CRITICAL THINKING 7.5  *What is wrong with Maslow and Herzberg?*

Sometimes, inaccurate theories which make a nice, memorable story become entrenched in the literature and are regurgitated from author to author long after they are disproved. Maslow's theory of motivation is a classic example. It is still taught on many management courses and described in many management textbooks. Maslow studied a group of atypical, very successful men and came up with a theory that there are five types of motivation and that they are arranged in a certain hierarchical order. None of this has been supported by academic research. Since 1977, it has been known that there is little evidence for either the existence of five types of motives or their hierarchical ordering (Korman, Greenhouse and Badin, 1977).

Similarly, the job enrichment theories developed by Herzberg are still taught on management courses and described in management textbooks. Herzberg claimed that there were two types of motivation: motivating factors and hygiene factors. Hertzberg's theory was enormously influential in enriching jobs. However, his conclusion was reached on the basis of poor research – he asked two questions and should not have been surprised that he received two separate types of answers. Further, the apparent existence of two types of motivation could have arisen from attribution theory rather than motivation theory: we tend to attribute good things to ourselves (motivation factors) and bad things to other people or our environment (hygiene factors) (Lock, 1976; Wall, 1973).

### Equity theory

Equity theory was put forward by Adams in 1965. It is a very simple theory which states that people try to balance what they put into a job with what they get from it. If the rewards from a job are less than the effort they expend, they will reduce their effort to restore the balance. On the other hand, if the rewards are noticeably higher than the effort they expend they will increase their effort in order to restore the balance. The implications of equity theory are straightforward. If an employer wishes to increase motivation, wages should be raised and employees will then increase their effort in order to maintain the balance. Unfortunately, research suggests that the situation is not quite so simple. It would seem that, while equity theory is correct in predicting that a decrease in rewards will be met with a decrease in effort, an increase in rewards does not necessarily guarantee an increase in effort.

### Expectancy theory

Expectancy theory is one of the dominant theories of motivation. It starts by noting that different people value different things. In an employment context, some people are motivated by money, some by status, while others are motivated by security. This means that one of the first steps in increasing motivation is to identify those rewards which are valued by a specific individual.

Expectations play a crucial role in determining how hard people will work. Two expectations are particularly important. The first is the expected probability of achieving the level of performance demanded. This is called the *effort–performance expectancy*. It is the answer to the question, "If I make the effort, how likely is it that I will achieve the performance required?" For example, a salesperson might have a target of 100 sales per month. The effort–performance expectancy is the chance a salesperson perceives that they have of achieving that target, provided they make the effort. They may believe that their chances are good (high effort–performance expectancy) and consequently they will work hard to achieve that target. However, the salesperson may believe that the target is too ambitious or the market is in recession, and consequently no matter how hard they work they will not achieve that target (low effort–performance expectancy). Consequently they will not be motivated to make the required effort.

The second expectation concerns the link between performance and reward (**performance– reward expectancy**). It answers the question, "If I achieve my target performance what is the likelihood that I will be given my reward?" For example, a salesperson might believe that achieving their target is certain to result in a large bonus (high performance–reward expectancy). On the other hand, the salesperson might believe that the organisation's word cannot be trusted and that, even if the sales target is achieved, a bonus will not be given (low performance–reward expectancy).The situation is shown in Figure 7.4.

Expectancy theory has clear indications for managers who wish to maximise the motivation of their staff:

- Do not assume that everyone is motivated by money. Work out the rewards that each person values and offer these as incentives.

- Make the performance required absolutely clear. Specify exact behaviours.

- Make sure that performance targets are considered to be reasonable and attainable with extra effort. Make sure that employees know that achieving the target performance will be rewarded. Never renege on a promise of a reward – it will lower, probably irrevocably, the performance–reward expectancy.

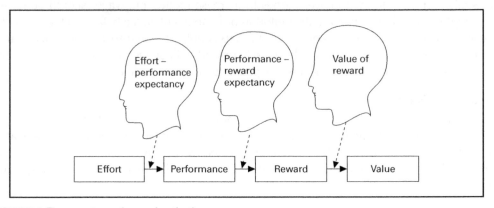

**FIGURE 7.4** The expectancy theory of motivation

### Goal-setting theory

The basics of goal-setting theory were developed by Locke (1968) and claims have been made that it has more scientific support than any other approach to motivation (Pinder, 1984). The basics of goal-setting theory are very simple: people are motivated and work harder when they are set difficult, but not impossible, goals. Goals focus people's attention on required behaviour and allow them to mobilise their efforts in a clear direction. Moreover, goals often boost people's commitment so that they will persevere longer in the face of difficulty.

The nature of the goals is a crucial factor in their ability to motivate. People are motivated when:

■ Goals are *difficult but realistic* and within the capabilities of employees. Often, goals should be set using the performance of existing employees as a guide. For example if the top 15 per cent of sales representatives obtain average monthly sales of £80 000, a target of £80 000 can be set for all sales representatives. *Vague goals* such as "work very hard" do not motivate people as much as specific goals that specify quantity, quality and timescale. A specific goal for a lumberjack might be to fell 40 trees (quantity) per day (timescale) with side branches removed and delivered to central logging depot (quality).

■ *People are committed to goals* and regard them as reasonable. Some researchers say that goals should be set in a participative way but others maintain that delegated goals are just as effective.

## 7.6 Staffing toolkit

*Toolkit*

■ Make absolutely sure that your methods of recruitment and selection are as fair as possible and that they do not discriminate against people on the grounds of gender, sexual orientation age or disability.

■ A great deal of effort can be saved if jobs are designed so that responsibilities are clear and motivating. Every job should have a job description and a personnel specification. Be careful to make sure that these documents are kept up to date and are used when making decisions about selecting staff or training them.

■ Use modern selection methods because they are much more accurate (but still far from perfect) than the classic trio: interviews, references and CVs. If you decide to use any of the classic trio for other reasons, put them at the end of the selection process where they can do least harm.

■ Ensure that staff are properly trained and that there is an adequate training budget – both for expenses and the time needed for training. Make sure that training is relevant to an employee's present job or a likely future job – consult the job description, the person specification and any other relevant documents such as recent appraisal forms.

■ Take responsibility for your own training. Do not leave it to your employer. It is more important to you than it is to them. You get a lifetime's worth of benefit from training and development. They only get a few years' benefit. In your first two years of employment this should be at least four weeks per year. Later, it should be at least two weeks per year. Above all else, make sure that you develop your ability to learn and adapt (check your learning style). If you can learn and adapt you will get maximum benefit from later experience

■ Pay employees reasonable rates. If you underpay they will become demotivated and reduce their efforts or engage in counterproductive practices. Set clear, ambitious but reasonable goals. Establish the things that motivate individual employees and then offer individualised incentives. Do not assume that everyone is motivated by pay. Make the links between effort, performance and rewards clear. Do not renege on rewards that have been earned.

# Activities and further study

## Essay plans

Prepare plans for the following essays:

1  Choose a job that interests you. Describe how you would recruit someone for this post. (This does not include the selection phase.)

2  Evaluate scientific research on the validity of different methods of personnel selection

3  What is fairness in recruitment and selection? How would you establish whether a selection method was unfair

4  Describe how three different theories of motivation can give practical guidance to managers wanting to motivate their subordinates

## Web activities

1  Look up the local website of Saville-Holdsworth Ltd (SHL), e.g. www.shl.com/shl/nz, www.shl.co.za or www.shl.com/SHL/hk *or* shl.com. Follow the trail site map; candidate helpline; practice tests; you will then be able to do some of their psychometric tests on line. The site also contains a lot of excellent information about selection and assessment.

2  Look up other sites that give information about recruitment. One good source is the site at the University of Cape Town: www.careers.uct.ac.za/students/careering/articles/selection.pdf. Often the sites of major employers give details of their selection methods. A good one is Qantas's site www.qantas.com.au/infodetail/about/employment/QTests.pdf. Beware: there are many poor sites offering unscientific tests or which use tests as a part of a sales ploy.

3  Go to the website http://www.nelsoncroom.co.uk and look at the material concerning online training.

4  Kolb and Fry's learning cycle may be the most well-known example. However, other good descriptions of how managers learn are available. Use the Internet to locate at least two other cycles. Evaluate the cycles you locate and identify their similarities and differences with Kolb and Fry's system.

## Experiential activities

1 Write two sentences about yourself under each heading of Roger's seven-point plan.

2 Think of a job that you would like to do in, say, three years' time. List the skills and knowledge needed to do that job. Then rate yourself on whether you have the knowledge and skills at present. For each area where there is a gap identify the training you will need and identify a suitable training method.

3 Imagine that you have been asked by your present employer, university or college to develop a one-day induction programme for people joining your organisation. Work out what training you would give.

## Recommended reading

1 Clarke, L.A. and Roberts, J. (2010) "Employer's use of social networking sites: a socially irresponsible practice", *Journal of Business Ethics*, 95, 507–525. This article discusses the unethical practice of using social networking sites such as Facebook to obtain information for hiring and firing decisions.

2 Mason, R. and Power, S. (2009) "360° appraisal: a simple pragmatic solution", *Clinical Governance: An International Journal*, 14(4). A straightforward, practical example of the use of 360-degree feedback to improve the performance of hospital consultants.

3 Eliott, E.M. and Williams, F.P. (1995) "When you no longer need Maslow: exchange professionalism and decentralisation in the management of criminal justice agencies", *Public Administration Quarterly*, 19(1). Pages 74–78 criticise need theories (such as Maslow's or Hertzberg's) and suggests that situational variables asre underemphasised.

# CHAPTER

# 8

# Leading and Leadership

## ❖ LEARNING OBJECTIVES

After studying this chapter you will have a realistic and detailed view of leading people in work situations. You will understand how leaders, followers and situations interact to influence the leadership. You will also appreciate the complexity of the subject. In particular you will be able to:

- ❖ **critically evaluate** the concept of leadership
- ❖ **describe in detail** types of leaders and leadership styles

- ❖ **explain in detail** the relationship between leaders and the characteristics of their followers
- ❖ **explain in detail** the relationship between leaders and the situations in which they operate

The management process of staffing aims to maximise the effectiveness and potential of employees. It uses four main methods. Three of these methods (selecting, training and motivating) were discussed in the previous chapter. The fourth main method of maximising the effectiveness of staff is leading. Fundamentally, leading is about one person changing the direction and behaviours of other people, often in times of adversity, by using personal influence.

## CASE 8.1: *Terry Leahy – Tesco's finest*

There are many surveys and books which attempt to define a business leader. A good place to start is to consider Terry Leahy, CEO of Tesco from 1997 to 2011.

In 1924 Jack Cohen bought tea from a supplier called T.E.S (T.E. Stockwell) and added the first letters of his own name (CO) to form the brand of Tesco. It operated at the bottom end of the market, by "piling it high and selling it cheap". Before Leahy took over, it was still firmly in the second rank of supermarkets below Sainsbury's and Marks & Spencer. He began to move it to its now well-established pole position in the supermarket sector with a number of significant developments. He introduced the Tesco's Clubcard and the upmarket "Finest' brand", and developed its market-leading Internet service. Today, from its headquarters in Cheshunt, it is the UK's largest private sector employer with 1000 stores and 23 7000 employees and is the second largest food retailer in the world when measured by profits.

Sir Terry was born in Liverpool and studied at what is now part of Manchester Business School – earning money during vacations by stocking shelves in Tesco stores. Almost by chance he obtained a junior management post at Tesco but rose to be marketing chief and finally CEO. He abandoned Tesco's strategy of apeing Sainsbury and Marks & Spencer's and devised the Clubcard scheme which both increased loyalty and yielded data that could be mined to reveal customer trends. He also led the way in international developments, with strategic alliances in India and China. In 2003, 2005, 2006 and 2009 Leahy and his "Cheshunt mob" were one of the most admired group of managers (*Management Today*, December 2009 – a very easy but interesting read).

Leahy's leadership style is not flashy – he defined a leader as someone "who takes you further than you would go on your own". Key aspects of his leadership philosophy include:

- *Vision, values and culture* are more important than strategies or marketing tactics and they should come from staff. He promoted listening to customers, specifically initiatives like cashiers calling for help if there is more than one customer in a queue, and made sure that all Tesco managers have access to customer concerns. He himself visited a store at least once a week to listen to staff and customers.

- *Encouraging and growing future leaders*. Leahy was quick to point out that Tesco's success was not all his own, acknowledging that it was a team effort. "I don't believe you can lead by central control or diktat; certainly we don't at Tesco. How can I sit in my office and micro-manage almost 350 000 people around the world?" He did not settle for one leader, he wanted thousands of them. As a result, Tesco devoted a great deal of time, energy and money developing staff. Leadership was also found in customers. Leahy said that if you allow them, customers will take you further than you can go on your own

■ *Keeping things simple*. People need to understand what is expected of them and how they can contribute. This does not come from management jargon but from simple thoughts, simply communicated in a way that relates to the jobs that people have to do. For leaders to grow and develop they need a clear framework.

Leahy's tenure is proof of his leadership. The average CEO remains for four years while Leahy was CEO of Tesco for 14 years. Further, when the Board sought to replace, him, they chose another Liverpudlian, Philip Clarke – except Leahy supported Everton while Clarke supports Liverpool FC! (*Economist*, 2010).

Henry Newbolt's poem "Vitai Lamparda" reflects the classic image of heroic leadership. There is a battle in the desert where the army has formed a defensive square that has been "broken" by the enemy:

66 The sand of the desert is sodden red -
Red with the wreck of the square that broke
The gatling's jammed and the colonel dead,
And the regiment blind with dust and smoke. 99

Clearly, the situation is dire. Annihilation threatens. Fortunately someone remembers how they were inspired by the captain of the cricket team on the playing fields of Eton and shows leadership, calling out to his fellow soldiers, "Play up! Play up! And play the game!" The men remember the stoicism and fortitude they learnt while playing cricket at school. They rally, reform the square and prevail over the enemy - all thanks to the call from a true leader of men.

Wow! If leadership can bring about fantastic changes like that, it is little wonder that every CEO on the planet wants more leadership. After all, you just select the right types and then send them on a week or so's outward bound course somewhere on Bodmin Moor or the Lake District and get them to play a modern equivalent of cricket. Voila! Even a pathetic organisation will be redeemed. Unfortunately, in reality, leading people is less heroic and much more complex. Further, not everyone realises that leadership has its dark side.

A competent worker who is motivated can produce acceptable results. When targets are easy and the situation is static they have the momentum to churn out results without intervention from others. However, the momentum is not enough when things become difficult or where a change of direction is needed. An external force is required to alter the direction or to continue in the face of adversity. One external force is leadership. Organisations are very keen to foster leadership; if teams are properly led they will achieve more. Managers therefore need to know about leadership.

## 8.1  Definition and concept of leadership

The central concept of leadership is *power to influence others and get them to do things they otherwise would not do*. It is often the ability to get people to follow a vision of a better state of affairs. Probably the best formal definition of leadership is:

> 66   . . . . a social influence process that involves determining a group's objectives, motivating behaviour in aid of these objectives and influencing group maintenance and culture.
>
> *(Lewis, Goodman and Fandt, 1995)* 99

### Differentiation from 'management'

Sometimes, a key role of a definition is to clarify it's distinction from something similar. Clearly, leadership and management are not the same things. Table 8.1 draws on the writings of Mintzberg (1998), Kotter (2001) and others to contrast *leadership* and *management*.

| Leaders' *strategies* | Managers' *strategies* |
|---|---|
| Having the *vision* to take a *long-term* view in order to shape the organisational *cultures* by persuading *followers* | Achieving the *objectives* in the *shorter term* and *enacting* requirements which *achieve stability* by *giving instructions to subordinates* |
| Leaders' *methods* | Managers' *methods* |
| Adopts a *proactive* approach using *charisma* and *passion* to make people *emotional* and *excited* so that they can be *sold* a mission which *transforms* their efforts towards work | Adopts a *reactive* approach using *formal authority*, *logical arguments* or *monetary rewards* which people will *transact* for their efforts towards work |
| Leaders' *motives* | Managers' *motives* |
| *Strives* towards future *achievements* | Takes *action* to achieve specific *results* |
| Leaders' *actions* | Managers' *actions* |
| Takes *risks*, *uses conflict* and frequently breaks *rules* | *Minimises risks, avoids conflict* and usually *devises rules* |

**TABLE 8.1**  A contrast between leaders and managers

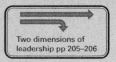
Two dimensions of leadership pp 205–206

## CRITICAL THINKING 8.1 *Management versus leadership – a false dichotomy*

Table 8.1 is clearly an oversimplification because it only has two categories. In fact there is a spectrum in which people can take intermediate positions. Furthermore, at a superficial level it gives a dangerous impression that management is bad and that leadership is good: the words used for leaders are less restrictive and more inspirational. This is unreasonable. Leadership deploying all the above characteristics has taken some organisations into zany, unpredictable, directions which destroyed value for stakeholders (e.g. shareholders, employees and government tax revenues). A closer inspection of the table indicates that leadership is primarily concerned with nice things such as dealing with people and liberating their potential, whereas management focuses on less exciting activities such as getting tasks done. As we shall see later in this chapter, there is considerable evidence that good leaders pay attention to both people *and* tasks. Mintzberg (1998 – an excellent read) points out that leading people, especially professional people, is a covert activity and that leaders do a lot more hands-on managing than one might expect. Covert leadership means managing routine things in a nuanced way. In 2009 Mintzberg asserted that "We're over-led and under-managed" and that "corporate America has had too much fancy leadership disconnected from plain old management". He turns the knife further by writing, "Too many leaders fancy themselves above the messy, but crucial work of managing".

In general, management is about coping with complexity and managing things, whereas leadership is about influencing people and coping with change. Most people dislike being managed but they want to be led.

## Main components of leadership

At first sight leadership might appear a single topic but as Figure 8.1 shows it is more complex and has at least three components.

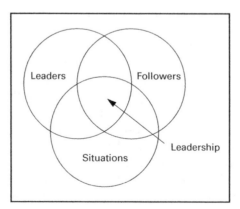

**FIGURE 8.1** The components of leadership

Obviously, there must be *leaders*. Second, there must be *followers* since it is impossible to lead no one. Third, leaders and followers do not exist in a vacuum – there must be a *situation*. The relationship between these components is shown in Figure 8.1. Leadership exists where these three components intersect. The next sections of this chapter examine each of these main components in greater detail.

## 8.2 Leaders

An assembly of strangers will have equal positions and it will be leaderless. Very soon, one or more people will start to take a more dominant role and **leaders will emerge**. These people will exercise more **power** over decision-making and the allocation of resources. The power these leaders exercise will arise from different sources and several **types** of leaders are possible. Further, leaders have their own **traits** (characteristics) and **style**. The sub-topic of "leaders" can therefore be divided into five subsections:

- leader emergence
- leader power
- leader traits
- leader types
- leader style

### Leader emergence

In many work settings the leader is appointed by superiors. These are **formal leaders** who have official power. Generally, their official power is sufficient to maintain their position. However, if a formal leader has the wrong characteristics or the situation becomes chaotic another member of the group becomes the de facto, **informal leader**. Informal leaders can emerge in other situations. For example, in a volunteer organisation, a formal leader might not be appointed and an informal leader will emerge. Similarly, a group of army recruits will have a formal leader (a corporal) but, among themselves, one private will emerge as the informal leader of the group.

Curtin (2004) used Tuckerman's (1965) framework of group development to explain the process of leader development. During the formation stage, a number of members announce their "candidacy" for the leader position. During the conflict stage two or more leaders pass the "candidacy threshold" and conflict with each other as they vie for position. Hollander (1961) suggested

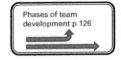

Phases of team development p 126

that these candidates build up "idiosyncrasy credits" by helping the group accomplish its task and meeting the group's expectations. The candidates must be both innovative and conformists (see Stone and Cooper, 2009): they must innovate to provide novel solutions but these solutions should not be so drastic that they appear impractical. The nature of the task can play an important part in deciding who emerges as a leader. If the task is very specialised and technical, the candidate with most expertise in the area will have a strong advantage. The candidate's social skills also play an important part. Emergent leaders tend to talk more and give more instructions to others. They are also careful to monitor their own behaviour and use the information to choose from a range of resactions (see Eby, Cader and Noble, 2003). They are also good at managing the emotions within their group (Pescosolido, 2002), clarify ambiguities and catalyse the group to act in a cohesive way. (Smith and Foti, 1998). They suggest that leaders who emerge show a strong tendency to be intelligent, dominant and have a strong belief in their own abilities to change things.

Several authors suggest that emergent leaders tend to have a narcissistic streak (Brunell *et al.*, 2008). In some ways narcissistic tendencies may be counter-productive once a leader is established. This demonstrates the important point that the qualities needed to emerge as a leader may be different from the qualities needed to be an effective leader.

## Leadership power

Leaders have power. They are able to deploy resources, decide which team members should reap the most rewards and, to a large extent, have the power to choose the tasks attempted by the group. It is important to understand the basis on which this power is derived. Writers (e.g. French and Raven, 1960) have distinguished four main sources of leadership power.

- **Position power** is sometimes called **legitimate power** or **formal power** and it stems from a manager's position in the organisation. Often this power will be written down and enshrined in job descriptions. Position power may overlap with other sources of power because a position in a hierarchy will usually give a person control of both intellectual and material resources.

- **Reward power** is the ability to bestow or withhold things that other people desire. Typical rewards are pay and promotion. Rewards also include the allocation of desirable jobs and recognition. Managers can use these rewards to influence behaviour. **Coercive power** is one particular type of reward power. It is the ability to dispense punishments. Typical punishments include verbal reprimands, pay penalties or even dismissal.

- **Expert power** is based on knowledge and special expertise. It is often derived from possession of a central position within a communication network which provides up-to-date and, often, confidential information. Expert power may not always reside with managers. Frequently, expert power resides with technical specialists. For example, a relatively junior IT specialist may eclipse a senior manager when a problem involving computers needs to be solved.

- **Referent power** is based on popularity and esteem. It is the power associated with interpersonal attraction, and often involves admiration and the willingness to accept someone as a role model.

It should be remembered that power in itself is neither good nor bad. It is the uses to which power is put that matters.

## Traits and skills of leaders

Managers are keen to identify the characteristics that leaders possess. If these leadership traits can be identified then organisations can either select people who have these traits or they can use training and development to give leadership traits to their employees. In this way the level of leadership in an organisation can be improved. Many researchers have tried to meet this need and identify the characteristics of leaders. Initially, this research was not very fruitful because different studies highlighted different characteristics. These differences led researchers to the initial conclusion that there was no single set of traits which leaders held in common. However, in 1991 Kirkpatrick and Locke reviewed the research and came to the conclusion that leaders tended to show the following traits:

- **Energetic and tenacious** – leaders tend to have a high need for achievement and want to get ahead in their work and career. They are prepared to take the initiative to make things happen.
- **Want to lead other people** – leaders are happy to assume responsibility and to seek power, not for its own sake, but in order to achieve their goals.
- **Honest, trustworthy and well organised** – leaders are good at obtaining and keeping the confidence of other people. They usually keep their word.
- **Intelligent and verbally fluent** – leaders are able to analyse situations accurately, solve problems and make sensible decisions
- **Self-confident and interpersonally skilled** – leaders are able to cope with setbacks and take hard decisions. Leaders are usually emotionally stable.
- **Commercially astute** – leaders understand their organisation and its business environment. They accumulate considerable information about their organisation's vision strategy, technologies and procedures.

Other researchers have built on this. Judge *et al.* (2002) examine the traits of leaders using the five-factor theory of personality. They found that leaders tended to be extroverted, conscientious, stable and open to experience. This combination of personality factors correlated fairly highly with holding leadership positions. Apparently, the agreeableness of a leader did not correlate with leadership success – leaders may well be self-centred monsters! Judge *et al*'s. (2002) research gives strong, quantitative support for the trait theory of leadership.

More recently, Sternberg (2007) suggested that leaders were not characterised by single traits but a confluence of traits that reinforce each other. They were **W**isdom, **I**ntelligence and **C**reativity (WICs):

- *Wisdom* involves having the right values and having tacit knowledge of the organisation and its business environment. It also includes being able to appraise social situations with accuracy.
- *Intelligence:* Sternberg did not use the term "intelligent" in a conventional sense. He used it to mean practical intelligence – the set of skills and dispositions needed to solve everyday problems. Practical intelligence requires the ability to apply previous experience in order to select, shape and adapt to environments – rather than solving academic or abstract problems.
- *Creativity* involves skills and dispositions for generating new ideas and novel products. Sternberg emphasised that there were many types of creativity which range from simply redefining the situation to reconstructing and redirecting the organisation.

Luthans and Aviolo developed the concept of an **authentic leader** which seems to be one of the emerging pillars of leadership research today. Authentic leadership is defined as "a process that draws from both positive psychological capacities and a highly developed organisational context, which results in both greater self-awareness and self-regulated positive behaviours . . . fostering positive self-development". Authentic leaders have four main characteristics:

1  **Balanced processing** is the way leaders objectively analyse data before making a decision.

2  **Internalised moral perspective** is the way that a leader is guided by internal moral standards and the way that a leader uses these same standards to regulate their own activities.

3  **Relational transparency** is an open and truthful way of dealing with other people. It also includes sharing information openly and having emotional responses that are appropriate to the situation – i.e. avoiding inappropriate displays of emotion.

4  **Self-awareness** is the extent to which a leader understands their own strengths and weaknesses and the way that they make sense of the world.

Scales to measure each of these four facets have been developed. Luthans and Aviolo's work is based upon positive psychology and aims to offer a more effective way of developing leaders.

Most of this research on leader characteristics can be summarised in the idea of **positive psychological resources** (Luthans and Avoilo, 2003). It suggests that leaders can build up a positive profile in many ways, i.e. intelligence, personality and experience. The lists given in previous paragraphs merely demonstrate the huge range of the possible components of positive psychological resources. This suggests that there are many ways in which leadership effectiveness can be improved. Luthans and Aviolo's positive resource approach is quite different to previous work, which was based on a deficit-reduction model, i.e. where it was important to discover a leader's weaknesses and then work out how they can be strengthened.

Excellent information on leaders is contained in a special edition of the *American Psychologist* in January 2007. In particular it contained an article by Stephen Zaccaro which helps make some sense of the plethora of lists of the traits of leaders. Zaccaro makes the distinction between *proximal* and *distal* traits. Distal traits are basic long-term characteristics that are difficult to change. Proximal traits are similar to skills. They involve distal traits which have been modified by experience. Figure 8.2 (based on Zacccaro, 2007) shows the traits of leaders which help them to develop appropriate skills and expertise. These skills and expertise, together with environmental factors, influence how well the leader manages their team. This in turn influences whether the person will emerge as a leader, their effectiveness while they are a leader and, ultimately, whether they will be promoted to higher leadership positions.

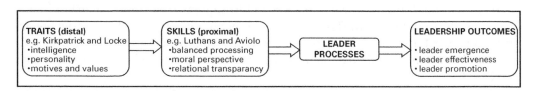

**FIGURE 8.2** Zaccaro's model of how traits affect leader performance

> ## CRITICAL THINKING 8.2 *Do researchers understate links between traits and leader effectiveness because they only think in straight lines?*
>
> The relationship between personality traits (both distal and proximal) with leadership may be understated. Researchers generally use statistics that can only detect linear relationships. They often miss more subtle, curvilinear relationships. A classic example concerns the trait of assertiveness. Ames and Flynn (2007) performed a subtle analysis on "what breaks a leader". They found that people in leadership positions who had either low assertiveness or very high assertiveness were not effective. Low assertiveness means that other group members set an agenda that may be against the team's interest. High assertiveness can bring instrumental rewards in the short term. In the long term they can be costly in relationships that are needed for success. This means that at least some traits have a curvilinear relationship with leader success. However, most research will miss such relationships because they only use statistics, such as correlations, which can only detect linear relationships.

Finally, there is the question of whether people are born with leadership traits or whether they learn them from their experiences. Arvey *et al.* (2007) suggest that approximately 30 per cent of the differences between leaders is hereditary. The remaining differences are caused by environmental factors such as the availability of role models and early opportunities for leadership development.

### Types of leader

Even though leaders may have many characteristics in common, there are many differences in the way that they carry out their role. Therefore authors have been able to identify many different types. One way of organising the types of leader is to categorise them according to three interrelated facets: the leader's source of authority, the change they produce or their style of behaving.

### *Leaders types classified by source of their authority*

Many distinctions between the different types of leader are focused upon their source of authority to act as leaders. Authority for leadership can arise from a *higher source or from God*. The classic example is a **hereditary ruler** or a religious leader such as the Pope or the Grand Ayatollah who are elevated to supreme religious leadership by the highest levels of our hierarchy. This type of leadership is not very important in commercial organisations but it is occasionally encountered in small, owner-occupied organisations. At one point it seemed as though the Ford organisation might be led by a hereditory ruler (see Case 8.2).

Other types of leader draw their *authority from their organisations*. The distinction between **formal leaders** and **informal leaders** has already been noted (page 194). The authority of formal

**CASE 8.2:**  *Edsel Ford: a rare example of hereditary leadership*

Edsel was Henry Ford's only child and it was Henry's wish that he should take over his father's business. In 1919 he became the company president. Unfortunately, key decisions were contested and overruled by his father but eventually he was able to persuade him to manufacture a new car which was a commercial success and helped reverse flagging sales. Edsel favoured faster and flashier cars and expanded the motor company's overseas car production. He died in 1943 and his father took back the presidency of the Ford Motor Company.

In 2009 Toyota needed to rejuvenate the company. Hereditary leadership came into action; the founder's grandson, Akio Toyoda became the company's president.

leaders arises from their official position within a hierarchy and the scope of their power is formally set out in writing. The weakness of formal leadership is that people in a formal role may not have characteristics such as intelligence, personality, training or experience to exercise leadership required of them.

Many types of leader draw their *authority from the consent of their followers.* Greenleaf (1977) identified **servant leaders** who devote themselves to fulfilling the needs and desires of their group. If they fail to do this there is a danger that they will be overthrown by someone who is better at this task. Servant leaders emphasise trust, understanding, co-operation and the ethical use of power. By fulfilling followers' needs servant leaders maximise their followers' potential and hence the achievements of the group. Perhaps the archetypal servant leader is the parish priest whose *raison d'être* is to serve his flock and lead them to righteousness. Most democratically elected leaders are also servant leaders. The characteristics of servant leaders have been well studied. Spears (2004) applied a scattergun approach and identified 10 traits: listening, empathy, healing, awareness, persuasion, conceptualisation, foresight, stewardship, commitment and community building. Russell and Stone (2002) were more structured. They suggested that the characteristics of a servant leader fell into two categories:

1  Functional characteristics, which help get the job done, include: honesty, trustworthiness, service orientation and appreciation.

2  Social characteristics (accompany attributes) maintain the social structure of the group and include: listening, credibility, encouraging others, teaching others and delegating.

The concept of a servant leadership is related to the **path – goal theory of leadership** proposed by House (1971). In essence, the theory maintains that a leader should adopt a style that helps subordinates attain their goals – provided the goals are consistent with the aims of the organisation. In general, this means that a leader should clarify a follower's *path to goals and increase the relevance of rewards* obtained when the goals are reached. Clarification of the path involves:

- helping followers define the goals they should reach within those roles
- increasing followers' confidence that they can achieve the goals

Increasing the relevance of rewards involves:

- learning the followers' needs
- ensuring that a follower receives his or her reward when goals are achieved

House believed that good leaders are capable of different styles and they vary their approach according to the followers' needs. The path–goal theory of leadership has several points in common with expectancy theory.

Cole (2004) also distinguishes **functional leaders** who secure their leadership position because they serve the purposes of their group. The source of their authority is also the consent of their group. However, the concept of functional leader is much narrower than the concept of servant leader. Functional leaders simply adapt their behaviour to meet the competing needs of the task at hand. Servant leaders look to the future well-being of their followers. Groups grant **situational leaders** authority for a short period of time when they are facing difficult circumstances. When circumstances return to normal, previous leadership roles are resumed. The classic fictional example is the butler, the Admirable Crichton, who assumes leadership over his lords and masters because, when they are shipwrecked, he is the only one with practical skills. When they are rescued he relinquishes leadership to his lords and masters.

Several types of leaders derive their *authority from themselves*. **Principle-centred leaders** gain their authority from their own moral and ethical values. Covey and Gulledge (1992) identified a type of leader who recognises and keeps to principles such as even-handedness, fair dealing, honesty and trust. It is practised from the inside to the outside at all levels (personal, group and organisational). The leader often exercises self-discipline and self-denial and tries to improve their own character and competence. People recognise the goodness of principle-centred leaders and therefore consent to follow them.

**Charismatic leaders** are sometimes called **visionary leaders** and they include great leaders of the past such as Alexander the Great, Boadicea, Churchill, Mother Theresa, Gandhi and Martin Luther King. Charismatic leaders draw their authority from their abilities to awe-inspire people. They have a personal "presence", a vision and the ability to enthuse followers towards that vision. These charismatic leaders can have a dramatic effect on the lives of their followers. Such leaders were first identified by Weber (1947) who defined charisma as a "quality of an individual personality by virtue of which he is considered extraordinary and treated as endowed with supernatural or exceptional forces or qualities". Both charismatic leaders and transformational leaders (see below) raise their followers' aspirations and activate their higher-order values such as altruism. The followers identify strongly with their leaders, which makes them positive about their work so that they try to exceed simple transactions and standard expectations (see Aviolo Walumbwa and Weher, 2009). The notion of charismatic leaders belongs to the "great man" (masculine intended) theory of leadership where great leaders are born and cannot be developed or trained. Often, in the fullness of time, charismatic leaders turn out to have fundamental flaws.

**Transformational leaders** are less exceptional and revered than charismatic leaders. According to Bass (1985), transformational leaders form a clear view of the future and they are able to achieve a step change in the performance of their followers. This is often achieved by radically changing the way that followers see a situation or their organisation. Transformational leaders usually raise the self-esteem of individual followers and pay attention to their development needs. This contrasts with charismatic leaders who require followers to sacrifice their own needs in favour of "the cause". The exact nature of transformational leadership is summarised in a paper by Bono and Judge (2004). Bono and Judge found that charisma was related to the leader's personality. Transformational leaders tended to be stable extroverts. Transformational leadership has five main components:

- **Charisma** consists of two sub-components: idealised influence and inspirational motivation. **Idealised influence** involves high standards of moral and ethical conduct so that transformational leaders are held in high regard and engender loyalty in followers. **Inspirational motivation** starts with a strong vision for the future which is based on values and ideals. This generates an enthusiasm among followers. Sometimes, idealised influence and inspirational motivation are combined to produce charisma.

- **Intellectual stimulation** involves challenging organisational norms and pushing people to develop inspirational strategies and challenging existing norms.

- **Individual consideration** refers to the way that leaders recognise the talent and also the concerns of group members.

- **Management by exception** refers to how a leader monitors performance and takes corrective action. Having set standards, the leader adopts a passive approach and only intervenes when problems become serious.

- Transactional leaders **establish** goals and then they guide their followers to pursue their plans – largely by means of giving rewards when the plans are executed properly.

Effective leaders can induce followers to do bad things. Ineffective leaders can let bad things happen. Lipman-Blumen (2005) identified a dark type of leader – the **toxic leader**. Toxic leaders are individuals who have destructive behaviours and dysfunctional personalities. They generate serious and enduring poisonous effects on the groups they lead. A classic example of an extremely toxic leader would be Adolf Hitler. Adolf is not an isolated example: think of leaders such as Robespierre, Stalin, Pol Pot and Sadam Hussain!

Toxic leaders are not necessarily proactive like Hitler, Stalin, Pol Pot or Radovan Karadzic. Some leaders may be toxic because they fail to act or are ineffective. Inactive toxic leaders are difficult to identify but British Prime Ministers such as Stanley Baldwin or Neville Chamberlin might be considered. Toxic, inactive leaders in commerce and industry are even harder to identify because they are sheltered by their organisations. Would any organisation be willing to admit it is led by an idiot? Kellerman (2004) identifies seven types of toxic leader:

- incompetent leaders who lack skill or motivation
- rigid leaders who reject new ideas because they are unbending
- intemperate leaders who lack self-control
- callous leaders who are uncaring and unkind
- corrupt leaders who lie cheat or steal
- insular leaders who disregard the welfare of people outside their group
- evil leaders who commit atrocities and who use pain as an instrument of power

## CASE 8.3: *Koresh's toxic leadership in Waco*

Another example of a more recent, proactive toxic leader is David Koresh, leader of the Davidian religious sect. Koresh had a borderline personality disorder and he manipulated people in very small increments. He pulled them deeper and deeper into his power without them knowing where they were going or being aware of the consequences. There were allegations of sexual abuse and other misconduct: he released a video claiming he had been told by God to procreate with the women of his group to establish a house of "Special People". Couples dissolved marriages so that Koresh could have sex with ex-wives. There was some evidence of child abuse. He believed that the government was the enemy of the Davidians. After a long series of legal disputes over his leadership, criminal activity and stockpiling of weapons, Texan authorities in Waco felt forced to act and attempted to execute a search warrant. Koresh anticipated the raid. He had prepared defences and ordered some followers to arm and take up defensive positions. Shots were exchanged and then a ceasefire was arranged. For 51 days the siege of Waco ensued during which Koresh allowed the "release" of some children. Texan authorities used proactive techniques such as sleep disturbance, crushing cars and driving tanks over the graves of sect members – not an especially bright move when dealing with people with border personality disorders! The FBI, fearing further atrocities such as abuse of children, planned a "relief operation". When Koresh's Davidians opened fire the FBI punctured walls so that people could escape and they used a lot of teargas. No one left. Fires broke out. Some say sect members were prevented from escaping. Many were buried alive by rubble or suffocated by the effects of fire. Seventy-five of Koresh's followers died. Nine survived. No doubt, Texan authorities were imperfect. But, no doubt more people would have lived without Koresh's toxic leadership.

One explanation for the behaviour of toxic leaders is that they believe they are specially chosen or have a special mission. On that basis they believe they should not be bound by normal rules or ethical standards.

A number of researchers have examined whether gender is relevant to leading people. There was a general assumption, promulgated by war films, novels and poems that leadership is a "man thing". Research by Powell, Butterfield and Bartol (2008) suggests this stereotype is not true. Indeed, in their study, MBA students judged descriptions of females who were transformational leaders more highly than identical descriptions of males who were also transformational leaders. However, research by Ryan *et al.* (2007) suggests that some differences do exist. When women achieve leadership positions they may experience "a glass cliff" – they tend to be put in more risky leadership positions where the chances of failure are higher.

### Leader style

Types of leader can also be based on the way that they treat subordinates. This is a very big topic which deserves its own section. The way that leaders treat subordinates is usually called leader style.

Many researchers have investigated leader style. At first, investigators studied a *single dimension* of management style – participation. As early as the 1930s Lewin, Lippet and White (1939) examined leadership style in boys' clubs. They distinguished three leadership styles:

1  **Democratic leaders** (sometimes called **participative leaders**) gave their group clear guidance but they did not dominate the situation. They encouraged input from group members so that they felt engaged. This lead members to be more motivated and creative. They were also careful to take the views of the group into account in any decision.

2  **Laissez-faire leaders** (sometimes called **delegative leaders**) played a minimal role. They made sure of the basics, such as venue and timing, but otherwise provided little input. They offered little guidance and left all decisions to the group members.

3  **Authoritarian leaders** provided very clear expectations. They told a group what it had to do and how it had to do it. They made decisions unilaterally.

Lewin *et al.* set up groups with these three types of leader. They then examined how productive the groups were. Democratic leaders had the most productive groups. Findings for autocratic leaders were mixed. When the leader was present the productivity of the groups was almost as high as the productivity of the Democratic group. However, when, inevitably, the leader was not physically present there was a dramatic fall in productivity. Consequently, their overall productivity was lower. The least productive was the laissez-faire group. More recent research (Skogstad *et al.*, 2007) has demonstrated how destructive laissez-faire leadership can be – especially in a stressful work situation where there was bullying.

In 1958 Tannenbaum and Schmidt refined Lewin *et al.*'s ideas. Instead of seeing leadership style in terms of clear-cut groups they saw it as a continuum stretching from authoritarian at one end to participative at the other. Further, Tannenbaum and Schmidt gave specific instances of the behaviour of managers at various points on this continuum. For example, a very autocratic leader would tell subordinates what to do; a fairly democratic leader would consult with his or her group and a very democratic leader would engage in joint decision-making.

A little later McGregor (1960) suggested that managers could adopt one of two leadership theories. **Theory X**, held by autocratic managers, maintains that workers are lazy, unreliable and need to be told what do. **Theory Y**, held by democratic managers, says that workers naturally enjoy work and are most productive when they have made a contribution to decisions.

Likert (1979) identified four management styles (which he called systems) that can be arranged on a single dimension:

■ System 1, **exploitative-authoritative style** where the leader is autocratic, rarely delegates, guards information jealously, manages by edict and uses punishment as the main way of motivating people.

■ System 2, **benevolent-authoritative style** where the leader adopts the same autocratic style but uses rewards to motivate instead of punishment.

■ System 3, **consultative style** where the leader has some trust in workers and permits some teamwork. Workers will be consulted over decisions but the final decision is taken by the leader.

■ System 4, **participative group style** where the leader has a high level of trust and confidence in workers. Decisions are made in a participatory way. Information flows in all directions.

The leadership styles identified by Lewin, Tannenbaum and Schmidt, McGregor and Likert are very similar, as shown in Figure 8.3.

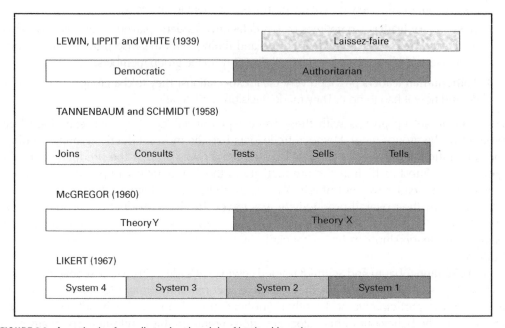

**FIGURE 8.3:** A synthesis of one dimensional models of leadership style

All four models have authoritarian at one end and democratic leadership at the other. They differ however in the number of categories. All except Lewin, Lippit and White imply that leaders must have a style. Lewin, Lippit and White's model has a management style that is close to nothing (laissez-faire). The one-dimensional approach to leader styles was an advance but it had two problems. *First*, as already been noted, these models of leading imply leaders must be active. *Second*, the dimension democratic–authoritarianism is complex and might be concealing more fundamental dimensions.

Two important studies into leadership style were conducted at Ohio State University and the University of Michigan. The Ohio studies looked for dimensions of leadership, while the Michigan studies looked for differences between leadership in high-performance and low-performance units. Although their aims were different the two studies came to much the same conclusion – that there are two major dimensions of leading: the emphasis a leader places on *people* and the emphasis a leader places on the *task*. As Figure 8.3 shows, other researchers have located similar dimensions but have used slightly different names. Blake and Mouton (1964) put the two dimensions into graphical form and created the well-known **managerial grid** (the diagrammatic part of Figure 8.4). There they were able to divide the grid

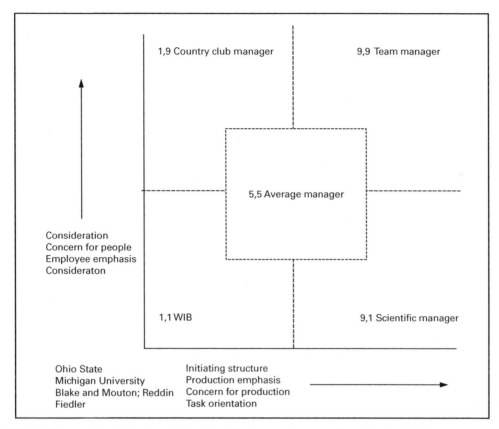

**FIGURE 8.4** Managerial grid showing relationship with other two-dimensional models of leadership

into five areas representing five main leader styles. A leader who stressed both the personal side of the team and the task was called a 9,9 "team manager". A leader who stressed task but ignored the personal side was called a 9,1 "scientific manager". A leader who stressed the personal side, ensuring that employees enjoyed their work while ignoring the task they were supposed to do, was called a 1,9 "country club manager". A leader who stressed neither the task nor the people was called a 1,1 WIB (weak inefficient bastard). Of course, most leaders were somewhere in the middle of the extremes and would be called a 5,5 "average manager".

Reddin (1970) adapted the basic 2 × 2 grid in two ways. He changed the names of the types of leader and then he added an extra dimension to show what the style would be for average, good and poor leaders. Reddin's grid is shown in Figure 8.5.

Thus, a "country club" manager in the 2 × 2 grid could be a "developer", helping people to exploit their talents or a "missionary", simply being nice to people – depending upon how effective they were as leaders. Similarly an effective "scientific manager" would be a "benevolent autocrat" whilst an inefficient "scientific manager" would be an autocrat. Reddin's 3D grid is useful in reminding us that most leadership styles can be made better or worse depending upon the skill of the leader.

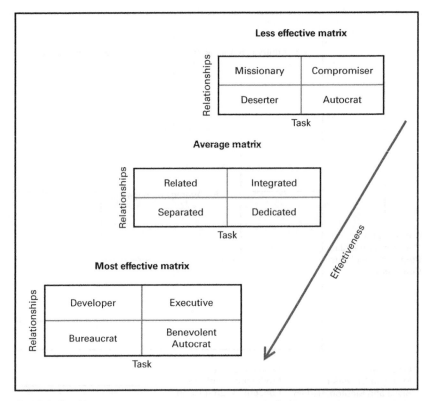

**FIGURE 8.5**  Reddin's 3D grid

## 8.3 Leaders and followers

Even a combination of leader characteristics *and* leader style fails to give a good understanding of leading in work situations. Something is missing. Sometimes a task-oriented style works, while at other times a person orientation (followers) is better. Hersey and Blanchard (1982) focused upon the importance of the followers.

Hersey and Blanchard started with the familiar two-dimensional grid inherited from the Ohio and Michigan studies which is based on task orientation and consideration. *First*, they translated the two dimensions into behavioural terms. Task-oriented leaders give explicit directions, whereas leaders with a lower task orientation let followers get on to work in their own way. Similarly, highly considerate leaders give followers lots of support. Figure 8.6a shows how this changed the basic $2 \times 2$ grid. *Third*, Hersey and Blanchard inserted the approach leaders should adopt to support their followers. The result is shown in Figure 8.6b.

*Fourth*, Hersey and Blanchard considered the development level of followers. Experience and commitment are key factors. Followers with neither experience nor commitment are poorly developed (D1), while followers who are both experienced and committed are highly developed (D4). Other combinations produce groups D2 and D3. Hersey and Blanchard matched the development level to the appropriate type of leadership support. The results are shown in Table 8.2.

*Fifth*, Hersey and Blanchard matched the appropriate support style for each of the four categories of follower. A key aspect of Hersey and Blanchard's approach is that all team members are *not* the same. An interesting but frequently overlooked implication of Hersey and Blanchard's work is that there is a category of worker who require no leadership (D4, the experienced and committed group). Following this one stage further might point to

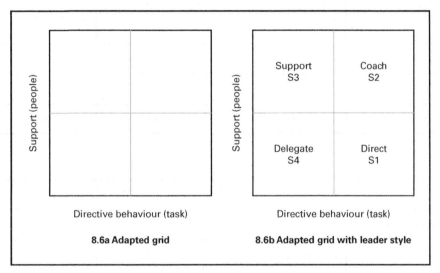

FIGURE 8.6a & b Hersey and Blanchard's integration of management style with support for followers

the conclusion that organisations should concentrate upon developing the experience and commitment of workers rather than developing the leader! However, the broad conclusion of Hersey and Blanchard's work is that different groups need to be supported with different styles. The **theory of vertical dyad linkage** took this notion a stage further.

The vertical dyad linkage theory is also known as the **leader–member exchange theory (LMX)**. Several theories imply that leaders relate to followers equally and as a whole as shown in Figure 8.7a. But, as everyone who has been a member of any group knows, this is untrue.

Liden and Graen (1980) suggest that leaders *behave* differently to different followers – a series of dyadic relationships. Each dyad is different: some are characterised by trust, others may be characterised by tolerance or hate or respect, etc. Further, an "in group" will receive confidential information, participate in decisions and be given extra responsibility. The "in group" believe they owe their membership to their competence rather than preferment. Leaders foster and protect their "in group". For example, when senior managers change jobs they often take members of their "in group" with them. Members of the "out group" may be treated differently – like temporary employees – within formal guidelines. They resent the "in group" and believe that they owe their position to bias or even nepotism. Dyads can

| Type of follower | | | |
|---|---|---|---|
| **Hersey Blanchard** **UNDEVELOPED (immature)** | | **DEVELOPED (mature)** | |
| D1 | D2 | D3 | D4 |
| **Enthusiastic beginners** Committed to their work but lacked experience and competence | **Disillusioned workers** Some experience and competence but lacking commitment and motivation | **Reluctant contributors** Some experience and competence but lacking confidence | **Peak performers** Experienced and competent, committed and motivated |
| **Suitable styles** | | | |
| **Hersey Blanchard** | | | |
| S1 – Directing | S2 – Coaching | S3 – Supporting | S4 – Delegating |
| **Tannenbaum and Schmit** | | | |
| Tell | Sell | Participate | Delegate |
| **Blake and Mouton** | | | |
| 9, 1 Scientific management | 9, 9 Team management | 1, 9 Country club management | 1, 1 WIB |

**TABLE 8.2** Hersey and Blanchard's matching of leader style to follower development (maturity) and comparison with other theories

have a self-fulfilling prophecy. The "in group" member receives more from the leader so, in accord with Adam's equity theory, they give more to the leader, perform better because of their inside knowledge and so receive more favour in return. A member of the "out group"

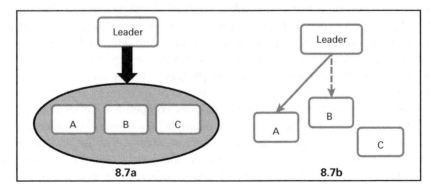

**FIGURES 8.7a & b** Simplistic leader-follower and dyad linkage leader-follower

receives less, gives less and then receives even less. Improving dyadic relationships is one key to good leadership.

The relationship between leader and follower starts as soon as they first meet. From then, the relationship proceeds in three main stages:

1  When a new member joins they are immediately evaluated by the leader and are given, what the leader considers, appropriate opportunities to demonstrate capability.

2  Leader and follower negotiate a role and the rewards that will ensue from its successful performance. Leader and follower extend trust. Subsequent perceptions, especially by the leader, that trust has been misplaced has critical consequences. If a leader feels betrayed, the follower will be demoted to the "out-group".

3  Successful relationships are routinised. The behaviours of leader and follower are consolidated so that each other's expectations are met consistently. Similarity between leaders and follower's personality and values are probably significant.

It is important to note that the vertical dyads may extend in chains. The leader will have a dyadic link with his or her leader and the follower may have a dyadic link with her or his followers. The network of dyads engulfs the whole organisation.

The vertical dyad linkage theory suggests that similarities of personality and values may be important in fostering a strong leader-follower relationship. Giberson, Resick and Dickson (2005) indicate a substantial correlation between leaders and followers in terms of:

- *personality traits* of agreeableness (.35), conscientiousness (.35) and extroversion (.34)
- *values* concerning benevolence (.42) and aesthetics (.35)

Similarities between leader and follower probably result from Schneider's ASA theory (**a**ttracting similar people, **s**ocialising new people to be similar and the **a**ttrition of people who differ). Research shows that followers are attracted to leaders on the basis of **prototypicality** – that is, they are drawn to leaders who are exemplars of the groups they belong to or want to join (Aviolo, Walumbwa and Weber, 2009).

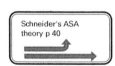

Schneider's ASA theory p 40

Some researchers (e.g. Bresnahan and Mitroff, 2007) liken the way relations between a leader and follower develop to the way attachment develops between mother and child – as described by John Bowlby (1988) in his classic book *A Secure Base: Parent Child Attachment and Healthy Human Development*. An "adult attachment" theory could set the concept of leadership on a stronger footing. An examination of any such similarities could produce a stunning dissertation or thesis.

In a similar vein, House's (1971) path–goal theory also emphasised relevance to vertical links and servant leadership. He suggests a major role of a leader is to help followers achieve individual and team goals. Leaders do this by clarifying goals and removing obstacles. The extent to which leaders enhance followers' paths to their goals varies from dyad to dyad. If leaders frequently default in minor situations, or catastrophically default in major situations, their position may become insecure. Deposing leaders has not been widely researched. It is another aspect of leadership that could form an excellent essay, dissertation or thesis.

Some writers (see Fulop and Linstead, 1999) suggest the traditional emphasis on leadership styles have been overzealous. They point to Peltz's (1952) comments, partly endorsed by Kanter (1983), that if a leader "has considerable influence within his organisation . . . he will achieve concrete benefits for them . . . not his good intentions, but his actual accomplishments are what pay dividends in employee satisfaction." It suggests that many followers may, like Machievelli, adopt the ethic that might is right and counsel a leader to "never mind your style, bring us results that justify the pain of being your follower!"

## 8.4 Situations and leading

An understanding of leading would be incomplete if the relationship between leaders and situations is ignored (see Figure 8.1). Several of the writers we have already cited include the situation in their models of leader style. For example, House (see above) believed that leaders are capable of different styles and they vary their approach according to the situation. He identified four leader styles, each appropriate for various situations. The four styles and the situations, which should be compared and contrasted with those suggested by Hersey and Blanchard, are:

- *Directive leadership* – providing instructions and guidance about methods, standards and rules. This is suitable in ambiguous situations where the leaders need to clarify situations to increase the probability of success.
- *Supportive leadership* – a friendly approach that is sensitive to the concerns and emotions of followers. This is suitable in stressful situations.
- *Participative leadership* – listening carefully to the opinions and suggestions of followers. This is suitable for complex problems where no single person has all the information or expertise.
- *Achievement-oriented leadership* – showing confidence in followers' abilities to meet challenges. This is suitable where creativity is important and where mistakes are accepted as an engine of growth and development

Fiedler's analysis of leader styles incorporated both follower and situations (such as whether the group's task was structured, the power of the leader's position, and the degree of control a leader has over the situation). Figure 8.8 illustrates the influence of the leader's situational control.

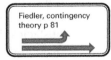

Fiedler, contingency theory p 81

If a leader has either low control or high control, a task-oriented leader style is indicated. If a leader has moderate control, a style emphasising consideration may be better. A great example of the integration of situational variables with leadership styles is given by Vroom and Jago's analyses of the way that leaders should make decisions.

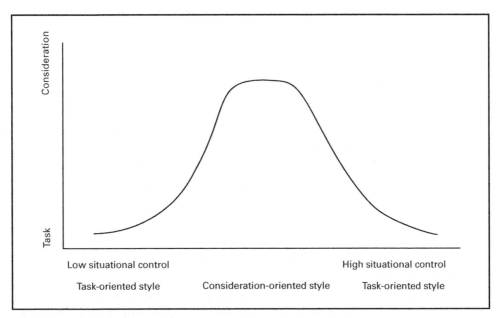

FIGURE 8.8 Fiedler's contingency theory of leadership style and situational control

Vroom and Jago's (1988) analysis of a leader's decision-making shows that situational variables such as: technical correctness, the structure of a problem and the adequacy of the information available to the leader are very important.

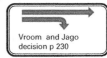

Vroom and Jago
decision p 230

To make matters even more complex, organisational variables can play a great part in determining a leader's success. This aspect of leadership has not been extensively researched but there is considerable anecdotal opinion. An exception is the work by Wasserman, Anand and Nohria (2001). They found that the leadership of chief executives has the greatest impact when there are few opportunities available but there are plenty of surplus resources. Presumably, under these circumstances skilled leaders are able to choose the right opportunity and then have the luxury of deploying massive resources to exploit it.

## CRITICAL THINKING 8.4 *Face-to-face leaders versus electronic leaders*

Today, one of the most stark situational factors is whether the leader meets their group on a face-to-face basis or whether they lead a virtual group communicating by emails and videoconferencing, etc. Zaccaro and Bader (2003) give an excellent overview of the similarities and differences in these situations. Xiao *et al.* (2008) found that when the team leader is physically present they have a great influence on communications. When the leader was communicating by electronic means, the balance of communications between the leader, senior members and junior members was more balanced. Followers in face-to-face groups are more cohesive, have more

> energy and have greater acceptance of group decisions than followers where groups communicate electronically.

Sometimes, situational variables may be called **leadership substitutes**, **leadership neutralisers** and **leadership enhancers** (Howell *et al.*, 1990). Other researchers use the term **moderator variables**. There are at least three kinds of substitutes for leadership:

- *Getting workers to lead themselves* by instigating self-managed work teams, obtaining guidance from colleagues and involving colleagues in making decisions. These establish group goal-setting.
- *Select and develop mature employees* who have motivation and experience (i.e. professional employees). These changes aim to remove the need for a leader by empowering employees.
- *Develop automatic (intrinsic?) reward systems* that motivate appropriate behaviour in a way that does not involve leaders. These establish highly formalised plans, standard operating procedures and clear areas of responsibility. These changes clarify the situation and so remove the need for a leader to arbitrate when there is ambiguity or role conflict.

Other ways of *enhancing* leadership include increasing employees' dependence upon the leader by giving the leader greater control of rewards and resources. Organisations may also enhance leadership by improving the image of the leader by involving them in important projects or bestowing symbols of approval.

## Post-heroic leadership

Notions of charismatic leaders and transformational leaders reached their height in about 1990. Doubts began to set in.

- Were there were enough people with charismatic qualities to be leaders in all organisations?
- Transformational leaders might change things for the worse (some transformational leaders became associated with greed, ruthlessness and lining their own pockets).
- There were examples were heroic leaders did not actually help the organisation to add value – some led their organisations to bankruptcy.
- Organisations were becoming too big and complex to be led by a single leader no matter how charismatic or transformational. This was particularly true of organisations in the knowledge industry.

Mintzberg (2010) is not impressed by the contribution made by heroic leaders. Top organisational performance is "a question of building strong institutions, not creating heroic leaders. Heroic leaders get in the way of strong institutions". Consequently, organisations started to think about leadership in more realistic terms. Their conclusions led to what is known as **post-heroic**

**leadership** or **distributed leadership.** The concept of post-heroic leadership was identified by Huey in 1994. It abandons ideas of leaders acting as heroes, single-handedly saving the followers from the perils of the organisational jungle (Pearce and Manz, 2005). The heroic image of leadership was fostered by the popular press, which prefers stories that are exciting, broad-brush and simple. It ignores the mundane reality where good leadership is boring, detailed, complicated and almost invisible to those outside the organisation. The square that broke probably reformed and won the day not because a brave soul had cried "play-up, play up and play the game". It probably won the day because a recruiting sergeant had conscientiously selected good cadets, lowly officers had spent hours training squaddies in defensive tactics and because some lowly clerk had remembered to order reserve supplies of bullets. The concept of post-heroic leadership has six main characteristics:

- Workers are encouraged to develop *their own expertise and commitment to their work*. Considerable resources are devoted to "growing" people and making them effective. Hence the organisation has a large proportion of "exemplary followers".
- Post-heroic leaders want other people to *take responsibility and become empowered*. They actively seek input from other people – even at the expense that they themselves may become dispensable.
- Exemplary followers have *the resources to solve their own problems*. They do not need a hero to intervene and save them.
- The post-heroic leader devotes time and effort to *develop an organisational culture* where information is widely shared and where people are expected to be exemplary in taking responsibility for adaptation and innovation.
- Exemplary followers take an *active part in determining strategies*.
- Followers *share the limelight* when there is success (and they also share some of the "ordure" when things go wrong).

An excellent introduction to post-heroic leadership is given by Crevani, Lindgren and Pakendoff (2007). Post-heroic leadership has major implications for leadership research. In the future, researchers will need to focus upon teams rather than individuals. Further, leadership will need to be investigated, *in situ*, by quantitative field studies rather than survey techniques (Lindgren and Packendorff 2009).

## CRITICAL THINKING 8.5 *Post-heroic leadership – Planet Utopia?*

It is easy to understand why the concept of post-heroic leadership has such allure. Management's romance with heroic leadership was clearly overheated. Overheated romances eventually come back down to earth. A theory on the rebound can be as unrealistic as a relationship on the rebound. Post-heroic leadership may work in a minority of situations familiar to academic writers: research groups, boards of studies, consultancy organisations. Such situations involve intelligent, educated, professional, motivated people. Further, there is the luxury of time for analysis (sometimes, to the point of paralysis). Such luxurious situations may not be abundant in practical situations. About 15 per cent of people find it easy to cope with day-to-day customer complaints but they find it difficult to comprehend longer-term strategies for preventing complaints. Soldiers might well appreciate opportunities to exercise the privilege of distributive leadership to weigh up the merits of two or more equal solutions. But, under fire, they do not want to form a discussion group. They want to unite under a single plan. A leader can provide this. The executives of a bank under a speculative attack have no time to debate. Delay probably means disaster. Even a mediocre decision by a leader offers a chance of success. If success follows, the leader becomes charismatic. If failure ensues, a guru can write a case study in favour of his or her chosen theory!

## Other important perspectives on leadership

A chapter of this kind can do no more than cover the main themes of a vast topic. However, it is important not to lose sight of a number of other issues. For example, it is interesting to speculate on the differences between *men and women leaders*. As more women earn well-deserved leadership positions, this is an issue of increasing importance. There is some evidence that women leaders are particularly good at motivating and communicating with their teams. They also tend to lead in an interactive, collaborative way. It has been suggested that the post-heroic type of leadership is linked to the way in which women leaders operate because it emphasises the skills of relating to other people. Another up-coming topic is the issue of *virtual leaders* and how they may differ from traditional leaders. Teleworking and other technological advances mean that more people are working away, sometimes continents away, from their leaders. Nobody yet fully understands how this affects leadership style.

CRITICAL THINKING 8.6 *Leadership – philosophical, cynical and scientific views*

Philosopher Noam Chomsky (1999) has a critical view of leading. The definition at the beginning of this section shows that, fundamentally, leadership involves one person influencing other people to do things they otherwise would not do. Put another way – *manipulation of other people is at the heart of leadership*. This manipulation can be for evil as well as good. It is questionable whether leadership should have received such positive, romantic attention during the last half century. Chomsky questioned whether it is right for us to abrogate our own responsibility to think for ourselves. Many people are happy to be "told what to do". Further, many people may believe that leaders are merely those who help them on the path towards their existing goals. Unfortunately, Chomsky argues, the social system has its ways of inducing people to adopt goals that most benefit the leaders. In essence, Chomsky argues that leadership is undemocratic.

Cynics attack leadership from another direction. They contend that good *leadership is merely a matter of good luck and attribution theory.* Leaders are highly visible and therefore they are thought to be responsible for the success or failure of the organisation whether or not they actually have power or influence. A clear example of the cynics' case is managers of football teams. If the team has a successful season, the manager is lauded. If the team has bad luck (injuries, bad draws against opponents or treachery from the club chairperson), the manager gets fired. More scientifically, Bligh *et al.* (2007) found that followers tended to heap blame on leaders if they thought that their work environment was poor even when their leaders were not particularly culpable. Cynics advise that leadership success boils down to: "first be lucky and then be very skilful in persuading others that your efforts were the most relevant factor". To cynics a good leader is merely someone who happens to be on the winning side and who is sufficiently guileful to claim the credit. And, as everyone knows, winners get to write history.

## CRITICAL THINKING 8.7 *Flaws in leadership research*

"Leadership agnostics" think that we know much less about management than we believe. Many "findings" about leadership are questionable. Research uses poor criteria. Most of the research depends on measuring subjective ratings of the satisfaction of followers. Yes, satisfaction of followers is very important – but so is the value added to resources consumed. Very few studies use objective measures such as the organisation's fitness to meet challenges from the environment or the value an organisation adds to the resources. Further, leadership is there to improve the bottom line measures. Few studies have even attempt to measure the *difference* (distance travelled) any leader makes to things that really matter.

## 8.5 New directions for leadership research

Researchers have been studying for decades the same questions about leading, such as: What are the qualities of leaders? What are the types of leaders? How do situations affect leadership? Hackman and Wagerman (2007) suggested reframing the topic of leadership:

1 Instead of asking "whether leaders make a difference" we should be asking *"under what conditions do leaders matter?"* Post-heroic leadership downplays the impact of leaders. They are merely a part of a system that is sometimes subject to so many constraints that not even the most charismatic leader can have any effect. The question therefore arises "under what circumstances can leaders play an important role?"

2 Instead of asking "what are the traits of successful leaders" we should be asking *"how do the personal attributes of leaders interact with the situation to influence the*

*outcomes?"* It is now agreed that neither traits nor situations are sufficient to explain leader effectiveness. It is the interaction between the two that matters. The interactions may be unbelievably complex. If there are just three traits and just three situational variables there are at least 243 different types of interactions. Is it humanly possible for leaders to have the brainpower to process all the combinations in a practical setting? If it is not possible then the value of this line of research is very limited!

3  Instead of asking "is there a single dimension that determines good leaders from bad leaders?" we should be asking *"is good leadership qualitatively different from bad leadership?"* There are many social and psychological phenomena where two different dimensions are needed to distinguish good from bad. For example, the effect of rewards upon people is qualitatively different from the effects of punishment. A similar situation may be relevant to leaders.

4  Instead of asking "how do leaders and followers differ?" we should be asking *"how can everyone in an organisation be considered to be both leaders and followers?"* Leaders must have followers. But lesser leaders must follow bigger leaders – and so on ad infinitum. Under some circumstances followers, such as the Admirable Crichton, emerge as leaders. There is no clear-cut line between leadership and followership.

5  Instead of asking "what should be taught on leadership courses?" we should be asking *"how can leaders be helped to learn?"* Leaders manage situations with the help of mental models they have built up over many years. Leaders need to be helped to build up mental models as accurately and as quickly as possible. Leadership training must teach managers to examine their own mental models, check their accuracy and the degree to which they transfer to novel situations.

Hackman and Wageman's questions are a fitting note on which to end this section on leadership. It is hoped that their questions are answered before the next edition of this book is due to be written.

## 8.6  Leadership toolkit

A leadership toolkit needs to give two kinds of advice: how to be a leader and how to manage leaders.

### Toolkit for leaders

- Have a clear vision about where and how you want your group to go. Communicate this vision enthusiastically and lucidly.
- Be a good role model. Act intelligently, energetically and with integrity.
- Do not rely on a single source of power. Usually you will need to supplement reward power with, say, expert power or referent power.
- Adapt your approach to the *situation* that you face. For example, in very easy or very difficult situations it may be best to be directive.
- Adapt your approach to the characteristics and, especially, the needs of your followers. Do not assume that all followers have either the same needs or the same relationships with you.
- Pay attention to the two main dimensions of leadership: focus on the task your group needs to perform and at the same time focus on personal issues such as the relationship between yourself and team members and also the relationships between the various members of the team.

### Toolkit for managing leaders

- Do not rely on leadership too much. There are many situations where even the best leadership makes no difference. If you rely on good leadership alone, there might be chaos if your leaders move to another, competing, organisation. It is safer to rely on good procedures that select and develop committed, mature and competent workers.
- Beware that leadership is much less effective in groups that communicate predominantly by electronic means.
- Be careful to align formal leadership with informal leadership by appointing formal leaders who have, or who can gain, respect.
- Arrange to select staff who have leadership qualities: intelligence, integrity, creativity, etc. However, it is often the combination of qualities that matters. The combination must add up to a significant level of competence that can deal with difficult situations.
- Make sure that leaders have effective control over rewards and sanctions which are valued by their followers.
- Beware "toxic leaders" who might influence their group to follow bad pathways that might damage the organisation.

*Toolkit*

# Activities and further study

## Essay plans

1 Choose a business leader and describe their career in the context of the issues raised in this chapter.

2 To what extent are leaders born not made?

3 What are the characteristics of effective leaders? (Top tip: inevitably this will involve regurgitating many of the lists of research findings but you need to do much more than this. Compare and contrast the lists, and synthesise them. You can add value with a short discussion about how leader effectiveness is defined at the start of the essay. You could also make the point, with examples, that leader effectiveness depends on the situation and the followers. You should then refer back to this discussion of effectiveness at least three times during the remainder of the essay.

3 What is post-heroic leadership and how did the concept arise?

4 The dark side of leadership.

5 Is leadership necessary?

6 What is the difference between management and leadership?

## Web activities

1 Use the Web to research successful business leaders such as Warren Buffet, John C. Bogle, Inguar Kamprad, Ratan Tata and Alan Bond. Also research the leadership of Rosa Parkes. Synthesise the information in a table and speculate on the commonalities of business leaders.

2 Use the Internet to locate and research the career of one toxic leader who interests you. List the ways that they have damaged their organisations and suggest ways that their colleagues and followers might have been able to limit the damage they caused.

3 Go to: psychology.about.com/library/quiz/bl-leadershipquiz.htm and complete the quiz on leadership style. Do not take the results too seriously but as you answer the questions try to identify the leadership dimensions they are attempting to measure. Also note that the quiz is fairly typical of those used on management development courses. Consider the psychometric properties quizzes like this should have.

4 Go to http://www.leadership-expert.co.uk/7-tips-to-transform-leadership/ and read seven useful tips on becoming a good leader. This site also has a range of good

information on other topics such as "how to gain your first loyal follower", and "do leaders and credit cards mix?"

5 Use the Internet to locate three examples of "toxic leaders" or "narcissistic leaders". The example of Adolf Hitler is too obvious to be counted amongst your examples. On the basis of your research, work out the advice you would give an organisation on how to avoid employing toxic or narcissistic leaders.

## Experiential activities

1 In a seminar, nominate four members and four business leaders (such as Michael Eisner, Harinda Singh, Gordon Wu and Meg Whitman). Allocate a business leader to each seminar member and arrange a balloon debate for the next seminar.

2 Choose an effective leader that you know well and list the personal qualities that you think helped them to be an effective leader. Compare your list with the list of characteristics of effective leaders that are given in this chapter. You can extend this experiential activity by doing the same thing with a leader who you consider to be ineffective.

3 Imagine that you are in a leadership position. What style of leader do you think you would be?

4 Go to your learning resources centre (i.e. library) and ask your learning resource facilitator (i.e. librarian) to direct you to a hard copy of *Annual Review of Psychology, 2009*. Turn to page 421 and browse the article on "Leadership: current theories, research, and future directions". This is not easy reading but it will help develop skills that will be useful throughout the remainder of your course and, maybe, the rest of your life. First, do not dwell on details. Look at the section headings and sample the odd paragraph, here and there. Next, choose a section (about a page long) that interests you most and read it carefully. You may need to read it several times, perhaps separated by a day or more. The style is abstract and very difficult for a newcomer to assimilate. Nevertheless, persevere. No pain, no gain! The skills you are learning will be of immense benefit when completing future assignments. Despite the difficult style, try to relate your chosen section to what you have heard in your lectures and what you have read in this or other books. Think how you could use this information and references in future assignments. Write down the names of three or four researchers whose publications are quoted. Look at other chapters and note those which may be relevant to your studies of management (hint: pages 451 and 475 – and there are at least two other chapters relevant to management). *Annual Reviews of Psychology* are the gold standard of concise, up-to-date information. Topics are renewed on a cycle of about three years. *Annual Reviews of Psychology* should be one of your top resources when researching an essay, assignment or work project. *Remember that!* There are annual reviews in other subjects relevant to management (e.g. sociology). Locate at least three of them.

5 Use this chapter to identify as many different types of leader as possible. Write each different type on a file card and then shuffle the cards. Ask a friend to arrange the cards

into groups so that the leader-types in each group are similar in some way. Then ask your friend to explain what the leaders in each type of group have in common. Repeat this exercise with several other friends, and finally on yourself. Then consider whether the many different types of leader mentioned in the literature could usefully be grouped into a smaller number of categories.

## Recommended reading

1 Curtin, J. (2004) "Emergent leadership: case study of a jury foreperson", *Leadership review*, **4**, 75–85. A delightful paper, available on the Internet, which describes how a leader emerged in a jury. It is an example of a methodology (participant observation) which is rarely used in management research.

2 Sternberg, R.J. (2007) "A system's model of leadership: WICS", *American Psychologist*, **62** (1), 34–32. This is the trait theory of leadership reincarnated in a modern, slightly more sophisticated, guise! The paper incorporates most modern theories of leadership. Many other excellent articles on leadership will be found in same issue of *American Psychologist*.

3 Zaccaro, S.J. (2007) "Trait-based perspectives of leadership", *American Psychologist*, **62** (1), 6–16. This is good account of the trait theory of leadership. It emphasises patterns of traits and gives a new model.

4 Mintzberg, H.H. (2009) "We're over-led and undermanaged", *Business Week*, 17 August, **4143**, 68. An iconoclastic article suggesting that too much emphasis has been placed on leadership. Stimulating thoughts!

# CHAPTER

# Decision-making

# 9

## Chapter contents

## ❖ LEARNING OBJECTIVES

After studying this chapter you should be able to **explain** why managers need to make decisions, the ideal way in which they should be made and **give some of the reasons** why the ideal is not always attained. In particular you will be able to:

❖ **list** two major ways that decisions may vary

❖ **distinguish** between programmed and non-programmed decisions

❖ **discuss in detail** different styles of making decisions

❖ **describe in detail** the seven main stages of rational decision-making

❖ **describe** five ways of generating alternative solutions to organisational problems

❖ **explain in detail** how alternative solutions to organisational problems can be evaluated

❖ **draw up** a decision matrix for a major choice you may need to make

❖ **describe briefly** six common faults in making decisions

Managers never have enough time, money, staff or other resources. If managers obtain what they think are enough resources, their minds turn to new, more demanding goals which require yet more time, money or staff, etc. This is a good thing. It means that managers are proactive and accept the challenge of continuing improvement. However, the perpetual shortage of resources requires frequent decisions between the available options. Decision-making is therefore an important management process.

---

### CASE 9.1:  *A good "bad decision" to clean microwave ovens*

Reckitt Benckiser's boffins devised a fantastic product to clean microwaves. A little sachet is placed into the microwave and when the oven heated, the sachet popped, spreading the cleaner around. When the cycle finished, the sachet could be used as a cloth to wipe the microwave oven. Decisions to develop and trial the product seemed brilliant. Reckitt decided to support the product, and because the organisation had several super-brands it was secure enough to innovate in this way. But sensibly, Reckitt Benckiser decided to limit the risk of launching a new product by thorough market testing. Unfortunately, consumer tests proved that people do not actually want to clean their microwaves very often – perhaps because microwaves are no longer expensive items. So the product failed. Reckitt Benckiser did not castigate those involved. The initial decision to support the product was not good. But, it encouraged innovation, developed management skills and fostered the right culture of market research. Not a bad decision after all.

---

Decision-making is not an isolated management process. It is closely linked to planning. Senior managers constructing strategic plans need to make important decisions which are often based on incomplete data and ambiguous situations, and they may have momentous outcomes. It may be many years before the outcome is known. A wrong strategic decision may cause severe pain such as dismissal of key executives or other employees. Junior managers following operational plans certainly make many more decisions but they are less significant and based on clearer, unambiguous information. Further, the correctness of their decisions will be obvious very quickly (sometimes within minutes) and if they are wrong it will be possible to take relatively painless remedial action.

Leaders also make many decisions. If he or she chooses, say, wrong goals, adopts the wrong style or decides to trust the wrong follower they are likely be replaced or usurped. Poor decision-making can affect many other areas of management. Wrong financial decisions can alienate shareholders. Wrong human resource (HR) decisions can affect employees. Wrong decisions are inevitable. Within limits they should be tolerated because organisations which relish "blamefests" discourage innovation. Organisations that control acceptable bad decisions can learn and prosper. Managers who make occasional bad decisions learn lessons and they work harder to redeem themselves. Decisions can also be both good and bad, as Case 9.1 illustrated.

Clearly decision-making is complex and involves many activities – especially making decisions in a rational way, using varied decision-making techniques and avoiding problems in making decisions.

## 9.1 Definition and types of decision

The definition of a decision is no intellectual challenge. It simply means:

66 Making a choice about something. 99

It usually carries connotations that the choice is significant and will have long-term consequences. Decisions can concern an object such as choosing the most cost-effective commercial software package. It can also concern people. For example, at the end of the selection process an employer must choose the most suitable candidate. A decision can also involve abstract notions and ideas such as strategic objectives or an organisation's moral standards.

The simplest decision is whether or not to accept a single possibility. A decision with only one option is often called **Hobson's choice**, after a sixteenth-century stable owner who had a local monopoly of hiring horses in Cambridgeshire. To make sure the best horses were not overworked Hobson rotated the position of the horses within the stable. Anyone wishing to hire a horse had to accept the horse in the stall nearest the door – "take it or leave it". A modern example of a single-option decision might be granting an employee compassionate leave. This is positive because it helps the individual and demonstrates social responsibility. However, it also has negative consequences for employees who need to cover for another's absence and, possibly, customers who may need to wait longer. Another example of a single-option decision is whether or not to purchase software at exorbitant prices from a monopoly supplier.

Most decisions involve a choice between several things. A decision between two things is usually called a **dilemma**. The two objects of a dilemma are not necessarily negative. In the fourteenth century the French philosopher Jean Buridan noted a dilemma between two positive things could have dire consequences. "Buridan's Ass" was both hungry and thirsty. Fortunately it was close to a pile of hay and an equal sized trough of water. Unfortunately, the ass was exactly halfway between the two positive rewards. The ass died because it could not decide whether it preferred the hay to the water and consequently did not move from the mid-point. A modern equivalent of Buridan's ass is a student who locates two very desirable job opportunities and who has only has enough time to apply for one of them. He or she takes so much time agonising over which one to choose that the deadlines for both applications are exceeded.

Dilemmas, however, are usually associated with a choice between two negative things. In Greek mythology captains of ships sailing the narrow strait of Messina between the toe of Italy and the island of Sicily had to make a choice between Scylla and Charybdis. On the one side of the straight there was a monster, Scylla, who regularly ate sailors who passed by and on the other side was a monster, Charybdis, whose huge mouth swallowed water to create an engulfing whirlpool. Modern negative dilemmas involve being caught between "the devil and the deep blue sea" or being "between a rock and a hard place". Modern managerial dilemmas often follow a dramatic fall in market share after which managers must choose between dismissing some loyal employees or running the risk of the organisation becoming bankrupt. A less sympathetic case is the dilemma facing directors of large banks, who must choose between facing a storm of public protest or the loss of key employees who might defect to the competition if they do not receive a large bonus.

A **false dilemma** arises when people think there are only two options when, in fact, there are more. A **trilemma,** for example, involves three options. The so-called **Warnock's dilemma** is actually a quintelemma. Warnock made a post on an intranet forum in the year 2000 but there was no response. He then had to decide between five possible alternatives in order to understand the lack of reaction. The five alternatives were:

1 The original post was perfect – no follow-up comments were necessary.
2 The original post was rubbish – no one could be bothered to reply.
3 Nobody read the original post – for various reasons.
4 Nobody understood the original post but would not ask for clarification - perhaps because they feared appearing stupid.
5 Nobody cared about the original post.

Warnock noted that the real reason why there was no response to the original post was probably an amalgam of all five alternatives. (Warnock's plight has even given rise to a new verb: to be "Warnocked" is to make a post on a discussion group or blog and not receive a reply.)

Decisions are sometimes described as a series of sequential activities, smoothly transforming into one another. In real-life situations decisions are characterised by lack of clarity, pressure and situation of factors such as risk-taking and politics. Consequently, much decision-making in innovation deviates from rationalists models. Decision-making often takes the form of garbage-can decision-making (Styhre et al., 2010). This brief description of the complications in making decisions discusses the dimensions of clarity, the decision situation and the pressure.

---

### CASE 9.2: *To tea or not to tea*

Elmwood Fine Teas started in 1990 as a tea room set in a mansion in Kentucky. In a short time it became a local institution and achieved recognition as one of the British Tea Council's best tea places in the world. Thousands of people went to enjoy a formal British tea of sandwiches, scones, cakes and, of course, tea. Two gift shops and an art gallery were added. They did well – visitors usually made purchases after drinking their afternoon teas. The owners diversified. They started wholesaling tea and published books with gourmet recipes. Soon the wholesaling and publishing became bigger than the tea rooms and the owners found that running all aspects of the business was too much. They had to make a decision whether or not to close the tea-rooms and concentrate on wholesaling and publishing.

Major factors in the decision were:

- The impact on the local community. The tea room had become a tourist feature, earning money for the local community.
- The tea room accounted for 40 per cent of the total income.

▶

■ Money would be needed for investment in the publishing and wholesale business.

■ The tea room was an important aspect of the brand.

After considerable deliberation the tea rooms were closed. The mansion was sold (with stipulations that tea rooms could not be re-opened and the mansion's image could continue as the company logo). The owners are pleased with their decision. The wholesale business is prospering and more books are being published.

*Source*: based on Wellner (2006)

## Clarity

Some decisions, such as the choice of a photocopier are straightforward. The objective is clear, the decision criteria well known, the information concerning the photocopiers is objective, the problem is well structured and the organisation has procedures for handling this kind of decision. This type of decision is called a **programmed decision**. Programmed decisions often require little thought and may be delegated to less senior employees. Usually:

■ they are repetitive and routine

■ they have existing precedents. Managers do not need to establish new methods and can rely on those which were successful in the past

■ they are well structured

■ they have solutions that are well known or obvious

■ they have a high degree of certainty of the outcome

■ most, if not all, of the required information is available

**"Non-programmed decisions"** are the opposite. They are non-routine, require original thinking and they are usually taken at a senior level. It has been argued that the increasing uncertainty and volatility of the business environment has increased the proportion of non-programmed decisions. Sometimes, non-programmed decisions can involve unusual or life-threatening situations. Strategic decisions are also usually non-programmed.

**CASE 9.3: *Healthy Pepsi***

Most people associate PepsiCo with the manufacture of sugary drinks, crisps and other fatty, salty snacks. In 2010, the boss of the company, Indra Nooyi decided that Pepsico should become a part of the solution to the public health challenge of obesity – not one of its causes. It was decided to reduce the salt in its biggest brands by 25 per cent within five years. Similarly, it was decided to withdraw sugary drinks from schools around the world within two years. In part, the decisions were motivated by social responsibility. In part, they were motivated by a wish to avoid the company going the way of tobacco firms and being held responsible by governments for health problems associated with their products.

These decisions are excellent examples of non-programmed decisions. They were the result of complex factors in the business and social environment. The company had rarely made such wide-raging changes in the formulation of its products. The decision was made at the very top of the organisation. Some of the production technology needed to bring about the change has yet to be perfected. The decision was made with incomplete knowledge of the relevant decisions by the company's arch rival Coca-Cola. Most important of all, the reaction of customers is uncertain and hence the reaction of investors might be jittery.

Reducing calorie, salt and fat consumption is only one aspect of preventing obesity. Increasing calorie burn is another. "Why aren't we going after computer and cable-TV companies for creating a sedentary lifestyle?" asks Ms Nooyi.

*Source: Economist, 25 March 2010*

In many cases managers cannot be certain of the outcome but they are able to calculate their chances of success or failure with some accuracy. The probability of failure is known as **risk**. Risk is not necessarily a bad thing – it is often associated with higher returns. However, it needs to be managed carefully. It often needs to be spread across different projects or investments so that the failures of some will be compensated for by the success of many others. A cardinal principle of risk management is that the combined level of risk should not jeopardise the fundamental stability of the organisation.

## CRITICAL THINKING 9.1 *Lehman Brothers' risk busts the bank*

Lehman Brothers provides a salutary lesson in accepting a combined level of risk that could jeopardise an organisation's existence. Lehman Brothers was once the fourth largest investment bank in the USA. It specialised in securitising the risks that people might default on their mortgages. Basically, this involved amalgamating lots of poor risks on the basis that only a small proportion would actually fail. The collective risk of these bundles can be quantified and the bundles can be sold to others or held as investments. It is not clear why Lehman held so many of these bundles (securities). Some say it was a deliberate investment decision. Others say that they could not sell all the securities they had created. The bank managed to hide its huge level of risk for a long time. But when the mortgage market turned, the truth leaked out. Lehman brothers had to devalue these assets which meant its reserves were so low that other banks would not lend it the money it needed to continue. The bank went bankrupt, hastening a global financial meltdown.

A decision-maker may have clear goals but may not be able to calculate accurately the risks attached to the alternative solutions. These situations are uncertain. **Uncertainty** is usually defined as the inability to calculate the probability of failure. It arises from two sources: the absence of information and the complexity of the environment. For example, a marketing manager may make an uncertain decision because the size of the potential market is not known. An uncertain decision may also be made when the size of the potential market is well established but there are so many factors influencing purchasing decisions that it is impossible to predict the number of sales.

**Ambiguity** represents the lowest level of clarity. It usually exists when a decision-maker is not clear about the goals. Ambiguity also arises when the alternatives are difficult to define. Sometimes, there is ambiguity in whether a manager should be making a decision at all. Ambiguity means that a manager cannot be clear whether he or she is tackling the right problem or evaluating the right alternatives. Hence it is impossible to even estimate the probability of success.

In general, decisions that are clear are likely to be successful. The relationships between the five concepts related to clarity (programmed decisions, certainty, risk, uncertainty and ambiguity) and other factors are given in Figure 9.1.

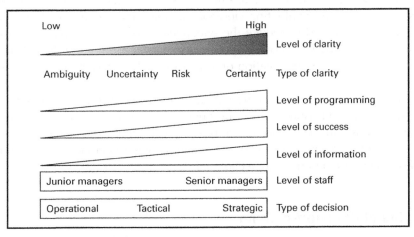

**FIGURE 9.1** Correlates of decision clarity

## Pressure

Decisions also vary according to the degree of pressure involved. Pressure is largely independent of clarity since a manager can be under pressure whether or not the decision involves a clear, programmed problem or an ambiguous, non-programmed problem. Pressure in decision-making has three main aspects: time, conflict and organisational politics.

Many decisions are made under **time pressure**. Sometimes the time pressure is caused by a decision-maker's lack of planning and foresight. Sometimes managers may not have the experience or ability to foresee a routine, predictable problem. Sometimes the time pressure is generated by an unpredictable event such as an accident or the resignation of a key employee. A crisis arises when there is a major threat which must be resolved quickly. Most managers find crises are stressful but many thrive on the excitement and activity. In crisis situations, decision-makers may not be able to consult others. Consequently, they may not be aware of all possible solutions and may not be able to reconcile differences of opinions. Many organisations attempt to reduce pressure on the managers in times of crisis by providing "disaster training". This aims to teach decision-makers how to remain cool under pressure and how to deal with the media. It also encourages them to anticipate how they would deal with a number of disaster scenarios.

Pressure may also be generated by **conflict** between opposing groups. Conflict may generate strong emotions that interfere with judgement. However, a moderate level of conflict may improve the quality of decisions because it tends to ensure that a wider range of alternatives is considered. Dealing with conflict situations needs a high level of social skill in order to avoid long-term antagonism between contenders.

Conflict is often the consequence of **organisational politics**. Ideally, decisions should be based on a totally objective analysis of facts. In many situations judgements are distorted by favouritism, coalitions, alliances and the desire to please superiors. In these circumstances the pursuit of power and influence may become more important than the correctness of the decision. Organisational politics are more likely to affect ambiguous and uncertain decisions where there are conflicting viewpoints. Dean and Sharfman (1996) found that organisational politics tend to reduce the effectiveness of decision-making. However, it is possible to defend the inclusion of "political factors" on the grounds that, if they are taken into account, the implementation of a decision will be easier because it meets less opposition.

The results of Dean and Sharfman support the generally held view that pressure interferes with decision-making. Pressure tends to produce tunnel vision and restrict the number of alternative solutions considered. Moreover, pressure uses up mental capacity so that less is available to diagnose the problem and evaluate alternatives. Other factors which reduce the quality of decisions are described in Section 9.5

## 9.2 Styles of decision-making

Managers approach decision-making in varied ways. Often, the decision-making style adopted by managers will reflect their personality. For example, some managers are cautious and favour solutions that carry little risk, while others are adventurous and favour decisions which carry a high risk. Similarly, some managers are decisive and reach conclusions swiftly while others take a long time and will not come to a conclusion until all the information is available.

Perfectionists tend to make decisions slowly. Rigid people often fail to consider all alternative solutions – especially those solutions which include novel elements. Intelligence has a major impact on decision-making. Generally, intelligent people make better decisions more quickly because they process a wide range of information speedily. However, a combination of intelligence and perfectionism can slow down the decision-making process. Such people like to gather vast quantities of information and analyse it exhaustively. Sometimes this can lead to "paralysis by analysis".

Rowe, Boulgarides and McGrath (1994) considered all these aspects and came to the conclusion that there are two main dimensions which govern decision style. They are shown as the axes in Figure 9.2. The first dimension deals with *tolerance for ambiguity*. Some managers like to deal with situations where the objectives are clear, the alternatives are easily understood and the information is objective. These managers dislike ambiguity. They value order and consistency. Other managers are happy to deal with situations that are ill-defined and which can be tackled in a large number of ways. They have a tendency to see problems in a wider perspective and they revel in the freedom which ambiguity may give. The second dimension concerns *rationality*. Some managers are very rational and stick to reasoning with objective information. They make their decisions in a logical and sequential way. Others are more *intuitive* and go by their "gut feelings". They tackle a problem from many angles and may use unorthodox, even zany, methods. Rowe, Bulgarides and McGrath used a combination of these two dimensions to identify the four decision-making styles shown in the quadrants of Figure 9.2.

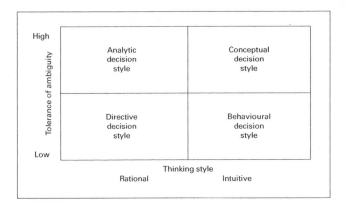

**FIGURE 9.2** Rowe, Boulgarides and McGrath four decision-making styles

A manager with an *analytical style* will collect as much data as possible – preferably objective data from a management information system. She or he will consider the alternatives in a clinical, objective way and try to choose the optimum solution. Their decisions will usually be technically very competent. A manager with a *conceptual style* will try to see a problem in perspective and will try to understand the general principles that will give a broad approach. They will collect a large amount of data but they will use information obtained from people as well as that obtained from a management information system. Their decisions will often be unusual and creative. A manager with a *directive style* will often appear efficient and practical. They usually make decisions very quickly because they simplify the situation, deal with a restricted range of information and consider only a narrow range of conventional alternatives. A manager with a *behavioural style* is usually concerned with other people's feelings and the impact a decision has upon colleagues and employees. They obtain the majority of their information by talking to others on a one-to-one basis.

It must be emphasised that few people are pure examples of these four styles. Managers may tend towards one of the styles, but they will generally adopt other styles when the situation demands. In fact, the situation in which a decision is taken has a considerable influence upon the style that is appropriate. Vroom and Jago (1988) tried to be more specific. Their work involves three main components: an analysis of decision styles, an analysis of decision situations and a procedure for linking styles and situations.

Vroom and Jago did not use the classification of management styles developed by Rowe, Boulgarides and McGrath. Instead, they developed their own classification based upon how autocratic or democratic a manager was:

- A **very autocratic** manager (A1) makes decisions entirely on their own using the information available.

- A **fairly autocratic** manager (A2) makes decisions on their own but will obtain information from subordinates.

- A **fairly consultative** manager (C1) discusses decisions with *individual* subordinates and will obtain their ideas. However, this manager will make the decision on their own and the decision may or may not incorporate the views of subordinates.

- A **very consultative** manager (C2) discusses decisions with *subordinates as a group*. However, the decision will be made by the manager on their own and it may or may not incorporate the views of subordinates.

- A **very democratic** manager (G2) is very group oriented. The group will play a major part in identifying the problem, diagnosing the situation, suggesting alternatives and choosing the final course of action. This manager accepts and implements the alternative chosen by the group.

When Vroom and Jago examined decision situations they identified eight important situational variables which are:

- the requirement for decision to be technically correct                     (DQ)
- the importance of employee commitment                                      (DC)
- the adequacy of the leader's information                                    (LI)
- the structure of the problem                                               (DS)
- probability of employees' commitment to autocratic decision                (EC)
- degree to which employees' goals are congruent with those of the organisation    (EG)
- the probability that employees will disagree among themselves over the preferred alternative                                                       (ED)
- the degree to which employees have enough information to make a good decision   (EI)

*Note*: the abbreviations have been changed from Vroom and Jago's diagram in order to make it clear which factors relate to the decision (D), the leader (L) or the employee (E). Vroom and Jago simplified these characteristics into two levels: high or low. They were then able to draw up the algorithm shown in Figure 9.3 to identify the appropriate decision style.

Vroom and Jago's diagram is very elegant but it is probably too complex to be of much use to practising managers. Two very general conclusions may be that structured decisions and employee commitment may slightly favour autocratic styles.

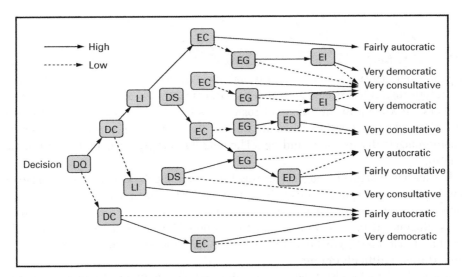

**FIGURE 9.3** Vroom and Jago's decision-making algorithm

Often, differences in decision-making style boil down to whether decisions are made by an individual or a group. **Group decision-making** has a number of advantages:

- Groups have a *greater resources* such as a "pool" of knowledge and experience that can be brought to bear on any decision. They have a broader perspective and many minds have more processing power than a single mind.
- Interaction between group members may result in *synergy* where ideas are cross-fertilised to produce a better result.
- People are *more likely to support a decision* if they are involved in making it.
- Group decision-making serves as an important *communication channel*.
- Group decision-making serves important *"political" functions*.

Unfortunately, group decision-making also has a number of *disadvantages*:

- Groups usually work much more slowly than individuals.
- Decisions made by groups may be less optimal because of many compromises that are necessary to maintain group cohesion. At its worst a decision made by a group may simply represent the "lowest common denominator".
- Group decision-making may undermine managerial authority.

The style of decision-making is important – especially for the way that a decision is accepted by other people and its appropriateness to the situation. But the style of a decision does not give an adequate picture. It does not give much detailed guidance on the practical details of *how* to make a decision. Fortunately, details of how to make an ideal decision are set out by the rational decision paradigm which is described in the next section.

CRITICAL THINKING 9.2 *What's the use of Vroom and Jago's model?*

Vroom and Jago's model of decision-making style is very elegant and intellectually interesting. It has spawned a great deal of research and comment from academic thinkers. However, do the practical results justify all the research time, the trees pulped to make paper or the carbon dioxide emitted as researchers jet from conference to conference to discuss their findings. The model is simply too complex for practical situations.

It is hard to imagine managers learning Vroom and Jago's decision tree to the extent that they can use it spontaneously. It is even harder to imagine a manager adjourning a meeting convened to make an important decision in order to consult Vroom and Jago's diagram. It may be argued that the value of Vroom and Jago's model is less direct and that it has a great deal of benefit for management training. The evidence to support this is difficult to find.

A search of the PsychLit database for the past decade (2000–2010) did not reveal a single case where the performance of actual managers was improved by training based on the Vroom and Jago model. Some findings based on simulations with MBA students or on people's perceptions of *satisfaction* were located – but not on the *actual performance* of managers. One study (Duncan, LaFrance and Ginter, 2003) found that commanding generals in the American Civil War who made decisions in a way that is consistent with the Vroom-Yetton model of decision-making were more successful in achieving the objectives of their campaign. This is interesting but of marginal relevance. Clearly generals in the American Civil War (1861–65) were not using this decision model and neither had they attended any training courses based upon Vroom, Jago or Yetton's work.

## 9.3 The rational decision paradigm – decision-making in ideal circumstances

Most organisations are keen to make rational decisions. The rational decision paradigm sets out what they should do under ideal circumstances. The rational decision paradigm is sometimes called the **classical decision-making process** and **the rational comprehensive method**. It is illustrated in Figure 9.4.

Each of the stages as identified in the rational decision paradigm needs to be discussed in detail.

### Detecting a problem

The most crucial step in good decision-making is to recognise that a decision needs to be made. It goes without saying that if the need for a decision is not identified then an appropriate choice of action cannot be taken. Most decisions stem from two main causes: a desire to exploit a new opportunity or a need to correct a problem.

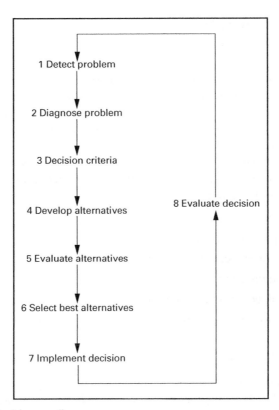

**FIGURE 9.4** The rational decision paradigm

*New opportunities* often arise from technological developments such as biotechnology. They can also arise from sociological developments such as changes in the age distribution of the population or in social attitudes.

*Problems* are situations where there has been a failure to meet established goals. It is easy to dismiss such failures as minor blips which should go away of their own accord. It is easy, and often justifiable, to claim that a failure is the result of someone else's actions and should be resolved by them. Problems needing decisions arise from four main sources:

- **a disturbance** caused by unpredictable factors such as a sudden resignation by an existing employee, the interruption of supplies by bad weather or the discovery of theft and fraud

- **a decline in performance** such as increased levels of waste, poorer machine utilisation, higher expenses. Gradual, insidious declines often present the greatest difficulties because they are easier to rationalise, overlook or deny

- **deviation from plan** such as a delay in commissioning new equipment, failure to achieve planned market share, or even an overproduction of merchandise

- **competitive threats** such as new competitors, the expiry of patents or the development of substitution products

## Diagnosing an opportunity or problem

Once an opportunity or problem has been recognised it must be *defined* and the nature of the problem *diagnosed*. Sometimes a problem is diagnosed at a very superficial level and a decision is made to treat the symptoms of the problem rather than its real cause. For example, a manager may conclude that a decline in sales is due to lack of effort by the sales force. He or she may then decide to retrain sales staff. However, the real cause of the problem may be that the product is out of date and competitors are offering products that are more market friendly.

A very simple approach to problem diagnosis is to ask, "*who* is doing *what to whom?*". A rather more sophisticated method is to ask what, where, when, how, who, what and why? Less cryptically the questions are:

- *What* is the evidence that a problem really exists?
- *Where* does the problem appear to arise?
- *When* does the problem appear to arise?
- *How* urgent is the problem?
- *Who* is most involved with the problem?
- *What* factors (people, departments, organisations, processes) are related to the problem?
- *Why* did the problem occur?

When a problem has been diagnosed, it is always worth checking the analysis with people who are not involved in the situation and who will not share the same assumptions. This results in a more robust diagnosis. It is very important to communicate the problem definition to people involved in subsequent stages, otherwise they will be basing their efforts on implicit and slightly different assumptions. Chaos may ensue.

## Establishing decision criteria

Establishing the criteria for a good decision is a vital stage of the decision-making process. It is often overlooked. Many people do not develop decision criteria until *after* alternative solutions have been identified. This has a big disadvantage. Decision criteria may then be distorted to favour one of the alternatives instead of being thought out in an objective way. Hence the decision may be subconsciously biased towards a faulty, subjective choice. Frequently used decision criteria are:

- financial costs or benefits
- physical resources needed
- human resources needed
- quantity (more production)
- quality (better products)
- certainty of desired outcome (risk)
- acceptability to others
- appropriate timescale
- reliability (e.g. low maintenance)
- compatibility with organisational culture and values

The combination of criteria used to decide between alternative solutions will depend on the exact nature of the problem. For example, an organisation deciding which photocopier to purchase may choose to base its decision upon cost, reliability, quantity (sheets per minute) and delivery time.

Once decision criteria have been established, their relative importance is assessed. For example, the weight given to the decision criteria for the photocopier might be: reliability 0.4, delivery time 0.3, quantity 0.2 and cost 0.1.

## Developing alternatives

It is important to generate several alternative solutions so that the best one can be chosen. If the decision is important, special techniques may be used to produce alternatives. The main techniques are:

- **Employee suggestion schemes** encourage everyone in the organisation to produce new ideas. Many suggestion schemes are moribund and either produce no suggestions or only trivial ones. Good suggestion schemes are usually found in organisations which stress creativity and which give substantial rewards for good ideas.

- **Idea quotas** are used to ensure a steady flow of new proposals. Some companies require each employee to propose at least one improvement to quality, efficiency or service every month. Idea quotas need to be supported by a range of incentives and a commitment by management to implement a large number of the suggestions made.

- **Brainstorming** was a very popular method of generating ideas in the 1970s and 1980s and is still used today. A meeting of, say, six people would meet specifically to generate a large number of ideas. Every member is expected to provide new thoughts – no matter how zany or bizarre. The *number* of ideas generated is emphasised. Participants are expected to "freewheel" and build on the ideas of others in a spontaneous, uninhibited way. Criticism, sarcasm or judgemental comments are not allowed. Since written notes appear formal and may slow the process, brainstorming sessions are often recorded. Some people doubt the value of brainstorming. They point to findings from social psychologists which indicate that creativity is often a solitary process. The presence of other people, even in a brainstorming situation, tends to increase the quantity of routine rather than truly novel ideas. In group situations many people are reluctant to make radical suggestions because they fear the disapproval or ridicule of others.

- **The nominal group technique** attempts to overcome some of the difficulties that arise from group dynamics and is more controlled than brainstorming. Members first write down their individual ideas. During this stage they are not allowed to speak to other participants. Each member then presents one idea to the group. The ideas are not discussed but are merely summarised on a flip chart. In the final stage group members rate each alternative. They are not allowed to speak to each other during this process. Nominal groups are useful when complex, controversial decisions need to be made. They are also useful in situations where assertive members are likely to dominate a discussion. Computer versions of nominal groups in which members communicate by email can also be used. An added advantage of using email is that contributions can be made anonymously.

■ **The Delphi technique** is similar to the nominal group technique. However, participants do not meet in person. Instead, participants write out their ideas, which are collated and fed back to the group in an anonymous form. Participants are asked to give revised estimates which, in turn, are again collated and fed back. The process is repeated until some kind of group consensus is achieved. Initially the Delphi technique used paper questionnaires but today it is more usual to use email.

## Evaluating alternatives

The fifth stage of decision-making involves *collecting and collating relevant information*. For example, data concerning reliability, productivity, delivery time and cost of photocopiers could be obtained from rival manufacturers. The accuracy of the information is important. It makes sense to cross-check information from several sources. It would be better, for example, to cross-check the details given by photocopier manufacturers with information from organisations which have already purchased their photocopiers.

More complex decisions such as where to site a factory or whether to develop a new product will require a great deal of information – often more information than a human brain can store. Consequently computers and *management information systems* may be used to assemble, collate and present the information. Generally **management information systems** track four kinds of information:

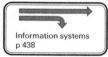

Information systems
p 438

■ **production data**, e.g. number of units produced, the number of clients processed, machine utilisation or levels of waste recovery

■ **financial data** such as present and future cash flow, invoices outstanding, investments

■ **commercial data** such as sales, stock levels and perhaps competitor activity

■ **personnel data**, e.g. employee numbers, seniority, location and training

Management information systems usually produce routine, monthly or weekly, reports and only alert managers when events deviate from a plan (**exception reporting**). However, managers who are making major decisions are able to request specific reports which contain the information they need. Programmes which produce these specific reports are often called "decision support systems". Decision reports have a tighter focus than general reports and they will attempt to filter out routine and irrelevant information. Decision reports need to deliver high-quality information which is up to date and comprehensive. Further, the information needs to be presented in a way that is easily understood by the people who are making the decisions.

Many decisions are made against an uncertain background. The data used by decision support systems often contain estimates containing a margin of error. Decision support systems may therefore include a "sensitivity analysis" (sometimes called a "what if" analysis) that will take account of a range of possibilities. Typically, a sensitivity analysis consists of three sub-analyses: first, the analysis is performed on the best estimates available. This will be called the "central prediction". Second, an analysis using optimistic estimates, which assume everything goes well, is performed. Third, an analysis using pessimistic estimates, which assume that things go wrong, is performed. Sensitivity analyses are vital if a wrong decision could jeopardise the survival of an organisation or have other very serious consequences. They allow the decision-maker to see whether a decision could send the organisation out of business.

Evaluating alternatives is a particularly crucial stage of the rational decision paradigm and a number of methods have been devised to help managers. The main methods are:

- gut feelings
- heuristics
- PMI analysis
- decision matrices
- hat analysis

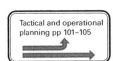

Decision techniques p 238

Each of these methods is a very important aid in choosing the best alterative and they are considered in detail in the next main section (9.4).

## Implementation

Even correct decisions are useless unless they are implemented. The first stage of implementation is to communicate the decision to those who need to take action. This is much easier if these people have previously participated in making the decision. One specific person should be made responsible for carrying a decision to fruition. Implementation is often a question of using the techniques of tactical and operational planning.

Tactical and operational planning pp 101–105

## Evaluation

The implementation process should be monitored to check whether a decision produces good results. Sometimes it may be necessary to adjust the way that the decision is implemented or it may be necessary to adjust the decision itself – in extreme circumstances it may even be necessary to abandon or reverse the decision in the light of subsequent events. The lessons learned during evaluation should be used to improve later decisions. The last disadvantage is very important. As long ago as 1957 the Nobel prizewinner Herbert Simon pointed out that people are not entirely rational. Their rationality is limited by their brainpower to store, manipulate and communicate with information. It is also limited by people's perceptions and emotions. In other words decision-making is limited by bounded rationality. Herbert Simon noted that managers tend to accept the first reasonable solution that occurs. This is called **satisficing** and it is very common. Satisficing means accepting a solution which meets minimum requirements. It is the opposite of **optimising** which is the acceptance of the solution that provides the best possible answer.

Ariel Rubinstein (1998, p.16) gives details of experiments which show how some decisions are not rational. They also shows how our limited memory, the sources of information we choose and working in groups puts boundaries on rational thinking when making decisions.

One consequence of bounded rationality is that decision-makers may try to simplify the situation and use "rules of thumb", called **heuristics**. Heuristics are simplifications and shortcuts which allow decisions to be made quickly without constantly stopping to ponder. Typical examples of heuristics are "never schedule activities for more than two-thirds of the

## CRITICAL THINKING 9.3 *What is wrong with the rational decision paradigm?*

The rational decision paradigm is very logical and systematic. In theory it will produce the best possible decision. However it has a number of disadvantages:

- It works best if the problem is clear and unambiguous. Further, it needs clear preferences which make it possible to order the criteria and then rank the alternatives upon the criteria.
- It works best if the problem and the problem situation are fairly stable over time.
- It is time-consuming.
- It requires a lot of information which is assumed to be accurate, measurable and accepted by all.
- It assumes that decision-makers are totally rational and that organisational politics do not impinge upon decisions.

time available" or "always allow a 20 per cent overrun on building projects". Gigerenzer and Selten (2002) cast an interesting light upon heuristics. They suggest that heuristics are a rational response to bounded rationality because they allow decision-makers to cope speedily with complex decisions. Further, they contend that heuristic rules often lead to better decisions than the rational decision-making paradigm.

The consequences of bounded rationality and other problems are discussed in a later section on the problems of decision-making.

## 9.4 Decision-making techniques

A large number of techniques have evolved to help managers make prompt and accurate decisions. The main methods are: gut feelings, heuristics, PNI analysis, decision matrices and thinking hats.

- **Gut feelings** are sometimes called **gut instincts**. They are usually vague feelings that something will turn out right or, perhaps, turn out wrong. They often arise from the brain subconsciously accessing memories of similar situations. They are also closely related to a person's values and beliefs. Gut feelings often have a high emotional content which originates from some of the primitive areas of the brain. Gut feelings are frequently encountered when a decision involves a high level of ambiguity. Many people can cite instances where their gut instinct led them to a good decision. This evidence is anecdotal and probably relies on selective memory of instances where successes are remembered and failures are forgotten. In fact, gut instinct probably has a slightly higher than chance probability of success. This may be due to a self-fulfilling prophecy where an emotional belief in a decision leads to greater effort and persistence which, in turn, leads to success. It would be a very rash manager who relied upon gut instinct to make major irreversible decisions.

- **Heuristics** are much better than gut instinct. They are simple rules based on experience. A classic heuristic is **the Pareto principle** (the 80/20 rule): 80 per cent of success is obtained from 20 per cent of activities – or, in this context, 20 per cent of the information will yield a decision that is 80 per cent accurate.

- **PNI analysis** is a very simple decision-making technique which can be used in decisions on whether or not to take up a single option. It involves constructing a table with three columns as shown in Figure 9.5. The positives, negatives and interesting aspects of the single option are inserted into the relevant columns. When the table is complete, a judgement is made as to whether the positives outweigh the negatives. If the difference is small, the entries in the "interesting" column are used as a tie-breaker.

- **Decision matrices** are a relatively sophisticated tool that involves five stages. First, criteria and their weights are arranged at the top of the matrix while alternative solutions are listed down the side. Figure 9.6 demonstrates how a decision matrix can be used to choose the best photocopier. The relevant criteria are: reliability (which, because of its importance, is given a weighting of .4); delivery time (weighting .3); quantity (sheets per minute, weighting .2) and cost. There are four potential photocopiers which in this example are labelled A, B, C, D. Second, using a nine-point scale, each photocopier is rated on each criterion. In the example, copier B is highly reliable and is given a rating of 9, while copier A is very fast and is also given a rating of 9. Third, the ratings are multiplied by the weight for each criteria. For example copier C has a rating of 3 for reliability which is weighted .4 and therefore they weighted reliability is 1.2 ($3 \times 1.2$). Fourth, the weighted ratings, are added and the total entered in the final column. In this example, photocopier B is the best choice because it has the highest total (6.0 = 3.6 + 0.9 + 1.4 + 0.1).

The decision matrix is very useful: it makes clear that copier B is the best choice but it might have been rejected because it is expensive and the delivery time was poor. A less systematic decision process might have chosen the poorer photocopier C because it was cheap.

- **Hat analysis** is a metaphor inspired by Gilbert and Sullivan's operetta, *The Mikado*, in which Pooh-bah, the "Lord High Everything Else" (General Manager?) has many roles:

| Positives | Negatives | Interesting |
|---|---|---|
|  |  |  |
|  |  |  |
|  |  |  |

**FIGURE 9.5:** A simple PNI table

| | Reliability (0.4) | Weighted reliability | Delivery (0.3) | Weighted delivery | Quantity (0.2) | Weighted quantity | Cost (0.1) | Weighted cost | TOTAL weights |
|---|---|---|---|---|---|---|---|---|---|
| Copier A | 5 | 2.0 | 1 | 0.3 | 9 | 1.8 | 3 | 0.3 | 4.4 |
| Copier B | 9 | 3.6 | 3 | 0.9 | 7 | 1.4 | 1 | 0.1 | 6.0 |
| Copier C | 3 | 1.2 | 9 | 2.7 | 1 | 0.2 | 9 | 0.9 | 5.0 |
| Copier D | 1 | 0.4 | 7 | 2.1 | 3 | 0.6 | 5 | 0.5 | 3.6 |

**FIGURE 9.6**  Example of decision matrix

first Lord of the Treasury, Leader of the Opposition, Paymaster General, etc., etc. To avoid confusion about the role he was occupying at any one time he would wear a distinctive hat. In decision-making, hat analysis is useful in complex decisions that must be viewed from many perspectives. Separate members of the decision team are given various "hats" and are asked to evaluate alternative solutions according to the perspective of their hat. Sometimes, however, a single person, like Pooh-Bah, is asked to wear several hats in succession. There are several versions of this technique. For example, in one version there is the "white hat" who is responsible for examining data and gaps in knowledge; the "red hat" inspects any alternative using gut instinct and emotion; the "black hat" inspects possible solutions with a dark mien (pessimistic, cautious, defensive) etc. A more managerial focus uses hats based on PESTLE:

PESTLE p 96

- Pink hat examines alternatives from a political (both internal and external) perspective.
- Emerald hat views things from an economic perspective.
- Silver hat considers the sociological point of view.
- Turquoise hat is responsible for exploring technological issues.
- Ebony hat considers environmental issues.
- Lavender hat examines legal issues.

Hat analysis does not lead to a specific decision in a mechanical way – as do decision matrices. But it does ensure that most of the relevant factors are taken into account so that decision-makers can integrate them in an organic way.

## CASE 9.4: *BodyCheck decides on its cardio equipment*

BodyCheck is the main gym in Glossop – a Pennine town between Manchester and Sheffield. It had a good number of exercise bikes, treadmills and cross-trainers that were in perfect working order and would last a good few years. However, the equipment was past its prime. Management recognised the need to make a decision about its replacement. External factors played a part in the decision: the economic climate was subdued so the gym would be able to negotiate a good price with suppliers and "state-of-the-art" machines would sustain the gym's premier status in the town. Replacing the cardio equipment involved a significant investment of over £120,000. It also required a subsequent decision about which machines to buy. But, how should that decision be made? Gut instinct was not appropriate – it was a major choice which could not be reversed with ease. Further, there are few, if any, heuristics concerning gym equipment. Gym equipment involves few political, economic, sociological, technological, etc. issues – therefore "hat analysis" was not appropriate. In this situation, a decision matrix is an ideal technique.

Soundings with other gyms and a scan of the trade press identified four possible suppliers: M, N, O and P. Staff at BodyCheck identified four decision criteria: safety, function (providing appropriate exercise), cost and reliability. Safety was identified as the most important criteria and it was weighted .5 so that no other factor could overwhelm it. Weightings given to other criteria were: function .3, reliability .1 and cost .1. These weights illustrate interesting points. *First*, some criteria are much more important than others – in this case safety is paramount. *Second*, it is better to limit the number of criteria, otherwise minor criteria have so little weight that they add more complications than their importance justifies. BodyCheck then rated suppliers on the criteria and multiplied the ratings by the weights to produce the decision matrix shown in Figure 9.7.

| | Safety (0.5) | Weighted safety | Function (0.3) | Weighted function | Cost (1.0) | Weighted cost | Reliability (1.0) | Weighted reliability | TOTAL weights |
|---|---|---|---|---|---|---|---|---|---|
| Supplier M | 9 | 4.5 | 6 | 1.8 | 8 | 0.8 | 9 | 0.9 | **8.0** |
| Supplier N | 9 | 4.5 | 9 | 2.7 | 6 | 0.6 | 9 | 0.9 | **8.7** |
| Supplier O | 8 | 4.0 | 8 | 2.4 | 6 | 0.6 | 6 | 0.6 | **7.6** |
| Supplier P | 9 | 4.5 | 8 | 2.4 | 5 | 0.5 | 7 | 0.7 | **8.1** |

**FIGURE 9.7:** BodyCheck's decision matrix

The decision matrix showed that the best equipment was provided by supplier N and the worst was provided by supplier O. The decision matrix also revealed some interesting aspects. All total scores were high and this indicates that generally cardio equipment is good. Although safety was strongly weighted, it played an insignificant role in the decision because the equipment of all suppliers was very safe. Further, cost on its own would not be a good basis for a decision because both the best equipment (supplier N) and the worst (supplier O) were in the middle of the range in terms of cost. In effect, the major determinant of the decision was the way the equipment functioned – the appropriateness of the exercise it provided and its ease of use by members. These results would provide a useful heuristic for future decisions of this kind.

The final aspect of BodyCheck's decision process was to evaluate its decision. The performance of the new cardio equipment was monitored and members were asked for their opinions. Fortunately, only fine-tuning of some aspects of the equipment was needed.

## 9.5 Common problems in decision-making

It is rare for the decision-making paradigm to be followed in its pure form. Sometimes certain phases will be omitted. Often it is necessary to cycle through the paradigm several times before the best decision is made. Frequently other factors intervene to create decision making faults. Managers may try to be logical but their efforts are bounded by the capacity of their thinking power and also by their emotions and attitude. Generally, there is more information than a human brain can process. Consequently people will choose to attend to some information and ignore other information. The way that people make this choice is often called "orienting response" and is a major influence on how decisions are made (see Weber and Johnson, 2009).

Another major issue is the way that people assess the probabilities of various outcomes. Recent research suggests that we process information in two ways. First, there is an automatic, intuitive and emotional process (gut feeling?). Second, there is a slower, analytical, deliberate and logical process. Kahneman (2003) suggests that the second system is used to supervise and correct wrong, intuitive, judgements made by the emotional system. There seem to be systematic errors in decisions about time and money: people are much more optimistic about the time they will have available in the future than the money that will be available. People also overestimate the difficulty of adjusting to lifetime changes such as moving home to somewhere 1,000 miles away, not achieving promotion, or receiving a big windfall. In general, people are not very good at predicting future events: the accuracy of political predictions made by pundits is not much better than chance (Tetlock, 2005). The decision-maker's characteristics can also influence the probabilities attached to future events. In many situations and contexts women are more risk averse than men – possibly because they are more aware of emotions, and emotional discomfort magnifies perceptions of risk. Risk-takers tend to have certain personality characteristics: they tend to be extrovert, stable and open people who have low scores on conscientiousness and agreeableness. Risk-taking is also associated with sensation-seeking. People who are good with basic mathematics and probability tend to have better judgement of probabilities (see Weber and Johnson, 2009 for references). Kahneman and Klein (2010) disagree about the use of gut feelings when making decisions but, in most circumstances, relying on "gut feelings" to make important choices is very dangerous. Kahneman and Renshon (2007) explain that in conflict situations there are systematic distortions of decision-making which mean that the hawks (the hardliners) usually win - often with disastrous consequences!

The list of individual findings seems endless and is of doubtful use for individuals with bounded rationality. Fortunately, a more useful list of common errors in decision-making have evolved over the decades. They are: procrastination, anchoring, escalation of commitment, groupthink and communication failure.

## Procrastination

Procrastination is the tendency to delay decisions without a valid reason. It is sometimes called dithering and is personified as the "thief of time". Procrastination usually results in indecisiveness and may make a problem more difficult because it has extra time to grow. Procrastination often arises from a fear of failure. It is most prevalent in organisations with a "blame culture" where avoiding mistakes is more important than achieving success. Probably the most effective way of overcoming procrastination is to divide a decision into smaller stages and to set a deadline for the completion of each smaller stage.

Avoiding procrastination does not mean that decisions must be rushed. It means that *unnecessary* delays should be avoided. Impulsive decisions are as bad as delayed ones. In most circumstances it is appropriate to allow time to "sleep" on a decision so that it can be subjected to a reasonable period of reflective thought. Procrastination only arises when a decision is delayed for several days without the prospect of new information.

## Anchoring

Anchoring refers to a tendency by decision-makers to give undue importance to information that is received early. It is sometimes called the "primacy effect". Early information tends to act as the standard by which other information is assessed. If later information is contradictory it will tend to be ignored or dismissed. Unfortunately, early information is often inaccurate because it was assembled in a hurry, without the time to perform cross-checks to ensure that it is comprehensive.

## Escalation of commitment

A decision may be made on the basis of early information; but as more facts emerge the original decision becomes untenable. By this time a decision-maker may have invested considerable time, effort and prestige in the original decision. To abandon it may appear to be a waste of past commitment and disloyal to their advisers. They may feel that abandoning the original decision would cause them loss of face. Consequently, they may become more and more determined to commit resources to ensuring the success of their initial decision. Up to a point, this may be justified. If a little extra effort is able to produce success then it is reasonable to give a little extra effort. The problem is that a little extra effort may not achieve success – it may require just a little more effort and so on – ad infinitum! There comes a point where it is necessary to cut one's losses and follow another course of action. Some of the worst decisions in history have been the result of the escalation of commitment. In the 1970s America escalated its commitment to the Vietnam war long after it was apparent that the initial decision was flawed. Many government projects have been continued to the point of absurdity because politicians are reluctant to admit mistakes and cut taxpayer's losses. Generally, it is better to avoid these situations by following the example of stock market investors and setting a "stoploss" – a clear point at which they will sell their investment and accept whatever losses they may have incurred.

## Groupthink

Participative decision-making has many advantages. A wider range of knowledge or experience and the synergy between members may produce ideas of better quality. However, participative decision-making has a number of disadvantages: it takes extra time, dominant members may distort discussions and the goals of individuals may detract from the goals of the organisation. A further problem with participative decision making is the phenomena of **groupthink**.

Groupthink is a mentality among members of a decision team to suppress their own disbelief in order to show solidarity and maintain agreement at any cost. Members suspend their critical judgements, which could lead to a better decision. Groupthink is particularly prevalent in closely knit groups, whose members come from similar backgrounds and who share similar goals. It is also prevalent in groups that have a high regard for each other. Groupthink is partly produced by the desire to conform. Dissenting members may suspend their personal judgement in favour of what they see as the consensus of the group. Unfortunately, other members may be doing the same. An *illusion* of agreement is created. Those who question this apparent agreement may be ridiculed or have their loyalty questioned. Groupthink often impairs a group's ability to generate a wide range of alternatives and to evaluate them effectively. Many disastrous political decisions such as the Watergate cover-up, the Bay of Pigs invasion and the 1986 *Challenger* launch disaster have been attributed to the negative influence of groupthink.

The effects of groupthink can be so catastrophic that a number of countermeasures have been devised Some organisations only take major decisions after appointing a **devil's advocate** who challenges assumptions and assertions. This forces decision-makers to consider a wider range of solutions. A similar technique is the use of **multiple advocates** where individuals are charged with arguing minority and dissenting viewpoints. Multiple advocacy is used by several governments to ensure that decisions are well argued and take a number of different perspectives into account.

Klein (see Kahneman and Klein, 2010) suggests that organisations should hold a **premortem** before it takes an important decision. Before an important project starts, managers should say "we are looking into a crystal ball and this project has failed; it's a fiasco. Now, everybody, take two minutes and write down the reasons why you think the project failed". Premortums are easy to conduct and they are good at identifying potential problems. They rarely cause decisions to be abandoned but implementation can be "tweaked" in beneficial ways. A premortum is a low-cost, high-payoff management technique.

## Communication failure

The final fault in decision-making is failure of communication. It is obvious that a decision needs to be communicated to those involved in its implementation. It is slightly less obvious that it should also be communicated to those, such as suppliers, customers and stakeholders, who will also be affected by the decision. Communication should not be confined to the actual decision. The need, the diagnosis and the range of alternatives underlying the decision must be explained. Particular effort is needed to explain the advantages and the disadvantages of the chosen alternative.

## 9.6 Decision toolkit

- Do not take decisions by default. Even if nothing is happening or things are going well, decisions may still be needed. Monitor external environment for impending events.
- Clarify and check the main factors involved. Ask "who", "what", "why", "where", "when" and "how" questions. Do not accept the facts as stated to you. Reframe them by looking at then from the other way round.
- Limit risk to a level that your organisation can survive if things go badly.
- If a decision is easily reversed do not procrastinate. Make it quickly.
- Establish standards and measures that you can later use to evaluate important decisions.
- Be creative in producing a number of alternative decisions (e.g. brainstorm).
- If a decision is important, evaluate alternatives using PNI analysis, decision matrices or "hat analysis".
- Communicate decisions extensively.
- Evaluate important decisions against criteria set earlier.
- Avoid groupthink and escalation of commitment.

*Toolkit*

# Activities and further study

## Essay plans

Produce essay plans for the following topics:

1  Why do people make bad decisions?
2  How do decisions differ from each other?
3  What different decision-making styles can managers adopt?
4  Is one decision style better than another?
5  What techniques and strategies would you use to ensure that decisions are properly implemented?

## Web activities

1  Use the Internet to obtain information about the following decision-making errors. For each error write two sentences about (a) what the error is, (b) why it is important and (c) an example:

- availability heuristic
- base rate fallacy
- loss aversion
- peak-end rule
- representativeness heuristic
- simulation heuristic
- status quo bias

2  Use the Web and other sources to find out about the phenomenon of "Risky shift".

3  Access the following website: http://www.mindtools.com/pages/article/newTED_00.htm. It gives details of the following decision-making tools:

- Pareto analysis
- paired comparison analysis
- grid analysis
- decision trees

- PMI (plus and minus implications)
- six hats analysis

Which tool do you think would be most helpful in making (a) simple, easily reversed decisions and (b) complex decisions with expensive implications?

## Experiential activities

1  Think of three managers (or other people you know well) and try to identify their decision-making style. Evaluate their success as decision-makers and summarise their impact on you and others affected by their decisions.

2  Analyse three decisions you have made in the last year. Identify ways that your decision-making process could be improved.

3  Identify an important decision (such as your choice of course options for next year). Perform a grid analysis to establish the best solution to the problem.

## Recommended reading

1  Kahneman, E. and Renshon, J. (2007) "Why hawks win", *Foreign Policy*, 158, 34–39. A readable but very informative article by a Nobel prizewinner, which explains why hardliners often influence decision-makers to make a wrong decision.

2  Kahneman, E. and Klein, G. (2010) "When can you trust your gut?", *McKinsey Quarterly*, 0047 5394, issue 2. An easy but an unmissable read where the role intuition should play in decision-making is debated by two top experts.

3  Clydesdale, G. and Tan, J. (2009) "Preparing students for front-line management: non-routine day-to-day decisions", *Journal of European Industrial Training*, **33**(7), 594–613. An article comprising criticisms of the way that decision-making is taught: inappropriate emphasis on models based on physics and too much emphasis on strategy. Highly recommended.

4  Rubinstein, A. (1998) *Modelling Bounded Rationality*, London: MIT Press. This book is freely downloadable. Do not attempt to read all of it. Read section 1.4 (pp. 16–21) which gives excellent evidence that human decision-making is not entirely rational.

5  Chung, J.O.Y., Cohen, J.R. and Monroe, G.S. (2008) "The effect on mood on auditors' inventory valuation decisions", *Auditing: A Journal of Practice & Theory*, **27**(2), 137–159. An empirical example of subjective factors influencing supposedly objective decisions. Do not get bogged down in statistics – skip complicated tables. There are lots of references. This is a good example of reporting empirical studies.

# CHAPTER 10

# Controlling

## Chapter contents

## ❖ LEARNING OBJECTIVES

After studying this chapter you should be able to **appreciate** the importance of control processes in ensuring that plans are effective. You should be able to understand the basic principles and stages of control systems and then describe the main types of control in organisations. Finally, you should be able to describe the advantages and disadvantages of control systems in organisations. In particular you should be able to:

❖ **define** control and give at least two examples of the dire consequences to organisations when control is lax

❖ **explain** why control is necessary

❖ **draw a diagram** of the components of a basic control system

❖ **describe in detail** how targets and standards are set

❖ **describe briefly** the following concepts:
  – hard outcomes, soft outcomes and distance travelled
  – the characteristics of good standards of performance
  – control variety and the law of requisite variety

❖ **describe in detail** the four main requirements of measures of performance

❖ **explain** how actual performance is compared with standards

❖ **explain** how corrective action can be taken to remedy any variance between standard and performance

❖ **describe in detail** different types of control system – especially feed-forward, concurrent and feedback control

❖ **explain in detail** the concept of a balanced scorecard

❖ **evaluate in depth** the dangers of control systems

Control is the final link in a chain of management. Without some form of control to ensure that end results are achieved, planning, organising, staffing and deciding will have been a waste of time. Therefore, control is sometimes called the "terminal" management process because it occurs after the other processes. Control is very closely linked to both strategy and planning. Control ensures that the right things are done at the right time and in the right way. As Case 10.1 shows, the consequences of poor control can be dire.

### CASE 10.1: *Poor control – Baring's banker, Toyota's troubles and Perrier's poison*

Barings Bank is a stark example of an organisation brought to its knees by poor control. It was founded in 1762 and established a venerable reputation until it collapsed in 1995. Nick Leeson, an ambitious securities dealer working in Singapore, decided to obtain outstanding results by using the bank's resources for unauthorised speculation in Japanese securities. Leeson made a small but manageable loss of "only" £2 million. Inadequate financial controls allowed him to cover his losses with a spiral of further unauthorised speculation until losses reached over £860 million. When the level of Leeson's, and his employer's losses became known, the bank almost collapsed and was ignominiously sold to a Dutch Bank, ING, at a token price. Poor financial control had ended 200 years of venerable banking history.

Dire consequences of poor control also happen outside the financial sector. For many years Toyota held an impeccable reputation for the safety and quality of its cars – largely built upon its system of total quality control. A founding principle was "getting quality right the first time". Any production employee had the authority to stop the production process if they saw a quality issue. Indeed Toyota's implementation of total quality management became a legend – it regularly headed the list of league tables for car quality control. But in 2006 reports began to emerge that it was not controlling manufacturing faults with sufficient rigour. In some cars the brakes had momentarily failed. Other cars had accelerated unexpectedly – causing accidents. There were allegations that 52 people had died in the USA as a result of these faults. Toyota handled the crisis very badly. It was adamant that its quality control system was invincible and that many of the reports were misleading. Evidence of faults became conclusive. Toyota's response was half-hearted and reluctant. However, in 2010 the company was forced to recall millions of cars for repair work. The company's president was forced to offer humiliating apologies to the US Congress. He admitted that during a period of rapid expansion, the company's priorities had become confused. He announced a complete review of quality control across the company and that he would personally oversee the process. It was estimated that the costs of lost sales plus the costs of repair work were in excess were about £1.23 billion

Fortunately, not all control systems are faulty. For years, Perrier had traded on the purity of its bottled water. Then an engineer inadvertently cleaned equipment using benzene (a potentially carcinogenic substance). Minute traces of benzene, well within the legal limits, found their way into the water. The control system quickly detected the fault. All bottles were withdrawn from shelves and destroyed but good control and an appropriate response enabled Perrier's reputation to remain intact.

## 10.1  Definition and need for control

At its simplest, control means "to have the power to make people or things to perform actions that are desired by the power-holders". While this definition serves a useful function in highlighting the link between control and power, it is not very useful in the management context. This simple definition is too wide. It has little discriminatory power because it encompasses many other management topics such as leadership, selection, planning, strategy, etc.

The definition can be improved by differentiating "command" from "control". Military terminology suggests that the distinction is useful because the terms "command *and* control" are frequently used together. **Command** can be thought of as "distal-control" reflecting the fact that it "makes people do things" from a distance in terms of place (the headquarters issuing a command may be miles away from the unit responsible for executing it), seniority (e.g. strategy set by top managers), or time (a command may be hatched several months before it is executed). Distal-control usually concerns making people and things take a certain direction. It is generally considered to be a part of strategy and planning. In many management contexts, the term "control" is solely concerned with getting the job done by ensuring efficient operation of procedures. **Procedural control** involves *maintaining efficiency* or enforcing *compliance* to standards within the transformation process. It is sometimes called "proximal control" because it happens close to the place where resources are transformed. This type of control will be exercised by managers who are only one or two levels above the people making the transformation; it is likely to be exercised by people in the same building and it is likely to be exercised within days, if not hours, of the work being done.

One of the leading writers on the subject, Merchant (1985), clearly sees control as a separate activity to planning (which encompasses strategy). He defines it as:

> ❝ The systematic process through which managers regulate organisational activities to make them consistent with expectations established in plans and to help them achieve all predetermined standards of performance. ❞

Merchant's definition has two advantages.

1 It emphasises that control is a systematic process rather than a haphazard collection of activities that may be started or stopped at whim.

2 It explicitly links control processes with plans and desired organisational outcomes.

Fayol's (1949) definition also views planning as a separate process from controlling. He defined control as:

> ❝ verifying whether everything occurs in conformity with the plan adopted, the instructions issued, and the principles established. Its object is to point out weaknesses and errors in order to rectify them and prevent recurrence. ❞

Fayol's definition has remarkable similarities with Merchant's. However, it highlights a major point that the goal of controlling is to identify errors so that they can be rectified and prevented.

## Need for control and its wide scope

There are several reasons why organisations and managers need to exercise control. Without control, products or services will be defective. Without control, there will be waste and inefficiency which will increase costs. Except in monopoly situations this means an organisation will be unable to compete. Without control, people will be uncertain about what is happening elsewhere in the organisation: this ambiguity may lead to confusion and dissatisfaction. These are compelling argument in favour of *some* control. In the longer term, however, the most important reasons why organisations and managers need to exercise **control** is that, as Fayol points out, good control enables managers to identify and eliminate things that cause error. In section 7.5, we show that control is not always good. It must be exercised to the right extent and in the right way.

## Need for control is ubiquitous

The need for control in functions such as quality, finance and operations is easy to understand. In fact, Table 10.1 shows it is relevant to all major functions – but the form of control varies. In some functions the control is very rigid and based on hard data. In other functions control is often subtle and based on subjective perceptions.

## Control and globalisation

Increasing globalisation makes control both more difficult and more important. There are both practical and cultural difficulties.

---

*Marketing function:* advertising effectiveness, PR effectiveness, market penetration, sales activities, customer retention, agent efficiency, etc.

*Operations function – supply chain management:* costs, quality of supplies, reliability of suppliers, social responsibility of suppliers, etc.

*Operations function – production:* costs, output (quantity and quality), product pipeline, machine (resource) utilisation, waste, etc – see pages 369, 373–377.

*Operations function – warehousing and distribution:* stock levels, wastage (obsolescence and deterioration), shrinkage (theft!), delivery times, etc.

*HR function – employees:* payroll, absences, lateness, labour turnover, employee performance, hours worked, satisfaction and motivation, equal opportunities, etc. – see pages 386–396.

*HR function – health and safety:* obedience to safety procedures, working environment (heat and ventilation), hygiene, hours worked, etc.

*Finance function:* administrative costs, income streams, expenditure, interest payable, debts, lending, capital, etc. – see pages 413–415.

*Information function:* costs, usage rates, serviceability (downtime)

---

TABLE 10.1 Some control ramifications in the five main organisational functions

Many of the *practical difficulties* arise from size and distance. Globalised organisations are usually big and *increased size* always makes sensitive and effective control problematic. Further, the *distance* between an organisation's units may be thousands of miles. It is difficult for a manager to visit all units on a regular basis. It is also difficult to convene meetings with representatives from these units. Often, despite the use of electronic media, a manager is less aware of the nuances that modify formal communications or alert them to malfeasance. For example, a senior manager of a merchant bank such as Barings, would find it much more difficult to monitor the actions of a trader in Singapore than a trader at headquarters in London. Global headquarters in the western world may genuinely abhor the use of child labour yet there are recurrent examples where they find it impossible to rule this out in subsidiaries or contractors. In this sense some global headquarters exercise "command without control" (Tallman and Koza, 2010). It is notoriously difficult for organisations to control their intellectual property, such as patents or copyright, in many countries that are skilled in making duplicates or fakes. Finally, globalisation makes control more important because the effects of errors are more difficult to contain. For example, American banks do not exercise adequate control over lending to sub-prime borrowers. When these loans went bad the global interconnections between banks meant that the "credit crunch" spread from America to the rest of the developed world.

*Cultural differences* also make controlling more difficult. For example, the culture of an organisation's headquarters may rely upon formal, quantitative control measures whereas a distant subunit may have a culture that achieves control via family links. Many global concerns are joint ventures where the partners have conflicting attitudes and objectives. Considerable energy may be needed to reconcile the differences – even before control processes are designed and implemented (Li, Zhou and Zajac, 2009). In general, globalisation means that billion-dollar companies originating in the USA, the UK and Canada will be losing control to other countries (Smith, 2009).

Control in even a single country or single location is not a simple process. It comprises at least four main components which are described in greater detail in the next section.

## 10.2 Components of control

The control process, in even a single country or single site is not a simple process. It can be viewed as a cycle which has four main components:

1 setting performance *standards*

2 measuring *actual performance*

3 *comparing* the actual performance with the standards

4 *taking action* to reduce significant discrepancies between standards and actual performance

Each of these components of controlling needs to be covered in greater detail. Further, in reality controlling is influenced by other factors, such as the impact of the environment and the possibility that standards are incorrect. Figure 10.1 illustrates how the components and other factors relate.

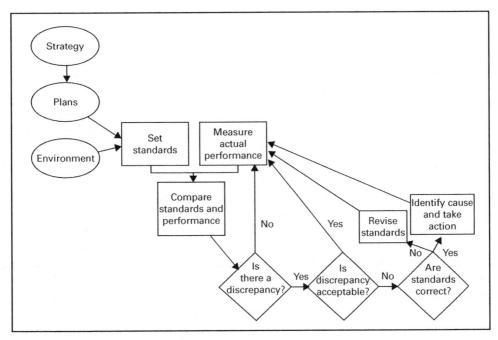

**FIGURE 10.1** The components of a control system

## Setting standards

Standards can take many forms and they are often called **targets** or **outcomes**. They are easiest to set in batch-manufacturing operations such as the production of DVD players. Here a standard might read "each month the Dundee factory will produce 300 000 DVD players that meet quality specifications". Standards are also easy to set in sales environments where a standard might read, "The Dubai outlet will achieve a turnover of AED 500 000 per month with a profit margin of AED100 000" or "capture 5 per cent of the UK confectionery market by September 2012". It is usually easy to set standards at a corporate level. Corporate standards might be "Value added per employee will be RMB7000 per year" or "the share price will increase by 5 per cent above the Dow Jones Index over the next three years". Such standards and targets are often called "hard" or "quantitative" standards. **Hard standards** are those which can be checked objectively. Hard standards usually have at least three components:

1 a **quantitative** component specifying how much is produced
2 a **qualitative** component specifying the quality of what is produced
3 a **deadline** specifying the time frame of production

Sometimes the standards of performance will have additional components such as the **margin of error** (i.e. the deviations or random fluctuations that will be tolerated).

In many contexts **hard standards** are not sufficient. A hospital, for example, may meet its hard target of 100 clinically successful operations per month but it would not be a success if it achieved its target by treating patients in a brutal, inconsiderate and impersonal way. In many situations hard targets need to be supplemented by "soft outcomes" (see Dewson *et al.*, 2000) such as "to the satisfaction of patients". In another situation a local authority in West Yorkshire, in the UK, was awarded a European Union (EU) grant for training disadvantaged minority groups. The EU controlled the project by setting hard standards (the number and types of people trained) *and* soft standards such as participants' self-confidence or their ability to work in a team. In education and training standards are often less concerned with absolute levels of, say, reading ability. A school in a very privileged catchment would find it easy to ensure that 50 per cent of pupils were above the national average for reading whereas a school in a deprived area would struggle to achieve the same target. In these circumstances standards are often set in terms of "distance travelled" – the actual *change* in, say, reading ability.

Many standards will *originate* in strategy documents, plans and organisational structures such as management by objectives (MBO). However, a substantial number of the standards will be imposed by the external environment. For example, motorists expect a certain level of reliability from their cars. If a manufacturer sets a lower level of reliability it will sell fewer cars and the manufacturer will be faced with a Hobson's choice between raising their standards or becoming bankrupt. In other instances the standards will be directly imposed by government – e.g. pollution and safety standards. For example, a UK molybdenum processing company will be obliged to control its emissions of SO$_2$ so that they are within the permissible levels set by the British government. Extra-territorial governments may also set standards. For example, a pharmaceutical manufacturer in the north of Dublin must meet the quality standards of the US Federal Drug Agency because it needs to sell its products in the American market.

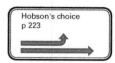

Hobson's choice
p 223

*Standards of performance* may have several characteristics. They should be **clear** and **easy to understand**. They also need to be written with care so that they are **precise.** For example, a teacher should not set students the standard of being "well prepared" for seminars. The teacher should specify that the student must:

- complete related assignments on time
- bring materials such as worksheets, books, paper and pencils
- arrive a few minutes *before* the start of the seminar, etc.

Multinational companies also need to take **cultural differences** into account when setting standards – especially when the standards relate to interpersonal relationships and dress codes. For example, it would be inappropriate to set a dress code of a skirt, blouse and jacket for women working in a Muslim country. This illustrates that standards of performance must be reasonable and acceptable to those expected to achieve them.

Control systems designed by committees are prone to having too many performance measures – each committee member may argue for the inclusion of measures that show their unit in a favourable light. Too many measures cause costs to rise, and people may spend more time measuring performance than performing productive work. Further, a large **number of measures** is likely to swamp management's ability to interpret the information and important information may be crowded out by less useful data. Generally it is better to decide first upon the number of indices that can be handled competently, then prioritise the potential measures before adopting those that are most important. Standards are **not permanent** or "carved in stone". They can and should be changed. Setting standards, especially "soft standards", is an art not a science. Soft standards are often first set by guesswork. Experience may prove them to be too difficult or too easy. They should then be changed so that they are more appropriate. So, many standards emerge by trial and error. In other situations changes in the business environment require changes of standards. For example, if a government enacts legislation to provide extra safeguards for investors, the added paperwork will mean that workers in the back offices of investment institutions will not be able to process the same number of transactions per hour and consequently their performance targets will need to be reduced.

## Measuring performance

Once standards have been set, measures of actual performance are needed. In many cases this is easy – what needs to be measured is obvious from the standard itself. For example, if the standard of performance requires a call centre to handle 300 calls per hour, it is clear that there should be a system for logging and reporting the number of calls answered. However, the situation is rarely so straightforward. Appropriate measures of performance will depend on five factors:

1 what is to be measured
2 number of measures
3 accuracy
4 reporting
5 costs

### 1 What is measured by performance standards?

Choosing what is to be measured is more difficult than it seems at first sight. The above example of the call centre illustrates that it is easy to identify quantitative, banal measures but, on their own, they are rarely satisfactory. Often the obvious measures are short-sighted and merely perpetuate the status quo. Instead the **measures should be linked to the call centre strategy**. If that strategy is to encourage callers to find the information they need on the Web, it would be much better for each operative to answer fewer calls and spend more time with each caller explaining the Web resources. In this case a better index of performance would be the number of callers who subsequently refer to the website.

There is also a tendency for performance measures to be chosen because they are **easy to collect** rather than because they provide useful control information. In fact, while it is easy to count the number of calls, the result is not very useful because a call centre which briskly fobs off each caller with an excuse will seem better than one which thoughtfully resolves the callers' problems. The call centre should collect performance data based on the number of enquiries *successfully* resolved per hour – a task which is much more difficult than simply logging the number of calls. A classic example of measuring what is easy to collect rather than what is important is often seen in education, where a committee will scrutinise a course outline and reference list but never attend lectures or observe a lecturer advising a student.

Sometimes, performance measures fail because they *do not* **monitor the external environment**. For example, a sales manager may monitor the sales figures of his or her team and discover a 10 per cent fall below target. The sales manager may then fire a large proportion of the team and recruit new sales people. However, data from the environment might show that in the country as a whole, sales had declined by 20 per cent and in relative terms the manager's sales team had been doing a good job. Failure to measure the environment probably led to firing high-performing staff and hiring recruits who would probably perform worse.

### 2 Number of control measures (metrics)

Control measures are sometimes called **metrics**. Control systems should have enough metrics to cover the main aspects of a system. However, it is not a good idea to have too many measures – otherwise the system becomes too cumbersome, time-consuming and bureaucratic, and gets in the way of the actual transformation of resources. As a very broad generalisation, it is better to limit the number of control measures to seven or fewer – perhaps only one or two per performance standard. This means that people will be able to remember, understand and observe the measures without constant references to books and charts. A small number also means that overlap between measures is likely to be spotted and eliminated. However, in large or complex organisations more than seven measures may be needed in order to give comprehensive control. For example, a handful of measures would not give proper control for a pharmaceutical giant such as GlaxoSmithKline. Such an organisation needs to have measures to cover its research laboratories, its production units, its sales force and its accounting procedures. The number of activities, processes and items that an organisation needs to control is referred to as **control variety**. In general, an organisation needs as many standards of performance as there are components to be controlled. This is known as the **law of requisite variety** (Ashby, 1964). It contends that a simple control system applied to a complex organisation will not be comprehensive and will miss important changes and developments.

### 3 Accuracy of control measures

*Accuracy* of control information is important. A stock control system which merely gives the total number of items in a food warehouse would not be very useful. It would be much better if the warehouse's contents were itemised by product and sell-by date. On the other hand, some control systems, especially those where data is automatically captured by computer, report actual performance to a ridiculous degree of precision. For example, the ink cartridge for a leading brand of bubble-jet printers contains 6 ml of ink plus or minus 0.05 ml, i.e. 5.95 ml–6.05 ml. However, at one time, the zealots in the quality control department measured the ink in cartridges to five decimal places and the control logs would be replete with figures such as 5.03462 ml. Printing the extra digits possibly consumed more ink than was measured by the last three digits! The unnecessary precision may make the information more difficult to interpret.

**CASE 10.2:** *Massaging control data in the British National Health Service*

An established index of the performance of a hospital is the time patients spend on trolleys waiting to be transferred to beds. In response to such targets, some hospitals merely removed the wheels from trolleys and claimed that patients were lying in beds. Another well-established performance measure is based on the time patients spend on waiting lists. Hospitals developed many techniques to manipulate this control measure. One ruse involved telephoning patients to enquire about their holiday plans and then, shortly afterwards, offering the patient an appointment during the period when they were known to be away. When the appointment was declined, the patient was removed from the list and the hospital's performance appeared to improve (Pitches, Berils and Fry-Smith, 2003). A spot survey revealed that about one-third of 41 health-care trusts in the UK were systematically fiddling their performance data (Audit Commission, 2003).

The accuracy of control metrics can also be undermined by conscious or unconscious **manipulation**. This is euphemistically termed "data massaging" or "performance optimisation". Goodhart, a high official in the Bank of England coined **Goodhart's Law** which, basically, says that "an index of performance ceases to be an accurate measure of actual performance within two months of its adoption". The reason is simple. Managers are rarely stupid. They know that if an index shows their performance is poor they, and their unit, will be penalised. Improving performance will probably involve a lot of hard work. On the other hand, massaging performance data on which the index is based involves less work. From their point of view, massaging data is a better investment of time. As the months and weeks go by skills in massaging performance data improve. Hence, after a short interval, more and more error is added by massaging and performance data become less and less accurate. There are stunning examples of Goodhart's Law in the British National Health Service (see Case 10.2).

The health sector is not alone, however, in fiddling performance. University departments are also masters. One index of performance is the number of research papers written by their academics. Some departments boost their performance artificially by encouraging staff with few publications to resign and head-hunting staff from other departments who have published more widely. **Smoothing** is a common form of "performance optimisation". It is very prevalent in sales and consultancy organisations. If, say, sales for one month considerably exceed a target, some of the sales will be "delayed" until the next month. Similarly, if sales fall below the target, some anticipated sales for the next month will be "advanced". Such ruses are used to maximise bonuses to managers and their teams. Manipulation is very widespread. It must be taken into account when designing control systems. It is essential either to choose performance measures that cannot be falsified or to install an audit system which will detect malfeasance. In many situations it is better to ensure that performance data are collected by someone who is totally independent of the people responsible for actual performance.

### 4 Reports of control measures

*Timeliness* is an important feature of control data. Information should be up to date so that prompt remedial action can be taken. In batch production of, say, microchips, data need to be collected every few minutes so that, should faults occur, corrections can be made quickly and only a few minutes' production will need to be scrapped. In other industries such as nuclear power generation, performance measures are instantaneous and problems can be identified very quickly indeed. However, in many circumstances it is better to base indicators of performance on longer time intervals. They will then be less contaminated by temporary factors. For example, it would probably be wrong to judge a sales force's performance upon a single week's, or even a single month's, sales figures. Such information will be inherently unstable. It will be influenced by exceptional events such as one or two very large orders or seasonal factors.

The *format* of control reports is important. A report should give the information needed to decide whether standards have been met. Its format should be compatible with performance standards and it should be consistent with the needs of those who will use it. Generally, a report should only contain information relating to factors which a person can change or influence.

### 5  Costs of performance measures

Finally, the *costs* of control measures should be kept within reasonable limits. These costs should certainly include the time of those who collect the information, prepare reports and decide upon appropriate action. It may also be wise to include the opportunity costs – the value of the work which these people would otherwise be performing. It is a fundamental rule of control systems that the cost of the system must be less than the cost of deviations which they seek to regulate. The rule can be illustrated by a trite example from libraries: it is wasteful to install a security system costing £20 000 per year when the cost of stolen books is £5 000 per year. A more realistic example can be found in one social service department where an administrator whose labour costs are £22 000 per year is employed to check expense claims of care assistants in order to avoid false travel claims amounting to £5 000 per year.

---

### CASE 10.3:  *Correcting MPs' expenses costs more than their fiddling!*

A recent saga involving British members of Parliament (MPs) is a classic example of a control system which costs more than the abuse it aimed to control. Members of Parliament are allowed substantial expenses. In 2009 the details of their claims became public and they showed that many MPs had made false claims. Once the control system (a democratic and free press) had detected the anomaly it was necessary to take corrective action by reviewing the system and clawing back money that was falsely claimed. Sir Thomas Legg asked 392 MPs make repayments. His work was deeply flawed – "lazy, incompetent and illogical" said one MP who had not made false claims. Many MPs were exonerated by a judge, Sir Paul Kennedy, who was asked to adjudicate appeals.

It later emerged that some MPs had, collectively, made false claims to the tune of £1.12 million. However, the Legg enquiry and the subsequent adjudications by Kennedy had cost the taxpayer £1.16 million. This control system had destroyed the value rather than creating it. This does not mean that malfeasance by MPs should be ignored. Rather it points to a need to design and execute a cheaper, more efficient control system.

## Comparing performance with standards

The diagram of a control system at the start of this chapter shows the third stage is a comparison of actual performance with the standard. It attempts to determine whether or not there is a deviation. In practice, the situation is more complex because many deviations are trivial and insignificant. Consequently, once a deviation has been detected it is necessary to make a further decision as to whether it justifies action. Deviations (sometimes called **non-conformities**) show up clearly on **control charts** that are used in production processes such as radiator manufacture. The nominal size of some radiators is 1 m but plumbers have no difficulty in using radiators that are 5 cm larger or smaller. The radiator manufacturer therefore sets the standard at 1m but is happy to ignore deviations up to 5 cm. It controls production by measuring every tenth radiator and plotting its length on a traditional control chart (see Figure 10.2).

Control charts show both the target performance and the actual performance (the length of every tenth radiator). They also show the region of unacceptable deviation. In the example of the radiator manufacturer it can be seen that production is proceeding smoothly, well within the region of acceptable performance. Then, for some reason, the radiators begin to get shorter. When they are 4 cm too short, a warning is activated and this triggers remedial action before the acceptance limit is breached. There is a time lag, and for a while the shortening of the radiators continues but the trend changes just before the deviation becomes unacceptable. The remedial action begins to take effect and the length of the radiators increases until it reaches the standard. It is quite usual for the correction to overshoot slightly before settling down at normal levels once more.

The radiator manufacturer set the level at which action should be taken (4 cm) on the basis of its experience. Other companies use "tectates" as their trigger for remedial action. A tectate is the level which contains 68 per cent of products when the system is working properly. The tectate equals one-half a **standard deviation** either side of the performance standard. In fact, the standard deviation is an important statistic in many statistical control processes. Some systems insist that faults occur less frequently than six standard deviations from the standard

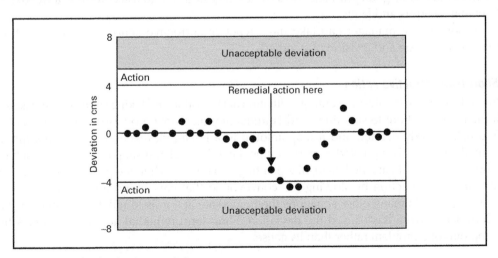

**FIGURE 10.2** Example of a classic control chart

(approximately three faults per 10 million instances). Such systems are usually called "six sigma" control systems. They are found most frequently in the manufacturing sector where many thousands of objects are produced and the control process is highly statistical, and in these instances the system will be called **statistical process control (SPC)**.

It is often assumed that a control process should only protect an organisation against **downside risk** (variation) – such as a failure to meet a production or a sales target. However, in many circumstances, the **upside risk** is just as important, if not even more important. A factory that produces too many goods will have had to pay extra costs for raw materials, etc. and then have to pay storage costs until a buyer can be found. It may even turn out that it will need to dump the excess production. Similarly, sales staff who take too many orders may cause an organisation to fail to meet its commitments. Such a salesperson may collect his or her commission before moving on to another job – leaving a trail of dissatisfied customers who then turn to competitors.

## Corrective action

The first three stages of a control are a waste of time unless some corrective action is taken. Many control systems only trigger action when there are significant deviations from standards. This is usually called **management by exception** – sometimes unkindly dubbed "the wake me if you need me school of management". While management by exception is economical and requires the least effort, it is usually misguided. Action should be taken when things *are* running to plan. For example, people maintaining production at satisfactory levels should be praised for their success. Furthermore, it might be advantageous to analyse why plans are implemented successfully so that they can be held as examples of good practice. For example, some university departments do detailed surveys if a course receives very good initial feedback from students. The aim is to identify the aspects of the course that make it so good. The results of the detailed survey are then used to improve other courses. This illustrates an important, but often forgotten principle: it is as important to use control as a fertiliser to enable good products and services to grow as it is to use control as a weedkiller to eliminate errors and faults.

In principle, a manager can take three types of corrective action: immediate action, longer-term action and revision of standards.

### *Short-term corrective action*

Immediate action involves accepting a situation at face value and taking short-term measures. It often called "trouble-shooting" and is frequently undertaken by junior management. It is usually clearly defined and it may amount to a knee-jerk reaction. Often appropriate immediate action is stipulated in an operational handbook. For example, a car manufacturer who discovers that cars are leaving the painting department while the paint is still tacky can take immediate action by slowing the conveyor so that cars spend longer in the drying compartment. In many other situations the immediate action is to talk to members of staff whose faulty work has caused the deviation. Short-term remedial action often treats the symptoms of a problem rather than its cause.

### Long-term corrective action

Sometimes a control system reveals either a large number of discrepancies or the frequent recurrence of the same discrepancy. It is then necessary to analyse the situation in order to identify the underlying cause or causes. Due to pressure of work some managers are unable to step back and take time to analyse the situation in sufficient depth. They may resort to more and more frequent use of immediate responses. However, it is much more efficient to identify long-term causes and take basic actions. For example, if cars frequently emerge with tacky paint, there could be underlying problems with either the chemical composition of the paint or the engineering specifications of the drying room. Both of these propositions will need to be investigated in depth. In other situations it may be necessary to redesign a job or equipment.

### Revision of standards of performance

When neither short-term nor longer-term action can resolve the discrepancy between a standard of performance and the actual outcome, it is usually necessary to re-examine the performance standards. For example, if a railway company cannot meet punctuality standards even after it has purchased new engines and retrained all staff, it would be appropriate to produce new timetables with slightly longer journey times. Unfortunately, revising standards of performance is often a soft option and may be used in preference to making hard decisions about equipment and staffing levels. If standards of performance are revised downwards, the strategic implications must be recognised and the organisation's strategy adjusted in an appropriate way.

## 10.3  Types of control system

The stages described in the previous section apply to all control systems. However, the nature of control systems and the way they are implemented varies widely. Control systems differ according to their location within an organisation, their orientation in time and the management function. Further, a recent trend is to view control as a system that encompasses the whole organisation.

## Control systems classified by *location* within organisations

As we saw at the beginning of this chapter, control is ubiquitous. A single control system is not appropriate to all situations and many different types have evolved. A major difference between types of control system depends upon whether it is located in a separate authority within an organisation (centralised control) or whether responsibility for control is widely dispersed throughout the organisation (decentralised control).

**Centralised control** exercises power along the lines outlined by Weber. It emphasises a hierarchical structure, rules, procedures and the uniformity of their application. Everything is well defined and standardised. Control resides in a formally constituted authority such as quality control or inspectors. Centralised control shares its philosophy with McGregor's Theory X – employees cannot be trusted and they will do things wrong unless they are closely supervised. However, employees can be

Weber p 73

channelled into doing things correctly using a mixture of threats (e.g. dismissal) and bribes (e.g. wages or promotion). Organisations using bureaucratic control tend to be rigid and produce high volumes of standardised products or services. Centralised control is sometimes called "bureaucratic" or "extrinsic" control.

**Decentralised control** has a more organic approach. It uses trust and shared values to guide the behaviour of employees. Power is dispersed throughout the organisation. It shares its philosophy with McGregor's Theory Y – employees want to do things right and can be trusted to monitor their own work. Organisations using decentralised control tend to be flexible, adaptive and produce one-off "creative" products or services. Decentralised control is sometimes called "intrinsic" or "organic" control. Authors such as Ouchi (1980) and Robbins and Decenzo (2003) refer to decentralised control as **"clan control"** because control is exercised by the group rather than an external authority. Table 10.2 compares and contrasts bureaucratic and decentralised control.

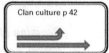
Clan culture p 42

| | **Centralised control** | **Decentralised control** |
|---|---|---|
| Organisational structure | Top down, formal, many levels, rigid, distrusting | Egalitarian, informal, flat, flexible, trusting |
| Control mechanisms | Rules and procedures that are systematically enforced | Socialisation, norms, values and self-control |
| Enforcement | Quality control, inspectors and auditors | Teams in which everyone monitors quality – especially their own work |
| Rewards | Extrinsic (e.g. pay, security, status, etc.) | Intrinsic (e.g. pride, satisfaction, work interest, self-development, etc.) |
| Outputs | High-volume, standardised, mature products and services | Small batch, novel or creative or individual products and services |
| Environment | Stable or slow changing | Volatile or quick changing |

**TABLE 10.2** Comparison of centralised and decentralised control

Few organisations are pure examples of either centralised or decentralised control: most occupy intermediate positions. However, the modern trend is to move away from centralised towards decentralised control. Decentralised control is a component of empowerment which means giving junior employees the ability to control their activities, take decisions within prescribed limits and assume responsibility for their actions.

## Control systems classified by *timing*

Control is frequently classified according to its timing and is divided into feed-forward control, concurrent control and feed-back control. Most organisations use a combination of all three types. Figure 10.3 shows how these types of control act upon inputs, the transformation process and on outputs.

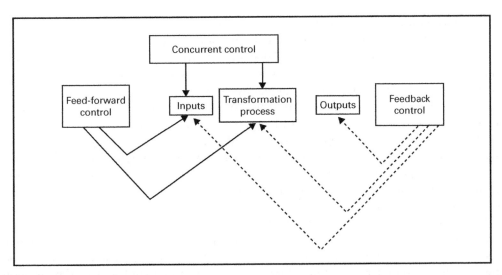

**FIGURE 10.3** The timing of control systems

**Feed-forward control** (Koontz and Bradspies, 1972) anticipates problems and attempts to prevent deviations from performance standards before they occur. It controls the resources an organisation puts into the transformation process. Generally, this means specifying the correct standards for inputs and then examining them to check that they meet those standards. The exact nature of feed-forward controls will depend upon the nature of the resource. For example, manufacturers of Blackberry palm computers will set a high specification for computer chips in order that the chips will perform the required functions reliably over a long period of time. They will then carefully inspect the chips from suppliers to ensure that they meet the specifications. Similarly, top-notch consultancy practices will attempt to control the quality of their future employees by recruiting people with high qualifications from prestigious universities and colleges. Another example of feed-forward control is the screening of potential borrowers by credit agencies to eliminate those who are likely to default on repayments. Feed-forward control is sometimes called "preliminary" control or "preventative" control. Unfortunately, it is impossible to anticipate all the problems, so other forms of control, concurrent and feedback, may be needed.

**Concurrent control** takes place at the same time as resources are transformed. Faults are never given the chance to "build up" and produce waste. A major feature of concurrent control is constant monitoring of the transformation process. Concurrent control is particularly important in continuous process industries such as refining oil. Instruments constantly measure the process and make adjustments if anything is going wrong. Instruments also alert a human when any major deviation from standards occurs. Another example of concurrent control is satellite tracking of a fleet of lorries to establish their progress at all times. Concurrent control occurs in many other situations – especially when a supervisor (sometimes called an "overlooker") works in the same room. The overlooker watches employees at work and, should something go wrong, takes immediate corrective action by steering and guiding the employee. Concurrent controls are sometimes called **"steering" controls**.

**Feedback control** evaluates products or services after they have been transformed. It focuses upon the end results. The archetypal form of feedback control is when a batch of completed work is sent to a quality control department, where an inspector checks each item and rejects any that are faulty. Faulty work is then returned to the operative for appropriate rectification or, if this is not possible, the faulty item is scrapped. Feedback control takes many forms. For example, many retail organisations employ "mystery shoppers" who make purchases while posing as members of the general public. They complete a report form on the service received. The report is logged and sent to the shop manager and the shop assistant. Other organisations use satisfaction surveys. For example, most colleges and universities use questionnaires at the end of a course to gather data on student satisfaction. Financial reports are also a form of feedback control since they give information on, say, a completed financial year.

Feedback control has two big *advantages*. First, it enables managers to compare actual outcomes with their plans. Hence, it gives useful information on the efficiency of the planning process and allows plans to be improved. Second, it gives employees clear information about how well they are performing. This information may be a powerful source of motivation. However, feedback control has one very major *disadvantage* – by the time faults have been detected a great deal of damage may have been done and corrective action may be very costly or impossible. A system that relies exclusively on feedback control will produce a great deal of waste. Sometimes feedback control is called "post"-control.

## Control systems classified by *function*

Although the components of control remain similar they are applied in different ways in different management functions.

For example, the *purchasing function* of an organisation will have specialised methods for ensuring the quality of its inputs. In some sectors of the manufacturing industry, such as metal refining, this will involve high-technology (high-tech) equipment and specialists who scientifically test the composition of the ores they use. Most organisations will also have some form of **inventory control** which aims to minimise the cost of maintaining large stocks of supplies. Some organisations, such as a large supermarket, will operate a system of inventory control using **economic order quantities**. They calculate the optimal size of an order in terms of transport and storage costs. They will then set a minimum level of stock and when the actual level of stock falls to this minimum level a new batch of items will be ordered. Because purchases are scanned at checkout, the processes can be automated so that a computer can generate the order which is sent to the supplier. The Argos chain of stores in the UK provides an excellent example of inventory control. Each store holds only a handful of each item in the catalogue – the exact number is determined by the previous buying patterns of its customers. As soon as an item is sold, a computerised system registers the sale and a replacement is immediately requisitioned from the warehouse. Perhaps the ultimate form of inventory control is *just-in-time* (JIT) scheduling. These systems, pioneered by Japanese industry, aim to use feed-forward control so that the need for an item is anticipated and an order placed so that the item will arrive "just in time" to be used. Just-in-time scheduling needs very careful planning and implementation but it can reduce stocks almost to zero, saving considerable amounts of money.

## CRITICAL THINKING 10.1  *Carpe diem gets control – for Goodhart!*

"*Carpe Diem*" meaning "seize the day" is a famous phrase coined by Horace the Latin poet. The phrase has many virtues; it is memorable, pithy, constructive and acceptably assertive. The fact that the phrase is in Latin adds valuable connotations: it is international, established and the people who use it are educated. In short it is an advertising agency's dream! Sage Software, based in Newcastle upon Tyne, specialises in business software and services. They call one of their programs, a timesheet used for tracking the time spent on projects, "Carpe Diem". It is an excellent, well-tested program, widely used by major corporations, IT firms and providers of professional services such as solicitors. Probably more than 30 per cent of the readers of this book will use Carpe Diem at some point in their careers. Organisations such as legal partnerships decide upon a time unit – usually six minutes (i.e. one-tenth of an hour). When, for example, a client telephones a clock starts and a client is billed for every six minutes, or part thereof. In due course, the client receives an invoice for the "billable hours" of service they have received. Initially, Carpe Diem was used as an administrative, back office, tool to collect data and generate invoices. Soon it started to be used as a control mechanism. Most individual solicitors are evaluated on the number of "billable hours" they log in a year. Their promotion, bonuses and even continuing employment are dependent, very largely, on the number of hours registered on the Carpe Diem system. Of course, solicitors and other professional people are not stupid. Following Goodhart's law, they soon learn to manipulate the system. A few pleasantries, a couple of hesitations and a caveat or two can turn a four-minute telephone conversation (1 unit) into a telephone conversation lasting six minutes and 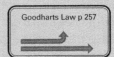 ten seconds (two units). This example demonstrates a number of common issues about control systems. *First*, it is common for data collected for different purposes and used at a later time for control purposes. *Second*, it demonstrates Goodhart's Law that indices of performance quickly degenerate after they are introduced so that they no longer reflect that performance with total accuracy. Third, it illustrates that collecting control data may alter people's behaviour in subtle but significant ways.

Next time you telephone your solicitor, investment adviser or IT consultant keep a check on the length of the call. There is a significant probability that it will last six minutes ten seconds, twelve minutes ten seconds, eighteen minutes ten seconds and so on. Of course, if you enjoy pleasantries, hesitations and caveats, it is money well spent!

*Production functions* usually have highly developed control systems that use both concurrent control and feedback control. In some sectors such as the pharmaceutical industry the control will involve high-tech methods where samples taken at each stage of the manufacturing process are subject to analysis in the laboratory. Even in less high-tech contexts the production function will carefully check its output. Techniques such as **total quality management (TQM)**, **statistical process control (SPQ)** and **quality circles** are common components of control systems in manufacturing operations.

Quality control in operations p 373

The *human resource (HR) function* has a distinctive set of controls to ensure that people meet performance standards. They may include feed-forward controls which specify the qualifications and licences that people in certain posts must possess. They include concurrent controls such as arrangements for supervision. The HR function will also control people's work behaviour through a system of appraisal and reward. Perhaps the final example of control systems concerning people will be disciplinary procedures that aim to correct major deviations from expected performance.

*Sales functions* use obvious controls such as sales turnover per month. They may also measure the profitability of sales. However, monitoring the performance of sales representatives presents particular problems: they operate away from the organisation and it is not easy to supervise their work. As noted earlier control of sales staff is made even more difficult because of their high turnover. A sales representative can make all kinds of exaggerated claims to close a sale, collect the commission and then quit before the consequences of her or his technique are realised. In the 1990s many UK insurance companies failed to exercise adequate control over their sales staff. As a result many members of the public were sold inappropriate insurance policies. When this was discovered, the insurance companies were required to compensate victims to the tune of £2 billion.

*Financial functions* are particularly keen on controls that reduce levels of fraud, theft or misappropriation. They establish comprehensive accounts which can be audited. The finance function will also control spending commitments to ensure that the organisation does not spend more money than it can afford. Further, the finance function will produce financial reports which management can use to control an organisation's financial health. Such reports use indices such as value added per employee, gross profit margin, return on equity and economic value added. These indices are described in more detail in Chapter 12, on budgeting.

## Control as an organisational system

Clearly, control is something that happens in all parts of an organisation. Recently, it has been understood that control should not be allowed to operate in an isolated, piecemeal way. It should be co-ordinated into a coherent system. Further, there are major differences in controlling ranks of employees performing the same monotonous tasks and the way that empowered, educated employees working on intricate tasks are to be controlled. Simonds (1995) identified four subtle levers of control for these people and, consequently, the whole organisation:

1 **Belief levers** use the key ethics and values of the organisation. They guide a large range of decisions and behaviours. To be effective they must be upheld by senior managers. Belief systems exercise control by obtaining people's commitment to the grand purposes of the organisation.

2 **Boundary levers** are often thought of as "minimum standards" which are set by management and consist of constraints on decisions and actions. Employees are free to be innovative and creative within these constraints. Boundary systems are particularly

important where employees are empowered to make significant decisions. Boundary systems exercise control by staking out the territory within which people can exercise freedom.

3 **Diagnostic levers** are close to the picture of controlling that has been given in the previous sections of this chapter. Diagnostic systems rely heavily on goal-setting, quantitative data, statistical analyses, etc. They are essential in getting the job done by transforming resources into something more valuable.

4 **Interactive levers** are the communications systems of the organisation such as the regular face-to-face contact between workers and supervisors. They also include reports, analyses and, particularly importantly, discussions in meetings. Interactive levers attempts to position the organisation for the future by clarifying strategic and other uncertainties. Interactive levers exercise control by ensuring that information flows freely throughout the organisation.

Simonds' levers of control are particularly appropriate in modern organisations where managers simply do not have sufficient time to supervise workers on a constant basis and were workers are empowered.

At about the same time that Simons was developing his levers of power, Beer (1994) was developing a slightly more complex view which he called the **viable systems model (VSM)** of control. The VSM envisaged five systems of control:

1 **the operational system** which controlled the performance of "productive" work

2 **the co-ordination system** which uses routines and standard operating procedures to ensure that individual units are stable, efficient and effective

3 **the management systems** which monitors performance, allocates resources and coordinates the activities of different units

4 **the intelligence system** which scans the environment and identifies opportunities and threats

5 **the policy system** establishes organisational values and objectives. It also balances the needs of the present situation with the organisation's likely future needs

Beer emphasises that all five systems are intertwined and linked to the business environment by **information channels and linkages**.

The work of both Beer and Simons was developed and synthesised by Ferreira and Otley (2009) into a framework for management control systems. It has three sorts of component:

1 **controls of performance** such as: targets, plans, performance indicators, evaluation and reward systems

2 **controls of strategy**

3 **controls of vision** which includes mission statements and key success factors

Ferreira and Otley note that their systems are linked by a series of feed-forward and feed-backward loops.

Excellent descriptions of the systems view of control are given by Herath (2007) and O'Grady, Rouse and Gunn (2010) and Taticchi, Tonelli and Cagnazzo (2010).

## 10.4  The balanced scorecard

L ord Kelvin, after whom the SI scale of temperature is named, is also famous for his statement "if you cannot measure it, you cannot improve it". In other words, "what you measure is what you get!" It follows that if a control system only measures financial information then you can only get improvements in financial results. In the past many control systems were based on financial data or data provided by management accountants. This is quite understandable since money is undoubtedly important. Some say that "money talks". They are wrong. Most practising managers know that "money *SHOUTS*!" Further, money is easy to quantify and measure. Nevertheless, emphasis on financial control means that many organisations are diverted from their wider goals. Every organisation has stakeholders who care about non-financial aspects such as social responsibility and its employees. To obtain balanced control of an organisation, financial controls need to be supplemented with controls that reflect other things such as customer and supplier image, the well-being of workers, innovation, etc. This basic idea was developed by Kaplan and Norton (1992 – a good read) into what is termed a balanced scorecard.

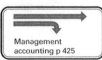

Management accounting p 425

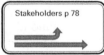

Stakeholders p 78

> 66 It is a set of measures that gives top managers a fast but comprehensive view of the business. It includes financial measures and complements them with measures on customer satisfaction, internal processes, and the organisation's innovation and improvement activities. 99

These measures were chosen because they were believed to be the drivers of future organisational performance. Kaplan and Norton encouraged people to think of the balanced scorecard as the indicators in an aeroplane cockpit. "For the complex task of navigating and flying an airplane, pilots need data and information on many aspects of the flight" such as fuel, air speed, altitude, direction, etc. A pilot who relies on just one indicator is an accident waiting to happen.

> 66 Similarly the complexity of managing an organisation today requires that managers be able to view performance in several areas simultaneously. 99

The balanced scorecard brings together, in a single management report, many of the elements that will determine the organisation's wider success. It forces managers to take a wider and more sophisticated view of controlling their organisation.

Kaplan and Norton recommend managers examine their organisations to identify key objectives in terms of:

1  What *financial objectives* must we achieve in order to satisfy our shareholders (or stakeholders)?

2  What *internal business process* must we excel at in order satisfy our shareholders and customers?

**3** How do we need to *learn and grow* in order to sustain our ability to change and improve in ways to achieve our vision?

**4** How do we need to *appear to our customers* in order to achieve our vision?

It should be noted that the contents of a balanced scorecard are closely linked to an organisation's vision and strategy. It is not necessary to have the same number of objectives in each category but there should be at least two. The total number of objectives should not be more than, say, 15, or complexity could lead to confusion (see Kaplan and Norton, 1996).

On their own, objectives are not enough to create a balanced scorecard. Each objective must be accompanied by a method of measurement (**outcome metrics**) and a target that should be achieved. Measures should be taken frequently, perhaps every three months, and the results displayed on a series of graphs representing dials (**the management dashboard**) that indicates clearly whether objectives are being met. Underperformance should evoke action or initiative to bring performance on that objective back to target.

Some organisations, especially local authorities and educational institutions, publish the results from their balanced scorecards on the Internet. A detailed explanation of how to produce a balanced scorecard is given by Niven (2006).

## 10.5  Dangers of control processes

Control processes are a vital part of good management. However, they have their dangers. The five main dangers are eliminating serendipity, cost, rigidity, distortion and ethics.

**1** Controls deploy power to ensure that plans are properly implemented. However, plans are the products of people's minds and it is not possible for people to anticipate all eventualities. Hence, from time to time, managers will encounter favourable situations produced by **good fortune (serendipity)**. If they are working in an organisational climate which has strict, rigid controls, they may eliminate serendipity. For example, modern control systems would have prevented Alexander Fleming from discovering penicillin. Modern quality assurance procedures would have made certain that the laboratory conformed to Heath and Safety requirements. Open windows would *NOT* be allowed. Consequently, dust containing the penicillin fungus could not enter a sterile environment to contaminate the agar jelly in a Petri dish – indeed an open Petri dish would not be allowed in any modern laboratory with half-decent controls. Further, had Fleming been subject to controls enforcing a production rate of experimental results, and writing "conformity reports" he would not have had the time to ponder the significance of a momentous chance event. In a similar vein many universities have instigated a system of committees to approve the content of courses. The time and effort needed to obtain consent to deviate from an "approved syllabus" inhibits teachers from making significant changes reflecting contemporary events. Eliminating serendipity has greatest consequences when an organisation's mission involves some kind of creativity.

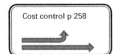

Cost control p 258

2 The dangers of control systems *costing* more than any errors was described in an earlier section.

3 Control systems may be appropriate when they are first installed. However, as the internal and external environments continue to change, control systems become *rigid* and less aligned with organisational needs. The tendency for control systems to stay the same over long periods inhibits *organisational change*.

4 Control systems are designed, on purpose, to alter people's behaviour. This would not create problems if all relevant aspects of organisational activity were covered. But they are not. So, they *distort behaviour* towards the "bits" that are. Shorter-term quantitative activities will be covered by robust controls while other activities will have either poor controls or none . This results in people being motivated to perform only those areas with visible controls. The control systems therefore *distort the behaviour* of employees. For example, where sales volume is the only area with controls, sales staff will concentrate only upon achieving high sales figures at the expense of profitability or customer loyalty. They may also forsake activities known as "organisational citizenship" such as training colleagues or public relations activities to promote the organisation in general. In universities and colleges there are highly visible control data for research activities (i.e. the number of published papers). Similar data for teaching activities are subjective and harder to collect. Consequently, there is a tendency for staff to focus upon research to the detriment of teaching. Students in such institutions should be quite vociferous in their support of staff who give teaching priority. Strict control systems can result in competitive organisations where there is a great deal of stress and tension (Jaworski and MacInnis, 1989).

Balanced scorecard
p 268

5 Control systems often raise *ethical issues* – especially privacy and freedom. For example, some organisations may wish to control the quality of their workforce by requiring all members of staff to be tested for drug use. Other organisations may wish to control the level of theft by insisting that all bags and purses are inspected by security staff when employees leave the premises. A few organisations monitor staff using closed-circuit television. Finally, some organisations check emails on work computers. The ethical issues involved are very complex. At a minimum, control systems that invade privacy should be explained to potential recruits at the time they make an application. Surveillance by closed-circuit television should be in the full knowledge of everyone who is observed. It must not be used where decency would be infringed (e.g. toilets or changing rooms). While the courts have upheld the rights of employers to inspect all emails sent from work computers, employees should be made aware of the policy when they apply.

Ethics p 466

Many abuses by controllers are covered up because the organisation is afraid that it might look stupid or incompetent or its reputation will be tarnished in some other way.

**CRITICAL THINKING 10.2** *Quis custodiet ipsos custodies?*

The close linkage between control and power was noted at the start of this chapter. Anyone in charge of an organisation's control system is a very powerful person. To a large degree they can exercise control over the behaviour of other people and thus over the organisation itself. Such power should not remain unchecked. The question arises "Who controls the controllers?" or as Plato might have said *"Quis custodiet ipsos custodies?"* ("Who will guard the guards themselves?"). Plato's answer was that they will guard themselves against themselves because of a noble lie: they believe they are better than other people and therefore have the responsibility to protect others. In other words, we must rely on the egotistical delusions of those in charge of the control system. Unfortunately some guardians are crooked and are not noble. Fraud by senior management is the hardest to detect; top managers know how to get around controls; very often they designed the controls and they *are* the control system. A classic example is the loss of £666 000 by the London Philharmonic Orchestra. Its general manager and financial director, Cameron Poole, used his knowledge and access to get round the system, devised by the auditors Deloittes, which in theory should have involved four people in raising a cheque. Poor control can also arise because the guardians are lazy, disinterested, inexperienced or simply looking the other way. The London Philharmonic Orchestra (LPO) had respected auditors checking the books, a chief executive and a board of "directors" plus an LPO trust which was full of distinguished business leaders. Many of these people had access to the fraudulent financial figures produced by Cameron Poole.

*Source*: (based on *The Times*, 23 March 2010)

The obvious answer to the *Quis custodiet ipsos custodies?* question is that "internal" guardians need to be controlled by bigger, external guardians or government regulators. Regulators, in turn, can be guarded by parliament or a democratic institution. The problem is that parliaments are rarely very good at exercising this control. In 2005 Europe's official financial watchdog, the European Court of Auditors, refused to sign off the European Union's accounts for the eleventh consecutive year because they are riddled with fraud and errors – especially the accounts for farm subsidies and regional development.

*Toolkit*

## 10.6  Control toolkit

Control is a very important aspect of managers' work. The following suggestions aim to provide useful guidance:

■ Investigate the costs and benefits of controls carefully. Remember to include less obvious costs such as increased workplace tension. Eliminate those controls where the benefits do not exceed the costs by a clear margin.

■ Examine the relationship between the organisation's strategy and plans and the control system. Eliminate those controls which are linked to neither. Introduce new controls where major elements of the plan or strategy are currently unrepresented. Produce a balanced scorecard.

■ Examine existing controls to determine whether they distort the balance of the organisation or if they could be manipulated with ease.

■ Examine cases of failures that have occurred in the past. Consider what extra feed-forward controls, concurrent controls or feedback controls will be needed to eliminate such failures in the future.

■ Reprimands to employees who do not meet standards should:
   – be immediate. Bad practice should not be given time to establish itself
   – be applied consistently each time standards are not met
   – focus upon actions and behaviour rather than the person's characteristics. They should emphasise the correct standards and behaviour rather than dwell upon incorrect and past behaviour. They should provide information which helps the person produce the correct actions
   – be given in a supportive and friendly way

   Some organisations adopt a policy of **progressive discipline** whereby the strength of any reprimand depends upon the severity of the deviation from standards and its frequency. A minor deviation which is an infrequent occurrence would receive only a light reprimand whereas a minor deviation which is frequent receives a strong sanction. A major deviation from standards or a minor one which has occurred frequently in the past would attract a very strong reprimand.

■ Adherence to standards should be recognised as actively as deviations from standards. People should be congratulated when they have achieved objectives as planned.

■ Above all, managers must remember that the vast majority of control systems cover less than 80 per cent of the performance of an employee. This 80 per cent of performance is unlikely to be measured with more than 70 per cent accuracy – especially if actual performance is gauged using subjective opinions of supervisors. It is therefore a simple arithmetical calculation that many control systems are, at best, about 56 per cent accurate!

# Activities and further study

## Essay plans

Produce essay plans for the following topics:

1 What are the characteristics of a good control system?
2 Give examples how feed-forward, concurrent and feedback control could be used in two named organisations of your choice (e.g. college, restaurant, hospital, charity, etc.).
3 How do modern frameworks for organisational control differ from earlier ones – and why?

## Web activities

1 Surf the Web to find extra reading on the subject of management control. The following sites are excellent places to start your search:

http://www.accel-team.com/control_systems/index.htm

www.businessballs.com/sixsigmadtifactsheet.pdf

http://www.sixsigmaiq.com/

2 Surf the Web to find information about famous failures of management control. The following sites are good places to start:

http://www.projectsmart.co.uk/avoiding_project_failure.html

http://www.ohnonews.com/perrier.html

Failures you might like to investigate include: failure to control the costs of the Scottish Parliament; the UN's failure to control granting of oil quotas to Saddam Hussein's Iraq; failure of insurance companies to control the selling tactics used by their salesforces.

3 Log onto the Sage website and read the promotional material for their timesheet program, Carpe Diem.

4 Research the ways that Rupert Murdoch, Conrad Black and Azil Nadir (of Polly Peck) abused their position as guardians of their organisational control systems.

## Experiential activities

1 Choose an important activity of your life. Design a simple system to monitor and control the way it progresses.

**2** Talk to two people from different organisations. Ask them about the control processes used in their work organisations and the effect that these processes have on them.

**3** Think of a control system you have experienced. List the way that you and others have used the system to your own advantage

## Recommended reading

**1** Herath, S.K. (2007) "A framework for management control research", *The Journal of Management Development*, **26**(9), 895–915. A good overview of control but probably too extensive. Focus on pages 896–898 (nature of control, control processes and need for control) and pages 904–911 (Whitley's dimensions of control systems: the relationship between control and organisational strategy, organisational structure, corporate culture and management information systems).

**2** Turner, P. (2010) "Primary schools braced for SATS tests boycott", *Financial Times*, 9 May. An example of how Goodhart's Law applies to exam results.

**3** Economist (2008) "Balanced scorecard" *Economist*, 26 December. A quick introduction to Kaplan's notion of the balanced scorecard and its benefits.

# Reporting and Communicating

## Chapter contents

## ❖ LEARNING OBJECTIVES

After reading this chapter you should be able to understand the importance of communication in all aspects of management. You should be able to avoid some of the problems of poor communications. In particular you should be able to:

* **define** and **explain** the concept of communication

* **explain in detail** each of the five main stages of communication derived from the work of Shannon and Weaver

* **contrast** verbal communication with non-verbal communication

* **list** and **briefly compare** seven different communication channels

* **explain** the effect of misuse in communication channels and list the changes a message is likely to undergo as it is repeated

* **draw a diagram** depicting at least three kinds of communication network

* **briefly describe** five important listening skills

* **explain** the modifications which have been made to Shannon and Weaver's communication model

* **give** at least seven practical tips for writing reports and at least seven practical tips for making presentations

Very simple communication failures can have disastrous consequences. For example, in November 1940 British air defence knew that a large air raid on either Coventry or Wolverhampton was imminent. On the 14 November a British boffin, Professor R.V. Jones, detected navigation beams guiding the German bombers and he correctly deduced that the target was Coventry. A clerk made an error and transposed some of the numbers of the grid reference given to him. Air defences were deployed to protect Wolverhampton. That night 554 citizens of Coventry died and a further 865 were wounded as a result of a very "successful" air raid on a city that was virtually undefended.

Communication errors also occur in commerce and industry but they are usually kept secret. An exception was the chief executive of Barclays who inadvertently admitted to a House of Commons committee that he did not use Barclaycard because it was too expensive! Whether or not poor communication is kept private, the consequences can be major: a boardroom split, a lost sale or the wrong service delivered to the wrong client. The classic example of a management communication gaffe was by Gerald Ratner.

### CASE 11.1: *Doing a "Ratner"*

Poor communication skills have been the downfall of many CEOs (Budd, 1993). Perhaps the most spectacular example is the case of Gerald Ratner, head of a chain of jewellers with shops in virtually every major British town. During a speech to the Institute of Directors he joked that one of his firm's products was "total crap" and that some of the earrings it sold were "cheaper than a prawn sandwich" and probably would not last as long. The media seized on the speech. Sales plummeted and £500 million was wiped off the company's value. Mr Ratner was forced off the board and the company had to spend huge sums on rebranding.

Ratner is not the only example of "foot in mouth disease". David Shepherd, marketing manager at Top Man, was asked to clarify their target customers and commented "Hooligans or whatever". He added "very few of our customers have to wear suits at work . . . They'll be for his first interview or first court case".

Asda's Andy Clarke "did a Ratner" in August 2010. In his first speech as their CEO he was asked to explain why its sales had fallen. He chose unfortunate words and admitted that his supermarket's food was not up to scratch! Critics commented that a mistake like this is unusual in one of a CEO's first speeches. Fortunately, the market took the benign interpretation that Andy had taken the first step in solving a problem – recognising that a problem existed. However, the incident does highlight the importance of good managerial communication.

Managers spend more time in communicating than in any other activity. Mintzberg (1973) estimated that managers spend 59 per cent of their time in scheduled meetings. They spend a further 10 per cent of their time in informal meetings and 6 per cent of their time telephoning. Thus, without counting the time they spend on written communication, managers spend no less than 75 per cent of their time communicating. Good communication ability is an essential skill for all managers.

## 11.1  Definition of communication and reporting

Communication may be defined as:

66    an interpersonal process of sending and receiving symbols that have messages
      attached to them.

*(Schemerhorn, 2002)*    99

A similar but less technical definition is given by Miller, Catt and Carlson (1996, p. 71)

66    The sharing of meaning between the sender and receiver of a message.    99

In a managerial and, rather starry-eyed, context communication may be formally defined as:

66    An interactive process of providing and passing of information that enables an
      organisation to function efficiently and for employees to be properly informed
      about developments. It covers all kinds of information and the channels of
      transmission.

*(After ACAS, 1982)*    99

All of these definitions make it clear that the essence of communication is the transfer of information from one person's mind to another person's or other people's mind. They also make it clear that the information is transferred using symbols (words, numbers, diagrams, gestures, etc.) using some channel (face to face, telephone, text message, newspaper, letter, etc.).

It is often implied, by definition such as that offered by ACAS, that transfer of information is a good thing. A moment's thought reveals that this is not necessarily so. Conmen are invariably good communicators, so are many dictators. In less dire situations, the purpose of much communication is to obfuscate. Governments, politicians, financial institutions and some industrialists expend a huge effort on communications designed to ensure that the public do *not* appreciate the "real" situation.

In hierarchical days, when Fayol first identified the management processes represented by the mnemonic POSOCRB (see page 72), communication was synonymous with reporting. Bosses needed information from subordinates in order to co-ordinate their activities and make grand decisions. Fayol grudgingly acknowledged that bosses needed to communicate to subordinates in order to give orders and instructions. Reporting therefore focused on upward communication. Nowadays, the communicating is much more complex. It also includes downward communication and horizontal communication. Further, increased use of teleworking, part-time staff and fixed-contract or short-term employees has made organisational communication much more difficult.

Communication, good or bad, pervades any organisation. Shannon and Weaver (1949) produced what is probably the most thorough analysis of the stages of communication, but subsequent researchers have modified their model.

**CRITICAL THINKING 11.1** *A good day to bury inconvenient information*

The ultimate example of using communication to obfuscate must be the email sent by Jo Moore (an information officer in the British government) to press officers. On the day that the jets had been crashed into the twin towers of the World Trade Center in New York (9/11) she realised that the tragedy would monopolise media attention and people would not notice unpalatable domestic news. She sent an insensitive and cynical email to information officers that: "It is now a very good day to get out anything we want to bury. Councillors' expenses?" Unfortunately the email was "leaked" (a salutary example of informal communication and the dangers of trying to hide information in a free society). Jo Moore's email is by no means an isolated example. Government information is sometimes awash with disinformation. When a head of state issues a press release, confirming his or her full confidence in a minister, it is very likely that he or she has authorised "an adviser" to talk to the Minister about ways their "retirement" can be arranged a little later, on health grounds or the need to spend more time with the family, etc. Company communications are also sometimes awash with disinformation. Chief executives of companies about to go bankrupt routinely assure shareholders of the organisation's financial health (it gives them time to sell their own shareholdings!).

## 11.2  Stages of communicating (Shannon and Weaver)

In theory, communication can be divided into discrete stages but, in practice, these often occur simultaneously. In fact, communication is a very dynamic process in which the message, the channels and people's perceptions are live and constantly change. Clampitt (1991) identified that one approach to communication can be likened to the flight of an arrow: information flows in a direct line from a sender to a recipient. Based upon the early work of Shannon and Weaver, the flight of information passes through six main stages:

1  **deciding** to communicate
2  **encoding** the message
3  **transmitting** message via a channel
4  **receiving** the message
5  **decoding** the information
6  **taking action** and **sending feedback**

### Stage 1: Deciding to communicate

People often assume that communication is always good but as we saw in Critical Thinking Box 11.1 this is not true. Communicating can be malevolent. Further, it can be counter-productive. Communicating nonsense merely blocks a communication channel so that other messages may not get through. As Aesop's fable about the boy who sent several nonsense messages about wolves illustrates, wrong or unnecessary messages desensitise a channel so that later, truthful messages are ignored. Some people are "communicaholics". They need to check situations and give instructions so frequently that it distracts others from their work. Communicaholics use their mobile phone on trains and in restaurants incessantly to "touch base" and check "whether anything has happened".

The dangers of over-communication are greatest when likely recipients are deluged with new information. Typical examples are bombarding new employees with the minutiae of long-term information when they are struggling to absorb information that will help them cope with the first week. It is silly to organise training seminars that start at 8 a.m. and continue to 8 p.m. Fatigue inhibits learning and later information tends to block out earlier information. This is called "retroactive inhibition". The speed and ease of email has increased the likelihood of irrelevant and unnecessary communication and spam.

However, the dangers of not communicating are greater. Sometimes people may not realise that they have information that is relevant to colleagues. Others may realise that their knowledge is relevant but they may fail to communicate because they assume that it is already known to colleagues. When this happens there is a total communication failure that is difficult to correct. In general, the balance of advantage lies in communicating information rather than withholding it.

Traditional models of communication (e.g. Shannon and Weaver, 1949) assume that people are clear about the messages they wish to transmit. In fact, this is often not the case. Holden (2001, page 257) points out that "the purpose of a communication is not always clear, and communication might have multiple goals for a single message".

## Stage 2: Encoding the message

Once the need to communicate has been recognised information needs to be put into symbols that can be transmitted. This is known as "encoding". It must be emphasised that information is never communicated directly. Symbols are communicated. Wrong symbols mean the message may be inaccurate. There are many types of symbols but, generally, they are divided into two types: verbal and non-verbal.

### *Verbal communication*

Verbal communication consists of words, numbers, diagrams or pictures – anything that could be traced or copied with a pen. It is the type of communication that naturally springs to mind when the topic of communication is mentioned. Verbal communication is the primary means by which we convey factual information. Verbal communication may also convey emotions such as the feelings of relatives in a deathbed scene in a novel. Verbal communication usually flows from a conscious decision to transmit information to other people.

Encoding suitable messages with numbers is usually very precise – provided both the sender and receiver are numerate. Encoding with words is less certain. Words have slightly different meanings to different people. A difference in meanings can be stark. "Knock me up in the morning" means one thing in Northern England and something quite different in northern USA. In French the word "demand" is a mild word that means "to ask": in

---

### CASE 11.2:  *Words versus numbers in communication*

Young and Oppenheimer (2009) presented people with information in either a verbal form, such as "very high risk", "high risk", . . . "very low risk" and numerical form such as ".05%", "1.0%". . . "50%", etc. They found that people overestimate possibilities that are described in verbal forms such as "low risk" or "people may occasionally experience". If people are verbally recommended new behaviours that have low risks they are unlikely to follow the recommendation. Young and Oppenheimer's research indicates that using words to indicate the risks of *not* doing new things (i.e. innovating) is better than using numbers. The moral of this research is to *encourage* people to do new things you should use numbers. To warn people about the *dangers* of avoiding new things, you should use words.

---

English it is strong and means "to insist". Differences in the shades of meaning frequently involve emotional connotations. For example, the factual meaning of the word "charity" is the free transfer of wealth from one person to another. To a capitalist it conveys the emotions of kindness and humanity. In contrast, to a communist it may convey a sly, capitalist attempt to assuage guilt. Such differences have huge implications for managers – especially those who are managing in a different culture or social group. It is important they use neutral words and avoid those loaded with emotional connotations. For example, it would be unwise for a manager of a multinational company in an Arab country to attempt to galvanise local employees in a "crusade" for efficiency. The scope for cultural misunderstanding is increasing in a world of increasingly diverse workforces (see Reilly and DiAngelo, 1990).

There are well-documented differences in the way that men and women select and encode messages (Borisoff, 1992). Women tend to encode messages with words indicating intimacy (sharing problems and responding to the needs of others) while men tend to use words that have connotations of status and independence. Women also tend to use more qualifying phrases such as "it seems to me" and "I understand" (Hirschman, 1975). Haag and Laroche (2009) found that chief executive officers who were good at understanding emotions were able to communicate more effectively within the boardroom in crisis situations.

Culture and gender are not the only reasons why people encode messages differently. Intelligent people, most managers and specialists, will feel the need to give a full and detailed explanation of their ideas. This may mean that the complexity of their messages will be too high. It is a very good idea to observe the KISS principle of communication – **K**eep **I**t **S**imple, **S**tupid. Good communicators give concrete examples which show the practical application of their abstract ideas. Personality also determines how people encode ideas. Introverts, for example, will encode ideas in a detailed, accurate and objective way, while extroverts will encode the same ideas in grand, colourful, sweeping terms that play upon subjective emotions. There is some evidence that the structure of an individual's brain influences the way a message is encoded. For example, if the left half of the brain is dominant, a message will be encoded in a way that emphasise facts and logic. If the right side of the brain is dominant the message will be encoded in terms of feelings and emotion. Similarly, if the part of the brain that processes visual information is well developed, the message will have lots of visual images such as "You can see that it is clear" and the speaker will use lots of diagrams and pictures. If the auditory part of the brain is well developed, the message will eloquent, fluent and contain phrases such as "I hear what you are saying". The study of the way brain structure influences communication is called **neuro-linguistic programming**.

Verbal communication, especially written communication, is under conscious control and is open to conscious manipulation. Verbal communications are therefore frequently mistrusted. People often look for non-verbal cues in order to cross-check what people say and write.

### *Non-verbal communication*

Non-verbal communication consists of postures, gestures and grunts (para-linguistics) and is usually unconscious. It is almost impossible to avoid sending non-verbal messages. For example, the lack of a response to a greeting will convey disapproval. Non-verbal communication conveys powerful but simple emotional messages. It is the carrier wave that sets the context for the details in verbal communications. If a non-verbal message conflicts with a verbal one, the non-verbal one will prevail. Actions speak louder than words.

Probably the most important non-verbal cue is *eye contact*. Humans are exquisitely sensitive to the eye movements of others and can identify their direction of gaze to within a few degrees. They can tell whether other people are looking at individual features of their face such as eyes or mouth. Avoidance of any gaze sends the message that a person desires no contact. This is a useful signal of avoidance in crowded situations such as lifts. Purposefully looking down while listening signals deference, a cycle of fleeting eye contact and looking sideways indicates guilt and shiftiness. Prolonged looking at someone's eyes can indicate confrontation or romance, depending on the exact context. During a one-to-one conversation, there is a delicate choreography of eye movements. Patterns of eye contact differ from culture to culture and this can be the cause of misunderstandings. In some cultures it is considered polite to look away while a superior is speaking but a western person might interpret this as shiftiness or insolence.

*Facial expressions* are keenly observed since they are not usually under total conscious control and frequently indicate a person's true feelings. For example:

- Raised eyebrows signal amazement or disbelief.
- Narrow eyes and pursed lips signal anger.
- Frowns signal unhappiness or hostility.
- Biting or trembling lips signal anxiety and worry.
- Smiling signals friendliness, pleasure, happiness and sometimes a desire to please.

A person's *voice* also gives information. A strong, clear, low voice without hesitations signals confidence and certainty. A high-pitched, shaky voice indicates nervousness. Broken, hesitant speech sends the message that the speaker is unsure of him or herself and is unprepared.

*Gestures* of limbs and fingers often indicate underlying emotional states. Nods are particularly important; they mean a person is paying attention and is in agreement, while shaking of the head signals strong disagreement. Shrugging shows indifference. Fidgeting, especially with fingers, touching face and hair with fingers and shifting from foot to foot indicate nervousness. Doodling can indicate either nervousness or boredom. Rubbing a finger around the collar is also a sign of guilty nervousness. Finger-pointing denotes authority. It also indicates displeasure. Repeated finger-pointing in males indicates anger and is often a precursor of a brawl. Gestures can be brought under conscious control and are often used effectively by politicians, celebrities and speakers.

*Posture* is another important non-verbal cue that is often called **body language**. Sitting upright on the edge of a chair and leaning slightly forward indicates active listening and interest. Sitting with legs slightly apart and arms slightly bent down one's side indicates openness. Hands on hips signals anger while folded arms indicate a determined unresponsiveness. Slouching generally shows boredom but this can be a source of confusion since some male teenagers use slouching to send a message that they are "cool" and relaxed!

*Dress* sends non-verbal messages. At one time one's school tie and the colour of one's collar (white or blue) sent crude and often erroneous signals about status and character. Today the signals are more complex, but probably equally erroneous, and are encoded by artefacts such as the exact brand of jeans or the ring tone on a mobile telephone as well as less subtle messages printed on a T-shirt. Most organisations have a dress code that sends messages about the organisation. The egalitarian ethos of some Japanese organisations is often signalled by all levels of the organisation wearing the same design of overall. In the armed forces rank is explicitly signalled by the stars or "stripes" on a person's uniform. In some creative advertising agencies the media people are expected to conform to the norm of non-conformity!

The *physical setting* (sometimes called **proxemics**) of any communication sends strong non-verbal signals. For example, a meeting with a superior manager in an office where he or she is seated behind a desk will be shorter and more formal and will tend to make a subordinate talk more about their own achievements than, say, a meeting in a pub. Indeed, the layout of offices (open plan or individual offices) sends signals about an organisation's culture. Hurdley (2010) gives an excellent, detailed account of the non-verbal signals given by the corridors in a large university building. Even the physical distance across which a dialogue occurs has implications. In Anglo-Saxon countries distances greater than 2 metres will communicate an impersonal, remote relationship, a distance of 1 metre will indicate a working, business relationship, while a distance less than 0.5 metre will indicate an intimate, emotional relationship of some kind. These distances may be different in other cultures. For example, they tend to be smaller in Arabic countries – the British are, literally, "stand-offish". Such cultural differences can cause complications, confusion and annoyance.

## Stage 3: Transmission via a channel

Once encoded, a message must be transmitted to another person or group via a channel. Many types of communication channels exist. The choice is important. Indeed, Marshall McLuhan (1964) claimed that the channel used can actually alter the message transmitted. He coined the famous phrase "the medium is the message". The form of a message (print, visual, musical, etc.) determines the way in which that message will be perceived – an important message scribbled on a scrap of paper will be perceived as inconsequential, whereas a trivial message beautifully typed on a large sheet of heavy paper will tend to be seen as important. Kira, Nichols and Apperley (2009) contrasted two different channels of communicating with customers. One channel consisted of face-to-face communication in the presence of a computer. The other channel consisted of a telephone link, again, in the presence of a computer. They looked at the differences that the channels made to planning a journey. The task was completed significantly quicker when the link was via telephone. Further, a telephone link induced participants to multitask: they would use the computer and talk at the same time. In the face-to-face situation subjects either used the computer or communicated to the other person. Surprisingly, there was little difference between the satisfaction of the people involved. It would seem that although telephone interaction has fewer communication cues, such as body language, it is not an impoverished channel of communication. But it is less time-consuming and more task focused.

As a rough approximation, communication channels can be divided into two groups: personal communications to one other person or a small group of people, and mass communications to large numbers of people.

### Personal communication

Personal communication can take many forms such as direct contact, telephone, email, fax and letters. The vast majority of communications involve "face-to-face contact" at a one-to-one level or a one-to-several level. Recent evidence of the importance **one-to-one** channels of communication is given by Bennett, Mousley and Ali-Choudhury (2008). They investigated the way that marketing specialists transferred knowledge to people in non-profit organisations. They found that knowledge transfer largely took place through face-to-face communication and occasionally through formal teamwork. Despite its importance, face-to-face communications can have many problems, which are listed in an excellent paper by Eppler (2007). After summarising the literature and conducting several focus groups he identifies five main types of problem that can arise when experts and decision-makers communicate:

- *difficulties caused by experts* such as the use of overly technical jargon, not relating the information to the problem facing the decision-maker and jumping into long-winded details before giving a general summary
- *difficulties caused by managers* such as not clarifying the aims of the meeting, a reluctance to discuss details and a lack of technical know-how – especially if they have technical but outdated background
- *difficulties caused by interaction between decision-maker and expert* such as inappropriate stereotypes on both sides and confusion about their reciprocal roles
- *difficulties caused by the situation* such as time constraints, distractions, external interruptions and information overload
- *difficulties caused by the organisational context* such as the differences in departmental or professional priorities. For example experts may emphasise quality and reliability whereas decision-makers may emphasise time and money.

Personal communication can also involve the **one-to-many** level where one person can communicate with thousands. Often the communicator will employ a charismatic appeal to core values. They make each person feel that they are speaking directly to them. The evangelist Billy Graham and the dictator Adolf Hitler were masters at this type of communication. In face-to-face contact both the originator and the recipient are physically present. The latter can hear the spoken words and see or hear all the non-verbal cues. Managers much prefer direct contact because it is quick, has immediacy and offers all the information contained in both verbal and non-verbal cues. Managers tend to dislike formal written documents. They feel that by the time they are written, checked and delivered the information may be out of date. Furthermore, they know that writers of formal documents will be careful and circumspect in what they write – omitting speculation and contentious information. In principle **video-conferencing** should be almost as good as face-to-face contact since participants receive all visual and oral cues. It also allows communication between people who are hundreds or thousands of miles apart without incurring huge travel costs. However, video conferences are more predetermined, formal and subject to more rigid time constraints. Participants in a video conference may also be suspicious that important things may be happening "off camera".

---

### CASE 11.3: *The medium is the message*

The classic example of the medium altering the message was the 1960 presidential election where the two contenders, Nixon and Kennedy, debated the issues. Radio listeners believed that Nixon won the debates with clearer, better informed, more coherent answers. However, voters who watched the same debate on television believed that Kennedy was better. In addition to hearing his answers they saw his young, handsome, clean-cut appearance. Nixon's suit merged with the studio and he appeared to need a shave. Kennedy won the election but if Nixon had worn a different suit and had had better make-up the result could have been very different. Nowadays, politicians often have "image consultants" in a studio to check the effects of the set, lighting, make-up and clothes before they go on air at a party conference or in a pre-election debate.

---

Managers like the *telephone* as a channel of communication. While there are no visual cues, there are many other non-verbal ones such as enthusiasm, hesitations, etc. that help put the overt verbal message into context. Providing the two people know each other, the telephone has the same immediacy as direct contact. *Letters* and *memos* are excellent channels for transmitting detailed, formal and important information. It has been said that memos are written not to inform the reader but to protect the backs of the writers. The letter heading, the quality of the paper and the format of the letter give important non-verbal cues about the writer and their organisation. A facsimile (fax) combines some of the qualities of a letter (minus some non-verbal cues such as quality of paper) and the immediacy and spontaneity of the telephone. As a channel of communication emails lack the non-verbal cues of the telephone or letter but they have a great deal of immediacy and spontaneity – perhaps too much spontaneity. In the heat of the moment it is far too easy to press the "send" button for an ill-considered and potentially incriminating email.

One of the most popular means to achieve personal communication is *workplace tours* where, typically, managers walk around their areas of responsibility, surveying the situation and apparently "chatting" to their team. This is often called "walking the job" or "Management by walking about" (MBWA). These tours provide a rich source of communication. A manager can grasp the situation in their area of responsibility directly. Tours make it easier for their team to communicate their concerns. They also provide informal opportunities to give the team specific and up-to-date information. Finally, tours are an essential way of building trust between the team leader and team members. Some organisations set up specific ways for managers to communicate with customers. For example, senior executives may timetable one day a month to talk to customers. This provides a communication channel where they can receive direct information about issues such as the reliabilities and capabilities of systems such as invoicing and servicing. Similarly, senior executives at some hotel chains spend time working as porters.

---

## CASE 11.4:  *The communication of Cafédirect*

Cafédirect was a fair trade pioneer. It was formed in 1991 by a consortium of Oxfam, Tradecraft, Equal Exchange Trading and Twin Trading. In order to communicate its ethical brand to consumers it carefully chooses both its message and its channels. Cafédirect, attuned its message according to the brand's stage of development:

- *Solidarity era (1993–99)* – use of simple packaging depicted the product's producers. It aimed to connect the consumer to the coffee growers. For example many posters showed farmers enduring hardship or illustrating pride. At the end of this period their communications implied that they were more ethical than their competitors and they attacked the "fat cat" approach of other organisations

- *Marketing development era (1992–2002)* – they tried to divest its charity image and establish itself as a quality product. The Fairtrade® mark was prominently displayed as a unique selling point. They changed their product's name to 5065 – the average height at which the coffee beans were grown. Many other products were displaying the Fairtrade® mark and it was no longer strong as a unique selling point. Consequently, CaféDirect reduced the symbol size on its packaging

- *Mass market era (2002 to date)* – widening its range of products (from budget to premium) but then constructing different communications according to the target market for each individual product. Communications also emphasised the organisation's percentage of profits that it hands back to producers. Its public relations effort has tended to emphasise stories of sustainability and shared ownership as reasons why people should prefer to buy its brand.

Cafédirect has obtained a strong image despite the surprising fact that it has never used television as a communication channel. Instead it has used a clever combination of volunteers, network associates, journalism and print advertising.

*Source*: based on Davies, Doherty and Knox (2010).

### Mass communication

Channels of mass communication have been studied extensively. Some old, but still very valid, studies by Hovland (1957) looked at the way mass messages should be encoded. In general such messages should not try to frighten people into doing things (the technique backfires because people have a tendency to shut out threatening stimuli). Both sides of an argument should be given (this makes the message more resistant to counter-propaganda) and messages should be given by authority figures and celebrities.

Hovland also discovered that a **two-step flow of information** operated in channels of mass communication. Mass messages are first detected by a relatively small number of opinion leaders who avidly attend to media in their area of interest. The opinion leaders digest and interpret the information and then pass *their interpretation* to a much larger number of people by informal conversation and other forms of direct contact. The opinion leaders act as **gatekeepers** who are a special kind of communication channel. They are particularly important when knowledge needs to be transferred across organisational boundaries. Gatekeepers need to be able to interpret and reinterpret lots of information – often by using concrete examples that are easy to understand. They also need to use their knowledge of the organisation to adapt information so that it is appropriate for the specific setting (Cranefield and Pak, 2007).

**Newsletters** and **company newspapers** are the traditional forms of mass communication in organisations. They aim to keep employees informed of new developments and make them feel that they are a key part of the organisation. They are characterised by downward communication, i.e. giving workers the information management wishes them to know. Many organisations try to soften this harsh fact with "talk back" columns where employees can express a view. Much of the content in newsletters and company newspapers is discounted as "management propaganda". Modern equivalents of newsletters and company newspapers are company websites, Facebook pages, bloggs and ebulletins. **Podcasts** and **presentations** by senior figures at "company days" or conferences are other organisational channels of mass, downward communication. Many companies are avid users of Twitter and tweeting to promote their ethos and company image. These channels have been found unsuitable for selling but they are useful in providing quick customer service and their analysis is a cost-effective way of gauging contemporary customer reaction.

Organisations can communicate to large numbers of workers using meetings. For example, in the 1980s many organisations set up intersecting **quality circles** (see Chapter 15). Information would be passed from circle to circle until it was known by most people in the organisation. **Team briefings** were also popular. The chief executive would brief department heads and the information would be cascaded down the organisation. The department heads would then brief middle managers who, in turn, would brief junior managers and the junior managers would brief operatives and so on, until everyone in the organisation had been briefed. A typical team briefing would be held at least once a month and would last for 30 minutes including time allowed for participants to ask questions. **Consultative committees** with trade unions or staff associations are another useful way of transmitting messages to large numbers of workers.

Managers often forget the existence of information channels outside their direct control. In most organisations there are **trade unions** or **staff associations** which communicate to their members on a regular basis. Indeed, some trades unions are better at communicating with their members than the management of an organisation is at communicating with its employees. When this happens management loses a lot of control and influence. It is said that a substantial part of the labour relations problems in the British car industry in the 1970s occurred because union communications prevailed over management communications.

The organisational **grapevine** is often overlooked. Traditionally information passes informally by word of mouth or email, from friend to friend or from organisational ally to organisational ally. An organisational grapevine is characterised by two features. First, it is very fast. A whole organisation can get news of an event within 24 hours – long before a newsletter is printed. Second, organisational grapevines are notorious for distorting the information they transmit. Nowadays, the internal grapevine has additional speed since employees can use electronic methods such as Facebook or Twitter to spread information and gossip. The ease with which employees can now communicate with each other without the information being "filtered" by management shifts substantial power from the managers of an organisation.

**External channels** of communication can also influence the flow of information within an organisation. For example, an organisation can issue newsletters, send emails and organise team briefings until it is blue in the face but claims of financial success will not be believed in the face of a critical article in a **prestigious newspapers** such as the London *Financial Times* or the Singapore *Business Times*. Similarly, a petroleum company's eco-friendly assertions can be dented by a well-researched report from an environmental pressure group.

**Professional grapevines** operate via informal chit-chat at conferences, meetings and telephone calls. They are largely outside management control, yet they transmit information both within and outside the organisation. In general, management communication is most credible when it deals with detailed, operational information. However, when more general and evaluative information is transmitted, managerial channels will often be discounted. Information sent by informal and external channels will have greater credibility. This may even happen in situations where the management version lies closer to the truth!

Channels of communication are also needed to **obtain information** *from* large numbers of people. They include suggestion schemes and attitude surveys. Often **suggestion schemes** exist in the minimal form of a box on the wall of the canteen to which little attention is paid. However, when they are publicised and when people receive large awards for suggestions that save the organisation money, they can be very effective. **Attitude surveys** may involve face-to-face interviews, telephone interviews, questionnaires and, nowadays, web questionnaires. Attitude surveys can yield quantitative and "objective" information about employee morale. They can also be used to track changes over several years or evaluate the success of various projects.

### Noise in communication channels

Shannon and Weaver (1949) noted that few channels of communication are perfect. They are subject to events and interference that either obscure or distort a message. This is called **noise** and consists of other signals that break up or interfere with a message. They can be either physical or psychological. Interruptions and mobile phones are prime examples of **physical noise**. For example, a CEO may be outlining a strategic plan to her board of directors when a business associate phones to check a future appointment. Even though she curtails the call, momentum is lost and the impact of the message is diluted. In a similar vein, many otherwise superb presentations have been ruined by the gauche arrival of coffee and refreshments at a key moment. Another source of noise is distraction – perhaps a loud conversation in the next room or the glare on a computer monitor. Common forms of **psychological noise** are fatigue, biases and prejudices, daydreaming and not paying attention.

Channels differ in the extent to which they are subject to noise. Written communications are less influenced by noise, while the noise present in an organisation's grapevine can make the original message unrecognisable. Communication where information is passed by word of mouth is especially susceptible to noise. Jablin *et al.* (1987) note that each individual in a chain filters and interprets information according to their perceptions, thought patterns, motives and attitudes. This filtering constitutes noise that changes the information before it is passed on to others. Jablin *et al.*'s thoughts were hardly new. They were noted, half a century beforehand, by Frederick Bartlett (1932), a famous British psychologist. As a part of his studies into in the phenomena of "remembering" he conducted a famous experiment on the way that a series of people remembered a spooky ghost story. The tale "War of the ghosts" was narrated to one person who narrated it to another and so on – rather like the party game "Chinese whispers". However, Bartlett very carefully noted the changes to the story as it passed from mouth to mouth. He identified three consistent changes:

■ With each telling, the message becomes **shorter**. A little of the contextual detail was lost with each rendition (possibly because it exceeded the short-term memory capacity of seven pieces of information that the average human mind can store – which is why it is important to "Keep It Simple Stupid!"). The phenomenon of shortening may be responsible for reducing a thoughtful, considerate management decision to a bald diktat by the time it reaches "ordinary" employees. Studies show that the loss in information as it passes down an organisation's hierarchy can be dramatic. Typical figures are:

    – CEO's understanding                 100 per cent (perhaps!)

    – director's understanding            63 per cent

    – senior manager's understanding   56 per cent

    – middle manager's understanding   40 per cent

    – junior manager's understanding    30 per cent

    – operative's understanding        20 per cent

These figures indicate that slightly less than one-third of a message's information is lost each time it is transmitted to another managerial level.

■ The message becomes **sharper**. The main point of the story is emphasised and minor themes are lost or are distorted so that they reinforce the main theme.

■ Frequently the message is **hijacked by irrelevant detail**. For example, just one line in a presentation by the CEO of a jewellery retail chain (see Case 11.1) might jokingly refer to "crap" products. However, after the speech has been relayed through a series of media interviews it appears that the CEO is confessing that his stores sold only "crap products". A misfortune of this kind forced the UK jewellers, Ratners, into closure.

### Direction of communication

Many writers classify a communication channel by its direction. Three directions, upwards, downwards and horizontal, are usually differentiated.

**Upward communication** towards top managers is called reporting and it was identified by Fayol as "R" in the acronym POSDCRB. Information is communicated upwards in reports giving performance data about areas of responsibility and actual or anticipated problems. Managers will also report the performance of their subordinates. Sometimes upward reports make suggestions for scheduling and other improvements. Upward reports usually rise only one level in the organisation because they are then integrated with reports of colleagues at the same level before being transmitted higher in a new report. Good upward communication requires an atmosphere of trust where mistakes are accepted and where there is support to help avoid further occurrences. If these are absent, employees will conceal negative facts, and decisions by senior managers are based on inaccurate information.

**Downward communication** is how top management let people know the organisation's strategy and the targets they must meet. Typically, downward communication takes the form of meetings, memos, policy statements, operating procedures, etc. Good downward communication helps build employees' organisational commitment. Unfortunately, as noted above, a great deal of information is lost before it reaches those at the bottom of an organisation.

**Horizontal communication** occurs between people at the same level. Sometimes it is called "gang-plank" communication. Horizontal communication tends to be informal and sometimes lengthy. It often starts with a conversation, telephone call or email, which is then followed up by a more formal memo or note. Good horizontal communication is vital if the activities of different departments or people are to be effectively co-ordinated. A large part of a middle manager's job involves horizontal communication. Quality circles and teamworking are specific types of horizontal communication. Bartels et al. (2010) investigated some of the properties of vertical and horizontal communication. They found that, in the Netherlands, vertical communication was important in achieving worker's identification with the organisation. Horizontal communication was more important in maintaining an employee's identification with their profession or trade. They also found that, in general, employees identify more strongly with their profession or trade than their organisation.

### Communication networks

Communication channels rarely exist in isolation. They are usually linked to other channels to form a network. As Figure 11.1 shows, there are four main types of network.

In the **star network** (sometimes called a **wheel network**) people at the periphery can only communicate with the person at the centre, who is able to communicate with everyone. Star networks are very efficient when dealing with very simple tasks that amount to little more than collecting and ordering easily understood information. They are hopeless at dealing with complex tasks, because the person at the centre becomes overloaded and those at the periphery are unable to help. The person at the centre of the star is usually highly satisfied with the group but those at the periphery are not.

The **line network** (sometimes called a "chain" network) is a little better at complex tasks because people in the middle of the line can share complex processing and they are usually satisfied with the group. People at the ends of the line are usually dissatisfied with the way a group works.

A **Y network** is a hybrid between a star network and a line network. They are notorious for fostering power struggles between the person at the fork of the "Y" and the person who is next down the "leg" of the "Y".

In a **ComCon** network (sometimes called an "all-channel" network) everyone is completely connected to everyone else. ComCon networks are poor at dealing with simple situations where the choice lies between two obvious actions such as an emergency

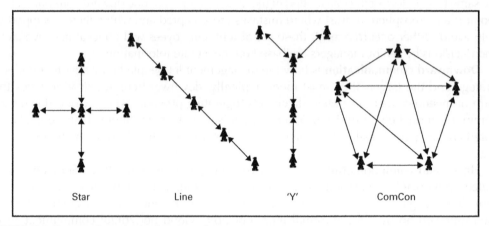

| Star | Line | 'Y' | ComCon |

**FIGURE 11.1** Patterns of communication channels

situation where it is necessary to choose which of two exits is better. In these situations a ComCon networks wastes time sending messages in haphazard directions while waiting for a consensus to emerge. However, ComCon networks are good in complex situations where a lot of information needs to be synthesised. They are also good at dealing with bottlenecks of information since messages can be re-routed through less congested channels.

In the past organisations tended to adopt star or inverted "Y" networks. Modern organisations tend towards the ComCon model. This change has been assisted by the development of information technology where employees have access to large amounts of information which, previously, was only available to management. The development of organisational intranets has also meant that anyone in an organisation is able to send messages to any other member of the organisation.

## Stage 4: Receiving the message

A message may be flawlessly encoded and sent via an appropriate channel but if a part or the whole of a message is not received there will be a breakdown in communication. This is analogous to a broadcaster producing a perfect programme and sending it from a powerful transmitter only to find that the television or radio at the other end is either faulty or tuned to a different wavelength. Sometimes, messages are blocked out of consciousness because they are painful to the recipient or the recipient does not trust the source. This is analogous to a viewer making a snack during advertisement because they believe that manufacturers' information is biased and not worth watching.

A message may not be received because a person is attending to other things. To a small extent this problem can be overcome by the sender clearly indicating the relevance and importance of the information. For example, an email can be allotted a high priority and a clear notification of the subject matter given. Further, the first few lines of the email should indicate the type of response required and the date, or time, that a response is due. Poor *listening skills* are often blamed for a poorly received message.

---

**CASE 11.5:  *Best advice – listen up!***

The august magazine *Harvard Business Review* runs a series of articles on the theme "The best advice I ever got". The issue in November 2008 carried an article by Maureen Chiquet who was the global Chief Executive Offficer of Chanel. She recalls that earlier in her career with another organisation, she proudly gave a presentation to the CEO and head of marketing. The head of marketing was supportive but the CEO proceeded to ask a series of penetrative questions. Maureen recalls that she was young, confident and knew what was cool. She argued her case with energy. But the CEO continued with questions that she failed to answer. Finally, she stopped talking and went back to her office. Shortly afterwards her CEO telephoned and said, "Maureen! I am going to give you some important to advice. You're a terrific merchant. But you've gotta learn to *listen*".

"20 years later his words continue to have a profound effect on how I . . . interact with employees, customers and other stakeholders". In many industries you have got to have a strong point of view and present it effectively. But to lead effectively and to achieve real business results . . . you have to listen. You have got to constantly ask questions and seek out diverse opinions, and remain humble enough to change your mind – whether about a product or a person".

Maureen Chiquet adds, "When I'm in a Chanel boutique, I ask the store employees what's selling, how customers are responding on what we should be doing differently. Their front-line observations help me find my own thoughts". It is also important to listen to direct reports, customers, suppliers and the public at large. Useful information can be gleaned from many sources such as YouTube and fashion sections in magazines.

Maureen Chiquet knows that listening has its drawbacks. Sometimes people are only telling you what you want to hear. Nevertheless she attributes a considerable part of her success to her boss's advice and learning to listen.

*Source:* based on an article in *Harvard Business Review,* November, 2008, p. 40.

---

Actually, making sure a message is received involves more than just listening, and it is better to refer to *receiving skills*. There are five main receiving skills:

- **Setting aside time to receive messages**. Often managers are so intent on sending signals that they leave no time to receive them. It has been said that in face-to-face situations the most important listening skill is to stop talking. The second most important listening skill is to stop talking. The third most important receiving skill is also **stop talking!**

- **Understanding the overt message,** i.e. comprehending what is actually said or written. Many factors, especially expectations, prevent proper reception of a message. An incoming message is immediately evaluated using our past experiences. This saves time by allowing us to skip detailed parts of the message because we can insert what we expect to hear instead. Whenever a decision has important and irreversible consequences it is vital to check that the overt message has been understood. With written communication this is as simple as rereading the message or asking others to read it. Where the message is a verbal report of a meeting – especially a report of what a third person did or said – it is well worth verifying the report with an independent source, preferably with the person whose speech is reported.

- **Understanding the motives for issuing** the message. It is often useful to ask why is *this message* being sent to *me* at this *time* in this *way*? These questions may reveal the sender's motive, which may place the message in context. For example, a notice read out at the end of a very long meeting under "any other business" signifies that the sender hopes the recipient will not place undue emphasis on the information given – either because the information is not, in fact, important or because the sender is Machiavellian and wishes to bury bad news. Similarly, an unexpected memo on the importance of observing proper personal relationships between managers and subordinates probably means that a manager somewhere has been having an improper sexual relationship that might harm the organisation's reputation.

- **Understanding the emotion** behind the message. Often a message might appear to convey no new information but it may be said in an angry voice or a happy voice. Similarly, a letter or memo that contains many underlined or emboldened words often indicates an angry or impatient sender. Sometimes when a communication seems to have no overt point whatsoever, it is carrying a very important emotional message "I want you to notice me and pay me more attention!"

- **Avoiding criticism**, evaluative judgements and arguments – before the full message has been delivered.

Receiving messages requires sensitivity to both verbal and non-verbal cues. It also involves paying attention to what a speaker or writer is trying to communicate rather than multitasking by trying to read an email at the same time as conducting a telephone conversation. Fidgeting or thinking about other issues may prevent the accurate reception of a message. Receiving information is not a passive activity – even though one should normally refrain from interrupting a speaker. If a part of a message seems unclear, there should be no hesitation in asking for clarification or for the message to be repeated. A fail-safe tactic, to be used if there is any possibility of ambiguity, is to relay one's apprehension of the message back to the sender using phrases such as "I want to be sure I have heard correctly . . . what you have just said is . . .". An active listener will detect and respond to the feelings behind a comment. For example, a colleague may say "we have had many new orders this week". A passive listener might reply "yes, there were 102", whereas an active listener would reply "yes, there were 102 and I guess you are concerned about the extra workload that is placed on you".

## Stage 5: Decoding the information

Once a message has been correctly received its meaning needs to be understood. This is called "decoding" and, in many ways, it is the mirror image of encoding described previous in stage 2. An important principle of decoding is to avoid over-reaction to individual words or phrases. For example, if a single sentence in a document refers to "policing" a regulation, it would be an over-reaction to draw analogies with jackboot authoritarian regimes. Similarly, if a two-page email about market competitiveness contains a short paragraph about costs it would be wrong to decode it to mean a programme of downsizing is imminent. Triandis (1977) identified a number of errors in decoding messages. Table 11.1 illustrates some of the decoding problems that may arise.

The actual example given by Triandis indicates that decoding problems are particularly acute when the sender and recipient of a message are from different ethnic origins.

The final stage in the chain of communication envisaged by Shannon and Weaver is deciding upon appropriate action. The process of decision-making was discussed in Chapter 9. Usually it is appropriate to signal to the sender of the original message that it has been received and acted upon. This feedback completes the communication loop, saves the effort of re-sending the same information and clears the channels for other messages.

| Actual words | Manager's/subordinate's intended meaning | Meaning decoded by subordinate/manager |
|---|---|---|
| "How long will it take you to finish the job?" | Please participate in setting your deadlines | He does not know what the job involves |
| "How are your family?" | I am interested in you as a person, not as a cog in the machine | She is trying to pry into my private life |
| "We should be able to meet the deadline" | There may be a problem with this deadline | He is confident about the deadline and needs no support |
| "Have you had a chance to read my report?" | Why haven't you come back to me about the report I worked overtime to write? | She is too arrogant to understand all the things I have to read |

**TABLE 11.1** Errors of decoding

## 11.3  Modifications to Shannon and Weaver's model

*S*hannon and Weaver's "arrow" model of communication has been very influential. It identifies a straightforward series of stages that can be explained easily. The model was based upon an analogy with radio communications where there is a mechanical, non-interactive flow of information from sender to receiver. However, as Schramm (1954) points out, human communication is rarely so simple – it is characterised by feedback. The recipient of a message is not passive like a radio receiver. As soon as a message comes in, a human being starts to react with, say, non-verbal frowns or questions.

Clampitt (1991) likens organisational communications to a *circuit of information* where, in response to feedback, the sender may modify the message she or he initiates. Unfortunately, the situation is still more complex. A radio transmitter simply sends its message and a radio receiver simply receives it. In human communication, both sender and receiver monitor their own activities and adjust their behaviour accordingly. A shy person may become embarrassed on hearing themselves speak and start to stutter. On realising that a message is complex for the listener a speaker may repeat key information. Thus it can be seen that human communications have many feedback mechanisms which generally help clarify messages. The feedback loops in human communications mean there is a constant cycle where messages go backwards and forwards between two people. Clampitt likens this to a *dance* where people need to make complementary moves. These moves are governed by a set of rules such as starting a conversation with a neutral or pleasant topic. For example, many telephone conversations start with the question "How are you?" to which the customary answer is "Fine. How are you keeping?". If one partner fails to make the expected steps (for example, by giving a long-drawn-out description of their state of health) the communication dance falters.

Herriot (1989) uses the recruitment process as a superb example of the interactive and reciprocal nature of communication. The process is divided into episodes where either the organisation or the potential recruit receives overt verbal, contextual and non-verbal information. At the end of the episode the person or organisation must decide whether to continue the recruitment "dance". For example, at the start of the process the potential recruit sees a job advert. It gives overt details about the job and the organisation. Placement in a quality newspaper, the layout, pictures and general tenor give contextual cues. Using this information the potential recruit decides whether to make an application. The application sends messages to the employer, and so on. As Figure 11.2 shows, both parties have power and both must choreograph a series of steps for the recruitment process to reach a successful conclusion.

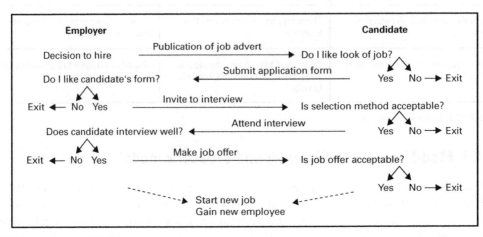

**FIGURE 11.2** The recruitment tango

Both the circuit and dance models of communication stress the importance of feedback and it is important to develop a good feedback technique. Some useful guidelines are:

- Give feedback **as quickly as possible** after the receipt of a communication or observing behaviour. However, if the feedback is negative it may be better to wait a little while until the recipient may be more receptive.

- Give feedback in **frequent, short episodes** rather than waiting for a number of issues to accumulate.

- Feedback should be about **specific** communications or behaviour rather than general attitude or approach.

- Whenever possible give **positive** feedback on things that people do or say correctly. Often good behaviour is assumed or overlooked. In many circumstances positive feedback is two to three times more powerful than negative feedback. Negative feedback often causes denial and defensive or other emotional reactions. Negative feedback tends to teach people to avoid getting caught rather than doing things right – with the possibility that they may reduce the amount they communicate so that there is less likelihood of attracting criticism.

Communication errors in operating theatres in hospitals can have lethal effects. Consequently they have been extensively researched. While the findings are particularly apposite to medical contexts, they are also relevant to managerial situations. Lingard *et al.* (2004) observed 48 surgical procedures and catalogued communications errors. The main ones were:

- poor timing (46 per cent) (too late, too early)
- poor content (36 per cent) where information was missing or inaccurate
- bad purpose (24 per cent) where issues were not resolved
- poor "audience" (21 per cent) where key individuals were excluded from the communication

There were 421 communication events and 129 (31 per cent) of them were failures. Some of the failures involved several errors. While many failures had only minor consequences about one-third of the failures jeopardised patient safety.

## 11.4  Communications toolkit

In the first chapter it was noted that good communication is the most important skill which organisations demand from new recruits. There are two communication activities that have a high profile and can have a long-term impact on the career of a manager. They are writing reports and making presentations.

### Writing reports

- **Reports differ from essays and assignments** because they have a clear purpose – to persuade the reader to *do* something. Consequently, the first step in producing a successful report is *to be absolutely clear about the action or actions the report needs to initiate.* Possible actions include: buying a product; making a change; stopping an unwise or unsafe practice.

- **Prioritise recommendations**, with the most important first. In many cases it is also useful to work out the approximate costs and timetable for implementation.
- **Identify the readership carefully**. In assignments you know precisely who the reader is and you can assume that they know a lot about the topic. The readers of management reports can be other managers, new recruits, general public, customers, suppliers or regulators, etc. They will differ greatly in their prior knowledge and reasons for reading your report. You must take readers' characteristics into account.
- **A short summary** (one or two pages) should be placed at the start of the report.
- **Use of short words and short sentences** is a key to a good writing style. It is also good practice to avoid long paragraphs.
- **Be careful with spelling and grammar**. Enemies will use small grammatical mistakes to "rubbish" a report. Some detailed guidance on how to avoid common grammatical errors is given in the website that accompanies this book.

### Making a presentation

There are three main types of presentation

- **briefings to two or three people**: e.g. a unit manager briefing the organisation's senior executives during their visit to the unit
- **presentations to between six and fifteen people**: e.g. consultants explaining their proposals to the management team of a client organisation
- **set-piece presentations to tens, if not hundreds of people**: e.g. a chief executive addressing all members of staff at the organisation's annual conference

Each type of presentation has its own tone and characteristics. It is vital to choose an appropriate style. Some detailed guidance on making a presentation is given in the website that accompanies this book.

# Activities and further study

## Essay plans

Produce essay plans for the following topics:

1 Draw a diagram of the communication process and then explain each stage.
2 What are the main barriers to good communication?
3 What is the importance of the "grapevine" to managers?

## Web activities

1 Use an information database such as AIB Inform or ProQuest to obtain longer articles on communication such as:

   Peter Richardson and D. Keith Denton (1996) "Communicating change", *Human Resource Management*, **35** (2), 203–217 (an excellent article giving specific instances where communication played an important part in changing organisations)

   Dorothy A. Winsor (1988) "Communication failures contributing to the challenger accident: an example for technical communicators", *IEEE Transactions on Professional Communication*, **31** (3), 101–108 (a good description of the way failures of communication led to the Challenger disaster)

2 Use your search engine to locate extra information on practical aspects of communication. Terms you could use are: communication; listening; non-verbal.

3 BBC Bitesize offers good but basic information that is useful in some cases. For example, if you have never written a memo, the advice on this site will help prevent basic mistakes.

4 There are a number of interesting websites which list the reasons why communications fail. A favourite is: http://youblog.typepad.com/the_youblog/2007/02/why_communicati.html

## Experiential activities

1 With a group of four friends, each write a topic concerning "communication" on a slip of paper. Allocate one slip to each person at random. Allow three minutes for thought and preparation. Then each person should give a two-minute talk on the subject written

on their slip of paper. At the end of each talk, friends should nominate three good aspects of the speaker's communication skills and two aspects that could be improved.

2  Plan a 10-minute presentation to, say, a group of careers advisers on the topic of "me and my future work".

3  Think of a recent communication (email, letter, phone call, face-to-face comment) which you sent that was misunderstood. Analyse the reasons for the misunderstanding and devise ways of avoiding these problems in the future.

## Recommended reading

1  (2008) "How to have effective meetings", *People Management*, 2 October, p. 45. Eight common-sense tips on effective meetings.

2  Eppler, M.J. and Mengis, J. (2009) "How communicators can fight information overload", *Communication World*, May–June, 4–5. Seven common-sense tips in communicating your message to people who are bombarded with information.

3  Clampitt, P.G., DeKoch, R.J. and Thomas, C. (2000) "A strategy for communicating about uncertainty", *Academy of Management Executive*, **14**(4), 41–58. This article discusses how executives' choices about what they communicate must be aligned with organisational strategy.

# CHAPTER 12

# Budgeting

## Chapter contents

## ❖ *LEARNING OBJECTIVES*

After reading this chapter you will be able to understand the importance of budgeting. You will be able to identify the main types of budget and have some understanding of the budgeting process. You will also be able to understand management ratios that are in common use. In particular you will be able to:

❖ **define** a budget and explain the key terms within it

❖ **list** four resources that usually need budgets

❖ **explain briefly** four main types of cash budgets

❖ **draw** and **explain** a cash graph

❖ **explain** the following aspects of budgeting:

  – "top-down" and "bottom up" budgeting

  – zero-based budgeting

  – activity-based costing and budgeting

❖ **explain** the formulae and use of nine different profitability ratios

❖ **explain** the concepts of gearing, leverage and debt ratio

❖ **explain** the formulae and use of four different debt ratios

❖ **explain** the formulae and use of two different operational ratios

It is rare to open the financial pages of a newspaper without seeing at least one article berating some organisational misfortune that was caused by poor budgeting. Case 12.1 illustrates poor budgeting at the BBC.

---

### CASE 12.1: *Bad budgeting at the Beeb*

The BBC is the world's largest broadcasting corporation and has an income of almost £5 billion, raised, compulsorily, from every house in the UK that has a television or radio. You might therefore think that it would have developed a robust system of budgets that would help it use the money wisely. Dream on! In 2010 the National Audit Office investigated the BBC's budgetary system for managing. It found that:

- There was no cost–benefit analysis of the programming options open to the BBC.
- It did not have a clear view of the total budget for the coverage of individual events because it has separate budgets for different media, i.e. radio, television and Internet coverage. Further, the fees of some celebrities were hidden among other long-term contracts.
- It did not compare its costs of covering major sporting and music events with the costs incurred by other broadcasters.

The BBC is not alone in having difficulty with its budgeting process. The government itself has encountered problems – especially in the way that it budgets for major IT projects. A controversial plan to computerise all National Health Service (NHS) patients' records had an original budget of £2.3 billion but the actual cost was in excess of £12.7 billion – a budget overrun in excess of £10 *billion!* Similarly, an IT project to set up a National Offender Management Information System shot up from £2 to £4 million in 2004 to £690 million in 2008 – even though the final system was not as good as the system planned at the start. Further, Fujitsu won a £146 million contract to provide a system for magistrate's courts. Eventually, the system was expected to cost in excess of £500 million – a 352 per cent budget overrun.

---

Budget overruns also occur in private industry and commerce. However, they are less visible because private organisations can use commercial secrecy to hide them. Budget overruns in government and public corporations have to be paid for or by a taxpayer or licence payer. Budget overruns in private industry or commerce have to be paid for by shareholders (including charities and pension funds). Sometimes bad budgets cause organisations to close down, with the loss of many jobs.

Clearly, budgeting is a vital management process which involves all managers in an organisation. Superficially, similar activities are performed by the finance function. The finance function will help individual managers produce their departmental budgets by providing information and expertise. It then collates individual departmental budgets into a master budget for the whole organisation. However, as Chapter 17 explains, the work of the finance function is more technical and

The finance function
p 409

involves other activities such as issuing stocks and bonds, producing financial reports for investors and ensuring that regulations are followed. It is *helpful* if individual managers have some understanding of these more specialised activities. However, it is *essential* that individual managers can budget the activities of their own departments.

## 12.1  Definition and concept of budgeting

Distributing an organisation's resources effectively, planning their use carefully and making sure that they are not wasted are vital to adding value. These activities are usually called budgeting. Budgeting may be defined as:

> **66** A single-use, numerical and time-limited plan that commits resources to a project or activity. **99**

This definition has four components:

- **Budgets are plans for future actions**. They are *single-use* plans to meet a situation at a given time – it is highly unlikely that exactly the same plan will ever be used again. Budgets are undoubtedly plans, so Fayol was technically wrong to make budgeting a separate management process. Nevertheless, treating budgets separately has practical advantages: it divides a very large process into two smaller, more manageable, parts and the division emphasises the importance of plans involving money.

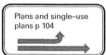
Plans and single–use plans p 104

- **Budgets always involve numbers.** This gives greater precision and enables progress to be tracked and controlled with greater accuracy.
- **Budgets have a fixed time interval** – usually a year but other time intervals of one month, three months, six months or two years are quite common. Sometimes, budgets are automatically refreshed and extended about halfway through their time interval. These are called **"rolling" budgets**.
- **Budgets commit resources to specific projects** (such as an advertising campaign) or specific classes of activity (such as travelling expenses).

Nearly always, responsibility for a budget is formally allocated to one person – a **budget holder**. For example, the budget for a whole unit will be the responsibility of the general manager. He or she may then delegate part of the budget to, say, the production director or the sales director, etc. Sometimes budget holders are called **responsibility centres**. In the context of management the word " budget" does not carry the negative connotations of meanness and skimping that are associated with common phrases such as "budget holiday" or "budget jeans". Quite the contrary, some budgets (such as the chairperson's entertainment budget!) might be very generous indeed. Budgets are not just simply plans, *they are also control devices*. Actual expenditure is compared to a budget and remedial action is taken if there

Controlling p 248

is a large "variance". For example, a consultancy organisation will usually compare its budget income against its actual income on a monthly basis. It will take action if the actual income is too low.

**Budgets have five main uses**. *Planning* the availability and use of money as well as *controlling* the availability and use of money have been noted already. Third, budgets help *co-ordinate* different parts of the organisation. For example, when the production budget and the marketing budget are integrated into a master budget, the activities of the two parts of the organisation will be syncronised. Fourth, budgets *enable managers to delegate many activities* while knowing that they will be performed in a way that is consistent with wider objectives. Fifth, good budgets can also *speed up decision-making*. By referring to the appropriate budget, many decisions can be made without the delay involved in referring them to senior levels.

---

### CASE 12.2: *Banks' advice on budgeting*

Banks are particularly keen to offer advice to new business start-ups. It may mean their customer will grow to use more banking services and pay more charges in the future. New businesses face many challenges in their first year of trading. The main reason so many fail is that they do not budget accurately, so most banks focus on this aspect. Good advice on budgeting may also avoid the heartbreak of a new company becoming bankrupt. A good budget forecasts costs, revenues, sales and how the business is to be financed.

A clear budget is vital. It should be derived from business objectives, and should identify what money is needed, why and where it will come from. Clear, detailed budgets targets help give security by:

- ensuring money is spent on the right things
- identifying loss-making areas
- identifying the need for remedial action if, for example, revenue is not meeting target or if costs are rising

A budget also establishes expected cash flow so the business can assess if its income will cover its expenditure. Difficulty with cash flow is common for new businesses because it takes time to build up a business and win new customers. Good budgeting systems can help manage the business by seeing if customers are slow in settling accounts. Managing cash flow may ultimately keep the business afloat.

---

## 12.2 Non-financial budgets

Budgets are used to plan, commit and control many different kinds of resources such as operations, materials, human resources and information. But, above all, they are used to plan, commit and control money and finances. The following section outlines that group of financial budgets. First, this section describes non-financial budgets, in order to emphasise the fact that financial budgets are only one resource that must be planned, allocated and co-ordinated. The main types of **non-financial budgets** concern operations, human resources (HR), materials and intellectual capital.

- **Operations (production) budgets** are detailed plans for the output of production units. They are necessary to ensure an organisation's output matches its sales. Short-term production budgets are often called **production schedules**. Some organisations draw up budgets for new products. For example, major drug companies will try to ensure that they introduce several new drugs to the market every year. This is often called a product pipeline.

- A **materials budget** is a plan for acquiring and storing parts or supplies which need to be available to the production department. It is closely linked with supply chain management.

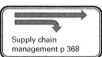
Supply chain management p 368

- **HR budgets** are detailed plans for employees who will be needed to fill various jobs. An HR budget will specify the skills and qualifications that are required by various groups of people. It will need to take into account the likelihood of employees quitting the organisation and the time-lags involved in training their replacements. A specialised HR budget is called a **management succession plan**.

- Some advanced organisations produce budgets for **intellectual capital**. For example, software developers draw up a plan to ensure a steady flow of intellectual property such as patents and new ideas. They may also try to quantify and systematically develop the value of the knowledge possessed by its employees, the value of its brands and the worth of its relationships with customers and suppliers. This is closely linked to knowledge management. It may involve budgets to ensure the intellectual capital of the organisation increases every year.

Knowledge management p 452

## 12.3 Types of financial budget

Money is a vital resource in any organisation. Money is the means by which resources and products are exchanged with the outside world. It is also the means by which the transformation process within the organisation is evaluated. This chapter focuses on the budgets and the way they affect *all* managers – *departmental budgets*. Managing money usually involves the finance function. *Financial budgets* attempt to predict and regulate the flows of money *to* and *from* an organisation, and they are generally constructed by financial experts.

Finance and accounting function p 409

Departmental budgets focus on the flows of money within an organisation and they are generally constructed, and observed, by all types and levels of manager. There are two main types of departmental budget: depertmental expenditure body and departmental capital budgets.

### Departmental expenditure budgets

An expenditure budget is a plan showing the money a department can expect to pay out. At the start of a financial period, departmental managers predict what they need to spend.

Expenditure will be detailed into various cost headings, such as labour costs, reorganisation costs, sales, materials, etc. In a large organisation the expense budget will show the anticipated and actual expenses for each responsibility centre such as production unit 1, production unit 2, sales, administration, etc. Departments usually have clearly defined expenditure budgets covering the next 12 months. They may have outline expenditure budgets for future years. Expense budgets will probably specify the outgoings for each month and the actual outgoings will be compared closely with the plan. If actual expenditure exceeds the budget, action, such as cutting costs, will be taken to eliminate the variance. If expenditure is less than the departmental budget, most managers will go on a spending spree to use up their budget so that it will not be cut in future years. The major expenditure budget headings are:

- salaries and benefits
- rent
- utilities (heating, light, power and water)
- business travel
- maintenance of equipment and building
- communications (post, telephone, Internet)
- equipment

## Departmental capital budget

The capital budget concerns the investment a department can make in equipment and new buildings. Ideally, these investments are made according to a predetermined plan that anticipates future needs and they will be scheduled in a way that maximises the return on the investment. Usually, an organisation will determine the amount of money it can invest in new building or equipment. It will then ask departments for suggestions on how this money can be invested. The most promising suggestions will be chosen after thorough scrutiny to see if they are practical, related to the organisation's strategy and whether they are likely to give a good return on the investment. Departmental suggestions that survive this scrutiny and which fit within the money available for the organisation as a whole will be given a departmental capital budget. Sometimes, capital expenditure is less controlled. Breakdowns of existing machines, new legislation or unexpected technological developments may force emergency capital expenditure.

## 12.4  The budgeting process

Departmental budgets (or project budgets) can be prepared in two main ways: a traditional "top-down method" and a more recent "bottom-up method". The **top-down** method of preparing budgets follows the formal lines of authority described by Weber. Senior management set overall budgets which are in line with the organisation's strategy. These overall budgets set out the broad parameters for each department (or project). Departmental managers then prepare more

Weber p 73

detailed budgets, within these limits, for each of their sections – and so on until there are detailed budgets for small units of activity or workers. The top-down method has the big advantage of following established lines of command and it usually produces an integrated set of budgets for the whole organisation. The top down approach to budgeting may use "standard costings" which have been in use since the Industrial Revolution and have been refined in the USA (Fleischman and Tyson, 1998 – a passable read). Standard costs are estimates of outlays such as materials, wages, fuel, etc. needed to produce routine components or services. Standard costs also include an element for overheads. The use of standard costs allows management to control expenditure by identifying situations that cost too much or opportunities where extra value can be added.

Top-down budgeting may appear autocratic and may alienate junior staff. **Bottom-up budgets** aim to remove these disadvantages. Junior members of staff are asked to anticipate their area's income, expenditure and capital needs. Senior management review the departmental budgets to identify crucial factors that will influence or limit departmental budgets. These factors are often termed **principal budget factors** or **limiting factors** or **key factors**. They are factors the organisation cannot change and involve raw materials, labour, finance or legislation. Finally, senior management then integrate all information into a **master budget** which is consistent with the organisation's strategy. The bottom-up approach empowers junior staff. It means that they are more likely to take ownership of the budgets and therefore they are likely to apply them more effectively (see Churchill, 1984).

Most departmental (or project) budgets are now produced by a cyclical process which starts with submissions from their main areas of business activity such as sales or operations, etc. Departmental budgets are synthesised into an initial master budget. The initial master budget is almost certain to be too large and is likely to be sent back to the original departments (or project leaders) with a request to decrease costs. Several iterations may be necessary before departmental budgets and the master budgets converge. This process may seem tedious but it does ensure that many people are involved, and therefore committed, to the final master budget.

Perhaps the easiest way to prepare a departmental (or project) budget is to take last year's budget, and increase each entry by a few per cent to take account of inflation and make other adjustments to accommodate foreseeable changes. This method tends to produce budgets that grow needlessly each year irrespective of needs. **Zero-based budgeting** (Pyhrr, 1973) was introduced to counteract this tendency and it has been adopted by most major organisations because it deploys resources more efficiently than simply adapting last year's budget. In zero-based budgeting all expenditure has to be justified as if it were a new project or activity. The assumption is that any expenditure is unnecessary *unless* a positive case can be made. This means that all activities and the priorities allotted to them are reconsidered at the start of each budgeting cycle. Zero-based budgeting is too radical and takes too much time to apply simultaneously to all budgets within an organisation. Recent history suggests that zero-based budgeting is very susceptible to political influence and pressures. In recent years it has fallen into disuse, at least outside the public sector. Nevertheless, used selectively it does restrain expanding budgets and it reduces the "entitlement mentality" towards budget increases.

Traditionally, budgets were produced on a departmental basis with separate budgets for the purchasing department, the HR department, the production department, and so on.

Since several different responsibility centres will contribute to a given item of production it is difficult to establish the costs or a budget for specific products or services. **Activity-based costing** *and* **budgeting (ABC)** was developed to overcome this difficulty (see Geri and Ronen, 2005 – a passable read; Pare, 1993).

 Activity-based costing traces all the costs incurred in generating and delivering a specific product or service. Armed with an accurate picture of the profits generated by a product, managers can expand production of those goods or services that add greatest value. Alternatively, they can try to increase profits by driving down the costs of unprofitable services. In some cases activity-based budgets and costings can point to products or services that should be discontinued. For example, it may be that it costs £20 to buy raw materials and manufacture a product that sells for £40 – a healthy profit of 100 per cent. However, activity-based costing might reveal that the product also requires an average of £10 advertising, £4 storage and £9 for customers' support. These additional costs are normally spread among departmental budgets so that the organisation is unaware that it is making a loss of £3 on each sale. Hoozee and Werner (2010) believe that worker participation and appropriate leadership style are an indispensable element of designing activity-based costing systems (ABCs).

## CRITICAL THINKING 12.1 *The problems of budget guesstimates?*

A finished budget, replete with columns of figures, looks authoritative and objective. However, budgets are often political and contain hidden assumptions. When preparing and approving budgets it is often valuable to list such assumptions and to question them. Further, many of the figures contained in a budget are estimates that can sometimes go wildly wrong because of political factors and other "unforeseeable" events. For example, Royal Dutch Shell and its Japanese partners experienced a massive £5.1 billion budget overrun in its project to develop an oilfield near the Russian island of Sakhalin in the Bering Sea, north of Japan. Some of the overrun was caused by Shell and its partners. However, a large proportion of the overrun was the result of political delays and harassment by the Kremlin which was keen to dominate negotiations over ownership of the development. Other expenses were added by the need to re-route a pipeline after environmental groups protested that the original route would damage the breeding grounds of a rare species of whale. Sometimes such factors can be anticipated by making comparisons with budgets from competitors – they may have experienced similar issues. Further, it is worthwhile considering previous budgets in the same organisation. For example, in the building industry there is a chronic tendency for projects to overrun budgets by 100 per cent. For example, the budget in 1997 for conversions to make Holyrood House suitable for the Scottish Parliament was £40 million. The final cost, in 2004, was £431 million – a *1000 per cent* budget overrun.

 It is prudent to take such factors into account when preparing budgets (especially budgets for buildings). Experienced managers are aware that budgets are sometimes guesstimates. They therefore take a defensive stance by overestimating costs. This conservative approach is likely to give them room for manoeuvre. However, if all managers take this approach a lot of money is reserved unnecessarily and the organisation will not be able to deploy its resources to maximum effect. A number of worthy projects will not go ahead because managers have added a safety margin to their own budgets.

## 12.5 Management ratios

Financial budgets and outcome figures are usually designed to control individual activities (or projects) at an operational level. Ratios are very useful summaries of aspects of efficiency – but it must be remembered that they are summaries that may hide important details. A list of ratios does not make exciting reading, but this is no reason to ignore them. The following sub-sections describe ratios, of which there are two main types, most frequently used by managers in general describe ratios of which there are two main types, most frequently used by managers in general: labour productivity ratios and operational ratios. There are many other financial ratios that are used by specialists in the finance and accounting function. It is often helpful if managers in general are familiar with them.

Financial ratios p 430

### Labour productivity ratios

**Labour productivity** is the effectiveness with which the efforts of employees are harnessed. There are two main indices: value added per employee and labour productivity. *Value added per employee* yields a monetary figure indicating how much each employee is adds. It is:

$$\text{Value added per employee} = \frac{\text{Net profit}}{\text{Number of employees}}$$

*Labour productivity* gives a percentage value of how much is added. It is useful because it can be compared with other percentage indicators. It is calculated by the formula:

$$\text{Labour productivity} = \frac{\text{Gross profit}}{\text{Labour costs}}$$

Usually indices of labour productivity are considered alongside indices of return on capital because employees who have lots of capital and equipment at their disposal *should* be expected to be more productive.

## CRITICAL THINKING 12.2 *Budget games*

Budgets are supposed to be objective and rational plans for deploying organisational resources – especially financial resources. However, it is quite rare for this to be 100 per cent true. People play budget games. Perhaps the four most common budget games are legacy building, empire building, budget circumvention and "back scratching".

■ The budget game *legacy building* is played by powerful people who want a memorial. They persuade their organisation to divert resources to a charitable institution, or other body, which bears their name, or the name of a cherished one. A classic example was the British magnate and MP, William Greenwood. Many years ago he convinced his cotton company to pay for a research institute, the Shirley Institute in Didsbury, Manchester, on condition that it be named after his daughter, Shirley. Greenwood's company, and the jobs it provided, no longer exist but the work of the Shirley Institute lives on in the Tog Ratings that describe the heat retention of gloves, duvet or anoraks! Powerful people often pre-empt organisational resources to fund a memorial in the form of a building named after them. Examples can be seen in most universities. Most vice-chancellors have an *edifice complex*: they know a new building will be a permanent legacy – unlike an improved education received by students working in a better equipped existing laboratory.

■ The budget game *empire building* is also played by powerful people but also by those who aspire to power. Empire builders manipulate themselves into positions where they hold key information and act as "gatekeepers". By restricting or enhancing the information in a selective way, gatekeepers divert budgets from rational deployment towards that which unnecessarily expands their own area of responsibility. This ploy has the useful function of denying resources to competitors.

■ The game of *budget circumvention* is played by experienced managers at all levels. They know how to get around budget rules. They craftily bring forward certain items of expenditure or income while delaying others. Budget limits can be circumvented by dividing up a large purchase (which would need to be approved by higher authority) into several smaller components and then sanctioning a series of smaller invoices, not needing approval.

■ The full title of the fourth budget game is *"you scratch my back and I'll scratch yours"*. It is a non-zero sum team game ubiquitously played at junior management levels. It is also rife at middle management levels. Its simplest form is seen where several junior managers direct similar production lines. One, through circumstances beyond his control, is unlikely to make his budget targets and will be "punished". Another, by happy chance is likely to exceed her targets and is likely to be "rewarded" with higher targets in the next budget round. Neither is stupid. She lends him machines or cedes him priority for the best jobs – knowing that in a month or two the position is likely to be reversed.

A variation is played by managers who control activities in a production sequence. For example, in banking, one manager may sell a service, the next may process the applications and a third manager may be responsible for delivering the service. If the latter seems to be falling behind their budget, it is highly likely that they contact their comrades. There is a good chance that their comrades agree to trim their activities – knowing that within days the tables may be turned. Back scratching also occurs at middle management levels – especially when budgets are being constructed. One manager may support another's budget "easing" on the basis that their budget may need "easing" next year. The legendary Davy Crockett used the term **logrolling** to mean the same thing. Logrolling is a metaphor of a North American sport where pairs of contestants need to move a floating log from one bank of an icy river to the other bank. It is to the pair's mutual advantage to move their feet in synchrony! Classical managers refer to "back scratching" and "logrolling" as "quid pro quo". It amounts to the same thing!

Seasoned managers know these and many other budget games. They take pains to ensure auditors, accountants and management information systems find it difficult to detect these activities. Budget games mean that any budgetary system is, at best, only 90 per cent accurate. It is wise to accept the imperfection in a tolerant way. Generally, budget games are used to overcome obstacles and inevitable flaws. They help the organisation provided they are played within reasonable limits. Intolerance leads to inflexibility, and may drive budget games underground where they can grow to an unacceptable level and endanger the organisation.

## Operational ratios

**Operational ratios** try to gauge how actively a department or organisation is using its assets. The main operational ratios are the activity ratio and the asset turnover ratio.

The **activity ratio** is sometimes called the "inventory turnover ratio". It is an index of how frequently completed goods or services are replenished ("turned over"). The formula is:

$$\text{Activity ratio} = \frac{\text{Sales turnover}}{\text{Average inventory}}$$

Usually the average inventory is obtained by combining the level of stocks at the start and end of the accounting period and dividing by two. A company that reports a yearly activity ratio of 1 is extremely poor since, on average, finished items languish on shelves a full year before they are sold. In general, a high activity ratio is good.

The **asset turnover ratio** shows how effectively an organisation is using its assets to generate sales. It is calculated by dividing sales revenue by total assets. The formula is:

$$\text{Asset turnver} = \frac{\text{Sales}}{\text{Total assets}}$$

A high figure indicates that the organisation is using assets in an intensive way (Brigham, 1985). However, there are substantial differences between industries. Low-technology operations often yield a high asset turnover because they are labour intensive rather than capital intensive.

The importance of management ratios in understanding management and managers was emphasised at the start of this section. However, it is equally important to remember that other aspects must be taken into account when arriving at a balanced assessment of an organisation. Taking some kind of corporate action solely on the basis of a collection of ratios is an accident waiting to happen. It is important to draw up a **balanced scorecard** that is made up of both financial and non-financial indicators. Managers often have the motivation and the means to distort and thwart the budgeting process (see Critical thinking 12.2). A safeguard against these aberrations (fraud) is to employ **auditors**. Auditors must be independent of the budgets they examine. They should have no family relations in the unit they are auditing, or any commercial interest in it. External auditors from another organisation, such as an accountancy firm are best, but a great deal of money can be saved by using internal auditors if their independence is guaranteed.

Balanced scorecard
p 268

## CRITICAL THINKING 12.3 *Disadvantages of budgeting*

Budgets are essential to good management and all managers will need to master the art of preparing and operating a range of budgets and management ratios. However, managers must also be aware of the disadvantages. Three particular disadvantages are costs, manipulation and restricted view:

- Good budgets take a *long time to prepare* and can be very *costly* – especially if the budget is zero based. The budget for a medium-sized department can easily consume four weeks of a manager's time which she or he could be spending on transforming resources rather than on paperwork. Budgets should not cost more than the benefits they bring.

- Unwise implementation of a budget can also lead to *manipulation*. If a manager has an unspent proportion of a budget at the end of an accounting period, there is a strong temptation to spend the residue on unessential purchases in order to make sure that the budget is not cut in future years.

■ Finally, budgets have the disadvantage that they might produce *tunnel vision* or *rigidity* and become an end in themselves. In fact, budgets never account for more than 80 per cent of an organisation's activities. They are a tool to help achieve goals rather than goals in themselves. Budgets should focus on organisational objectives rather than the costs of individual items.

### CASE 12.3: *How budgeting helps First Luggage*

Gideon Kasfiner launched First Luggage, a door-to-door luggage collection and delivery service, in 2004. The business now employs nine people and turns over £2 million a year. Here Gideon explains how financial planning has helped him grow his business in a controlled way.

#### Annual and monthly timetable

"I start doing my annual budgets three months before the year end. I look at the current year and see whether we are going to increase sales, and if we are how it's going to increase our costs, and so on. My accountant actually sets the budgets though, from the figures I give. Then, every month, I sit down with my management accounts. I look at my actual income and expenditure, compare them with my projections and look at the variance. I can see under every budgetary heading where things have gone up or down and I can make appropriate decisions.

So, for example, we may have budgeted sales of £200 000 for one month but only made £170 000. I might, for example, look at the marketing budget and do some more advertising. I might take a service out where costs are high, or even put prices up. It's all about juggling."

#### Detailed picture business

"I work with as many budget headings as I can. On the sales side, I break the figures down into the different products we deliver – suitcases, prams, golf bags, and so on. Then I can see exactly where revenue is coming from. I'll also look at the top 15 countries I'm delivering to. On the cost side there are all sorts of headings, from transportation to fuel surcharges, office rent, salaries, and PR and marketing. It's not easy doing things this way, but it gives me a better picture of my business and I have more areas to juggle with. Flexibility is very important. Initially, I did the monthly reviews on my own and then I started doing them with a commercial colleague. Ideas are better when you have two heads looking at the same thing."

#### Basic sensitivity analysis

"After doing the annual budgets, I do them again with a 20 per cent drop in sales to see what the impact would be on the cashflow if there are any changes in the market. I want to make sure I'm being as prudent as I can be with my cash. My mind is always looking at the downside as well as the upside. If I have a month that hasn't come up to where it should, my comfort zone is that I can do something about it."

## 12.6 Budgeting toolkit

- Money is not the only resource which requires a budget. Ensure your organisation has budgets for other resources such as operations, materials and HR. Make sure that *you* have a personal budget for the most precious resource – **time**.

- Make absolutely sure that you have a cash budget that ensures you have enough cash to meet likely bills. Review this budget on a weekly basis.

- Make an expenditure budget so that it shows categories of spending. Review this budget frequently with a view to reducing costs in categories with large expenditure.

- Make a capital budget and review it to ensure that assets under your control are earning a competitive return.

- Involve as many people as possible in the preparation of budgets

- Choose a maximum of seven budget ratios which give appropriate information (your personal dashboard) about how each subunit of your area of responsibility is performing. Build up a time series of these ratios. Review these ratios on a monthly basis. Draw conclusions about the efficiency of your subunits. Check your conclusions after including other information, and then take appropriate action.

# Activities and further study

## Essay plans

Write essay plans for the following questions:

1 What are the main types of budget used by organisations?
2 Explain in detail the main disadvantages of using budgets within an organisation.
3 Evaluate the advantages and disadvantages of budgets.

## Web activities

1 Most organisations view their budgets as commercially sensitive and do not publish them. However you should spend 15–20 minutes trying to locate sites containing some kind of budget. You are most likely to achieve success with international, national and local government sites. These organisations often have a legal obligation to divulge some budgetary information. A good site is: http://www.jointreviews.gov.uk/money/Financialmgt/1-23.html#1-231-councils

2 Locate sites that give guidance on the preparation of budgets. A good site is: http://www.duncanwil.co.uk/cash.html

3 Locate and examine a website with a complicated budget. One possibility is: http://www.enzt.co.nz/~yesweb/_files/Student%20Resources/Finance%203%20 Cash%20Budget.doc

## Experiential activities

1 Obtain budgets for an organisation you know (college, workplace, club, charity). Examine the budgets and compare the range with that given in this chapter.

2 For an organisation you know well, list the budget ratios that would be relevant if you were managing that organisation.

3 Draw up your personal income, expenditure and cash budget for each of the next 12 months.

4 Talk to someone you know well and who trusts you. Ask them what impact budgets have on the way that they work and the methods they use. Enquire what methods they would use to ensure budgets work to their own and their team's advantage.

## Recommended reading

1  Fleischman, R.K. and Tyson, T.N. (1998) "The evolution of standard costing in the UK and the US: from decision-making to control", *Abacus*, **34**(1), 92–119. A detailed history of cost accounting showing how managerial techniques evolve in response to problems and pressures of the time.

2  Geri, N. and Ronen, B. (2005) "Relevance lost: the rise and fall of activity-based costing", *Human Systems Management*, **24**, 133–144. A critical review of ABC (pages 134–135): a case study of use of ABC (pages 138–140); and an evaluation of ABC (pages 140–141).

3  Ogden, D.M. (1978) "Beyond zero based budgeting", *Public Administration Review*, **38**(6), 528–530. An old, short, but very useful paper putting zero-based budgeting into context.

# PART 3
# Management Functions

## Part Contents

# Introduction to Management Functions

**13**

## Chapter contents

## ❖ *LEARNING OBJECTIVES*

This short chapter is a brief introduction to management functions and puts the contents of this section of the book in context. The five chapters in Part 3 explore the five largest functions in greater depth:

- ❖ marketing
- ❖ operations
- ❖ human resource management (HRM)
- ❖ finance
- ❖ information management

Marketing, operations, HRM and finance have long been acknowledged as major functions in most organisations. They are presented in the order of their appearance in a theoretical chain as follows:

1  In principle, the first function of an organisation is to **explore a market and identify business opportunities**.

2  Secondly, it should then establish an operations function that will **produce a product or service that will exploit the market opportunity**.

3  Then it is vital for an organisation to find the **right people to work in it**.

4  And of course, it needs to **manage the money it earns and uses**.

For many years these were regarded as the "big four" management functions. However, now there is a fifth function: the information function has expanded so much that many people include it in the "big five" organisational functions.

The previous part was devoted to *management processes*: activities performed by practically all managers as a part of managing their own areas of responsibility. Management work can also be viewed in terms of management functions: specialised activities performed only by some managers. Functions involve specialised knowledge and they have an impact on the organisation as a whole – outside a manager's direct area of responsibility. For example the human resource function will be responsible for ensuring enough recruits and trained workers for production and marketing etc. Similarly, the finance function will ensure the supply of money to all functions within the organisation.

Management functions and processes frequently overlap. For example, there is apparent overlap between staffing processes and the human resources management (HRM) function. However, examination reveals important differences. The staffing process involves everyday activities such as leading and motivating subordinates. The HRM function (outlined in more detail in Chapter 16) concerns specialist activities that are performed by a much smaller sub-set of managers who have relevant professional qualifications such as membership of the Chartered Institute of Personnel and Development (CIPD). The HRM activities will include issuing employment contracts, succession planning and aspects of employment law. Similarly, there is apparent overlap between budgeting and the finance function. Again, however, closer examination reveals significant differences. Most managers will engage in the process of forming and monitoring budgets. The finance function, on the other hand, will involve a special cadre of people who will be accredited to an organisation such as an Institute of Chartered Accountants in England and Wales (ICAEW). They will be involved in specialist activities such as raising finance, the preparation and auditing of accounts and devising financial systems.

Figure 13.1 shows it is possible to identify at least 14 management functions – although not all will be found in every organisation. They can be grouped into three main types:

1  **Line functions** have a direct part in producing the goods or services.
2  **Enabling functions** provide services and support which help line functions.
3  **Control functions** ensure that standards, regulations and laws are kept.

This distinction is not exact. The finance function, for example can act as an enabling function (making sure money is available) and as a control function (checking for fraud).

Each function forms a part of the organisational system and interacts with other functions. In that sense all functions are equally important. However, there is research which suggests that some functions may make a bigger contribution than others. One of the best studies was conducted by Paterson *et al.* (1997). They visited 67 UK manufacturing companies and looked at five management functions: human resources (HR), quality, research and development (R&D), strategy and technology. They spent two days talking with directors and managers and inspecting documents. At the end of the process they gave a rating to each of the five functions. Patterson *et al.* returned a year later and collected data on productivity from each company. This is a particularly strong feature of Paterson *et al.*'s research (data

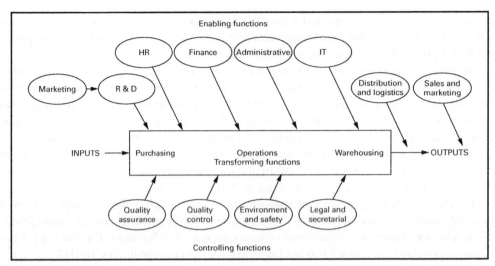

**FIGURE 13.1** Management functions

collection was prospective – in most research it is retrospective). Finally, they compared the ratings for the functions with productivity during the year. The results for productivity are given in Figure 13.2.

Such clear-cut results were a surprise. The contribution of HRM to *future* profitability and productivity was much greater than that of the other four functions. Research and development and strategy also made a significant contribution to the future performance. The authors were surprised that the contribution made by the quality function was low and they believe that the results arose due to a ceiling effect – the quality in all firms visited was already so high that it did not differentiate between them.

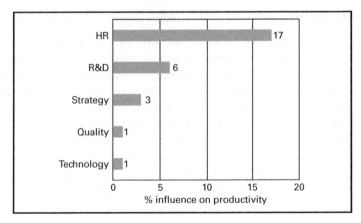

**FIGURE 13.2** Influence of five functions on productivity

## 13.1  Line functions

Line functions are those that play a direct part in making a product or service, i.e. marketing, R&D and operations (which includes supply chain management). Both marketing and operations are covered in the next two chapters. The remaining line functions (after marketing and operations) are research and development.

### Research and development (R&D)

The purpose of the research and development function is to invent or improve new products or services. In small companies the function may rely upon one or two ingenious people. At the other end of the scale, organisations such as GlaxoSmithKline or Hutchinson Communications have large, dedicated R&D establishments. Research and development is also present within the service sector. For example, there was a great deal of R&D before Barclays Bank introduced the world's first credit card.

Governments usually fund a large proportion of R&D activity – especially in the development of weapons. Research and development laboratories can usually be divided into three types: *research laboratories,* which carry out basic and applied research – often situated away from manufacturing units; *development laboratories*, which are more closely related to particular products or services and act as support functions to local units; and *test laboratories*, which are usually responsible for monitoring the quality of chemicals, energy and materials bought by an organisation and the quality of output – e.g. medicines. The latter type may be subsumed under the technical services function. Smaller organisations that cannot afford laboratories may either manufacture goods that are licensed from research laboratories or they may outsource their R&D function.

## 13.2  Enabling functions

Enabling functions provide other functions' specialist services so that they can operate more effectively. For example, the HR function will help a production manager recruit new workers. This means that less of a production manager's attention is diverted to activities outside his or her main task or area of expertise. The three largest enabling functions, finance, HR and IT, are considered in later chapters. Most organisations have two further enabling functions: technical services and secretarial services.

### Technical services

The technical service function can take many forms. It can include the maintenance of buildings and equipment – especially where it is of a specialised or scientific nature. In these situations the technical services function will be responsible for testing, calibrating equipment and maintaining its usability. For example, an oil refinery might have a technical department that tests pilot plants before they go into service. In a chemical company the technical function may be responsible for neutralising dangerous chemicals before handing them on to external disposal contractors. The technical function often includes design and drawing-office work and is closely related to the R&D function. Where a product or service has a technical element the technical services may be called on to solve customers' problems. For example, paint manufacturers usually have a technical service department to investigate why paint may not have worked on the surface chosen by a customer. Sometimes, the technical service function is subsumed under the operations function.

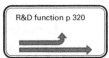

## Secretarial function

The secretarial function is found in most organisations. However, it is usually dispersed among the other functions and may not have a clear identity. In large organisations there will be a single department that is responsible for servicing meetings by producing agendas and publishing minutes. For example the House of Commons has a large secretarial function that is responsible for producing agendas and minutes of meeting and producing Hansard. With the advance of word processors and photocopiers the secretarial function as a separate entity has contracted and other employees have absorbed this work into their jobs. The secretarial function is most relevant to financial institutions and government bodies. Classic examples of a secretarial function is the registrar's department in a large university and a department that sends documents to a company's investors and shareholders.

## 13.3  Controlling functions

Controlling functions have a responsibility to prevent misuse of the organisation's resources. There are three main controlling functions: quality assurance, quality control and legal services. Parts of the finance function (discussed in Chapter 17) also perform control activities.

## Quality assurance

This is a *proactive* activity to arrange things in a way that ensures products and services are produced according to standards. It involves a series of systematic procedures designed to prevent "non-conformities". Quality assurance is a continuous process undertaken by all employees.

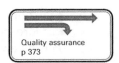

## Quality control

This is a *retroactive* activity to check production after various stages have been completed and extract defective products or services. It is usually the responsibility of a team of inspectors who may form a separate department within the production function.

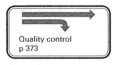

## Legal and administrative functions

Legal and administrative functions are also control functions. They exist to stop employees, and the organisation, from performing undesirable acts. In a large organisation the *legal function* will be "in-house" but in a medium or small organisation the legal function will be outsourced. The function will generally be staffed by a few highly trained and specialised staff. Their job is to ensure the organisation complies with external laws and regulations and does not enter into unfortunate contractual obligations. The legal function may also undertake litigation to advance or defend the organisation. Legal functions are particularly important in government organisations and quangos. Most large organisations have some kind of legal department to defend intellectual property such as patents, trademarks and copyright. The *administrative function* is responsible for ensuring that internal regulations and procedures are upheld. The administrative function is very important in governments and educational organisations and in bodies that award permissions, allowances and grants.

Finally, some organisations will have other control functions. For example, a chemical company may have a small unit to control the rate of noxious emissions from its chimneys and ensure that pollution laws are respected. Often, these specialised control functions are contained within a technical service function or the operations function.

# Marketing

## ❖ LEARNING OBJECTIVES

After reading this chapter you should understand some of the purposes and the position of the marketing function within organisations. You should be familiar with ways of analysing markets and understand the ideas behind the marketing mix. You should also be familiar with some of the general criticisms of the marketing function. In particular you should be able to:

- ❖ **define** both markets and marketing and explain key terms such as size, niches, segmentation and relationship marketing

- ❖ **explain** concepts such as competition, barriers to entry and exit and market dynamism

- ❖ **discuss in detail** market strategy and market positioning

- ❖ **contrast** briefly markets research and marketing research

- ❖ **list** seven uses and four methods of market research

- ❖ **discuss in detail** each of the five main components of the marketing mix

- ❖ **differentiate** between marketing and public relations

- ❖ **outline** some of the techniques and methods used in advertising

- ❖ **evaluate** at least four criticisms of marketing

In theory at least, marketing has prime place in the sequence of management functions because it identifies needs an organisation can exploit with a product or service. Once this need has been recognised, the other functions – operations, human resource management (HRM), finance function, etc. – can work together to produce the product or service. In fact, the marketing function also plays an important part at the end of the process – selling the finished product. Some people find it difficult to distinguish between marketing and sales. As a simplification, marketing is "having something you can get rid of" while selling is "getting rid of what you have!"

---

### CASE 14.1: *Marketing Red Bull*

You are late for a lecture, and feeling exhausted after last night's party. What you need is a pick-me-up. You pop into the nearest corner shop and scan the fridge which is full of cans of various fizzy drinks. You soon see that the shop has a promotion on a brand of cola (buy one get one free), but it's not your preferred choice. Luckily, it does sell your favourite energy drink which you eagerly buy, even though the smaller can represents relatively poor value. After a few swigs, the caffeine kicks in and you're feeling almost human again.

When you're shopping like this, do you ever wonder why does this shop sell one type of fizzy drink but not another? Do you wonder why they packaged the drinks in that way, or why one costs more than another? All these decisions have been made as part of somebody's marketing strategy, involving a complex mix of pricing, competition, promotion and positioning. And Red Bull is an excellent example of this.

In the early 1980s, Dietrich Mateschitz came across products known as "tonic drinks" while travelling in the Far East, including one, from Thailand which local workers used to stay awake during their shifts. It was called Krating Daeng or "Red Bull". Mateschitz bought the foreign licensing rights and decided to target young professionals, rather than factory workers, as they were more affluent and open to trendy marketing campaigns. The firm focused on "buzz marketing" or word of mouth, and the brand image was linked to youth culture and extreme sports, such as motor sports, mountain biking, snowboarding and dance music. Red Bull's target consumer segment began to adopt nicknames for the product such as "liquid cocaine" or "speed in a can", thus spreading its "left-field" appeal. Red Bull is now a leading player in the energy drinks field, yet still maintains an anti-corporate image.

The marketing of Red Bull involves a lot more than spotting a gap in the market and then developing an excellent brand image. It also included developing a marketing strategy based upon a great deal of market research. A sophisticated marketing mix was also developed to make Red Bull a competitive product. Last, but by no means least, it needed a large and well-motivated salesforce to get the product "on the shelves" so that the ultimate consumers could make their purchases. This chapter gives a greater understanding of all these aspects of marketing.

*Source*: based on: http://www.bized.co.uk/compfact/redbull/redbullindex.htm

## 14.1  Definition of marketing

Typical definitions assert that marketing is:

> 66 An organisational function and set of processes for creating, communicating and delivering value to customers and for managing customer relationships in ways that benefit the organisation and its stakeholders.
> *(American Marketing Association, 2004)* 99

> 66 Responsible for identifying, anticipating and satisfying customer requirements profitably.
> *(Hannagan, 2005)* 99

> 66 The management process responsible for identifying, anticipating and satisfying customer requirements profitably.
> *(Chartered Institute of Marketing [UK], 2010)* 99

Each of the definitions has disadvantages. The first is so megalomanic that it includes practically everything in an organisation. It does not differentiate between marketing and other essential functions such as production or finance. Two of the definitions imply, quite wrongly, that marketing only applies to commercial, profit-making, organisations. A definition which escapes these problems and which commands some consensus is:

> 66 A product or service's conception, pricing, promotion and distribution in order to create exchanges that satisfy consumers, organisational objectives and the interest of other stakeholders.
> *(See, for example, Health Advantage, 2004; Pride and Farrell, 2000; Quintessential Careers, 2004)* 99

This definition has a number of key features:

- It centres on the exchange relationship between consumers (in the broadest sense) and organisations.
- It emphasises that these exchanges should be satisfactory to all parties.
- It specifies the activities which constitute marketing.
- It implicitly accepts that other functions in the organisation play an important part in a satisfactory exchange.

Many writers emphasise the importance of adopting a marketing orientation where everyone in an organisation has a marketing role. For example, when a driver of a company van parks discourteously it tarnishes the company's image and affects its relationship with a customer. Similarly, an operative making a poor-quality product, an off-hand customer service assistant, a tardy accounts clerk and an arrogant chief executive all affect an organisation's relationship with customers and clients. The management guru, Peter Drucker (1999) takes the view that:

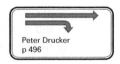

Peter Drucker
p 496

> 66    The purpose of business is to create and keep customers . . . it has only two
> functions – marketing and innovation. The basic function of marketing is to
> attract and retain customers at a profit.    99

This view is overstated. It makes marketing synonymous with everyone in an organisation so the term is therefore redundant. Further, there are many non-profit organisations where customer satisfaction is not the only organisational objective (e.g. the prison service). Nevertheless, most organisations need to have a **market orientation**. This is also called being "consumer centred" or being "consumer driven".

## 14.2 Successive views of the marketing function

Robert Keith (1960) argued that marketing functions had experienced a revolution. His ideas have been updated: current "periodisation" divides the marketing revolution into five phases (see below), and plentiful examples of of each phase still exist. Petkus (2010) suggests that practical outcomes can arise from a study of marketing history:

- **Production** orientation was the first phase – at its height from, say, 1870–1950. This marketing strategy emphasised producing as much of any product as cheaply as possible so that as many people as possible would buy it. This orientation is appropriate when a large, under-supplied market exists and where consumer tastes do not alter very quickly. A classic example would be Sunlight Soap, developed in 1884. There was a huge market but incomes were low. Further, there was not an over-supply of soap; there was a credo that "cleanliness is next to godliness" and smoke-filled skies guaranteed continuing demand. The manufacturers, Lever Brothers, only had to make huge quantities of soap at a low price and get it to the shops. They and their workers in Port Sunlight were "well off".

- **Product** orientation was very prominent from, say, the 1920s until the 1960s. This strategy emphasised the quality of a product in the belief that well-made products would dominate. This strategy is appropriate when a market is aspirational, incomes are rising and where other products are of dubious quality. A classic example would be the Hoover vacuum cleaner whose quality features included a "beater bar" and a headlight.

- **Selling** orientation was important during the 1950s and 1960s. It emphasised high sales and promoting products as much as possible – with relatively little attention to product design. It required good salespeople, advertising and points of display. A classic example would be the selling of washing powders where there was little difference between the products but they were heavily advertised in order to gain brand recognition and to encourage consumers to perceive the differences.

- **Marketing** in its current form gained importance in the 1970s. It is the dominant orientation today. It focuses on detecting and satisfying consumer needs. It is characterised by high levels of market research and good customer services. *Societal marketing* is now considered a major aspect of the marketing orientation. It emerged in the 1960s and is based on the idea that products should meet the needs of customers and also promote the well-being of society by refraining from products or selling methods that would be harmful. A good example of societal marketing would be the development of the Fair Trade organisation and the development of investments that are ethical. Much of the rest of this chapter is based on this orientation. However, the next edition of this text will probably need to include a section on academic advances in galactic marketing!

■ **Relationship marketing** stresses satisfying, and preferably long-lasting, links with customers. Quality products which satisfy customer needs remain important, but consultants and academics advise that a positive customer experience engendered by close attention to customers and good customer service is paramount. The aim is to develop customer loyalty so they repeat their purchases. A classic example of relationship marketing is Marks & Spencer's emphasis on good quality products, which used to be made in Britain for use by British people, at a sensible price and with good customer service which would not make exchanges or refunds difficult. Marks & Spencer's ubiquitous phrase "Your M&S" clearly exemplifies *they* have "bought into" relationship marketing. It is often thought that relationship marketing emerged during the 1970s but it has been present longer (see, Tadajewski and Saren, 2009).

---

**CRITICAL THINKING 14.1** *Are "stages" marketing's own QWERTY keyboard?*

The stages of the marketing "revolution" are reproduced in most contemporary textbooks. Yet, decades ago, Fullerton (1988) and Hollander (1986) disputed them. A recent analysis by Jones and Richardson (2007) shows that the other marketing orientations were clearly in existence during the period known as the production era. Jones and Richardson attribute the persistence of periodisation to "sloppy scholarship to plagiarising the work of other textbook authors". Perhaps there is an analogy with keyboard production. As noted earlier, while it is known that the QWERTY keyboard is very inefficient, it is so familiar that no manufacturer would dare to be the first to market something better – what a pity for us all!

---

## 14.3 Markets

*A market* (in contrast to *marketing*) may be defined as:

> 66 The actual or potential buyers of a product. 99

This means a market is wider than individuals: it includes private and public sector organisations, supplier groups and purchasing groups. It is also wider than present or past buyers: it includes anyone or any organisation that is reasonably likely to buy a product in the future. Kotler (1986) defined a product broadly as:

> 66 anything that can be offered to a market for attention, acquisition, use or consumption that might satisfy a want or need. It includes physical objects, services, persons, places, organisations and ideas. 99

An organisation that hopes to sell its product needs to study its market very carefully and may commission extensive market research. It needs to examine the characteristics of its market such as:

Market research p 335

- the *people* and *organisations* that make up the market
- the *product* or *service* it offers
- the *purpose* for which the product is bought and the *needs* it satisfies
- the *times* and *occasions* (e.g. birthdays, setting up a new home or everyday purchases) when the product is bought
- the *method used to buy* the product (e.g. retail outlet, regular order, telephone order or Internet shopping)

People and organisations do not buy products for their own sake. Products are bought because they *solve a problem* or confer *benefits* upon their owners. For example, organisations do not purchase a car for a sales representative because they want to own a car. It will be purchased because the organisation believes it will benefit from the sales representative's ability to visit more customers and it can be sure its image will not be damaged by its representative arriving in a clapped-out old banger.

Markets can differ in many ways. The main differences are size, competition, barriers and dynamism.

## Size, niches and market segmentation

Markets differ markedly in size. Some markets, such as detergents and cleaning materials, are vast and international. Global companies such as Proctor and Gamble have developed to meet the needs of such markets. In principle, large markets are good and lead to very cost-effective products because development costs are shared among millions of customers. However, these benefits accrue only if the large market is *homogeneous* (every consumer is quite similar and has comparable needs). It is difficult to mount an effective marketing campaign for a large, *heterogeneous* market (where there are distinctive groups with distinctive needs). It is usually better to target a smaller, more homogeneous group. by focusing upon a restricted range of products or consumers, i.e. a niche market.

A **niche market** is "a portion of a market whose needs are met by a restricted range of specialised products". A classic example is the Tie Rack chain. It operates within a wider market for clothing, but it sells only ties, scarves, handkerchiefs and other accessories. Appropriately, many of Tie Rack's outlets occupy physical niches at airports or railway stations. WesternGeco, a subsidiary of the American company Schlumberger, also operates within a niche market. It provides technically sophisticated seismic imaging services for oil companies. Catering for a niche market means an organisation can develop highly specialised expertise and project a distinctive image.

Another way to produce a homogeneous market is *market segmentation* where a wider market is divided into subgroups whose members have similar needs. Typical methods of market segmentation divide customers according to factors such as loyalty, age, gender, neighbourhood or social economic status.

Perhaps the most important way to segment a market is to divide it into *past customers* (i.e. loyal customers) and *new customers*. In the late 1990s there was a craze to focus upon past customers. The craze arose because, with the development of the Internet, customers had a much greater ability to "shop around" and become "promiscuous consumers". Many organisations therefore concentrated on establishing a dedicated base of existing customers and developing a long-term relationship that would prevent loyal customers switching to other suppliers. This is called "relationship marketing". It was supported by claims such as:

- Costs of acquiring a new customer are 10 times higher than keeping an existing customer.
- Loyal customers spend more than new customers.
- Past, satisfied customers tell others about their satisfaction.
- Past customers are more profitable because they are willing to pay a premium for a service they know.

The principles of relationship marketing were embraced by organisations trading with other organisations. For example, a computer software company would develop a close marketing relationship with its customers. Specific programmers would be devoted to specific clients so personalised assistance would be available if needed and they would help establish a deep, long-term and profitable relationship. Initially these concepts were applied to business organisations (**B2B transactions**). However, their relevance to retail transactions was quickly appreciated. Very successful examples of **customer management** and relationship marketing include the Tesco Clubcard scheme and Airmiles. A fundamental aspect of customer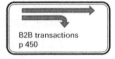

B2B transactions
p 450

management is the concept of **client life-cycle**. A new client needs to be welcomed, perhaps by email, and assured that they have made the correct choice. An established customer needs to be told that they are important and that the organisation wishes to attend to their needs. A long-established client needs to be made aware of new products.

Some of these basic beliefs have not withstood scrutiny. Werner and Kumar (2002) suggest that loyalty is not as profitable as the gurus of the 1990s suggested. For example, long-term customers tend to demand more favourable contracts. Further, many long-term customers make disproportionate demands in terms of customer support.

Market segmentation by *age* is also very common. Classic examples are the UK travel organisation Club 18–30 which markets lively Mediterranean holidays to youthful consumers, and the SAGA Group which markets holidays and financial products to people aged over 50 years. Market segmentation by age is widespread in the fashion and entertainment industries.

Market segmentation by *gender* is widespread in the publishing industry. For example magazines such as *Woman's Weekly* and *Cosmopolitan* are marketed for women, while *FHM* and *What Car* are marketed for men. Similarly, cars offered by major manufacturers will include some cars designed to appeal to women and other cars designed to appeal to men.

Market segmentation by *neighbourhood* is very common. For example, billboards in prosperous areas will depict luxury goods purchased out of discretionary income, while billboards in less affluent areas will advertise basic products. Probably the most extensive classification of residential areas is the ACORN system (CACI, 2010). Readers in the UK can obtain the ACORN classification of where they live by visiting the Internet site http://www.caci.co.uk/acorn-classification.aspx. The ACORN classification starts with five major categories:

1 wealthly achievers

2 urban prosperity

3 comfortably off

4 moderate means

5 hard-pressed

These are then subdivided into 17 major groups. For example, the wealthy achievers are subdivided into three groups: wealthy executives, affluent greys and flourishing families. The hard-pressed are divided into four groups: struggling families, burdened singles, high-rise hardship and inner-city adversity. The groups are further divided into subgroups. For example, the affluent greys, who comprise 7.7 per cent of the British population, are subdivided into older affluent professionals (1.8 per cent), farming communities (2.0 per cent), old people in detached homes (1.9 per cent) and mature couples (2.0 per cent). A manager marketing sophisticated financial products such as shares or annuities would target neighbourhoods containing many affluent greys, while a government department trying to ensure proper take-up of welfare benefits might target neighbourhoods containing many people experiencing high-rise hardship.

Markets are often segmented by *socio-economic status*. This system classifies markets according to the work performed by the head of the household. The categories are:

- A upper middle-class (e.g. directors, senior managers and senior civil servants)
- B middle-class (e.g. lawyers, doctors, middle managers and higher professional workers)
- C1 lower middle-class (e.g. teachers, nurses, junior managers and lower professional workers)
- C2 skilled workers including technologists and many engineering workers
- D working class
- E subsistence workers and unemployed people

Market segmentation by socio-economic status groups consumers who have similar spending power and preferences. This discussion covers only the most popular ways of dividing a large market into homogeneous groups. Many other methods exist. Markets are often segmented by lifestyle using categories with cute acronyms such as "YUPPIES" (young upwardly mobile persons), "DINKIES" (dual income no kids) or "GRUMPIES" (grown-up mature persons).

## Competition

In a captive market customers must purchase from a single supplier or do without. For a supplier a captive market is ideal because very little effort is needed to sell products. But, captive markets are like magnets to other organisations that set up in competition. Captive markets are very rare. A market is generally regarded as being a captive when there are fewer than four suppliers. Sometimes captive markets are called **monopolies** or **duopolies**. A market which has, say, more than 12 suppliers is generally called a "fluid market".

## Barriers to entry and exit

Captive markets exist in situations when it is difficult for competitors to enter. For example, in the aerospace industry there are often only one or two suppliers (e.g. Boeing or Airbus). Few organisations can afford the immense costs of setting up huge and complicated factories or build up the technical knowledge and expertise. **Barriers to entry** also exist in the form of laws and regulations such as patent laws, copyright laws and planning permissions. Distribution channels can also constitute entry barriers. Commercial practices by competitors may present further entry barriers – especially the practice of **predatory pricing** (OECD, 1989), whereby a large, established business cuts its price below its costs so that new competitors must sell at a loss and therefore eventually be driven out. **Exit barriers** prevent organisations withdrawing from markets. Usually they wish to exit because a market because it is unprofitable or it is no longer fits an organisation's strategy. Typical exit barriers include losing the capital already invested, the costs of making staff redundant, loss of prestige or government pressure.

---

### CASE 14.2: *Rockefeller's predatory pricing*

A classic case of predatory pricing is given by John D. Rockefeller's oil interests (Tarbell, 1950). A new entrant, the Pure Oil Company, was driven out of business when Rockefeller's Standard Oil Company drastically lowered its price, knowing that its vast reserves could survive a short-term loss in order to reap a long-term benefit of having the market to itself. Another example of predatory pricing is the way established airlines cut the price of their air fares in the 1970s to force a new entrant, Laker Airways, out of the transatlantic passenger market.

---

## Dynamism

A growing market is called an "expanding market". A market that is shrinking is called a "declining market" and one that stays the same is called a "static" or "stagnant market". It is generally easiest to operate in an expanding market. Organisations operating in a declining market need to pay very close attention to costs in the hope that they will be able to drive out less efficient competitors.

These characteristics are not the only factors that differentiate markets. In order to predict and anticipate markets it is necessary to understand six further influences such as those indicated by a PESTLE analysis. **Cultural factors** are also important characteristics of markets. For example, the French culture and traditions made it much more difficult for the McDonald's hamburger chain to enter the French market.

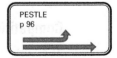

PESTLE
p 96

## 14.4  Market strategy and market positioning

Organisations often consciously decide, the type of market they prefer to serve. This is called "**market strategy**", "**market positioning**" or "**portfolio planning**". PESTLE analysis was developed to aid market positioning. Other schemes include the Boston matrix, the General Electric matrix and the Anscoff matrix.

The **Boston Consulting Group Matrix** (**BCG matrix**) focuses on two aspects of a market, its *dynamism* (growth rate) and relative *share of a market*. This allows products or services to be categorised into the four types shown in Figure 14.1.

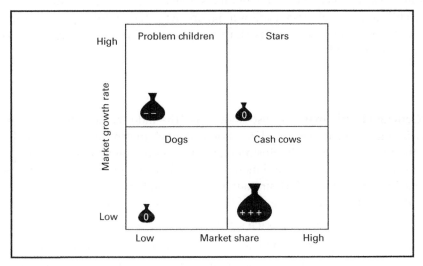

**FIGURE 14.1** The BCG matrix

If a product has a low market share in a slow-growing market, the product is classified as "a dog" because it is doing poorly in a weak market. The outlook is poor and an organisation might be well advised to consider eliminating the product from its range – preferably by selling it to someone else or, in the worst case, shutting it down. If the product has a low market share but operates in an expanding market, the organisation has a "problem child" because the outlook is mixed. The expanding market bodes well but the low market share implies a struggle to keep up with market leaders who will be able to obtain greater economies of scale. In these situations an organisation must decide whether to inject substantial resources. This may be risky. Sometimes, products categorised as "problem children" are called "cash hogs" because, like some adolescents, their potential is uncertain but they require large and frequent injections of cash. A product which commands a high share of a slowly growing market is categorised as a "cash cow". Its high market share means that economies of scale are achieved and a lot of money is generated. This money can be used to promote other projects such as "a problem child" or a "star". Organisations may become complacent about their "cash cows" and pay more attention to new products. Because of lack of investment the "cash cows" lose their competitiveness and turn into "dogs". A "star" is a product that has a high share of an expanding market. Generally, it will generate most of the funds needed for its own development and promotion but, from time to time, this may need supplementing by injections of resources from a "cash cow".

## CRITICAL THINKING 14.2 *What is wrong with the Boston matrix?*

The Boston matrix provides a reasonable basis for the allocation of development funds. However, it has its disadvantages (Morrison and Wensley, 1991). It oversimplifies markets by focusing upon just two aspects: market growth and market share. This may lead an organisation to ignore other important aspects (Haspeslagh, 1982). Moreover, the Boston matrix simplifies the two dimensions into just two crude categories; high and low.

The **General Electric matrix** is also known as "The Industry Attractiveness/ Business Strength" matrix or the "Directional Policy" matrix. It overcomes some of the disadvantages of the Boston matrix by incorporating *more factors* and allowing *three levels* for each dimension. The General Electric matrix has two composite dimensions: "industry attractiveness" and "business strength". **Industry attractiveness** is an amalgam of five characteristics, resembling PESTLE:

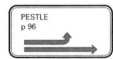

PESTLE
p 96

- *market forces* – size, growth, price sensitivity and bargaining position
- *competition* – as types of competitors or substitution by new technology
- *financial and economic factors* – economies of scale, profits, entry and exit barriers
- *technology* – market maturity, patents, copyrights and manufacturing technology
- *socio-political factors* – pressure groups, legal constraints and unionisation

The General Electric matrix then evaluates on factors reflecting **business strength**. Using these two dimensions an appropriate strategy is determined. In practice, this process is quite complicated because an intricate system of weights is applied to the characteristics of the industry and the strengths of the business or product. Figure 14.2 indicates appropriate strategy for products or sevices in each cell.

For example, a weak product in an unattractive market should be discontinued, preferably by its sale to another organisation. A strong product in a similarly unattractive market should be milked for all the cash it can generate. The case of a weak product in an attractive market is interesting. The organisation should either quit or take a gamble and invest many resources in the hope the product or service can be a market leader. It is similar to the "problem child" category of the BCG matrix.

Unfortunately, even a system as sophisticated as the General Electric matrix does not capture the full complexity of product positioning. For example, an established market leader can be positioned in a number of ways. It could try to obtain an even greater market

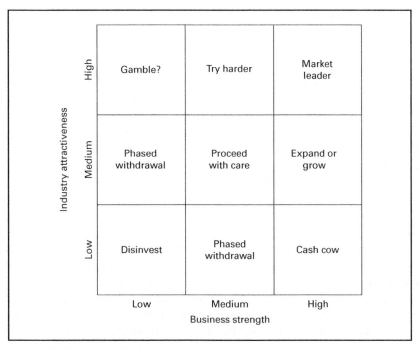

**FIGURE 14.2** The General Electric matrix

share. Alternatively, the product can be adjusted so that it appeals to a new market. Ansoff (1989) developed a matrix to aid these decisions. An Ansoff matrix focuses upon whether both the markets and the products are new or established. Figure 14.3 shows Anscoff's recommendation for each combination.

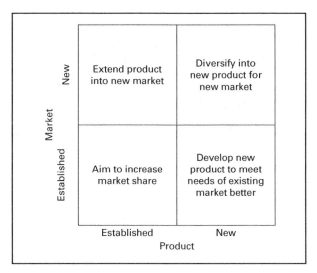

**FIGURE 14.3** The Ansoff matrix

Once a suitable market has been identified it is necessary to decide the organisation's position. It is often assumed that organisations should be market leaders or **pioneers** – devising new methods, opening up new markets and devising new products (Pettinger, 1997). They frequently have a high esteem. However, being a pioneer can be risky. There may be unknown difficulties. Pioneers carry substantial development costs. If the ideas are successful they can be copied, at less cost, by other organisations. An alternative, often more successful, marketing strategy is to adopt a "follow the leader" approach: keeping a keen eye on developments and maintaining a capability to quickly exploit the advances made by others. Other organisations adopt a strategy of building up a competitive advantage through **technical excellence**, or quality.

A marketing function must consider the maturity of their organisation's products or services and try to ensure their portfolios contain goods at different stages of the product life cycle. In general, product life cycles have five main phases, as shown in Figure 14.4.

The continuous line shows the "natural" progression of sales. When a new product or service is introduced, there is a period of slow growth of sales, followed by a rapid increase as the product or service is adopted by opinion leaders and then a wider range of consumers. At maturity, growth is either slow or there is a small decline as the product loses some of its "novelty value". At this point the product has wide acceptance. During the saturation phase, sales may decline because, although the market may be expanding, new competitors emerge. Finally, the product declines and sales generate little cash. This pattern varies greatly. In fashion items and children's toys, the whole life cycle is less than a year. In other cases such as "big ticket" items (e.g. televisions) the life cycle can be more than a decade. Organisations try to predict the life cycle of their products or services to ensure that they have new products "in the pipeline" to replace saturated or declining products. The life cycle

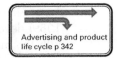
Advertising and product life cycle p 342

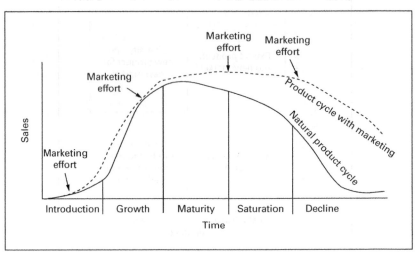

**FIGURE 14.4** Product life cycle

of products is particularly important in industries such as pharmaceuticals where it can take decades to develop new medicines. Marketing functions monitor the life cycles of products for a second reason. By mounting a marketing effort, such as advertising, new packaging or restyling at key times, sales can be boosted to extend the product life cycle. The effect of a marketing effort on a product life cycle is demonstrated by the dotted line in Figure 14.4.

## 14.5  Understanding markets (market research)

**M**arket research is defined by the American Marketing Association (2004) as:

> ❝ the function that links the consumer, customer and public to the marketer through information – information used to identify and define marketing opportunities and problems; generate, refine and evaluate marketing actions; monitor marketing performance; and improve understanding of marketing as a process. ❞

The terms "market research", "markets research" and "marketing research" sound very similar. **Market research** refers to *any* information about markets. **Markets research** is looks at the characteristics of markets. **Marketing research** looks at information concerning a specific product or service. It is useful to divide market research into two main activities: *markets research* and *marketing research*.

## Markets research

Research on markets is sometimes called "market intelligence". It obtains information, usually quantitative, on the size of a market, its growth, its use of technology, its dynamism and the level of competition. Often markets research is based on existing (secondary) data compiled by government and industry sources such as census figures, the retail price index and the value of imported goods. It may also use journal and newspaper articles to build up a picture of competitors.

## Marketing research

Marketing research is information that will be useful to organisations who wish to sell specific products. It is the research which, say, the brand manager for Coca-Cola uses to devise an advertising campaign. Marketing research overlaps with research on markets but its focus is narrower and is closer to the point of sale. Marketing research can, perhaps, best be considered under two headings: usage and methods.

### *Uses of marketing research*

Marketing research can play a vital role in bringing to market a product valued by customers and which is presented to them in an enjoyable way. Marketing research's main uses include:

- *Product generation* – identifying new products by listening to consumers, brainstorming sessions with designers and marketing executives.

- *Product improvement and embellishment* – again, the source of suggestions can be consumers or brainstorming. Ideas may also be generated by examining competitors' products or even products and services in other markets.

- *Product testing and refinement* – prototypes of products and services can be tested on small groups of consumers. Their reactions and comments are usually incorporated in a modified product.

- *Consumer targeting* – pinpointing the people who are most likely to buy the product or use a service.

- *Sales forecasting.*

- *Packaging and advertising design* – various suggestions for packaging or adverts can be tested on consumers and the most effective chosen.

- *Point-of-sale displays and procedures* – developing and then refining point of sale displays, brochures, etc.

### Marketing research methods

The main sources of marketing research are:

- **Existing internal data** – sales records, call reports and especially quotations that have been not been taking up by customers. Customer loyalty schemes routinely gather vast amounts of information on consumers. **Surveys** have many forms. The simplest is a questionnaire returned by a purchaser when she or he registers a guarantee. Many organisations also use **questionnaire surveys**. Questionnaire surveys are administered by market researchers who approach customers, who fit their **quotas**, as they visit shopping malls, etc. Alternatively, they may be administered in a more rigorous way to a **random sample** of people. Random samples are much more expensive than quota samples. Questionnaires *may also* be distributed via the post but this method may result in a very poor response rate. The telephone and the Internet are also used to administer questionnaires. However, the sample of respondents may be very unrepresentative.

- Questionnaires need to be constructed to ensure that questions are "neutral". A series of questionnaires administered to the same group of people is called **consumer panel**. Consumer panels have the advantage that they can track changes in customer preferences. Unfortunately, repeated questioning of the same people can sensitise them to issues so that they gradually become unrepresentative. Some unscrupulous organisations use questionnaires as a way of introducing themselves to people, getting them to divulge information and then attempting to sell them a product. This is called "SUGGING" (selling under the guise). Charities also use surveys as a ruse to raise funds. This is called "FRUGGING" (fund-raising under the guise). Both practices are unethical.

- **Focus groups** or **group discussions** are frequently used in market research – especially when customers' underlying attitudes to new or changing situations are relevant. Focus groups consist of, say, 12 people representing different types of consumers plus a leader who ensures they cover the required topics. Focus groups may attempt to assess "emotions" and "deep attitudes". Some techniques are exotic and perhaps silly. Partricipants, might be asked to nominate a type of tree that they associate with a certain public figure. In better situations, a focus group is asked to taste a new drink and compare it to existing drinks. **Experiments** are used infrequently. Usually they are employed to study the impact of advertisements and packaging and they often take the form of observing consumer behavior. For example, a supermarket may stock shelves in a different ways and videotape the behaviour of customers. The videotape will be analysed to establish which shelf layout generates most purchases.

## 14.6  The marketing mix

Successful marketing involves an appropriate combination of five main factors. This combination is called the **marketing mix** and is based on the "5 Ps": **p**roduct or service, **p**rice, **p**ackaging, **p**romotion and **p**lace of purchase.

## Products

A product can be either a physical entity or a service. Ownership of a physical entity changes hands when a *product* is purchased. When a *service* is purchased ownership is not transferred. From a marketing viewpoint, the most important feature of either is the *benefit* it bestows upon the customer. An engineer, a technologist, and a design specialist may eulogise about the product's features or its technical sophistication. However, these are only important if the consumer believes that they confer some benefit. Benefits may be a saving of time, enabling a previously impossible task, a feeling of well-being and attractiveness or an increase in status. In other words a product or service must solve or ease a problem for the consumer. For example, consumers do not buy computers because they can add up numbers quickly or because they are high technology. They buy computers because the machines solve problems such as communicating with others, writing assignments, keeping accounts or storing information. If a product or service confers benefits its competitors do not, the product has a "**unique selling-point**".

Consumers frequently judge products on the basis of their **quality** – freedom from imperfections and an implication of exclusivity or "class". Marketeers imply quality when they offer "fine wines", "prime beef", "select cheeses", "high-calibre education", and so on. Generally products must also offer **durability** – functioning satisfactorily for an acceptable time. However, in some products (razors, pens, live entertainment, etc.) durability is not expected.

**Brand** is important. Marketing functions give their brands close attention. Brands started when farmers burnt distinctive marks into the flesh of their cattle so that they could be identified should they stray or be stolen. Farmers who produced good cattle were particularly keen on branding because their brand would be recognised at market and their cattle would command a higher price. In the early days of mass production good producers of products such as cornflakes (Kelloggs) or soap (Pears) would mark their products with a distinctive mark. As the brands of cornflakes or soap became better known, manufacturers took steps to ensure other people could not use the same mark. They also promoted brands via advertising that made them instantly recognisable and invoked positive associations in consumer's minds. Kellogg's, for example, developed a brand which is associated with freshness, sunshine and vitality. Today, most major products carry brands, some of which are so well known that they are very valuable. Some of the most famous brands in the USA include Coca-Cola, Ford, McDonald's, Microsoft and GAP. Other world-famous brands include BP, Cadbury, IKEA, Nintendo, Qantas and Rip Curl.

The major advantage of brands is that they add benefits to a product. A classic experiment by Penny, Hunt and Twyman as long ago as 1974 neatly demonstrates the point. They asked consumers who normally used brand B to try two products without knowing their brand. A majority (61 per cent) preferred brand A while 39 per cent preferred brand B. Another group also tried the same two products. For this group the brands were known. 35 per cent were found to prefer brand A while 65 per cent preferred brand B. A brand may be defined as:

> 66 A symbolic construct created by a marketeer to represent a collection of information about a product or group of products. This symbolic construct typically consist of a name, identifying mark, logo, visual images or symbols or mental concepts which distinguish the product or service. 99

A brand projects a product's "promise" and differentiates it from competitors, and may attempt to give a product a "personality". To be successful, a brand must have several characteristics (see iboost, 2005). These include:

- *Simple, clear messages.* A campaigning message or one which seems to go against the "Establishment" (e.g. the themes of the Benetton and FCUK branding) are often a "cheap" way to success.
- *Credibility* – so claims are believed.
- *Motivation of customers* which increases the enjoyment of purchasing products with the brand. This makes it more likely that purchases will actually take place.
- *Creation of strong user loyalty.* This is, perhaps, the most important aspect of branding.

Once a brand has been established, it can be extended to other products. This reduces the cost of a new project gaining a place in the market. However, extension to weak or inappropriate new products can cause significant damage to a brand image.

## Price

As a broad generalisation, a marketing function will set the price of its goods at a *level* above its costs and as much as the product or service can command.

Exceptions to this rule are almost as many as adherents. The ability and willingness of consumers to pay for a product is important. It is pointless marketing a product or service at a price beyond the means of customers. The variation in supermarket and petrol prices from region to region or town to town is a clear example of how the ability of the consumer to pay influences prices: in affluent areas prices are usually higher than in poorer areas. Luxury goods are a classic example where people are willing to pay substantially more than the production costs. The price of diamonds, for example, has, for over a century, been maintained at an artificially high level. Superb branding (a diamond is forever) and a superb cartel (DeBeers) meant that the price of diamonds could be controlled so that the very affluent and starry-eyed men would pay high prices (*see* Economist, 2004).

Sales of some products respond very quickly to changes in price while the sales of other products change very little if the price increases or decreases (this is called **price sensitivity** or **elasticity of demand**). The price of vegetables such as broccoli is very price sensitive because people will switch to another vegetable such as cauliflower if there is a small price increase. On the other hand, many medicines are price insensitive. People will cut back on other purchases in order to have money to buy medicines that might save their life. If a product or service has an inelastic demand, the marketing function of an organisation can engage in **price-skimming** – supplying only the upper fraction (those who can afford high prices) of the market. They can charge very high prices which quickly recover development and production costs. Price-skimming enables an organisation to build a considerable surplus so that, should a competitor enter the market, they can afford to engage in predatory pricing. Branding can also raise prices. Classic examples are the pharmaceutical industry where branded, well-advertised products supported by an excellent sales force can cost several times more than an equally effective generic medication. For example, the painkiller Neurofen costs more than the equally effective generic drug Ibuprofen. However, the generic drug Ibuprofen does not have to bear the marketing, sales and advertising costs incurred by the branded version.

The price of products is heavily influenced by marketing strategy. For example, new products, such as plasma screen televisions, are introduced at a very high price to establish an aspirational position at the top of the market. This confers prestige that will help sustain a higher price among naive and impressionable consumers.

The price of a product or service may be concealed. For example, people can visit many tourist attractions such as museums, parks or educational "lectures" without any fee. However, someone, somewhere, will be paying higher taxes to sustain their enjoyment. In fact, a marketing function's dream is to separate the person who uses the product from the person or organisation that pays – that way the demand will stay high despite high prices.

## Packaging

Packaging is not often considered as a separate aspect of the marketing mix and it is usually subsumed under the heading of "promotion". In practice, the marketing function of most organisations will pay considerable attention to the way goods are packaged because it can make a very substantial difference to sales. Further, packaging has the important purpose of ensuring a product is delivered in prime condition. Packaging can also be used to increase the perceived benefit. For example, some items are packaged in an oversized box in an attempt to make the customer believe that the product is bigger than its actual size. Similarly, some products such as jewellery, are packaged in grossly expensive cases made of embossed leather and silk in order to enhance the perceived value of their contents.

The characteristics of good packaging include:

- *It is distinctive* from its competitors.
- *The colours are appropriate to the product's benefits.* For example, the packaging of a valuable item is likely to be coloured in gold and silver, while the packaging of a fun item is likely to be coloured in vivid reds, oranges and yellows.

- It *displays the brand name* in a prominent position.
- It contains a *flattering picture of the product* where happy people (sometimes, animals) clearly enjoy the benefits of a purchase.

## Promotion

Promotion is also called "**marketing communications**" and may be defined as:

> 66 Any type of persuasive communication between the marketing function and one or more of its present customers, potential customers or stakeholder groups which aims, directly or indirectly, to increase the likelihood that time, product or service will be purchased. 99

This definition has four important components. *First*, it emphasises the central concept of persuasive communication. *Second*, the aim of communication is to increase purchases. *Third*, communications are directed at a target that is wider than the organisation's present customers. *Finally*, some communications may be closely linked to the sales process in the short term, while other communications may be designed to have an indirect, longer-term effect.

### Public relations

Public relations (PR) is also known as "**perception management**" and critics such as Chomsky (2002) have called it "manufacturing consent", "media control" or "spin". It may be defined as:

> 66 A part of the promotional mix that communicates with stakeholders, the media and the public in general in order to achieve broadly favourable and supportive attitudes towards a product, organisation or cause. 99

A shorter and less technical definition for public relations might be "the management of an organisation's image". Both definitions emphasise that public relations is a general activity and is only loosely tied to the sale of a specific product. It aims to obtain a generally favourable attitude so that subsequent, more specific communications are likely to succeed. Often, an organisation's marketing function will employ specialist public relations consultants to maintain its image. Public relations experts use six main methods:

- **Press conferences** are public or quasi-public events where speakers provide information on newsworthy items. They are stage-managed and attended by selected journalists and television reporters.
- **Press releases** are also called "news releases" and may consist of short fax statements sent to the media.
- **Publicity events** are contrived situations designed to attract media attention. Outrageous publicity events are sometimes called "**guerrilla marketing**".
- **The circuit** refers to the "talk-show circuit" where public relations consultants attempt to get their clients or spokespersons to appear on these programmes.

- **Books, brochures** and other writings are sometimes commissioned and published on behalf of clients.
- **Press contacts** are developed assiduously so that they can be fed information about the organisation in the hope that the reporter will write a favourable story.

Public relations experts often identify opinion leaders and powerful people ("movers and shakers"). They then attempt to develop friendships by offering corporate hospitality at events such as the Chelsea Flower Show, the Happy Valley racecourse in Hong Kong or Australia's prestigious Telstra motor rally.

Sometimes public relations organisations engage in "cause-related marketing" – giving a proportion of their profits to a good cause in the hope that their generosity will reflect positively on them.

### CASE 14.3:  *Cause-related marketing*

A classic example of cause-related marketing is given by Christmas card manufacturers who hope to promote their sales by promising to give 10 per cent of their profits to charities. A clever and ingenious example of this is provided by Tesco's "Computers for Schools" campaign in which shoppers are given vouchers to pass to their local school. However, cause-related marketing can backfire. In 2003 Cadbury sold chocolate bars with tokens which a school could exchange for sports equipment. The scheme caused uproar. It was criticised by the Food Commission for encouraging obesity rather than a healthy, sporty lifestyle.

### Internal promotion

Internal promotion aims to alter the attitudes of the organisation's own workforce. It is particularly relevant when new products are being launched. Internal communications tend to foster the "team spirit" within an organisation. Further, staff become an unofficial salesforce who talk about the new product with their relatives, friends and acquaintances.

### CASE 14.4:  *Guerrilla marketing*

A good example of guerrilla publicity occurred in August 2002 when Vodafone arranged for two men to "streak" at an international rugby game with the Vodafone logo painted on their backsides. The men's magazine *FHM* provides another good example of guerrilla marketing. The magazine cover featured a nude photograph of a former children's television presenter. After doctoring the photograph to preserve her modesty, *FHM* projected it onto one of the towers of the Houses of Parliament. Both stunts earned considerable free publicity. World Cup authorities take guerrilla marketing very seriously indeed. Perhaps they do not wish to endanger the money earned by official sponsorship. The official beer sponsor for the 2010 World Cup was Budweiser. However, a Dutch brewery, mystifyingly called Bavaria, decided to impinge with some very mild guerrilla publicity. Thirty-six blonde beauties attended a match wearing orange tops and miniskirts – no slogans, just the colour of the Dutch team. The FIFA marketing police were enraged. The orange-clad blonde beauties were escorted from the terraces and two of them were arrested, carted off to jail and arraigned with criminal charges. Of course they were subsequently released. The Dutch brewery must have been over the moon because comparable publicity would have cost a lot of money. FIFA officials and the South African police did their own reputation some harm.

In 2010 the British Conservative Party anticipated the route that the outgoing prime minister would take on the way to seek the Queen's approval for a general election. They also anticipated that the media would film his progress from helicopters. So, they arranged supporters to be along the route. They held aloft big placards promoting the Conservative cause. Few television newscasts could resist the images.

### Advertising

Advertising *promotes specific goods and services*. It may be defined as:

> Attracting public attention to a product, service or issue using non-personal methods of communication with a view to persuading the targets to adopt certain behaviours or thought patterns. Usually the desired behaviour is to purchase a product and the advertising organisation usually pays for the advertisement to be put before the target audience.

It should be noted that advertising is impersonal. There is no one-to-one contact between buyer and seller. This distinguishes advertising from selling. Moreover, advertising concerns specific products or services. This distinguishes it from public relations.

An advertising campaign can have a number of objectives depending upon a product's position in the product life cycle. If the product is new, the campaign is likely to focus on making target customers aware that the product exists. It may also try to establish the new product's position in the market and its brand. Advertising a new product will also emphasise its unique benefits and appeal to people's needs for novelty and the status from being an early adopter. During the growth stage, advertising may seek to reassure tentative purchasers and boost confidence in the product. In the maturity and saturation stages, advertising will seek to differentiate one brand from another. At this stage the main objective will be to increase, or at least preserve, market share. Organisations may engage in either defensive or offensive advertising. Offensive advertising ("knocking copy") points out weaknesses of competitors' products.

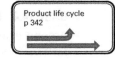
Product life cycle
p 342

Advertisers use many media including: **billboards** ( "poster hoardings") (lorries, taxis or buses); **leaflets** (also known as "flyers") (distributed in the street); **direct mail** (magazines) newspapers, skywriting, Web-banners; **radio, cinema** and **television**. The exact choice depends on the product and target audience. For example, luxury goods are unlikely to be advertised using leaflets distributed in the street. They are more likely to be advertised in upmarket magazines.

An advertisements first job is to **a**ttract attention, then develop the **d**esire for the product and finally to encourage consumers to take **a**ction and purchase the product (ADA). Methods may include:

- *Repetition* – very important with new products where the aim is to make people remember the name.

- *Bandwagon campaigns* implying everyone is purchasing the product or service and to be without it would be odd. This tactic is frequently used during a product's growth stage.

- *Testimonials* appeal to people's propensity to obey authority. They may quote sources of authority such as "five out of six doctors eat product X".

- *Pressure campaigns* often take the form of "buy now, before stocks are gone" or "buy now, before a tax increase". This tactic is frequently used during a product's maturity stage.

- *Association campaigns* try to link products with desirable things and attractive or famous people. Association campaigns are often used in conjunction with testimonials.

---

**CASE 14.5:** *Misleading advertisements*

In 2002 the Chinese State Drug Administration estimated that 89 per cent of advertisements for drugs and medical services were illegal. Specific examples of misleading advertisements are found throughout the world. In 2003 the American Federal Drug Agency (FDA) ordered Purdue Pharma to withdraw advertisements for a painkiller, OxyCotin, because they failed to mention a fatal side effect. A rather different criticism was levelled against the American milk industry's campaign "got milk" featuring celebrities with "milk moustaches". Physicians complained that the advertisements ignored data linking high milk consumption with heart disease and prostate cancer. Their complaints were supported by the Department of Agriculture (USDA).

---

## Place

Place is the fifth and final component of the marketing mix. It is the location where ownership of goods is transferred or where a service is performed. The place where a product is marketed depends on two main factors: distribution channels and customer expectations.

### Distribution and place

Transporting goods to market, storing them until requested by a customer, employing sales staff and providing a setting which the customer finds conducive can cost as much as the production of an article or service. Few organisations can afford to provide these facilities on a national or regional basis; hence they need to rely on other people, wholesalers and retailers. Since wholesalers and retailers act on behalf of many producers the costs can be shared. Moreover, wholesalers and retailers develop specialist expertise so distribution costs are minimised. Historically, the location of the transfer of goods and services happened in marketplaces at the centre of towns and cities. Then it took place in shops in the centre of towns and cities. Now, with motor transport, goods and services are exchanged for money in an often purpose-built **shopping mall** or **retail park** on a motorway circling a large town.

However, a traditional *shop* or a *department store* is not always appropriate or convenient. **Catalogue sales**, for example, are more convenient for people in isolated communities or those who are confined to homes by disability. Some organisations have deliberately developed alternatives to the traditional chain of retail distribution. Tupperware developed a new distribution structure by *selling its products in people's homes* at Tupperware parties. This reduced costs and used social pressures. **Catalogue showrooms**, pioneered by Argos, reduce the need for space to display merchandise. Consequently catalogue showrooms offer a wider range of products at a keen price. However, they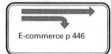

E-commerce p 446

require superb logistics to ensure that a replacement article is sent from a central store on the same day one is sold. With the Internet a growing number of transactions take place in *cyberspace*.

### Customer experience and place

Customers have clear images and expectations about where they will buy goods. If these expectations are not met they do not buy. They expect to buy cabbages at a greengrocer and not at a newsagent. They expect to buy expensive jewellery in a plush setting where they receive a great deal of personal attention. Consequently, a marketing function will pay great attention to the image of the place where its goods or services are exchanged, This is known as the "**merchandise assortment**". The merchandise assortment must be consistent with the ideas of the consumer otherwise they are unlikely to enter the store to find a suitable article. Another important factor image is *location*. People expect stores to be located among other stores selling similar or complementary products. For example, it is expected that a store selling chairs and tables will be near a store that sells carpets, which in turn will be near a store that sells curtains. Stores arranged in a line next to a large parking area are called a "strip". Stores that are arranged around a central area designed for sitting, strolling and perhaps taking light refreshments are called, especially in America, a "mall".

The interior of a store will be laid out so it gives a customer an experience which is consistent with the image of the organisation. The physical characteristics such as decor, displays and layout are called "atmospherics" or "ambiance". Most important, the exterior atmospherics, which indicate the type of things a store will sell, exert a strong influence on a customer's willingness to enter. Interior atmospherics, which may include music, influence a customer's movement and mood. A primary concern will be to draw potential consumers to the back of a store by using a particularly attractive display or moving image. Once drawn to the back of a store a customer will be encouraged, perhaps by appropriate music or exotic displays, to tarry. As they tarry, they are more likely to make a purchase. A way for supermarkets to draw customers to the further reaches of their stores is to place essential items such as bread at the furthest distance from the entrance. Supermarkets have long appreciated the importance of layout. For example, sales are increased if essential items are positioned either on high shelves or on low ones. Discretionary items are placed on shelves at eye level. As consumers reach for essential items they are likely to see, and purchase, discretionary products. Similarly, supermarkets know that the ends, between aisles, are positions where products are most likely to be selected.

## CRITICAL THINKING 14.3 *The charges against marketing*

Marketing is more controversial than other management functions. Its intentions – to interpret and fulfil customer demand – are impeccable. It also plays an undeniable role in creating mass markets which bring economies of scale that in turn drive prices down to the benefit of most people. However, its critics also have a strong case. Their indictment includes misleading advertisements, manipulation, encouragement of antisocial behaviour, creation of false markets and dumbing down.

Use of *misleading advertisements* is a frequent criticism. The malpractice seems to be particularly prevalent in the pharmaceutical and food industries where advertisements may claim spurious health benefits. In some countries the problem seems endemic. The marketing function is often accused of *underhand manipulation*. Advertisements may not openly state a product's benefits. They may be implied by information of which the consumer is unaware. In other words, consumers are induced to buy products by messages outside their awareness or logical control. This reflects an imbalance in power and resources. A consumer buying an everyday product can only devote seconds to their choice. A multinational organisation marketing the same product to millions of individuals can devote a team of a dozen or more experts for several months to devise ways to induce a consumer to make a purchase. One tactic is to target people with fewer evaluative powers. For example, makers of a breakfast cereal may *target adverts at children* knowing that, in turn, they will pressurise their parents.

Another tactic might be **subliminal advertising,** which involves projecting a message at a very low level so that people are not conscious of the message being there. For example, an advertiser might project a very faint advertisement during a soap opera programme. The advert is so faint that the viewer does not realise it is there but the message is registered subconsciously. Initial experiments showing subliminal advertising could be effective were seriously flawed. Modern research shows that subliminal advertising does not work. Subliminal advertising is illegal in many countries. Underhand manipulation is not limited to the use of children or subliminal adverts. It can arise from non-verbal messages. An advertisement may not explicitly state that a product will bring wealth and power. It may, however, imply these benefits by including images of wealthy and powerful people. For example, a business school prospectus might include photographs of successful business people boarding an aeroplane en route to a meeting on international strategy. However, it may know, full well, that most of its MBAs work within the domestic economy. One of the first people to note manipulation by the marketing function was Packard (1957).

Criticisms of the marketing function for using misleading advertisements are by no means restricted to the pharmaceutical or food industries. The travel industry, especially companies selling air fares, is frequently admonished for misleading, bait and switch tactics. Hectares of Sunday newspapers are covered with offers of cheap flights. Yet, when even the nimblest consumer telephones, there are no remaining seats at the cheapest rates. They are encouraged to switch to more expensive, and presumably more profitable, flights.

Some people criticise marketing for *encouraging antisocial behaviour*. Attracting attention is a major problem. There is so much advertising and so much media coverage that an organisation's message may get lost. An easy solution is shock tactics. But many shock tactics involve antisocial behaviour. For example, an organisation producing crisps (chips) might draw attention to its product with an advertisement depicting a pupil successfully deceiving a teacher during a mathematics lesson to eat crisps. The advertisements would probably increase the sales of the crisp manufacturer. However, it would make classroom discipline more difficult. It might mean the skills of a future generation are impaired so that a country has a reduced ability to provide social goods such as transport or health care.

The marketing function will usually seek to maximise the benefit for its own organisation rather than the community. It may benefit the organisation to develop and market a new product that is unnecessary and which will, in the long term, damage people and their society. In essence, this criticism accuses the marketing function of *developing and exploiting unnecessary and dangerous consumer needs*. For example, the market research of the company Masterfoods (MARS) revealed a marketing opportunity for a large wafer, chocolate caramel cream confectionary bar for women. It developed a product, Mars Delight, which was launched in Ireland. A marketing spend of £15 million was devoted to promoting this product. However, in the light of increasing obesity in the developed world, Mars was criticised for developing a needless and, possibly dangerous, product.

Perhaps the most important criticism against the marketing function is its *impact on society*. Because of its economic power and its expertise, the influence of the marketing is very widespread and pervasive. This leads to two further criticisms. First, it promulgates a capitalist, market ethos which ignores other social, cultural and aesthetic considerations. Probably more important is the impact on intellectual standards – *dumbing down*. The marketing function will wish to appeal to as many people as possible. This behaviour might lead to a society with low standards.

Many of these criticisms may be unfair because they are directed at the image of the marketing function. The marketing function may be partly responsible as a victim of its own hype. Further, many countries have enacted legislation that curb marketing's worst excesses.

## 14.7 The sales function

The sales function is ignored by many textbooks. However, practising managers such as Henry Ford knew the value of the sales function. He is reported to have said that *nothing* has value until it is actually sold. Strategy can be superb, production can be lean, finance can be sophisticated and the human resources function can be inspirational, but a commercial organisation will die unless it sells its products or services.

### CRITICAL THINKING 14.4 *Why do textbooks shun sales?*

Most management textbooks wax lyrical about marketing and marketing strategy and devote endless chapters to them, but sales is all but ignored except for a brief mention of sales promotion. This is clearly unbalanced since many of the top organisations such as Marks & Spencer, Tesco, B&Q, Amazon, John Lewis, IKEA, Carphone Warehouse and DSG (formerly Dixons) are predominantly sales organisations. How does this imbalance come about? Why do academics and researchers tend to shun the sales function? There are at least three possible reasons:

1 Academics and researchers work in universities and colleges where income is provided by the state and the sales function, if any, is small. They are unaware of its importance.

2 They have a negative view of sales as the mere pursuit of profit and lucre – this, they believe, is so much less worthy than the pursuit of truth, knowledge and learning.

3 The topic of sales is less congenial to academic study. An understanding of sales requires more than reading a few books and research papers. It may need some actual experience. Further, sales requires more than analysis and contemplation. It requires practical, emotional and social skills.

A cynic might maintain that people who are interested in sales avoid academic life, with its writing and research, because so much more money can be earned working in sales than writing about it.

The sales function covers a huge range of situations – from someone on a street corner selling the *Big Issue* to a very high-powered executive selling an inter-continental computer system. There are many instances of heinous sales methods. The techniques to sell timeshares and the methods employed by consultants and advisers in the finance and pension industries are sometimes very questionable indeed. Often, the common link in bad sales is a highly geared bonus or commission system. Nevertheless, these examples of sales give an inaccurate caricature. The vast majority of sales staff are oriented to providing a service to provide a benefit to the community. For example, without the activities of pharmaceutical company's sales representatives many GPs would remain ignorant of medications that would be good for their patients.

Most sales situations can be fitted into one of two categories: B2C (business to customer) and B2B (business to business) sales There are at least two general approaches to **B2C sales**. At the lower end, where the product is worth less than, say, £2, or where local enthusiasts for a charity aim to raise contributions, a pushy approach may yield benefits. People will contribute £1 or £2 to avoid hassle. However, a pushy sales approach soon reaches its limits. Sales people selling big-ticket items need to adopt a much more thoughtful approach. Within seconds, they need to evaluate the best way to approach a customer and to elicit their likely needs. It is often said that a good salesperson sells with their ears, not with their mouths! When needs are clarified a salesperson needs to suggest appropriate purchases and the **benefits** that the purchases will provide. Inexperienced sales staff often make the mistake of pointing out the technical features of a purchase such as a television screen with a faster refresh rate. An experienced salesperson, on the other hand, emphasises the benefits of a better viewing experience of, say, a soccer match where a football in flight is smooth rather than juddering. The sales function will be responsible for training sales staff. Much of this training will be on-the-job training but most sales staff will attend a course on selling techniques. Many different approaches are available. Perhaps the best known is the AIDA method which has four stages:

E-commerce B2C and B2B p 450

- First, **Attract** the customer's attention in a pleasant and civilised way.
- Second, **Interest** the customer in a product.
- Third, develop the customers **Desire** to own the product (anticipating the benefits).
- Finally, induce the customer to take a vital **Act** of making the purchase.

**Business-to-business sales** can be very sophisticated. In essence, a sales representative will aim to establish a long-term relationship where they are regarded as a trusted adviser. Again there are many methods and training courses. Perhaps the best known is "**the seven steps of the sale**" which is also known as PSS – professional selling. The seven steps are:

1 *Plan the approach carefully.* The larger the organisation the greater the need for research about its structure, suppliers and the organisation's strategy, etc. Gaining access can be a major problem. It is usually vital to establish a good rapport with a decision-maker's personal assistant since they can grant or deny access. They can also provide information that is very useful at a later stage.

2  *Prepare a friendly, professional and confident introduction* to the first meeting and set the scene by asking how much time is available and if it is acceptable to start by asking questions and taking notes. In some situations a *brief* description of your own organisation and its capabilities might be appropriate at this stage.

3  *Use thoughtful questions* to determine the needs of the organisation. Often there is a major need plus subsidiary ones. Questioning should be done with empathy and the responses should be listened to most carefully. Body language is important. Questions should also cover how the organisation might prefer to develop your relationship. *Make a presentation* which focuses upon how the benefits of the product match the needs of the organisation. The presentation should also show an understanding of the organisation. *Overcome* objections and comments. Often the first response should be to clarify the issue by asking questions such as "what makes you say that?" Many objections are merely requests for further information. Use questions and objections to develop a constructive discussion.

4  *Close the sale* – but not too early! A standard closing is, "Are you happy that we've covered everything and would like to go ahead?" – but many other ploys exist.

5  *Follow-up* depends on the type of product or service. At the very least it should be a call to confirm that they customer is happy with the product and its delivery. Follow-up may provide good opportunities for extending a network of contacts.

Business-to-business sales may involve other activities. It may, for example, include advising customers how to display your products. It may involve explaining the product to your customer's staff and perhaps training them to use it. Above all else, sales representatives gather a great deal of intelligence about the market – its trends and opportunities – which the marketing function and the organisation as a whole might exploit.

## 14.8 The marketing plan

Many marketing functions formalise their intentions into a marketing plan for the next three or more years. The process is a special version of planning in general, which was explained in Chapter 4. Typically, the plan starts with the corporate mission which is translated into a future strategy incorporating customer needs and the resources, especially financial technological and human, available. Marketing strategy is usually formed after reviewing:

Planning
p 89

- the marketing environment
- the organisation's marketing mix
- the organisation's marketing function – its experience and capabilities

This information is used to devise an appropriate marketing mix which will contain specific targets for major objectives. Tactical plans are constructed to enable the achievement of the major objectives. They will include goals such as advertising campaigns, sales efforts and, say, point-of-sale material. Finally, there will be operational plans to determine, for example, exactly which advertisements will be placed in which magazines on what dates. The process is rarely so linear. For example, a strategic marketing plan is revised when operational plans make it apparent that there is no realistic prospect of achieving a strategic objective.

---

### CASE 14.6:  *Sleigh Bells' marketing plan*

Sleigh Bells is a new American duo who specialise in noise, dance punk and lo-fi. The contract is with Columbia Studios which are owned by Sony. In 2010 they released their debut album, *Treats*. Marketing is a vital component in the success of performers. A label will have a strategic marketing plan that involves maintaining existing stars and launching a number of new performers each year (launch pipeline).

The marketing department at Columbia devised a tactical marketing plan for Sleigh Bells – only parts of which are public. The department went into top gear to implement its front-line tactical marketing. A lead single was planned to step up publicity in preparation for the release of an album. The next tactical event was a campaign in the UK where the awareness of the duo was thought to be strong – partly because the plan had staged a series of events and articles with *NME*, *Sunday Times Culture* and *Q*. Specialist radio support was scheduled to include John Kennedy at XFM, Zane Lowe and and Huw Stephens at Radio One. A whole year was a careful marketing plan.

---

Marketing plans and, indeed, the whole of the marketing function are useless unless they are properly implemented and the product or service is formed. This can be a complicated operation. The next chapter therefore gives details of the operations function.

# Activities and further study

## Essay plans

Write essay plans for the following questions:

1 How might markets differ?
2 What models might organisations use to locate a profitable market? To what extent are these models consistent with each other and how useful might they be in practice?
3 Why do organisations undertake market research? What methods could they use?
4 What is meant by "the marketing mix"?
5 What are the main criticisms against marketing? To what extent are these criticisms valid?

## Web activities

1 Look up the websites of:

Chartered Institute of Marketing – http://www.cim.co.uk/home.aspx

  Marketing Week – http://www.marketingweek.co.uk/

  Marketing Institute Singapore – http://www.mis.org.sg/

  Marketing Association of Australia and New Zealand – http://www.marketing.org.au/

2 Look up postgraduate courses in marketing such as:

  http://www.prospects.ac.uk/

  http://www.whatuni.com/degrees/courses/Postgraduate-list/Marketing

  http://www.masterstudies.com/MBA-MSc-Masters-Degree/Business-Economics-and-Administration/Marketing/Sweden/

## Experiential activities

1 It is possible to gain some first-hand experience of marketing or sales with vacation work or, perhaps, a management training scheme with short periods of work in different functions ("Cooks Tours").
2 Talk to a manager who works in marketing or sales. Try to get detailed answers to the following questions: what type of organisation is it? What are its goals? What is its basic

transformation process? What are the future challenges marketing and sales functions are likely to face?

## Recommended reading

1 Smith, M. (2002) "Derrick's Ice Cream Company: applying the BCG matrix in customer profitability analysis" *Accounting Education*, **11** (4), 365–376. A practical example of how the BCG matrix can be used.

2 Friel, M. (1999) "Marketing practice in small tourism and hospitality firms", *International Journal of Tourism Research*, **1**, 97–109. A description of the way small firms in the English tourist industry market themselves.

3 Cooper, L. (2010) "Small business digs in deep into marketing mix", *Marketing Week*, **33** (28), 26–29. Discusses the marketing activities of small and medium-sized businesses.

## CHAPTER 15

# Operations

## Chapter contents

## ❖ LEARNING OBJECTIVES

After reading this chapter that you will be able to understand why the operations function should follow marketing and why the name of the function was changed from "production". You should appreciate why "operations" applies to both the manufacture of physical goods and the provision of services. You should also have a clear idea of the way in which operations systems are devised and managed. In particular, you should be able to:

❖ **define** the operations function and related concepts such as "lean production"

❖ **list** the six main "critical success factors" for an operations function

❖ **compare and contrast** operations functions in manufacturing and service industries

❖ **describe in detail** both product design and production methods

❖ **describe** at least two main types of work layout

❖ **explain** supply chain management

❖ **define** what is generally meant by "quality" and **evaluate** the criticisms made of the "quality movement"

❖ **explain** the concepts of "quality control", "quality assurance" and TQM

❖ **list** and **explain** four ratios that can be used to assess the efficiency of an operations function

Two hundred years ago the Industrial Revolution was in full swing but most people were making do with very basic, meagre possessions. Labour and capital were readily available. Under these circumstances the production function was the dominant function. If a product could be manufactured, it could be financed and would be bought by a ready market. Since then, many things have changed. Scientific advances have made available new products such as cars, vacuum cleaners and radios. There is also greater competition both at home and abroad. In advanced countries manufactured goods such as cars no longer account for the bulk of economic activity. Instead, the majority of products now involve a element of service. The production function has changed in major ways. In particular, its name has changed to "operations" in order to encompass both physical products and intangible services.

---

### CASE 15.1: *Life is a roller-coaster – managing operations at Thorpe Park*

Thorpe Park is a large leisure complex near London. The operations manager signs on before 9.00 a.m. in time to check the estimated number of visitors for the day. Next, costumes and appearance of "cast members" (costumed staff who walk around the park to help and entertain visitors) are inspected to ensure that they meet standards. Then there is a discussion with the admissions supervisor to check that the pay kiosks are ready. If all is well, the operations manager gives the signal for the park to be opened – all this must happen before 9.30 a.m. Once admissions are going smoothly it is time for a "management walkabout". During the walkabout, the operations manager chats to "cast members" receiving and giving information and, probably more important, maintaining their motivation and reaffirming standards. The walkabout also provides other supervisors with the chance to brief the operations managers on aspects such as the cleanliness of certain areas. The walkabout is liable to frequent interruptions – 100 of the 600 cast members have a radio and any incidents can be reported, and receive a response, almost instantly. Often the response involves a visit to the site of the incident. Walkabouts occur several times a day. In between, there are times in the office. One important task is to monitor the number of visitors in the park and compare them with those of the day before, the previous week and the previous year. The information from the walkabouts and the computer provides a continuously updated picture of the activities of visitors. The deployment of "cast members" and other resources is frequently adjusted to ensure that visitors encounter as few queues as possible and have an enjoyable experience at the park.

*Source*: adapted from Hannagan (2005, p. 41). With thanks to R. Boaden.

---

## 15.1 Definition of operations and general characteristics

The operations function may be defined as:

> " The function that manages the part of an organisation that is directly involved "
> in the transformation of resources into higher value goods or services.

This definition emphasises that the operations function involves people who do the actual transformation of inputs into the organisation's output. Operations is a central part of any organisation. The aim of many organisations is to make the transformation process as efficient as possible. This is known as **lean production**. Organisations will also try to make the transformation process as flexible as possible so that it can adapt or change its product should customers' needs change or if the organisation can find a more profitable product. This is known as **agile production**. In a successful organisation the whole of the transformation process is geared to the needs of the customer. Generally, customers make the following demands, often known as **critical success factors** (Slack *et al.*, 2001):

- a *keen price* requiring a tight control of production costs
- *high quality* requiring quality assurance and quality control
- *fast, flexible* and *reliable delivery* requiring either high (and costly) stocks or speedy production, a delivery system free from breakown
- products and services that offer *variety* and *innovation* requiring a creative and flexible production system
- the *right volume* of goods or services requiring a production system with the appropriate capacity

Except in very small organisations the customer can be another department or section – often the next step in the production process. In many organisations departments are encouraged to purchase goods and services from other organisations if they can be supplied at the same quality but lower costs. This is called "outsourcing". It means that **internal customers** are as important as external ones and an inefficient section is unable to survive by relying upon a "captive market" in its own organisation. Treating each stage of production as a customer also means that a value can be placed on each stage of production. It helps identify stages that add little value and these activities can be eliminated. In other words, the production process can be seen as a chain of events that add value to the "raw materials" and which culminate in a product or service that is purchased by a consumer. The idea of a "**value chain**" was advocated by Porter (1998) as a means of creating and sustaining a superior production system. A technique called "process value analysis" (Hammer, 1997) may be used to streamline the operations function.

In many organisations, operations is the largest function and employs the most people. Further, operations function may involve dangerous tools such as metal-cutting equipment and chemicals such as acids, which can harm employees and others. The operations function must be aware of, and heed, regulations dealing with safety and employment.

## 15.2 Types of operations (manufacturing, services and product-service systems)

Operations functions are often divided according to whether they produce a product or service. As we shall see later, this distinction is becoming blurred. Nevertheless it is important to compare and contrast product and service operations.

## Comparison of operations functions in service and manufacturing

There are at least six major differences between manufacturing and service operations:

■ *Manufacturing is more physical.* Transformations in the manufacturing organisations are tangible (i.e. the end result can be touched, seen and perhaps heard). As a generalisation, products in the service sector are not tangible. It is, for example, impossible to touch or see the learning that has taken place in the mind of a student. However, there are many exceptions. For example, it is possible to touch and see the transformation which a hospital brings about when it cures a patient.

■ *The product in services is more varied.* For example, a large organisation manufacturing cars may have 200 000 employees and produce a range of 50 different cars in a year. On the other hand, a gourmet restaurant with, perhaps, a staff of 20 may produce 1000 different dishes during the year.

■ *Production and consumption are usually simultaneous in service operations.* Transformation in manufacturing organisations is usually clearly separated from consumption. For example, an MP3 player may have been manufactured several months before it is purchased. On the other hand, the provision of a massage occurs at exactly the same time that the massage is enjoyed by the customer. The *simultaneous production and consumption* in service transformations has three important consequences:

– It makes it very *difficult for service organisations to stockpile products* in order to even-out peaks and troughs of demand. Products of a service organisation are therefore very perishable. The ultimate example is given by air travel. If a seat it is not sold at the close of check-in, a part of the airline's revenue is lost for ever. On the other hand, the manufacturers of Christmas cards can continue to print cards during the summer and stockpile them until they are needed in December.

– Simultaneous production and consumption found in service operations usually means that *the consumer is present when the service is produced*, will play an interactive part and can help to make the product a success or failure. For example, a responsive audience can help to make a theatre production a success. Similarly, lack of preparation and participation by students can ensure that a seminar is a failure.

– The simultaneous production and consumption found in service operations usually means that the *service must be provided in a place close to the location of the consumers.*

■ *Operations in a service organisation usually involve a higher level of personal ability and judgement.* Operations in manufacturing organisations are usually systematised and controlled to the point where the identity of the exact employee performing the transition does not matter: a plasma screen produced in Scotland by Ivan Robertson will be identical to one produced by in China by Yuan Zi. However, this is not the case with services. A song performed by Mike Smith at a party in Glossop will be quite different from the same song performed by Jay-Z at a nightclub in Dubai! High personal judgement and ability are important ingredients in service organisations such as legal advice, film production, cooking, hairdressing and nursing. The personal factor in service operations is even more significant because service operations are usually much more labour intensive than manufacturing operations.

■ *Demand in manufacturing is more predictable*. For example, the monthly demand for mobile phones is fairly predictable and rarely differs from the average by more than 20 per cent. "Spikes" in demand, such as Christmas, are predictable and can be managed by building up and drawing down stocks. In contrast, a service industry such as package holidays needs to cope with huge swings in demand. Some of this, such as seasonal variations, is easy to predict. However, a great deal also depends upon random factors such as weather, exchange rates and fashions in destinations. To make matters worse, the travel trade cannot draw upon reserve stocks of flights and hotel rooms.

■ *Operations in manufacturing are easier to evaluate*. Physical output in manufacturing can be checked against very detailed specifications concerning size, reliability and other technical qualities. In service organisations, this is much more difficult. For example, it is very difficult for an accountancy organisation to measure quality. It can show "due diligence" – that appropriate steps and procedures have been followed, – but the ultimate check on quality is the fairly crude measure of whether the accounts are accepted by the tax authorities. Similarly, surgeons may be evaluated on the percentage of patients who die in their operating theatres. However, the evaluations may be very faulty since the best surgeons are usually allocated the more difficult cases!

## Operations functions in service industries

Metters and Marucheck (2007) note that, although services are now a larger portion of the economy than manufacturing for every nation on earth, the majority of operations' research focuses on manufacturing issues. They suggest this arises because it is difficult to define services and they tend to be small scale. Further, operations functions differ even within the service industry. For example Schmenner (1986) noted that products in the service industry differed on two major dimensions: the degree of labour intensity and consumer orientation (consumer interaction and customisation). The notion of degree of **labour intensity** is self-explanatory: it is the number of people needed to provide a service. Low labour intensity is often characterised by the use of expensive equipment and tight scheduling to ensure the service is delivered on time. High labour intensity requires hiring, training, scheduling and controlling large numbers of widely dispersed staff. **Consumer orientation** is the degree to which customers deal, face to face, with the staff and how much the service must be changed to meet the needs of individual customers. These two dimensions allow the operations function of service organisations to be placed in one of four categories, as shown in Figure 15.1.

## Varieties of operations functions in manufacturing industries

There are huge differences between the operations functions in manufacturing industries. They are often divided into projects, small-batch, large-batch and continuous production.

■ A **project** is a one-off product. They are difficult to automate and incur high costs. Sometimes this is called project management. Project management is typical in industries such as construction and film-making, and it is appropriate for situations that

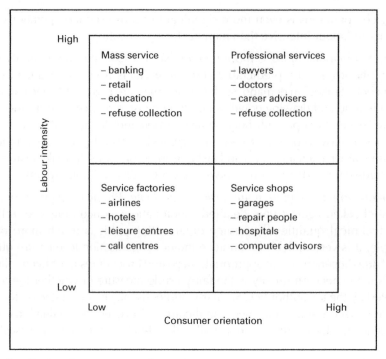

High

Labour intensity

| Mass service | Professional services |
|---|---|
| – banking | – lawyers |
| – retail | – doctors |
| – education | – career advisers |
| – refuse collection | – refuse collection |

| Service factories | Service shops |
|---|---|
| – airlines | – garages |
| – hotels | – repair people |
| – leisure centres | – hospitals |
| – call centres | – computer advisors |

Low

Low                                    High

Consumer orientation

**FIGURE 15.1**    Classification of consumer operations

require flexibility and a quick response in a dynamic environment. It usually requires clear deadlines and specialised skills. People with the appropriate skills are assembled as a team, on a temporary basis, led by a project manager.

- **Small-batch operations** are sometimes called **jobbing**, **unit** or **one-off** production. This is characterised by small orders: for example, a small-batch operation may be to supply a hotel with 50 chairs, 10 settees and 10 tables in the hotel's colour scheme. Small-batch operations often have a "craft" quality about them. While there is some element of standardisation, it is labour intensive and individual employees make a significant contribution. They can see the end result of their work and take pride in their achievements. Small-batch operations are flexibile but costs are high. Further, they depend upon the co-operation of skilled employees.

- **Large-batch** operations are typified by mass production. A classic example might be a factory that makes mince pies. During a year, the factory might make 10 million pies that are almost identical. A large factory will contain expensive, advanced equipment that makes a narrow range of products (for example, during the summer months the equipment might be able to produce apple pies). Examples of large-batch operations include the manufacture of glassware, underpants or weighing machines. Because many identical items are produced, the costs of each item are reduced to an absolute minimum. Large-batch operations are usually very efficient and easy to control,

Fordism p 66

but are inflexible. It takes a great deal of time and money to obtain new specialised machines, train workers in new, specialised tasks and to work out a new system. Sometimes large-batch manufacturing is also known as "repetitive production" or "the assembly-line system".

■ **Continuous process** operations are typified by oil refining where there is a continuous flow of crude oil into the bottom of a distillation column. As the raw material passes through the process, which usually involves heat and/or treatment by chemicals, it is transformed into more valuable commodities such as refined oils and, say, butane gas, which are continuously extracted from the top of a distillation column. Other examples of continuous process operations are the glass industry, steel-making, electricity generation and water supply. Continuous process operations are characterised by a high use of energy and technology. Since high costs are involved in heating up the process, operations are continued on a 24-hour basis, seven days per week. This implies shift work. Often processes are highly automated and are controlled by a relatively small number of highly educated employees. Inputs and outputs need to be planned very carefully to avoid interruptions.

---

**CASE 15.2:** *Manufacturing operations at Patak's Foods*

Patak's manufacture a wide range of products including fresh breads, frozen ready meals and snacks. It is perceived by consumers as being the most authentic brand of Indian food available in mainstream grocery outlets. Patak's is also a significant supplier of products to Indian restaurants throughout the world and its products are available in more than 40 countries, including continental Europe, Japan, Australasia and North America.

Pataks' manufacturing plants are based in Dundee (frozen foods), Glasgow (breads and chilled snacks) and Wigan (products packaged in jars, cans and packets). The Wigan factory is believed to be the largest factory in the world manufacturing solely Indian food and it employs *c.* 350 employees. Within the UK factories, nearly 50 per cent of the workforce is employed in direct manufacturing. They are managed by dedicated and focused management teams. At each site there are strong technical functions, which work closely with manufacturing to ensure the highest possible standards of housekeeping, hygiene, etc. Within each production facility, considerable autonomy is given to individual manufacturing lines, but clearly defined ambitious key performance indicators are established and performance is measured against these indicators on a consistent and hourly basis.

---

Different types of operations function reflect an underlying dimension. At one pole the focus is on the *products* made. Functions at this end make a small range of goods in high volumes using special-purpose machinery. At the other pole, the focus is on the *processes* used. Functions at this end of the spectrum make a wide range of goods but in low volumes. Process-focused functions are usually flexible. Figure 15.2 shows how the different types of production can be located on this dimension.

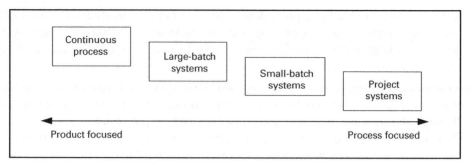

**FIGURE 15.2** Product versus process operations

## Product-service systems

The traditional distinction between operations that make a product and those that provide a service is becoming less clear with the advert of product-service systems (see, for example, Spring and Araujo, 2009; Zomersijk and Voss, 2010). Product-service systems take a wider view and integrate operations into a system designed to deliver a benefits that require less effort for the user. Sometime product-service systems are called **servicisation**. Case 15.3 gives an example from the humble washroom to make the concept clear.

---

### CASE 15.3:   *The development of a product-service system in the washroom*

Once, a textile manufacturer could earn a profit by making towels for public washrooms. A salesperson would visit an organisation, sell a dozen or two boxes of towels (product) and then revisit several months later to see how many towels need to be replaced.Somebody noticed that washrooms were often a mess with unhygienic towels lying all over the place. The manufacturer exploited the situation by developing a dispenser (additional product) which provided a clean length of towel and rolled away the used section. It then realised that it could make more profit by arranging for someone to visit the organisation every day, remove the used towel and install a clean one (service). This had environmental benefits. With economies of scale it could launder the towels using less energy and fewer chemicals than its individual customers used when they were laundering their own towels. Further, when the towels came to the end of their life they would be properly recycled (at a profit) rather than dumped in the nearest bin. The company soon realised that while its employees were visiting organisations to change the towels they could also check the supplies of toilet paper (service) which, of course would be contained in their own dispenser (product). The employees could also provide periodic "deep cleans" (service). The deep cleans maintained a healthier environment and also used fewer chemicals that might damage the environment. Initially, the company was a typical textile manufacturer. But, by the time it was operating a "full washroom service" it had morphed and about one-third of its employees were involved in production and about two-thirds were providing the service.

Other examples of servicisation are:

■ Xerox started by manufacturing and selling photocopiers. Now they offer finance services (leasing photocopiers), consultancy (advising organisations on document handling and storage), business software and translation.

- Phillips Medical started as a manufacturer of diagnostic machines for hospitals. Now they offer finance services (leasing, etc.), staff training, maintenance of the rooms where diagnosis takes place and online back-up.
- Wilkahan (Germany) makes office furniture that is easy to repair and reuse. They also offer a service which inspects the furniture and replaces worn out components.

The basic idea behind servicisation is that consumers do not actually want products. What they want is the *use* of the product and the enjoyment of its benefits. As Case 15.3 indicates, companies did not actually want roller towels. They wanted decent washroom facilities and were delighted when someone could provide an integrated service – thereby leaving them to get on with their core business. Another clear example of servicisation is given by the music industry. Few people wanted cluttered piles of vinyl and CDs everywhere. They wanted to listen to music of their choice and were happy to download it from the Internet. This demonstrates a further aspect of product-service systems – **dematerialisation**, where the product hardly exists in a physical form. University libraries are an excellent example of dematerialisation. Instead of buying thousands of journals and storing them on miles of shelving, they now subscribe to an electronic journal database and pay the database a small fee each time a journal is accessed. This is another important change – **payment is per use**, not for physical possession. It means that students can access a bigger range of journals and they do not have to spend time travelling. Servicisation can have a big impact on the environment. It often uses fewer resources more efficiently because the service provider reaps the benefits of specialisation and the economies of scale. Further, dematerialisation means that there is less need to move products around and generate $CO_2$.

## 15.3  Designing operations

Designing an operation from scratch is rare. It is more likely that a facility will need to be grafted onto an existing function. Nevertheless, it is useful to follow the ideal paradigm where a function is being established on a greenfield site. There are three main stages: product definition and design, system definition and design, and choosing a suitable location and organising the work layout. The following outline of these stages focuses upon the manufacturing sector. However, there are equivalent stages when designing a new service.

### Product definition and design

Defining and designing a new product starts with the organisation's mission statements and strategic plans. Several products may be considered and each evaluated on their likely market and the resources they will need, etc. Good ideas may be suggested by existing employees. The activities of competitors must also be taken into account. Whenever possible, new products which competitors would find it difficult to copy are chosen. Only a small number of potential products survive this examination. Each survivor then goes into to the **product development cycle** which will narrow the range further. The product development cycle follows five stages:

- development of prototypes
- testing of prototypes, evaluation and modification
- piloting revised prototypes – with market research
- evaluating revised prototypes and adjustment
- trial production of fully functioning products

Co-ordination between departments at each stage of the cycle is an important ingredient of success. For example, it is argued that the close co-ordination and consultation between departments in Japanese organisations enables them to develop new products 30 per cent faster than comparable American organisations. Each activity involved in producing the new product is examined in fine detail so that unnecessary actions and features can be eliminated and the most efficient **work process** identified. Often this results in **re-engineering** the product. During trial production, fully functioning workflow will be set up. **Workflow** is the movement of work from one point to another in a production system. An examination of workflow establishes the most efficient order of performing tasks.

Development of a new product can take months or years. The process can be accelerated with **computer-aided design (CAD)**, which speeds the process by drawing designs more quickly. Sophisticated computer packages incorporate information such as physical constraints, government regulations and the properties of materials. A good system will alert designers to features that are impossible or illegal. It may be able to construct large parts of the design from a few basic instructions. A good CAD system will build a model of the new product. Variations of the model can be tested with computer simulations so that the optimal design can be identified. Computer-aided design is usually followed by some form of computer-aided manufacture (CAM).

## Production methods and design

Product definition and methods of production are very closely related – often the product is changed to make it easier or cheaper to produce. The main factors influencing production methods are product flow, capacity and the level of automation.

Products and services *flow* at different rates. Some, usually those produced by continuous processes, flow at a steady rate and differences in demand are dealt with by maintaining extra stocks. This is a sensible approach when the costs of closing down and starting up are higher than the cost of maintaining stocks. In other situations the flow is predictable but uneven. For example, there

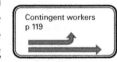

Contingent workers
p 119

are more letters to be collected, sorted and delivered during the Christmas period and there is more soft fruit to be picked during summer months. In these cases the system will need to carry either a high level of surplus capacity, or hire equipment or employees on a temporary basis at periods of high demand.

The demand for some products and services escalates at times of crises. Typical examples are the armed forces, firefighters and the police. Organisations that need to meet crises often maintain high levels of staff but deploy them to non-core activities when demand is low. For example, during wet weather when there are few fires, firefighters will spend their time maintaining machinery and advising on fire prevention. Another tactic is to train a large reserve of people, on a part-time basis. For example, mountain rescue organisations rely on trained volunteers. A final way of dealing with a peak demand is to pool resources with other organisations that have complementary requirements – on the basis that they are unlikely to need to draw on the pool at the same time.

The flow of work has an important influence on the *capacity* of operations. This should be estimated accurately since it is expensive to upgrade inadequate capacity or carry surplus capacity. Often, different parts of the transformation process have different capacities. For example, a factory may be able to assemble 2000 units per week, store 2500 units a week and distribute 1800 units per week. In this case the capacity of the whole operation is 1800 units because total capacity is determined by the sub-process with the lowest capacity – the **bottleneck**.

The *level of automation* is a further major factor in the design of an operational facility. A high level of automation brings advantages. Machines are more reliable, accurate and consistent than human beings. Further, they can be used in dangerous environments. In some cases specialist equipment is designed and commissioned. This is appropriate in mass production where equipment costs can be set against the income from millions of items. However, there is the danger that circumstances may change and expensive, specialised equipment cannot be adapted. Generally, it is better to purchase multifunctional equipment.

Fortunately, developments in robotics have meant that it is practical to design very flexible equipment that can be reprogrammed quickly to produce other products. This is called **flexible manufacturing**. Computers may be used to plan and control operations. They may receive information from people or machines. They may then monitor the transformation process and provide alerts (when things go drastically wrong) or provide reports. In some situations a computer will be able to initiate corrective action. When computers are highly involved in operational systems the process is usually called **computer-assisted manufacture (CAM)**. This is a misnomer because computers may have an equally high involvement in the provision of services. A better term might be **computer-assisted operations (CAO)**.

Automation has relieved humans of the burden of many tedious, repetitive, alienating and debilitating activities (see Pettinger, 1997). In the short term *individuals* may have lost their livelihoods but in the longer term the *community* has benefited from cheaper goods and greater prosperity.

Computers confer another benefit. They make it easier to share information throughout an organisation. In the past, an individual, even the chief executive, could only be aware of a small fragment of the information generated. However, information technology and knowledge management mean that all employees can have access to, say, the organisation's order book, the progress of major projects and major financial indices such as an organisation's share price. Sharing information produces a greater "team spirit" and "empowers" people at all levels. It encourages people to take responsibility and it reduces the need for more formal methods of control.

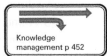
Knowledge management p 452

Information technology and robotics usually involve high "set-up" costs. The operations function will become dependent upon the calibre of a small number of systems analysts and computer staff. Moreover, high investment in current IT systems produces a reluctance to adapt to changes in the environment. New and nimbler competitors who depend upon the wit, ability and adaptability of human systems may be able to gain a competitive edge while the programmers and analysts are still testing new programs.

## Selecting a suitable location

The nature of the product or service will be a major factor in selecting a suitable location. The received wisdom that services need to be in close proximity to the market is still largely true but telecommunications have weakened the link. A television programme may be bounced around the globe from satellite to satellite before it reaches a distant viewer. Similarly a resident in Brisbane may have her enquiry about her electricity bill answered at a call centre in Bombay.

A major consideration will be the cost of land. In turn, this will reflect a number of other factors such as the proximity to a city centre. The price of land is also affected by the prestige and image of the neighbourhood (land within 1 km of Buckingham Palace is much more expensive than land within 1 km of the marshalling yard to the rear of London's Euston station). There are many local variations to these trends. The classic example is the location of organisations offering logistics services. They prefer premises that are located at the centre of motorway networks. Transport companies are prepared to pay higher prices for land at the hubs of the UK motorway networks in, say, Northampton or Warrington than for land in the centre of London or Manchester. Minimising transport costs is important for many other organisations – especially when they transform heavy raw materials or heavy finished products. Organisations that use a lot of energy need to be near to energy resources. A host of political and cultural factors also impinge upon location decisions. Organisations prefer to site their operations facilities where there is:

- political stability
- freedom to move capital in and out
- lower taxes
- fewer regulations such as planning permissions

A classic example of the importance of these factors was the decision of many American pharmaceutical and electronic corporations to site facilities in the Irish Republic; which was politically stable and had a convenient transatlantic position and relatively few restrictions on capital moments. The Irish government also offered several years "tax amnesty" to certain types of incoming investment.

Culture, language and the availability of *skilled labour* are other significant factors. A classic example was the choice by Japanese companies to site factories in the UK. Other governments offered equivalent tax incentives. However, the UK is an island nation similar to Japan and has the advantage of skilled labour which speaks English. The Japanese companies were, however, careful to site these operations away from traditional UK centres of car-making in order to avoid "inheriting" bad labour relations and restrictive practices.

Since so many factors can influence the suitability of a site, a decision of where to locate an operations facility is usually very complex. These decisions may be made on an intuitive basis but many organisations use more scientific methods. If transport costs are important, an organisation may use the **centre of gravity** method – identifying the midpoint of journeys its supplies, products and people will make. Other organisations use a **weighted scoring system** similar to a decision matrix.

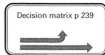

Decision matrix p 239

## 15.4 Operations layout

Machines, workstations and office space can be configured in many ways. Some configurations will be efficient. Others will waste space and time. There are four main types of work layout: fixed position, process layout, cell layout and product layout.

- **Fixed-position** layout is where the objects to be transformed are not mobile and must be processed *in situ*. This often causes confusion because the name may be misinterpreted to mean an operations facility that is fixed. The objects that must be transformed *in situ* are usually static because they are too large or too fragile to move. For example, most houses must be constructed *in situ* where the house will stand. Unfortunately, fixed-position layouts also have strong disadvantages. Often, the layout of these sites is fraught with problems: there may not be enough space to receive and store materials and equipment; there may not be enough space to carry out a transformation efficiently. Every job is unique so unit costs are usually high. (Slack *et al.*, 2001).

- **Process layout** is where location is determined by the transformation process. It is also called "job-shop layout" or "layout by function". Similar processes are grouped, usually into departments. For example, a small manufacturing firm may make components for hydraulic pumps. The components are made from small blocks of aluminium that need to be shaped, drilled and polished. The company adopts a process layout whereby, once the blocks are received, they pass to the grinding department where they are turned on lathes until they are the correct shape. The blocks then pass to the drilling department where the appropriate holes are bored. Finally they are sent to the polishing "shop" where the appropriate finish is applied. Although the shapes, holes and finish may vary from batch to batch, all components pass through the same sequence of departments. The optimal sequence can be established by counting the number of moves that a product makes between processes. Process layout has a number of advantages. It can be very *efficient* since employees have a chance to specialise in a narrow range of tasks. Moreover, the *utilisation of equipment is good* since it is concentrated in one specific area where its use can be maximised. However, it can become parochial and the work can be monotonous.

- **Cell layout** is also called "group technology layout" or "team layout". Cell layout is where the raw materials are bought to a closely defined area. For example, a beauty salon might devise an operational structure to transform ugly ladies into beauties. One layout would be for customers to arrive at the manicure department to have their nails polished. After this, they would walk to the hairdressing department for colouring and tints. Finally, they would walk to the facial department for a make-over. The workflow in this salon would be a process layout. Another beauty salon might arrange things differently. A lady would arrive and be allocated a cubicle where she would be attended by a team who would polish her nails, tint her hair and provide a facial without the customer having to move. Within this cell there are the same processes as those in the former salon. The advantages of the cell layout include good team spirit and fast through put – the product does not waste time being transported. The main disadvantages are the high set-up costs and lower utilisation of equipment (the manicurist and others waste their time moving between customers).

■ **Product layout** occurs when each input to the system follows an identical prearranged path in which each transforming process is performed in a logical sequence. A product is usually transported along the sequence using mechanical devices such as a conveyor belt. Product layout is also called "line layout" and "assembly layout". Classic examples include traditional car assembly and slaughterhouses where carcasses are processed in a strict sequence. Often product layout will entail several "production lines" that are literally parallel. Product layouts are notoriously sensitive to bottlenecks. The activities of workstations must be carefully calculated to ensure that the tasks can be completed before, say, the conveyor moves on. If an operation cannot be completed at the rate of the conveyor belt, it will be necessary to allocate more employees or machines. This is called **line balancing**. Product layout has distinct advantages. If the volume of product is high, it is likely to yield lower costs. However, it is not very flexible and disruptions cause severe problems. From an employee's perspective, work is monotonous and demotivating.

There is an approximate relationship between the type of operational function and work layout as shown in Figure 15.3. The layout in most operation functions does not follow any one pure type. Usually a hybrid of several types is used.

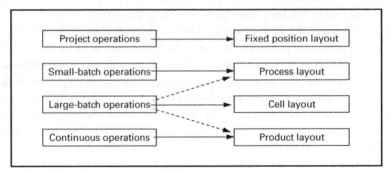

**FIGURE 15.3**   Type of operation and work layout

## 15.5  Managing operations

Once an operation has been established it must be maintained and managed. This involves three main components: *scheduling, cost control* and *quality issues.*

## Scheduling

Two crucial concepts in scheduling are "demand lead time" and "supply lead time". **Demand lead time** is the time that a customer is prepared to wait between ordering a product and receiving it. In many situations, especially retailing, the demand lead time is zero – if a product is not on the shelf, a competitor's product will be purchased. In other situations, such as white goods (e.g. washing machines and refrigerators), the demand lead time will be about one week. With specialised goods such as furniture the demand lead time is, perhaps, three months. In engineering and infrastructure, such as a nuclear submarine or new motorway, demand lead time may be several years. Demand lead time for services is less than that for goods but there are some spectacular exceptions. For example, people are prepared to wait years for certain kinds of education and health care. **Supply lead time** is the time between a decision to produce something and its delivery. Supply lead time also varies considerably but it is always longer than demand lead time. The whole point of scheduling within the operational function is to reduce supply lead time so that it approximates as closely as possible to demand lead time. Figure 15.4 (after Boddy, 2002b) shows the relationship between the two.

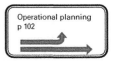

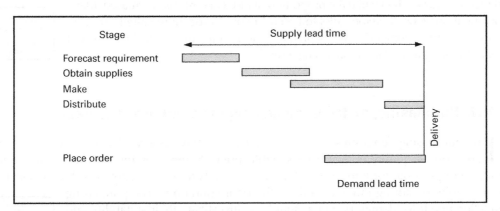

**FIGURE 15.4**   Demand lead time and supply lead time

Most organisations have "forward plans" which are sometimes called "aggregate plans" and cover a long period – as far ahead as the organisation can usually see. In oil prospecting the planning horizon can be 20 years – the supply lead time between deciding to prospect for oil in an area and a time when petrol will be sold to a customer. More frequently, forward plans have a time horizon of one to three years. These plans are not very precise but have general goals which ensure an organisation does not take on too many commitments. **Master production schedules** are drawn up for relatively short periods of time. Often they cover only a week but more frequently they cover three months, six months or a year. A master production schedule will be very detailed and it will specify exactly how many items of each kind need to be produced in a time interval (e.g. per day, per week or per month). In many organisations the master production schedule will be subdivided into a production schedule for each unit or line which must be integrated with each other.

Despite great care and effort, it is impossible for schedulers to anticipate every possibility. It is inevitable that production is disrupted by events such as non-delivery of supplies or problems with employees. Consequently, most experienced planners overestimate (sometimes by a factor of 100 per cent) the time needed to achieve production goals. This extra time, which is available to cope with emergencies, is often called *"**float time**"*.

## Controlling costs

Controlling costs is particularly important to the operations function. Its extensive use of energy, materials and equipment means that it is likely to be one of the largest cost centres. Poor control of costs can have expensive consequences. An organisation may need to borrow or it may need to increase its prices and risk losing customers. For example, poor cost-control forced Network Rail to borrow an extra £10 billion (*Financial Times*, 18 October 2003).

Organisations usually have clear and accurate information concerning direct costs such as raw materials, wages and energy. They also have good data on indirect costs such as administration, buildings, insurance, etc. However, it is notoriously difficult to apportion indirect costs to specific products. This is particularly important because, in recent years, direct costs have fallen while the proportion of indirect costs has increased. Many organisations have therefore adopted a cost control procedure called "activity-based cost management" (ABC) which aims to specify and control the costs of manufacturing a product or providing a service.

Activity-based costing p 306

## 15.6 Purchasing, distribution and supply chain management

The **purchasing function**'s job is to ensure a timely supply of raw materials of an appropriate quality and at a reasonable price. Sometimes the purchasing function may be responsible for transporting the raw materials from their suppliers. It may also be responsible for storing raw materials in the right conditions. The purchasing function needs to identify potential suppliers, investigate their suitability and then negotiate contracts. There is often a close relationship between purchasers and suppliers and this may involve some degree of integration of the two organisations' IT systems. The purchasing function has a very close relationship with the operations function and in some organisations it is viewed as a part of operations. Purchasing is sometimes called "**procurement**". The aim of the **distribution function** is to store goods in conditions which maintain their quality and then to move them efficiently to the customers.

Distribution and transport p 370

The **supply chain management (SCM)** concept was born at the beginning of the the 1980s (Alfalla-Luque and Medina-Lopez, 2009). As products became more complex and quality standards more stringent, four difficulties arose. *First*, it might not be possible to find anyone able to supply very specialised or complex equipment and it might be necessary to enter a **strategic partnership** to encourage someone to produce the particular components. *Second*, continuity of supply could not be guaranteed: a supplier who signed an initial contract might, at a crucial moment, be unwilling to sign a subsequent contract. *Third*, the quality of components or services procured from off-the-peg suppliers might be very variable – perhaps because suppliers did not have the expertise. *Fourth*, it became socially unacceptable to ignore the more distant damage that can be done to the environment or society by suppliers. For example, some furniture manufacturers were castigated for buying wood from importers who sourced their raw materials from unsustainable lumbering. These difficulties led organisations to look further back into the chain leading to their purchases and to manage it more systematically. Hence the field of SCM was born (see Oliver and Webber, 1982).

Figure 15.5 shows that in essence, SCM involves starting with raw materials that are farmed, quarried or invented and tracing their path down to the point where they reach the organisation ready for transformation into something of higher value. It also involves tracing products or services within the organisation. The internal supply chain is usually called **logistics**. In principle, SCM continues to where goods or services reach the customer, who may not, in fact, be the actual consumer. In practice these onward movements are usually called distribution, warehousing and sales. Case 15.4 illustrates many of the characteristic features of supply chain management.

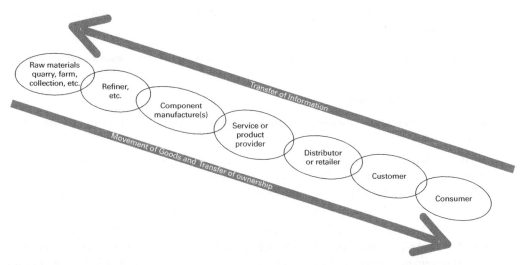

**FIGURE 15.5**  A simplified supply chain

## CASE 15.4: *Beefing up the supply chain*

When a Victorian cockney wanted a nice sirloin steak of Argentinean beef he would walk to his local butcher and, provided other customers had not got there first, he could buy one. Success would also depend upon whether the butcher had happened to go to Smithfield market that morning and there happened to have been a delivery from a ship. The arrival of the ship and its cargo would have depended upon it being loaded, several weeks earlier with meat that happened to be at Buenos Aries dockyard. The availability of carcasses would depended upon a gaucho (Argentinean cowboy) happening to drive his stock to the slaughterhouse at an appropriate time. This, of course would have depended upon the gaucho calving and rearing enough animals several months earlier.

This long chain of haphazard events would break down frequently and the Victorian cockney would have to go without his favourite steak. Sometimes, even though the steak was available, the Victorian cockney would have to do without because currency fluctuations would make it too expensive.

Today's cockney is much more certain to obtain her favourite steak. She will go on line to check which supermarket offers the best price and order steaks for home delivery. There is little chance that she would be disappointed. Using data from her "loyalty card" and the weather forecast (sunny weather means barbecues!) a computer program will predict demand and steaks will be withdrawn from a large warehouse owned by a specialist cold storage company. A fleet of refrigerated container ships will have been chartered to provide regular shipments. Their schedule will have been calculated so that consignments arrive just-in-time to meet demand. There will always be enough carcases at the Buenos Aries dockyard because the gauchos' farmer's co-operative will have predicted demand so that the correct number of animals will be calved and reared. All the interlocking contracts with the supermarket will have been signed months in advance and any currency risk will have been hedged on the exchanges. Not only delivery of the steak but also its price will be almost guaranteed!

The main features of SCM are:

- It deals with the **whole sequence of transformations** from farming or quarrying to the final customer.

- There is a **close relationship** between an organisation and its suppliers. *Goods and services move forward* from the suppliers **to** the organisation. *Money and*, equally importantly, *information* **flows back** from the organisation to suppliers. This includes information of the market demand, quality standards and, sometimes, specialist production knowledge.

- **Timing** is a key element of all supply chains. If the timing is poor, extra inventory (stock) will need to be held as a buffer for late deliveries. Worse, customers can be disappointed and the organisation's reputation tarnished. The most extreme illustration of the importance of timing in supply chain management is the **just-in-time** (**JIT**) technique. A major proponent of JIT is the car-maker Toyota. Taken to its extreme, JIT aims to deliver all materials, components and services just one second before they are needed. This saves the cost of inventory (stores) and the costs of warehousing them. Just-in-time has other benefits – delays cause major disruptions and departments or processes that cause them are cruelly exposed. To everyone's benefit, they quickly learn to become more efficient. The penalties of delay meterd out by JIT often mean there is better design and better control. Further, production scheduling is synchronised with demand.

- **Distribution** is also called **transport**. People in the distribution function are usually involved in route planning, stock rotation and the efficient use of warehouse space. Distribution of utilities such as electricity, water and public transport are special cases that involve unique challenges. The distribution function is particularly important in manufacturing industry, but it is also important in the delivery of some services such as social care or financial services. For example, Reuters sell information, especially financial information. They transport their product via fibre-optic cables that must have the utmost speed and reliability. **Warehousing** is important in most supply chains. Specialist warehousing is needed for many perishable products, chemicals and pharmaceuticals. This service may be outsourced to an organisation which caters for several companies in the same industry.

The supply chain needs managing at three levels. *Strategic level* SCM involves major decisions such as ensuring organisational strategy is consistent with the organisation's supplies. It will also include strategic decisions on such as who should be strategic partners. Further, strategic SCM will involve major decisions on the number, location and size of distribution centres. At the *tactical level* SCM will involve deciding stock levels and the

## CRITICAL THINKING 15.1 *What is wrong with just-in-time?*

Just-in-time creates many bureaucratic problems and has a number of other disadvantages:

- It *does not necessarily save inventory costs, it merely moves them down the supply chain*. This is fine if you are Toyota. If you are a small organisation that supplies one of the suppliers of their suppliers, the chances are that you will need to increase *your* inventory. The problem is clearest when farming is at the bottom of the supply chain. Crops will *not* grow just-in-time. If your major customer (sorry, your major partner!) is a sausage manufacturer, which uses your wheat as a filler and has a just-in-time system, you will have few options other than pay for your corn crop to be stored for months on end.

Disadvantages of bureaucracy p 73

- It often *ignores transport costs*. In most industries there are huge economies of scale in moving supplies in bulk. Yet, JIT often requires suppliers to make frequent smaller deliveries – sometimes several deliveries per day Resources are wasted by the traffic jams caused by extra deliveries and the environment is assaulted by needless carbon emissions.

- It is often unrealistic because it *assumes level prices*. The prices of many things go up and down. Just-in-time means that some organisations are at the mercy of the market. Shrewd organisations will buy and stockpile when the market is low and deploy its stockpile when the market is high.

- It *needs a stable, uncontroversial environment* because it needs a consistent workflow. This is a gift to a disruptive pressure group or trade union. They can extract concessions almost as big as the JIT savings by threatening a serious disruption. Further, the disruption may not be the result of malevolent intention. A fire at a supplier's factory can have catastrophic effects unless the organisation, such as Toyota, has been careful to source from several suppliers. In that case, the slack at the other suppliers could be used to make up the shortfall.

timing, placing and pricing of specific contracts. It will also involve tactical decisions about methods of transport (boat, air, rail, road, Internet, courier, mail, fibre optics), scheduling and routes. At the *operational level* SCM will involve daily distribution plans, inventory audits, goods reception and dispatch.

When SCM was established in the 1980s there was a great deal of emphasis on **electronic data interchange** (**EDI**) whereby the computer systems of an organisation would be linked to the computer system of the supplier. Information about markets, production schedules and inventories would be passed to the supplier who would use this information to adjust their production to meet likely future orders. During the same period, the pace of globalisation increased and supply chain managers needed to cope with the challenges of obtaining components or services from other countries, with different currencies, working practices, legal systems and outlooks.

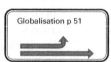
Globalisation p 51

The core competencies of many organisation do not include SCM. They therefore outsource it to specialist supply and logistics organisations. A good case study of the way that Tesco outsourced parts of its supply chain for petrol to TGD (a major European logistics company) is given at http://www.tdg.eu.com/documents/Tesco.pdf. Other well-known specialist supply chain organisations are the (Eddie) Stobart Group and Wincanton. An interesting aspect of SCM is the **reverse supply chain** – the way that an organisation manages the return of its goods. Although only a small proportion of goods are returned, the processing of warrantees or the recycling of products to a second-hand market can be a substantial cost which needs proper management (see Lavassani, Movahedi and Kumar, 2008).

## 15.7 Quality and the operations function

### Definition and concept of quality

Quality, like motherhood and apple pie, is a good thing. Most texts and learned journals accept this axiom. Quality alone is believed to be the reason for Japan's success since 1945 (the industriousness of its workers, its strategic position, import controls and a favourable exchange are, apparently, incidental). However, it is a difficult concept to define. One straightforward and objective definition might be:

66   Of high standard and free from defects.   99

This is generally taken to mean that a quality product or service should:

- conform to high expectations of consumers
- be safe to use or consume
- be reasonably priced and give the impression of a higher-priced product – but without signs of cutting corners
- be durable for a reasonable period. "Reasonable" is very dependent upon the product. A reasonably durable bouquet of flowers should last, say, 10 days whilet a reasonably durable set of cutlery should last a lifetime

- be aesthetically appealing. However, "aesthetics" is a very subjective term
- be delivered intact at the appropriate time and place

Delivering a quality product or service can incur extra costs because organisations must invest more money in equipment and procedures to prevent failures. Further, extra costs will be involved in checking goods or services for defects. However, it is generally believed that the savings from reduced waste, reduced effort in rectifying defects and greater customer loyalty outweigh these extra costs. Indeed, Crosby (1979) contended that "quality is free". It is getting things wrong that costs money. Quality control may be viewed as a special case of "controlling". From the viewpoint of the operations function, quality can be considered under five headings: quality control and quality assurance, continuous improvement, quality circles, benchmarking and total quality management. The criticisms of the "quality movement" are also important.

Controlling p 261

## Quality control and quality assurance

Traditionally, organisations would attempt to give customers a quality product using **quality control**. Finished items, or a sample, would be sent to the quality department for checking. Any unsatisfactory items (or batch) would be sent back to the production department for remedial work. In extreme cases, bad work would be scrapped. When samples of work are inspected for defects, it is often called "statistical quality control". Quality control has a number of undesirable features. First, it does nothing to prevent defects occurring in the first place. Second, a quality control department is rarely able to detect all faults. Some get through to the customer and cause dissatisfaction. To counter these problems many firms take a preventative approach and install a quality assurance system.

**Quality assurance** is a systematic set of activities to ensure quality is built into products. It operates throughout the whole process of producing goods or services and is not confined to the end product. Quality assurance tries to ensure that each stage of the transformation process (raw materials and the processes used) is adequate so that a satisfactory end product is guaranteed. Quality assurance is usually the responsibility of all workers who perform the transformation rather than of an external department. Quality assurance is an advance over quality control but it can be interpreted in a very static way. In the worst situation, quality assurance on its own would merely help to churn out the same product that would eventually become obsolete.

## Continuous improvement

In a competitive environment it is not sufficient to use the same (perhaps, initially, very efficient) process endlessly to produce the same (perhaps, initially, very innovative) product or service. Other organisations will try to capture a market by adopting better methods. Consequently, organisations and their workers must adopt an attitude of constantly seeking ways to enhance quality. The idea of continuous improvement became prominent in Japan in the middle of the twentieth century and was known as "**Kaizen**".

## Quality circles

Quality circles are small groups of eight to ten employees and their supervisor(s). They were first developed in the 1960s by **Kaoru Ishikawa** in Japan. The aim of the group is to identify, analyse and solve quality-related issues. The members of a quality circle first attempt to identify the problems which are then examined in detail. The last step in a quality circle is to identify solutions. The solutions are then presented to management for action. Quality circles increase communication in the organisation and motivate employees. Quality circles were very popular during the 1980s but their use has since declined – partly because management failed to take up many suggestions and partly because some managers felt that they undermined their authority.

## Benchmarking

Benchmarking consists of comparing operations against the operations of other organisations that are recognised as leaders in their industry. The technique, developed by Xerox, took the traditional practice in which companies had informally compared themselves with others and developed it into a more rigorous process. A benchmarking team first identifies the key processes of its operations. Next it establishes ways of measuring the effectiveness of the processes. Finally, it enlists the co-operation of leaders in its industry and obtains results for its own "and their" effectiveness. If the results show that one of its processes is noticeably poorer than that in comparable organisations, the cause of the poor performance will be identified and corrective action taken.

## Total quality management (TQM)

Total quality management is not a precise technique. It is a philosophy, which aims to produce zero defects and 100 per cent customer satisfaction. It is often associated with the phrase "doing the right thing at the right time". It is also associated with phrase "getting things right first time". An earlier form of TQM was **statistical process control** developed by **W.E. Deming** in America in the early 1950s. He visited Japan to explain his ideas, which received an enthusiastic reception, and they were implemented widely by Japanese industry. Deming's approach was much more than a statistical method – it was a philosophy which pervades a whole organisation. Deming's ideas were developed and expanded by others, such as **Juran** and **Crosby**.

According to Deming, everyone in the organisation – from top to bottom – must be committed to providing goods or services of the highest possible quality. The approach stretches even beyond the organisation. Suppliers, wholesalers and retailers must also share the commitment. The relationship with customers consists of a chain of events (called "**quality chains**") to deliver a high-calibre product or service. This, like all chains, is no stronger than its weakest link. Hence, everyone in the organisation and its suppliers need to be conscious of the quality of the contribution they make. Employee involvement in the quality system is vital. Total quality management aims to prevent defects rather than detect them at a later stage. The exact nature of TQM will vary from organisation to organisation, but will, have six common features:

Supply chain management p 368

- Absolute priority, throughout the organisation, to providing the customer with a quality product.
- Top management strongly supports the TQM programme.
- An ethos of continuous improvement.
- Fast responses to the changing needs of the customer. This implies a short product-development cycle.
- Actions based on facts rather than opinions, i.e. measurement, the collection of statistics and interpretation of trends.
- Involvement of all employees.

Some organisations such as the US Department of Defense divide TQM into seven stages:

- Establish a management and cultural environment that has vision and long-term commitment to quality.
- Define the mission of each unit within the organisation.
- Set performance-improvement goals and priorities and provide opportunities for improvement.
- Establish projects and plans to detect and devise improvements.
- Implement the improvements.
- Evaluate the improvements.
- Review the situation and start the cycle again.

Perhaps the culmination of the "quality movement" was the development of ISO 9000. It is an international standard that shows an organisation has a "quality" quality system. In order to attain ISO 9000 accreditation an organisation must subject its quality system to auditing by an external, independent, certified body. An organisation that has ISO 9000 accreditation can supply other organisations, such as large car manufacturers, that are themselves accredited. Hence, ISO 9000 offers enormous commercial advantages. Now that most organisations have ISO 9000 accreditation, an organisation without it operates at a huge commercial disadvantage.

---

**CRITICAL THINKING 15.2** *Quality, bureaucracy and mediocrity – criticisms of the quality movement*

Most organisations still value quality highly – although possibly less highly than in the heady days of the 1980s and 1990s – but there are three main criticisms: too much emphasis on documentation (bureaucracy), a lowering of standards mediocrity and failure to produce benefits.

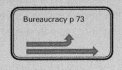
Bureaucracy p 73

Many quality systems such as ISO 9000 depend upon *documentation* to prove that standards have been met. They rarely involve an evaluation of the actual product or service. Hence, organisations will pour enormous resources into improving their documentation rather than improving their product or service. For example, schools may cancel classes and extra-curricular activities so that staff have time to prepare a perfect paper submission for its inspectors.

Quality systems worked well in production environments where the outcome was an objective, measurable product. However, they are more difficult (but not impossible) to implement in personal services where there is an interaction between the provider and the customer. For example, a quality system may evaluate a teacher partly on the basis of questionnaires from students. Hence, a teacher will have a vested interest in giving high marks so that students will rate them highly. Unfortunately, this may lead to the quality of education being driven downwards rather than upwards as the designers of the system intend. *Standards may be driven* down even in manufacturing. An experienced production manager may have witnessed the sacking or humiliation of a colleague who has failed to meet quality standards. Therefore, a shrewd manager will set lower standards that he or she knows can be met.

The value of TQM has been questioned very severely. A survey by Arthur Little indicated that only 36 per cent of 500 companies implementing TQM felt it was having a significant impact on their competitiveness. Another survey by A.T. Kearney of 100 British firms indicated that only 20 per cent believe their quality programmes have achieved tangible results. A further survey of 30 quality programmes by McKinsey & Co found that two-thirds had not yielded the expected improvements (Hendricks and Singhal, 1999). Hendricks and Singhal surveyed the financial results of 3,000 companies and compared their performance before and after obtaining quality awards. They found that companies obtaining quality awards had better stock market performance, better sales, better operating income and higher total assets in the period after implementing quality programmes than in the previous period.

## 15.8 Measuring the effectiveness of operations

It is not surprising that indices have been devised to measure performance of the operations function. They are similar to financial ratios. Fundamentally, productivity is the ratio of inputs to outputs in a given period of time. It should be noted that production is not the same as productivity: *production* is the number of units made, *productivity* is a comparison of inputs to outputs. The latter is an index of how effectively resources are transformed. For whole organisations, productivity is relatively easy to measure:

Management ratios
p 307

$$\text{Productivity} = \frac{\text{System outputs}}{\text{System inputs}}$$

However, the outputs and inputs can only be compared using a common scale – money. The basic formula for productivity then becomes:

$$\text{Productivity} = \frac{\text{Value of sales}}{\text{Cost of materials} + \text{Labour} + \text{Capital}}$$

This formula works well for the organisation as a whole but it is less useful when evaluating a function such as the operations function. Some of the value of sales will have been contributed by marketing, distribution and others. When judging an individual function, the inputs and outputs of others need to be evaluated. Often this is a subjective process that leads to debate.

An alternative approach is to use the number of hours that workers need to spend making an object. These are called "indices of labour productivity". In principle the procedure is very simple. A record of the number of hours worked is kept and the following formula applied:

$$\text{Hours per unit produced} = \frac{\text{Total hours worked}}{\text{Number of units produced}}$$

For example, if a computer manufacturer employs a group of people for a total of 400 hours and they produce 100 computers, the hours per unit produced will be 4. Such indices are particularly useful because they permit comparisons across time and across facilities. If an earlier calculation had shown that a year previously it had taken five "person hours" to produce a computer, the managers of the production unit can congratulate themselves on having raised productivity by 20 per cent. Similarly, they can compare their performance with computer-makers in other countries. If they find that competitors in Taiwan produce computers in three hours, they can be less sanguine. Such comparisons need to ensure that like is being compared with like. The increase in productivity in the previous year could have occurred because the company had invested in better equipment. Similarly, competitors in Taiwan may be making computers to a lower specification. The use of hours worked as an index can also lead to problems when work is performed by teams. A skilled circuit designer earns considerably more than the person who packs the computer, and it is wrong to count their work per hour as equivalent.

To overcome these difficulties many organisations use a further index of labour productivity – the "added value index". First, they calculate the added value by subtracting all costs from sales revenue. Next, they compute the index using the formula:

$$\text{Added value index} = \frac{\text{Sales revenue} - \text{Materials and service costs}}{\text{Employment costs}}$$

This is a very useful index of labour productivity. The added value index should be greater than 1, otherwise workers are destroying value rather than creating it. The differences in specifications are taken into account, because a higher specification should be reflected in the prices of computers. Further, inclusion of employment costs automatically adjusts for the fact that one firm might be using a lower-calibre, but cheaper, labour.

All indices, including the added value index, should be used with care since they can be affected by factors outside the control of the operations function. For example, productivity can be affected significantly by government regulation, sudden changes in customer demand and new entrants to an organisation's market.

# Activities and further study

## Essay plans

Write essay plans for the following questions:

1 What is an operations function? How could it differ between organisations – especially between those making a tangible product and those providing a service?

2 What considerations would you take into account if you were asked to set up an operations function for a social work department of a local council?

3 What considerations would you take into account if you were asked to set up an operations function for a factory producing LCD television monitors?

4 What are the characteristics of servicisation and how will it develop in the next decade?

5 Compare and contrast "quality control", "quality assurance", and "total quality management".

6 What criticisms are levelled against quality systems? Are these criticisms valid?

7 How would you assess the effectiveness of an operations function?

## Web activities

1 Visit the following websites:
http://www.iomnet.org.uk/ (Institute of Operations Management)
http://www.sapics.org.za/ (Professional Society for Supply Chain Management)
· www.logistics.ust.hk (Hong Kong Logistics and Supply Chain Management Institute)

Consider whether the views of these professional organisations take an objective or a self-serving view of their contribution to management.

2 Look up postgraduate courses in operations such as: http://www.whatuni.com/degrees/courses/Postgraduate-list/ or Google 'Operations postgraduate courses'.

3 Use Wikipedia to find out more on the gurus of quality management: Demming, Duran and Ishikawa.

4 Go to http://www.cfsd.org.uk/events/tspd6/tspd6_3s_cases.html#cas and consider the list of product-service systems. Try to identify common themes in product service systems.

## Experiential activities

**1** It is possible to gain some first-hand experience of operations with vacation work or, perhaps, a management training scheme with short periods of work in different functions ("Cooks Tours").

**2** If possible talk to *two* operations managers one from manufacturing and one from services. Try to get detailed answers to the following questions. What type of organisation is it? What are its goals? What is its basic transformation process? How does the function operate? What are the future challenges the operations function is likely to face?

## Recommended reading

**1** Baines, T.S., Lightfoot, H.W., Evans, S., Neely, A., Greenough, R. *et al.* (2007) "State-of-the-art in product-service systems", *Proceedings of the Institution of Mechanical Engineers – Part B – Engineering Manufacture*, **221** (10) 1543–1553. A literature review which gives a good definition, features, applications and named examples of product-service systems (PSSs).

**2** Alfalla-Luque, R. and Medina-Lopez, C. (2009) "Supply chain management: unheard of in the 1970s, core to today's company", *Business History*, **51** (2), 202–221. Good background to the development of SCM (page 207 onwards).

**3** Hackman, J.R. and Wageman, R. (1995) "Total quality management: empirical, conceptual, and practical issues", *Administrative Science Quarterly*, **40** (2), 309–343. An old, but still very useful explanation of the major concepts of TQM. Best used for reference or as a primer rather than an article. Highly recommended.

**4** Rieple, A. and Singh, R. (2010) "A value chain analysis of the organic cotton industry: the case of UK retailers and Indian suppliers", *Ecological Economics*, **69** (11), 2292–2303. A detailed example of value chain analysis. Start reading at section 6. Do not get bogged down in details and statistics.

## CHAPTER 16

# Human Resource Management

## ❖ LEARNING OBJECTIVES

After you have read this chapter you will have an understanding of the human resource (HR) function and the crucial role it plays in many organisations. You will know the main methods employed by the human resource management (HRM) function to produce an effective workforce. In particular you will be able to:

❖ **define** HRM and **differentiate** this function from the process of staffing

❖ **explain** how the HRM function should be linked to an organisation's strategy

❖ **list** six areas (and give a specific example of each) where there are legal requirements the HRM function must obey

❖ **explain in detail** HRM's role in organising pay and compensation

❖ **explain in detail** the concept of HR planning and **give** two ratios of employee turnover

❖ **explain** the HRM function's contribution to recruitment and selection and training and development

❖ **explain in detail** how an HRM function might organise "performance management" and appraisals

❖ **explain in detail** HRM's role in employee relations

❖ **describe** the welfare role of HRM

The HRM is one of the five major management functions. It is certain to be found in any medium or large organisation, such as the South African publishing organisation, Media24.

---

### CASE 16.1: *The HR function at Media24*

Media24 is Africa's biggest publishing group. It provides entertainment, information and education 24 hours a day. Newspapers (including South Africa's largest, the *Daily Sun*), magazines, books and web publishing and complemented by printing and distribution for private education businesses. Media24 employs about 7100 people in over 60 subsidiaries and divisions.

Each division has an HR function. Typically it has one specialist for every 150 employees who will implement HR policy and provide operational HR support to line managers in fields including recruitment, selection, performance management, employee relations, salary administration and employee relations. The corporate HR function, based in Cape Town, has about 22 specialists. They set the strategic direction and best-practices management across the group. They give specialist HR expertise in the fields of talent management, recruitment, assessment, selection, training, mentoring, succession planning, transformation (specifically black economic empowerment through affirmative action and skills development), remuneration management, payroll administration, employee relations and employee assistance (some of which is outsourced).

The HR function in Media24 is slightly atypical, because Media24 is operated in a strongly decentralised fashion and approaches to HR may differ from business to business within the group. A major challenge is recruiting and developing talented specialists needed to meet a strategy of rapid growth within South Africa and elsewhere on the continent, as well as in Asia.

*Source*: We are grateful to Shelagh Goodwin of Media24 for providing this case.

---

Some aspects of HRM are dealt with elsewhere in this book – in Chapter 7 (Staffing – selecting, developing and motivating people) and Chapter 19 (Social responsibility and ethics).

## 16.1 Definition and history of human resource management

Human resource management is an enabling function that represents "the human side of enterprises" It focuses on the relationships between employees and organisations that add value and help attain goals. Human resource management may be defined as:

> 66 The productive recruitment, development, deployment and motivation of people at work in order to achieve strategic business objectives and the satisfaction of individual employees. 99

Since people are an integral part of the definition of management, it follows that the function that deals with the human side of the organisation is a pivotal function. All managers play a part in the productive use of people, and in Chapters 7 and 8 we looked at the aspects of managing people – selecting, training, motivating and leading – that involve all managers. The HRM **function** involves a higher level of technical expertise that is only required by *some* managers. In particular the HRM function provides a high-level input to the organisation's *infrastructure for managing people*. In other words:

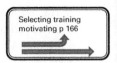
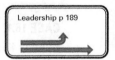

- It formulates policies, strategies and plans concerning the workforce – especially strategies to help organisational change.
- It devises the style and standards of managing people.
- It provides rules and procedures for implementing the two previous activities.
- It provides a service (advice) function for maintaining and improving a workforce.

As an enabling function, the primary mission of HRM is to help other functions – especially the line functions – achieve their goals. Unlike some other functions, HRM is concerned with the whole organisation, so its managers need to know about all parts of the organisation – its strategy, market position, operations, legal requirements, and so

---

### CASE 16.2:  *The human resource function at Enterprise Rent a Car*

Enterprise Rent a Car is an international company with over 750 000 cars for hire and its success depends upon providing superb customer service. This means that it must ensure it has high-quality, well-motivated staff. The role of its HR function is to make proper arrangements for hiring, training and developing staff, and to ensure proper arrangements for occasions when it is necessary to discipline or dismiss them.

The function goes beyond existing employees: it develops an HRM strategy which is closely linked to the organisation's strategy, anticipating likely developments (e.g. growing into new markets such as truck rental) and technological changes (e.g. global positioning devices for vehicles). The HR function also keeps an eye on likely retirements or promotions, and notes the skills needed by people who will fill the gaps. There is a policy of promoting managers from among existing employees. The workforce planning at Enterprise is developed to take all of these, and other factors into account.

*Source*: Based on *Times 100 Case Studies*

---

on. While the HRM function is primarily an enabling function, it also has a minor role as a control function. It will usually monitor key indices such as absences, turnover, wage costs and compliance with employment legislation.

There is plenty of evidence that HRM is a function crucial to an organisation's prosperity. There are plenty of CEOs who make comments such as "people are our most important asset". These assertions are backed by empirical research (see Baron and Kreps, 1999; Pfeffer, 1998).

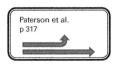
Paterson et al.
p 317

Human management has a long history dating back at least as far as such caring industrialists such as Robert Owen and Joseph Rowntree. Their philosophy of enlightened self-interest led them to provide decent conditions for their employees on the basis that a well cared for worker would be more productive. These efforts were often called "industrial betterment". In 1900 there were about a dozen "professional" welfare workers in the UK, but by 1913 there were about 1300 – enough to form a Welfare Workers' Association. In the inter-war period negotiations with unions became a major issue and these were often conducted by "labour managers" or "employment managers". Large companies such as ICI, Pilkingtons and Marks & Spencer formed specialist personnel departments to manage recruitment and absences among hourly paid workers. During the Second World War the Ministry of Labour insisted that all establishments producing war materials had a welfare worker or a personnel officer.

By 1945 personnel management had taken the form that is just recognisable today. Employment legislation from 1960 onwards added further emphasis to the personnel function. Further, new management techniques for improving worker productivity were suggested by behavioural scientists such as McGregor in the USA. However, personnel management was often seen as a low-status function better suited to amateurs and women! The term "human resource management" began to be used in the USA. The term had useful connotations. It emphasised the fact that human resources were just as important as financial and physical resources, and implied that the people who managed these resources were as important as production managers and finance managers. In addition, the term "human resource management" clearly required personnel managers to take on a strategic role within their organisations. Many people regarded this change of name as superficial spin – "old wine in new bottles!" Others resented the term because it implied that the people in an organisation should be used, manipulated and discarded when necessary like other resources such as metal, machines and a mortgage. As the field of personnel management grew, specialisms started to arise. Larger HR functions may now have special groups devoted to diversity, recruitment, industrial relations or pay.

In the mid-twentieth century many HR departments were highly *centralised*. They formulated a set of procedures that were imposed throughout an organisation. This could mean that policies and procedures would be applied where local conditions made them inappropriate. Moreover, managers often felt alienated by procedures in which they had played no part. It was easy for them to blame their own shortcomings on, say, a subordinate appointed largely at the behest of the centralised HR function.

The HR function in many of today's organisations is *decentralised* and operates in a "devolved" way with general guidelines and advice from the central HR function. This structure has its dangers too. Devolution may mean that complicated procedures are set up and operated by non-specialist staff – some of whom deliver a poor-quality service. The image of the organisation may suffer. Further, devolved units may duplicate the work of other units.

## 16.2  Components of the human resource function

The components of the HR function can be fitted in a logical framework shown in Figure 16.1

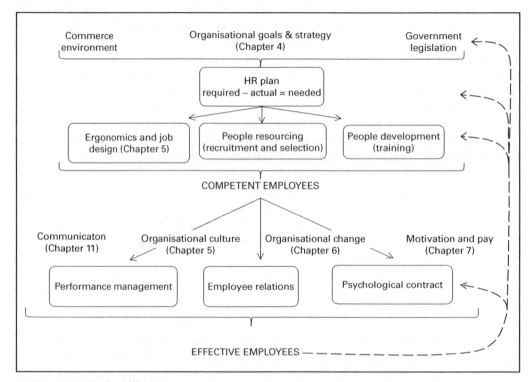

**FIGURE 16.1** An idealised HR system

Human resource management starts with organisational goals and strategy that are influenced by both market conditions and government legislation. The HR function must interpret the organisational goals in terms of the numbers of employees, occupations and skills. This interpretation is sometimes called the "people requirement". The HR function then establishes its present number of employees, their mix, occupations and skills. The difference between the future requirements and the present complement is the gap that the HR function must fill. It can be filled in three main ways: ergonomic job design, resourcing people and developing people. Generally it is better to redesign a job ergonomically so that it can be performed by most people – there will then be less need for selection or training and the results are more certain. However, it may be impossible to redesign a job to this extent. The HR department should then attempt to select people who already have the skills and competences needed. This will mean that there is no delay or failure in training people. Unfortunately, selection is not perfect. In many situations the ideal person for a job may not exist and some people offered jobs will turn out not to have the skills they

Job design and ergonomics p 117

claimed. It will be necessary to employ people who have only some of the skills and develop the rest by training.

Well-chosen, well-trained people working in a well-designed job are *competent workers*. They are *able* to do the job, but this does not mean that they *will* do the job. There are a wide range of factors which help transform competent workers into effective workers. Some of these factors, such as organisational climate, motivation and communication, have been covered in earlier chapters. However, the HR function will also need to arrange performance management (e.g. pay, promotion and discipline), and employee relations in order to transform competent workers into effective workers. There are, of course, feedback loops. The success or failure of the HR function to produce effective workers will feed back into the organisation's aims and goals and other aspects of its own function.

## People resourcing

People resourcing is known as **recruitment and selection** or **inplacement**. The responsibility for people resourcing lies with individual managers and is a part of the staffing process (see Chapter 7) The HR function must remember that, except when recruiting its own staff, it is offering a service. Responsibility for selecting an employee must lie with the head of the department where he or she will work. So, the main recruitment and selection responsibilities of the HR function are:

- establishing a system for approving and filling a vacancy
- training staff in selection techniques and legal aspects
- advising on a job description and other information for applicants
- preparing and placing advertisements
- approving and liaising with recruitment agencies
- corresponding with applicants (invitations to interview, etc.)
- making arrangements for an interview or other selection methods
- assisting with interview or other selection method
- advising on starting salary and conditions of employment
- communicating the formal job offer and writing to unsuccessful candidates.

## People development

People development is also known as **training and development**. Again it must be remembered that, except when training and developing its own staff, it is offering a service. Responsibility for training and developing an employee lies with the head of the department where she or he will work. So, the main development responsibilities of the HR function are:

- establishing and maintaining a system that ensures all employees are fully developed and properly trained
- advising on the development needs of specific individuals
- monitoring and maintaining a list of training providers

- co-ordinating the training offered to employees within the organisation
- developing and providing training courses on topics specific to the organisation or where there are advantages in providing training "in house"
- evaluating the effectiveness of the training

## Performance management

Competent employees are generally motivated to perform well and are capable of learning. If suboptimal behaviour is noted and discussed, most workers will improve their behaviour. There are many methods of performance appraisal.

### Methods of performance appraisal

In an archetypal appraisal system, a subordinate and his or her boss meet at regular, say three-monthly, intervals to discuss performance. Ideally the meeting will have no other purpose than improving performance; the boss will have an intimate knowledge of the job and the subordinate's actions. Ideally, the subordinate will be totally open, prepared to accept that his or her performance is less than perfect and be willing and able to make substantial changes in the way that he or she works. After "deep and meaningful discussion" the subordinate and the boss will be able to identify the correct way forward and produce a realistic plan that the subordinate will implement with assiduity.

---

### CRITICAL THINKING 16.1 *Why appraisal systems often fail*

There are four main reasons why appraisal systems often fail:

1 Subordinates manipulate information. They are not stupid. They know that, even with assurances that "our conversation will only be used for purposes of your development", information will leak into decisions about pay rises, promotion and, perhaps, dismissal. They will spend time preparing for the appraisal rather than doing their normal work. They will pursue their own targets rather than being a good organisational "citizen".

2 Attribution theory has a big impact on the way an employee interprets, and thus implements, the outcome of appraisals. They almost always attribute good results to their own skill and effort. On the other hand, bad results are attributed to other people or to unfavourable circumstances. Hence a good appraisal merely confirms present behavior while a bad appraisal is likely to focus attention on things that are wrong with the work situation – including the support and effectiveness of the supervisor!

3 A boss will not usually have sufficient time to conduct a comprehensive appraisal. A thorough appraisal, together with the attendant paperwork, might involve a boss in two days' effort. A boss who has, say, eight subordinates will therefore spend 16 days per quarter (about 20 per cent of available time) on

performance appraisals during which time they need to ignore production crises and other "marginal" matters.

4 Bosses are rarely fully informed about their subordinates' jobs and their performances; the jobs may have changed quite dramatically since the bosses were promoted from them. The average boss spends less than 10 per cent of their time with any single subordinate. Further, it is difficult for a boss to be objective. They have their own styles and preferences.

Organisations have tried to minimise such problems in two main ways: by making the appraisals more quantitative and obtaining **metrics** by using rating scales.

Although rating scales, especially behaviourally anchored rating scales, look scientific, there is a problem when they are used in appraisal systems. They lack discrimination, because most employees are placed in the top two positions. This is partly because superiors may wish to be kind to subordinates. It may also occur because superiors do not wish to admit that they manage their unit in a way that tolerates average or below-average performance. Furthermore, some managers want to save their time for other activities they consider more productive. They know that any subordinate who receives an average or below-average rating is likely to contest the judgement and they will need to spend hours justifying their view and placating the aggrieved subordinate. Moreover, the aggrieved subordinate will continue to work in their unit. It may be a more cost-effective use of time to give an acceptable rating and invest the time saved in solving another problem.

Problems with superior ratings led to the development of a technique called 360-degree feedback. **360-degree feedback** gets its name from the fact that feedback is provided from all directions (Figure 16.2). Questionnaires are distributed to a range of people including the boss, colleagues, subordinates and perhaps customers.

The questionnaire is completed on a confidential basis and analysed by someone with no vested interest in the results. The average of the ratings will then be fed back to the employee and their boss so that the appropriate lessons are learnt. 360-degree feedback is not without its own problems. People generally dislike rating their colleagues. The actual rating that they give can be distorted in many ways. Sometimes colleagues come to a mutually advantageous agreement that they will not give each other poor ratings. In other cases rivals for promotion can seek to improve their own chances by criticising their competitors.

### *Consequences of performance appraisal*

With luck, a performance appraisal will reveal that a person is working competently and adding value to the organisation but there will be some points that can be improved or developed. The boss and subordinate should note the generally favourable appraisal and produce an action plan to address the development points. This plan should be reviewed after, say, three months to check that the plan has been, or is being, fulfilled. In a minority of cases, an appraisal might reveal problems. This always causes rancour and a great deal of emotion. The subordinate is likely to contend that he or she has been the victim of misunderstandings, bias or stereotyping. These claims may be true and they should be considered fairly.

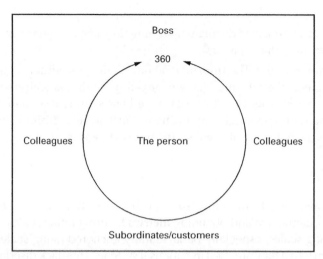

**FIGURE 16.2** 360° feedback

If the claims are groundless, it is important to tackle the reason for poor performance. If the problem arises from lack of training, additional training can be provided. If the problem arises from a mismatch between a person's abilities and those required by the job, the person can be moved to a more suitable position. A *transfer* that is perceived as demotion will be resented and it is likely that the person will resign from the organisation within a short time. If they remain they are likely to experience frustration, loss of confidence and may transmit discontent to others. Transfers may offer a solution when poor performance arises from poor relationships. For example, if there are frequent personality clashes between colleagues or with a boss it may be better to transfer the person to another job of equal status.

It is quite rare for people to be dismissed for poor performance. Usually *dismissal* only takes place when there has been a clear failure to perform the job. For example, people may be dismissed for *gross misconduct* such as dishonesty, a clear neglect in duty or a blatant refusal to obey an instruction. Dismissal may also occur if a worker *breaches* their *contract of employment* by going on strike, or disrupting the work of others or putting other workers in danger. Dismissal is a major step and normally only taken after considerable thought. The employees should be notified (preferably in writing) of their poor performance, warned of the potential consequences and given reasonable opportunity to make changes. Dismissal procedures and legal requirements must be followed to the letter. In some circumstances, such as theft, drunkenness, the imminent threat of damage to property or the safety of others, it may be possible to **summarily dismiss** an employee without notice. If an employer obstructs an employee and makes it difficult for him or her to do their job, the employee may resign and claim a **constructive dismissal**. This means that the employer has shown that they have no intention of fulfilling their side of the employment contract. The employee may then claim compensation for **wrongful dismissal**.

## Pay and compensation

The HR function plays a key role in determining the compensation packages for employees. It will establish a salary structure that other departments must operate. If a salary structure is not in place, different departments will pay different salaries for equivalent work. There will be a great number of anomalies and a lot of time and effort will be spent dealing with complaints. Further, the lack of a sound salary structure is likely to lead to an infringement of employment legislation where different groups are paid different salaries for equivalent work. Most pay structures are based on some form of grading or job evaluation. In the past the tasks involved in a job would be evaluated and allotted points. The number of points would determine the salary band appropriate for the job. Someone's salary would be within that band but other factors such as experience, seniority or recognition for good work would determine the exact placement. Probably the best-known points system for job evaluation is the Hay-MSL system for evaluating senior management jobs.

In the past, a salary system of a large organisation would have many, perhaps seven or more, narrow bands. People would sometimes start employment at the bottom of the lowest band and work their way up to the top of the highest band by the time they retired. **Narrowband** salary structures give workers the sense of progression but they have their disadvantages. First they are complex to administer; every little change in a job's content means the job needs to be regraded. Every time someone moves to a slightly different job they might change salary bands. Because small changes could make a difference to an employee's pay, the HR function was forever wrangling with people who contested the positioning of their job. In recent years there has been a trend towards **broadbanding** where there are fewer, wider bands. As Figure 16.3 shows broadbanding produces a simpler and more flexible salary structure. Some organisations maintain that it is less divisive and more motivating for employees.

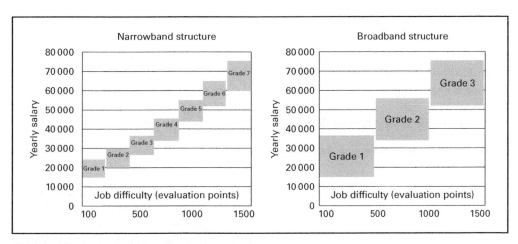

**FIGURE 16.3** Narrowband and broadband salary structures

Now it is more likely that jobs are evaluated in terms of the *skills* needed to perform the tasks. Again there is usually a point system. Jobs that demand higher skills, more experience or higher physical demands are generally higher paid. The labour market will also play its part. People in occupations that are in short supply will generally be paid more.

Many firms have moved to a system whereby people are paid according to their *performance*. Such systems are often called *incentive schemes* and they can take many forms, but they are all based on the expectancy theory of motivation. Some jobs are paid on a strict commission basis where there is a direct relationship between salary and output. These schemes produce high motivation for ambitious people who are not concerned about security. However, they have the disadvantage that they encourage selfishness and discourage organisational citizenship. They also encourage people to exploit short-term possibilities and then move on to another job before the long-term consequences are apparent. A less aggressive regime entails a reasonable basic salary plus commission when performance exceeds a pre-set limit. These systems often attract better employees than those solely working on commission. However, they too tend to encourage selfishness and discourage teamwork.

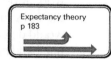

Expectancy theory
p 183

### CASE 16.3:  *Reckitt Benckiser's remuneration*

Reckitt Benckiser has a remuneration committee which sets the salaries for the company's top managers. It aims to devise a scheme that fosters an innovative and entrepreneurial culture. Top managers' pay consists of three parts: a base salary, short-term incentives and long-term incentives. If a top manager made all their targets, they receive an additional 40 per cent of their base salary. A manager who does extremely well (double targets) can earn a bonus of 144 per cent of the basic salary. Long-term remuneration takes the form of stock options and is based on indices such as three-year corporate growth and earnings per share.

In 2010 the CEO, Bart Brecht, received a basic salary of £987 000 plus a bonus of £3.52 million, making his total salary £4.5 million. In the preceding 10 years he had amassed share options worth £87 million. Bart Brect donated shares worth £110 million to a personal charitable trust that specialises in humanitarian, educational and environmental causes.

(See also Case 2.4 on Reckitt Benckiser's globalisation page 52.)

Performance-related pay (PRP) has many conceptual advantages: in theory, it ties remuneration to the contribution an individual makes to organisational goals. In practice, the achievements of PRP are much less impressive. Outside sales and other readily quantifiable occupations, it is very difficult to assess accurately an individual's contribution to organisational goals – most jobs are too complex and multifaceted. Performance-related pay often engenders distrust. A survey by Towers-Perrin (1999) revealed considerable dissatisfaction in companies that had tried to install the system. Indeed, 84 per cent of companies had experienced problems some writers suggest that PRP reduces employee motivation. A meta-analysis by Perry, Engbers and Jun (2009 – an especially good read for those completing an assignment on PRP) found that recent research largely supported earlier findings that individual financial incentives are ineffective – especially in the public sector. However, contrary to expectations, they found that it could have some effect in lower-paid jobs, where there was a high level of trust and where the appraisal system was objective.

A third system is to pay a basic salary plus a bonus that is based upon the performance of the *team*. In principle, this should promote teamwork while still providing motivation for individuals. Unfortunately, some members of a team may decide that it is better to provide

---

## CRITICAL THINKING 16.2 *Why are so many performance-related pay schemes ineffective?*

Performance-related pay schemes were in great favour a few years ago and governments started to introduce them into the public sector in order to drive up productivity. They are now less popular. Many believe that PRP was a major cause of the credit crunch. Many bankers were rewarded by a very aggressive system of PRP and this led them to take enormous risks and to lend unwisely. Furthermore, research findings indicated that, at best, the success of PRP is very patchy. There are four main reasons why PRP schemes may not work:

1  A sizeable minority of employees are very hostile to PRP schemes because they believe the schemes are a tool of management manipulation.

2  The allocation of rewards is perceived as unfair. This is particularly true when appraisals are based on supervisors' opinion and where there is considerable ambiguity in the definition of a job or where the indicators of success are ambiguous or subjective. These situations mean that the links required by the expectancy theory motivation are broken

3  Many employees are already working hard and cannot improve their performance even if offered more pay

4  Performance-related pay might increase motivation but motivation on its own may not be enough to increase performance. Management should first remove other limitations before introducing PRP.

Some people maintain that even the patchy successes of PRP are an artifice because it necessarily involves clarifying employees goals. These sceptics argue that it is the clarification of the goals which produces the partial success or PRP, not the incentives of the payment system.

---

a moderate performance and rely on other members of the team to earn bonuses for them. Another system involves profit, where by employees are given a reasonable basic salary but there is an additional element based on profit in the preceding year.

## Other benefits

Benefits are the non-cash rewards that a person receives. They are similar to **perks** or **perquisites** and can form a substantial proportion of the total remuneration. For example, when contribution to state schemes are included, most employers pay employees an additional 15 per cent over and above salary in terms of medical, sickness and retirement benefits. "Benefits in kind" include:

- employee share schemes
- membership of professional bodies
- travel accident insurance
- company car (especially in the UK)
- free car parking
- personal training (e.g. pre-retirement courses)
- counselling
- subsidised childcare
- life insurance
- tuition fees for employees and dependants
- recreational clubs
- subsidised canteens and catering

Benefits can add 30 per cent or more to an employee's total remuneration. Organisations offer these benefits because they help attract and retain people of the calibre they need. Many employees value these benefits more than a marginal increase in salary. They are, therefore, an economical way of motivating employees – especially when benefits receive favourable tax treatment. Some employers offer "flexible benefit packages" where the value of the total remuneration package is fixed but employees have considerable choice about how it is distributed between salary and their own mixture of benefits. An organisation's remuneration system is closely linked to the organisation's maturity, and more details are given in the website that accompanies this book.

## Employee relations (industrial relations)

### Definition and concept of employee relations

The topic of employee relations (ER) is more widely known as **industrial relations (IR)**. It is also known as **labour relations** and **staff relations**. The term "employee relations" is preferred because in most modern economies only a minority of people work in industry. Similarly, "labour relations" has strong and possibly misleading connotations with physical labour which now forms only a small part of economic activity; the term is more frequently used in the USA. Staff relations implies that the topic is only relevant to people employed in "staff" positions. The term "employee relations" makes it clear that the topic is relevant to everyone who is employed in an organisation. Employee relations may be defined as:

" The study of institutions and processes controlling the mutual dealings between an organisation and its employees – especially the mutual dealings between an organisation and collective worker groups. "

In many situations ER concerns the mutual dealings between an organisation and a trade union, but it also encompasses dealings with staff associations and informal groups. The nature of ER is usually a feature of the management style and the industrial or commercial sector. Generally three main philosophical approaches to ER are distinguished – confrontation, concensus and pluralist:

- **Confrontation** arises from beliefs that organisations and employees have irreconcilable objectives. There is a great deal of mistrust between the two parties. Employee relations are often seen as a battleground in which the employees or the organisation seeks supremacy in dictating terms of employment, etc. Such conflicts can be mutually destructive. For example, workers may strike and picket an organisation with such success that the organisation is forced into bankruptcy and closes, leaving the employees worse off and without employment. Confrontation tends to be seen in traditional organisations with a long history of poor ER – often in traditional and declining industries where competition (perhaps international competition) is fierce. Confrontation is based on a *radical philosophy* derived from Marx: there is a fundamental conflict between employing organisations (capitalists) and the workers (the proletariat). Employers will maximise profits at the expense of the workers. Since employers have more power than an individual employee, workers need to band together so that their collective power is equal to or greater than the power of the employer. The ultimate goal will be for the workers to own the organisation collectivity or to control it by controlling the government. This philosophy was once very prevalent in some trade unions – albeit in a watered down and more sophisticated form.

- **Consensus** is sometimes called the **unitarian approach and** is the mirror image of the confrontation. Employees or their representatives form a genuine partnership working towards mutually beneficial solutions. In practice, a fully consensual approach is very rare and is, perhaps, only seen in co-operatives and small organisations. The consensus approach is based upon a *unitarian philosophy* which believes that there is a set of goals and objectives which serve everyone's interests. The well-being of the organisation is therefore paramount and everyone must work towards pleasing its customers. The **conformity approach** focuses on achieving *harmony between various subgroups of employees* – avoiding demarcation disputes where one group takes industrial action to pre-empt another group trespassing on its traditional territory. The conformity approach tries to set objectives and procedures that allow different groups to rise above their own vested interests. The conformity approach is based on a *pluralistic philosophy* that acknowledges that different workers and groups of workers will have a variety of objectives that may not be totally compatible. Since potential conflict may be mutually harmful, it is necessary to have a system of rules and procedures to resolve it. Workers must conform to the system so that the organisation remains productive.

Employee relations in public service and government are usually based on a pluralistic philosophy.

Employee relations usually involves a sophisticated interplay between *formal* and *informal* systems. The formal part of the system will con*sist of* "official" documents, meetings, agendas and timetables. The formal part of the system legitimises and crystallises ER. However, the formal system is often inflexible and prone to developing into "stand-offs". The informal part of the system consists of networks of respected people in both camps. It often operates via informal meetings in corridors and in "off-the-record" telephone conversations. The informal network oils the informal network and helps it function.

Employee relations usually involves the most senior managers in an organisation. The head of the HR function will have a very important advisory role but final decisions will be made by the CEO or the board of directors. The HR function will play an important role in setting up and maintaining the ER system and may be given executive powers with regard to minor decisions. More information on the people involved in bargaining and the phases of the bargaining process are given in the website that accompanies this book.

### Types of unionisation

An organisation will face big disadvantages if its workers are not organised in some way. For example, it will need separate negotiations with each employee or it must ignore employees' wishes. A workforce can be organised in many ways. At the bottom of the scale are **non-union organisations**. Non-union organisations usually occur in small, recently established businesses which are experiencing favourable trading conditions. If the organisation encounters difficulties and employees feel they are ignored they will either join a union or leave the organisation en masse – at a time when the organisation needs to devote its attention to other things. Some non-union organisations establish a **staff association** to represent workers and conduct negotiations. Some organisations try to avoid demarcation disputes between unions by coming to a **single-union agreement** where the whole workforce is represented by one union. It drastically simplifies ER and often means that a more logical and systematic approach to ER can be established. Single-union agreements may be accompanied by **no-strike agreements** whereby both union and organisation agree a method, usually arbitration, of resolving conflicts without strike action.

Many large organisations with a workforce that is very diverse in terms of its skills and trades and which has long history of unionisation are, necessarily, **multi-union**. Multi-unionism can require a great deal of effort managing rivalries between unions. Organisations are usually keen to avoid a sequence of never-ending negotiations where each trade union attempts to impress its own members and poach members of other unions by "leapfrogging" earlier agreements. In these circumstances the organisation may attempt to instigate **single-table negotiations** where all the unions are present and where one comprehensive agreement can be made. Needless to say, single-table negotiations are often very protracted and complicated.

## 16.3 The psychological contract

The idea of a psychological contract has been around since the 1960s. It is an unspoken understanding between an employee and their employer about what they can expect from each other – "I have promised to do this and my employer has promised me that he or she will do that". Usually the employee understands that she or he has promised effort, loyalty, trustworthiness, etc. in return for training, pay, job security and promotion from the employer. Psychological contracts in the past could be summed up by the phrase "I will give total commitment to the company and the company will look after me until I retire". Robinson and Rousseau (1994) defined the psychological contract in a more long-winded way:

> 66 An individual's belief regarding the terms and conditions of that reciprocal exchange agreement between that focal person and another party . . . a belief that some form of a promise has been made and that the terms and conditions of the contract have been accepted by both parties. 99

Note that it is the individual employee who believes that the contract has been accepted by both parties. An employer may intend to keep the contract but knows full well that it is unenforceable. A new manager installed after a takeover or merger may have no such intention. The HR function plays a crucial role in managing the psychological contract. A classic paper by Sims (1994 – a good read) indicates that the HR function should:

- arrange realistic job previews
- arrange training sessions devoted to the contract during the early stages of employment
- clarify organisational ethics and values

In general, the HRM department should make sure that the contract is communicated as clearly as possible. Guest and Conway (2002 – a good read) discussed the views of 1036 senior managers about the promises made by the organisation and the extent to which the promises were met. Table 16.1 is based on their data and uses an index where 100 is the maximum possible score. The list in the table is a good indication of the areas of employment included in the psychological contract.

It is unsurprising that when fewer promises are made fewer promises are broken. Indeed, when fewer promises are made they tended to be exceeded! Promises are frequently made about training and development, safety, feedback and fairness. Yet in all these areas there are shortcomings in their fulfilment.

Rousseau (1995) identified two main types of psychological contract: transactional and relational. The *transactional psychological contract* is nearest to a normal commercial contract. Workers agree to do certain things such as work overtime or move to a new location in return for a specific reward such as extra money. Transactional psychological contracts are often seen in clearly defined jobs that are relatively short term. They tend to centre upon specific outputs and specific rewards. *Relational psychological contracts*

| Aspects of employment | Promises made | Promises kept | Difference |
|---|---|---|---|
| Training and development opportunities | 88 | 63 | −25 |
| Safe environment | 87 | 39 | −47 |
| Feedback on performance | 81 | 60 | −21 |
| Fair treatment | 78 | 49 | −29 |
| Open two-way communication | 72 | 67 | −6 |
| Fair rate of pay | 65 | 48 | −16 |
| Opportunities for promotion | 55 | 67 | +12 |
| Avoiding unreasonable demands | 54 | 69 | +15 |
| Attractive benefits | 54 | 50 | +4 |
| Recognition for innovation and ideas | 49 | 68 | +18 |
| Pleasant working environment | 49 | 53 | +4 |
| Job security | 47 | 49 | +2 |
| Interesting work | 43 | 64 | +22 |

**TABLE 16.1** Promises made and promises kept in the psychological contract

are usually seen in long-term employees where the work is only defined in a general way. As their name implies, relational psychological contracts centre upon the way that the parties behave to each other. In the past, this was usually a paternalistic relationship where the employee would be loyal, compliant and adopt the organisation's values in return for secure employment and the knowledge that they would be looked after in times of misfortune. Modern psychological contracts where organisations can no longer offer long-term employment tend to stress a worker providing flexibility and a willingness to learn in return for high pay, the acquisition of marketable skills and a high quality of life.

Although the psychological contract implies a mutual agreement, there is a huge power differential between the two parties – the employer's viewpoint prevails. Workers then feel that the contract has been violated. This happened to large numbers of employees during the downsizing and restructuring of organisations in the 1980s and 1990s. Many workers felt cheated: while they had kept their part of the bargain, many employers had reneged on their part by increasing workloads and making many peoples' jobs redundant. In one study, 54 per cent of graduates claimed that their employers had violated their psychological contracts within the first two years of employment. The most frequent violations involved training, pay and promotion. The reactions of employees who believe that their psychological contract has been violated have been extensively researched. They experience feelings of injustice, deception or betrayal.

There are cultural differences too. For example, workers in Singapore who are used to short-term contracts are less aggrieved by violations than employees in the USA. Violations of the psychological contract usually affect workers' attitudes and behaviour towards their employers. The most obvious response is to leave the organisation and work for another employer. Some people, probably a small minority, complain to their employers. Probably most employees adopt the third option of keeping quiet and focusing tightly on their official duties while cutting back on more discretionary behaviours such as doing extra hours. Some employees attempt to get even. Revenge can take many forms and may include pilfering, neglecting duties that are hard to monitor, denigrating their employers in public, divulging trade secrets and even sabotage or destruction of the employer's property.

## CRITICAL THINKING 16.3 *The bizarre nature of the psychological contract*

Lawyers would regard the psychological contract as a very strange contract indeed. It is bizarre in a number of ways:

- *It is rarely written down.* Only a part of the expectations on both sides are made explicit. Some of the expectations are conscious but others are subconscious and the contracting parties may not be aware of their existence.

- *It is based on perceptions.* Consequently, there are as many psychological contracts as there are employees in the organisation.

- *It is dynamic* and will change over time. In a sense the psychological contract is under constant renegotiation.

Because the psychological contract is so dissimilar to other contracts some people believe it needs to be renamed "transitory employee perceptions of their employment". This would emphasise the subjective, individualistic and non-permanent nature of the psychological contract. Guest (1998) complains that, in practice, we should not take the concept seriously because it involves so many variables interacting in unknown ways.

**CASE 16.4:**  *Revenge for reneging on the psychological contract*

Palmer (1999) gives examples of the revenge people can take. Employees sometimes take revenge when employers renege on their psychological contract. For example, one 50-year-old from Wales tells how a new senior position was created in the service department where he had worked alone for more than four years. "I applied in writing for the new position, setting out my achievements. I was not granted even a brief interview despite the fact that I was on the premises. On the last afternoon of my resignation notice I destroyed all the test rigs I had built and the notes I had made to speed up the job. Subsequently I learned that three staff had been taken on to do the work . . . I had previously done myself."

Another example includes a 25-year-old publishing assistant who "rearranged" her boss's files, and did it so effectively that important documents were lost for several months. A final, ingenious example is a disgruntled word-processor operator who changed all the screens in her department to black characters on a black background. The organisation had purchased several replacement monitors before it located the real cause.

## 16.4 Employee engagement

Employee engagement is a current concern of HR departments yet it has a long history. In 1975 Csikszementkihalyri identified the concept of "flow" – a holistic sensation (presumably a good sensation) that workers feel when they are totally absorbed in their job when there is little difference between their own identity and goals and those of the organisation. Workers in a state of "flow" do not need to make any conscious effort to do the work needed to fulfil the mission and vision of their organisations. In 1990, Kahn coined the term engagement to describe a situation where the very *selves* of organisational members are harnessed to perform their jobs. Engagement integrates the ideas of job satisfaction and organisational commitment. It can be thought of as an employee's involvement with, commitment to and satisfaction with work. Engagement, it is claimed, unlocks people's potential so that they prepared to "run the extra mile" in order to help the organisation. Gatenby *et al* (2009) define engagement as:

> 66 creating opportunities for employees and their colleagues, managers and wider organization. It is all about creating an environment where employees are motivated and want to connect with their work and really care about doing a good job . . . It is a concept that places flexibility, change and continuous improvement at the heart of what it means to be an employee and employer in the 21st century workplace. 99

Employee engagement is often measured using a 12-item questionnaire devised by the Gallup organisation. MacLeod and Clarke (2009) report that employee engagement is related to:

- lower pilfering
- lower accidents

- higher productivity
- higher profitability
- higher innovation

Wow! It seems that employee engagement might be an *even* better managerial panacea than leadership! Unfortunately studies suggest that few workers are highly engaged. In high-scoring companies 24 per cent of employees are highly engaged and in low scoring companies only 3 per cent of employees are highly engaged. The main methods of increasing engagement include:

- Give *strong, transparent leadership* which gives employees a clear link between their jobs and the organisational vision.
- Managers who *clearly appreciate the employees' work* and who treat them as individuals. The managers must also be efficient and ensure that workers are equipped and supported to do their job.
- Employees should know that they are *free to express ideas* about how they do their job and how decisions are made in their department. Problems and challenges should be shared. Further, employees should know that their views will be carefully considered.
- The organisation should have a *sense of integrity* and live up to its values.

Unfortunately, there are several barriers to raising the levels of employee engagement. MacLeod and Clarke note that senior managers may not be aware of the need for employee engagement and do not understand the benefits it can bring. Even when senior managers are enthusiastic, middle and junior managers may not share their beliefs. Further, managers may not not know how to increase engagement and they may be ill-equipped to implement engagement strategies. As a result the organisational culture is unable to deliver engagement.

## CRITICAL THINKING 16.4 *Doubts about employee engagement*

The arguments in favour of employee engagement seem almost as strong as the arguments that were made by Herzberg in favour of motivators and hygiene factors. Yet, in due course Herzberg's theories were found to be based, to a considerable extent, on methodological flaws (see page 183). MacLeod and Clarke (2009) present a great deal of evidence in favour of employee engagement but, although there is a lot of evidence, much of it has very poor scientific value. There are four main doubts: poor definition, overreliance on case studies, poor quality measures and ambiguous experimental design and analysis.

1 *Definitions of employee engagement are vague.* If those given in MacLeod and Clarke are copied onto file cards and people are asked to nominate the construct

they are defining, a very wide range of answers are obtained. Guest (see MacLeod and Clarke, 2009, p. 8) points out that much of the discussion on engagement tends to get muddled and he suggests that "the concept of employee engagement needs to be more clearly defined . . . or it needs to be abandoned".

2  Much of MacLeod and Clarke's report consists of over 40 repetitive *case studies*. Yet, elsewhere in the this book (page 179) it was noted that case studies are a very weak form of evidence and depend on the background, experience and motives of the writer. There is often a **publication bias** in favour of examples that have worked. After all, what HR director who had invested tens of thousands of pounds in a programme to improve employee engagement that had failed would be keen to allow the results to be published? Many of the case studies are produced by organisations such as consultancies that have a vested interest in promoting employee engagement. It should be remembered that Harvard Business School was using case studies to extol the methods of Enron and the Royal Bank of Scotland.

3  The validity of the scales measuring employee engagement is not high. The most frequently used measure of employee engagement is the Gallup Q12 survey. (http://www.gallup.com/consulting/12153/Employee-Engagement-Overview-Brochure.aspx). A large-scale "in-house" study (Harter *et al.*, 2009) assessed the validity of the Q12 against nine criteria such as customer loyalty, profitability, turnover, safety and quality, etc. The validity correlations were not high. The median coalition was .23 which means that the things measured by the scale captured only 5 per cent of the differences between business units on these outcomes. A validity of .23 can be compared with validities of .58 and .4 for intelligence tests and personality tests, respectively.

4  Many studies of employee engagement are poorly designed and do not differentiate between cause and effect. For example, they show that employee engagement is correlated (slightly) with profitability. However, it is perfectly feasible that working for a profitable company causing people to be engaged rather than the other way round. Further, many studies use weak statistics. For example they divide organisations into high-scoring units and low scoring units. It is virtually certain that employee engagement is a continuum. Analysing a continuum in separate slices wastes information and may produce misleading results.

## 16.5  The legal background to human resource management

Governments have passed laws concerning the employment of people for almost 200 years. Initially these laws concerned the basic contract between employer and employees such as how wages must be paid (in cash, not in kind) and about the rights of workers to belong to trade unions. Broadly, between, say, 1900 and 1950, governments passed legislation concerning health and safety at work. Since 1960 they have passed legislation concerning social issues and the rights of individuals. As Table 16.2 shows, there is a raft of legislation concerning workers.

---

**Categories of employees**

- Employment of minors – to prevent exploitation of children
- Part-time workers and fixed-term employees – to prevent their exploitation

**Anti-discrimination (to ensure fairness)**

- Race, ethnic origin, colour
- Gender, pregnancy, sexual orientation
- Disability, age
- Rehabilitation of offenders – relatively minor offences need not be disclosed after five years (usually!)

**Health and safety**

- Place of work – must be safe, clean and at a reasonable temperature
- Working hours – must not be excessive
- Injuries to health

**Benefits**

- Form of payment – not as tokens to be exchanged at employer's shop
- Written statement of wage calculations – to check payment is accurate
- Minimum Wage Act – to ensure workers are not exploited
- Holidays – granting minimum statutory (Bank holidays) and other leave
- Parental leave – paid and unpaid time off work for mother and father
- Pension benefits – to ensure that people have retirement income
- Written employment contracts – to ensure clarity about duties and responsibilities
- Time off for study – to allow people the opportunity to gain qualifications

**Redundancy or dismissal**

- Reasons for dismissal – clear, written notification is required
- Consultation on closure – to ensure that workers' viewpoints are heard
- Redundancy –prevents victimisation at times of closure or redundancy
- Period of notice – gives stability of employment
- Continuation of employment if organisation changes hands (TUPE)

**Trade unions**

- Trade union membership – the right to belong or not belong to a trade union
- Picketing –the circumstances under which picketing may take place

---

**TABLE 16.2** Areas of legislation on the employment of people

Clearly this is not an exhaustive list. Legislation may vary from country to country and from time to time. It is usually the job of the HR function to check the legislation in the territories where they operate. Usually, they maintain a file with this information. They will also give guidance to other managers, perhaps as oral advice, memos on specific cases or periodic guidance notes. Failure to observe the legislation can have serious consequences. Infraction of safety regulations, for example, might result in a temporary closure of the organisation. The organisation might also be fined and its senior managers imprisoned. Failure to uphold employment law may involve an appearance at a tribunal which has the power to fine the organisation, award compensation or order an employee's reinstatement. Cases of this kind are nearly always attended by unfavourable publicity.

---

### CASE 16.5:  *Lloyds TSB earns disability benefits*

Lloyds Bank is a venerable institution stretching back to 1765. However, neither its age in nor its size and financial might mean that it can pay lip-service to employment legislation such as the UK's Disability Discrimination Act 2005. This Act covers more than obvious disabilities (e.g. physical impairment). It also covers disabilities that are not visible such as diabetes dyslexia, epilepsy or asthma. The Act means that employers must make "reasonable adjustments" to cope with disability on a person-by-person basis. Lloyds TSB has a strategy to deal with disability which has won numerous awards. The measures which the bank takes to create an inclusive working environments include:

- arranging flexible working hours
- providing software to read Braille
- installing chairs that give extra back support
- personal development programmes for employees with disabilities
- a disability resource toolkit
- software which reads out a computer screen (JAWS)

Such changes have clear benefits. The bank is able to recruit from a wider range of people and, in general, disabled people stay in jobs longer. It also enjoys strategic benefits by making its employees more representative of the community and improving its image – not least among customers who themselves may have a disability.

*Source*: Based on *Times 100 Case Studies*

---

## 16.6  Human resource strategy and manpower planning

An HR plan is often a very complex document. It is often produced in four stages. *First*, the future staffing requirements must be established. The process starts by examining the organisation's strategic plan to establish the impact of any changes, such as:

- new equipment
- new legislation
- new working procedures

- expansion or contraction
- centralisation, decentralisation
- reorganisation or mergers

This establishes the kind of job the organisation will need to fill together with the skills and competences that will be demanded. An organisation may wish, at this stage, to specify the number of various groups such as men, women, ethnic minorities, disabled people it would like to have on the payroll at a future date. At the end of this stage the organisation will have a **future staffing requirement**.

The *second* stage is to establish similar information for the **present staffing levels**. This is sometimes called a **human resource audit** and the result is sometimes called a **workforce profile**. Many organisations conduct HR audits on a systematic basis so that the information will be to hand if it is needed. The information can often be obtained from the organisation's IT system which calculates various indices of labour turnover. The simplest is the **crude percentage turnover** which is calculated according to the following formula:

$$\text{Percentage turnover} = \frac{\text{Number holding posts in year}}{\text{Number of posts}} \times 100$$

Another index of turnover is the **average length of service**. Both the crude index of labour turnover and the average length of service have the disadvantage that a poor result can be produced by the rapid turnover by a few individuals in a few posts. A more sophisticated index that does not suffer this disadvantage is the **labour stability index (LSI)** which is calculated by the formula:

$$\text{LSI} = \frac{\text{Number of people with more than a year's service}}{\text{Number of people employed 12 months before}}$$

Very low labour turnover might indicate a stagnant organisation that is not receiving enough new people and ideas. The problem of a high turnover is even less desirable and more common. An organisation with high turnover will be spending a lot of money recruiting and training people, which is wasted when they leave. Further, a high turnover disrupts the work of the people who stay with the organisation. High turnover is often a symptom of problems elsewhere in the HR function, such as monotonous work, poor communications, poor management style or poor wages. However, labour turnover must be interpreted in the light of information from other comparable organisations. Some industries such as hotel and catering have a notoriously high labour turnover.

It is difficult to determine the exact reason why people leave the organisation unless exit interviews are conducted. **Exit interviews** should be held within a day or two of an employee's resignation. It is no use waiting until the last day when attitudes have mellowed by fond farewells, mending of fences and anticipation of appreciative ceremonies and presents. Exit interviews need to be as close as possible to the point at which an employee decides to leave. They should be conducted by an independent and sympathetic person from the HR function. They *must not* be conducted by line management or people associated with them.

The *third* stage is to subtract the actual staffing levels from the future staffing requirements to produce a "skills gap" – an estimate of the number of new employees that will be needed in order to meet the organisation's strategic plan. Sometimes the comparison of actual and required staffing levels produces a surplus. This can occur if, say, a branch is to be closed or if new equipment will require fewer workers. Identifying surpluses is as important as identifying gaps: it often takes longer to resolve and needs early detection.

In the *fourth* stage gaps or surpluses are carefully inspected and appropriate action taken to ensure that the future supply of workers is equal to the number of workers demanded by the organisation's strategic plan. This is sometimes called "**right sizing**".

It is often possible to fill gaps for junior jobs by recruiting people from outside the organisation, and the time needed to train new employees must be taken into account. Recruitment for jobs with long training times needs to be scheduled ahead of recruitment for jobs with short training times. Senior jobs are often filled by promoting people from within the organisation. This is often a long-term process and it requires careful planning. It is called **succession planning** and almost all large organisations use it. Ironically, succession planning is more important for small organisations. In large organisations there is a much greater probability that someone suitable can be found. Simple arithmetic means that this is much less likely in small organisations, which can be reduced to chaos if a senior member of the management team resigns and no one is ready to take his or her place.

A succession plan starts with the organisational chart and works on a "falling under a bus" basis. This asks the question "who would take over if the CEO fell under a bus tomorrow?" When the successor is identified, other questions are asked: "how ready would the successor be?" and "what extra experience or knowledge would they need?" Of course, there would then be the problem of filling the post vacated by the person promoted to the CEO. Consequently, the process would be repeated for every position within at least two levels of the CEO. A succession plan is completed by drawing up schedules for the training and development of successors.

Succession plans are fraught with problems – which is why they are shunned by many small and medium-sized organisations. If they become public, as they probably will, they become organisational dynamite. The putative successor develops an initial mien of a "crown prince". Rivals to the succession may not acquiesce to their fate. They may set out to undermine the crown prince. They may tear the organisation apart in an attempt to seize the succession.

Staff surpluses often result in retrenchment, which is much less pleasant to deal with than organisational expansion. However, ignoring worker surpluses is great folly. A delay will mean an organisation will decline further, a bigger surplus will accumulate and a further round of unpleasant measures or emergency, traumatic, action will be needed later. It is much better to deal with surpluses promptly.

Potential surpluses can be managed by "freezes on recruitment", early retirements or redundancies. Short-term surpluses can be managed by "overtime bans" or short-time working. A freeze on recruitment may mean that the organisation is cut off from new people and new ideas. Further, unfilled vacancies may accumulate in certain departments that are already overloaded. Bottlenecks that impair the organisation's effectiveness may develop. Early retirement schemes can cause a haemorrhage of valuable expertise.

Redundancy schemes can cause great disruption and cause the motivation of workers to plummet. The HR function may seek to mitigate the effect on morale by offering voluntary redundancy. This too has great dangers. It is virtually certain that the majority of those who volunteer are those the organisation can least afford to lose. Some organisations manage redundancy situations by adopting a policy of last in, first out. At a superficial level this seems fair but it may be that people who have been recruited recently have competencies that are a better match to future needs. Needless to say, all of these problems are easier to solve if they have been detected early and there is plenty of time available to find a solution.

## 16.7 The welfare role of human resource management

At the start of the chapter it was noted that HRM had some of its roots in the welfare movements of the nineteenth century. The intervening sections of this chapter may have given the picture that HRM is now a mere management tool for controlling and manipulating workers. In fact, HRM has never totally lost its welfare role. In most organisations the HR function has a genuine concern in improving the lives of its employees. The welfare actions an HRM function might take are:

- Helping employees *solve personal problems*. Employees encountering problems often go to the HR department for help. At its simplest this help might consist of a sympathetic ear plus some common-sense advice. In other situations it might take the form of a transfer, a change in working hours or a modification of the job. At its most sophisticated level the help might take the form of an **employee assistance programme (EAP)**. In an employee assistance programme the workers are given the telephone number or other contact details of a counselling service they can consult if they have personal problems. While the company will pay for the service, the counselling will be totally independent and conducted on a confidential basis. It is argued that the independent nature of an EAP will encourage people to seek help at an early stage before a problem becomes too difficult to solve. An EAP is usually able to help employees who have problems involving debt, marital and family relationships, a poor work–life balance or a drug problem.

- Help *employees' careers*. Many HR functions try to structure jobs into patterns that provide careers for their employees. They may also offer training that has no direct or immediate relevance to an employee's current job but which will enhance his or her employability. In many cases an HR function will liaise with schools to provide work experience for scholars. Sometimes, the HR function will create temporary posts in order to help unemployed people make the transition into work.

- When an employee encounters a serious and acute crisis such as illness or bereavement, it is usually the HR function that instigates and *co-ordinates the organisation's compassionate response* such as arranging extra leave or sending condolences. In some countries where there is inadequate health care the HR function may take the lead in raising money to pay for treatment.

- The HR function usually takes the lead in the *social life of an organisation*. It often manages an organisation's sports and social clubs. Generally, it also organises social events, parties and celebrations. Further, the HR function will usually have responsibility for the organisation's catering services.

All of these contributions are usually considered peripheral activities, but their sum total improves the quality of people's working lives.

A final aspect of the HR function – *its advocacy on behalf of employees* – is often overlooked. In a majority of organisations HR personnel act as a buffer between the demands of other functions and employees. For example, a production manager may, perhaps to further his or her personal career, wish to instigate a very demanding schedule that involves high targets and a great deal of overtime. The marketing and financial functions may lend their support to the changes. It is likely to be someone in the HR function who draws attention to the impact these changes will have on employees. Similarly, the HR director will be present at board meetings where an organisation's strategy and tactics are first discussed. He or she is almost certain to make a significant contribution to ensure that the strategy and tactics are as "employee friendly" as possible.

# Activities and further study

## Essay plans

Write essay plans for the following questions:

1   What are the main laws that affect employment of people in your country? What steps can the HR function take to ensure that they are observed within an organisation?

2   What is HR planning and how does it contribute to achieving an organisation's goals?

3   What is the role of an HR function in *recruitment and selection* and how does this differ from the staffing procedures performed by managers in other departments?

4   What is the role of an HR function in *training and development* and how does this differ from the staffing procedures performed by managers in other departments?

5   Outline some of the factors that need to be taken into account by an HR function when it sets out to devise a salary and remuneration structure.

6   What are the main approaches and components to employee relations?

7   To what extent does the HR function, in an organisation you know well, still perform a traditional welfare role?

## Web activities

1   Look up the website of professional bodies in HRM such as: http://www.cipd.co.uk/default.cipd (Chartered Institute of Personnel and Development) and http://www.nipm.in/ (National Institute of Personnel Management India).

2   Look up postgraduate courses in HRM such as http://www.whatuni.com/degrees/courses/Postgraduate-list/ or Google "HRM postgraduate courses".

## Experiential activities

1   It is possible to gain some first-hand experience of HRM with vacation work or, perhaps, a management training scheme with short periods of work in different functions ("Cooks Tours").

2   If possible talk to a manager working in the HR function. Try to get detailed answers to the following questions. What type of organisation is it? What are its goals? What is its basic transformation process? How does the function operate?

3 Write a list of four topics that you think will be particularly relevant to the HR function in the next decade. Consider how they might change the way an HR department is structured.

## Recommended reading

1 Perry, J.L., Engbers, T.K. and Jun, S.Y. (2009) "Back to the future? Performance related pay, and the perils of persistence", *Public Administration Review*, **69** (1), 39–52. An analysis of factors relevant to PRP and a review of research that draws practical conclusions.

2 Sims, R.R. (1994) "Human resource management's role in clarifying the new psychological contract", *Human Resource Management*, **33** (3), 373–383. This describes the HR functions's role in clarifying and forming the psychological contract.

3 Guest, D.E. and Conway, N. (2002) "Communicating the psychological contract: an employer perspective", *Human Resource Management Journal*, **12** (2), 22–37. Most research views the psychological contract from the employee viewpoint. This considers it from an employer's viewpoint.

4 Reed-Woodard, M.A. (2010) "Maximising employee value", *Black Enterprise*, **41** (2), 56. An interview with the HR director at Wal-Mart on how it leverages human capital for profits.

# Finance and Accounting

## Chapter contents

## ❖ LEARNING OBJECTIVES

After reading this chapter you should be able to appreciate the contribution to an organisation made by the finance and accounting function (FA function). You should be able to identify the four specialist activities that the function performs – over and above the budgeting processes undertaken by all managers. In particular you will be able to:

❖ **describe** how the finance and accounting function:
- records transactions
- manages theft and fraud
- tracks commitments
- manages information
- controls costs
- raises money

❖ **explain in detail** the difference between debt financing and equity financing

❖ **list** five major considerations, including depreciation, that affect investment decisions

❖ **list** four ratios used to evaluate potential investments

❖ **interpret** a company's profit and loss account

❖ **interpret** a company's balance sheet

❖ **interpret** a company's cash-flow statement

❖ **differentiate** between financial reporting and management accounting

❖ **describe** different ways of categorising costs and **give examples** of each category

The finance and accounting (FA) function looks after an organisation's money but is sometimes bitterly resented. Accountants in particular may be castigated "as knowing the cost of everything and the value of nothing". Others dismiss people working in FA function as mere "bean counters", implying that they have a narrow and myopic view. Nevertheless, the function is found in *all* organisations because all organisations need to look after their money. This chapter aims to give non-accountants or non-financial experts a general introduction. As Case 17.1 demonstrates, the FA function is very extensive.

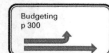

Budgeting p 300

---

### CASE 17.1: *The job of financial accounting*

The Financial Services Skills Council (FSSC) is an employer-led organisation which aims to improve the skills of people who work in finance functions in UK organisations, so it should be in a good position to describe what goes on. It regards financial accounting as a strategic, administrative and support role, involving extracting information from financial records such as budgets and interpreting what they mean. This information is used to help an organisation to see whether it is meeting targets. A true picture of an organisation's finances is an essential basis for strategy and any forward plans which might be available to stakeholders such as shareholders, potential investors, bankers, employees, creditors and government departments.

A chief financial officer (CFO) is likely to have overall control of the financial management systems which control working capital and relationships with debtors, creditors and suppliers. Chief financial officers prepare and sign off the annual reports and need to ensure that the company is complying with all financial legal requirements and professional codes. Specific activities include:

- preparing financial statements and accounts, such as profit and loss accounts or income statements
- monitoring the companyís financial performance on a constant basis
- advising board members and directors on strategic direction and advising managers on daily financial decisions
- advising the business managers and stakeholders about future trends and economic challenges
- reporting on variances between actual performance and budget performance, recommending corrective action
- preparing and reviewing organisational budgets
- advising managers on all aspects of financial policy and control

This chapter gives a deeper explanation of all these activities.

*Source*: based on Financial Services Skills Council's job profile for "Financial Accountant". The website contains many other profiles such as: Credit Management, Financial Control, Management Accountancy and Anti-fraud.

## 17.1  Managing the organisation's money

Most people in the FA function will be involved with managing its money. This involves a wide range of activities such as managing credit, recording transactions, tracking commitments, etc.

### Managing credit

Most customers obtain goods on credit – either short-term credit (30 days from invoice) or long-term credit where interest is charged and special arrangements are made. One of the main reasons why organisations fail is that a customer goes bankrupt owing a substantial amount. In turn, this loss may force the organisation itself into bankruptcy. In turn this may make a supplier bankrupt . . . and so on. Credit control is clearly a vital activity. The finance and accounting function will be responsible for establishing a system that checks customers' credit ratings quickly but unobtrusively with credit reference agencies such as Experian or Equifax. Credit reference agencies provide information about individuals, companies and organisations. On the basis of this information, a sensible credit limit will be set. If this limit is exceeded the customer will only be supplied if cash is provided. In some industries, such as the building industry (which is notorious for bankruptcies), supplies may only be provided in return for cash.

### Recording and expediting transactions

The FA function will also need to keep records of its transactions with customers and suppliers – probably by computer. An organisation must have mechanisms for claiming money from its customers by sending invoices and bills. This must be a systematic process that operates quickly. An organisation can get into financial difficulty by focusing on output but ignoring collecting "money due" until there is a cash crisis. Then it may have difficulty obtaining supplies or it may need to borrow money at a high rate of interest. Invoices for payment therefore need to be sent to customers either at the same time as, or shortly after, they have been sent goods. Some organisations calculate the following ratio to check whether it is paying its bills faster than it is receiving payments from customers:

$$\text{Debt Credit Ratio} = \frac{\text{Debtors}}{\text{Creditors}}$$

Similarly, the FA function must make arrangements to make payments to suppliers (**disbursements**). If these payments are not made promptly the organisation may be refused supplies. In particular wages and taxes must be paid promptly.

### Managing theft and fraud

In some organisations, such as supermarkets, large amounts of cash need to be stored and transported. The finance and accounting function needs to ensure the security of cash while it is stored and in transit. In most organisations, prevention of theft and fraud is a major issue. A key element is the fidelity of the staff who handle money. References and other checks must be made to establish trustworthiness. Some organisations take out insurance to guard against embezzlement or fraud by employees who handle money and who have access to financial records. This is often called a "fidelity bond" or a "dishonesty bond". The FA function must also control access to documents such as chequebooks and to computer systems. The use of the Internet by customers and the growing practice of allowing customers and suppliers access to selected parts of an organisation's information system have made computer security particularly important. Key security principles are:

- No one in an organisation should be able to authorise payments to him or her self.

- Large payments must involve authorisation by two independent people.

- Financial records need to be checked (audited) by independent people. **Internal audits** will be conducted by people from the same organisation but who work in a different department or branch and who have no connection whatsoever with the person responsible for maintaining the cash or the records. Internal audits are conducted relatively frequently, say, once every three months. **External audits** are usually conducted by personnel from an accountancy firm or organisation. External audits will be conducted, say, on an annual basis and the external auditors will be required to state whether they believe the accounts and records are an accurate reflection of the true situation.

## Tracking commitments

The FA function is responsible for checking that the organisation's commitments are within its ability to pay. Large projects will be tracked individually and require specific authorisation. Smaller, more routine acquisitions will be delegated to managers who will have strict limits of authority. A junior manager, for example, may be permitted to authorise expenditure up to £500 whereas a director may be able to authorise expenditure up to £10 000.

## Financial information and budgets

All managers in an organisation will be involved with budgets. A finance and accounting function will give individual managers and departments guidelines and advice. They will also have responsibility for co-ordinating and collating departmental budgets into a master budget. Finally, the accounting and finance function will play the lead role in collecting key financial information and preparing reports for management.

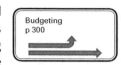
Budgeting
p 300

## Controlling costs

Organisations must contain costs. In some organisations there is a separate sub-function to look after "cost accounting". When organisations were small, costs were originally considered as "fixed costs" in the sense that they did not vary with the volume of work – they were much the same during quiet or busy times. For example, a blacksmith's costs of staffing and managing a forge did not change very much according to the number of horses that were shod. However, as organisations became more complex, the importance of "variable costs" was recognised. A workshop producing 20 railway carriages per year would incur more costs than the same workshop producing 10 carriages per year: it would use more materials, consume more power and employ more staff. As organisations, particularly service organisations, became still more complex, a method of "standard costing" was developed. In standard costing, the fixed costs are divided by the number of items produced and the result is then added to the other variable costs to arrive at a cost per item. The method works particularly well when the organisation has only one product or service. Where there are several outputs the allocation of costs is more complicated and requires estimates such as the time spent to produce an item or the percentage of resources used. Some people prefer the terms "**direct costs**" and "**indirect**" costs to the terms "variable" and "fixed" costs. The main variable costs are wages for casual workers and raw materials. A final development in costing has been the use of **activity-based costing**.

This section has outlined the "bread-and-butter" work performed by the FA function. There are, however, other more specialised areas such as raising money, investing money, financial reporting and management accounting.

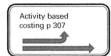

Activity based costing p 307

## 17.2 Raising money

Often an organisation can profitably use more money than it has to hand. When this occurs, the FA function will be asked to raise money. This is often called "financial management". It generally involves raising capital plus creating and managing an organisation's financial structure. Capital can be raised in two main ways: as debt or equity. The main distinction between them is that debt must be paid back at some time and it increases the organisation's liabilities, whereas equity is not paid back but some of the ownership of the organisation is transferred to the person owning the money.

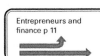

Entrepreneurs and finance p 11

### Debt financing

Debt financing involves a loan for a fixed period at the end of which the money (the principal) is repaid and the lender receives interest during the loan. However, the lender does not gain any ownership rights and debt financing is therefore favoured by people who have strong proprietorial feelings about their organisation. Debt is often classified into **short-term debt** (up to one year – often to cover operating costs such as rents and salaries), **medium-term debt** (between one and five years – often to cover the purchase of new equipment or other medium-sized assets) and **long-term debt** (which is usually used to purchase buildings). Normally, lenders will need to see a credible business plan, a cash-flow forecast and a projection of the financial position in future years. A lender also needs to have confidence in the organisation's senior management. A lender will charge an interest higher than that which could be obtained by leaving the funds on deposit in a government bank. Lenders are "risk averse" and ask for higher rates ("a risk premium") if they believe the risks are greater than leaving their money in a government bank. Main sources of debt finance are:

- Loans from *other parts of the same organisation* which are making lots of money (**positive cash flow**). They are the easiest types of loan to arrange because there is a commonality of interest and the parties to the loan will know each other well.

- Loans from *individuals* such as wealthy people who have assets they do not need for their immediate purposes. These lenders are sometimes called "**Angels**" – especially those lending money to fund a theatrical or cinema production. Individuals making substantial loans are likely to require a formal agreement and guarantee or collateral that, should things go wrong, they can sell to recover their loan. The most usual form of collateral is a claim on buildings or land but it may take other forms such as securities. Owners of small companies are often required to offer their private residence as collateral. Often, very small businesses are set up using loans from family members or friends. In some parts of the world the extended family is *the* main source of funds for small organisations. Loans from family are likely to be informal and impose less rigorous conditions.

- Loans from *finance companies* are also available. Perhaps the most famous finance companies are Warren Buffett's Berkshire Hathaway Investment Company (in 2002 it loaned Wal-Mart $125 million to restructure its finance) and General Electric Capital Fund. Often finance companies specialise in certain industries where they have particular expertise. Finance firms may also specialise in lending to companies at various stages of development. **Venture capitalists** specialise in lending money to business start-ups that have little or no trading history. **Mezzanine capitalists** lend to companies who are likely to seek their stock market quotation in the near future.

- *Banks* are a traditional source of finance and are available in most localities. However, banks have a reputation for being very conservative lenders.

- Loans from *governments* may also be available for organisations in certain areas that meet policy criteria such as maintaining a rural economy or offering work to groups of people who find it difficult to obtain employment.

- Government, local government and very large organisations may be able to raise loans from the *public*. Typically, they are for terms of 10 years or more. Because these loans are usually safe, the interest payable (the **coupon**) will not be high. Government loans are called "gilts" or "consols" (consolidated annuities – an old form of indefinite loans to the British government). Such loans to large companies are often called "debentures".

If the money is needed to acquire an asset such as land, buildings or equipment it can be financed in a rather different way. It can be **leased** rather than bought outright. The organisation never owns the asset but it pays the **lessor** a regular rent. This means that it does not have to find the whole cost "upfront" and the rent can be paid out of current earnings. The length of a lease varies considerably. For equipment such as a photocopier or a computer the lease may be as short as one year. Buildings and land, on the other hand, frequently involve leases as long as 25 or 99 years. Leasing rather than outright purchase may be better. *First*, it reduces the risk of obsolescence. The risk is transferred to the lessor since, if the machinery becomes outdated, it is returned to the lessor and the lease is terminated. *Second*, there may be tax advantages.

## Equity finance

With equity finance the loan does not receive interest and there is no promise that it will be repaid. Instead a proportion of the ownership of the organisation is exchanged. If the borrowing organisation is a success there will be a share in the increased value. This may be some combination of an increase in dividends or the value of the share which, ultimately, can be sold to someone else. If the borrowing organisation is a failure, dividends will be cut and the value of the share (equity) will decrease. In equity finance, the lender is taking a risk on the success of the borrower. Consequently, a lender will look for substantial returns. In equity finance, lenders frequently exercise considerable hands-on control of the company. When shares of the company can be bought by members of the public, individual shareholders are often passive investors but their interests are protected by legislation, and big shareholders such as insurance companies who may insist on being represented on the board of directors. A public company must send investors accurate reports and hold a meeting at least once a year (**annual general meetings – AGMs**) in order to appoint directors, approve accounts, approve major changes and appoint auditors. A canny investor could buy one share in 52 companies and dine out every week at a series of well-timed AGMs!

Equity finance has a number of *advantages*. It limits an organisation's exposure to financial risks such as changes in interest rates. New equity partners often bring useful contacts and wider expertise. However, equity finance also has *disadvantages*, especially loss of control. In a private company with only a few equity partners there may be personality clashes between the original owner and investors. There may also be acute difficulties when one equity partner wishes to sell their share of the company. Equity financing is often provided by **venture capitalists** who will seek to achieve high returns within, say, five years. 3i is a classic venture capital organisation.

Larger companies have the option of raising money on a stock market. Usually, these are companies that have outgrown mezzanine finance and their "initial public offering" (IPO) is for the **Alternative Investment Market** (**AIM**), which is specifically tailored to the needs of a growing company. The AIM provides the benefits of a public quotation but it has a more flexible approach and fewer formalities than a **full stock market listing**. When a company joins a stock market, the accounting and finance function together with its advisers issue a prospectus that states the maximum number of shares (**share capital**) and the basis of its existence. In the UK the latter consists of a **Memorandum and Articles of Association**. They set out the company's constitution and the rights of shareholders. The shares are given a "nominal value", which is usually £1. The actual value of a share will change immediately they are traded and will be determined by market forces.

There are different types of shares. **Ordinary shares** are closest to the common understanding of shares. They confer ownership of a small part of a company and they carry full voting rights. If the company fails, these shareholders are the last to receive proceeds from its break-up and may receive nothing at all. There is no promise that the shares will ever be redeemed and their value will depend upon what a buyer is prepared to pay. **Preference shares** are a safer investment because there may be a redemption date and they may receive higher dividends. Further, should the company fail, holders of the preference shares are paid before ordinary shareholders. However, preference shareholders are not usually entitled to vote at general meetings unless there has been a default in paying dividends.

**CASE 17.2:  *3i – The doyen venture capitalist***

Before 1945 it was difficult for small, growing companies to obtain credit. In 1946 the government joined forces with major banks to form "Investors In Industry", subsequently known as 3i. Its job was to lend money to small, promising organisations that were too high a risk for commercial sources of lending. Because it involved several banks and lent to a large number of organisations, the average risk was minimal. Indeed, some of the investments were huge successes. 3i bought shares in the ownership of British Caledonian Airways for £4.5 million and later sold its holding for £100 million. Generally 3i was a huge success and it was floated on the Stock Exchange. It is now a world leader in private equity and venture capital. It has a team of over 250 investment professionals whose work spans three continents. Examples of organisations obtaining venture capital from 3i are given on the company website: www.3igroup.com/shareholders/about/business/venture/venture.pdf.

The accounting and finance function of a publicly quoted company will monitor its share price very closely because it reflects the market's opinion of the company's performance. If the share price "underperforms" the market, the company may become a target for a takeover in which the senior management, including the CFO, may lose their jobs.

When an organisation needs to raise money the FA function will consider the advantages and disadvantages of each source and, with outside specialist help, select the type that is most appropriate. It will then seek to locate a shortlist of specific individuals and organisations. The exact mix of equity finance, long-term debt and the organisation's reserves is known as the "**capital structure**". Probably the most important aspect of an organisation's capital structure is its gearing (leverage). Gearing is a ratio of long-term debt to equity.

Gearing
p 434

## 17.3 Investing an organisation's money

### Types of investment

When an organisation has more money than it needs to meet running expenses, it should spend the surplus wisely on projects that will add value. The FA function will be deeply involved in assessing possible uses. This is often called **"investment appraisal"**. Investments may include:

- plant and equipment
- marketing and brand development
- improved systems, especially IT systems
- stocks of materials or land
- staff training, selection and motivation

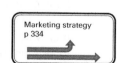

Marketing strategy
p 334

## Four major investment considerations

Investment projects sometimes arise from current operational demands such as the need to replace existing equipment or move to larger premises. They can also arise from strategic decisions The initial screen of investment projects will involve four major considerations.

The *first* is whether the investment will further the *strategic vision*. Those that lie outside the vision will cause the organisation to lose focus: it may not have the necessary expertise and it may not be able to concentrate on a number of disparate activities.

*Second*, the likely **rate of return** on the new investment (**ROI**) will be considered. This is effectively the same as **return on capital** (**ROC**) and **Return on Assets** (**ROA**) and its calculation is explained later. **Payback period** is often used to evaluate projects that generate some kind of income. As its name implies, it is the period of time that will need to elapse before the net income received equals the capital invested. Although the concept is simple, the calculations can be quite complex because they involve compound interest. Further, income needs to be discounted to take inflation into account since investment takes place in the present while the income will be received in the future when the money will be worth slightly less. The **net present value** is also based on forecasts of future earnings. Future cash flows are discounted for inflation using present value tables. All the cash flows from a project are then added. If the sum is greater than the initial investment the project goes to the next stage of consideration. If the sum is less than the initial investment, the project is abandoned. If early calculations show that a new investment cannot achieve this target the project is likely to be abandoned.

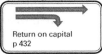

Return on capital
p 432

The **level of risk** is the *third* major consideration. The finance and accounting function will be asked to forecast outcomes based on three sets of assumptions: unfavourable assumptions, likely assumptions and favourable assumptions. If the results of projections based upon the unfavourable assumptions are dire and suggest that an investment may endanger the whole organisation, it is likely that the project will be abandoned unless some of the risk can be offset by insurance or other means.

*Finally*, initial considerations of any project will take **affordability** into account. An investment should fit comfortably within the reserves of the organisation – or at least within its borrowing powers. Further, it should not place an unreasonable strain upon the organisation's working capital and cash flow.

## Depreciation

The FA function will also estimate the rate at which a proposed investment will depreciate. Equipment will not continue working for ever: it will wear out and become obsolete. The rate at which this occurs plays a crucial role in investment decisions: the costs (which include set-up costs and training, etc.) must be written off by the time the asset comes to the end of its working life. Assets depreciate at hugely different rates. A computer system, for example may need to be written off within three years, while agricultural land may not need to be "written down" at all – indeed, it may appreciate. The rate at which an organisation depreciates its assets is, to some extent, a subjective decision based upon the predicted life of the asset. There are usually regulations governing the rate at which assets can be set against tax liabilities. The level of depreciation is shown on a balance sheet and this may affect an organisation's financial standing.

There are several ratios based upon the rate of return of potential investments. They include **yield**, **discounted rate of return** (**DRR**) and **net present value** (**NPR**). The same measures are used in management accounting to guide managers on how well they are using assets.

## 17.4 Financial reporting

The finance and accounting function prepare reports on the state of an organisation's finances. Many of these reports are legal requirements. They include tax returns and returns for sales tax or value-added tax. These must be completed correctly and to a deadline otherwise the organisation will incur (in theory) heavy financial penalties. Reports also need to be made to the owners of the organisation so that they can check that the organisation is being managed effectively. For private organisations these reports will be sent to a few people who have a stake in the organisation and they can be in almost any format that these owners consider proper. Charities will need to prepare reports for their trustees. Public bodies will need to prepare reports for the appropriate authority. Companies *must* prepare reports for shareholders and potential investors. Reports, except those for the owners of private companies, are publicly available. The financial reports usually include three specific sets of accounts: profit and loss account; balance sheet; and cash-flow statement.

### The profit and loss account

The profit and loss account (also called "**income statement**") is arguably the most important of the three main accounts. It shows the extent to which an organisation is adding value to the resources it consumes. If an organisation is making a healthy profit the chances are that it will also have a healthy balance sheet and cash flow. The profit and loss account also gives some insight into how a company is making its money. An example of a profit and loss account for Tesco is given in Case 17.3.

---

### CASE 17.3: *Tesco profit and loss account*
Tesco's profit and loss account (Table 17.1) is fairly traditional. There is a clear title, date and a statement of the period covered and the units used – £ millions. There are then two columns of figures: present year and previous year. Any significant changes between the years are noted in a narrative report. There are also reference numbers to a series of notes contained elsewhere in the accounts.

The profit and loss account shows that in 2009 Tesco made a healthy and growing after-tax profit of £2166(*) million. This is probably the most important conclusion to be drawn from the profit and loss account. It is also important to note that Tesco contributed £788 million to the community in taxes.

| Tesco Group Income Statement (adapted)<br>53 weeks ended 28 February 2009 | Notes | **2009**<br>**£m** | 2008*<br>£m |
|---|---|---|---|
| **OPERATIONS** | | | |
| Income from Sales | 2 | **54,327** | 47,298 |
| Cost of Sales | | **(50,109)** | (43,668) |
| **Gross profit** | | **4,218** | 3,630 |
| | | | |
| Administrative expenses | | **(1,248)** | (1,027) |
| Profit arising on property-related items | 2/3 | **236** | 188 |
| **Operating profit** | 2 | **3,206** | 2,791 |
| | | | |
| **FINANCE ACTIVITIES** | | | |
| Share of post-tax profits of joint ventures and associates | 13 | **110** | 75 |
| Finance income | 5 | **116** | 187 |
| Finance costs | 5 | **(478)** | (250) |
| | | | |
| **Profit before tax** | 3 | **2,954** | 2,803 |
| Taxation | 6 | **(788)**¶ | (673) |
| **Profit after tax** | | **2,166*** | 2,130 |
| | | | |
| | | | |
| **Non-GAAP measure: underlying profit before tax** | | | |
| | notes | **2009**<br>**£m** | 2008*<br>£m |
| **Profit before tax** | | **2,954** | 2,803 |
| Adjustments for: | | | |
| IAS 32 and IAS 39 'Financial Instruments' - Fair value remeasurements | 1/5 | **88** | (49) |
| IAS 19 Income Statement charge for pensions | 28 | **403** | 414 |
| 'Normal' cash contributions for pensions | 28 | **(376)** | (340) |
| IAS 17 'Leases' - impact of annual uplifts in rent and rent-free periods | 1 | **27** | 18 |
| IFRS 3 Amortisation charge from intangible assets arising on acquisition | 1 | **32** | - |
| **Underlying profit before tax** | 1 | **3,128** | 2,846 |

**TABLE 17.1** Tesco profit and loss 2009

The profit and loss account starts with Tesco's income: its sales of £54 327 million. It then gives the costs of its supplies (£50 109 million). However, there were other costs – administrative expenses of £1248 million. Note that both supplies and expenses need to be subtracted from the money Tesco made, so they are shown in brackets. Tesco manages a great deal of property, buying and selling stores and land as well as granting and taking on leases. In 2009 it made a profit of £236 million. on these activities. The total of all these figures shows the operating profit (£3,206 million). In other words, Tesco's main operations were adding value at a rate of 5.9 per cent. In order to run its business Tesco needs to participate in a number of financial activities. For example it receives profits from partnerships and joint ventures with other organisations (£110 million). On many days it will have spare cash which it can loan to banks and others on a short-term basis (e.g. the **overnight market**) and receive interest (£116 milion). It also has long-term borrowings on which it paid £478 million in interest. These sums are added and subtracted from the operating profit to yield a pre-tax income of £2954 million which falls to £2166 million when tax is extracted.

There are many ways that Tesco could have calculated the figures and presented the results. Adopting its own, idiosyncratic, method could confuse investors. Instead, Tesco prepared its accounts according to standard methods – the **generally accepted accounting principles** (**GAAP**). However, Tesco felt that accounts prepared in this way gave a slightly misleading picture of its underlying profitability. Consequently, it supplied extra information about its pension fund, investments, leases and "payments" made on acquiring new assets. In order to make it easy for investors Tesco has made these additional calculations using proven methods such as the **International Accounting Standard (IAS)** or the **International Financial Reporting Standards (IFRS).** The final result indicates that Tesco's underlying profit before tax was £3128 million – a noticeable increase on the previous year.

## Balance sheet

The balance sheet is an essential tool for understanding the financial position of an organisation usually at the end of an accounting period. It is like a snapshot of organisational health. In essence a balance sheet shows what an organisation *owns* and what it *owes*. It indicates whether an organisation is in a position to expand, whether it can handle the normal ebbs and flows of revenues and expenses, and whether it has sufficient cash reserves. It also indicates whether it is collecting debts quickly or whether it is slowing down its payments in order to avoid a cash shortage. Together with profit and loss accounts, balance sheets are the most important reports the accounting and finance function will need to prepare. The profit and loss account of Tesco is explained in Case 17.3.

---

### CASE 17.4:  *Tesco balance sheet*

An asset is any item of value owned that could be converted to cash. Like most companies Tesco divides its assets into current assets and non-current assets (Table 17.2).

**Current assets** are possessions that are expected to be sold or used up in the near future, probably within the next year. In Tesco's accounts current assets are:

- Inventories – stocks of goods waiting to be sold. It is not surprising that Tesco holds £2669 million worth of stock.

- Trade and other receivables – invoices Tesco is expecting to receive from financial institutions for, say, franchises etc. (£1798 million).
- Receivables – it is perhaps surprising that Tesco is owed as much as £4836 million by customers, banks and the taxman in the form of tax credits.
- Short-term investments such as overnight loans to banks are worth £1233 million.
- Cash in the bank to the value of £3509 million is needed to ensure that suppliers are paid promptly.

Clearly, Tesco had plenty of current assets. They totalled £14045 million.

**Non-current assets** are longer term. They are assets that are likely to be kept longer than, usually, a year. Tesco's non-current assets include:

- goodwill and other intangible assets such as trademarks and intellectual knowledge (£4027 million)
- property, plant and equipment. Tesco has oodles - a whopping £23 152m
- longer-term investments (£1 860m)
- longer-term loans and financial instruments including tax credits (£29 948 million)

Tesco's longer-term assets total £32 008 million. When they are added to current assets, Tesco possesses £46 053 million.

This does not mean that Tesco is worth over £46 000 million, because it also has substantial liabilities. Liabilities are negative. They are usually shown in accounts by enclosing negative figures in brackets. Liabilities are categorised as current or non-current. The main **current liabilities** are:

- invoices and other payable bills to suppliers and for services such as insurance, etc. (£8522 million)
- financial bills such as repayment of loans and financial derivatives (£9508 million)
- a contingency fund of £10 million to guard against various problems and challenges which, individually, are difficult to foresee

In total, Tesco has current liabilities in excess of £18 000 million. Tesco also has **non-recurrent liabilities**. These include:

- *financial liabilities* such as borrowings and financial derivatives (£12 761 million )
- *pension liabilities* (post-employment benefit obligations) of £1494 million
- liabilities that it has been *able to defer* for more than a year (£696 million)
- a *contingency fund* of £67 million to guard against longer-term, unforeseen problems

In total, Tesco has long-term liabilities of £15 018 million. When this is added to the short-term liabilities, the grand total of Tesco's liabilities is £33 058 million. This liability may seem massive. However, it must be remembered that its assets are very, very big. When liabilities are subtracted from the assets it emerges that the net assets of Tesco are £12 995 million – that is what the company was worth on 28 February 2009.

| Tesco Balance Sheet (adapted)<br>28 February 2009 | notes | 2009<br>£m | 2008<br>£m |
|---|---|---|---|
| **ASSETS** | | | |
| **Current assets** | | | |
| Inventories | 15 | **2,669** | 2,430 |
| Trade and other receivables | 16 | **1,798** | 1,311 |
| Loans, advances & other assetts | 17 | **4,836** | 411 |
| Short-term investments | | **1,233** | 360 |
| Cash and cash equivalents | 19 | **3,509** | 1,788 |
| | | **14,045** | 6,300 |
| | | | |
| **Non-current assets** | | | |
| Goodwill and other intangible assets | 10 | **4,027** | 2,336 |
| Property, plant, equipment | 11 | **23,152** | 19,787 |
| Investments | 12 | **1,860** | 1,421 |
| Loans and financial instruments | 17 | **2,969** | 320 |
| | | **32,008** | 23,864 |
| | | | |
| **TOTAL ASSETS** | | **46,053** | |
| | | | |
| **LIABILITIES** | | | |
| **Current liabilities** | | | |
| Trade and other payables | 20 | **(8,522)** | (7,277) |
| Financial liabilities (borrowings, liabilities, derivatives) | | **(9,508)** | (2,982) |
| Provisions | 26 | **(10)** | (4) |
| | | **(18,040)** | (10,263) |
| | | | |
| **Non-current liabilities** | | | |
| Financial liabilities | | **(12,761)** | (6,336) |
| Post-employment benefit obligations | 28 | **(1,494)** | (838) |
| Deferred tax liabilities | 6 | **(696)** | (802) |
| Provisions | 26 | **(67)** | (23) |
| | | **(15,018)** | (7,999) |
| | | | |

| TOTAL LIABILITIES | | (33,058) | |
|---|---|---|---|
| **BALANCE** | | | |
| Net assets | | 12,995 | 11,902 |

**TABLE 17.2** Tesco balance sheet, 2009

## Cash-flow statements

A cash-flow statement indicates how an organisation obtains funds and how it spends them. They are sometimes called "funds flow statements", "sources and uses of funds statements" and "statement of changes in financial position". They should conform to accepted standards such as **IAS7** (**International Accounting Standards 7**) developed by the International Accounting Standards Committee (IASC).

Cash-flow statements are needed because a simple balance might not give a useful picture of an organisation's cash position. It is not uncommon for healthy companies to have a negative cash flow – spending more than their income. It is a nightmare for many smaller organisations. Such companies may be spending a lot of money developing new products and buying new machines. This spending will generate cash in the future. Very unhealthy companies usually have a negative cash flow – they may be wasting resources on opulent offices, champagne receptions and private jets. Without a cash-flow statement it is difficult to differentiate between the two types. Cash-flow statements have two other major uses:

- Indicating whether an organisation is likely to have **enough money to pay future expenses**. If there is more than enough money the organisation should consider how it can use the surplus to add maximum value. If a deficit is likely, the organisation will need to cut costs or arrange extra finance.
- Helping **business planning and control**. A **cash-flow forecast** can be compared with the cash outcomes. This may provide an early warning that things are going wrong. It also helps future planning. The reasons for deviations from the forecast can be identified and incorporated in future plans.

An organisation may yield a 10 per cent profit on its products, but it will need money to buy raw materials, rent premises and pay workers before it receives any money from sales. A company may be fundamentally sound but if it cannot pay its bills promptly its creditors may foreclose. In a more realistic case, the situation will be less dramatic but there will still be some months where expenditure outstrips income, and vice versa. The cash budget is a plan to ensure that money is available when needed to pay bills. Most organisations draw up a cash budget on a monthly basis for a year in advance. Some organisations might budget on a weekly basis and others, especially those in the finance sector, will budget cash very carefully indeed, on a daily basis. The cash flow is sometimes presented as a cash graph. Figure 17.1 gives a cash graph for a holiday company whose cash flow is extremely seasonal.

It can be seen in Figure 17.1 that for the year as a whole, the company will be highly profitable and in most months the cash flow will be positive (colloquially known as "up north"). However, few people take holidays in November and January. The cash flow is likely to "go south" in these months. Indeed, the cash budget indicates that the cash flow will be so negative in these months that it will exceed the organisation's overdraft limit and the CFO must arrange extra credit facilities and place strong constraints upon purchases during November and January. On the other hand, the strong cash flow between June and September means that major purchases should be made at this time and arrangements should be made to invest the surplus "cash pile". Figure 17.1 demonstrates an important point: often, the meaning of financial information is clearer when expressed in a chart.

It is sometimes claimed that cash flow is a better gauge of profitability than reported income. The latter depends on many arguable accounting decisions such as when revenue is recognised and how much to allow for depreciation, etc. Cash flow is more objective – it is the amount of money "in the bank" (and other places) on one specific date minus the money "in the bank" on another specified date. Cash flow is much harder to fudge than reported income.

### Types of cash flow

It is customary to organise cash flows under three headings: operating activities, investing activities and financing activities:

■ **Operating activities** usually give the largest single flow of cash. The main exceptions to this rule arise in financial organisations such as banks and investment companies. In a healthy company, operating activities provide a positive inflow of cash. Examining the cash flow for operating activities is very important because it may give three clear signals that an organisation may be heading for trouble.

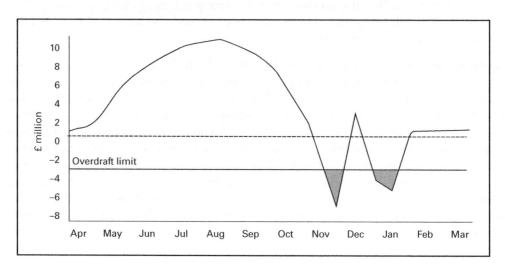

**FIGURE 17.1** A cash graph

- If operating cash flow (OCF) is negative the organisation is spending more money than it is creating. This may be justifiable during short periods of expansion and investment. A sustained negative OCF is bad. The organisation may be reporting an income but it may not be making any "real" money.
- If income exceeds cash flow (or if income is increasing while OCF is falling) the organisation is piling up assets that may not be worth what is claimed. For example, it may be counting stocks of unsold goods or income due from customers that have not actually been collected.
- It is often useful to look at OCF alongside sales and accounts payable (money owed to suppliers). If OCF is static or declining while accounts payable are increasing, the organisation may be attempting to ward off difficulties by delaying payments.

Some companies such as Amazon.com emphasise a variant of OCF: the "**free cash flow**". Ordinary operating cash flow does not usually include capital investments a company must make in premises and equipment in order to stay competitive. Further, for many retail organisations, such as Tesco, growth is mainly in the form of opening up new stores – which takes a lot of cash. Free cash flow takes these factors into account. In essence free cash flow is what is left over from OCF when funds for expansion and continuing operations are subtracted. In Amazon's case, free cash flow is the OCF minus operating interest and the costs of software and website development.

■ **Investing activities** include cash received or spent on purchases or sales of land, subsidiaries or equipment. Most companies have some form of long-term investments which are often called "financial instruments". The cash spent when these are bought or received when they are sold is also listed under investing activities. Monies that arise from participation in joint ventures are also usually reported under this heading.

■ **Financing activities** include cash obtained by long-term borrowing from the sale of bonds, stocks, shares and preference shares. If these are redeemed payments are shown as a negative cash flow.

## 17.5 Management accounting

### Uses of management accounting

Financial reports (section 17.4) are primarily designed to inform people outside the organisation so that they can decide whether their investments are used correctly and efficiently. However, a great deal of the work of the FA function is concerned with providing people *within* the organisation with information that helps them make day-to-day decisions and manage the organisation in the short and medium terms. This is usually called "management accounting". Management accounting is internal and usually confidential. It is therefore subjected to a lower level of external auditing and legislation. Management accounting often includes subjective data. Because managers need to take frequent decisions, management accounting reports are produced more frequently than financial reports – perhaps on a weekly or monthly basis,

**CASE 17.5:** *Tesco cash-flow statement*

It can be seen in Table 17.3 there was a healthy inflow of cash (£3960 million) to Tesco from operating activities – even after it had paid interest (£562 million) and corporation tax (£456 million).

However, in 2009 Tesco had a spending spree. It had a massive outflow of £5 974 million to investments. This was largely the result of purchases of property, etc. amounting to £5982 million and investments in joint ventures, etc. (£1263 million). This was a bigger spending spree than the previous year – presumably because Tesco was taking advantage of lower prices caused by the credit crunch. Some of the spending spree was balanced by sales of property, etc. amounting to £1354 million. Money for the spending spree was also obtained from investing activities. It issued more shares (£130 million) and it borrowed a massive £7387 million. However, its total borrowings did not rise by this much because it also repaid £2733 million worth of other borrowing. It also paid £889 million in dividends.

The cash statement ends with a summary. In 2009 Tesco had a net cash flow of £1601 million. This was twice the level of its cash flow in 2008 – mainly because it repaid fewer borrowings. It also had £1788 million cash from the previous year and a useful contribution from gains from changes in the exchange rate. On 28 February 2009 Tesco could lay its hands on cash to the value of £3509 million – more than enough to stop its creditors worrying!

| TESCO CASH FLOW STATEMENT (adapted)<br>53 weeks ended 28 February 2009 | notes | 2009<br>£m | 2008*<br>£m |
|---|---|---|---|
| | | | |
| **Cash flows from operating activities** | | | |
| Cash generated from operations | 33 | **4,978** | 4,099 |
| Interest paid | | **(562)** | (410) |
| Corporation tax paid | | **(456)** | (346) |
| **Net cash from operating activities** | | **3,960** | **3,343** |
| | | | |
| **Cash flows from investing activities** | | | |
| Purchase of property, plant and equipment, intangible assets, aquisitions | | **(5,982)** | (3,769) |
| Proceeds from sale of property, plant and equipment, investments | | **1,354** | 1,056 |
| Increase in loans to joint ventures | | **(242)** | (36) |
| Investments in joint ventures and associates, short-term | | **(1,263)** | (421) |
| Proceeds from sale of short-term investments | | | |
| Dividends and interest received | | **159** | 216 |
| **Net cash used in investing activities** | | **(5,974)** | **(2,954)** |
| | | | |

| Cash flows from financing activities | | | |
|---|---|---|---|
| Proceeds from the issue of ordinary share capital | | **130** | 154 |
| Increase in borrowings | | **7,387** | 9,333 |
| Repayment of borrowings | | **(2,733)** | (7,593) |
| New finance leases | | **-** | 119 |
| Repayment of obligations under finance leases | | **(18)** | (32) |
| Dividends paid | | **(889)** | (795) |
| Own shares purchased | | **(265)** | (775) |
| **Net cash from financing activities** | | **3,615** | **412** |
| | | | |
| **Net increase in cash and cash equivalents** | | **1,601** | 801 |
| Cash and cash equivalents at beginning of year | | **1,788** | 1,042 |
| Effect of foreign exchange rate changes | | **120** | (55) |
| **Cash and cash equivalents at end of year** | 19 | **3,509** | 1,788 |

**TABLE 17.3** Tesco cash-flow statement, 2009

## CRITICAL THINKING 17.1 *Are financial statements accurate? Watch out for restatements and lies*

Hundreds of eminent people have spent thousands of hours working on august committees to produce stringent standards such as the general accepted accounting principles and the international accounting standard. Further, public financial statements are audited and signed off by expensive external experts. There are also huge penalties when executives are discovered "fiddling the books". So you might feel you can rely on the financial statements of large organisations. Maybe, but don't bet your shirt on it. Table 17.4, which is only a small selection of examples, shows that there have been plenty of financial irregularities.

There are plenty of other examples. iSoft is known around the world for its software for the health-care industry. In 2010 Ian Storey, its ex-financial controller, was ordered to pay £20 000 and banned from practising as a chartered accountant for eight years. The granddaddy of financial irregularities was Enron which collapsed in 2002. It employed very gifted accountants to stretch the limits of accounting principles. They were the "smartest guys in the room" and they accumulated bad habits such as:

- inflating income by adopting *mark to market accounting* by estimating future income and including it in one year's figures
- *special purpose entries* which hid debt by keeping bad transactions off the balance sheet

> ▶

- *allowing its own CFO to deal, indirectly in ENRON shares*
- *pressurising its auditors* to apply reckless standards – the firm Arthur Anderson did not want to lose the $50+ million per year it was earning in audit and consultancy fees
- *failing to remove cancelled orders from its balance sheets* – on the basis that official cancellation letters had not been received

Many companies have audit committees to scrutinise their financial statements. It is best not to put too much faith in them. Enron's audit committee included a professor of accounting, a former president of a state bank, a congresswoman and a former UK Secretary of State for Energy!

When finance and accounting scandals come to light, professionals in the function sometimes congratulate themselves that they have revealed fraud! These professionals also have a euphemism for glossing over misleading financial statements; they issue corrections and call them "*restatements* of accounts".

| Company | Irregularity | Auditors |
|---------|-------------|----------|
| AIG (insurance) | Misreporting deals | PricewaterhouseCoopers |
| Anglo-Irish Bank | Hidden loans | Ernst & Young |
| AOL | Inflated sales | Ernst & Young |
| Bristol-Myers Squibb | Inflated income | PricewaterhouseCoopers |
| Haliburton | Booking unconfirmed agreements | Arthur Anderson |
| World Com | Overstated cash flow | Arthur Anderson |
| Xerox | Falsifying results | KPMG |

**TABLE 17.4** Some irreglarities in financial statements

rather than a yearly or half-yearly basis as for financial reports for shareholders. Management accounting data uses include:

- developing business strategy
- controlling
- improving performance and enhancing value

## Cost accounting

Management accounting is closely related to **cost accounting**, which is the process of tracking, recording and analysing costs associated with the activities of an organisation. The quantification and control of costs is a key element in ensuring that managers add value. Often, the first stage of cost accounting is to classify costs. One very simple classification involves dividing costs into materials, labour, power, rent, etc. This information can be collected for individual products and it can be compared with equivalent costs in the past or equivalent competitors. These comparisons point to areas where savings can be made. Many situations benefit from a more sophisticated approach where the costs are subdivided and then grouped according to abstract criteria:

- **Direct costs** are those costs that can be *specifically* and *exclusively* associated with a particular product or service (a **cost object**). For example, the direct costs for a television remote control will include the costs of components (raw materials), the labour costs of the people that assemble the remote control and the costs of packaging, etc. Generally direct costs are objective and easy to measure with great accuracy. **Indirect costs** cannot be identified specifically and exclusively with a cost object (Drury, 2005). Indirect costs are often called "overheads" and they include things like marketing and general expenses such as telephone bills and secretarial costs. Indirect costs also include a special category of **facility-maintaining costs**, which are expenditures on the organisation's infrastructure such as property taxes, lighting and heating. They are completely independent of business volumes but are necessary if the organisation is to stay in business.

- Some organisations allocate indirect costs to products or services using a **blanket overhead rate**. They may calculate the total indirect costs and the total of direct labour hours for the whole organisation and then divide the former by the latter. For example, a large organisation may have indirect costs of £30 million and the direct production of its services may involve 2 million labour hours. Consequently, each labour hour will carry an overhead charge of £15. A service which involves three hours' direct labour will incur a charge of £45 in addition to the direct costs. Blanket overhead rates are sometimes unfair and give a distorted view of true costs – especially where the indirect costs of departments differ drastically. For example, science departments in universities and colleges have much higher indirect costs than arts departments because they require more premises for laboratories, more support staff and higher insurance premiums. It would therefore be wrong to allocate the same blanket overhead rate to each hour of teaching in, say, arts and science.

- **Fixed costs** remain the same irrespective of the number of units produced. They are often closely associated with indirect costs. For example, if the rental of an assembly machine is $1000 a week to produce up to 4999 units, the same rent is paid irrespective of whether it is used to produce one unit or a thousand units. **Variable costs** change with the number of units produced. They are often closely associated with direct costs. For example, if the components for a television remote control cost $1, the variable costs will be $1000 in a week where 1000 remote controls are produced but will be $4 999 in a week where 4 999 remote controls are produced.

- **Incremental costs** are the extra amount needed to produce one extra item and they are closely related to the variable cost of each item. They are sometimes called **marginal costs**. If something can be sold for the same price and variable costs are low, extra production will mean a substantial increase in profits. Sometimes, however, incremental costs can be so high that extra product will result in a loss. For example, if an assembly machine can produce a maximum of 4 999 remote controls a week at a total cost of $5 999, the production of 5000 remote controls would cost $7000 (6000 plus $1000 to hire another assembly machine). The marginal cost of $1001 indicated by the management accounting system would probably dissuade managers from producing the extra unit.

■ **Opportunity costs** are the value sacrificed when one choice is sacrificed in favour of another. Opportunity costs only apply to scarce resources. For example, an organisation may consider selling a vacant plot of land for a profit of €4 million. If, however it could use the land to build a factory worth €6 million, the opportunity cost of selling would be €6 million. Management accounting information of this kind would help managers make the right decision.

## Management ratios

A finance or accounting function may also calculate ratios which indicate an organisation's efficiency. There are many ratios and some, ratios to gauge labour productivity and the likely worth of new investments, have been encountered earlier. These are the ratios that are most useful at the operational level. However, many other ratios are used at a strategic level, to see how well the organisation as a whole is doing. Management ratios are very useful summaries – but it must be remembered that they are summaries that may hide important details.

Labour productivity p 307

Clearly, a list of ratios does not make exciting reading, but this is no reason to ignore them. Everyone who is a manager or who needs to communicate with managers needs to be familiar with these indices. They usually form the basis of many senior management decisions and are a dominant influence on the way that senior managers think. If you cannot make sense of a senior management decision it is probable that *you* are at fault because *you* do not know, or understand, the ratios they are using. For example, if an organisation is making a takeover bid for your company it is highly likely that its senior managers have found that your productivity ratios are poor and they think they can make a profit by improving them. If a bank refuses your employer a loan for new machinery it is highly likely that it has computed debt ratios and found them too high. If you dislike figures and you think you can ignore ratios you will not last long as a senior manager – even if you have the charisma of an arch-angel. Scores of management ratios exist. Each has its own purpose. The following subsection contain some of the most frequently used ratios. They can be grouped into two main categories: profitability ratios and debt ratios.

Return on investment p 417

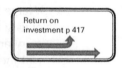

## Profitability ratios

Profitability ratios are global indices that show how well an organisation or unit is using resources. The five main global measures of profitability are:

1 **Gross profit**, also called **gross profit margin** or **profitability ratio**, is the organisation's mark-up on the sale price. It is probably the best single measure of an organisation's overall ability to add value when transforming inputs into outputs. It is the most

frequently used measure of profitability. Gross profit is the difference between income from sales and the cost of the goods sold, all divided by the value of the sales and multiplied by 100 to produce a percentage:

$$\text{Gross profit} = \frac{\text{Sales income} - \text{Costs}}{\text{Sales income}} \times 100$$

A comparison of the profit margins over a number of years reveals a great deal about an organisation.

*Declining profit margins* mean that the organisation is being forced to lower its prices – or is having difficulty in restraining costs, or both. For example, in 2004 the Chinese mobile phone maker, TCL, increased its profit by 30 per cent but its profit margin fell from 27 per cent to 22 per cent. Increased competition had forced it to reduce its prices, hence it was adding less value to each phone it made. Fortunately, TCL was able to sell more phones. In 2009 the bus and train operator, Stagecoach, reported a sharp fall in the gross profit of its train business from a margin of 6.5 per cent to a margin of 2.9 per cent. The company had been hit by falling sales to commuters during the credit crunch (lower income) and higher fuel costs.

*Increasing profit margins* mean that the organisation is able to command higher prices for its products (perhaps by improving them or shifting to more valuable markets) or is better at controlling its costs. The ideal situation is where a company's profitability increases for several years. This indicates a culture of innovation and cost control. The Compass Group is the largest support service company in the UK. It provides contract catering and other services to many organisations and runs the restaurants in prisons, banks, schools and airports. Its profit margins in 2007, 2008 and 2009 were 5.1 per cent, 5.8 per cent, and 6.5 per cent, respectively. The continuing improvement is attributed to tight control of costs and a move into more profitable markets such as cleaning and reception services. Comparisons of gross profit margins between companies in *the same sector* can indicate which companies have the best management.

2 **Profit after tax**, often known as "net profit margin", is very similar to gross profit margin except that it takes taxes into account. Sometimes it is called "net profit tax". It is a useful index for people who are interested in how much money an organisation is making for itself. It is calculated as follows:

$$\text{Profit after tax} = \frac{\text{Income} - (\text{Costs} + \text{Taxes})}{\text{Income}} \times 100$$

Profit after tax is an index of how well an organisation is able to transform inputs plus the effectiveness with which it is able to arrange its financial affairs in order to minimise tax. Organisations with high net profit margins will have more money to spend on other business operations such as research and development or marketing, or for distribution to shareholders and others. Comparison of the net profit margin for the same company over several years and comparisons between different companies in the same sector are as useful as those involving the gross profit margin. However, such comparisons need to be made with care where the tax regime differs between companies or financial years.

The previous indices focus on sales and revenue. But, in some circumstances sales and revenue are not the crucial factors. A factory which produces a profit margin of 5 per cent using six machines is probably better than a similar factory that has a profit margin of 8 per cent using 20 machines – the former's margin may be lower but each machine is producing a higher number of goods and more value is being created from the money used to buy the machines. In other words the management of the first factory is making capital work harder. A number of indices measure how efficiently capital is used (i.e. productivity). They include rate of return, return on equity, economic value added and payback periods. Indices of labour productivity are also relevant.

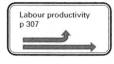

Labour productivity
p 307

3 **Return on capital** (**ROC**) is the traditional, most widely used index of how effectively a company is using its capital resources. Return on capital is sometimes called "**return on assets** (**ROA**)" and it is very similar to return on investments. It is calculated using the formula:

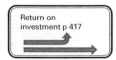

Return on
investment p 417

$$\text{Return on capital} = \frac{\text{Net profit}}{\text{Total assets}} \times 100$$

It should the noted that interest on loans is subtracted from net profit and that the index is usually calculated using profits after tax (i.e. net profit). The result depicts the actual benefit to the organisation. However, in some circumstances – when comparing organisations subject to different tax regimes – the index will be computed using the pre-tax figures. Unfortunately, the overall return on capital can sometimes be a misleading index because it includes capital borrowed from other sources. The following index takes borrowing into account.

4 **Return on equity** indicates how well the organisation is transforming the resources provided by the owner. It is calculated by the formula:

$$\text{Return on equity} = \frac{\text{Net profit}}{\text{Owner's equity}} \times 100$$

For example, the owner of a health club may have purchased a gym with £200 000 of her savings plus £100 000 loan from a bank. After deducting costs (including interest to the bank) and taxes, the gym makes a profit of £15 000 per year. This means that the return on equity is 7.5 per cent (15 000/200 000 × 100) which is more than the 5 per cent owner could have earned by leaving her £200 000 in a savings account. However, the extra interest will have been gained by accepting a higher level of risk.

5 **Economic value added** (**EVA**) was developed by Stern Stewart & Co. It compares a company's profitability with a minimum level of profitability elsewhere. It is usually the

difference between the return achieved by an organisation and the rate of interest on a standard loan from the bank (other comparators such as a stock index can be used). Economic value added is often used as an index of how well a company is creating wealth for its owners. The formula for calculating EVA is:

$$EVA = \text{Net operating profit after tax} - [\text{Capital} \times \text{Rate of interest}]$$

For example, a computer manufacturer in Singapore spent S\$100 million, which it could otherwise invest in securities at 9 per cent, on a new factory. The new factory produced a net operating profit of S\$11 million. An S\$11 million profit seems most acceptable. However, the EVA by the new factory is:

$$EVA = 11m - [100m \times 0.09] = 11m - 9m = 2m$$

In other words, taking the opportunity costs into account the new factory added an extra 2 per cent value to what could have been earned by keeping the money on deposit – not a big improvement considering the effort and risk involved.

## Debt ratios

Debt ratios are just as important as profitability ratios because a large number of organisations operate on credit. This is true of governments, charitable organisations and commercial companies. In itself, debt is not a problem – it can increase productivity. For example, a government may realise that a new school will improve literacy and, in the long run, the welfare of the population. However, it may not have sufficient funds in its current budget and it may be unable to increase taxes. In these circumstances it may make sense to borrow money and make repayments in future years when the benefits start to feed through to the community. Similarly, a bio-technology company may calculate that a new laboratory will be able to obtain a return of 17 per cent on capital employed. A bank may be prepared to lend the capital at 11 per cent. Again, in these circumstances, it would be sensible to borrow money to build the new laboratory. However, debt has its dangers. The greatest danger is that organisations borrow more money than they can repay (service). Debt ratios aim to provide information to help organisations avoid taking on too much debt and to warn lenders against unsound loans. There are four main debt ratios: gearing, interest cover, liquidity and "the acid test".

1  **Gearing** is also called "leverage" or "debt ratio". The basic principles of gearing were described in the previous paragraph: organisations may be able to generate a higher rate of return than the interest they would be required to pay. Gearing indicates the proportion of an organisation's assets which have been purchased on credit. The most usual index of gearing is:

$$\text{Gearing} = \frac{\text{Long-term debt}}{\text{Shareholder's equity}}$$

The level of gearing shows considerable variation from industry to industry. For example, in the transport industry the average gearing ratio is 150 per cent, in the building industry it is about 130 per cent while in a service industry gearing is about 100 per cent. Organisations that operate in very stable, predictable environments, such as public utilities or brewing, can service high rates of debt. On the other hand, lenders will be wary of loans to organisations operating in dynamic but turbulent environments, such as the building industry. A high gearing ratio means that an organisation will experience a greater profit in favourable times. Conversely, high gearing means that an organisation will suffer disproportionately when times are hard and interest rates increase.

2 Sometimes, the level of debt is evaluated using an index known as "**interest cover**" or "times interest earned". This ratio portrays the interest needed to service a debt as a proportion of the organisation's income. The formula is:

$$\text{Interest cover} = \frac{\text{Profit before interest and tax}}{\text{Total interest payments}}$$

Obviously, if the income of an organisation is much greater than its interest payments it is a good proposition for potential lenders.

3 **Liquidity** is a property that allows material to flow freely between one point and another. In financial terms, it refers to the ability to transfer money. Some assets, such as cash, are very liquid and can be transferred from one owner to another in a matter of hours. Other assets, such as property, may take years before a buyer is found and its value can be liberated for transfer. An organisation's liquidity is very important to its debtors because it indicates the organisation's ability to meet its short-term debts. There are several ratios showing an organisation's liquidity. The most important is the **current ratio**:

$$\text{Current ratio} = \frac{\text{Current assets}}{\text{Current liabilities}}$$

Current assets include cash, invoices that have yet to be paid (accounts receivable) and the inventory of goods that lies waiting to be sold to customers. Current liabilities include invoices from suppliers that are waiting payment (accounts payable), accrued expenses and tax liabilities. The current ratio for commercial organisations varies from industry to industry but for manufacturing organisations it is generally about 2.

4 Some organisations apply a stricter liquidity ratio. It is generally called the "**acid test**" but also the "quick ratio" because it indicates how quickly an organisation can make payments, i.e. meet its short-term liabilities without selling its inventory of goods waiting to be sold. The acid ratio is:

$$\text{Acid test} = \frac{\text{Current assets - inventory}}{\text{Current liabilities}}$$

This chapter has only provided a brief introduction to the FA function. However, it has shown that the function is vital to any organisation and the people working in it contribute far more to an organisation than "just counting beans"!

# Activities and further study

## Essay plans

Write essay plans for the following questions:

1 What measures can an organisation take to protect itself from the risk of bad credit and fraud?

2 What is the role of the finance function in raising money for an organisation?

3 How can the finance function guide an organisation in the investment of its resources?

4 Using the published accounts of an organisation that interests you, explain the organisation's profit and loss account, its balance sheet and its cash-flow statement.

## Web activities

1 Look at the sites of professional bodies in finance and accounting such as:

http://www.icaew.co.uk/ (Institute of Chartered Accountants in England and Wales)

www.cipfa.org.uk (Chartered institute of Public and Finance Accounting)

www.icai.ie (The Institute of Chartered Accountants in Ireland).

2 Look up details of finance and accounting scandals, e.g.: http://www.corporatenarc. com/accountingscandals.php

3 Watch some youTube clips on the Enron scandal, e.g. "Enron, the smartest guys in the room" (10 clips), "The effects of Enron Fraud".

## Experiential activities

1 It is possible to gain some first-hand experience of finance and accounting with vacation work or, perhaps, a management training scheme with short periods of work in different functions ("Cooks Tours").

2 If possible talk to a manager working in the FA function. Try to get detailed answers to the following questions: What type of organisation is it? What are its goals? What is its basic transformation process? How does the function operate? What are the future challenges the FA function is likely to face?

3 Choose the financial statements contained in the annual report of a company that interests you. Most can be found on the Internet: http://www.hemscott.com/help/ company-reports.do. Compare the financial statements with those of Tesco.

## Recommended reading

1 Mattessich, R. (2003) "Accounting research and researchers of the nineteenth century and the beginning of the twentieth century: an international survey of authors, ideas and publications", *Accounting Business & Financial History*, **13** (2), 125–170. A reference source rather than a read, this is a good place to start tracing ideas in accounting and finance. Useful for seminars, tutorials and assignments.

2 The Financial Services Skills Council's website.
www.fssc.org.uk/484808 13.html?i=8. This has a wealth of information on jobs in finance:
- auditing
- anti-fraud
- business advisory
- corporate finance
- financial control
- forensic accountancy
- insolvency
- payments and receipts
- tax accountancy

3 "Tales from the sharp end", *Financial Management*, August 2010, 20–24. Four interesting vignettes of people working in finance and accounting (business consultancy, Africa; orchestra, UK; book-keeping, UK; shipping finance, Sri Lanka), which contain a lot of tacit knowledge.

CHAPTER 18

# Information Management

## Chapter contents



## Learning Objectives

After reading this chapter, you will have an understanding of the increasingly important function of managing information and its role within the organisation. In particular you will be able to:

- **describe** briefly the basic components of an IT system
- **explain** the following concepts: expert systems, management systems, decision support systems, executive information systems
- **list** some of the factors that may cause the installation of IT systems to fail
- **describe** ways in which IT functions may be structured within an organisation
- **describe** in detail the two main types of e-commerce
- **describe** the difficulties and problems of e-commerce
- **outline** likely trends in e-commerce
- **describe** reasons why knowledge management is important
- **explain** the two main types of knowledge and **list** the main characteristics which differentiate knowledge from other resources
- **explain** the methods by which knowledge can be managed
- **list** the reasons why knowledge management is sometimes considered a current management fad

Recent developments in information management and computing have major implications for the way that many organisations, even very small ones, structure and use information and IT functions.

---

### CASE 18.1:  *Cloud computing and small fish*

The University of Bari in Southern Italy has a cloud computing project to help local businesses. Their small businesses do not need a large and expensive mainframe computer. They have a simple computer linked via the Internet to a large IBM System z mainframe whose services they can rent as and when they are needed. This has lowered the barrier and has helped local business benefit from advanced IT.

For example, when local fishermen haul in their nets, they use simple touch-screen systems to enter the details of their catch. They can then use complex databases to determine the demand and prices of the fish in local markets. Sometimes, they can enter the type and quantity of fish that were caught minutes ago, and start an Internet auction with wholesale companies. A further refinement means that packing details can be sent to the boat so that the catch can be placed in appropriate boxes as the ship sails towards the dock. This saves time and means the consumer has fresh fish. If prices are too low the catch can either be thrown back into the sea or donated to a charity.

The cloud solution uses the Linux operating system and complex software from IBM such as WebSphere and Tivoli middleware.

*Source*: based on *Mainframe Computing*, **23** August 2010, (8) 4–5

---

The classical view that there are the big four functions – marketing, operations, finance and human resources – is becoming less accurate each year. There is now a fifth large function, the information function. The influence of the information function and its associated IT is very widespread: its tentacles penetrate all other functions. Indeed many functions, especially operations and finance, could hardly function without good IT support. Practically all organisations have at least one computer to manage information for essential tasks. In comparison, there are organisations with no operations function or sales function. For example, DABS.com, the Internet computer supplier, is purely a retail marketing organisation. It does not manufacture or provide a service except selling things. Similarly, tax collectors have no marketing or sales function.

The information function is more distinctive than the other big management functions in two main ways. *First*, it is more heavily dependent on one specific technology (computing). Hence, it is heavily loaded with technical terms and knowledge, which this book does not even attempt to cover. *Second*, it experiences a rate of change which is many times faster than that experienced by the next most changeable function – operations.

The widespread use of computers has meant that people can trade using the Internet. **E-commerce** has quickly become an accepted aspect of both sales and marketing, but it is not a simple activity. The requirements of B2B trade and B2C trade can be quite different.

Further, salutary lessons have been learned from the dotcom bust and boom. Since e-commerce depends fundamentally on both information management and IT, it has been included in the same chapter.

The information function is also closely involved with **knowledge management**. Knowledge is probably the most important asset of any organisation and it needs to be managed as systematically as other organisational assets.

## 18.1 Historical context of IT

The IT function is not very old – it started only slightly more than 50 years ago, on the birth of computers. One contender for the first of these would be the Colossus machine built by the British intelligence services in 1943. Colossus could be programmed to search intercepts of German codes for certain words which, if located, would enable that day's codes to be deciphered. Some people define a computer in terms of its ability to store programs – in which case the Small-Scale Experimental Machine (SSEM) at the University of Manchester was the first true computer.

Information technology was once a small, expensive function concentrating on performing routine tasks with speed and accuracy and directly involved only 1 or 2 per cent of people in very large organisations. Now it is a function whose growth has shaped the way organisations have developed. For example, greater control and number-crunching has enabled large organisations to develop more sophisticated products and services. Better communications have made globalisation easier. Access to vast amounts of information has enabled employees to make decisions that were once the preserve of managers. Finally, connections between organisational networks permit more efficient links between an organisation, its suppliers and its customers.

The development of ever more ingenious input devices such as Apple's iPad, wireless communications and social networking have transformed everyday life. In health care, for example, doctors can use their mobile phones and laptops to obtain instant information on

---

**CRITICAL THINKING 18.1** *Are we collecting too much information?*

For most of human history information was scarce – rather like trying to find a cup of water in the middle of a desert. Today, we collect so much information that finding what we want will be just as difficult – rather like being at the bottom of Niagra Falls and trying to fill a cup with water – there is so much at such speed that gallons of water hit the cup and immediately splatter out. This knowledge can be an organisation's greatest asset and knowledge management is closely linked to the IT function. Indeed, many chief knowledge officers are at the head of the IT function.

Knowledge management p 452

Wal-Mart handles more than 1 million customer transactions every hour and 2.5 petabytes of information (the equivalent of 167 times the books in the library of Congress) are sent to databases. Facebook contains 40 billion photographs. When the Large Synoptic Survey Telescope in Chile starts operating in 2016 it will acquire a fantastic 140 terabytes of information every five days and is likely to outstrip available storage. Huge improvements in information management and interpretation are needed. The future is also likely to bring vast improvements in the speed at which information can be sent on the Internet. Google is already experimenting with fibre optic networks that aim at speeds of a gigabit per second – 200 times faster than present speeds. More data is not necessarily a good thing. For example, data on arrests for prostitution in Oakland, California, is available on the Internet. A simple analysis showed that police never made arrests on Wednesdays. So, guess what happened?

*Source*: based on Economist (2010a).

drug interactions and treatment recommendations. The Continua Health-Care Alliance is developing gadgets such as a carpet that senses erratic movements that can predict whether a patient will fall. They are also developing electronic devices which remind people to take medication (Economist, 2010b).

## 18.2  Uses of IT systems

Information technology starts by analysing organisational goals, tasks and procedures (often called systems analysis) and determines the hardware and the software (programs) an organisation needs. An IT system can be used in five main ways:

1  To provide quick and efficient *processing of routine transactions* such as payroll, invoicing and bookkeeping, and to monitor processes *reliably and frequently* so remedial action can be taken. For example, IT systems can be used to monitor the temperature, pressure and output of an industrial retort to ensure that medicines are produced exactly to their specifications. This was one of the earliest uses of IT.

2  To *communicate* with other computers allows people in the same organisation (**intranet**) to share electronic databases. For example, a customer may contact the organisation with a request for a bespoke product. After entering the request, the customer service department transmits it to the design section which prepares plans, etc. that are returned to the customer service department to check they meet customer needs. Revised plans are then forwarded to the production department. When the product is manufactured, details are sent to the dispatch department and finance department so that they can prepare invoices, etc. **Extranets** are computer networks that allow people outside the organisation, such as suppliers, to communicate. Often the extranet will use the World Wide Web. In some cases commercial extranets require security provided by firewalls, digital certificates and encryption. Companies use extranets to exchange large volumes of data, share product catalogues or collaborate on joint development efforts.

**3** To provide information to *guide decisions*. Computers can model the business process and predict likely outcomes. It can also calculate "what if" scenarios which can indicate the sensitivity to external buffeting. Decisions may be improved in two ways: decision-makers may be given more accurate and timely information and computer modeling may help decision-makers understand the problem.

*Expert knowledge systems* simulate judgements of experts. Typically, these systems contains a knowledge base and a set of rules to apply the knowledge. A classic example of an **expert system** is a computer program that plays chess. A further example is given by the British Council, which uses an expert system to help students, especially overseas students, navigate the complex process of applying for a university place in the UK. Many expert systems use **fuzzy logic**. Fuzzy logic is needed because information is often unclear and incomplete. Moreover, there may be several possible answers to a managerial problem. Fuzzy logic is an approach developed by Dr Lofti Zadeh in the 1960s (Zadeh, 1965). It computes "degrees of truth" rather than coming to a clear-cut true or false conclusion. Rather like the operation of the human brain, a number of partial truths are averaged to form higher truths until the conclusion is strong enough to warrant action. An expert system that approximates the operation of a human brain is called a neural network. A **neural network** is trained by inputting large amounts of data and rules. Once trained, advanced neural networks can extend rules to new situations and perhaps, even, develop new rules. Neural networks are widely used in oil exploration and weather forecasting.

---

**CASE 18.2: *Computer battles***

We are accustomed to airlines and hotels using computers to adjust rates and prices to maximise their profits. Recently it has been possible for consumers to retaliate using similar technology. "Bing" (Microsoft's search engine) helps consumers decide when to buy an air ticket. It uses a database on the prices of 225 billion flights to predict when the cost of a flight will be lowest. It is likely that similar programs will be written to help consumers book hotel rooms or buy cars. Of course, airlines will not take this lying down. They will program their computers to predict the predictions made by Bing and adjust their prices accordingly. The battle between computers may be endless. Microsoft may then predict the predictions of the predictions made by the airlines – and so on ad infinitum.

*Source*: based on Economist (2010b).

---

## Types of information systems and causes of failures

**Management information systems** (**MIS**) use information technology to collect, collate and use simple analytical tools to produce routine reports so that structured, day-to-day activities can be performed more effectively. Management information systems may also solve straightforward problems and are most useful to operatives and first-line managers. **Decision support systems (DSS)** are computer applications that analyse business data so that users can make business decisions more easily. For example DSS might produce a report comparing sales figures between one month and the next or it might project the quarterly income. Decision support systems are most useful for middle managers. **Executive information systems (EIS)** are very similar but the term is usually reserved for systems that support senior management. An EIS contains more data concerning the external business environment – such as information about competitors, legislation and market trends. Executive information systems are less likely to report raw data, and more likely to interpret information and present it in graphical form so that the main points can be understood very quickly.

### CRITICAL THINKING 18.2  *Why IT systems fail*

Information systems can be very useful but many, perhaps half, fail. For example, a consortium including Hilton Hotels, Marriott International and Budget Rent a Car commissioned an IT system to confirm bookings. After *four* years and *$125 million* spent in development costs, the project collapsed when it became clear it would miss its deadline by two years. The consortium ended in acrimony with their members suing each other for breach of contract. Information technology failures are more visible in the public sector. The National Health Service commissioned a system to computerise health records which has become the greatest government IT white elephant in history. Costs have escalated, suppliers have walked away and the project is running years behind schedule (Savage, 2010). The National Insurance Recording System encountered problems which meant that 170 000 pensioners may have been underpaid by up to £100 a week (The Times, 1999).

These are not isolated examples. A survey by the Standish Group (2009) showed that only 32 per cent of all projects were completed on time, on budget and with the required features. Indeed, 24 per cent of projects were cancelled prior to completion or delivered and never used. Some of the reasons why information systems fail are (Cringely, 1994):

- Users do not understand their own requirements.

- Technical teams fall in love with a technology and are determined to apply it – no matter who needs it.

- Businesses change during the design phase – such as the sale of a division or a merger of the entire company.

- Project duration is underestimated. A rule of thumb is to double the expected project duration.

- Organisational politics cause project delays while departments argue it out.

## 18.3  Structure of the IT function in an organisation

The head of an IT function is often called the chief information officer (CIO) and sometimes also called chief knowledge officer (CKO). Information technology functions may be divided into four sections: maintenance, projects and applications, relationship management, and infrastructure.

### Maintenance

A manager in charge of *IT maintenance* (operations) is responsible for making sure that the IT system works. Colloquially this is known as "keeping the lights on". In some organisations, especially those providing financial information, this can be an immensely important task.

---

### CASE 18.3: *Keeping the lights on at Reuters*

Reuters, now merged into Thomson Reuters, is a global company which provides data from around the world for news organisations and financial institutions. It trades upon its ability to provide information reliably and instantaneously. It sells online stock market and other information to 327 000 financial professionals working in equities, fixed income, foreign exchange, money, commodities and energy markets around the world. Reuters's IT system enables its customers to search, store and integrate information from its database. It is totally dependent on the smooth and uninterrupted operation of its IT system. If Reuters's IT system failed there would be a huge risk that stockbrokers throughout the world would make massive losses which they would seek to recover from their information supplier. If Reuters's IT system was even suspected of being unreliable, its customers would rush to competitors, such as Bloomberg.

---

Information technology operations managers are responsible for having a plan to deal with malfunction or calamitous disaster such as a terrorist attack. Indeed, all IT functions will have a section devoted to the security of their organisation's network. They will use firewalls, content filtering and intrusion prevention systems to prevent unauthorised access. The Cabinet Office, for example, has a special office for cyber security to counter methods of a cyber attack such as:

- *Espionage* – penetration and theft of secret information. Cyber attacks steal passwords, contracts and proprietary information from companies such as Merck and Paramount pictures.
- *Vandalism* – defacing web pages or harming programs. In 2010 there was an attempt to implant malicious software (**malware**) on Google's computers. Many sources claimed that the attacks emanated from China. Sometimes pornography or political propaganda can be left on a website.
- *Denial of service* – so many messages are sent to a target system that it cannot cope and it collapses. Recent targets have included the New York Stock Exchange, Amazon and Yahoo. In 2007 Russia unleashed a three-week cyber attack on Estonia in retaliation for relocating a Soviet war memorial.

- *interference* with critical infrastructure can be achieved if, say, power, water or communications are computer-controlled.

Many of the cyber attacks emanate from China and Russia. Attackers often gain access by enticing employees to click on contaminated websites – or even adverts offering to clean up viruses. In the case of the attack on Google's computers, it was thought that the attackers received help from a Google employee.

## Projects and applications

**A head of IT solutions and applications** will be responsible for specific projects such as the development and maintenance of computer programs that manage, say, an organisation's supply chain. Typically this will involve identifying the requirements and then co-ordinating a team of programmers to write the computer code. The programs will then need thorough testing and debugging before they are installed. After installation, work will be needed to modify the program in order to keep it up to date.

## Relationship management

**Relationship managers** (**RMs**) will report to the Head of IT Solutions and Applications. These people have to manage the way the system relates to groups of either internal or external customers. For example, a large catering company may have a hotels RM whose job is to ensure that the hotel division has appropriate IT systems compatible with the IT system of the organisation, its suppliers and its customers. The hotel RM will be responsible for liaising with senior management in the hotel division and identifying IT requirements. He or she will determine whether the requirements should be met by a bespoke program or by an existing package. The hotel RM will liaise with project teams who write or install the programs. In this organisation there would be IT staff managing relationships with restaurants, pubs, clubs and bistros, and relationship managers for headquarters departments such as HR and Finance. Some organisations provide IT services for external clients. In this case the RMs would be organised according to types of client and have titles such as RM Internet Organisations, RM Retail Organisations or RM Wholesale Organisations.

## IT infrastructure

The **Head of IT Infrastructure** will be responsible for the hardware (i.e. computers and peripherals such as printers or networks). She or he may also be responsible for installing intangible things such as access rights, passwords and security. The rate of change in computers makes it very difficult to keep an organisation's computer system up to date. **Moore's Law** states that the power of computers doubles every two years (sometimes quoted as every 18 months). On the one hand, a Head of IT Infrastructure will need to keep up with new technologies and up-to-date equipment. On the other hand, in reality, a great deal of money will have already been invested in equipment that cannot be jettisoned each time there is new technology. The Head of IT Infrastructure will often face the task of grafting new equipment onto a "legacy system" in a way which meets the organisation's needs.

### *Cloud computing*

In the early days of electricity, manufacturers needing electric power built their own generators on site – even though they had to build substantial generators to cope with peak demand and despite the fact that, for most of the time, it would be runing at less than half capacity. Transmitting electric power improved. Shrewd generating companies offered contracts to a substantial number of organisations. The generating companies "only" charged for the electricity consumed so a manufacturer did not, in good times, have the burden of installing extra generators or, in bad times, carry the burden of paying for idle capacity. Further, manufacturers were relieved of worries about changes in electricity generating technology, the supply of coal or government intervention. Computer geeks will shudder at the analogy. But a very similar thing is happening to IT functions. This is called **cloud computing**. A cloud is an allegory of the Internet. Years ago, a strange shaped bubble was used to symbolise abstract infrastructure of an electronic network.

An increasing number of organisations have ceased to own a mainframe computer. Instead they use what is probably a much larger computer owned by a specialist company which is also providing computer services for many other organisations. Amazon was one of the leaders in this development. It needed huge capacity to cope with occasional spikes of activity but, most of the time, it was using less than 10 per cent of its computing resources. With some ingenuity, it could rent out spare capacity. In 2006 it launched the Amazon Web Service. Watchers (e.g. as Google, IBM and many universities) piled in with imitations and innovations. Microsoft's CEO has wagered Microsoft's prosperity on cloud computing saying that in 2010 75 per cent of their employees computed in a cloud and in 2011 it will be 90 per cent. Cloud computing will mean that organisations will not need to buy big mainframes. They can lease relatively cheap terminals and then pay when, and only when, they use the computers of their suppliers. This has advantages which include:

- Less capital is needed to buy big computers.
- Less effort is needed to keep up to date with machinery and software. All this is a part of the service provided.
- It is easy for a small organisation to increase its IT capability and for a large organisation in temporary trouble to reduce its IT provision.
- An organisation's IT capability is not located in a vulnerable place that is liable to terrorist threats or industrial action.

Cloud computing exists in two main forms: a **private cloud** where only a few organisations use the same computer and facilities; and a **public cloud** where, in principle, any organisation may join. Of course, there are hybrid clouds combining the two main types.

Information technology functions have many very skilled professional managers. To their dismay, cloud computing will decimate their numbers in the way that middle managers were decimated in the 1990s. It is important to remember that a deviant organisation, Enron, was able to use its position as a power generator in California to distort the supply to manufacturers, service providers and consumers because their "customers" had, long ago, forsaken their independent generators. Cloud computing has a lead lining!

**CRITICAL THINKING 18.3**  *Computer clouds' Lead linings*

Computing clouds are exposed to some of the following problems:

■ Like banks, they are based on the principle that risks are not correlated – one organisation's peak will be counterbalanced by another organisation's trough. For many years this will certainly be true. But, sooner or later peaks will coincide and there will be a crash. In banking, serious crises occur every couple of decade and major crises occur every 80 years or so. In IT things move faster – expect a cloud crunch within a decade!

■ The Gestapo would have loved cloud computing. It would have given them access to organisational and personal information about most organisations and people. Cloud computing involves issues of security of information and privacy.

■ Cloud computing is often provided on an international basis and work is shifted between different countries according to unpredictable demand. This makes security more difficult. Further, there can be intense legal difficulties if your organisation is seriously wronged. Under whose legal jurisdiction could you seek redress – India, the USA, the UAE, Singapore, Australia, Russia?

## 18.4  E-commerce

### Definition and extent of e-commerce

The US Economic Census defines **e-commerce (electronic commerce)** as:

> 66  Any business transaction whose price or essential terms were negotiated over an online system such as an Internet, Extranet, Electronic Data Interchange network, or electronic mail system. It does not include transactions negotiated via facsimile machine or switched telephone network, or payments made online for transactions whose terms were negotiated offline.  99

It is sometimes called "**e-business**" and is a relatively new form of economic activity. In the past decade it has grown more than 50 per cent per year. It accounts for about 10 per cent of non-financial transactions in the UK (Figure 18.1) but it is still much smaller than traditional "bricks and mortar" trading in conventional buildings.

These figures need to be seen in context – the vast majority of commerce still takes place in the old "bricks and mortar premises" (Markillie, 2004). As we shall see later most "brick" companies combine selling from premises with e-commerce. This is colloquially known as **bricks and clicks retailing**.

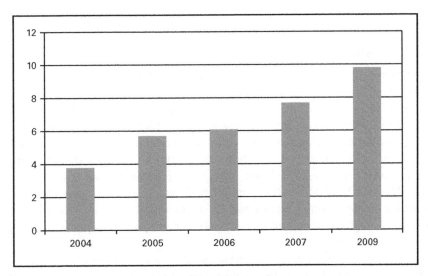

**FIGURE 18.1** Internet sales as a percentage of non-financial transactions

E-commerce typically involves desktop computers, but it can also involve personal digital assistants (PDAs) and pagers that distribute information such as stock market prices. Web-enabled mobile phones may also be used to conduct e-commerce.

## 18.5 B2C (Business to Consumer) e-commerce

**B**2C trading is when organisations use the Internet to trade directly with consumers. The classic example is Amazon.com which started Web trading in 1995. Amazon has been so successful that its range of products now includes clothing, electronics, toys and hardware. Indeed, Amazon now sells its B2C *systems* to companies such as Toys 'Я' Us and Target. Amazon's example attracted organisations such as Wal-Mart into retail e-commerce (**e-tailing**). Other early adopters were in the travel industry. Firms such as Expedia (American), Lastminute.com (British) and eDreams (Spanish–Italian) are well established. **E-booking** is another sector where B2C e-commerce flourishes. Another major player in B2C is the *recruitment industry*. Perhaps the best-known recruitment website is the "Monster" board that operates globally. E-commerce has also been used for less savoury transactions – especially unauthorised *pharmaceutical* sales and *pornography*. In 2003 Americans spent $700 million buying cut-price Viagra and prescription drugs from across the border in Canada. In the same year over $2 billion was spent in the USA on e-porn (Markillie, 2004). However, the growth of B2C e-commerce has not been smooth. The dotcom boom ended in a series of e-fiascos.

B2C retailing depends heavily on an organisation's *website* and the ease with which it can be located and navigated. One, costly, way of leading consumers to an organisation's website is to sponsor links on search engines such as Google. A more subtle approach

CRITICAL THINKING 18.4   *E-fiascos and dotcom bubbles*

E-commerce has had a roller-coaster ride since the mid-1990s. For about five years it experienced a meteoric rise where venture capitalists flocked to finance quite zany ideas such as pyjamas for pets. Shares in many dotcom companies rose to astronomical levels despite low earnings. Investors, apparently, could see growth potential and future earnings in a "new economic paradigm" centred upon e-commerce. In 2000, however, reality set in. Valuations of many dotcom companies were seen to be ridiculous. A classic example of a dotcom disaster is given by Boo. com (see Case study 18.4). Venture capitalists drew four main lessons: (1) ensure that some senior managers have experience; (2) avoid a concept that is too advanced; (3) avoid over-sophisticated technology; (4) control costs strictly – especially champagne, caviar and Concorde

The dotcom bubble burst. E-commerce contracted. Investors and customers became wary. However, with better management and a more considered view of the possibilities, the advantages of e-commerce re-emerged. Within three years e-commerce was expanding rapidly again.

is to embed in the website key words likely to be detected by search engines. Website design is crucial. It must be distinctive, yet convey an appropriate image. It must offer relevant information that can be reached with only three clicks of a computer mouse.

A website has inbuilt advantages in reaching some groups. For example, teenagers and young men spend more time online than watching television (Markillie, 2004). In theory a website should mimic the experience of seeing and entering a "bricks and mortar" outlet.

E-commerce finds it difficult to emulate the psychological experience of customers entering a "bricks and mortar" store. In many cases websites are little more than catalogues with an ordering mechanism. Despite valiant attempts, websites find it difficult to mimic a customer's state of mind when entering a store emblazoned with "sale" signs and littered with bargain bins. E-tailers also find it difficult to emulate the opulent trimmings of upmarket shops selling Gucci and Chanel. The ultimate website will use anecdotes, pictures and other alluring content to attract and keep people. In bricks and mortar retailing a potential purchaser has to make the effort to walk or drive to a competitor. In e-tailing a competitor is only three clicks away. Some *good* examples of e-tail websites include Galeria-kaufhof.de's system that tells shoppers when products are unsuitable for children (this promotes trust) and the Fnac.fr system that allows users to order books or CDs in advance of their release. Fnac.fr's system also notifies customers of authors' and artists' visits to stores.

E-tailing has an impact on bricks and mortar shops. For example, it is a common experience to visit a store and find a desired garment in the wrong size. In some stores it is already possible to take the wrong-sized garment to a scanner, scan its tag and order a garment of the correct size. The Internet is also used to lead customers to bricks and mortar shops. Computer users already ask search engines such as yell.com to locate, say, plumbers, tailors or grocers in their vicinity. In some areas global positioning systems (GPS) are already able to deliver similar information to mobile phones. Three major trends in B2C are apparent:

■ *More people are making purchases using the Internet*. In 2008, 55 per cent of all adults had, at some time, purchased goods or services over the Internet. Of these 81 per cent had purchased within the last three months (Office for National Statistics, 2008).

■ *E-buyers are purchasing a wider range of goods*. In the early days, e-buyers bought standard products such as CDs and books. As consumer confidence in e-commerce has grown, they purchase complex products. In 2008 the most popular Internet purchases were: travel, accommodation or holidays (48 per cent), clothes or sports goods (42 per cent), films or music (41 per cent), household goods (40 per cent), books and magazines (37 per cent) and tickets for events (37 per cent).

■ *Purchases downloaded are increasing*. This mainly concerns the purchase of films, music, computer software and, recently, electronic reading material. This means that products are dematerialised.

Dematerialisation
p 361

E-commerce is changing consumer behaviour. Many customers research products online before visiting a bricks and mortar outlet to make the actual purchase. In the USA, one in five customers of electrical goods research products online and will know the exact price. Seventy-five per cent of Americans research car purchases online before buying from a traditional dealer (Markillie, 2004). Customers are better informed and able to negotiate a keen price. They routinely compare prices in their local stores with online prices. They may even compare domestic prices with those abroad and then use a Web-based service to import them at a lower price. The process can work the other way around. Consumers frequently visit a bricks and mortar store to see and touch a product before returning home to buy online. This may mean that some shops become little more than showrooms. Both trends signify a decoupling of product information and the actual purchase. They also encourage consumers to be less loyal.

Some e-tailers, especially catalogue retailers, have adopted a strategy of using multiple channels which allow customers to complete different parts of a transaction in different ways. Argos is a superb example. It has used its well-developed competencies at distance selling and it allows customers to, say, check prices and availability online and have goods delivered to the customer's home.

Other excellent e-tailers include Amazon, Laredoute.fr, Alaplage.fr, Screwfix.co.uk and Otto.de. This list is interesting since, with the exception of Amazon, none are traditional dotcom companies. The largest group of e-tailers are catalogue retailers (Argos, Laredoute, Screwfix and Otto). They already had relevant skills, brand strength, distribution systems and customer service departments. Traditional organisations such as Tesco.com, Fnac.fr and Bahn.de are also having successful e-tailing. It would seem that, in the longer run, success in B2C e-commerce requires an evolutionary approach by large stable companies with experienced management rather than innovative start-ups by young caviar-eating and champagne-drinking entrepreneurs.

### CASE 18.4: *Boo.com disaster – how not to e-tail*

Boo.com was launched in November 1999 by two Swedes, Kajsa Leander, a model, and Ernst Malmsten, a 28-year-old poetry enthusiast. They found it easy to persuade venture capitalists to provide hundreds of millions of pounds to fund an Internet company selling designer clothing and accoutrements. They targeted trendy young people who had lots of money but little spare time. Boo's website was very advanced – so advanced that many personal computers (PCs) of the time had difficulty gaining access. On entering the site, shoppers were greeted by Miss Boo, a virtual shop assistant in trendy clothes and funky hairstyle. Shoppers could also see their purchases displayed on a three-dimensional virtual model of themselves. Leander and Malmsten used a very high profile to promote the company and themselves: lavish parties, private jet and transatlantic trips on Concorde to meet further venture capitalists.

The lavish lifestyle (fuelled by the three Cs – champagne, caviar and Concorde) plus the huge advertising campaign and advanced technology consumed $1 million each week but sales languished far below this level. In May 2000 the company went bust, having spent £178 million of investors' cash achieving very little. Subsequently Boo has been held as an example of how *not* to set up a dotcom company.

Boo's collapse was not an isolated event. Other dotcom companies such as Pets.com and Webvan.com also went into liquidation. As its name implied, Pets.com sold pet supplies. It was so heavily advertised that it was spending $179 to acquire each customer and, unfortunately, each new customer spent far less! Webvan.com offered an online delivery service and lost $35 million on sales of only £395 000 in its first six months.

## 18.6 B2B (Business to Business) e-commerce

While B2B e-trading shares many characteristics with B2C e-tailing, there are notable differences. In many areas, a B2B trading a website is less important. Customers know their suppliers. They are much less likely to use a search engine to locate the domain addresses. They are also less likely to be impressed by clever, eye-catching gimmicks that take time to download. B2B customers are more likely to be attracted by a straightforward, functional system. In many cases, there is an even closer link between customer and supplier in B2B trades. There is a growing tendency for orders to be generated automatically and sent to the supplier's own computing system – known as an **integrated supply system**. Such advantages have considerable cost savings. One disadvantage is the extra burden placed upon suppliers, who are forced to adopt its customers' systems. For example, all suppliers to Wal-Mart must conform to its computerised ordering system.

Argos, the world's biggest catalogue distributor, maintains tight control of its supply chain. It introduced a "track and trace" system for high-value goods. A "tote" (a bag) of, say, jewellery is given a **radio frequency identification (RFID)** tag and barcode label. Radio sensors at various stages of transport system automatically log the movement of each tote. In addition, hand-held sensors can track goods at other points. Tracking information is stored on a database.

### CASE 18.5: *B2B integration*

Recreational Equipment Inc. (REI) is a major retailer of sports and outdoor equipment. It sells goods made by many suppliers. In the past, it would send an order when stocks of a product fell below a certain level. It now uses an integrated supply chain where orders are generated and sent to suppliers over the Internet automatically. Further, approved suppliers can log into certain areas of REI's computer system and view information such as the current stock levels, buying trends and the profit margin. Suppliers, such as Cascade Designs, makers of tents and snow equipment, can anticipate REI's needs. They can start the production process in advance and ensure that goods are available when they are ordered. Cascade Designs can plan their production programme more efficiently. It also means that they can carry less stock.

Supply chain management p 368

## E-fraud

Fraud is a major threat to e-commerce. If customers feel that they will be tricked they will resort to traditional shopping. The problem of **phishing** (sending a fraudulent but official looking email requesting details such as passwords) is particularly threatening. In October 2004 there were over 1000 known phishing sites. In 2005 fraudsters stole $2.6 billion. This represents about 2.5 per cent of Internet sales – an increase of 37 per cent over the previous year (Tedeschi, 2004). AOL and eBay already provide software that alerts customers when they enter a known fraudulent site. AOL has developed "Chrome Mail" that allows subscribers to differentiate its official emails from fraudulent ones. **Spyware** is a program surreptitiously placed on a PC to capture and send back information that includes passwords. Many financial institutions are considering using **dynamic passwords** to defeat spyware. Dynamic passwords change each time they are used. One system is a version of a spy's "one-time pad". The bank sends customers a series of four-letter codes that are added to a static password. Once a code is used it is discarded and the next in the series is used. Since the bank also knows the correct series it can identify unauthorised attempts to access an account.

*Overpayment scams* are another type of Internet fraud. The buyer sends a cheque or bankers' order for much more than the purchase price of goods. The buyer then asks the seller to send back immediately the excess amount – which the buyer withdraws immediately. When the seller presents the original cheque, it turns out to be false. By then the buyer will have disappeared and it will be impossible to claim the money sent for the apparent overpayment. Some people are duped by **chain emails** that promise big returns but are very unlikely to return even the original investment. In some countries it is illegal to start or send on a chain email. In the **domain name scam** a fraudster obtains the details of a site's owner. Just before the renewal date, they send an official-looking invoice asking for the renewal fee – hoping that it will be paid.

## 18.7  Knowledge management

Knowledge management applies to all organisational functions. But, for three reasons, it has a particularly close relationship with the IT function. *First*, some of the key knowledge which must be managed concerns the IT system itself. *Second*, computers are the major tools for mining data and creating new knowledge. *Third*, the IT system is a major way of storing organisational information (but its importance is surpassed, by a huge margin, by the knowledge stored in the brains of its employees).

Management gurus such as Peter Drucker (1997) suggest that knowledge is the major asset of organisations. Senge's (1990) book, *The Fifth Discipline*, emphasised the need to structure an organisation so it maximises its ability to increase its intellectual capital.

The importance of knowledge was highlighted in the 1990s. Many companies had attempted to become lean organisations and had used techniques such as business process re-engineering to downsize. Many long-serving employees were made redundant. Some took revenge by destroying vital information or equipment before they left (see page 400). Others simply left – taking the knowledge in their heads with them. Organisations then realised their loss. They were forced to repair the damage by rehiring managers on a more expensive, consultancy basis. Greater organisational complexity, new technology, increasing competition and changing client demands added extra emphasis. Organisations recognised that a competitive advantage based on technology is transient and that longer-term competitive advantage is based on the knowledge of their employees (Martensson, 2000 – an excellent read). Skandia, a Swedish insurance company, made an innovative appointment – the world's first Chief Knowledge Officer to manage its intellectual capital.

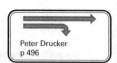
Peter Drucker
p 496

As its name implies knowledge management can be considered as two parts – *knowledge* and *management*!

## 18.8  What is knowledge?

Knowledge is a complex topic which can be divided into four sections: knowledge and similar concepts; tacit knowledge and explicit knowledge; the characteristics of knowledge; and the sources of knowledge.

### The concepts of data, information and knowledge

A chief knowledge officer's main responsibility is to maximise an organisation's "intellectual capital". The main components of intellectual capital are:

- skills and abilities of employees
- methods
- routines and procedures
- databases on clients and suppliers
- technologies
- organisational culture (knowledge culture) – see page 458

- patents[‡]
- copyrights[‡]
- brand name*
- reputation*
- relationships with suppliers, customers and opinion leaders*

Only some intellectual assets involve knowledge within the organisation. Other assets are legal protections ([‡]) and, probably more importantly, knowledge in the minds of people who are not a part of the organisation (*).

Data and information are not the same as knowledge – although the distinction between the concepts is rarely as clear. **Data** is merely a statement of an event or situation – such as "19 analyses conducted" or "20 units sold today". **Information** is is derived from data when it is manipulated in some way (collated, compared, analysed, etc.) so that a pattern emerges. For example, when the sale of 20 units is compared to the data revealing 15 units, 16 units and 18 units for the previous three days it reveals a pattern of short-term increase. **Knowledge** is produced when this information is:

- *Filtered* to eliminate irrelevant data which may shroud key data or provide an unnecessary distraction.
- *Placed in context and evaluated.* A claim that seven out of ten customers are very satisfied is less impressive given the context that nine out of ten consumers of a competing product are very satisfied.

Knowledge is produced when people use their experience, thinking, learning and understanding of the context to interpret what the information means. Knowledge allows people to exploit information in order to achieve organisational goals. For example, knowing that a product is increasing demand might lead a manager to realise a market is strong and that it will be possible to increase production or raise the price.

## Tacit knowledge and explicit knowledge

Polyani (1966) was one of the first to identify an important distinction between tacit knowledge and explicit knowledge.

- **Tacit knowledge** resides in the minds of people, usually arising from human interactions and evolving in an unplanned way. It also requires subtle skills and practice. Such knowledge is often hidden and is not easily represented in writing or electronic form, It often consists of hunches, intuitions and insights. Tacit knowledge is generated in a dynamic way and is based on personal interactions and experience. It may be organised illogically or chaotically, and is very sensitive to an organisation's culture and context.
- **Explicit knowledge** usually exists as documents or in an electronic form (e.g. customer database). It is conscious, documented and available to a wide range of people in an organisation. Explicit knowledge is usually well structured in a logical way. Information technology is good at sharing explicit knowledge.

The quantity of tacit knowledge is usually much greater than the quantity of explicit knowledge. However, the two types of knowledge interact (Nonaka and Takeuch, 1995).

People share their tacit knowledge by socialising and interacting. Over time a body of common knowledge evolves and is written down or formalised in some other way – the tacit knowledge has morphed into explicit knowledge. People internalise the explicit knowledge and start to use it in their own context – in turn, this generates more tacit knowledge, and so on. Figure 18.2 portrays the relationship between four components of organisational knowledge.

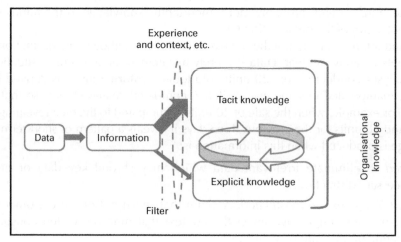

**FIGURE 18.2** Components of organisational knowledge

### Characteristics of knowledge

It would be lazy to think that organisational knowledge is similar to other resources such as financial capital, plant or machinery – although it shares many facets with human resources. Knowledge has distinctive characteristics (Martensson, 2000):

- It is *difficult to store*. It cannot be stacked in a warehouse. Much is in the minds of individuals who can be forgetful.
- It is often *disorganised and fuzzy*. Allee (1997) outlined numerous qualities. It is messy: multi-modal, multi-dimensional, evolves organically, is often slippery because it travels on language and it is often open-ended.
- *Context is important* because it can change the interpretation.
- It is *ineffectual if it is not actively used*.
- It *loves to escape organisational boundaries*.

Intellectual assets are rather like human resources but, from many standpoints, a lot worse!

### Sources of knowledge

Knowledge does not appear out of nowhere. At the most obvious level it is either created or collected. Madsen and Desai (2010) suggest that employees gather most knowledge from projects which fail. Other source good sources of knowledge are suppliers, clients, trade press, quangos and professional organisations. Two more recent sources of knowledge are data mining and cloud computing.

Organisations are now collecting such vast amounts of data on suppliers, employees and customers that Orwell's 'Big Brother' would salivate (see Critical thinking 18.1). **Data mining** accepts that such data is very low grade and out of context. For example, a loyalty card may yield data on how many units of alcohol the card holder purchases each week. But, it will not know how many units are purchased elsewhere or the number of people who consume the alcohol (e.g. frequent entertaining). Despite lack of quality, the sheer quantity of information allows sophisticated statistics to dig down to establish general trends that are useful.

Until recently the reliance on fixed and expensive media such as print, film, radio and television has meant that organisations only promulgated the knowledge of a privileged, articulate elite. Web 1.0 supported this is status quo – the same elite dominated websites. For example, experts provided information that was checked before inclusion on the Web version of Encyclopedia Britannica. Web 2.0's interactivity (about 2003) changed this. Instead of merely downloading information non-experts can make a contribution. For example, the participatory Web allows people without formal authorisation to share their, sometimes erroneous or calculating, knowledge via the Web. The classic example is Wikipedia. Bloggs and Twitter can be very effective ways of communicating tacit information (or disinformation). Consultants, training organisations, software developers, academics and authors are good at exploiting Web 2.0's interactivity. Widespread, useful but unchecked knowledge on the Internet is often called "cloud knowledge". Despite its drawbacks, "cloud knowledge" is an important source of organisational knowledge – provided it is used intelligently!

## 18.9  Managing and using knowledge in organisations

Research by KPMG (quoted by Warren, 1999 – an excellent read) indicates that poor knowledge management can have severe consequences. For example, 43 per cent of companies admitted that poor management of knowledge had damaged at least one relationship with a key client or supplier. More than 10 per cent said that their organisation had lost significant income. Clearly, good knowledge management is far from automatic. Figure 18.3 includes the final stages needed for knowledge management to be useful.

Knowledge is important because it can help organisations to add value. For example it can help capture best practice and ideas as well as helping make better strategic decisions and reducing costs. (Martensson, 2000). Warren (1999) identifies four practical ways where knowledge management is used:

- *Processing transactions* such as sales, purchases, expenses stock levels, etc. These may be mundane, but they are vital in any organisation. Errors or delays can damage efficiency. Even minor glitches cause intense irritation for employees, suppliers and customers.
- *Communications and collaboration* is helped by systems such as electronic bulletin boards, threaded discussions, best practice databases or learned-lesson databases. They help build relationships between people and emphasise a "sharing culture".

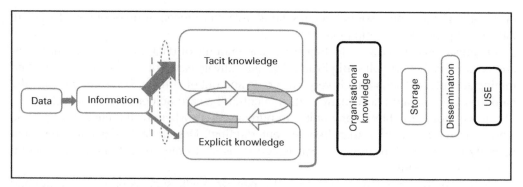

**FIGURE 18.3** The complete management knowledge process

- *Document management systems* which capture, store and make documents readily available help make quick decisions and respond to customer enquiries effectively.
- *Business intelligence software* helps search for information and then synthesise it into value-adding knowledge. A particularly useful development, now available in many universities and libraries, are systems which search multiple databases initiated by a single question. Some business intelligence software incorporates "fuzzy searching" and "automatic indexing".

The culture of the organisation is important. It can either help or hinder the management of an organisation's knowledge. **Knowledge cultures** encourage employees to:

- *Share the same vision of the organisation*. They will have participated in the formation of the vision.
- *Understand how the whole organisation operates*. This helps maintain a sense of perspective.
- *Be willing to discard old ways* – in particular, managers think of control as a co-operative process. Rather than controlling subordinates, managers exercise control *with* subordinates. People are not costs. Their knowledge, experience and creativity are seen as a main asset.
- *Feel confident* and able to discuss ideas openly and frankly.
- *Have wide access to information available*. Everyone can obtain information about budgets, expenses, schedules and other databases. People can see for themselves how their actions and ideas contribute to organisational goals.

Chief knowledge officers also need to foster a chain of orgainisational practices that creates and harvests knowledge, stores knowledge and disseminates knowledge. If this chain does not exist knowledge will have little use.

- **Knowledge creation and harvesting**: the main methods of creating knowledge are similar to those which is generate alternatives in decision making. Harvesting knowledge is equally important. People may believe that withholding tacit knowlegde suits their interests

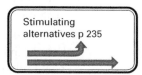

Stimulating alternatives p 235

better than sharing – after all, do senior managers share information about their salaries? Often employees do not share knowledge because they believe that their knowledge is unimportant (Martensson, 2000). A significant part of knowledge harvesting involves separating corn from weeds and preventing bad information entering the system.

- **Knowlege warehousing**: when knowledge is created or harvested it must be stored safely in an organised way so that the correct knowledge can be retrieved accurately and easily. This means that it must be archived in several separate, peferably anonymous, locations that are "bomb proof". It must also be carefully indexed and tagged

- **Knowledge dissemination** imposes contradictory demands. On the one hand, as many employees as possible should be able to use the knowledge. On the other hand, knowledge must be witheld from ill-wishers who might damage the organisation. Recent methods of dissemination include emails, internal twitters and internal wikis. Knowledge dissemination has a less positive side. Chief knowledge officers will spend a substantial proportion of their time preventing knowledge falling into the hands of compedtitors or enemies such as disgruntled ex-employees.

Knowledge management (KM) is not straightforward. There is a tendency to focus on the capabilities of IT and other technologies. In fact, there is strong evidence (Bassi, 1997; Warren, 1999) that KM systems based purely on a technological system usually fail. Time is another major enemy of good knowledge management. Employees have a natural tendency to attend to immediate matters rather than longer-term activities such as knowledge harvesting, etc. It is therefore important to give them dedicated time where they can record what they know. Many companies hold **post-project reviews** (PPRs) which have the explicit aim of recording and organising both the tacit and explicit knowledge that has been gained. Goffin *et al.* (2010) note that written reports are not very good at communicating tacit

## CRITICAL THINKING 18.5 *Is KM business salvation or "the emperor's new clothes"?*

Martensson (2000) wonders whether KM can ever be a big sucess because it largely involves tacit knowledge which, as noted earlier, is messy and largely unmanageable. Further, many of the concepts of KM are ill-defined and slippery. For example, some experts use the term "intellectual capital" while others use the snazzy phrase "competitive intelligence" (unfortunately a title CCIO does not have an alluring ring!). Knowledge management is also very costly and its outputs are very uncertain. It is often assumed, but rarely proved, that knowledge is a "good thing" in itself.

Bacon (2008) lists reasons why KM, as practised in many organisations, is no longer effective. Much of the information that is valuable to an organisation lies outside its own boundaries but KM usually focuses on the less significant portion it can control and often engages in the sterile activity of publishing information on its Intranet. Knowledge management developed at a time when the Internet was quite crude.

> Web 2.0 and Web 3.0 are much more interactive and powerful. Google, Lindekin and Facebook do a much better job than company systems at the qintessential KM tasks of linking people to information and people to experts. With the exception of proprietary and commercial information, internal systems show little advantage. Centralised KM has already outlived its usefulness! As early as 1999 Warren questioned whether knowledge management was just another office in the C-suite.

knowledge collected at PPRs and it needs to be supplemented with other mechanisms such as mentoring schemes and knowledge brokering. Finally, it is often necessary to overcome the reluctance of employees to share knowledge. Sucess is more likely if there is a clear expectation to share tacit knowledge. Further, willingness to share information can be taken into account when selecting employees, and making promotion and salary decisions.

Some people are sceptical about the current emphasis on knowledge management. They say that, like the quality movement in the 1980s and business process re-engineering in the 1990s, knowlege management has the hallmarks of a management fad. Chapter 20 discusses management fads and outlines the scientific principles against which claims for any management technique can be judged.

# Activities and further study

## Essay plans

1  Should IT be regarded as one of the "big" functions in modern-day industry and commerce?

2  What do you think the next generation of IT will bring? (Hint, engage in "blue sky thinking" and then relate it backwards to the development of previous generations of IT.)

3  Compare and contrast one named B2C organisation with one named B2B organisation.

4  What are the main types of e-commerce? For each type give detailed, specific examples and compare and contrast each type of e-commerce.

## Web activities

1  Visit the website of the British Computer Society (http://www.bcs.org/), the Australian Computer Society (http://www.acs.org.au/) or the IEEE computer society (http://www.computer.org/portal/web/guest/home).

2  Look up postgraduate courses in IT such as: http://www.prospects.ac.uk/ or http://www.whatuni.com/degrees/home.html.

3  Visit the website of major computer manufacturers to see if you can spot recent and pending developments in IT. Some useful sites are: http://www.oracle.com/us/sun/index.html or http://www.cisco.com/ and http://www.microsoft.com/en/us/default.aspx.

4  People are already aware of the problems posed to the security of information by cloud computing. Search the Internet to locate information on the rules and regulations that have been implemented or suggested.

5  Visit the US government's small business guide to e-commerce: http://www.whatuni.com/degrees/home.html.

## Experiential activities

1 It is possible to gain some first-hand experience of the IT function with vacation work or, perhaps, a management training scheme with short periods of work in different functions ("Cooks Tours"). You could also obtain similar experience working in an e-tailing organisation.

2 Try IT *and* knowledge management using the Internet.

3 If possible talk to a manager working in IT. Try to get detailed answers to the following questions: What type of organisation is it? What are its goals? What is its basic transformation process? How does the IT function operate? What are the future challenges the operations IT function is likely to face?

4 If possible talk to a manager working in e-commerce. Try to get detailed answers to the following questions: What type of organisation is it? What are its goals? What is its basic transformation process? How does e-commerce operate? What future challenges is e-commerce likely to face?

5 In a group of up to six colleagues, brainstorm products that you could set up as an e-commerce venture: (a) a B2B product or service and (b) a B2C product or service.

## Recommended reading

1 Monideepa, T. and Qruflech, S. (2010) "Examining tactical information technology–business alignment", *Journal of Computer Information Systems*, **50**(4), 107–117. Aligning IT function with the strategy and tactics of an organisation, this is moderately technical and difficult to read. Focus on the findings (section 4.1, pages 109–113). Abstract main ideas; do not get bogged down in details at this stage.

2 "Clash of the clouds; computing", *Economist*, (2009), **391**(8625), 66 and "Google on a cloud; move into operating system could change computing", Financial Times, 9 July 2009. Two short aricles that give some insight into the titanic commercial battle that developments in cloud computing are causing between Microsoft, Google and, to a lesser extent, IBM.

3 Nonaka, I. and von Krogh, G. (2009) "Tacit knowledge and knowledge conversion: controversy and advancement in organisational knowledge creation theory", *Organisational Science*, **20**(3), 635–652. This article gives the distinction between tacit and explicit knowledge, and describes the process which converts tacit knowledge into explicit knowledge. This is difficult to read because it is theoretical and is over-referenced. Focus on sections 2.1, 3.2, 4.1 and 4.2.

# PART 4
# Personal Perspectives on Management

In the previous sections we have examined the nature of management, management processes and management functions. While these are important, *your* personal perspectives are also important. *You* should be aware of *your* responsibilities and *your* approach. Some of these personal perspectives are covered in earlier chapters. For example, Chapter 1 has a section that is relevant to *your* career and Chapter 7 has a section on training and development which is relevant to *your* personal improvement. Further, most chapters end with toolkits, development activities and recommended readings which you can use to extend *your* personal competencies. However, two major personal perspectives need to be considered in depth. They are:

- *your* ethical and social responsibilities
- *your* ability to evaluate and criticise management fads, gurus and scientific reports

## Part contents

# Social Responsibility and Business Ethics

## ❖ LEARNING OBJECTIVES

After reading this chapter you should understand the main aspects of ethics and social responsibility that should guide managers, organisations and individuals. In particular you should be able to:

* **define** the concepts of ethics and social responsibility
* **briefly** describe five philosophical approaches to ethics
* **name** and **give at least one example** of three ways in which managers may act unethically
* **list** nine ethical principles that should guide the behaviour of managers

* **describe** in detail strategies for upholding ethical principles
* **list** eight ethical principles that should guide the actions of organisations
* **list** four ethical principles that should guide the actions of consumers and citizens

Many management decisions and actions involve ethical issues: if an organisation is making a loss, is it ethical to make employees who have given loyal service for many years redundant? Is it ethical for a marketing manager to increase sales by placing sweets at eye-level at checkouts? Is it ethical to manage an inefficient organisation that makes a loss and can only exist by receiving a government subsidy? Other professions, especially medical professions, have a clear code of ethics to help guide them in equivalent decisions. Indeed, practitioners of these professions take an oath before they are admitted to a professional institution. Managers face a wide variety of ethical issues yet they do not have an equivalent oath – although the idea has been mooted.

---

### CASE 19.1:  *Harvard MBAs renounce greed*

In 2009, in the wake of a series of huge corporate scandals (e.g. Enron and WorldCom) MBA students at Harvard Business School formed a broad coalition to develop a code of ethics for managers. They hoped that the oath would make a difference to their lives and improve the public image of managers. They also hoped that the oath would challenge MBAs to work to a higher professional standard so that managers would become respected for their integrity and professionalism. Some of the key pledges were to:

- manage resources to create value that no single person could create alone
- promote the well-being of individuals inside and outside an organisation
- avoid using position to advance their own interests at the expense of others
- uphold the laws in letter and in spirit
- refrain from corruption, unfair competition or harmful business practices
- uphold human rights and dignity of all people affected by the organisation
- report performance and risks accurately and honestly
- develop oneself and others, help their management profession to advance and create sustainable and inclusive prosperity

Is a code like this really necessary? There are already laws against embezzlement, harming others, discriminating against people and submitting fraudulent reports. The words are fine and lofty but would it be practically possible to prove that someone was to blame for not advancing management as a profession or creating inclusive prosperity? Is the oath anything more than glorified PR?

---

Managers tend to have a poor ethical reputation because they are thought to follow the ethic that "greed is good" and pursue profit irrespective of everything else. Without doubt, this view is largely unfair and pessimistic. There are certainly some unethical managers. But, some doctors are unethical and so are some lawyers, architects and politicians! However, the ethical issues that affect managers are very varied and not well known. Lau (2010) provide strong evidence that ethics education improves student's ethical awareness and moral reasoning. The following chapter aims to explain the basic concepts of ethics and social responsibility as they apply to people who are managing others. This chapter also aims to identify ways that organisations, managers, individuals and consumers can uphold high ethical standards.

## 19.1 Definitions and concepts of social responsibility and ethics

The basic idea behind social responsibility is that organisations exist within a community or social structure. Therefore they should contribute to wider activities to help their communities flourish. Social responsibility may be defined as:

> 66 An organisation's voluntary activities which go beyond formal laws, regulations and economic goals and which help their community or society meet longer-term or wider needs in fields such as the environment, arts, education and health. 99

The term "voluntary" is important. Organisations must already observe regulations to protect the environment and safeguard people's health. This is not social responsibility – it is merely complying with the law.

People such as Milton Friedman (1970) argued that managers are not well equipped to make decisions about the wider society. Whenever managers are using the organisation's resources for "social good" they are adding to costs which must either be passed on to the consumer or withheld from the dividends paid to shareholders, such as pension funds. Friedman, famous economist and Nobel Laureate, maintains that business ethics should be interpreted quite narrowly. He argues that the main social responsibility of managers is to operate their organisations efficiently so that they add the greatest value to resources they consume – within the law – and engage in free competition without deception or fraud. Friedman takes the view that corporate social responsibility beyond enlightened self-interest is a subversive form of taxation. Companies who devote resources to other activities are being unethical because they are jeopardising their competitiveness and inviting bankruptcy, where shareholders lose their savings and workers lose their jobs. Stone (1990) argues that companies have no mandate or special ability to make decisions except on the basis of long-term profits. Shaw (1991) goes further and points out that social responsibility is a covert attempt by government to shift its own responsibilities to commercial organisations.

Stakeholders
p 78

Bernstein (2010) notes that companies in competitive environments confer great benefits to society simply by going about their normal commercial business by:

- providing goods and services that people need and are willing to buy. Ordinary people have access to luxuries that were out of the reach of previous generations

- offering lower prices and better quality than competitors in order to stay in business

- shareholders (especially pension funds and frugal savers) can usefully deploy surplus assets until they need them

- employees earn wages and suppliers win contracts

- the taxes that companies pay finance schools, hospitals, roads, etc.

Environmental laws are nice for butterflies, birds and baboons but they delay the building of homes or power stations, etc. In countries such as South Africa, such laws mean that people suffer "rolling blackouts" and live in shacks. Corporate social responsibility can inhibit investment in poor countries such as Chad. It took Exxon more than six years, straining every sinew, to meet, "Equator Principles" – and pressure groups still remained dissatisfied. Other investors (and their bankers) have taken note and concluded that investment in Chad is not worth the effort. Chad has lovely butter files but its people remain poor.

Mintzberg (1983) and Carr (1968) argue that organisations should take a broader view. They should be socially responsible in order to head off government legislation. Socially responsible behaviour enhances an organisation's public image and this has a direct impact on its long-term viability. Organisations do not operate in a vacuum. They draw resources from the wider society and business decisions may have an impact on many people.

Advocates of corporate responsibility urge organisations to adopt a "triple bottom line" that includes profits, environmental protection and social justice. In practice this is quite difficult because whilst profits are objective and quantifiable, environmental protection and social justice are often subjective and nebulous. Nevertheless, advocates of corporate social responsibility have a very powerful argument. Wider stakeholders, such as politicians and government bodies, control legislation or trading conditions which the organisation may need. If an organisation behaves in a socially responsible way, the wider stakeholders are more likely to grant access to these resources. If an organisation helps its community it is likely to flourish. If a community flourishes it will buy more goods produced by the organisation and so the organisation will flourish too. Kim et al. (2010) point to the added advantage that a firm's corporate social responsibility (CSR) helps foster positive relationships with their employees. Furthermore, an organisation's CSR should have a sound ethical basis.

---

### CASE 19.2:  *The Co-op is the UK's ethical favourite*

GfK NOP is a market research organisation, based in London, which has strong German links. One of its specialisms is gauging people's opinions about ethical organisations. Its research suggests that, for UK consumers, the most important aspects of ethical companies are:

- fair treatment of employees – both at home and abroad (79 per cent)
- promoting the environment (77 per cent)
- ensuring good working conditions for local producers and suppliers (75 per cent)
- treating suppliers fairly and paying a fair price (73 per cent)

The least important factors in defining an ethical company were making charitable donations, promoting balanced body image and selling organic or GM-free products.

Every year GfK NOP asks a sample of people to rate companies' ethical standing. Table 19.1 shows the results for the UK, the USA, France, the Netherlands and Spain.

| Country | Ethical brands in rank order |
|---|---|
| UK | Co-op, Body Shop, Marks & Spencer, Tradecraft and CaféDirect |
| USA | Coca-Cola, Kraft, Procter & Gamble, Johnson & Johnson, Kellogg's |
| France | Danone, Adidas, Nike, Nestlé, Renault |
| Netherlands | Adidas, Nike, Puma, BMW, Demeneter |
| Spain | Nestlé, Body Shop, Coca-Cola, Danone, Corte Inglés |

**TABLE 19.1** International rankings of ethical brands

The Co-op has scored a hat trick and has been ranked as the most ethical British organisation for three successive years. Its ethical stance is based upon a clear set of values such as self-help, self-responsibility and solidarity. The next stage is to clearly identify its stakeholders, both internal and external. For example, its internal stakeholders include employees but, unusually, its customers are also internal stakeholders. To some extent, its suppliers are also internal stakeholders because the Co-op works in a close partnership with them. For example, by working very closely with its supply chain, the Co-op has been able to introduce a welfare standard for indoor-reared chickens from UK farms – without huge additional costs. It also supports external stakeholders such as local communities by contributing to charities such as "Street Games".

The Co-op recognises that, inevitably, some ethical activities may not be commercially viable and managers have to make choices that some members do not like. However, the reasons for the decision are always clearly communicated so that dissenters can understand why these decisions were made.

## Definition and concept of ethics

Ethics is a fuzzy, subjective concept. Lewis (1985) likened defining ethics to "nailing Jello to a wall"! A valiant and simple definition of ethics is:

> The code of morals that set standards as to what is good or bad, right or wrong, in the decisions made by individuals and groups or organisations.

This definition implies that right or wrong are universally agreed properties that are either inherent or set down via religious beliefs. However, ideas of right and wrong differ from person to person and from culture to culture. Hence, ethics can only apply to those notions of right or wrong which are shared between people or groups. On a global scale ethics may be defined as:

> The established customs, moral and human relationships which people in general believe are right.

Ethics are inextricably linked with values. Values are "relatively permanent and deeply held beliefs of the ideal states of affairs". They play a great part in shaping attitudes and they govern many of our personal choices.

## 19.2 Philosophical bases of ethics and social responsibility

An understanding of philosophical approaches helps identify the main themes of ethical thought. This is easier than treating each ethical problem in isolation and it is often useful to compare and contrast the different approaches. The major philosophical approaches to ethics can be grouped under four headings: sophists and sceptics, enlightened self-interest, utility, and rights.

### Sophist and sceptic views of ethics

**Sophists** were philosophers who wandered through ancient Greece giving talks and instructions for a fee. **Sceptics** were also from ancient Greece and they questioned the grounds of accepted beliefs. Sophists and sceptics noted that ethics are very subjective: what is considered ethical by one person may be regarded as unethical by another. The division of opinion is along the lines of self-interest: while a lower-paid worker might consider an income tax rate of 50 per cent ethical, a higher-paid worker might consider the confiscation of half of his or her hard-earned income by other people as unethical. In addition, ethical standards can change dramatically over time. Each successive generation rewrites ethical history.

Modern sceptics and sophists argue that received ethics are often little more than the values held by committee members of a professional body at any meeting. Indeed, a cynic might define ethics as a mechanism by which a temporarily influential group seek to impose their values on others.

Kohlberg (1976) suggested that moral development passes through three stages. The *first* centres on avoiding pain and achieving pleasure. The *second* involves meeting the moral standards of others and society. The *best* stage, only achieved by some people, is the post-conventional stage where behaviour is centred upon personal, abstract principles.

Cynics are not impressed with such reasoning. They retort that an action can be either unsuccessful or successful. Success puts a person in a position to impose their values on others. Accordingly, ethics follow the law of **might is right**. If you have power, you determine what is and is not ethical and you get to write the history books that prove your view is justified. If the cynics and sceptics are correct, stop bothering about the nature of goodness, find out what the dominant people think is good and follow their ideas!

### CRITICAL THINKING 19.1 *What is wrong with "might is right"?*

Superficially, "might is right" may not be a bad thing. After all don't people become mighty because they are better suited to their environment? Therefore, is it not in society's interests that they prosper? Unfortunately there are two related problems. *First*, it leads to a very nasty, brutish society. *Second*, a "might is right society" is unstable. A "might is right" leader must always look over his or her shoulder. A loss of "might" for only a day or two due to, say, influenza, might allow a "coup" by a second or third in command. The leader of the coup will then dread catching influenza and a "putsch" by the third or fourth in command. In these turbulent situations, sensible people devote their energies to saving their skins rather than, say, inventing new things, exploiting new markets or helping others.

## Enlightened self-interest

**Enlightened self-interest** is a ubiquitous ethical principle. It is associated with the philosopher **Hobbes** and his notion of the **social contract**. Many beneficial community activities would be impossible if everyone followed their own short-term goals. For example, long-term self-interest means that we should not steal books from libraries. If everyone did so, libraries would cease to exist and we would all be deprived of their benefits. Confucius identified the principle of *reciprocity* as an important aspect of ethics. Unless, perhaps, you are dealing with a masochist, you should not do things to other people which you would not like them to do to you. A good rule of thumb is that when making a decision about other people ask, "would I think it reasonable if this were done to me?" Another Confucian principle is "Do no harm". One should not leave the world a worse place than one found it. Improving the world a little is a bonus.

Many business ethics such as honesty, integrity, keeping one's word and ensuring the safety of employees are based on enlightened self-interest. If such ethics are followed, business and commerce prosper. Enlightened self-interest is not served by activities such as:

- giving wrong or misleading information
- refusing to honour a freely agreed contract or agreement
- giving or accepting a bribe to secure a business deal
- stealing the property of others – including intellectually property

Many commercial laws are based on the principles of enlightened-self interest and tend to punish behaviour which would disrupt orderly trading.

## Utilitarian approach and consequentialism

The utilitarian approach is probably the dominant approach towards organisational ethics today and it is used to justify many management decisions. It emphasises efficiency and effectiveness. The utilitarian approach was based on the belief that right and wrong stem from the will of God. God wills the happiness of his creatures and whatever increases the sum total of happiness is right and whatever decreases the sum of total happiness is wrong – the greatest happiness for the greatest number. This is sometimes called **hedonism** because it is concerned with maximising pleasure.

**Consequentialism** is very similar to utilitarianism. It can be summed up by the famous phrase "ends justify the means" and it does not matter who makes the decision. A major issue in consequentialism is whether ethics should be judged by *intended* consequences or the *actual* consequences. Imagine a situation where a manager attempts to hinder a competitor by putting her or him in charge of a prominent task that most people expect to end in a big failure. But, with hard work and luck the project is a conspicuous success. Was the original decision ethical or not? A consequentialist from the expected consequence school would decide that it was unethical, while a consequentialist from the actual consequence school might decide it was one of the most ethical decisions ever made. In this case, the issue might be decided by another perspective – the virtue approach.

In essence, the **virtue approach** says that the ethics of an act depends on the virtue of the manager that takes the decision, irrespective of the decision. In the unlikely event that the heavenly Mother Theresa had tried to hinder her competitor the decision would have been ethical. However, had the evil Hitler made exactly the same decision in very similar circumstances it would have been a heinous act. Lewis (1985) clearly understated the difficulties when he wrote that grappling with ethics is like trying to nail jelly to a wall.

Consequentialism is relatively modern. Its precursor, the **utilitarian approach**, is associated with the philosophers Bentham and John Stuart Mill. Bentham made a radical claim for his time. When calculating the net effects of good or bad, each person (male or female, black or white) should be counted equally. Bentham's ideas are fundamental to democracy. Majority interests are always paramount because this produces the greatest good. The majority can therefore bestow or extract whatever it wishes from a minority. Stuart Mill demurred in an aristocratic way. He introduced the notion of quality. He suggested it was better to be a Socrates dissatisfied than a fool satisfied.

Many management decisions are made in a utilitarian way. An organisation may decide to shed 10 per cent of its workforce in order to protect the jobs of the remaining 90 per cent. A government may decide to promote a vaccination programme to safeguard the health of the majority, although it might make some people ill.

## CRITICAL THINKING 19.2   *What is wrong with utilitarianism?*

Utilitarian ethics can be criticised on three grounds:

- It is usually very difficult indeed to perform an accurate cost–benefit analysis. The calculations may be too complex. The data may be unobtainable or inaccurate.
- Who may legitimately perform the calculation and what weights may they attach to the valuation of various outcomes?
- The harm to the individuals in the minority may be so great or so intense that it may be unacceptable. Utilitarianism's friend, consequentialism, implies that

ends justify the means. If 6 million people need to be exterminated in order to safeguard the health of 60 million people then, according to an extreme consequentialist, so be it – the 6 million people need to be exterminated. Some people consider such ethics as *the tyranny of the majority*.

## Deontology and rights

**Deontology** is based on the Greek word for duty, deon. Deontology is regarded as the foil to the worst excesses of consquentialism. The basic belief is that ethical choices cannot be evaluated by their consequences because there are higher values. Hence moral judgements should involve higher principles than maximising pleasure. The morality of any act is largely determined by whether it is motivated by "good will", i.e respect for a moral law. A manager whose acts to hinder a competitor happen to turn out to favour the competitor is not acting in a moral way – even though the outcome is good.

A major problem with deontology is how can the worthy higher principles (categorical imperatives) be determined? Kant believed that an act would only be moral if it would be right to apply it to everyone and that the well-being of people is a proper end in itself. Another famous principle is non-aggression where no one may threaten or commit violence – unless it is used defensively. Other major *prima facie* duties are:

- self-improvement and making ourselves better people
- helping people who have helped us (gratitude)
- keeping both explicit and implicit promises – e.g. the implicit promise to tell the truth (the right to be told the truth)
- ensure people get what they deserve and recompense someone if you have harmed them (the right to have rewards that are fair)
- help other people and avoid doing harm (the right to peacefully go about one's life)

## CRITICAL THINKING 19.3 *What is wrong with deontology?*

Deontological principles can lead to moral paradoxes. Imagine that a runaway railway carriage is hurtling down the track and will kill five people. However, it is possible to divert the carriage down a branch track where one person would be killed. It would be immoral to change the points since it would ensure that the person on the branch track is killed. Yet it would also be a moral act because it would avoid harm to five other people. Utilitarians would, in theory, have no hesitation in changing the points.

Deontology also gives no guidance over which principle should have precedence over another in the situations where they conflict. Perhaps the strongest criticism is that deontology is essentially a dressed up version of popular morality because it is impossible to prove the ultimate rightfulness of a principle.

Deontogical principles emphasise the rights of other people. The concept of human rights is a bulwark against the *tyranny of the majority*. According to Locke an individual is born with certain rights and she or he does not surrender all of these to the community. Thomas Jefferson, a major contributor to the American Declaration of Independence, listed the unalienable human rights as life, liberty and the pursuit of happiness. Since then scores of additional rights have been claimed, discovered or invented. Two important codes of human rights are the UN Declaration of Human Rights and the European Convention on Human Rights.

Much employment law is based on the concept of rights. The right of workers to have a safe working environment was recognised almost 100 years ago. Recent legislation covering rights include consultation before a major redundancy, compensation after a redundancy, belonging to trade unions and protecting workers from unfair dismissal. Equal opportunities legislation aims to protect the rights of women and minorities. More recently, the right to privacy has become an ethical issue.

---

### CRITICAL THINKING 19.4 *What is wrong with rights?*

Individuals or minorities use the idea of rights to extract benefit from others. Often the idea of rights can lead to "the tyranny of the minority" where a minority extracts unreasonable concessions on the basis of their own perceptions of their inherent dues. In fact we have no inherent rights. They are granted by those in power. Rights change when others cease to concur. In the past monarchs and their subjects believed in the Divine Right of Kings – until, that is, Parliament did not concur and beheaded one of them.

---

## Justice

Some people regard justice as a type of human right but it is often treated separately. Gilliland (1993) identified two main aspects of justice: procedural and distributive.

**Procedural justice** is the consistency with which decisions are applied. In employee selection, for example, it is unethical to treat some people in a favourable way because, say, they are relatives of senior managers. All candidates should be treated similarly and asked questions that are clearly relevant to job performance (Smither *et al.*, 1996). Procedural justice is also involved in promotion decisions, setting salary levels, disciplinary matters and granting contracts.

**Distributive justice** is the correctness of decisions in terms of a balance between what a person puts into a situation and the rewards they receive. Distributive justice involves evaluations of inputs and outputs, and these evaluations will vary from person to person.

## CRITICAL THINKING 19.5 *What is wrong with justice?*

The problem with procedural justice is that people and their situations may differ greatly. For example, one job applicant may be new to the job market and another may have worked in the very same firm for years. Should their interviews be identical? If they are, the market entrant, who is likely to be a member of a minority group, may be disadvantaged because they will be unfamiliar with technical terms used. Contrarywise, dumbing down interviews would disadvantage old hands because they may not be able to demonstrate their experience. Distributive justice is often subjective and heavily dependent upon cultural norms. What is fair in one society is unfair in another. An hourly wage of £4 is regarded as unfair exploitation in the UK in 2011 but it was a good rate of pay in the UK in 1907. Today, an hourly rate of £4 would also be regarded as very fair payment in Angola. Fairness is in the eye of the beholder. Unemployed people existing on state benefits may regard a top rate of tax at 62 per cent (50 per cent income tax plus 12 per cent NI contribution) to be fair but a city solicitor who has trained for seven years and who now works 14 hours each day on difficult, high-pressure problems may regard the same tax regime as exorbitant. A cynic might contend that fairness is whatever you can fool others into believing.

Another example illustrating the intense questions concerning fairness would be a worker who has exceeded targets every month for 10 years until the last year when he has consistently failed to achieve them – his wife was very ill. His boss is under pressure to achieve his goals by firing subordinates. What, in this case, would be the fair course of action? The outcome would depend on the tenure of the boss. If the boss has been in post 11 years and has benefited from previous high performance, the subordinate would probably keep his job. If the boss had been in post for a year it is probable that the subordinate would be fired. Is it fair that an individual's future should depend on the tenure of his or her boss?

Procedural justice and distributive justice are, in fact, highly correlated (Brockner and Wiesenfeld, 1966; Leck, Saunders and Charbonneau, 1996; Sheppard and Lerwicki, 1987).

## 19.3  Business ethics for individual managers and professional workers

### Examples of bad ethical behaviour by individuals

Bad ethical behaviour by individuals can take many forms. The three most frequent problems are bribery, conflict of interest and abuse of authority.

### *Bribery*

Bribery is unethical because it is a secret pact that is not open to examination (rights) and it undermines fair competition (enlightened self-interest). It results in excessive costs or purchase of inferior goods or services (utilitarianism). In 2010 the British government made bribery illegal and a company may be held liable for bribery committed by an employee – even if the company is unaware (OPSI, 2010). The maximum penalty is 10 years in prison. The only defence is if a company can demonstrate that it has adopted proper procedures and training. Transparency International rates countries' propensity to offer bribes. A score of 10 indicates no bribery and a score of 1 indicates ubiquitous bribery. The results for the 2008 are shown in Table 19.2.

| Country | Score | Rank | | Country | Score | Rank |
|---------|-------|------|---|---------|-------|------|
| Belgium | 8.8 | 1 | | Spain | 7.9 | 12 |
| Canada | 8.8 | 1 | | Hong Kong | 7.6 | 13 |
| Netherlands | 8.7 | 3 | | South Africa | 7.5 | 14 |
| Switzerland | 8.7 | 3 | | South Korea | 7.5 | 14 |
| Germany | 8.6 | 5 | | Taiwan | 7.5 | 14 |
| Japan | 8.6 | 5 | | Brazil | 7.4 | 17 |
| UK | 8.6 | 5 | | Italy | 7.4 | 17 |
| Australia | 8.5 | 8 | | India | 6.8 | 19 |
| France | 8.1 | 9 | | Mexico | 6.6 | 20 |
| Singapore | 8.1 | 9 | | China | 6.5 | 21 |
| USA | 8.1 | 9 | | Russia | 5.9 | 22 |

**TABLE 19.2** Prevalence of bribery in 20 countries

## CASE 19.3: *Olympic ideals, bribery and whaling*

An attempt was made to bribe certain members of the **International Olympic Committee (IOC)** to vote in favour of Salt Lake City as the venue for the Winter Olympics in 2002. In August 2004 a BBC programme, *Panorama*, set up a sting operation where its reporters posed (unethically?) as promoters and filmed a Bulgarian member of the IOC, Ivan Slavkov accepting a bribe. He was immediately suspended by the International Olympic Committee. It was suspected that more than 30 of the 124 committee members were open to bribes. Ivan Slavkov explained that he only accepted the bribe in order to uncover the identities of corrupt sports promoters. In 2010 The Sunday Times (24 October) accused senior members of FIFA of accepting bribes in order to favour certain venues for 2018 World Cup.

Recently six countries with seats on the International Whaling Commission were accused of selling their votes to permit whaling in response to bribes emanating from the government of Japan (Sunday Times, 13 June 2010).

Bribery is most rampant in construction and public works, arms and defence, and in the oil and gas industries. In many situations bribery is unclear. Part of the problem is the difficulty of distinguishing bribery from a legitimate business fee. It often masquerades as "a success fee", "an introduction fee", "an arrangement fee" or, even, "a gift".

---

### CASE 19.4: *A silly duchess solicits a bribe*

Prince Andrew, Duke of York, was not lucky in matrimony and divorced his wife Sarah Ferguson, known as "Fergie". Her divorce settlement and her entrepreneurial efforts at writing children's books and endorsing slimming products did not sustain the lifestyle she wished. The Queen refused to bail her out. So, Fergie tried a little bribery. For half a million pounds she offered to introduce a businessman to her ex-husband, who was, at that time, heading British trade missions. He was totally unaware of his ex-wife's exploits. His ex-wife was unaware that the businessman was a reporter from the *News of the World* newspaper who was recording the transaction and his deceit was likely to increase his career and the circulation of his employer's newspaper.

---

A gift may place the recipient in a situation where they feel an obligation. For example, a medical practitioner who accepts free flights and accommodation for a conference at an exotic location from a pharmaceutical company may, at a subconscious level, be more likely to prescribe one of that company's medicines.

Bribery has a cultural aspect. In some cultures giving gifts is a routine activity denoting respect. Under these circumstances refusal to accept a gift causes offence. In other cultures a small bribe to a lowly paid government employee is an accepted method of "expediting" the progress of a form. Pressure from developed countries to abandon these practices is often viewed as **ethical imperialism**. Companies from countries where giving bribes is illegal complain that their commercial activities, and hence jobs at home, are handicapped because they are not competing on a "level playing field".

Despite protestations, gifts and bribes should not be sought or accepted. They damage free competition and trade. Consumers do not get the best goods or services at the best price (utilitarianism). Where exchange of gifts is necessary in order to maintain friendly relationships, gifts should be open and their value should be proportionate. Usually a gift which costs more than a good lunch should be declared in an appropriate register. It may also be prudent to donate such gifts to others.

### Conflict of interest

People should have only one paymaster because this makes their duty clear. In practice, however, the situation is not straightforward and people sometimes find themselves in situations where they have two or more sets of obligations. They therefore need to resolve a conflict of interest (rights and justice). Examples of conflicts of interest are given in Case 19.5.

Transactions involving land or property are particularly prone to conflicts of interest. For example, a member of Manhattan City Housing Authority was fined $2250 after admitting that he had used his office to help his daughter get a job. Estate agents (realtors) attract many complaints. For example, some estate agents have been known to refuse to communicate offers made by purchasers who will not also take out commission-earning services such as insurance.

---

### CASE 19.5: *Conflicts of interest – Merrill Lynched?*

Analysts belonging to the merchant bank **Merrill Lynch** wrote reports recommending investors to *buy* or sell shares. They also had an investment banking division which, for a fee, helped companies *sell* stocks. The huge salaries of their analysts depended upon the fees earned by the investment division. In 2003 the Securities and Exchange Commission complained that the analysts' reports were not independent and that the analysts had allowed their banking colleagues to influence advice to clients. New York State Attorney Eliot Spitzer said that the investment advice was biased and distorted in order to secure and maintain lucrative banking contracts. Emails emerged which indicated that the analysts "said" one thing in public and another thing in private. These comments were angrily rebutted by Merrill Lynch, which was outraged that emails were taken out of context. Without admitting wrongdoing, it later paid $100 million, agreed to apologise and severed all links between analysts' pay and investment banking activities.

---

The best defence against conflicts of interest is **avoidance**. For example, many law firms will not accept instructions if they already have any legal dealings with people already in a legal dispute with the prospective client. Another mechanism, often used by politicians and public officials, is to place assets in a "**blind trust**". For example, it is quite permissible for the Prime Minister to hold shares – even though the decisions he or she makes can directly affect their value. Trustees of a blind trust act without any communication or information from the Prime Minister. Since he or she will not know the composition of his or her portfolio the Prime Minister can make decisions without any conflict of interest.

Some companies avoid conflicts of interest by constructing **Chinese walls** and **cones of silence**. After the Merrill Lynch affair, many financial institutions separated their research analysts from their investment bankers and do not allow information to pass between them – as though the Great Wall of China has been extended through their organisation. A "cone of silence" exists when contractors or their lobbyists are forbidden to contact officials (whether they are a few important people at the top of the cone or many people lower down). Often, a cone of silence is imposed once a shortlist of contractors has been drawn up. A cone of silence may be enforced by fining organisations or dismissing their bid if they attempt to break through the cone.

Conflicts of interest in public life can be mitigated, but not avoided, by **recusal** – abstaining from voting on any issue where one has a conflict of interest. In some circumstances a stronger form of recusal, **physical absence**, is needed. For example, in university examination boards, if a candidate is a relative, friend or business associate of an examiner, that examiner is required to leave the room. If all else fails, conflicts of interest can be mitigated by a **declaration of an interest**.

## CASE 19.6:  *Abuse of power – the Challenger space shuttle disaster*

The US government inaugurated the Space Shuttle Programme in order to beat the Russians in space. The contract to build the booster rockets was given to a company called Morton-Thiokol. Between 1980 and 1984, 45 launches were planned – but there were only 17. Moreover, NASA was facing unforeseen commercial competition from the European Space Agency. In November 1981 potential weaknesses were found in seals that contained the gases of the booster rockets. A launch in 1985 provided actual evidence that the vital seals, the "O rings", could actually fail – especially when the temperature was low. NASA management was told about the problem.

In January 1986 a launch was delayed three times due to bad weather – delaying the programme further. Another launch was scheduled but the weather forecast was again bad: an outside temperature in the region of –1°C was predicted. Thiokol management asked engineers for advice and a three-way telephone conference was held between Thiokol in Utah, Cape Canaveral in Florida and the Space Flight Control in Alabama. The presentation by Thiokol engineers lasted over an hour and ended with the recommendation that the launch be delayed. The project manager at the flight control centre said that the evidence was inconclusive. He bypassed the actual engineers and referred the matter to the most senior manager at Thiokol. He supported his engineers and did not recommend a launch. In a heated discussion NASA staff said they were appalled by the recommendation not to launch. The conference was interrupted for five minutes while the evidence was reviewed by Thiokol personnel. Despite continued opposition by the engineers, the managers (the engineers were excluded from the vote) decided that the launch should go ahead. NASA accepted the new decision.

Fifty-nine seconds after the launch the seals failed. The rocket exploded. Seven crew members died.

### Improper use of authority and power

Managers and people in professional positions have considerable authority and power which can be abused in many ways. A classic example of misuse is given by the Challenger episode (Case 19.6). Was NASA justified in insisting on a launch decision? Were the four members of Thiokol management justified in reversing their initial decision and excluding the engineers from the crucial vote? Did the engineers fail to use their authority by allowing themselves to be overruled by management?

Consequences of improper use of authority are rarely as dramatic or as well documented as the Challenger case. However, unethical use of authority arises quite frequently. A common abuse is to deny subordinate staff proper recognition for their work and claim their staff's achievement's for themselves. This occurs in academic life where members of staff publish students work without giving appropriate credit.

## Ethics and social responsibility for managers and professional workers

Many professional bodies have developed their own ethical codes. Managers should be familiar with the relevant ethical codes of their vocation and country. Most ethical codes cover nine main areas:

1 fair advertising
2 competence
3 self-regard
4 informed consent
5 freedom to withdraw
6 confidentiality
7 respect for social codes and multicultural sensitivities
8 professional relationships between colleagues
9 principles of fees and financial arrangements

### Fair advertising

There is nothing wrong with promoting goods and services. Indeed advertising increases market size leading to economies of scale and less expensive products. However, advertising needs to be socially responsible. In general:

- Qualifications, training and affiliations should be represented accurately.
- Information should not be withheld in order to promote misunderstandings.
- Employees of the press, radio television or other media should not be paid in return for publicity. Paid advertisments should be clearly identified as such.

The principle of fair advertising extends to the statements of others – especially those who are paid to promote the service or product. If they make a deceptive or false statement on behalf of an organisation it must issue corrections.

### Competence

The principle of competence means that managers should operate to high technical and professional standards. Difficult decisions are often necessary and cannot be shirked. The managers who make them should be competent and qualified. They should not get involved in situations where they could not cope should things go wrong. This means being able to cope with the worst case. Nevertheless there is also a need to extend competence but it should be gained in a way that does not harm others.

### Self-regard and welfare

Human dignity should be upheld. People should not be harmed except in very exceptional circumstances. This includes psychological harm. Actions involving *humiliation* should be avoided. If such tactics seem *absolutely* necessary a *second opinion should be obtained*. This may be provided by an impartial senior colleague or by an "ethics committee". In this context, humiliation or embarrassment must be seen through the eyes of laypeople, not through the eyes of managers or professionals who may have become blasé or burnt out after years of work in the field.

### Informed consent

People have the right to know what they are letting themselves in for before they commit themselves. They should have reasonable information on: the identity the people and organisations; the processes; the "ownership" of information and the uses to which the information will be put.

### Freedom to withdraw

People are expected to keep agreements that have been willingly agreed. However, there may be a problem over the definition of the term "willing". For example, is a parent taking out a second mortgage in order to buy medical treatment for their child a willing vendor? However, rather different rules apply to professional services and participation in experiments. People are free to withdraw from professional relationships after giving due notice and paying appropriate fees. People are free to withdraw at will from experiments.

### Confidentiality

In most circumstances, information obtained on a confidential basis should not be divulged to others without explicit, preferably written, consent.

There are, however, some situations where the principle of confidentiality should be breached. They include situations where people are likely to be a danger to themselves or others. They also arise when people are involved in illegal activities. Even in these cases a second impartial opinion should be sought. Information should only be disclosed to authorities when there is clear legal authorisation. In almost all circumstances the law must be obeyed – even if you have formed your subjective opinion that the law of the land is silly!

### Respect for social codes

People should show sensible regard to the *social codes* and *moral expectations* of the community in which they work. For example, a manager acting as a consultant in a monastery should not engage in blasphemous behaviour that causes gratuitous offence. If one cannot be tolerant and courteous to the people in an organisation it is better not to accept work in that organisation in the first place.

### Relationships with others

Many aspects of relationships with others are covered elsewhere. However, it is worth pointing out that managers should avoid body contact with employees or clients other than customary greetings such as shaking hands or giving "a pat on the back". Any form of activity with clients which could be construed as sexual or likely to reduce objectivity must be avoided.

Ethics relating to professional colleagues usually concern boundaries and roles. A general principle is to make, in advance, an explicit arrangement concerning roles, rights and obligations. Harassment of other people, especially junior colleagues, should be avoided. A professional worker should avoid interfering with the work of another professional. While the ideas, theories and data of another person can, and should be, scrutinised, personal *ad hominem* attacks should be avoided.

### Fees and financial arrangements

There is a cardinal ethical principle concerning fees: *fee structure and terms of payment should be made clear during, or immediately after, an initial meeting or consultation* (Francis, 1999). Sometimes broaching the matter of fees can be "delicate" and it is often appropriate to send a short letter confirming acceptance of an assignment together with a sheet setting out the fee rate, the estimated length of the assignment and the terms of the payment. A client should be notified immediately if it seems that costs are likely to exceed the initial estimate. Fees for missed appointments and cancelled meetings often need clarification. As a general rule, some level of fee is appropriate for second and subsequent cancellations. Invoices should be paid promptly.

## Ethical dilemmas

Many, possibly the majority, of ethical problems are not simple question of right and wrong but are a dilemma between two sets of ethical rights. Dilemmas can often be resolved by placing ethical obligations in order of precedence.

The rights of a *client* (i.e. the person across the desk) have the highest priority. In this context the client may not be the person who commissions the work or pays the bill. For example, an HR director of an organisation may commission an outplacement organisation to offer careers guidance to managers whose job is redundant. The outplacement organisation may employ a consultant psychologist to administer and interpret tests. In this case, the outplaced manager is the psychologist's client, not the outplacement organisation or the previous employer.

The interests of *the profession* are generally placed in second position (see Francis, 1999). This may give rise to acute problems in organisations such as the army where a person might be ordered by a senior officer to divulge information. Such dilemmas can be resolved by creating a specific corps of, say, doctors. A senior officer within the specialist corps may, for example, demand information whereas a senior officer outside the specialist corps may not.

There is much less agreement on the precedence of other rights. Much depends on the precise circumstances. Perhaps the rights of the person commissioning the work and paying the fee should generally rank third and the rights of the manager or professional should rank fourth.

## Upholding ethical principles

The most obvious way of upholding ethical principles is to avoid violating them oneself. You should also set an example to junior colleagues and members of the public by being seen to be ethical – *without* behaving like a sanctimonious prig! Difficult situations can arise when unethical behaviour is witnessed. Much depends upon the severity of the breach. The main objective must be to ensure that the unethical behaviour is discontinued.

With *minor and occasional ethical breaches* it is best to take low-level, informal action. Many, probably most, minor unethical acts arise from enthusiasm or ignorance. Here a light-hearted and informal comment will often be a sufficient remedy. In *more serious cases* the appropriate action is a substantive conversation. The dangers of the unethical act can be explained in a helpful way. It is often easiest to emphasise the dangers to the perpetrator (the victim might complain to professional body – certification might be withdrawn – the organisation will suffer from bad publicity, etc.). The intervention will be more effective if positive hints about how the ethical principles *can* be maintained are given. It is also possible offer a copy of the appropriate code of ethical conduct. With *very serious unethical behaviour* (i.e. premeditated, mendacious, frequent or serious), stronger action must be taken. The perpetrator should be told, point blank, preferably in writing, to desist forthwith. For example, one personnel manager in an organisation where interviewers had received equal opportunities training would bluntly tell erring interviewers, in front of colleagues and interviewees that "You know you cannot ask that or similar questions – stop now". A violent reaction must be expected. The unethical person is likely to make accusations of unreasonableness, nosiness, bossiness and attempting to put them down! Nevertheless it may be appropriate to "blow the whistle".

## CRITICAL THINKING 19.6 *"Blowing the whistle"*

Revealing one's employer's unethical or illegal behaviour is called "whistle-blowing" (Miceli and Near, 1994). It raises big issues because the whistle-blower, acting in the interests of the wider community, can bring serious sanctions upon themselves. Whistle-blowers may be fired or their promotion prospects blocked. In some countries there are laws protecting people against such retaliation but they are hard to enforce and financial awards by the courts are usually small. Some organisations view whistle-blowers as assets (Near, 1989) who help identify problems at an early stage. The problems can then be rectified before becoming a major issue that could threaten the organisation's future.

If an organisation does not have "whistle-blowing" procedures, it is probably wise to confide in a third person who can take the matter further. If the unethical behaviour has caused, or is likely to cause, serious damage, it should be reported to the appropriate professional organisation or victims. Except in emergency situations, whistle-blowers should make absolutely sure that they understand the situation correctly. In most situations it is preferable to wait two days between observing an unethical act and reporting it to others; the delay will help to put the facts into perspective. Whistle-blowers should stick to specific observations that they can prove. They should beware of hearsay evidence and should ensure the complaint is neither libellous nor slanderous. Whistle-blowers should not assume that the law will protect them. It may be advisable to take legal advice before reporting major ethical breaches. It is important to make accurate notes and gather documentary evidence which are stored outside the organisation's premises. Although it may be very tempting, it is usually a mistake to involve the media as a first step.

## 19.4  Ethics and social responsibility for organisations

Ethics is not just a matter for individuals. Organisations sometimes behave unethically by giving misleading information, exploiting less-developed countries and exploiting emotions:

- Giving *misleading or untrue information* to shareholders, clients and employees is a serious breach of ethics. Issuing misleading financial information by concealing debt from the balance sheet is particularly heinous. It has caused spectacular problems for organisations such as Enron and Madoff Investment Securities (Case 19.7).

- *Unethical exploitation in under-developed countries* is quite common. Nike, for example, has been accused of employing children in Pakistan at a very low wage to stitch footballs. Nike is not alone. GAP has been accused of employing child labour in Cambodia, and Benetton has been accused of paying low wages to children employed in Turkey. Unethical and socially irresponsible activities in underdeveloped countries are not restricted to the use of child labour – as Case 19.8 shows. The issues involved in these cases are complex. In many countries child labour is traditional and is an essential contribution to family budgets. Sometimes the children provide fake evidence of their age so that they can work in a factory. A wage of 50 pence per hour may not buy many luxuries in a country where the average wage is £30 000 but it buys a lot of essentials in a country where the average annual wage is £250! Further, unethical activity is often conducted by indigenous subcontractors and is discontinued when drawn to the attention of the multinational company. Nike, for example, withdrew contracts from their Cambodian subcontractor. It stipulated that other contractors must check birth certificates more carefully and enforce a minimum age of 18.

---

### CASE 19.7: *Mercenary Madoff*

Bernie Madoff was a pillar of the New York financial establishment. He was chairman of the second largest stock exchange (NASDAQ) in the USA and he handled many of the investments of stars such as Kevin Bacon and film-maker Steven Speilberg. He had earned a reputation as a trusted money manager whose funds made profits year in year out. But it was all a sham that was made possible by manipulating and inventing financial information. In fact, Madoff, had hardly dealt in shares at all. He merely used the capital of new investors to pay generous dividends to existing investors. This is called a **Ponzi scheme**. It works beautifully *provided* it is kept secret and there are lots of new investors to pay the old ones. Boston accountant, Harry Marcopolos, blew the whistle to the Securities and Exchange Commission as early as 1999. His repeated claims were ignored for many years. In 2008 Madoff confessed to a senior employee. Prosecutors estimated that he had swindled people out of $68.4 billion – the greatest fraud in history. He was sentenced to 150 years in prison. The celebrities who had invested in this fund lost money but survived. Others had few alternative investments to fall back on. French financier, Rene-Thierry Magon, lost more than $1 billion of his investors' money and committed suicide.

## Emotional exploitation

Emotional exploitation and shock tactics may be used by organisations to pursue their goals. "Shock and awe" advertising is used by some charities who are passionately convinced of their cause. The logic is easy to understand. For example, so many people die of lung cancer it may be justified to use graphic television adverts portraying diseased lungs or putrid blood vessels. Nonetheless, a larger number of innocent non-smokers may feel bad when they are bombarded by these images. The charity values their feelings as zero. Further, the majority of cigarette smokers do not die of lung cancer and the shock campaigns may have caused them unnecessary anxiety. Children and other relatives of occasional smokers may become unnecessarily unhappy. The charity, for laudable reasons, believes it is justified. Details of another example of shock and awe advertising, by Benetton, is given in the website that accompanies this book.

The cynical use of shock tactics by celebrities and the media is less ethical. They may use the plight of others to increase their own reputations by providing publicity for the cause. But, the publicity may have made the plight worse – leaving a divided community with a poorer image. A similar situation sometimes occurs with emergency aid. The aid may make local farms or businesses uncompetitive and they may cease to exist. When the aid stops, the community may not be able to support itself. Sometimes organisations are accused of exploiting ethical issues for commercial gain. Case 19.8 identifies some of the problems encountered by Apple.

---

### CASE 19.8:  *A gadget to die for*

In spring 2010, Apple launched its much acclaimed iPad, with a touch screen and amazing apps – a gadget to die for! The launch was tarnished when the *Independent* newspaper (27, 28 and 29 May 2010) revealed that working conditions in its assembly plants in China were causing some employees to commit suicide. The owners of the factory, Foxconn, were not impervious. They immediately ordered the construction of nets around its dormitories that would "catch" attempted suicides. Foxconn also assembles electronic products for Dell, Hewlett Packard and Acer. Almost all companies supplied by Foxconn have ethical codes to avert the exploitation of workers in developing countries. Almost all of us who purchase the products are delighted that we can buy such wonderful products so cheaply.

---

## Ethics for organisations

About 90 per cent of organisations with over 500 employees have a formal code of supplier conduct. However, organisations are diverse. It is difficult to provide an authoritative list of ethics and social responsibilities that apply to, say, a financial services company in London, a health-care organisation in Sydney or a computer manufacturer in Shenzhen, China. The following list gives eight ethical principles that apply to most organisations.

1 **Adding value**: organisations exist to add value. If they destroy value, by making unwise acquisitions or wasting, they should close or be transferred to another organisation that is able to add value. Organisations that destroy value often exist on subsidies from government or other units in the organisation. However, drastic retrenchment must not be applied too quickly. It is normal for a healthy organisation to encounter a "bad patch" that will justify, say, three years of support while it reorganises. Further, the social contribution an organisation makes must be taken into account. For example, it might be proper to provide a long-term subsidy for activities such as health or education. But, such exemptions should not be used too widely – otherwise the community will be handicapped by inefficient public services.

2 **Transparent governance**: an organisation's governance should be clear. At the very least people should know the identity of its owners, senior managers, its location and the nature of its business. Transparency in public companies needs to be higher. People should know the position of its finances, its assets, income, debts, prospects and the remuneration of senior officials. One of the issues in the Enron debacle was secret payments to top employees to prevent them from leaving the company and drawing attention to dire financial secrets.

3 **Accurate information**: an organisation must give accurate information. Its annual reports must be accurate. Public statements should contain the truth, the whole truth and nothing but the truth. The information provided about products must be realistic. Further, communications with the community, suppliers, employees and their representatives must be sincere.

4 **Contribution to the community**: at the very least, organisations must obey international agreements, the national laws and any local regulations, and pay their taxes. Many organisations choose to do more by supporting cultural activities such as theatres, operas, orchestras and sporting events. At a more mundane level other organisations support community projects and local charities.

5 **Environmental sustainability**: may be defined as "development that meets the needs of present generations without compromising the ability of future generations to meet their own needs" (Brundtland, 1987). The classic example involves ocean fishing. It may suit today's fishing fleets to catch as many fish as the market will buy, but this would mean that too few fish are left to breed. Other examples of sustainability involve forestry, the extraction of minerals and the emission of gasses. Fortunately, there are many instances where technology and control systems mean that organisations are making fewer demands upon the environment. For example, thanks to technological advances, today it takes less water and electricity to make a car than it did five years ago.

6 **Fair trade** has two main aspects. Trade with *customers* and trade with *suppliers*. Bribery, cronyism and other unfair processes should be avoided. Customers should be given accurate, not exaggerated, information. The product or service should be fit for the purpose intended. Agreements must be honoured in full. Organisations with a powerful market position should avoid "bullying" smaller suppliers. Invoices from suppliers should be paid promptly – normally within 30 days. Finally, organisations should not thwart open competition by participating in price rigging or a cartel.

7 **Fair employment**: an organisation should seek to create jobs which have reasonable security and which enhance the quality of employees' lives. The health and safety of employees is paramount. Employees should be treated with respect irrespective of their ethnic background, gender, age or religion. Employees should be consulted, or at the very least informed, of any major changes affecting their **work–life balance**.

8 **Whistle-blowing** (informing appropriate authorities when unethical or socially irresponsible actions are observed) should be encouraged. It is one means by which an organisation can become more ethical. Whistle-blowers should be protected from retaliation.

## Managing organisational ethics

### Detecting ethical problems

Probably the most difficult step in dealing with ethical problems is to recognise they exist. Unethical practices evolve slowly and become an accepted way. One way to identify unethical problems is to ask:

- Would I wish this to be done to me or my family?
- Would I be ashamed if my family or friends knew of this?
- Is this against my long-term self-interest?
- Will an individual or group of people be harmed rather than helped?
- Will the rights of any person or group be diminished?
- Will the majority of people regard the act as unjust or unfair?

If the answer to any of these questions is "yes", then an ethical problem probably exists. Once an ethical problem has been recognised, the next stage is to collect facts that can form the basis of generating corrective actions that can discussed and checked with senior colleagues, an ethics officer or an ethics committee.

### Creating an ethical organisation

Probably the most vital stage in creating an ethical organisation is to ensure top management understands the importance of social responsibility. Top management can be role models for other employees. A section on ethical values can be included in a vision statement. Finally, managers can establish systems that reward ethical behaviour. With top management support, an organisation can employ some of the following methods.

### Code of organisational ethics

Major organisations often develop a formal code of ethics which often *start* with a statement of general ethical principles, sometimes called **organisational "credos"**.

The *second* section of ethical codes often focuses upon specific situations and gives specific ways of dealing with activities such as bribes, kickbacks, political contributions, hiring employees or harassment. Unfortunately, an organisational code is no guarantee of socially responsible behaviour. Enron had an excellent code of ethics – but the board of directors decided to suspend it when it became inconvenient!

### Ethical structures

Some organisations create structures to manage ethical issues. The three most common structures are: ethics committees, ethics officers and whistle-blower protection schemes.

**Ethics committee** and **ethics ombudsmen** are responsible for taking proactive steps and drawing up an ethics strategy. They may also arrange **ethics training** or organise an **ethics audit**. Finally, the ethics committee or ethics ombudsman will devise ways to *detect violations* of the code and impose *penalties* on their perpetrators.

## 19.5 Business ethics for citizens and consumers

Managers are citizens and consumers who deal with other organisations in their private lives. Private commercial transactions should also be ethical. However, this aspect of ethics and social responsibility is barely recognised by academics and writers – individual consumers rarely offer lucrative consultancies or research grants! The information that does exist is less than reassuring. It might be that, to make the world more ethical we should start closer to home and consider unethical and socially irresponsible behaviour ourselves as consumers.

Vitell and Muncy (1992) developed a scale to measure people's tolerance of unethical behaviour. They found that in the USA rich, young and well-educated people tend to have the lowest standards of consumer ethics. Babakus *et al.* (2004) modified Muncy and Vitell's scale to make it internationally appropriate and collected data in six countries. Their scale included situations such as "drinking a can of soda in a supermarket without buying it", "not saying anything when a waitress (*sic*) miscalculates a bill in your favour" and "jumping a queue". On a scale where 0 per cent represents no tolerance and where 100 per cent total tolerance, the average score was 36 per cent. The results, from lowest to highest tolerance to unethical consumer behaviour were: USA (26 per cent), Brunei (28 per cent), Hong Kong (36 per cent), France (37 per cent), Austria (37 per cent) and UK (49 per cent). Older people were more principled than younger people and people with religious affiliation, especially Muslims, had higher standards than those without religious affiliation. Some of the most frequent ethical abuses by citizens involve CVs, insurance claims, benefit fraud and abuse of free services and plagiarism.

### CVs and application forms

Curricula vitae (CVs) and application forms are almost always the first sieve in the process of getting a job (Smith and Abrahamsen, 1992) and they frequently contain lies. It has been said that there are "lies, damn lies and CVs" (Walley and Smith, 1998). Typical inaccuracies involve the manipulation of dates of employment, exaggeration of work experience, false qualifications or hiding a criminal record.

### Unethical insurance claims

Insurance fraud seems to be an international occupation. Possibly the biggest insurance scam of all time was attempted by 12 Russian businessmen – mainly accountants and solicitors in New York. They helped stage car accidents in order to make claims on medical insurance policies. It is estimated that their activities cost US insurance companies up to $500 million. Insurance frauds are often justified on the grounds that they do no harm. In fact the cost is borne by other policy-holders. It increases the cost of insurance so that it is beyond the reach of the poorest and most needy members of society.

### Benefit fraud

Benefit fraud often attracts the attention of the media, and cases receive widespread coverage. People making fraudulent claims always have a rationale such as: "everybody does it", "I am entitled to it but the rules are stupid" or "it is only government money". Nevertheless, benefit fraud is unethical. It increases taxes (which damages the economy) or it means that people in genuine need receive less help. **Cuckoo working** bears some resemblance to benefit fraud but the victims are employers rather than taxpayers. In cuckoo working, someone does another job, often a freelance sideline, while they are paid by an employer.

### Abuse of free offers

Commercial organisations often make free offers to give a risk-free opportunity to evaluate whether their products are suitable. Consumers often exploit these offers. A clear example of this abuse is where a company's representatives sell the free offers rather than giving them away. Similarly, it is unethical to ask consultants to prepare proposals and then use the ideas in their brief to perform the work oneself. Harris (2010) found widespread and recidivist abuse of customer returns policy – the cost of which is paid for by genuine customers.

### Plagiarism

Plagiarism is unethical. It involves copying other people's work and pretending that it is one's own. Students must not do this. Anything copied from books, the Internet or other sources must be acknowledged and referenced. Many universities and colleges have sophisticated methods and software to detect plagiarism. Students caught plagiarising the work of others often forfeit their qualifications.

## Ethical principles for citizens and consumers

Ethics and social responsibility for citizens and consumers is not well developed but at least three principles are involved:

1 **Fair trade** with organisations that provide goods and services. This means:
  - Appointments should be kept.
  - Questions should receive frank and honest answers – even if the answer is "I am sorry I cannot reveal that to you".
  - Payments should be made promptly and at the agreed rates.
  - Trivial, facetious or mendacious complaints should be avoided.

Fair trade also involves ensuring that custom is only given to ethical organisation. Questions they should ask include:

■ Where are the goods made and how do you check the welfare in factories?

■ What do they do when they find underage workers – fire them or pay for schooling until they reach working age?

2 The need to **respect property** is obvious and stems from the utilitarian view of ethics. If property were stolen on a widespread basis, no one would have the incentive to work, build new facilities or invent new processes. Everyone would suffer. Respect for property is especially relevant with intellectual property. It is wrong to steal other people's ideas, writing or creations. It is unethical to make "pirate copies" of computer programs, video games and music tracks.

3 **Respect for others**: consumer transactions frequently involve frustration where you cannot get the deal, product or service to which you feel entitled. It is a well-known psychological fact that frustration often boils over into some form of aggression towards the nearest target – usually a representative of the organisation with which one is dealing. However, it is both unethical and often counterproductive to use physical or verbal aggression. While it is permissible to state a case forcefully and eloquently, physical and verbal abuse must be avoided. Even in the fraught situation of a hospital Accident and Emergency Department it is irresponsible to abuse staff. Similarly, it is unethical to abuse check-in staff if a flight is cancelled. This does not mean that redress for an error should not be sought. What it does mean is that any redress should be sought from the organisation responsible. The same holds true for "political" protests such as animal rights. Everyone has a right, within the law, to express their views and bring pressure to bear. However, it is totally unethical to subject employees of the organisation – or, worse, their families – to abuse. It is also wrong to intimidate employees of suppliers or customers.

## 19.6 Rights of managers and professional workers

Managers have a right to expect colleagues, employees and members of the public to:

■ Make and keep appointments.

■ Behave with courtesy and dignity.

■ Give frank and honest replies to questions.

■ Avoid making trivial, facetious and mendacious complaints.

■ Avoid commissioning two managers or professionals for the same assignment. If this is absolutely necessary both parties should be informed.

■ Avoid altering specifications of work without renegotiating fees.

■ Pay promptly and at agreed rates for products and services received.

## CASE 19.9:  *Heinous Enron*

Enron was an energy company based in Houston, Texas. In 1985 it had assets of about $12 billion – not enough to be included in the top 500 US companies – a significant but not outstanding organisation. Under aggressive new management that emphasised results and which used sophisticated financial structures it experienced phenomenal growth. By 2001 it was the seventh largest US company with assets of $33 billion and a share price of $90. It employed over 22 000 people and for six years the prestigious magazine *Fortune* nominated Enron as the USA's most innovative company. Academics flocked to Enron to write case studies.

It was an illusion. Enron was a hotbed of unethical practices. For example in 2001 it surreptitiously caused 38 "rolling blackouts" in California in order to bargain higher prices for the electricity (listen to http://www.youtube.com/watch?v=_dm61gVae-I). Its organisational culture encouraged staff to be cut-throat. One employee explained "If on my way to my boss' office to talk about compensation and stepping on someone's throat doubled my pay – well I would stomp on the guy's throat" (watch http://www.youtube.com/watch?v=E3dullclhoE).

Financial fraud and misrepresentation was also rife. Enron's founder (Kenneth Lay), its CEO (Jeffrey Skilling) the CFO (Andrew Fastow) constructed sophisticated financial structures and special arrangements which kept losses out of Enron's main accounts. Financial statements left a lot to be desired and analysts started to ask questions. In April 2001 Skilling verbally abused a New York analyst, Richard Grubman when he asked why Enron did

Financial statements
p 420

not publish a balance sheet as well as an earnings statement. In August an analyst for a French Bank (BNP-Paribas), Daniel Scotto, downgraded Enron's stock as "all stressed up and nowhere to go". The share price fell (partly because Skilling had been privately selling many of his own shares). Eventually Enron's concealed losses became common knowledge and its stock was downgraded by rating agencies in October. Bankruptcy proceedings started a few weeks later. The share price plummeted to zero.

Two employees were initially lauded as whistle-blowers but, in true Enron style, even the whistle-blowers were not quite what they seemed. Sherron Watkins was a Vice President and wrote an email to Lay warning him of potential irregulaties and advised him how they could be managed. Her whistle-blowing email only became public five months later and helped Lay's legal defence. Lynn Brewer was another celebrated Enron whistle-blower who has written books, given speeches and founded the Integrity Institute. She claims that in her executive role as head of risk management inside the legal department she wrote protesting emails to her bosses. However, an investigation by *USA Today* (14 November 2007) alleges that she was never an Enron *executive* and her boss says that she never saw Brewer's alleged report and never discussed it with her – especially since banking matters were outside their department's remit.

Kenneth Lay died of a heart attack. Skilling and Fastow were eventually given sentences of 24 and 10 years respectively. About 400 000 people lost their jobs – 150 000 of these employees had invested the majority of their savings in, now worthless, Enron shares. The grief caused by Enron did not stop there. Its auditors, Arthur Andersen, probably the most prestigious auditors in the world, were deemed negligent. They were caught shredding evidence and have since gone out of business. Perhaps the people who suffered most were private shareholders – including Enron employees who had loyally invested their retirement savings in the company.

*Toolkit*

## 19.7  Ethics toolkit

Ethical problems are usually complex, and this chapter does not cover all complexities. Proposed actions to deal with ethical problems can be evaluated against the following questions:

- In the long term, is this action against my own interest (enlightened self-interest)?
- Would this action add to or subtract from the well-being of human beings or other living things (utilitarianism)?
- Would this action infringe the accepted rights of any individual or group (rights)?
- Would this action involve unjust methods (procedural justice)?
- Would this action involve an unjust outcome (distributive justice)?

It is fervently hoped that everything in this book satisfies these standards.

# Activities and further study

## Essay plans

Write essay plans for the following topics:

1 To what extent does the study of the philosophical roots help our understanding of social responsibility and ethics?

2 What are the ways in which both profit and not-for-profit organisations behave unethically?

3 What are the ways in which individuals, both as employees and private consumers, behave unethically?

4 What measures can senior managers take to ensure that their organisations are ethical and socially responsible?

5 How should individual employees react when they encounter a breach of ethics by other people at work?

## Web activities

1 Surf the Web to locate the ethical code of the professional body for a management function that interests you. Compare this with the equivalent ethical code for a similar professional body in another country.

2 Use your search engine to locate the annual reports of four organisations. Find out how they report their commitment to ethics and social responsibility. At least one of these organisations should be renowned for its ethical approach (e.g. the Co-op). Another of the organisations should be not-for-profit (e.g. your local authority).

3 Use the Web to locate as much information as you can about ethical controversies involving one of the following organisations:

- Benetton
- Haliburton
- Nestlé
- sporting events (e.g. the Olympics, World Cup)

## Experiential activities

1 Write out a code of your own personal ethics.

2 Locate an ethics statement for your place of work or study. In addition identify the ethical structures that exist in your place of work or study.

3 Think of a socially irresponsible or unethical act that you have witnessed in the past and ask yourself the following questions:

   ■ What was it that made the act socially irresponsible or unethical?

   ■ Which philosophical principle of ethics was involved?

   ■ Who was involved?

   ■ What were the results?

4 Imagine that there was a major ethical breach by a senior person at your work or place of study and that you were the only witness. Work out ways that you would handle the situation.

## Recommended reading

1 Skapinker, M. (2010) "Should MBA students do the perp walk?", *Financial Times*, 20 September, and Sridhar, A. (2010) "The troubling aspects of an oath for business" *Financial Times*, 15 February. News on the ethics oath proposed by Harvard MBA students. The oath can be accessed at: http://mbaoath.org/about/the-mba-oath/

2 Reich, R.B. (2008) *The Case against Corporate Social Responsibility*, Goldman School Working Paper Series, Berkeley, CA: University of California. A freely downdoadable version (http://ssm.com/abstract=1213129) of Reich's iconoclastic battle against what he sees as the humbug of CSR. Easy to read but very long; worth a quick read to extract the main arguments and some examples. More detailed study is essential for assignments and preparation for tutorials.

3 Pava, M. (2008) "Why corporations should not abandon social responsibility", *Journal of Business Ethics*, **83**(4), 805–813. A riposte to many of Reich's criticisms.

## Chapter contents

## ❖ LEARNING OBJECTIVES

After reading this chapter you should have improved your ability to criticise and evaluate the merits of different claims by researchers and experts. You should have a framework for analysing evidence and you should be more resistant to the passing fads and confidence tricks in management. These skills will enable you to participate in seminars or write essays and examination answers that have more insight and earn higher marks. In particular you should be able to:

❖ **define** fads and give examples of an classic historic fad

❖ **decide** whether business process re-engineering is a recent management fad

❖ **define** what is meant by a management guru and **list** the three main types

❖ **critically evaluate** the work of Peter Drucker, Tom Peters and Michael Porter

❖ **briefly describe** five techniques used to support false claims for management techniques

❖ **compare and contrast** three main approaches in management research

❖ **describe** two main measurement problems in management research

❖ **list** three main characteristics of good management research

❖ **compare and contrast** a research study in management with a research study in medicine, chemistry, physics, psychology or engineering

Management is complex, open-ended, ill-defined and open to many interpretations. It is a role that is likely to cause anxiety (see Huczynski, 1993). Managers can never be sure that they are discharging their duties adequately. They are always faced with the possibility that they have ignored some new idea that would improve their organisation's competitiveness. At a more personal level, ambitious managers will want to show that they are more worthy of promotion than their colleagues by being more up to date. Managers also tend to be moderate extroverts – easily bored and liking change even when change is not strictly necessary. The heady concoction of angst, ambition and craving for change leads many otherwise shrewd managers to be gullible consumers of fads and gurus. Shapiro (1998) coined the phrase "Fad Surfing" to describe the penchant of managers to latch on to ephemeral fashions and "flavours of the month".

---

### CASE 20.1:  *Business process re-engineering: a recent management fad*

Business process re-engineering (BPR) was a fad of the 1990s (Micklethwaite and Wooldridge, 1996). It analyses an organisation into its component parts and examines the contribution each unit makes to the key processes. Business process engineering promised to result in a more efficient and profitable organisation. It is easy to understand why hoards of organisations lined up for BPR. However, it had classic characteristics of a craze – lots of dodgy "spin" and dubious results. It is a salutary warning that in order to avoid falling for a fad or a craze managers should apply scientific scepticism to what they read and what they are told by management gurus.

*The dodgy BPR spin*

A prestigious consultancy with close links to the Sloan School of Management at the Massachusetts Institute of Technolgy (MIT), CSI, earned fees for helping organisations implement BPR. Its consultants, Michael Treacy and Fred Wiersema (1995) published *The Discipline of Market Leaders* which extolled BPR's virtues. Their book shot into the best-seller list and demand for CSI's consultants soared – until malpractice was revealed. The consultants, their employers and some business associates were buying tens of thousands of copies of the book themselves – especially from bookshops thought to be used to compile the best-seller list.

*The dubious results*

First, the cost benefit of BPR was questioned. Clients were reluctant to reveal the exact details and analyses were conducted by people who had a vested interest in proving the technique was a success. Independent is analysts such as Hammer (1995) found that 70 per cent of BPR projects had failed. Further, an independent analysis showed that, while the shares of downsizing (sometimes called "rightsizing") organisations outperformed the market in the short term, in the longer term (three years later) they underperformed. People started to recognise the dysfunctions of "anorexic downsizing".

Whole business units were often obliterated and many middle management jobs were eliminated. Managers were demotivated. Many re-engineered organisations were forced to hire back their previous middle managers – as more expensive consultants. The company became an efficient but inflexible machine that made a static product but BPR had engineered-out the capacity to adapt and devise a better product (Dougherty and Bowman, 1995).

Management fashions cannot be ignored because most fads have powerful advocates who interpret any non-conformance as a sign of being out of date. This chapter aims to outline some aspects of management "fashions" so that they can be identified and handled appropriately. Developing a critical and scientific approach is the paramount objective of studying management. If this is achieved you will be able to cope with new research that did not exist when this book was written. The chapter is organised into five main sections:

## 20.1 Fads and crazes

A *fad* is "a craze or a peculiar, senseless, idea that is adopted capriciously and uncritically – perhaps because others have recently adopted it or perhaps because it satisfies some temporary psychological need". Fads are not new. Some of the earliest recorded fads involved finance. This is probably because financial records often survive. A well-known example is the seventeenth-century phenomenon known as "Tulipomania" (see Case 20.2). It demonstrates the classic recipe for a speculative craze. The main ingredients are:

- an unfamiliar or new product that seems scarce
- liquid assets (perhaps borrowed money) available to fund purchases
- a widespread belief that demand is infinite
- individuals who believe that they are among the first to know of the opportunity

---

### CASE 20.2: *Tulipomania – a classic fad*

Tulipomania occurred in Holland in 1637. Tulips had been recently introduced to Europe and were a status symbol. Their price rose inexorably and people bought tulip bulbs at high prices, not because they valued tulips but because they believed that someone else would pay a much higher price in the future. Many borrowed money to buy ever-more expensive tulips. Bulbs reached such giddy prices that very few people could afford to buy them – other "mugs" could not enter the market. At that point people realised that the price of tulip bulbs was way above their intrinsic value. There were lots of sellers and very few buyers. Many sellers, especially those who had borrowed, feared that they would not be able to obtain even a fraction of their original purchase price. In fear, they panicked and unloaded tulip bulbs onto an already glutted market. Prices dropped like a stone. Many speculators "had their fingers burnt" and cynics were again able to claim that markets are driven "by greed and fear".

Other classic fads have been documented, including the famous "South Sea Bubble" which is explained in the website that accompanies this book.

---

Some of the major critics of fads are Collins (2000), Huczynski (1993) and Micklethwaite and Wooldridge (1996).

## 20.2  Management gurus

The term "guru" is applied to spiritual leaders who solve problems by discerning fundamental truths. A guru has power and authority over devotees. In Europe, the term "management guru" is used, pejoratively, to imply someone who makes lofty pronouncements that do not take account of the practical constraints that apply to ordinary people. Some people (for example, Collins, 2000) believe that management gurus are the managerial equivalent of *carpet-baggers*. Huczynski (1993) noted that gurus fell into three types:

■ **Hero-managers** are gurus with first-hand, practical experience of managing and who have achieved outstanding things. They have no systematic approach or theory. They "fly by the seat of their pants" and "dabble" in the running of organisations. Classic examples of hero-managers who have become gurus include Sir John Harvey-Jones, former chairman of ICI, and Anita Roddick, the founder of the Body Shop.

■ **Consultant gurus** usually start working for a major firm of consultants such as McKinsey & Co. Unlike hero-managers, consultant gurus are members of a profession and they will have had specialist training. Their prestige and intellectual power is often derived from their early work with world-class organisations. Classic examples of consultant gurus are Tom Peters, Robert Waterman and Richard Boyatis.

■ **Academic gurus** hail from prestigious universities such as Harvard but may lack substantive experience of first-hand management. Their advice is based on theory and high-level abstractions which may have little relevance to managers facing practical challenges. Examples of academic gurus are Peter Drucker, Michael Porter and Charles Handy.

In 2003 Accenture ranked management gurus. The top 10 gurus were as listed in Table 20.1.

| Rank | Name | Specialty | Example Publication |
|---|---|---|---|
| 1 | Michael Porter | Strategy | *The Competitive Advantage* |
| 2 | Tom Peters | Excellence | *In Search of Excellence* |
| 3 | Robert Reich | Workers' rights | *Work of Nations* |
| 4 | Peter Drucker | Management | *The Effective Executive* |
| 5 | Gary Becker | Behavioural economics | *Human Capital* |
| 6 | Peter Senge | Organisational learning | *The Fifth Discipline* |
| 7 | Gary Hamel | Strategy and innovation | *Competing for the Future* |
| 8 | Alvin Toffler | Futurology | *Future Shock* |
| 9 | Hal Varian | Information systems | *Information Rules* |
| 10 | Daniel Goldman | Emotional intelligence | *Primal Leadership* |

**TABLE 20.1**  Top management gurus

Gurus specialise. Drucker offered advice on (among other things) the knowledge society. Peters's early work searched for organisational excellence, while Porter offered advice on organisational strategy. Nevertheless they have three common characteristics – vision, research and action (Huczynski, 1993). In keeping with the Sanskrit notion of a guru as a far-sighted religious leader, most gurus have a *vision that offers salvation* – often salvation from foreign competitors operating in low-cost countries. The vision must appear to have *clear, simple benefits* such as identification of new markets, faster innovation or improved quality. The guru's vision will be more attractive if it overturns a cherished, commonly held idea (Clarke and Salaman, 1993).

Management gurus usually promote *active research* in the sense that they encourage managers to experiment with new ideas and methods. They also tend to suggest recipes involving *short–term actions* that bring success. A specific example of short-term, standard recipes would be Parinello and Gottfried (2004) *10 secrets I Learned from the Apprentice*. Sometimes actions suggested by gurus are outrageous and "over the top" (Collins, 2000).

Gurus usually have an engaging and interesting style. However, it is important to see beyond their presentational skills to evaluate critically what they say and write. The influence of a "seductive" lecturing style was demonstrated long ago at Doctor Fox's Lecture.

## CASE 20.3: *Doctor Fox's seductive lectures*

In 1973 Nauflin, Ware and Donnelly staged a spoof lecture on "Game Theory As Applied to Physical Education". An actor was coached to present the topic with excessive use of double talk, non sequiturs, contradictory statements and meaningless references to unrelated topics. However, "Dr Fox" was introduced to well-qualified educators as an authority ("the real McCoy"). An evaluation questionnaire was distributed at the end of the lectures. The expert audiences evaluated the spoof Dr Fox highly. Over 90 percent reported that he had stimulated their thoughts and one member of the audience claimed to have read his previous publications!

It is impossible to consider all gurus. However, as a sample, we are going to look at the contributions of Drucker, Peters and Porter. Drucker has pride of place because his writings have influenced managers over decades; Peters is a good example of a flamboyant guru from a background of management consulting; while Porter is a classic example of a serious academic guru.

## Peter Drucker

Few people have had as much influence on the theory of management as Peter Ducker. Indeed, he has been so influential he has been called "the guru's guru". (Micklethwaite and Wooldridge, 1996). Some people regard Drucker as the person who established "management" as a discipline in its own right. (Taylor would not agree!) Nevertheless, Drucker has changed the world with his ideas of privatisation and knowledge work.

### Drucker's ideas

Drucker tackled three main issues: management as a discipline, managing organisations and the shape of society.

Perhaps Drucker's greatest contribution has been his focus on *management as a discipline*. Before Drucker, management was a hodgepodge. Drucker forged disparate components into a more coherent whole. He emphasised the importance of rational and clear management. In *The Practice of Management* Drucker (1954) pointed out that organisations are not ends in themselves but exist for a purpose – providing a product or service that has more value than the resources the organisation consumes – the theme of this book. Organisations should be designed carefully so that they fulfil their purpose. He emphasised the importance of outputs rather than inputs – management by results rather than management by supervision.

Drucker urged managers to view labour as a *resource* rather than a cost. *People* are *the* source of ideas for new products. *People* identify and exploit markets. *People* assemble parts into finished goods. *People* collect money and prepare accounts. If the *people* in an organisation are good the organisation prospers. People are not machines. Many have talents that are not utilised. The assembly line was inefficient because it could only move at the pace of the slowest individual and prevented others from using their talents. Drucker suggested that in many situations properly trained workers can manage their own activities better than an expert or manager. He emphasised the idea of "a responsible worker". These ideas are now obvious and commonplace. They were not so obvious in the 1940s and 1950s when managers viewed employees as a difficult and troublesome kind of machine that should be replaced by a mechanical device whenever possible. Drucker urged managers to spend more time engaging employee's minds rather than devising ways to control their hands. It can be argued that these ideas of Drucker were the beginnings of "employee engagement", "empowerment" and "team-manufacturing".

His second book emphasised the social aspects of organisations. He attracted the attention of the General Motors corporation. In 1946 *The Concept of the Corporation* quickly became a best-seller. It covered both the economics of General Motors and its sociological aspects – especially "the corporation as a social institution" and the way people interact. *The Concept of the Corporation* noted that General Motors's decentralised structure made it easier to find solutions to changes as they moved from wartime to peacetime production. Decentralisation works because it creates workers who feel that *their* contribution matters. It creates "farms for growing talent".

Drucker (1969) commented extensively on the *future shape of society*. He identified three main sources of **discontinuity**: the growth of the knowledge society, globalisation and disenchantment with government:

- In 1959 Drucker noted the importance of **knowledge workers** who collect, synthesise and evaluate, and create new ideas. Societies and governments should not shore up old industries against cheaper competition abroad. Instead, they should ensure a knowledgeable, skillful, experienced workforce that can invent better, higher-value, products or services. Drucker foresaw the increasing importance of knowledge workers would change management in significant ways. A large part of the information knowledge workers use is in their own brains. This asset is owned by employees – not the organisation. Knowledge workers are at liberty to change jobs and use their knowledge for another organisation. Knowledge workers are responsible for developing their own skills and abilities. The freedom of knowledge working can be both liberating and destabilising. New patterns of employment, training and even pension provision are needed.

- Drucker predicted greater **globalisation**. Drucker's global vision has been realised: the same goods are sold in very similar shopping malls in Manchester, Miami, Melaka, Melborne and Xian.

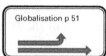

Globalisation p 51

- Drucker predicted that the third source of discontinuity would be people's **disenchantment with government**. He felt that governments should stop meddling with the economy and that their job was to govern by (*some*) legislation, regulation and the occasional provision of funds. Government should leave commercial and economic activities to others. He believed governments had no business managing telecommunication companies, airline companies and utilities. Drucker talked about re-privatisation. Some of these ideas of "privatisation" were taken up by British governments in the 1980s and is were later copied throughout the world.

Drucker's discontinuous society would thrive on innovation and entrepreneurship. Change would be risky. However, all economic activity involves an element of risk – "and defending yesterday – that is, not innovating – is far more risky".

---

## CRITICAL THINKING 20.1 *What is wrong with Drucker?*

Despite his pre-eminence, Drucker's work has been criticised – especially by academics. They complain that, after *The Concept of the Corporation* he does not support his ideas with rigour or with detailed evidence. Many academics regard him as a journalist rather than scholar because he only states the obvious in a readable way. This is unfair. His observations only seem obvious because they have been so influential that they have been adopted widely. However, some of Drucker's dictums are clearly silly. For example, he exhorts organisations to avoid an overemphasis on profits and that: "There is only one business purpose – namely to create a customer". In which case anyone can be a tycoon: millions of customers can be created overnight by offering £10 notes at a cost of £5! Finally, Drucker has few insights about small businesses and yet these are the organisations that he expects to flourish in a discontinuous, post-capitalist society.

---

## Tom Peters

Tom Peters the "management guru" rose to prominence in 1985 as a consultant with the prestigious consultants, McKinsey & Co. They asked him and a colleague to identify the common features of successful organisations. Peters and Waterman interviewed executives from 32 organisations such as IBM, Atari and Wang Laboratories. They published their findings in a book, *In Search of Excellence* (*ISoE*) (1988). The book was a best-seller. It appeared at a time when Japanese industry was making great inroads into the American market. Managers in their millions read the book hoping to find a way to halt or even reverse the Japanese advance.

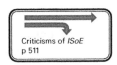

Criticisms of *ISoE*
p 511

As we shall see later in this chapter, both the methodology and the conclusions of *ISoE* were faulty. Nevertheless, the book was very readable and has had enormous influence. Tom Peter's other books include: *A Passion for Excellence* (Peters and Austin, 1985) *The Pursuit of Wow!* (1995) and *The Circle of Innovation: You Can't Shrink Your Way to Greatness* (1997).

### Peters's ideas

Many of Peters's ideas have been discredited but they still circulate widely and it is important to know the main concepts. *In Search of Excellence* identified eight common characteristics of excellent companies:

- *Bias for action*: excellent companies are willing to take swift action, try out new ideas and take some risks. Excellent companies avoid "paralysis by analysis". They also avoid forming committees that have a brief to "talk" about action.

- *Being close to the customer*: excellent companies link all their activities (e.g. strategies, organisational structure, procedures and systems), identifying customer needs and fulfilling them.

- *Autonomy and entrepreneurship*: excellent companies encourage key members of their organisation to act as entrepreneurs. Excellent companies avoid huge departments that hinder informal networking, contact and alliances.

- *Productivity through people*: excellent companies go beyond lip-service to the idea that people are an organisation's biggest assets. They invest heavily in employee development.

- *Hands-on, value driven*: in excellent companies senior staff act as leaders not managers. They keep a high profile and lead by example.

- *Stick to the knitting*: excellent organisations have a clear idea of their key skills and markets. They stay within their key competencies. They build on their strengths rather than trying to master all products and all markets.

- *Simple structure, lean staff*: excellent organisations have a clear sense of purpose and employ skilful and committed people. Consequently, they do not need a complex organisational structure to monitor or control employees.

- *Loose–tight controls*: excellent organisations allow employees freedom and discretion – especially to innovate. This means that creative abilities of employees can be harnessed.

Later, Tom Peters focused on the *chaos and uncertainty* of modern times. Peters believed that the world was changing so fast that organisations needed to reinvent themselves at regular intervals. He believed that the pace of change was so fast that it was impossible to predict the future with any certainty. Indeed, the rate of change has produced a business environment that is close to chaos. Peters set out to stop organisations whingeing, to accept chaos and learn to flourish in its opportunities. He counselled, "if you aren't reorganising, pretty substantially, once every six to 12 months, you're probably out of step with the times". At the end of each day managers must ask, "what exactly and precisely and explicitly is being done in my work area differently from the way it was done when I came to work in the morning?" Peters asserts that the modern business environment is crazy and not susceptible to rational and purposeful management – he advocates "crazy" actions such as "getting fired", "racing yaks", "taking off one's shoes", "making mistakes" and "taking breathing-relaxation exercises".

Organisational change
p 143

## CRITICAL THINKING 20.2 *What is wrong with Peters?*

Tom Peters is possibly the world's most criticised guru. At an emotional level he has been called "a professional loudmouth", "hype-meister" and "Prince of Disorder". Some employees dread the possibility that their boss may attend a second Tom Peters seminar – fearing that it will produce a trail of chaos, confusion, and inanities (Wade, 2003). Others point to Peters's confession that he faked data in *ISoE* (Kellaway, 2001). Peters's work has not stood the test of time. His later books are not based on research. They consist of anecdotes, "war stories" and personal views (Collins, 2000). The latter books are often inconsistent with earlier writings. Indeed, Micklethwaite and Wooldridge (1996) exclaim that he has "contradicted himself even more often than the average politician"! Research underlying Peters and Waterman's *In Search of Excellence* was far from rigorous. Perhaps the most damning criticism is that about two-thirds of the firms that ISoE extolled in 1982 have fallen from grace and became corporate basket-cases and some (e.g., Atari, Data General, Lanier) are moribund or do not exist today. Chapman's (2006) very readable book, *In Search of Stupidity* parodied Peters and Waterman and the disasters which subseqently befell the companies they considered excellent).

## Michael Porter

Reputedly the world's most famous business academic guru (Handy, 2005), Porter specialises in business strategy. His work is academic, carefully argued and supported by evidence. Michael Porter has played a part in creating the *Global Competitiveness Report* (Porter et al., 2004) which ranks countries according to their ability to defend their competitive position against other nations. He has advised many governments including those of the UK, Ireland, Portugal and New Zealand. Porter began (1980) by examining the individual organisations. Then, like Drucker, he widened his scope and went on to study the *Competitive Advantage of Nations* (1990) before looking at the problems of specific areas such as inner cities.

### Porter's ideas

Porter draws a clear distinction between strategy and efficiency. Modern organisations, he suggests, have focused exclusively on the latter by using techniques such as total quality management and BPR in an attempt to be more efficient than their competitors. However, if an organisation is doing essentially the same thing as its competitors, it is unlikely to be more successful in the longer run: it is arrogant to believe that it can perpetually outsmart others. Strategy is about choices and setting limits on what an organisation can accomplish. An ideal strategy places organisations where there are few competitors and where start up is difficult.

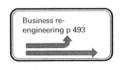
Business re-engineering p 493

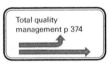
Total quality management p 374

According to Porter, there two main factors in gaining competitive advantage: industry type and forces of competition. The five *industry types* are:

- *Fragmented*: many suppliers and none have a dominant position. Fragmented industries are usually *very* competitive.

- *Emerging*: considerable potential for growth and very good profitability – at least for a short time. However, they attract domestic and foreign competitors.

- *Mature*: control of costs is vital.

- *Declining*: are best avoided but they can be managed by a strategy of innovation or brand development of "cult status" It may call for end-game strategies such as divestment or downsizing.

Globalisation p 51

- *Globalising*: provides economies of scale and can extend the life cycle of older products by selling to less-developed countries.

Porter's *five forces of competition* are:

- *Existing competitors* who provide intense rivalry – especially when there is no clear market leader, high fixed costs or where exit barriers are high. If competitors follow an aggressive growth strategy in a mature market, rivalry will be intense. If competitors simply "take profits" rivalry will be less.

- *New companies* always raise the level of competition – especially if there are high exit barriers. Some industries, such as motorcar production, have high entry barriers which deter new entrants.

- *Substitute products* bring competition which reduces prices. The impact may be lower if costs of switching are significant, e.g. manufacturers of industrial gases such as liquid oxygen or nitrogen can beat off substitutes because customers find it too expensive to change the connections of meters and regulators.

- *Supplier bargaining power* makes an industry unattractive.

- *Bargaining power of customers* can also make an industry unattractive. Customers have high bargaining power when products are standardised and when there are a few dominant customers. For example, the British supermarket, Asda, has enormous bargaining power when it negotiates fresh food products. Asda can make even a strong supplier such as Kerry Group's subsidiary Wall's Sausages quake by threatening to set up its own brand.

The type of industry and forces of competition combine, according to Porter, to identify three main organisational strategies.

- *Cost leadership*: making things cheaper than rivals (e.g. Aldi). This is the least favoured strategy.
- *Product leadership*: making a product or services that have special features for which customers will pay a higher price (e.g. Porsche cars).
- *Market leadership*: operating in a particular market or niche and dominating that market so the organisation's position cannot be challenged (e.g. Apple computers).

Gaining a competitive advantage involves more than determining the appropriate strategy. Organisations must examine their operations to establish which are efficient at adding value – i.e **value chain analysis**. In essence, value chain analysis systematically takes each step in the production of a product or service and determines what it adds to the final value. The value of individual steps culminates in the total value. Porter divided organisational activities into two groups: primary activities and support activities. The primary value chain shown in Figure 20.1, which is a major component of the functions depicted in Figure 13.1 (page 000).

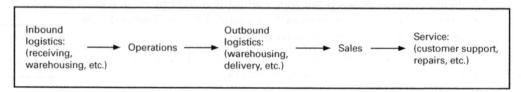

**FIGURE 20.1** Porter's primary value chain

The secondary value chain consists of support activities such as purchasing, human resource management, technology development and the firm's infrastructure.

Porter also wrote *The Competitive Advantage of Nations* (1990). The four key factors that make a country competitive are:

1 *Competition* between its companies that makes them improve.
2 *Demanding consumers* who force organisations to innovate.
3 *Resources,* especially human resources such as the skills of workers
4 *The cluster phenomenon*, where suppliers, etc. are grouped into a critical mass such as computer design in Silicon Valley, financial services in the City of London and knitwear in Tiruppur, India.

Since 1995 Porter has analysed ways of revitalising run-down *inner-city areas*. Instead, of providing aid and welfare, people should try to foster viable economic communities whose products can compete in the marketplace. Inner-city taxes tend to be high in order to pay for welfare programmes. This produces a vicious circle in which employers relocate elsewhere, jobs are lost, the need for welfare increases and local taxes are raised to even higher levels and so more employers leave. The real need is to develop wealth-creating companies by relaxing regulations and by keeping local taxes low.

CRITICAL THINKING 20.3 *What is wrong with Porter?*

Porter rarely takes people into account. He focuses too much on strategy and market forces while assuming that behaviour will follow. In over 500 pages of *Competitive Strategy* he devotes only two paragraphs to the management of people (Handy, 2005). One of the most serious criticisms of Porter's work is that it is out of date. Downes (2005), for example, claims that Porter's theories may have worked in the 1980s when the structure of industries was relatively stable and business cycles were predictable. However, Porter's assumptions are no longer accurate in the Internet Age which has resulted in hyper-competition where things change very fast. Organisations analysing strategy, as recommended by Porter, would react too slowly. They would suffer "paralysis by analysis". Rather than obtain competitive advantage from cost leadership or quality leadership, competitive advantage, etc., today it may stem from developing long-lasting relationships with more mobile customers.

## 20.3 Witch doctors' cons

Micklethwaite and Wooldridge (1996), liken management gurus to witch doctors who have tricks and cons that make them to *appear* effective. Some main tricks are: hindsight, the fortune-teller and Barnum effects, self-fulfilling prophecies and capitalisation on chance. Knowledge of each of these tricks will help readers avoid falling into the hands of gurus, academics and consultants who offer poor advice, such as BPR.

### Hindsight

Gurus love hindsight – subjective and selective hindsight at that! A corporation experiencing difficulties may consult a leading authority who examines the recent facts and then diagnoses why the organisation is in trouble. The gurus act as deathbed doctors pronouncing the reason for an imminent death. What corporations really need are hygienists that help them avoid trouble in the first place. Examples of deathbed witch doctoring occurred in the USA and Europe during the 1980s when organisations were awash with consultants explaining why they were in imminent danger of losing their markets to Japanese firms. Explanations varied according to area of expertise: sometimes it was teamworking, sometimes it was quality procedures and sometimes it was just-in-time delivery systems. Very few had given warning of the Japanese threat in advance. Further, few warned of the slow-down and stagnation of Japanese organisations during the 1990s. This illustrates the dangers of driving by the rear-view mirror and *"post hoc"* explanations.

    *Case studies* are hugely contaminated by hindsight and subjectivity. They may be produced by people who have a vested interest in an area such as finance, logistics, human resources or quality. They visit an organisation and, as human beings, can only access a small proportion of relevant information. They then sift this information – often in a subjective way according to their own mental filters, coloured by their own motives and training. Case study writers then interpret a selected range of information and arrive at a diagnosis. Other diagnoses may be equally valid but case study writers rarely consider or test alternatives. Because case studies are so full of subjective hindsight, they are often characterised as "shared ignorance" and they must be evaluated carefully. Questions which should be asked of any case study include:

- Who is the person(s) conducting the case study? What are their qualifications, expertise and motives?
- What range of relevant information was actually available? Was the information filtered in some way?
- To what extent does the diagnosis follow from the data? Were alternative diagnoses given proper consideration?

Case studies *are* a useful tool in management education and they do help captivate attention. However, they should only be developed to illustrate prior research.

## The fortune-teller effect

For example, Barnum was a circus entertainer who told fortunes. He foretold gullible members of his audience that "you will be going on a journey" or "you will hear from an old friend". He then watched their faces for clues which he used to embellish with more specific detail. At least some of the statements came true. Gullible members of the audience then believed Barnum's mystic powers were proven.

## Self-fulfilling prophecy

Sometimes a guru may harness a self-fulfilling prophecy. This occurs when making a prediction determines the outcome. Self-fulfilling prophecies are seen clearly in the financial markets. For example, the stock of a company may be progressing in line with similar companies. It might then, by chance, attract the attention of, say, Warren Buffett – one of the greatest stock market gurus and investors of all times. If Buffett were to suggest that the stock of this randomly chosen company would rise, it will increase dramatically. Buffett has such a powerful reputation that others will buy the stock – the price will rise as a result of the prediction rather than any improvement in the value of the company. Self-fulfilling prophecies operate within organisations. For example, the strategy department may predict that the sales of a certain product will decline. This would result in a cutback in the replacement budget and goods would be produced on progressively older machines. Moreover, because of the prediction itself, sales staff will promote the product less energetically. Thus, sales of the randomly chosen product are almost certain to decline. The strategy department will then victoriously quote the decline as their prowess of predicting the future!

Self-fulfilling prophecies are often called the "Pygmalion effect". In a famous experiment, Rosenthal and Jacobson (1992) arbitrarily divided pupils into two groups and told teachers that one group was bright and the other was dull (the two groups were allocated at random and scored about the same). When the groups were measured again, the "bright group" had made more progress than the dull groups. The false information had influenced teachers at a subconscious level. They gave more attention and set more demanding tasks to the "bright" group and this caused them to shine. The Pygmalion effect operates in organisations. A manager may arbitrarily decide that a subordinate is not very able. He or she then makes subconscious decisions that cause their expectations to be fulfilled. A low-expectation employee may find he or she is:

■ located in a low-prestige office, far from the manager
■ given less attention in business meetings – fewer smiles, less eye contact, less time to state their opinions and gets interrupted more frequently
■ given less information about what is happening and poorer feedback about their performance
■ less likely to be allocated to special products or high-profile activities

The cumulative effect will handicap the subordinate and prevent them making progress – thus confirming the manager's original arbitrary judgement.

## CRITICAL THINKING 20.4 *Is the Hawthorne effect the real cause of many improvements?*

The Hawthorne effect is a great friend of charlatans. It enables useless changes to masquerade as effective. It was discovered during famous "lighting" experiments at the Hawthorne factory (Mayo, 1933). They showed that *any* change is likely to bring about an improvement in productivity – not because the change is any good but because employees are influenced by the extra attention that they receive. Managers need to be very careful to take the Hawthorne effect into account. The unwary manager might conclude that any new project causes an improvement. The Hawthorne effect has enormous implications. Every claim for a management innovation must prove that benefits really are due to the innovation and not the Hawthorne effect. At the very minimum an evaluation of any innovation needs to have two groups. One (**control group** or **placebo group**) should receive exactly the same attention and consideration. In medical contexts they take a tablet which has the same colour, shape and size as the other group but it lacks the active ingredient. The other group (**experimental group**) is treated in the same way except the tablet contains the active ingredient. Scientifically, it is important that these studies are conducted on a **double-blind** basis – neither the subjects nor the people who evaluate their progress or productivity know to which group they belong. We are reluctant to take a medicine which does not meet these standards but we allow managers to follow ideas, fatal to many people's jobs, without such scrutiny.

Hawthorne effect p 75

## Capitalisation on chance

Charlatans and witch doctors capitalise on chance to produce evidence that seems to support their theories. They use three main tricks: the numbers game, regression to the mean and riding piggyback.

The easiest way to capitalise on chance is to play *the numbers game* because, in fact, most things *could* happen as flukes. For example, if enough chimpanzees tapped at random on a typewriter one of them would reproduce a Shakespearean sonnet. Imagine a firm of management consultants based in Boston but with branches in Birmingham, Bombay, Baltimore, Brisbane and Beijing. It encounters hard times when its consultants' time is "fee-earning free". A couple of wayward employees come up with a spurious management technique called "a New Post Porter Paradigm for a Lean, Customer Driven Organisation with Employee Engagement" (NPPPLCDOwEE or N–E for short). Impressed, the partners write personal letters to the CEOs of 120 world-class organisations saying that their N–E model predicts that their corporation will beat the industry average in the next three months. After three months the partners write to the 60 corporations who have, by chance, beaten the industry average and predict that they will continue to beat the industry average in the following three months. After that three months, the partners write to the 30 corporations who have, by chance, beaten the average and predict that they will beat the industry average in their next three months. They then write to the 15 corporations who have beaten the industry average for a year and point out that their consultancy has a solid track record of identifying success. The partners then offer consultancy services at £2000 per day to guide the corporation to continued success. If only a few gullible CEOs took up the offer, rewards would be great. Capitalising on chance would have produced a handsome income for the cost of producing and posting just 225 letters!

Witch doctors frequently con their patients by *misinterpreting chance events*. If, by chance, the chief of a tribe gets a disease, it will be interpreted as a sign of the anger of the gods. Incantations and sacrifices (interviews, meetings and PowerPoint presentations) will be made in appeasement. In all probability the chief recovers naturally – clear evidence that the witch doctors were accurate. In modern organisations chance events are misinterpreted in more subtle ways. Two particular cons concern minority positions and regression to the mean. They both depend upon the fact that practically all measures in management are subject to some random error. As Case 20.4 demonstrates, the margin of error is often very large.

High levels of random error mean that *minority positions are often overstated* (Paulos, 1998). Suppose that it is known for certain that 5 per cent of workers are clinically depressed but researchers do not know this. However, a well-meaning sponsor arranges for a sample of 100 workers to meet a doctor who diagnoses whether each is depressed. Suppose that the doctor's diagnoses are 80 per cent correct which, in the light of evidence (Visweswaran, Ones and Schmidt, 1996), is a generous assumption. There will be five people who are genuinely depressed but, because of the errors of measurement, the doctor only identifies four (true positives). There will be 95 people who, actually, are not depressed, but because of the errors of measurement (20 per cent), the doctor concludes that 19 are depressed (false positives). Thus, the result of the investigation is that 23 (19 + 4) per cent of workers are depressed when, in fact, the true figure is 5 per cent! Random error has produced a result that is almost five times the true figure! Managers of this imaginary organisation could be fit and well and waste a million dollars buying valium and paying for unnecessary counselling. Managers should be very wary of results based upon subjective judgements and where results suggest that less than 25 per cent of people experience problems.

---

**CASE 20.4:** *Huge errors in management judgements*

An example of huge measurement error in management is given by Viswesvaran, Ones and Schmidt (1996). They studied the evaluations that bosses make of their subordinates. They obtained data for a total of 14 650 subordinates, each of whom had been evaluated by two independent superiors. They then correlated the two sets of ratings and obtained a correlation of 0.52. This indicates that the consistency between two superiors is only 27 per cent true and the remaining 73 per cent is caused by random error. (Note: to obtain a percentage agreement from a correlation, square the correlation and multiply by 100.)

---

*Regression to the mean* is a con frequently used to promise to rescue organisations from a bad situation. It is a con that is particularly relevant to "before and after" studies. This con depends on measurement error. When any group is chosen, some people are selected by mistake. For example, suppose an organisation selects 100 of its poorest performers for a training course to improve their performance. Possibly 60 of those chosen are genuinely poor workers and the other 40 are chosen by mistake – a fairly conservative assumption in the light of Viswesvaran *et al.*'s results. Suppose that the training is useless but the 40 initial mistakes are evaluated a second time. By chance alone 24 of the 40 false negatives (60 per cent × 40) are correctly classified (the remaining 16 suffer the misfortune of being double false negatives). However, this evaluation of a useless training course would "prove" that it was worthwhile because it had reduced the percentage of poor workers by no less than 24 per cent. "Before and after" studies in commerce and industry are very susceptible to "regression to the mean" when the study involves a selected group of any kind.

The final con used by "management witch doctors" does not, technically, involve capitalising on chance but, since it may affect "before and after" studies, it is considered here. Riding *piggyback* involves taking credit for an improvement, caused by other factors that would have occurred in any event. For example, an ingenious traffic engineer might invent some device, say a new kind of speed hump, and claim that it will reduce accidents. The engineer might well persuade a gullible local authority to install the humps. When the figures are compared a year later, it might be found that the number of accidents has decreased by 2 per cent. Given that human consequences of an accident can be dire, an improvement of 2 per cent is well worth having. Consequently, the gullible local authority is likely to install the speed humps, willy-nilly, throughout its area. However, it might be wasting money. There has been a consistent decline in the rate of road accidents over many years. It is probably caused by better design of cars (especially brakes and tyres) and greater driver awareness. In fact, it would only be worth the local authority investing in speed humps if the traffic engineer could show a change that is significantly greater than the trend.

## 20.4    Scientific management research

### Types of scientific research in management

Scientific research into management takes four main forms: observation, experiments, field experiments and surveys.

Observation *is* frequently used. For example, supermarkets keenly monitor the way customers progress through aisles and the points at which they are most likely to pause to make a purchase. Observations of actual behaviour give very realistic information that is relatively free from bias.

*Experiments* are rarely used in management research. Occasionally an organisation will commission *laboratory research* into, say, the way that customers open different types of packaging or use different computer interfaces. They are tightly controlled so laboratory studies are very good at determining cause and effect. But experiments tend to be artificial and their results may not be generalisable to operational situations. The artificial situation in a laboratory overemphasises factors under investigation – because other influences are cancelled out. *Field experiments* overcome some of these problems. They are more realistic and produce results more applicable to "real life". For example, an operations function may vary the production system in half of their units and assess the effects objectively. Sometimes a finance director will vary a payment system to check whether it motivates staff. Field experiments are better than laboratory experiments in the sense that they yield more realistic **effect sizes** and produce results that are **generalisable**. However, field experiments are not very good at distinguishing between cause and effect. In the field, so many uncontrolled factors operate it is impossible to distinguish whether a change is due to the differences investigated or unknown influences.

*Surveys* are widely used in management research. They are relatively quick and cheap to conduct and they are good at exploring a wide range of factors. For example, a single survey would be able to investigate employee satisfaction with pay, working conditions, hours worked, job security and several other factors. In contrast, an experiment into job satisfaction would be able to measure just one or two of these factors. Surveys have a crucial problem: they investigate **epiphenomena** (*what people say* about a subject) not the phenomena themselves (the real situation – what people actually do). Often there is a gap between the two. For example, 85 per cent of people claim that their sense of humour is better than average and 80 per cent of men claim that they are excellent drivers. The results of surveys can also be strongly influenced by the exact wording of the questions.

### Special difficulties faced by management researchers

Research into many management phenomena is not straightforward. Researchers are challenged in two ways: measurement problems and the interactive nature of the subject matter.

**Measurement problems** in management research arise because many of the variables are intangible and difficult to manipulate. For example, if an engineer believes that a machine will work faster at a higher voltage it is relatively simple to increase the voltage precisely and measure the speed of the machine very accurately. However, a manager who believes that workers will be more productive if they are more motivated will find it very difficult to measure people's level of motivation. The situation with regard to outputs is similar: they too are difficult to measure in a totally reliable and objective way. Such problems mean that management researchers need to check the accuracy of their measures – especially their reliability and validity:

**Reliability** assesses whether a measure gives consistent results. For example, large corporations often use intelligence tests to select new employees; but if a test gives different results when a person is tested a second time, the test would be useless and it would not be sensible to rely on the scores it produces (in actual fact, intelligence tests are *very* reliable. The scores from two administrations, separated by a month, would correlate about 0.9).

Unfortunately a measure can be very reliable but is still useless because it does not measure what people may mistakenly think it measures. For example, verbal fluency can be measured fairly reliably (0.9) but, contrary to some stereotypes, it would be useless in selecting salespeople because it would not measure a key sales skill – listening to customers in order to establish rapport and determine their needs. The degree to which a measure gauges what it is supposed to measure is called **validity**.

The concepts of reliability and validity are not restricted to measures in psychology and human resources. Researchers in economics, marketing and organisational analysis must also ensure their measures are reliable and valid. Difficulties in obtaining accurate measures mean results of management research are much less certain than those in physical sciences such as biology and chemistry.

The **interactive nature** of management research (i.e. other people) makes scientific analysis problematic. For example, a sheet of glass does not change its refractive index simply because a physicist uses it as a part of his or her study. However, there is ample evidence that people change their behaviour when are a part of research. Subjects often try to please the researcher by trying to guess the purpose of the investigation and then behaving in a way that they believe will help.

---

### CASE 20.5:  *Client interaction foils accurate evaluation*

A manager may invent a new way of delivering pizzas and decide to assess any improvement by interviewing 50 clients. Although the manager is careful not to state their vested interest, they give enthusiastic non-verbal cues. Customers detect these cues and some decide to help by overemphasising the advantages of the new delivery system. This bias affects the results and an unduly favourable picture emerges. The new system may be adopted even when it might be slightly less effective than the existing one. In some cases, the **demand characteristics of an investigation** work in the opposite direction and subjects try to obstruct the purpose of the researcher. Demand characteristics of research were extensively studied by Rosenthal and Rosnow (1969).

The fact that people are the subject matter in management research produces yet further problems. For example, most management research depends on *volunteers*. A typical response rate for a management survey is about 30 per cent. The minority who reply are a self-selected group who may not be typical of the "population" as a whole. This might bias the results and mean that conclusions from an atypical minority are wrongly applied.

### Characteristics of good scientific management research

Good scientific investigations into management will pay close attention to five characteristics: choice of variables, choice of sample, good measures, good analysis and good reporting. A response to an assignment to evaluate research or gurus' advice should take these five characteristics into account. The adequacy of measures was discussed previously in this chapter. Standards for reporting scientific studies were also outlined earlier. The three remaining topics, choice of variables, choice of sample and analysis of results, need to be discussed further.

### Choice of variables

A variable is any attribute (characteristic) that can be measured and yields a range of values. For example, in a study of employees, variables might be: number of widgets produced per hour, age, educational qualifications, IQ, personality or the number of siblings. In a study of an organisation, the variables might be number of employees, turnover, type of industry, level of centralisation, number of levels in the management hierarchy and level of innovation. A good scientific study will ensure that all relevant variables are included. If important variables are omitted, investigators can never be sure their findings are true or whether they are the result of variables they have missed. Variables that investigators are most likely to miss are those that measure the context (background) of the investigation.

### Choice of sample

A scientific study will involve a large systematic sample that is free from bias. **Sample size** is crucial. Management researchers habitually use small samples. It is an immutable statistical law that results based on small samples are very volatile. Another investigator using another small sample is highly likely to get different results. Sample size is important because, as noted earlier, all measurements are subject to error. With a small sample this error does not have an adequate opportunity to cancel out. For example, with only three tosses of a coin it is not that unlikely that the error is in one direction and the result will be three heads. However, if the coin is tossed 30 times it is virtually impossible that they will all be heads: the most likely outcome is 15 heads and 15 tails.

The size of an adequate sample is determined by two main factors: the effect size and the range of differences between people. **Effect size** means the strength of the phenomenon studied. A strong phenomenon can be detected with a smaller sample than a weak one. The **range of differences** between people is a measure of how much people deviate from the average. This is usually expressed in terms of a statistic called the "standard deviation". When people differ from each other in a substantial way, a large sample is needed. When people are very similar, a smaller sample may be sufficient. Statisticians use complex formulae to determine the proper size for a sample. Schmidt, Hunter and Urry (1976) calculated that a sample of 172 is needed to detect a moderately strong phenomenon. Very few studies in management have samples remotely near this scientific standard. Two dodgy papers based on small samples give a better CV than one proper paper. In practice, many researchers and academics adopt a rule of thumb that the minimum sample size for a scientific study is 30.

## Analysis of results

The results of any investigation should be analysed rigorously. There are two main types of analysis: descriptive statistics and inferential statistics. **Descriptive statistics** include means, percentages and standard deviations for every variable. **Inferential statistics** give a higher level of analysis that checks for relationships between two or more variables. Probably the most frequently used inferential statistics, in ascending order of desirability are chi square, t-tests and correlations. Some investigators analyse data to produce a regression equation or trend-line that states exactly how one variable is related to another. Inferential statistics are usually accompanied by a level of significance – the probability that the results could have occurred by chance alone. Usually scientists only accept findings if their probability of occurring by fluke is less than 1 in 20 (less than 5 per cent).

---

### CASE 20.6: *Comparing scientific method in management and pharmacology*

This case contrasts the way that the long-term effects of a drug for Parkinson's disease, L-Dopa, were evaluated (Fahn, 1999) with the famous management study *In Search of Excellence (ISoE)* by Tom Peters and Bob Waterman (1988). Fahn's study is thorough and scientific but by no means exceptional in its field. *ISoE* was quite exceptional in its impact on many managers. This section is only concerned with *ISoE*'s methodology, which is set out in Table 20.2. Its origin and impact are described on page 501.

| *In Search of Excellence* | Evaluation of L-Dopa |
|---|---|
| *Choice of variables*<br><br>*ISoE* included variables such as strategy, structure, systems, nature of the staff, management style, organisational skills and super-ordinate goals. However, crucially, measures of contextual factors (technology, patents, geography, trade barriers) were omitted (Guest, 1992). So, there is no way *ISoE* could be sure excellence was caused by the variables studied. Excellence might result from strong patents and strong trade barriers, etc. | All variables closely related to the drug itself, the chemical formulation, dosage rates, improvement in the patients' health, etc. were included. The study also captured contextual variables such as patient's age, severity of illness, time since onset, etc. Consequently these variables could be ruled out as causes of any changes |
| *Sample*<br><br>75 organisations were selected by an ad hoc and subjective process on the basis of the organisations' reputation (and probability of future consultancy fees?). Some companies were then, subjectively, eliminated. Eventually, 21 organisations were chosen using a range of financial and other indicators. The study also included 12 companies who were considered to be "near misses"<br><br>The study had only one group, the organisations deemed to be excellent. This meant that *ISoE* could not be sure whether the factors identified as important in excellent organisations were not also present in awful organisations | 360 participants were enrolled and divided, at random, into 4 groups of 120 people (high dose, medium dose, low dose and control group). This arrangement gave added power and meant that the magnitude of levels of treatment (effect sizes) could be gauged. The study also included a "washout" period at the end of the experiment to see how patients reacted when no drug was administered |

| | |
|---|---|
| The samples in *ISoE* are, by no means, the worst samples in management research. Maslow constructed his hierarchy of needs on a smaller sample. Nevertheless, the *ISoE* sample is very inferior to the samples used in scientific investigations such as clinical trials | |
| *Measurement of variables*<br><br>Measurement consisted of interviews with an ad hoc group of senior executives and journalists. It is not known how these people were selected. Scientifically, they should be a systematic (random?) sample of employees and customers of the organisations studied. Senior executives were interviewed without measures developed by an independent source. Reliability and validity of the information obtained was not reported.<br><br>Clearly, measurement of variables falls a long way short of scientific standards. The way *ISoE* measured variables is probably poorer than most research in management | *Progress of patients was assessed using an established scale, the United Parkinson's Disease Rating Scale (UPDRS), developed by people unconnected with the study. The reliability and validity of UPDRS is reported in the scientific literature. Consequently, the investigators could not be accused of perverting their results by using a favourable standard. The L-Dopa study was also careful to avoid contamination by the Hawthorne effect. Patients were "blind" in the sense that they did not know whether they were in the placebo group or the dosage level they were receiving. Further, doctors judging their progress were also "blind" about the treatment of those they were evaluating. "Double-blind" studies of this kind are routine in scientific investigations* |
| *Analysis*<br><br>Analysis in *ISoE* is at the descriptive level using raw counts and sometimes percentages – based on far less than 100 data points. It rarely, it ever, gives standard deviations or uses any kind of inferential statistics | Means and standard deviations for all variables are reported. Inferential statistics are used to check whether there were any significant differences in patients' responses to different doses. A trend-line between dose and patient reaction was also calculated |
| *Reporting*<br><br>Peters and Waterman first gave their results at a presentation to colleagues at McKinsey Consulting. After several well-received presentations they decided to publish their results in a book which was not subject to peer review | Results of the study were submitted to the peer-reviewed journal, *Archives of Neurology*. The article was anonymously evaluated and the reviewers decided that it had sufficient scientific merit to justify publication |

**TABLE 20.2** A comparison between Peters and Waterman's study *In Search of Excellence* and Fahn's rigorous scientific study into the long-term effects of L-Dopa

Case 20.6 shows that management research does not always match the best standards of science. *In Search of Excellence* is by no means the worst example of management research – although it is, probably, somewhere in the bottom half. Many well-known findings are based on small samples, poor measures and inadequate analyses. Double-blind studies are virtually non-existent. You must therefore evaluate pronouncements and claims of researchers and management gurus in a critical way. The aim of this chapter was not to catalogue the inadequacies of management research, but to engender a critical outlook and inspire better research by future generations. We saw earlier that Porter's work on strategy suggests that demanding consumers are a requirement of competitive advantage. The same is true of management research.

*Toolkit*

## 20.5 Toolkit for evaluating scientific papers

It is virtually certain that at some time during your studies you will be asked to evaluate a scientific paper reporting research into management. The following toolkit aims to help you in this task. It might also help you if you are asked to write a research report. You should ask the following questions:

- Does the report have *any scientific or practical* **merit**? Does it make a significant advance in what we know about management or does it help us be better managers?

- Are the **authors** *clearly identified*? Are their affiliations given? Are all of their vested interests clearly stated?

- Does the *report link to* **existing theory** *or practice*? Does the introduction or literature review give accurate citations of important studies and include recent references?

- **What** *variables are measured*? Are they clearly defined? Have any relevant variables, especially contextual variables, been missed?

- **How** have the *variables been measured*? Are they sensitive, reliable and valid?

- Is the **sample appropriate?** Does it sample the right people? How was the sample chosen? Is the sample big enough? Is there a control sample?

- Is the **research procedure** *clearly stated* in sufficient detail for others to replicate the work?

- Is the **data reported** *in sufficient detail* so that it can be evaluated independently? Generally this means that the sample size for each variable and its meaning and standard deviation are given.

- Is the **statistical analysis** *appropriate and rigourous*. Generally, the weakest statistic is chi square. T-tests are better. Analysis of variance, regressions and correlations are good. Multiple correlations and factor analyses are excellent. But all of these must be appropriate for the data that is actually collected. Does the analysis consider the possibility of curvilinear relationships?

- Do the **conclusions** follow from the analyses?

- Are the **wider implications** *of the research described*? Are the conclusions integrated with existing literature? Are pointers for future research given?

- Is the **reference list** *adequate*? Does it include publishing details of all the papers cited? Are the publishing details comprehensive and given in a systematic format such as the American Psychological Association's (APA) style of referencing?

- Is the **style of writing** clear? Are the sections in a logical order? Is it concise? Is it as easy to understand as possible?

# Activities and further study

## Essay plans

1  With the aid of classic examples define a craze and describe the phases through which a craze is likely to pass.
2  Describe and evaluate Drucker's contribution to the understanding of management.
3  Describe and evaluate Michael Porter's contribution to the understanding of strategic management.
4  Outline the ways that apparent improvements may really be the result of chance factors.

## Web activities

1  Search the Web for more information on the work of gurus listed in Table 20.1 (page 497).
2  Surf the Web for more information on fads and crazes. A good site on crashes and crazes is www.stock-market-crash.
3  Search the internet using the terms "Ben Goldacre" and "Bad Science" to find topical and entertaining examples of fads and poor research. Watch Amazon Video http://www.amazon.co.uk/Bad-Science-Ben-Goldacre/dp/0007240198. It concerns use of fish oil to help learning in schoolchildren. Principles are relevant to many evaluations of management training.

## Experiential activities

1  Take 10 separate coins and flip them in the air. Count the number of "tails" (fails) that result. Remove all coins that were heads. Place all the tails in a circle and say "hocus pocus" or some other incantation and breathe on each coin twice. Flip these coins again and count the number of tails. If there are fewer tails than previously, evaluate whether your incantation and breath were the cause or whether it is some other phenomenon. What is this other phenomenon called?
2  Take a recent paper published by a professor in management (preferably from your own college or university). Evaluate that paper and compare its scientific merits with the work of Peters and Fahn – see Case 20.6, page 513.

**3** Discuss with your friends which of today's management trends will turn out to be irrational fads.

**4** Discuss with your friends which of today's markets is about to crash. The housing market? China? Greece? India?

## Further reading

Goldacre, B. (2008) *Bad Science*, London: 4th Estate Publishers. A lively book that exposes cons used in medical sciences. Most of the cons are relevant to management research.

## Recommended reading

**1** Hindle, T. (2008) *Guide to Management Ideas and Gurus*, London: Economist Books. An essential reference.

**2** Locke, E.A. and Latham, G.P. (2009) "Has goal setting gone wild, or have its attackers abandoned good scholarship", *Academy of Management Perspectives*, **23**(1), 17–23. Reveals four bad tricks used by some academics to make an argument. Do not get bogged down in details of goal-setting. Identify the tricks and see how they can be used.

**3** Keller, E. (2006) "The premises and pitfalls of market studies", *Manufacturing Business Technology*, **24**(4), 16, and Sinikas, A. (2007) "Finding a cure for survey fatigue", *Strategic Communication Management*, **11**(2), 11. Both articles are short but identify commmon methodological problems in using surveys.

# References

**Adair, J.G.** (1984) "The Hawthorn effect: a reconsideration of the methodological artefact", *Journal of Applied Psychology*, **69** (2), 334–345.

**Adams, J.S.** (1965) "Inequality in social exchange", in *Advances in Experimental and Social Psychology*, L. Berkowitz (ed), New York: Academic Press.

**Advisory, Conciliation and Arbitration Service (ACAS)** (1982) *Workplace Communications*, Advisory Booklet No. 8, London: ACAS.

**Alder, P.S.** (1993) "Time-and-motion regained", *Harvard Business Review*, **71** (1), 97–108.

**Alfalla-Luque, R. and C. Medina-Lopez** (2009) "Supply chain management: unheard-of in the 1970s, core to today's company", *Business History*, **51** (2), 202–222.

**Allee, V.** (1997) "12 principles of knowledge management", *Training & Development*, **51** (11), 71–74.

**American Marketing Association** (2004) "AMA adopts new definition of marketing", *Marketing News*, **15** (1), September.

**Ames, D.R. and F.J. Flynn** (2007) "What breaks a leader: the curvilinear relationship between assertiveness and leadership", *Journal of Personality & Social Psychology*, **92** (2), 307–325.

**Ansoff, I.** (1989) *Corporate Strategy*, Harmondsworth: Penguin.

**Arthur, M.B. and D.M. Rousseau** (1996) *The Boundaryless Career: A New Employment Principle for a New Organisational Era*, Oxford: Oxford University Press.

**Arvey, R.D., Z. Zhang, B.J. Aviolo and R.F Kreuger** (2007) "Developmental and genetic determinants of leadership role occupancy among women". *Journal of Applied Psychology*, **92**, 693–706.

**Ashby, W.R.** (1964) *Introduction to Cybernetics*, New York: Wiley.

**Audit Commission** (2003) *Waiting List Accuracy*, London: Audit Commission.

**Aviolo, B.J., F.O. Walumbwa and T.J. Weber** (2009) "Leadership: current theories, research, and future directions", *Annual Review of Psychology*, **60**, 421–449.

**Babakus, E., B. Cornwell, V. Mitchell and B. Schlegelmitch** (2004) "Reactions to unethical behaviour in six countries", *Journal of Consumer Marketing*, **21** (4), 254–263.

**Bacon, M.** (2008) "Knowledge management systems in the future", in *Virtual Futures for Design, Construction & Procurement*, P. Brandon and T. Kocaturk (eds), Oxford: Blackwell.

**Banks, D.** (2008) *An Introduction to Thermogeology: Ground Source Heating and Cooling*, Oxford: Blackwell.

**Barker, J.R.** (1993) "Tightening the iron cage: concertive control in self management teams", *Administrative Science Quarterly*, **38** (3), 408–437.

**Baron, J.N. and D.M. Kreps** (1999) *Strategic Human Resources: Frame-Works for General Managers*, New York: Wiley.

**Baron, R.A. and Greenburg, J.** (1990) *Behaviour in Organisations*, London: Allyn and Bacon.

**Bartels, J., O. Peters, M. de Jong, A. Pruyn and M. van de Molen** (2010) "Horizontal and vertical communication as determinants of professional and organisational identification", *Personnel Review*, **39** (2), 210–226.

**Bartlett, F.C.** (1932) *Remembering: an Experimental and Social Study*, London: Cambridge University Press.

**Bass, B.** (1985) "Leadership: good, better, best", *Organisational Dynamics*, **13** (3), 26–40.

**Bassi, L.J.** (1997) "Harnessing the power of intellectual capital", *Training & Development*, **51** (12), 25–30.

**Becker, S.O. and W. Ludger** (2009) "Was Weber wrong? A human capital theory of Protestant economic history", *Quarterly Journal of Economics*, **124** (2), 531–566.

**Beer, S.** (1984) "The viable system model: its prominence, development, methodology, and pathology", *The Journal of the Operational Research Society*, **35** (1), 7–26.

**Belbin, R.M.** (2004) *Management Teams: Why They Succeed or Fail*, 2nd edn, Oxford: Elsevier Butterworth-Heinemann.

**Bennett, R., W. Mousley and R. Ali-Choudhury** (2008) "Transfer of marketing knowledge within business-non-profit collaborations", *Journal of Non-Profit & Public Sector Marketing*, **20** (1), 37–17.

**Bernstein, A.** (2010) *Case for Business in Developing Economies*, New York: Viking Press.

**Birch, J.** (2000) quoted in Daft, R.L., *Management*, Fort Worth, TX: Dryden Press.

**Blake, R.R. and J.S. Mouton** (1964) *The Management Grid*, Houston, TX: Gulf.

**Bligh, M.C., J.C. Kohles, C.A. Pearce, J.E.G. Justin and J.F. Stovall** (2007) "When the romance is over: follower perspectives of adverse leadership", *Applied Psychology*, **56**, 528–557.

**Boddy, D.** (2002a) *Managing Products: Building and Leading the Team*, Harlow: Financial Times Prentice Hall.

**Boddy, D.** (2002b) *Management: An Introduction*, London: Pearson Education.

**Bono, J.E. and T.A. Judge** (2004) "Personality and transformational and transactional leadership: a meta-analysis", *Journal of Applied Psychology*, **89** (5), 901–911.

**Borisoff, D.** (1992) "Gender issues in listening", in *A Listening in Everyday Life: Personal and Professional Approach*, D. Borisoff and M. Purdy(eds), Lanham, MD: University Press of America.

**Bowlby, J.** (1988) *A Secure Base: Parent Child Attachment and Healthy Human Development*, London: Routledge.

**Boyatzis, R. E.** (1982) *The Competent Manager*, New York: John Wiley.

**Brecht, B.** (2010) "How I did it: building a company without borders", *Harvard Business Review*, April, 103.

**Bresnahan, C.G. and I.I. Mitroff** (2007) "Leadership and attachment theory", *American Psychologist*, September, **62** (6), 607–608.

**Brigham, E.** (1985) *Financial Management: Theory and Practice*, Chicago, IL: Dryden Press.

**Bristow, M.** (2001) "Management competencies", unpublished MSc thesis, Manchester School of Management, UMIST.

**Brockner, J. and B.M. Wiesenfeld** (1966) "An integrative framework for explaining reactions to decisions: interactive effects of outcomes and procedures", *Psychological Bulletin*, **120**, 189–208.

**Broughton, P.B.** (2008) *What They Teach You* at *Harvard Business School*, London: Viking Press.

**Brundtland, G.** (1987) *Our Common Future: The World Commission on Environment and Development*, Oxford: Oxford University Press.

**Brunell, A.B., W.A. Gentry, W.K. Campbell, B. Hoffman, K.W. Kunert and K.G. DeMarree** (2008) "Leader emergence: the case of the narcissistic leader", *Personality and Social Psychology Bulletin*, **34** (12), 1663–1676.

**Budd J.F. Jr** (1993) "12 CEOs found guilty of poor communications", *Public Relations Quarterly*, **38** (1), 4–5.

**Bullock, R.J. and D. Batten** (1985) "It is just a phrase we're going through: review and synthesis of OD phase analysis", *Group and Organisational Studies*, **10** (4), 383–413.

**Burns, B.** (2004a) *Managing Change: A Strategic Approach to Organisational Dynamics*, Cambridge: Pearson Education.

**Burns, B.** (2004b) "Emergent change and planned change–competitors or allies?", *International Journal of Operations & Production Management*, **24** (9), 886–902.

**Burns, T. and G.M. Stalker** (1961) *The Management of Innovation*, London: Tavistock.

**By, R.T.** (2005) "Organisational change management: a critical review", *Journal of Change Management*, **5** (4), 369–380.

**CACI** (2010) *New Acorn Classification Map*, http://www.caci.co.uk/acorn-classification. aspx (accessed December 2010).

**Cameron, K.S. and R.E. Quinn** (2006) *Diagnosing and Changing Organizational Culture: Based on the Competing Values Framework*, San Francisco, CA: Jossey-Bass.

**Campion, M.A., E.M. Papper and G.J. Medsker** (1996) "Relations between work team characters and effectiveness: a replication and extension", *Personnel Psychology*, **49** (2), 429–453.

**Campion, M.A., G.J. Medsker and A.C. Higgs** (1993) "Relation between workgroup characteristics and effectiveness: implications for designing effective workgroups", *Personnel Psychology*, **46**, 823–850.

**Carr, A.Z.** (1968) "Is business bluffing ethical", *Harvard Business Review*, January–February, 143–153.

**Castrogiovanni, G.J. and R.T. Justis** (2007) "Franchise failure: a reassessment of the Bates (1995) results", *Service Business*, **1** (3), September, 247–256.

**Chan, A.** (1997) "Corporate culture of a clan", *Management Decision*, **35** (2), 94–92.

**Chapman, M.R.** (2006). *In Search of Stupidity: Over 20 Years of High-Tech Marketing Disasters*, New York: Springer-Verlag.

**Chartered Institute of Marketing** (2010) *What is Marketing? CIM's Definition*. http://www.cim. co.uk/resources/understanding market/definitionmkting.aspx (accessed December 2010).

**Chartered Institute of Personnel and Development** (CIPD) (2009a) *Learning and Development Survey 2009*, London: CIPD.

**Chartered Institute of Personnel and Development (CIPD)** (2009b) *Factsheet on Teamworking,* London: CIPD.

**Chartered Institute of Personnel and Development (CIPD)** (2010) *Factsheet on Change Management,* London: CIPD.

**Child, J.** (2005) *Organisation: Contemporary Principles and Practice,* Oxford: Blackwell.

**Chomsky, N.** (1999) *Profit over People: Neoliberalism and Global Order,* New York: Seven Stories Press.

**Chomsky, N.** (2002) *Media Control: The Spectacular Achievements of Propaganda,* New York: Seven Stories Press.

**Churchill, N.** (1984) "Budget choice: planning versus control", *Harvard Business Review,* July–August, 150–164.

**Clampitt, P.** (1991) *Communicating for Managerial Effectiveness,* Newbury Park, CA: Sage.

**Clarke, T. and G. Salaman** (1993) "Telling tales: management gurus and the construction of managerial identity", *Journal of Management Studies,* **35** (2), 137–161.

**Cole, G.A.** (2004) *Management Theory and Practice,* London: Continuum.

**Collins, D.** (2000) *Management Fads and Buzzwords,* London: Routledge.

**Collins, J.C. and J.I. Porras** (1994) *Built to Last: Successful Habits of Visionary Companies,* New York: HarperBusiness.

**Contu, A.** (2007) in D. Knights and H. Willmott, *Organisational Behaviour and Management,* London: Thomson Learning.

**Cook, M.** (2009) *Personnel Selection: Adding Value through People,* Chichester: Wiley-Blackwell.

**Covey, S.R. and A.K. Gulledge** (1992) "Principles centred leadership", *The Journal for Quality and Participation,* **15** (4), 70–79.

**Cranefield, J. and Y. Pak** (2007) "The role of the translator/interpreter in knowledge transfer environments", *Knowledge & Process Management,* **42** (2), 95–103.

**Crevani, L., M. Lindgren and J. Packendoff** (2007) "Shared leadership: a post-heroic perspective on leadership as a collective construction", *International Journal of Leadership Studies,* **3** (1), 40–67.

**Crews, F.C.** (2003) *The Pooh Complex,* Chicago, IL: University of Chicago Press.

**Cringely, R.X.** (1994) "When disaster strikes: how to forfeit millions in exchange for nothing", *Forbes Magazine,* 29 August, 60.

**Crosby, P.** (1979) *Quality Is Free,* New York: McGraw-Hill.

**Csikszementkihalyri, M.** (1975) *Beyond Boredom and Anxiety: Experiencing Flow in Work and Play,* San Francisco, CA: Jossey-Bass.

**Curtin, J.** (2004) "Emergent leadership: Case study of a jury foreperson", *Leadership Review,* **4**, 75–88.

**Curver, B.** (2003) *Enron: Anatomy of Greed,* London: Arrow Books.

**Dana, L.P., T. Hamilton and K. Wick** (2008) "Deciding to export: an exploratory study of Singaporean entrepreneurs", *Journal of International Entrepreneurship,* **7** (2), 79–87.

**Daniels, K. and J. de Jonge** (2010) "Matchmaking and match breaking: the nature of match within and around job design", *Journal of Occupational and Organisational Psychology*, **83** (1), 1–16.

**Dannemiller, K.D. and R.W. Jacobs** (1992) "Changing the way organisations change: a revolution in common sense", *Journal of Applied Behavioural Science*, **4**, 480–498.

**Davies, I.A., B. Doherty and S. Knox** (2010) "The rise and stall of a Fair Trade pioneer: the CaféDirect story", *Journal of Business Ethics*, **92**, 127–147.

**Deal, T.E. and A.A. Kennedy** (1982) *Corporate Cultures: The Rites and Rituals of Corporate Life,* Reading, MA: Addison-Wesley.

**Dean, W.J. and M.P. Sharfman** (1996) "Does decision process matter? A study of strategic decision making effectiveness", *Academy of Management Journal*, April, 368–396.

**Dewson, S., J. Eccles, N.D. Tackey and A. Jackson** (2000) *Guide to Measuring Soft Outcomes,* Brighton: Institute for Employment Studies.

**Diaper, G.** (1990) "The Hawthorn effect: a fresh examination", *Educational Studies*, **16** (3), 261–268.

**Dougherty, D. and E.H. Bowman** (1995) "The effects of organizational downsizing on product innovation", *Californian Management Review*, **37** (4), 28–44.

**Downes, L.** (2005) "Beyond Porter", *Context Magazine*, http://www.contextmag.com/setFrameRedirect.asp?src=/archives/199712/technosynthesis.asp (accessed 12 January 2005).

**Drucker, P.F.** (1946) *The Concept of the Corporation*, New York: Mentor.

**Drucker, P.F.** (1954) *The Practice of Management,* New York: Harper and Row.

**Drucker, P.F.** (1969) *The Age of Discontinuity*, London: Heinemann.

**Drucker, P.F.** (1985) *Innovation and Entrepreneurship: Practice and Principles*, London: Heinemann.

**Drucker, P.F.** (1997) "The future that has already happened", *Harvard Business Review*, **75**, 20–24.

**Drucker, P.F.** (1999) *Innovation and Entrepreneurship*, 2nd edn, Oxford: Butterworth-Heineman.

**Drury, C.** (2005) *Management Accounting for Business Decisions*, London: International Thompson Business Press.

**Dubrin, A.J.** (2003) *Essentials of Management*, 6th edn, Mason, OH: South-Western.

**Dumaine, B.** (1993) "The new non-manager manager", *Fortune*, February, 80–84.

**Duncan, W.J., K.G. LaFrance and P.M. Ginter** (2003) "Leadership and decision-making: a retrospective application and assessment", *Journal of Leadership Studies*, **9** (4), 1–20.

**Eby, L.T., J. Cader and C.L. Noble** (2003) "Why do high self-monitors emerge as leaders in small groups? A comparative analysis of the behaviours of high versus low self-monitors", *Journal of Applied Social Psychology*, **33** (7), 1457–1479.

**Economist** (2004) "The cartel isn't forever", *Economist*, 15 July.

**Economist** (2010) "Tesco and the case against diversity", *Economist*, 10 June.

**Economist** (2010a) "Data, data everywhere", *Economist*, 25 February.

**Economist** (2010b) "When your carpet calls your doctor", *Economist*, 8 April.

**Eisnér, M.** (2010) *Working Together: Why Great Partnerships Succeed*, New York: Harper-Collins.

**Elliott, J.** (1991). *Action Research for Educational Change*, Buckingham: Open University Press.

**Eppler, M.J.** (2007) "Knowledge communication problems between experts and decision-makers: an overview and classification", *Electronic Journal of Knowledge Management*, **5** (3), 291–300.

**Fahn, S.** (1999) "Parkinson disease, the effect of Levodopa, and the ELLDOPA trial. Earlier versus later L-DOPA", *Archives of Neurology*, **56**, 529–535.

**Fayol, H.** (1949) *General and Industrial Management*, trans C. Storrs, London: Pitman Publishing.

**Ferreira, A. and D. Otley** (2009) "The design and use of management control systems: an extended framework for analysis", *Management Accounting Research*, **20** (4), 263–283.

**Fiedler, F.E., M.M. Chemers and L. Mahar** (1978) *The Leadership Match Concept*, New York: Wiley.

**Fisher, N.I. and V.N. Nair** (2009) "Quality management and quality practice: perspectives on their history and their future", *Applied Stochastic Models in Business and Industry*, **25**, 1–28.

**Fitzroy, P.** (2001) *Living with Globalisation*, http://www.abc.net.au/money/currency/features/feat8.htm (accessed 3 December 2010).

**Fleischman, R.K. and T.N. Tyson** (1998) "The evolution of standard casting in the UK and US: from decision-making to control", *Abacus*, **34** (1), 92–119.

**Follett, M.P.** (1941) *Collected Works*, New York: Harper and Row.

**Francis, R.D.** (1999) *Ethics for Psychologists: A Handbook*, Leicester: British Psychological Society.

**French, J.R.P. and B. Raven** (1960) "The bases of social power", in *Group Dynamics: Research and Theory*, D. Cartwright and A. Zander (eds), New York: Harper and Row.

**Friedman, M.** (1970) "The social responsibility of business is to increase its profits", *New York Times*, 14 September.

**Fullerton, R.** (1988) How modern is modern marketing: marketing's evolution and the myth of the "production era", *Journal of Marketing*, **52**, January, 108–125.

**Fulop, L. and S. Linstead** (1999) *Management: A Critical Text*, Basingstoke: Macmillan Business.

**Gatenby, M., C. Rees, E. Soane and C. Truss** (2009) *Employee Engagement in the Context*, London: Chartered Institute of Personnel and Development.

**Geri, N. and B. Ronen.** (2005) "Relevance lost: the rise and fall of activity-based costing", *Human Systems Management*, **24**, 133–144.

**Giberson, T., C.J. Resick and M.W. Dickson** (2005) "Embedding leader characteristics: an examination of homogeneity of personality and values in organizations", *Journal of Applied Psychology*, **90** (5), 1002–1010.

**Gigerenzer, G. and R. Selten** (2002) *Bounded Rationality: The Adaptive Toolbox*, Cambridge, MA: MIT Press.

**Gilliland, S.W.** (1993) "The perceived fairness of selection systems: an organisational justice perspective", *Academy of Management Review*, **18**, 694–734.

**Goffin, K., U. Koners, D. Baxter and C. van der Hoven** (2010) "Management lessons learned and tacit knowledge in new product development", *Research Technology Management*, **53** (4), 39–52.

**Grant, A.M., Y. Fried, S.K. Parker and M. Frese** (2010) "Putting job design in context: introduction to the special issue", *Journal of Organisational Behaviour*, **31**, 145–147.

**Greenleaf, R.K.** (1977) *Servant Leadership: A Journey into the Nature of Legitimate Power and Greatness*, Mahwah, NJ: Paulist Press.

**Guest, D.** (1992) "Right enough to be dangerously wrong: an analysis of the in search of excellence phenomenon" in *Human Resource Strategies*, G. Salaman (ed), London: Sage.

**Guest, D.E.** (1998) "Is the psychological contract worth taking seriously?", *Journal of Organisational Behaviour*, **19**, 649–664.

**Guest, D.E. and N. Conway** (2002) "Communicating the psychological contract: an employer perspective", *Human Resource Management Journal*, **12** (2), 22–39.

**Haag, C. and H. Laroche** (2009) "Dans le secret comités de direction, le rôle des émotions: proposition d'un modèl théoretique", *M@n@gement*, **12** (2), 82–117.

**Hackman, J.R. and G.R. Oldham** (1980) *Work Redesign*, Reading, MA: Addison-Wesley.

**Hackman, J.R. and R. Wageman** (2007) "Asking the right questions about leadership", *American Psychologist*, **1** (62), 43–47.

**Hage, J. and M. Aiken** (1968) "Organisational interdependence and intra-organisational structure", *American Sociological Review*, **33**, 912–930.

**Hage, J. and M. Aiken** (1969) "Routine technology, social structure and organisational goals", *Administrative Science Quarterly*, **14**, 366–375.

**Hage, J. and R. Dewar** (1973) "Elite values versus organisational structure in predicting innovation", *Administrative Science Quarterly*, **18**, 297–290.

**Hall, D.T.** (1996) "Protean careers of the 21st century", *Academy of Management Executive*, **10** (4), 8–16.

**Hall, E.T.** (1976) *Beyond Culture*, New York: Doubleday.

**Hammer, M.** (1995) *The Re-engineering Revolution: The Handbook*, London: HarperCollins.

**Hammer, M.** (1997) *Beyond Re-engineering*, New York: Harper Business.

**Handy, C.** (1989) *The Age of Unreason*, London: Pan Books.

**Handy, C.** (2005) *Management Gurus: Michael Porter*, http://www.bbc.co.uk/worldservice/learningenglish/handy/porter.pdf, (accessed 3 December 2010).

**Hannagan, T.** (2002) *Management Concepts and Practices*, Harlow: Prentice Hall.

**Hannagan, T.** (2005) *Management Concepts and Practices*, Harlow: Pearson Education.

**Harris, L.C.** (2010) "Fraudulent consumer returns: exploiting retailers' return policies", *European Journal of Marketing*, **44** (6), 730–738.

**Harter, J.K., F.L. Schmidt, E.A. Killham and S. Agrawal** (2009) *Q12 Meta-Analysis: The Relationship between Engagement at Work And Organisational Outcomes*, Washington, DC: Gallup.

**Haspeslagh, P.** (1982) "Portfolio planning: uses and limitations", *Harvard Business Review*, **60**, 58–73.

**Health Advantage** (2004) http://www.healthadvantage-hmo.com/customer_service/terms.asp#m

**Hendricks, K.B. and V.R. Singhal** (1999) *Quality Progress*, **32** (4), 35–43.

**Herath, S.K.** (2007) "A framework for management control research", *The Journal of Management Development*, **26** (9), 895–899.

**Herriot, P.** (1989) "Selection as a social process" in *Advances in Selection and Assessment*, J.M. Smith and I.T. Robertson (eds), Chichester: Wiley.

**Hersey, P. and K.H. Blanchard** (1982) "Leadership style: attitudes and behaviours", *Training and Development Journal*, **36** (5), 50–52.

**Hirschman, L.** (1975) "Female–male difference in conversational interaction", in *Language and Sex Differences and Dominance*, B. Thorne and N. Henley (eds), Rowley, MA: Newbury House.

**Hoff, R.** (1995) *Business Week*, 13 February, 67.

**Hofstede, G.** (1980) *Culture's Consequences: International differences in Work Related Values*, Beverley Hills, CA: Sage.

**Hofstede, G.** (2002) "Dimensions do not exist: I replied to Brendan McSweeney", *Human Relations*, **55** (11), 1355–1361.

**Hofstede, G., with G.J. Hofstede** (2005) *Cultures and Organisations: Software of the Mind*, New York: McGraw-Hill.

**Holden, L.** (2001) "Organisational communication", in *Management Concepts and Practices*, T. Hannagan (ed), Harlow: Pearson Education.

**Hollander, E.P.** (1961) "Emergent leadership and social influence", in *Leadership and Interpersonal Behaviour*, L. Petrullo and B.M. Bass (eds), New York: Holt, Reinhardt and Winston.

**Hollander, S.C.** (1986) "The marketing concept: a déjà vu", in *Marketing and Management Technology as a Social Process*, G. Fisk (ed), New York: Praeger.

**Honey, P.** (1982) *The Manual of Leadership Styles*, Maidenhead: Peter Honey.

**Hoozee, S. and B. Werner** (2010) "Identifying operational improvements during the design process of a time-driven ABC system: the role of collective worker participation and leadership style", *Management Accounting Research*, **21** (3), 185–199.

**House, R.J.** (1971) "A path-goal theory of leader effectiveness", *Administrative Sciences Quarterly*, **16**, 321–338.

**House, R.J. and J.R. Rizzo** (1972) "Towards the measurement of organisational practices", *Journal of Applied Psychology*, **56** (5), 388–396.

**Hovland, C.J.** (1957) *The Order of Presentation in Persuasion*, New Haven, CT: Yale University Press.

**Howell, J.P., D.E. Bowen, S. Kerr and P.M. Posdsakoff** (1990) "Substitute for leadership; effective alternatives to ineffective leadership", *Organisational Dynamics*, Summer, 20–38.

**Huczynski, A.A.** (1993) *Management Gurus: What Makes Them and How to Become One*, London: Routledge.

**Hurdley, R.** (2010) "The power of corridors: connecting doors, mobilising materials, plotting openness", *The Sociological Review*, **58** (1), 45–64.

**Hussey, D.E.** (2000) *How to Manage Organisational Change*, London: Kogan Page.

**Iboost** (2005) http://www.iboost.com/promote/marketing/branding/20025e.htm.

**Jablin, F., L. Putham, K. Roberts and L. Porter (eds)** (1987) *Handbook of Organisational Communication: an Interdisciplinary Perspective*, Newbury Park, CA: Sage.

**Jaworski, B.J. and D. MacInnis** (1989) "Marketing jobs and management controls: towards a framework", *Journal of Marketing Research*, **26**, 408–419.

**Jay, A.** (1967) *Management and Machiavelli*, New York: Holt, Reinhart and Winston.

**Jones, E.G.B. and A.J. Richardson** (2007) "The myth of the marketing revolution", *Journal of Macromarketing*, **27** (1), 15–24.

**Jones, M.L.** (2007) *Hofstede – Culturally Questionable*, Oxford Business and Economics Conference, Oxford, 24–26 June, http://ro.uow.edu.au/commpapers/370.

**Judge, T.A., J.E. Bono, R. Ilies and M.W. Gearhart** (2002) "Personality and leadership: a qualitative and quantitative review", *Journal of Applied Psychology*, **87** (4), 765–780.

**Kahneman, D.** (2003) "Maps of bounded rationality: psychology for behavioural economics", *American Economic Review*, **93** *(5), 1449–1476.*

**Kahneman, E. and G. Klein** (2010) "When can you trust your gut?" *McKinsey Quarterly*, 0047 5394, issue 2.

**Kahneman, E. and J. Renshon** (2007) "Why hawks win", *Foreign Policy*, **158**, 34–39.

**Kanter, R.** (1984) "Managing transitions in organisational culture: the case of participating management at Honeywell", in *Managing Organisational Transitions*, J.R. Kimberley and R.E. Quinn (eds), Homewood, IL: R.D. Erwin.

**Kanter, R.M.** (1983) *The Change Masters: Innovations for Productivity in American Corporations*, New York: Simon and Schuster.

**Kanter, R.M., B.A. Stein and T.D. Jick** (1992) *The Challenge of Organisational Change*, New York: Free Press.

**Kaplan, R.S. and E.P. Norton** (1992) "The balanced scorecard – measures that drive performance", *Harvard Business Review*, **70** (1), 71–80.

**Kaplan, R.S. and E.P. Norton** (1996) "Linking the balanced scorecard to strategy", *California Management Review*, **39** (1), 53–80.

**Katz, R.L.** (1974) "Skills of an effective administrator", *Harvard Business Review*, **52**, (5), 90–102.

**Kay, J.P.** (1996) *The Business of Economics*, Oxford: Oxford University Press.

**Keen, P.** (1981) "Information systems and organisation change", in *Implementing New Technologies*, E. Rhodes and D. Wield (eds), Oxford: Open University Press.

**Keith, R.J.** (1960) "The marketing revolution", *Journal of Marketing*, **24** (1), 35–38.

**Kellaway, L.** (2001) "A boast too far", *Financial Times*, 3 December, 16.

**Kellerman, B.** (2004) *Bad Leadership: What It Is, How It Happens, Why It Matters*, Cambridge, MA: Harvard Business School Press.

**Kim, H., M. Lee, H. Lee and N. Kim** (2010) "Corporate social responsibility and employee-company identification", *Journal of Business Ethics*, **95**, 557–570.

**Kira, A., M. Nichols and M. Apperley** (2009) "Human communication in customer-agent-computer interaction: face-to-face versus over telephone", *Computers in Human Behaviour*, **25** (1), 8–20.

**KOF** (2010*) Index of Globalisation*, Zurich: KOF Swiss Economic Institute.

**Kohlberg, L.** (1976) "Moral stages and moralisation: the cognitive–development perspective", in *Moral Development and Behaviour: Theory, Research and Social Issues*, T. Likona (ed), New York: Holt, Rinehart and Winston.

**Kolb D.A. and R. Fry** (1975) "Towards an applied theory of experiential learning", in *Theories of Group Processes*, C. Cooper (ed), New York: Wiley.

**Kondratiev, N.** (1935) "The long waves in economic life", *Review of Economic Statistics*, **17** (6), November.

**Koontz, H. and R.W. Bradspies** (1972) "Managing through feed-forward control", *Business Horizons*, June, 25–36.

**Korman, A.K., J.H. Greenhaus and I.P. Badin** (1977) "Personnel attitudes and motivation", *Annual Review of Psychology*, **28**, 175–196.

**Kotler, P.** (1986) *Principles of Marketing*, 3rd edn, Englewood Cliffs, NJ: Prentice Hall.

**Kotter, J.P.** (1995) "Leading change: why transformation efforts fail", *Harvard Business Review*, **73** (2), 59–68.

**Kotter, J.P.** (1996) "Successful change and the force that drives it", *Canadian Manager*, **21** (3), 20–24.

**Kotter, J.P.** (2001) "What leaders really do", *Harvard Business Review*, **79** (11), 85–91.

**Kotter, J.P. and J. Heskett** (1992) *Corporate Culture and Performance*, New York; Free Press.

**Latham, G.P. and L.M. Saari** (1979) "The effect of holding goal difficulty constant on assigned and participatively set goals", *Academy of Management Journal*, **22**, 163–168.

**Lau, C.** (2010) "A step forward: ethics education matters!", *Journal of Business Ethics*, **92** (4), 565–585.

**Lavassani, M.K., B. Movahedi. and V. Kumar** (2008) "Evolution of supply chain theories: a comprehensive literature review", *Production and Operations Management Society*, California: POMS.

**Lawrence, R.R. and J.W. Lorsch** (1969) *Organisation and Environment*, Homewood, IL: Irwin.

**Leck, J.D., D.M. Saunders and M. Charbonneau** (1996) "Affirmative action programmes: and organisational justice perceptive", *Journal of Organisational Behaviour*, **17** (1), 79–89.

**Levinson, D.J.** (1986) "A conception of adult development", *American Psychologist*, **41** (1), 8.

**Levy, D.L. and D. Egan** (2003) "A neo-Gramascian approach to corporate political strategy: conflict and accommodation in the climate change negotiations", *Journal of Management Studies*, **40** (4), 803–829.

**Lewin, K.** (1947) "Frontiers in group dynamics", *Human Relations*, **1**, 5–41.

**Lewin, K.** (1951) *Field Theory in Social Science*, London: Harper.

**Lewin, K., R. Lippit and R.K. White** (1939) "Patterns of aggressive behaviour in experimentally created social climates", *Journal of Social Psychology*, **10**, 271–301.

**Lewis, P.S., S.H. Goodman and P.M. Fandt** (1995) *Management: Challenges in the 21st Century*, St Paul, MN: West.

**Lewis, P.V.** (1985) "Defining 'business ethics': like nailing jello to a wall", *Journal of Business Ethics*, **4** (5), 377–383.

**Li, J., C. Zhou and E.J. Zajac** (2009) "Control, collaboration, and productivity in international joint ventures: theory and evidence", *Strategic Management Journal*, **30**, (8), 865–885.

**Liden, R.C. and G. Graen** (1980) "Generalisability of the vertical dyad model of leadership", *Academy of Management Journal*, 23, 451–465.

**Lievans, F., J.I. Sanchez, D. Bartram and A. Brown** (2010) "Lack of consensus among competency ratings in the same occupation: noise or substance?" *Journal of Applied Psychology*, **95** (3), 562–571.

**Likert, R.** (1967) "From production and employee centredness to systems 1–4", *Journal of Management*, **5**, 147–156.

**Lindgren, M. and J. Packendorff** (2009) "Project leadership revisited: towards distributed leadership perspectives on project research", *International Journal of Project Organisation and Management*, **1** (3), 285–308.

**Linguard, L., S. Espin, S. Whyte, G. Regehr, G. Baker, R. Reznick, J. Bohnen, B. Orser, D. Doran and E. Grober** (2004) "Communication failures in the operating room: an observational classification of recurrence types and effect", *Quality and Safety of Health Care*, **13** (5), 330–34.

**Lipman-Blumen, J.** (2005) "Toxic leadership: when grand illusions masquerade as noble visions", *Leader to Leader*, **36**, 29–35.

**Litwin, G.H. and R.A. Stringer** (1968) *Motivation and Organisational Climate*, Cambridge, MA: Harvard Graduate School of Business.

**Lock, E.A.** (1976) "The nature and causes of job satisfaction", in *Handbook of Industrial and Organisational Psychology*, M.D. Dunette (ed), Chicago, IL: Rand McNally.

**Locke, E.A.** (1968) "Towards a theory of task motivation and incentives", *Organisational Behaviour and Human Performance*, **3**, 157–189.

**Locke, E.A., K.N. Shaw, L.M. Saari and G.P. Latham** (1981) "Goal setting and task performance", *Psychological Bulletin*, **90**, 225–252.

**Luecke, R.** (2003) *Managing Change and Transition*, Boston, MA: Harvard Business School Press.

**Luthans, F. and B.J. Aviolo** (2003) "Authentic leadership: a positive developmental approach", in *Positive Organisational Scholarship: Foundations of a New Discipline*, K.S. Cameron, J.E. Dutton and R.E. Quinn (eds), San Francisco, CA: Berrett-Koehler.

**MacLeod, D. and N. Clarke** (2009) *Engaging for Success: Enhancing Performance through Employee Engagement*. Kew: Office of Public Sector Information.

**Madsen, P.M. and V. Desai** (2010) "Failing to learn? The effects of failure and success on organisational learning in the global orbital launch vehicle industry", *Academy of Management Journal*, **53** (3), 451–478.

**Markillie, P.** (2004) "A perfect market: e-commerce is coming of age", *The Economist*, **15**, 3–6 July.

**Marshak, R.J.** (1993) "Managing the metaphors of change", *Organisational Dynamics*, **22**, 44–56.

**Martensson, M.** (2000) "A critical review of knowledge management as a management tool", *Journal of Knowledge Management*, **4** (3), 204–216.

**Maslow, A.H.** (1970) *Motivation and Personality*, 2nd edn, Cambridge, MA: Harvard University Press.

**Mayo, E.** (1933) *The Human Problems of an Industrial Civilization*, New York: Macmillan.

**McClelland, D.C.** (1971) *The Achieving Society*, New York: Irvington.

**McGregor, D.** (1960) *The Human Side of the Enterprise*, New York: McGraw-Hill.

**McLuhan, M.** (1962) *The Gutenberg Galaxy*, Toronto: University of Toronto Press.

**McLuhan, M.** (1964) *Understanding Media*, London: Routledge and Kegan Paul.

**Medawar, P.B.** (1975) Victims of Psychiatry, *New York Review of Books*, 23 January, 17.

**Merchant, K.A.** (1985) *Control in Business Organisations*, Marshfield, MA: Pitman.

**Metters, R. and A. Maruchek** (2007) "Service management – academic issues and scholarly reflections from operations management and researchers", *Decision Sciences*, **38** (2), 195–214.

**Miceli, M.P. and J.P. Near** (1994) "Whistle-blowing: reaping the benefits", *Academy of Management Executive*, **8** (3), 65–74.

**Micklethwaite, J. and A. Wooldridge** (1996) *The Witch Doctors: What the Management Gurus are Saying, Why it Matters and How to Make Sense of It*, London: Heinemann.

**Miles, R.E. and C.C. Snow** (1978) *Organisational Strategy, Structure and Process*, New York: McGraw-Hill.

**Miller, D.S., S.E. Catt and J.R. Carlson** (1996) *Fundamentals of Management: A Framework for Excellence*, St. Paul, MN: West.

**Mintzberg, H.H.** (1973) *The Nature of Managerial Work*, New York: Harper and Row.

**Mintzberg, H.H.** (1983) "The case for corporate social responsibility", *Journal of Business Strategy*, **4** (2), 3–15.

**Mintzberg, H.H.** (1987) "The strategy concept II: another look at why organisations need strategies", *California Management Review*, **30**, 25–32.

**Mintzberg, H.H.** (1994) "Rethinking strategic planning. Part I: pitfalls and fallacies", *Long Range Planning*, **27** (3), 12–21.

**Mintzberg, H.H.** (1998) "Covert leadership: notes on managing professionals", *Harvard Business Review*, **76** (6), November–December, 140–148.

**Mintzberg, H.H.** (2009) "We're over-led and under-managed", *Business Week*, 17 August, 68.

**Mintzberg, H.H.** (2010) "Managing on three planes", *Leader to Leader*, **57**, 29–34.

**Morrison, A. and R. Wensley** (1991) "Boxing up or boxed in? A short history of the Boston Consulting Group Share/Growth Matrix", *Journal of Marketing Management*, **7** (2), 105–129.

**Mousa, T.T. and D.J. Lemark** (2009) "The Gilbreths' quality system stands the test of time", *Journal of Management History*, **15** (2), 198–215.

**National Audit Office** (2010) *Reorganising Central Government*, London: National Audit Office.

**Near, J.P.** (1989) "Whistle-blowing: encourage it", *Business Horizons*, **32** (1), 2–6.

**New Mexican** (1994) "Slogans often lose something in translation", *New Mexican*, 3 July, 1–2.

**Niven, P.R.** (2006) *Balanced Scorecard Step-by-Step*, Chichester: John Wiley and Sons.

**Nobes, C. and R. Parker** (2006) *Comparative International Accounting*, Harlow: Pearson Education.

**Nonaka, I. and H. Takeuch** (1995) *The Knowledge Creating Company*, Oxford: Oxford University Press.

**O'Grady, W., P. Rouse and C. Gunn** (2010) "Synthesising management control frameworks", *Measuring Business Excellence*, **14** (1), 96.

**Office for National Statistics** (2008) *Internet Access 2008: Households and Individuals*, Newport: Office of National Statistics.

**Oliver, R.K. and M.D. Webber** (1982) "Supply chain management: logistics catches up with a strategy", *Outlook*, New York: Booze Allen and Hamilton. Reprinted in Christopher, M. (ed) (1992) *Logistics: Strategic Issues*, London: Chapman Hall.

**OPSI** (2010) *Bribery Act 2010*, London: Office of Public Sector Information.

**Organisation for Economic Co-operation and Development (OECD)** (1989) *Predatory Pricing*, Paris: OECD.

**Ouchi, W.G.** (1980) "Markets, bureaucracies and clans", *Administrative Science Quarterly*, March, 129–141.

**Packard, V.** (1957) *The Hidden Persuaders*, New York: Random House.

**Palmer, C.** (1999) "Work: revenge: it's sweet but risky", *Observer*, 4 December, 19.

**Pare, T.C.** (1993) "A new model for managing costs", *Fortune*, **14**, June, 124–129.

**Parinello, A. and D. Gottfried** (2004) *10 Secrets I Learned from the Apprentice*, New York: Chamberlain Bros.

**Parker, S.K., T.D. Wall and P.R. Jackson** (1998) "That's not my job: developing flexible employees work", *Academy of Management Journal*, **40** (4), 899–930.

**Parson, H.M.** (1974) "What happened at Hawthorne?" *Science*, **183**, 922–932.

**Paterson, M.G., M.A. West, R. Lawthom and S. Nickell** (1997) *Impact of People Management Practices on the Business Performance*, London: Chartered Institute of Personnel and Development.

**Paulos, J.A.** (1998) *Once upon a Number*, Harmondsworth: Penguin.

**Payne, R.L. and Pheysey, D.C.** (1971) "G.G. Stern's Organisational Climate Index: a reconceptualisation and application to business organizations", *Organisational Behaviour and Human Performance*, **6**, 77–98.

**Pearce, C.L. and C.C. Manz** (2005) "The new silver bullets of leadership", *Organisational Dynamics*, **34** (2), 130–140.

**Peltz, D.** (1952) "Influence: a key to ineffective leadership in the first-line supervisor", *Personnel*, **29**, 209–217.

**Perrow, C.** (1979) *Complex Organizations: A Critical Essay*, Glencoe, IL: Scott Foresman.

**Perry, J.L., T.K. Engbers and S.Y. Jun** (2009) "Back to the future? Performance related pay, and the perils of persistence", *Public Administration Review*, **69** (1), 39–52.

**Pescosolido, A.T.** (2002) "Emergent leaders as managers of emotion", *The Leadership Quarterly*, **13** (5), 583–599.

**Peters, T.** (1995) *The Pursuit of Wow! Every Person's Guide to Topsy Turvey Times,* London: Macmillan.

**Peters, T.** (1997) *The Circle of Innovation: You Can't Shrink Your Way to Greatness,* London: Hodder and Stoughton.

**Peters, T. and R. Waterman** (1988) *In Search of Excellence,* New York: Harper and Row.

**Peters, T.J. and N. Austin** (1985) *A Passion for Excellence,* New York: Warner Books.

**Petkus, E.** (2010) "Historical perspectives in marketing education: justification and implementation", *Journal of Marketing Education,* **32** (1), 64–74.

**Pettinger, R.** (1997) *Introduction to Management,* 2nd edn, London: Macmillan.

**Pfeffer, J.** (1998) *The Human Equation: Building Profits by Putting People First,* Boston, MA: Harvard University Press.

**Pinder, C.C.** (1984) *Work Motivation,* Glenview, IL: Scott Foresman.

**Pitches, D., A. Burls and A. Fry-Smith** (2003) "How to make a silk purse from a sow's ear – a comprehensive review of strategies to optimise data for corrupt managers and incompetent clinicians", *British Medical Journal,* **327** (7429), December, 1436–1439.

**Polyani, M.** (1966) *The Tacit Dimension,* London: Routledge and Kegan Paul.

**Porter, M.** (1980) *Competitive Strategy: Techniques for Analysing Industries and Competitors,* New York: Free Press.

**Porter, M.** (1990) *The Competitive Advantage of Nations,* London: Macmillan.

**Porter, M., K. Schwab, I.M. Sala and A. Lopez-Claros** (2004) *Global Competitiveness Report 2004–2005,* Basingstoke: Palgrave Macmillan for the World Economics Forum.

**Porter, M.E.** (1996) "What is strategy?", *Harvard Business Review,* November–December, 61–78.

**Porter, M.E.** (1998) *Competitive Advantage: Creating and Sustaining Superior Performance,* New York: Simon and Schuster.

**Porter, M.E.** (2001) "Strategy and the Internet", *Harvard Business Review,* March, 62–78.

**Powell, G. N., D.A. Butterfield and K. Bartol** (2008) "Leader evaluations: a new female advantage", *Gender in Management: An International Journal,* **23** (3), 156–174.

**Pride, W. and O.C. Farrell** (2000) *Marketing: Concepts and Strategies,* Boston, MA: Houghton Mifflin.

**Pugh, D.S. and D.J. Hickson** (1976) *Organisation Structure in Its Context: The Aston Program,* Aldershot: Gower Press.

**Pyhrr, P.** (1973) *Zero Base Budgeting, a Practical Management Tool for Evaluating Expenses,* New York: Wiley.

**Quintessential Careers** (2004) http://quintcareers.com/jobseeker_marketing_glossary.html.

**Reddin, W.J.** (1970) *Managerial Effectiveness,* New York: McGraw-Hill Book Company.

**Reilly, B.J. and J.A. DiAngelo** (1990) "Communication: a cultural system of meaning and values", *Human Relations,* **43**, 129–140.

**Reimann, B.G.** (1974) "On dimensions of bureaucratic structure: an empirical reappraisal", *Administrative Science Quarterly,* **19**, 462–476.

**Ricks, D.A. and A. Mahajan** (1984) "Blunders in international marketing", *Long-range Planning,* **17** (1), 78–83.

**Rizzo, J.R., R.J. House and S.I. Lirtzman** (1970) "Role conflict and ambiguity in complex organizations", *Administrative Science Quarterly*, **15**, 150–163.

**Robbins, S.P.** (1998) *Organisation Theory: Structure, Design and Application*, Englewood, NJ: Prentice-Hall.

**Robbins, S.P. and D.A. Decenzo** (2003) *Fundamentals of Management*, Upper Saddle River, NJ: Prentice Hall.

**Robinson, S.L. and D.M. Rousseau** (1994) "Violating the psychological contract: not the exception but the norm", *Journal of Organisational Behaviour*, **15**, 245–459.

**Roethlisberger, F.J., W.J. Dixon and H.A. Wright** (1939) *Management and the Worker*, Cambridge, MA: Harvard University Press.

**Roger, A.** (1953) *The Seven-Point Plan*, London: National Institutes of Industrial Psychology.

**Rogers, R. and J.E. Hunter** (1991) "Impact of management by objectives on organisational productivity", *Journal of Applied Psychology*, **76** (2), 322–326.

**Rosenthal, R. and L. Jacobson** (1992) *Pygmalion in the Classroom: Teacher Expectation and Pupils' Intellectual Development*, New York: Irvington.

**Rosenthal, R. and R.L. Rosnow** (1969) *Artefacts in Behavioural Research*, New York: Academic Press.

**Rouleau, L. and J. Balogun** (2010) "Middle managers, strategic sense making and discursive competence", *Journal of Management Studies*, early view, 30 March.

**Rousseau, D.M.** (1995) *Psychological Contracts in Organisations: Understanding the Written and Unwritten Agreements*, London: Sage.

**Rowe, A.J., J.D. Boulgarides and M.R. McGrath** (1994) *Managerial Decisionmaking: Modules in Management Series*, Chicago, IL: SRA.

**Rubinstein, A.** (1998) *Modelling Bounded Rationality*, London: MIT Press.

**Russell, R.F. and A.G. Stone** (2002) "A review of servant leadership attributes: developing a practical model", *Leadership and Organisational Development Journal*, **23**, 145–157.

**Ryan, M.K., S.A. Haslam, C.K. Hersby and C. Atkins** (2007) "Opting out all pushed off the edge? The glass cliff and the precariousness and women's leadership positions", *Social and Personality Psychology Compass*, **1** (1), 266–279.

**Savage, M.** (2010) "Labour's computer blunders cost £26bn", *Independent*, 19 January.

**Schein, E.H.** (1978) *Career Dynamics: Matching Individual and Organisation Needs*, Reading, NH: Addison-Wesley.

**Schein, E.H.** (2004) *Organisational Culture and Leadership*, San Francisco, CA: Jossey-Bass.

**Schemerhorn, J.R.** (2002) *Management*, 7th edn, New York: Wiley.

**Schmenner, R.W.** (1986) "How can service businesses survive and prosper?", *Sloan Management Review*, Spring, 21–32.

**Schmidt, F.L. and J.E. Hunter** (1996) "The validity and utility of selection methods in personnel selection: the practical and theoretical implications of 85 years' research findings", *Psychological Bulletin*, **124** (2), 216–274.

**Schmidt, F.L., J.E. Hunter and V.W. Urry** (1976) "Statistical power in criterion-related validation studies", *Journal of Applied Psychology*, **61** (4), 473–485.

**Schneider, B.** (1987) "The people make the place", *Personnel Psychology*, **40** (3), 437–453.

**Schramm, W.** (1954) "How communication works", in *The Process and Effects of Mass Communication*, W. Schramm (ed), Urbana, IL: University of Illinois Press.

**Senge, P.** (1990) *The Fifth Discipline: the Art and Practice of the Learning Organisation*, London: Doubleday.

**Senior, P. and J. Fleming** (2006) *Organisational Change*, London: FT Prentice Hall.

**Shannon, C. and W. Weaver** (1949) *The Mathematical Theory of Communication*, Urbana, IL: University of Illinois Press.

**Shapiro, E.** (1998) *Fad Surfing in the Boardroom: Reclaiming the Courage to Manage in the Age of Instant Answers*, Oxford: Capstone.

**Shaw, W.H.** (1991) *Business Ethics*, Belmont, CA: Wadsworth.

**Sheppard, B.H. and R.J. Lerwicki** (1987) "Toward general principles of managerial fairness", *Social Justice Research*, **1**, 161–176.

**Simonds, R.** (1995) "Control in an age of empowerment", *Harvard Business Review*, **73** (2), 80–89.

**Sims, R.R.** (1994) "Human resource management's role in clarifying the new psychological contract", *Human Resource Management*, **33** (3), 373–383.

**Skogstad, A., S. Einarsen, T. Torsheim, A.M. Schanke and H. Hetland** (2007) "The destructiveness of laissez-faire leadership behaviour", *Journal of Occupational Health Psychology*, **12** (1), 80–93.

**Slack, N., S. Chambers, C. Harland, A. Harrisson and R. Johnston** (2001) *Operations Management*, London: Financial Times Prentice Hall.

**Smith, J.A. and R.J. Foti** (1998) "A pattern approach to the study of leader emergence", *Leadership Quarterly*, **9** (2), 147–153.

**Smith, K.** (2009) "Losing (ownership) control", *Harvard Business Review*, **87** (6), 18–20.

**Smith, M.** (1981) *British Telecom Survey Item Bank (Volume 2, Organisational Measures)*, Bradford: MCB University Press.

**Smith, M. and M. Abrahamsen** (1992) "Patterns of selection in six countries", *The Psychologist*, **5**, 205–207.

**Smither, J.W., R.E. Millsap, R.W. Stoffey, R.R. Reilly and K. Pearlman** (1996) "An experimental test of the influence of selection procedures on fairness perceptions, attitudes about the organization and job pursuit intentions", *Journal of Business and Psychology*, **10**, 297–318.

**Spears, L.C.** (2004) "The understanding and practice of servant leadership", in *Practising Servant Leadership: Succeeding through Trust, Bravery, and Forgiveness*, L.C. Spears and M. Lawrence (eds), San Francisco, CA: Jossey-Bass.

**Spring, M. and L. Araujo** (2009) "Service, services and products: rethinking operations strategy", *International Journal of Operations & Production Management*, **29** (5), 444–467.

**Standish Group** (2009) *Chaos Report 2009*, Boston, MA: Standish Group.

**Sternberg, R.J.** (2007) "A system's model of leadership: WICS", *American Psychologist*, **62** (1), 34–32.

**Stone, C.** (1990) "Why shouldn't corporations be socially responsible?", in *Business Ethics: Readings and Cases in Corporate Morality*, W.M. Hoffman and J.M. Moore (eds), New York: McGraw-Hill.

**Stone, T.H. and W.H. Cooper** (2009) "Emerging credits", *The Leadership Quarterly*, **20** (5), 785–798.

**Styhre, A., L. Wickmalm, S. Olilla and J. Roth** (2010) "Garbage-can decision-making and the accommodation of uncertainty in new drug development work", *Creativity & Innovation Management*, **19** (2), 134–147.

**Super, D.E.** (1990) "Career and life development", in *Career Choice and Development*, 2nd edn, D. Brown and L. Brooks (eds), San Francisco, CA: Jossey Bass.

**Tadajewski, M. and M. Saren** (2009) "Rethinking the emergence of relationship marketing", *Journal of Macromarketing*, **29** (2), 193–206.

**Tallman, S. and M. Koza** (2010) "Keeping the global in mind", *Management International Review*, **50** (4), 433–449.

**Tang, J.** (2010) "How entrepreneurs discover opportunities in China: an institutional view", *Asia-Pacific Journal of Management*, **27** (3), 461–480.

**Tannenbaum, R. and W.H. Schmidt** (1958) "How to choose a leadership pattern", *Harvard Business Review*, **36**, 95–202.

**Tarbell, I.** (1950) *The History of the Standard Oil Company*, New York: Peter Smith.

**Taticci, P., F. Tonnelli and L. Cagnazzo** (2010) "Performance measurement and management: a literature review and a research agenda", *Measuring Business Excellence*, **14** (1), 4–18.

**Taylor, F.W.** (1911) *The Principles of Scientific Management*, New York: Harper and Row.

**Tedeschi, R.** (2004) "Trying to reach customers in an era of e-mail suspicion", *New York Times*, 6 December, 16.

**Tetlock, P.E.** (2005) *Expert Political Judgement: How Good Is It? How Can We Know?* Princeton, NJ: Princeton University Press.

**The Times** (1999) "Passport to Farrago", *The Times*, 28 June, 21.

**Towers-Perrin** (1999) *Euro Rewards: Rewards, Challenges and Changes*, London: Towers Perrin.

**Treacy, M. and F. Wiersema** (1995) *The Discipline of Market Leaders*, Cambridge, MA: Perseus Books.

**Triandis, H.C.** (1977) *Interpersonal Behaviour*, Monterey, CA: Cole.

**Trompenaars, F.** (1993) *Riding the Waves of Culture: Understanding Cultural Diversity in Business*, London: Nicolas Brealey.

**Tuckerman, B.W.** (1965) "Developmental sequence in small groups", *Psychological Bulletin*, **63** (6), 384–399.

**Tuckerman, B.W. and M.A.C. Jensen** (1977) "Stages of small group development revisited", *Group & Organisational Management*, **2 (**4), 419–427.

**Tyler, W.B.** (1973) "Measuring organisational specialisation: the concept of role variety", *Administrative Science Quarterly*, **18**, 383–393.

**Velthouse B. and Y. Kandogan** (2007) "Ethics in practice: what are managers were really doing?", *Journal of Business Ethics*, **70**, 151–163.

**Viswesvaran, C., D.S. Ones and F.L. Schmidt** (1996) "Comparative analysis of the reliability of job performance ratings", *Journal of Applied Psychology*, **81** (5), 557–574.

**Vitell, S.J. and J. Muncy** (1992) "Consumer ethics: an empirical investigation of factors influencing ethical judgements of the final consumer", *Journal of Business Ethics*, **11**, 585–597.

**Vroom, V.H. and A.G. Jago** (1988) *The New Leadership*: *Managing Participation in Organisations*, Englewood Cliffs, NJ: Prentice-Hall.

**Wade, D.** (2003) "Torture of Tom Peters! Inanities", *Sunday Times*, 9 February, 7.

**Walker, E. and B. Webster** (2006) "Management competencies of women business owners", *Entrepreneurship Management*, **2**, 495–508.

**Wall, T.D.** (1973) "Ego-defensiveness as a determinant of reported differences in sources of job satisfaction and job dissatisfaction", *Journal of Applied Psychology*, **58**, 125–128.

**Walley, L. and M. Smith** (1998) *Deception in Selection*, Chichester: Wiley.

**Warren, L.** (1999) "Knowledge management: just another office in the executive suite?", *Accountancy Ireland*, December.

**Wasserman, N., B. Anand and N. Nohria** (2010) "When does leadership matter? A contingent opportunities view of CEO leadership", in *Leadership Theory and Practice*, N. Nohria and R. Khurana (eds), Cambridge, MA: Harvard Business Press.

**Weber, E.U. and E.J. Johnson** (2009) "Mindful judgement and decision making", *Annual Review of Psychology 2009*, **60**, 53–85.

**Weber, M.** (1947) *The Theory of Social and Economic Organisations*, New York: Free Press.

**Weick, K.E.** (2000) "Emergent change as a universal in all organisations", in M. Beer and N. Nohria (eds), *Breaking the Code of Change*, Boston, MA: Harvard Business School Press.

**Weick, K.E. and R.E. Quinn** (1999) "Organizational change and development", *Annual Review of Psychology*, **50**, 361–386.

**Wellner, A. S.** (2006) "Business was booming, but the Richardsons were seriously burned out", *Boston*, **28** (4), 52–55.

**Werner, R. and V. Kumar** (2002) "The mismanagement of customer loyalty", *Harvard Business Review*, **80** (7), 86–97.

**White, J.K. and R.A. Ruh** (1973) "Effects of personal values on the relationship between participation and job attitudes", *Administrative Science Quarterly*, **18**, 506–507.

**Winter, R.** (1987) *Action Research and the Nature of Social Enquiry: Professional Innovation and Educational Work*, Aldershot: Gower Press.

**Womack, J.P., D.T. Jones and D. Roos** (1990) *The Machine that Changed the World*, New York: Rawson Associates.

**Woodward, J.** (1965) *Industrial Organisation*: *Theory and Practice*, Oxford: Oxford University Press.

**Wrege, C.D.** (2008) "F. W. Taylor's lecture on management, June 4, 1907", *Journal of Management History*, **14** (3), 209–213.

**Xiao, Y., F.J. Seagull, C.F. Mackenzie, K.J. Klien and J. Ziegert** (2008) "Adaptation of team communication patterns: exploring the effects of leadership at a distance, task and urgency and shared team experience", in *Leadership At a Distance: Research in Technologically-Supported Work*, S. Weisband (ed), New York: Erlbaum.

**Yoo, J.W., D.J. Lemak and Y. Choi** (2006) "Principles of management and competitive strategies: using Fayol to implement Porter", *Journal of Management History*, **12** (4), 352–368.

**Young, S. and D.M. Oppenheimer** (2009) "Effect of communication strategy on personal risk perception and treatment adherent intentions", *Psychology, Health & Medicine*, **14** (4), 430–442.

**Zaccaro, S.J.** (2007) "Trait-based perspectives of leadership", *American Psychologist*, **62** (1), 6–16.

**Zaccaro, S.J. and P. Bader** (2003) "E-leadership on the challenges of leading E-teams: minimising the bad and maximising the good", *Organisational Dynamics*, **31**, 377–387.

**Zadeh, L.** (1965) "Fuzzy sets", *Information and Control*, **8**, 338–352.

**Zomersijk, L.G. and C.A. Voss** (2010) "Service designed for experience-centric services", *Journal of Service Research*, **13** (1), 67–82.

# Index